Religious Education 5–11

CW00558133

Religious Education has returned in the limelight of education. *Religious Education 5–11* deals with present-day debates and issues at the heart of this important subject. It provides systematic, holistic and unified guidance on teaching RE in primary school. The guide features vignettes, case studies, extracts and viewpoints from experts for deeper engagement. *Religious Education 5–11* offers ample guidance and suggestions for the classroom.

The main areas covered include:

- ■ Historical, legal and contemporary perspectives
- ■ What is RE about?
- ■ Aims, purposes and the field of enquiry
- ■ RE in the Early Years, Key Stages 1 and 2
- ■ Knowledge in RE
- ■ Concepts, attitudes, skills, dispositions and SMSC
- ■ Planning and structuring the curriculum
- ■ Theories, classical and contemporary pedagogies and multidisciplinary approaches
- ■ Assessment and progression
- ■ Subject leadership and the thriving community
- ■ Research and lifelong learning in RE

This book is an indispensable resource for all student educators, early career teachers and classroom practitioners interested in teaching Religious Education in an ambitious, contemporary and challenging way.

Imran Mogra is a senior lecturer in Religious Education and Professional Studies at Birmingham City University. He is the author of *Jumpstart! RE* (Routledge, 2018) and *Understanding Islam: A guide for teachers* (SAGE, 2020).

The *5–11* series combines academic rigour with practical classroom experience in a tried and tested approach which has proved indispensible to both trainee PGCE students and to practicing teachers. Bringing the best and latest research knowledge to core subject areas, this series addresses the key issues surrounding the teaching of these subjects in the primary curriculum. The series aims to stay up to date by reflecting changes in government policy and is closely related to the changing curriculum for the primary core subjects.

Each book contains lesson planning guidance and methods to develop pupils' understanding as well as offering creative and innovative ways to teach subjects in the primary classroom.

Titles in this series include:

Physical Education 5–11, Jonathan Doherty and Peter Brennan

History 5–11, Hilary Cooper

Modern Foreign Languages 5–11, Jane Jones and Simon Coffey

English 5–11, David Waugh and Wendy Jolliffe

Science 5–11, Alan Howe, Chris Collier, Dan Davies, Kendra McMahon & Sarah Earle

Maths 5–11, Caroline Clissold

Religious Education 5–11, Imran Mogra

Religious Education 5–11
A Guide for Teachers

Imran Mogra

Routledge
Taylor & Francis Group

LONDON AND NEW YORK

Cover image: Getty Images

First published 2023
by Routledge
4 Park Square, Milton Park, Abingdon, Oxon OX14 4RN

and by Routledge
605 Third Avenue, New York, NY 10158

Routledge is an imprint of the Taylor & Francis Group, an informa business

British Library Cataloguing-in-Publication Data
A catalogue record for this book is available from the British Library

ISBN: 978-0-367-25768-2 (hbk)
ISBN: 978-0-367-25769-9 (pbk)
ISBN: 978-0-429-28974-3 (ebk)

DOI: 10.4324/9780429289743

Typeset in Bembo
by KnowledgeWorks Global Ltd.

Contents

Tables

Boxes

Figures

Acknowledgements

I would like to thank the following:

Rudolf Eliott Lockhart and Mary Myatt for their quotes. Thanks are also due to Giles Freathy, Rob Freathy and the University of Exeter for permitting the use of the material on *The RE-searchers* approach. The Religious Education Council of England and Wales and Culham St Gabriel's Trust for their materials. Teachers who willingly shared their journey into the world of RE and who intend to lead the subject. I am most grateful for the permission granted by McCrimmons, Bloomsbury Academic, Taylor & Francis Informa UK Ltd, John Catt Educational, SAGE Publishing and RE Today Services. I also appreciate the consent from Buckinghamshire SACRE, Wokingham Borough Council, Birmingham City Council, Cumbria Development Education Centre, Diocese of Norwich and Norfolk SACRE. To my family for their love and support with RE. May Allah bless them.

Introduction

This book is intended to be a foundation in Religious Education (RE) for student teachers and early career teachers. It provides you with an overview of current developments in the subject and engages you in the debate regarding the future of the subject. It will help you understand why changes happen. It invites you to examine the nature of RE and consider the kinds of knowledge needed to provide coherence, sequence, integrity and challenge to this important curriculum area. It informs you about the various disciplines and dimensions of religion that can influence the teaching of RE. It seeks to involve you in considering and determining the purpose and aims of the subject for contemporary Britain. It assists you to think about your aims and purposes for the subject. It offers you an opportunity to consider, thoughtfully, some of the recent recommendations made by the Commission on Religious Education, and the curriculum expectations from the Religious Education Quality Mark framework and locally agreed syllabi. The book proffers some models of RE pedagogy based on well-established models and contemporary ones. The book also provides you with a range of teaching strategies to deliver high quality, ambitious and successful lessons. It analyses the role of planning, curriculum design and assessment in RE in primary settings and the potential of discrete subject teaching and cross-curricular work. The aim is to enable you to rationalise why you teach what you teach and how you teach it. The book suggests various ways of meeting the learning needs of pupils who have special educational needs and disability. To end, the book explores the role of subject leadership and research in RE.

RE, as a subject, is facing many challenges when contextualised in the operative formal curricula in schools and in its legal and structural situation. Thus, in Chapter 1, the historical and legislative legacy of RE is charted to offer you a nuanced understanding of the problematic nature of RE in England. This is an attempt to answer a common question 'Why is RE like this'? It highlights that the subject has not remained stagnant but has evolved from being faith-based to an educational endeavour. It also examines the legal requirements of RE.

Chapter 2 critiques and reviews developments from 2010 until 2020 to help you use this as a basis to think about the way forward, if any, for the subject. Probably, the most contested issue in the subject is that of the legal right of parents to withdraw their children from RE. The question of dedicating time for RE is a matter of concern as well. Consequently, both appear in this chapter. Chapter 3, 'What is RE all about?', focuses on the nature of RE as a subject and some of its vital characteristics. There is a brief consideration of the ideological standpoints of RE and RE from an international perspective. There is an analysis of the compulsory requirement of the subject and the importance of establishing the intent of RE. Moreover, from a philosophical stance, you will have an opportunity to examine your beliefs and values about each subject. A rationale for the subject is discussed. An interesting section invites your reflections on the name of the subject. Frequently raised concerns related to the teaching of RE have been included to reassure you.

DOI: 10.4324/9780429289743-1

Chapter 4 debates the question about knowledge in RE in the context of the 'knowledge-rich' curriculum and summarises three different types of specific knowledge that pupils are to learn in RE. A section is devoted to the current debate around Religion and 'Worldviews'. RE is faced with the issue of representation and breadth in its contents, which is why it is included within this chapter. Chapter 5 outlines the expected learning. The new Early Years Framework has been incorporated to show how RE can support its Early Learning Goals. The Key Stage 1 and 2 material reflects the contents from the non-statutory curriculum framework for RE in England published by the Religious Education Council of England and Wales. Chapter 6 is about the development of concepts, attitudes and skills and the activities to support these. Chapter 7 is about the spiritual, moral, social and cultural (SMSC) development of pupils as well as the development of dispositions and the activities to support these. The organisation, planning and mapping of the RE curriculum are looked at in Chapter 8. It covers elements such as cross-curricular, thematic, discrete and other approaches to planning. It draws attention to some of the principles and Big Ideas for curriculum design. The stages of planning are exemplified as well.

Chapter 9 is about becoming a thinker of your teaching. Some of the main theories of learning are sketched. It also re-visits and synthesises some of the famous pedagogies of RE, some of which were developed following research and each contributed towards understanding the nature of RE in the UK. Chapter 10 examines and exemplifies some well-established and contemporary pedagogies to develop your repertoire of teaching approaches. The aim is to demonstrate the rigour expected in the use of strategies. It invites you to be in search of pedagogies to improve your teaching and the success of your pupils. In Chapter 11, an attempt has been made to present multidisciplinary pedagogies for RE. These include theology, philosophy and human/social sciences in RE, artistic, dramatical, geographical, historical, linguistic, mathematical, multi-sensory, musical, poetical RE and theological approach and hermeneutics in RE. The purpose of Chapter 12, which is about pupils with Special Education Needs and Disability, is to emphasise the need for high ambitions for all pupils. It problematises definitions and underlines certain values and expectations to inform your thinking, and teaching. Thus inclusion in RE forms an important part of this discussion. RE is then brought to the service of pupils with SEND with many strategies suggested to support them. All pupils attending a special school will, so far as is practicable, receive RE unless their parents express a wish to the contrary, and so, a section deals with RE in special schools. RE is also brought to the service of the pupils with higher prior attainment. In Chapter 13, the two interrelated elements of assessment and progression are delineated. It discusses the problematic nature of assessment in RE. It sets out the key principles, purposes and categories of assessment. The chapter then offers a range of assessment techniques and tools to use for RE. It draws attention to and details new models of assessment. It presents examples of the mastery approach, age-related expectations and descriptor-based assessments.

Leaders play a crucial role in schools. In Chapter 14, the landscape of leadership and management is outlined. It considers concepts of mission and vision. The chapter also analyses the role of the RE lead practitioner. Policy content is described and the issues of inclusion and quality. A section is dedicated to the criteria for achieving a gold award from the REQM. An important aim of this chapter is to outline the national and local organisations and networks that sustain RE. Chapter 15 aims to promote your identity, autonomy and being reflective in a professional context. It highlights the need for engaging in continuous professional learning. It offers models to facilitate reflection. It emphasises the need for teachers as researchers. One of the sections deals with research in education at UG, PG/MA and PhD/EdD levels and explains the process of research. A section considers the areas of potential research in RE. An invitation is extended to you to join and contribute to the ever-growing RE research community.

The book consists of vignettes. These are insider narratives of student teachers and a reflection of the conception of their identity and subjective lived experiences elicited as part of their journey into teaching and RE subject leadership. Self-knowledge is useful for teachers as it unlocks the opportunities to shape and re-shape what teachers know about themselves as learners and what they might learn about their profession and subject. These should stimulate discussion and act as a catalyst for reflection. There are some viewpoints from experts in the field of RE to inspire you to take these as models for you to position yourself concerning some of the issues in RE and its teaching. Extracts have featured to engage you deeply with the material and to present a critical perspective of some issues. These can be used for discussion and reflection independently or with your peers and to relate these to your own positionality in regards to the subject. Case studies and reflections offer insights, depict examples and represent key ideas and practice to help you develop a nuanced understanding of the aspect under consideration.

Historical and contemporary RE

1

Yesterday, today and tomorrow

Introduction

Religious Education (RE) is facing a huge challenge as a subject when contextualised in the operative formal curricula in schools and within its own legal and structural situation as evident in current debates, many of which are a legacy of its history. Therefore, you need to reflect and be aware of its history to gain a nuanced understanding of RE. This chapter attempts to answer a question, often asked by students and teachers alike, 'Why is RE like this'?

One of the purposes of sketching the outline of this journey is to demonstrate the problematic nature of the subject, its uniqueness and its challenges, rather than being an apologia; it highlights the fact that the subject has not remained stagnant but has evolved, albeit in different ways, from being faith-based to an educational endeavour. It will also assist you to be better informed and use this as a basis to critically evaluate the proposed way forward for RE. Current RE in schools has resulted from long-standing issues as well as a consequence of present-day government policy. Therefore, to move the subject forward, Freathy and Parker (2015) urged all stakeholders to look more closely at both changes and continuities in the subject's past and the contexts in which they occurred.

The subject has been described as the most ecological subject on any curriculum because it changes and adapts to different times and places (Stern 2018:3). This is seen in Box 1.1. It has also been responsive and influenced by current and past events to serve sociopolitical and cultural purposes. The reason for characterising it as ecological is that RE will change from place to place and time to time, while several school topics are considered more universal: the same in all places and, other than being updated by new discoveries, the same subject always.

BOX 1.1 THE ECOLOGY OF RE

RE has never been like that. Perhaps other subjects are changeable too, but RE seems to be the most variable. One religion or many? Non-religious ways of life or just religious? Children taught amongst other children of the same religion or mixed? Religious groups involved in creating the curriculum or not? Attempting to bring people into religion or not? Connecting religion to the personal lives of children or studying religions using the methods of the social sciences? Incorporating moral education or an alternative to it? Compulsory or voluntary, and/or with a parental opt out? Is the subject even called RE, or is it 'religious instruction', 'religious education', 'religious and moral education', 'religious studies', 'worldviews education', 'religious literacy', 'theology and philosophy', 'philosophy and ethics', 'beliefs and values', 'sophology', or something else? (Stern 2018:4).

Source: Stern, J. (2018) Teaching Religious Education: Researchers in the Classroom, Bloomsbury Academic, an imprint of Bloomsbury Publishing Plc.

DOI: 10.4324/9780429289743-3

Many students and teachers often ask why RE is like this. Understanding its peculiar characteristics requires a review of the historical development of this traditional subject. Understanding the historical tensions in RE is essential to assist any teacher, especially the RE teacher to navigate the nature and purpose of the subject (Lundie 2012:23). Importantly, to search for good RE means to critically examine the factors which have influenced and affected current RE. A major area of influence is government legislation, which is the focus of this chapter. You will read about how researchers, academics and practitioners have developed pedagogical approaches to teaching RE in the forthcoming chapters.

History of religious education

This section briefly outlines the history and the legislative origins of the subject in chronological order. You need to recognise that the subjects of the curriculum have been influenced by their history. However, Copley (2008), who thoroughly documented sixty years of the history of RE, stresses that RE has had multiple influences acting upon it. This includes its history, the particular national identity of the UK, the unique cultural and legal position of the Church of England, the experiences and views of senior politicians, the attitudes of the public to religion and the rapid social change over the decades (Copley 2008:1). However, the influence of one faith group, the Church of England, has been most profound and deep-seated (Gearon 2013; Parker, Allen and Freathy 2020:60–61). The historiography of RE presented in this chapter is selective. However, Freathy and Parker (2015:24) provide a detailed historical case study drawing upon previously unutilised published and unpublished documentary sources. Therefore, to fully understand the conclusions and recommendations contained within these and other publications, or why they became so influential, it is important to know and understand the legislative and policy context in which they were written. Thus, they recommend that researchers and practitioners should recognise the complex circumstances in which these publications were produced.

The 1870 Forster Education Act

The provision for Religious Instruction was written into the Forster Act of 1870. This legislation made the subject as secure as it could be. Watson and Thompson (2007:54) note that there was uncertainty as to whether Parliament was going to agree to it. Moreover, there were fears that legislation might remove it. Similar anxieties have emerged at several points in subsequent history, recently Chater and Erricker (2013) expressed anxiety about its future existence because of reformist educational policies.

In the 1931 Hadow Report, *The Primary School*, it is noted that for some syllabuses: 'The teaching of religion is at the heart of all teaching' (Hadow 1931:154). There was a conviction that religious teaching should be an integral part of national education. The statement of the 1938 Spens Report on secondary education was more cautious '… no boy or girl can be counted as properly educated unless he or she has been made aware of the fact of the existence of a religious interpretation of life' (HMSO 1938:208). It argued that the traditional form which that interpretation took in this country was Christian. The 1931 report reflected the fact that religion in Britain has always been closely linked with education (Watson and Thompson 2007:54). Thus, you see religion and education are intricately connected.

However, Erricker, Lowndes and Bellchambers (2011:7) question whether such an assumption should be made today. Nevertheless, Christian churches have continued to be at the frontline of schooling and education in this country (Parker and Freathy 2020). James and Stern (2019:23) emphasise that by 1744, the Society for the Propagation of Christian Knowledge had established 2,054 schools and from 1791, Roman Catholic churches began setting up schools; in the late eighteenth century the Sunday school system was established; and the early nineteenth century saw Church of England, Roman Catholic and Free Church organisations setting up Teacher Training Colleges. This was well before the state became involved in education.

Unsurprisingly, therefore, Christianity retains the focus of RE in the UK and the Church of England has been directly interested in shaping the nature of RE, its curriculum and provisions and worship in schools. This close relationship continues to manifest itself today and is one of the reasons for education and religion going hand in hand in this country. Moreover, the historic relationship between the Church of England and the state continues to have a profound influence over the education system. Successive legislation has protected the privileged status of Christianity in RE. The 1870 Act had provided the withdrawal clause from Religious Instruction, not so much to protect atheists as those Christians who found their children in a school belonging to a denomination that they did not support (Copley 2008:30). As a matter of practice, the withdrawal clause was agreeable to Roman Catholics and Nonconformists, because it protected their children from the proselytism of Anglicans, particularly in single school areas. Many among the denominationalists opposed it because it appeared to separate education *per se* from RE. On the other hand, it was supported by some – Anglicans and Dissenters alike – because it protected religious freedom (Parker, Allen and Freathy 2020:553).

The 1938 report, with its less 'confessional language', nonetheless found it difficult to envisage education without an understanding of religion (Watson and Thompson 2007:54). Religious Knowledge was thought of mainly as religious or moral education and Religious Instruction or 'Scripture' was only a part of RE. Spens emphasised the teaching of religion was not, and cannot be, examinable; except in teaching the Scripture provided a right principle was adopted. Those who believed the Bible to be 'an inspired record of a unique revelation' were expected to welcome the systematic study of the Bible as providing essential background for religion. Those who believed otherwise had to admit that Christianity had played the most important part in the development of our civilisation (Spens 1938:170). Thus, the Bible took centre stage as the basis of the structure of Christian faith and worship in schooling (Watson and Thompson 2007:54) and children were given a Bible (Erricker, Lowndes and Bellchambers 2011:7).

In the important *1870 Elementary Education Act* (the Forster Education Act), the government accepted responsibility for the education of the nation's children. The 1870 Act had not made Religious Instruction universally compulsory (Copley 2008:30). From the beginning, RE had been controversial and continues to be so, although its reason has changed and varied. As denoted in Box 1.2.

BOX 1.2 POLITICALLY CHARGED RE

In 1870, comparatively few would have disputed that Britain was a Christian country. Also, the Christian churches were instrumental in bringing about compulsory education. It made sense that if you were intending to educate all young people for the first time, education in their religious heritage was essential. But what sort of Christianity should be taught? There was no love lost between the Church of England (the Established Church) and influential non-conformist groups such as Methodists. The latter were instrumental in seeking the education of the poor and increasing literacy among the working classes, which was an important aspect of their seeking rights within an exploitative industrialised society. The right of children to be educated, rather than simply used as cheap labour in factories, provides the backdrop within which RE formed a part of the state education. Education in religion, as part of providing literacy to the population, was controversial because it was highly politically charged. The wider social context was one in which radical reformers such as Robert Owen, and new democratic ideals were pitted against the traditional hierarchical ordering of society. If you taught children

> religion in elementary (primary) schools, to what purpose were you doing it? Was it to produce orderly and compliant citizens who knew both the catechism and their place, or to empower young people through making them literate and aware of the powerful teachings to be found in scripture? The former dominated, but many feared the latter being a result (Erricker, Lowndes and Bellchambers 2011:7).

The churches were divided and there was anxiety that RE in schools would be used to 'convert' potential members towards their own branch of Christianity. It threatened to make impossible any teaching about religion in the increasing number of local authority schools (Cox 1984:18–19). The solution appeared in what became known as the Cowper-Temple clause which provided for compulsory Religious Instruction to be restricted to undenominational teaching, or none at all, in the 'county school' (board school). It stated that in board schools 'No religious catechism or religious formulary which is distinctive of any particular denomination should be taught in the schools' (Forster 1870:448), meaning that while teaching about Christian denominations such as Anglicanism and Methodism could take place, explicit teaching through a specific denomination would not. Thus, there would be no Hail Marys in a community school (James and Stern 2019:25). Moreover, from its inception the unique character of this subject in its English version was established, i.e. religion was seen as an essential component of public education. Lundie (2012:23) notes that this was unlike the Irish, Spanish or Norwegian education systems where the subject nurtures in the state religion. Schools that were supported by ratepayers' money were prohibited from using distinctive religious systems (Webster 2010:8). In brief, this seemed to settle the issue of what was *not* to be taught.

RE has been a part of the primary curriculum in England and Wales ever since public schooling began, but its role has changed. Elementary education was made compulsory under the 1870 Education Act, with arithmetic, basic literacy and RE subjects. It continues to be compulsory. The inclusion of RE among the compulsory subjects has been debated. In contemporary times, there is a debate, and some have questioned whether RE should be compulsory and if so, for what reason (Cush 2007; Erricker, Lowndes and Bellchambers 2011:70; White 2004; Wright 2004). White (2004) argued that religion does not deserve a whole curriculum subject to itself as it is of a minority interest in the twenty-first century. Cush (2007) notes that others think that RE could be provided in faith-based schools for the minority that is interested so that the schools for the majority could follow a secular citizenship curriculum (Jackson 2004). The compulsory nature of RE, from a practical point of view, presents its own predicaments. Some senior leaders and teachers reported that RE and organising its resources and timetables would be much more convenient if the compulsory status of the subject were rescinded (Conroy et al. 2013:53).

This historical context may be lost to the majority of primary school teachers. Simultaneously, secularisation has marginalised the importance of religion, which again makes its purpose unclear and its presence on the curriculum questionable, if teachers themselves are not religious. As a result, the subject is often badly taught and, to some degree, avoided or handed to a religious member of staff to manage it (Erricker, Lowndes and Bellchambers 2011:7).

The 1944 Butler Education Act

The political climate of the 1930s, when there was the increasing influence of totalitarian systems of belief – Nazism, Fascism and Communism, had a bearing on the subject. The Spens Report suggested that the solution lay in RE (White 2004:153). Concurrently, a firm association had been made between the Christian religion and the cause of democracy itself when the 1944 Education Bill was being debated. After the war, organised Christianity in Britain enjoyed a recovery. In those times, national leaders from church and state agreed on compulsory RI as a way of strengthening people's moral commitment and attachment to democracy. In addition to moving beyond denominational particularism in Religious Instruction, discussed above, the case for RE in state schools was influenced by the huge support among teachers (White 2004:153).

However, contrary to what was assumed later by many religious educators (Copley 2008), the 1944 Act had a concept of RE as well as religious instruction. The phrase 'religious education' was not a later invention but is present by name in the 1944 Act. RE in the Act is held to embrace Religious Instruction, i.e. the classroom subject, and also the whole-school act of worship at the start of the day (Copley 2008:30). Hence, there may be a need to distinguish between RE as a curriculum subject and RE, which incorporates worship (Parker and Freathy 2020).

Thus, the Education Act 1944 made Religious Instruction with its non-denominational character compulsory (Butler 1944). It also continued a dual system of schools affiliated to, and partially funded and controlled by Christian churches and County schools controlled solely by Local Education Authorities (LEAs) (Freathy and Parker 2015:7). It also laid out other statutory requirements for the subject. These requirements applied to county and voluntary schools and included the following:

- The school day should begin with Collective Worship.
- Religious Instruction shall be given in every county and every voluntary school.
- All pupils should be provided regular Religious Instruction which would be according to an Agreed Syllabus.
- Parents had the right to withdraw their children from worship and Religious Instruction.
- Teachers had the right to withdraw from worship and from teaching religion.
- An LEA had the power to constitute a Standing Advisory Council on Religious Education (SACRE) to advise the authority upon matters connected with the Religious Instruction.
- RI was subject to inspection.
- An LEA would give no direction as to the secular instruction to be given to pupils in attendance at a voluntary school so that there was no interference with the provision of Religious Instruction in the school.

Non-denominational teaching as envisaged in the Cowper-Temple clause of 1870 was retained (Copley 2008:31). Interestingly, the most peculiar aspect of the Act was that it did not state which religion or religions were to be taught (Cox and Cairns 1989:3). The Act does not specifically mention Christianity as the religion to be taught. However, it suggested that it was tacitly assumed that Christianity was the only faith that pupils were likely to encounter, the only faith about which they, therefore, needed to be educated (Cox and Cairns 1989:3). As such, the intended religion among legislators was Christianity (Cox and Cairns 1989:46) as reflected in all the syllabuses (Cox 1966:16). Copley (2008:32) suggests that at the time, the words Christian and religious were nearly synonymous in a way that is no longer the case. The agreement to include this clause was far from the satisfactory outcome – a state from which the subject would not recover unless the specific mention of Christianity is to be removed from the Act. It put RE back in time rather than moving it forward (Grimmitt 2000:12).

The government and the Christian churches were now publicly recognised as equal educational and financial partners. The content for RI previously being taught in schools fell under the guise of Moral Education and Christian Education. However, once the 1944 Act made RI compulsory, a syllabus was attached to it and with it inspection was made a requirement. Webster (2010:8) suggests that this top-down change was mainly due to the government's view that the provision of moral guidance was needed to counteract changing social values and the disintegration of the family unit, both directly resulting from the Second World War.

In 1944, there was a recognition that a syllabus of RI might be needed, which was appropriate for children from Jewish families (Watson and Thompson 2007:54). Thus, as can be seen from the above, first, schools continued to attribute significance to Christianity, and second, the subject, as far as possible, would respond to the needs of the children receiving it. Subsequent legislation accepted these two principles as discussed below (Watson and Thompson 2007:54).

As to the content of the syllabi, for most, it was Scripture since it was considered the starting point for many denominations. It also seemed to focus more on religious knowledge than on religious understanding. One of the significant shifts was the configuration of RI as an academic subject, which utilised multiple skills as in other subjects (Webster 2010). But the 1944 Act, retained from the 1870 Act (Copley 2008:31), had the provision for parents to be able to withdraw their children from taking part in any teaching which may have been from a denominational viewpoint which they did not share (Louden 2010). This presented itself as a contradiction. On the one hand, RI had been made compulsory, yet, at the same time, parents could still remove their child from RI lessons on religious grounds. This is commonly known as the 'Conscience Clause'. This clause appeared to undermine RI's academic and equal status with other subjects since a child even today could not be removed from other subjects of the National Curriculum (NC) (Webster 2010:6). Nevertheless, significantly, the effects of the 1944 Act were that RE became a classroom subject among other classroom subjects (Copley 2008:35).

During the mid-twentieth century, education authorities sought agreement among various religious and professional groups about what material should be covered in RI and, thus, began the development of the 'Agreed Syllabus', made mandatory by the law. As the only subject that had to be taught by law, this legal requirement meant that schools supported their pupils' spiritual development (James and Stern 2019:25). However, the provisions of the Education Act 1944 which remained in force were repealed by the Education Act of 1996 (Meredith 1996).

Developments in the 1960s

Sometime around the middle of the 1950s, educationalists disagreed regarding the content of RI. Those within the subject detected that the appeal of Bible-based Christian instruction was fading (Christopher 2020:85). The 1960s came to be regarded as a significant decade by historians of British dechristianisation, as there was a loosening of ties between Christianity, the churches and other cultural institutions that played a part in the perpetuation of Christian culture (Parker and Freathy 2011). Some argued that RI did not reflect the changing social values: RI was being taught as a way to instruct every child into the Christian faith, even if the child did not belong to the Christian faith. Nationally, there was a huge increase in the range of beliefs, religions, 'alternative spiritualities' and worldviews accessible to the majority of the population.

Towards the end of this decade, some LEA syllabi began to address the issue of 'ethnicity' by providing examples of plans that suggested methods that encouraged religious enquiry (Webster 2010:9). Moreover, the 1960s witnessed the development of more personal and social education, and child-centred learning became increasingly important. There was a decline in teachers of RE for Christian 'evangelism' and students desire to engage with questions of meaning (Christopher 2020:85). Consequently, the appropriateness of Bible-centred teaching came under scrutiny (James and Stern 2019:25). The issues of immigration and 'racial' integration also became highly significant stimuli for reconsidering the aims and content of RE as the ethnic and religious diversity of post-Second World War England had increased dramatically (Parker and Freathy 2011). It was argued from a sense of natural justice that immigrant children had just as much of a right to learn about their own faith(s) as the 'indigenous' children had to learn about theirs (which was assumed to be Christianity). It was also argued that the separatist approach of distributing pupils into religiously differentiated classes or schools was to be avoided because it might lead to increasing 'racial' tension (Grosvenor 1997; Parker and Freathy 2011).

Educators became intensely interested in developmental psychology of the likes of Piaget and Bruner, the publication of *Readiness for Religion* (Goldman 1965) and the Plowden Report (1967), both of which were mainly grounded in the work of Piaget. Significantly, slowly, education began to change from being the 'authoritarian imparting of facts which the teacher knew, and the pupils respectfully accepted' (Cox 1983:17) towards a child-centred approach. For example, the West Riding syllabus was created in 1966 which advocated thematic, child-centred teaching (Hull 1990).

The Fourth R – The Durham Report

The discussion of the content and pedagogy of RI was extended in the 1970s. There was concern that the subject was indoctrinatory and therefore morally questionable. The second concern was about developing RE in the context of education rather than religion, in the sense of religious nurture (Copley 2008:96). The Church of England Board of Education and the National Society commissioned a report, known as *The Fourth R*, to be published by the Commission on Religious Education in Schools in 1970. The commission considered the position of RI in schools (Webster 2010:9).

The report tried to show the complex historical and political background against which RE in the UK had developed and which had shaped its character. It also looked to consider Christian concern about education as a whole, not just RE. It argued for replacing the concept of Religious Instruction with Religious Education, and for retaining school worship as an essential component of 'religious education'. It wanted to see RE acknowledged on educational grounds, not merely on grounds of legal compulsion, admitting that the cultural climate was so different from that of 1944 (Copley 2008:97).

The commission had consulted widely with various religious leaders and Secular and Humanist societies (Parker and Freathy 2020). The Report recommended that at least two periods a week should be dedicated to RE. It also stressed that the role of the subject was not instruction into one faith, but an exploration of personal belief systems, and, thus, it would be part of the general education programme offered in schools. However, Webster (2010:9) notes that throughout the 1970s, there was opposition to this change in focus of RI in schools. Some argued that such teaching was not in tune with the requirements of the 1944 Act (Webster 2010:9).

The country had undergone considerable changes by the 1980s. So, unlike the 1970s, there was little controversy in the 1980s. The influential *Swann Report* of 1985 highlighted the importance of the child at the centre of RE and emphasised that they should be seen as a valuable resource (DfES 1985). It also considered the nature and purpose of RE and separate schools for Black, Muslim, Sikh and Hindu groups. It strongly favoured 'non-denominational and undogmatic' approaches to RE (Parker and Freathy 2020). The *Professional Council for Religious Education* was also created in 1985, it produced the *REToday* and *REsource* magazines for schools, and you will read about this in Chapter 14.

The 1988 Education Reform Act (ERA)

This provided the legal basis for the practice of RE in England and Wales (Conroy et al. 2013:65). As the only mandated subject in law before 1988 (White 2004), ostensibly, the current legal context for RE in England and Wales is based on the 1988 ERA (DES 1988).

The Act intended to shake up the education system making schools accountable to the taxpayer (Webster 2010). The basic requirements and much of the language of the 1944 Act were repeated. However, the most momentous change appeared to be in the renaming of the subject from Religious Instruction to Religious Education. The compulsory nature of RE and the right of withdrawal for parents continued and it affirmed teachers' refusal to teach RE (Conroy et al. 2013:65; Lundie 2012:23).

Further new demands included:

i   That any new syllabus for RE shall reflect the fact that the religious traditions in Great Britain are in the main Christian whilst taking account of the teaching and practices of other principal religions represented in Great Britain;

ii RE must not be denominational in the county (now 'community') schools, while making it clear that teaching about denominational differences is permitted (Conroy et al. 2013:66);

iii Standing Advisory Councils for RE (SACREs) *must* be established;

iv Further, SACREs were required to convene a statutory Agreed Syllabus Conference (ASC).

You will learn about SACREs in detail later. All these provisions were retained by the Education Acts of 1996, 1998 and 2010 (James and Stern 2019:25; Lundie 2012:23–24).

Following the 1988 ERA, the debate continued within the RE community and others about what it meant for a syllabus to acknowledge that Britain's religious traditions are 'in the main Christian'. Questions were asked about the way to decide the other 'principal' religions and how to 'take account' of them was debated. It also led to further questions being raised regarding – how many religions were to be studied? How much time was to be devoted to Christianity and how much to other religions? Should students learn about the traditions and customs of other religions, or are they expected to get personal insight from the teachings of each of the religions? (Lundie 2012:24). The eventual agreement between the lobbyist and government was seen to hold the balance of interest between the Christian lobby and those of other faiths (Grimmitt 2000:12). It was a compromise between those wanting to restore Christian confessionalism as a basis for RE and those mindful of the impact of such legislation in a multi-faith society. Lundie (2012:24) emphasised that this legislation was imposed, in part, as a recognition of the increasingly secular nature of British society and for the need of a multi-faith approach to RE, which rejected the implicit Christian faith formation of previous approaches. Thus, some argued that no syllabus would meet the requirements of taking account of other principal religious traditions represented in the UK unless it included the teachings and practices of Judaism, Islam, Hinduism, the Sikh faith and Buddhism (Hull 1989:61). On the other hand, some (Thompson 2004; Thompson 2007) regarded this as an undue departure from what is, on the face of it, legislation requiring RE to be in the main Christian.

The 1988 ERA introduced the NC. Before 1988, all schools determined their own curriculum; what they taught in English, maths and science was completely up to individual schools or teachers. The one exception was RE; maintained schools had to follow a Local Agreed Syllabus. This was an indication of the sensitivity at the time surrounding what should be taught to children about faith and religion. The content had to be agreed upon by the community and not just left to the individual teacher (McCreery, Palmer and Voiels 2008:2). At the time when the first NC was introduced, Parliament decided to maintain the status quo rather than set a NC for RE, a decision which some have since regretted. An unfortunate consequence of this local location of the syllabus is that RE is often side-lined in school because it is not in the NC (McCreery, Palmer and Voiels 2008:2).

Nevertheless, the unique position of RE in the school curriculum was safeguarded in law. It was not a foundation subject, and so it was not at risk of being taken out of the compulsory curriculum as other subjects were (at least in principle); nor did it, for the same reason, come within the provisions for assessment (Leonard 1988:17). This was seen by many as problematic. On the one hand, RE was compulsory and, as such, protected. On the other hand, as it sat outside the NC, it was not expected to have the structural requirements of the NC; thus, there was the anxiety of RE being marginalised.

Even though RE was not a subject within the NC and was not required by the 1988 ERA to conform to its framework of attainment targets, programmes of study and levels of attainment, it came under enormous pressure to do so. Schools in England and Wales had accommodated the assessment and standards-driven ideology in all the other curriculum subjects. Initially, the pressure to bring RE within this managerial style of learning stemmed from a desire to prevent the subject from being marginalised from the rest of the curriculum (Grimmitt 2000:10). In the Lords' debate during the ERA 1988, the churches had expressed deep concern that if RE were outside the NC it would be marginalised (Copley 2008:137).

Kenneth Baker (then Secretary of State for Education and Science) explained that RE had to be positioned alongside the NC because the churches did not want the content of RE to be decided by the National Curriculum Council (a secular body), who decided the content of the other subjects (Webster 2010:10). As every LEA had a different ethnic makeup, the churches wanted each LEA, with their SACREs, to decide the content of their individual curricula, which would be produced through an LEA syllabus. Although it was acknowledged that RE had status and made part of the basic curriculum, the churches were not satisfied, as they wanted it to be part of the NC (Copley 2008:137). The creation of SACREs was seen as raising the profile of RE and impetus for the creation of new syllabi and bolstering existing ones (Copley 2008:139).

The resulting Bill stipulated that since the country was 85 per cent, Christian, most of the content would be Christian-based; the other faith traditions would still be represented but would not be given as much time. The SACRE of every LEA would create and review the syllabus every five years; thus, the purpose of RE was related to the societal needs and makeup of each local authority. The right of withdrawal (the 'Conscience clause') of 1870 and 1944 was retained.

McCreery, Palmer and Voiels (2008:3) discuss three significant differences between the 1944 Act and the 1988 ERA. In the 1944 Act, religion in school was referred to as instruction whereas under the 1988 Act, it was changed to education. The circular 1/94, influential at the time, reinforced the idea that RE was education, and with the decree that Agreed Syllabuses *must not be designed to convert pupils or to urge a particular religion or religious belief on pupils* (DfE 1994:15).

Second, an Agreed Syllabus shall *reflect the fact that the religious traditions in Great Britain are in the main Christian while taking account of the teaching and practices of the other principal religions represented in Great Britain* (DfE 1994:45). Previously, the 1944 Act did not mention Christianity because it was assumed that RI would be Christian. However, the subsequent explicit reference to Christianity has probably been the most controversial aspect of the law. Chater (2018:78–79) considers this to be at the heart of impasse for the subject and its vulnerability. He questions the meaning of 'reflect the fact' in a statutory document and the content for RE being reflected by the religious demography of Great Britain alone and also what constituted as 'principal'.

Moreover, studies by Loukes (1961) and Goldman (1965) suggested that children were not understanding the subject matter and were finding it irrelevant. Consequently, from the early 1970s onwards there was a move away from Bible-based syllabuses of earlier years to syllabuses that prepared children for the understanding of religious concepts, and then, in later years, to syllabuses that embraced the increasingly multicultural society. Rather than being a sharing of one faith, some syllabuses became the examination of worldviews. The shifts brought about a backlash among those who were concerned that children were failing to understand the Christian culture and religious heritage and who feared that national identity would be lost. Their lobbying ensured that an explicit reference was made to Christianity in the new act of 1988. The justification for the predominance of Christianity was largely a cultural one rather than to do with RE (McCreery, Palmer and Voiels 2008:3). Even if Christianity ceases to be a majority religion, Chater (2018:80) suggests that there would still be historical and constitutional reasons for ensuing its place in the RE curriculum.

The third significant change was that the law made explicit for the first time that all children should learn about the other principal religions practised in Great Britain. It thus recognised and valued the increasing presence of people of non-Christian religions in the UK, an indication of a hope that knowledge and understanding would lead to mutual respect between members of different faiths (McCreery, Palmer and Voiels 2008:3).

Model Syllabi of 1994

Over time, in addition to legal statutes, various non-statutory guidelines for RE were published.

Changing social and political policy in areas such as community and 'race' relations, citizenship and community cohesion impacted RE. The 1990s brought an interest in promoting democratic citizenship in schools, which influenced RE (Jackson 2013:122). In 1993, an attempt was made to capture an overview of the general learning and teaching of RE. 98 out of 107 SACRE inspection reports showed that there was no equity of learning experience and provision of RE throughout the different LEAs (SCAA 1994). The main reasons for this included the loss of advisory teachers in RE or not having one; general funding cuts; shortage of specialist teachers and a general lack of awareness of the syllabus and its requirements (Webster 2010:10).

The principal religious groups advised the School Curriculum and Assessment Authority (SCAA) about appropriate teaching materials and themes emerging from their religions for the different stages of schooling. This consultation led to the development of two 'model' syllabuses for RE in 1994. One of these began with pupils' questions and the other with religious material. This signified two different approaches to teaching RE (James and Stern 2019:26). They offered knowledge across six religions. These syllabuses were the first expressions of any national content for RE; although non-statutory, they had influenced initial teacher training and agreed syllabuses (Brine and Chater 2020:22).

By 1994, the view that RE should consist of the study of six religions including Christianity became established, both in classrooms and in official circles. This view appeared to be approved by the government which published *Circular 1/94* (DfE 1994) and two 'Model' syllabuses by the School Curriculum Assessment Authority. These were meant to exemplify the good practice of what should be taught to pupils across the Key Stages. Model 1, entitled *Living Faiths Today*, followed the phenomenological tradition (SCAA 1994a). This was later seen as Attainment Target 1: Learning about religions. Model 2, *Questions and Teaching*, focused on religious beliefs and practice and had more of a focus on skills (SCAA 1994b), which later became Attainment Target 2: Learning from religions.

This reflected a further significant shift in the meaning of 'local determination' of the agreed syllabuses for RE, as this national determination and the representation of faith leaders, professionals and policy makers was akin to that at the local level but promulgated by a national body with responsibility for NC subjects (Conroy et al. 2013:67; Lundie 2012:25). The model syllabus was used by LEAs as a guide, as it had become apparent that RE provision varied from Authority to Authority. These two Attainment Targets, when taught together, encourage pupils to develop knowledge about different religions as well as exploring personal attitudes and beliefs. The models identified skills such as interpretation, reflection and empathy and encouraged a skills-based approach to learning (Webster 2010:10).

It has been suggested that these model syllabuses of the then Conservative government gradually tightened its hold on RE, despite the subject being outside influence of the Secretary of State for Education and a matter for LEAs to decide. It also explains how RE became a victim of ideological manipulation, religious domestication and further marginalisation from other curriculum subjects (Grimmitt 2000:11).

Education Act 1996

Unlike the current NC (DfE 2013), strangely, the revised NC of 1995 had not referred to RE. Nevertheless, the status of RE within the curriculum was retained. Section 352 of the Education Act 1996 reiterated the distinctive place of RE as part of the basic curriculum alongside the NC. RE was to have equal standing with the core and foundation subjects within the school (Editorial 1996). It continued to differ from the subjects of the NC in that it was not subjected to national prescription in terms of attainment targets and programmes of study. Such matters were left for the ASCs to recommend locally prescribed procedures for their LEA concerning attainment targets, assessment and programmes of study.

The landmark publication in 2004

The Department for Education published two non-statutory guidance on RE in 2004 and 2010. The former had far-reaching consequences for the subject than the latter.

The *Non-Statutory National Framework for Religious Education* (NNFRE) jointly published by the Qualification and Curriculum Authority and the Department for Education and Skills (QCA 2004) was an attempt to address some of the uneven provisions experienced by RE. It was designed to supersede and extend the 1994 SCAA model syllabuses, with a similar lay-out to the new NC of 1999, which recognised the distinctive contribution that RE makes to the school curriculum (DfEE 1999:19). It made progress explicit through the use of Level Descriptors and also emphasised the importance of assessment within the subject. Schools and RE professionals received this document favourably, as it brought greater clarification of some aspects. It had secured widespread support across the RE community and played an important role in shaping the development of agreed syllabuses although its impact on the faith sector was less clear. It was greeted with approval from all the professional associations and faith communities (Gates 2005). It had aims, objectives and skills-based assessment but it did not define questions of content and approach (Brine and Chater 2020:28).

LEAs differed on the content of their syllabus; however, on the whole, the impact of the NNFRE had been huge as most followed this guide to create, enhance or improve their syllabus, which formed the basis for RE curriculum planning in state schools. There had been a general trend towards reflecting two dimensions of RE identified in the RE Model Syllabuses which now appeared in the NNFRE (Erricker, Lowndes and Bellchambers 2011:23).

The purpose of the NNFRE was to guide ASCs; establish entitlement and standards and to promote continuity and coherence and public understanding (QCA 2004). This national guidance was welcomed as non-statutory support for the delivery of RE nationally, although it did not replace the statutory guidance of the locally agreed syllabi. The NNFRE was neither itself a syllabus nor was it expected to be used as such. It was a framework that needed to be expanded before it could be used to support the development of locally agreed syllabi. However, the NNFRE proved very influential and continues to inform aspects of RE in some local authorities.

Given contemporary debates in religion and worldviews, it is interesting to consider that whilst the NNFRE retained the overall emphasis on the study of six principal religions, with the study of Christianity advocated at each key stage, simultaneously, it recommended that there should be opportunities for all pupils to study other religious traditions such as the Bahá'í faith, Jainism and Zoroastrianism and secular philosophies such as humanism, 'to ensure that all pupils' voices are heard and the religious education curriculum is broad and balanced' (QCA 2004:12), although SACREs were not obliged to respond to its recommendations (Watson, 2010). However, the law determines that the content of RE should be 'religions', and legal precedent defines humanism as not being a religion (Jackson 2013:132).

Be that as it may, some felt that the NNFRE conceived the subject as being instrumental-ist, which took account of social reality and the context of religion seriously. However, along these lines, some questioned whether the form of RE recommended by the NNFRE actually contributed to social cohesion or exacerbated the alienation felt by some pupils from minority communities (Barnes 2012:2). Moreover, despite the local determination of RE remaining a legal reality, on some practical levels, the influence of the NNFRE furthered the trend towards central influence and control of the RE curriculum (Conroy et al. 2013:68). This was one way through which RE got itself captivated by political and religious alliance (Grimmitt 2000).

RE in English schools: Non-statutory guidance

The second guidance was the *RE in English schools: Non-statutory guidance 2010* (DCSF 2010) published to support the provision of high-quality RE in maintained schools in England. It targeted a wide range of audiences. It was issued because RE continued to be an important curriculum subject in its own right and made a unique contribution to the spiritual, moral, social and cultural development of pupils and supported the wider community cohesion agenda of the time.

It offered guidance about RE in the curriculum and the roles of those involved in the subject. It is important to note that it did not constitute an authoritative interpretation of the law, which is a matter for the courts. However, this guidance replaced elements of *Circular 1/94* that relate to RE and explained that RE is a distinctive but core part of the basic curriculum for maintained schools in England. It did not contain details of the content for RE; rather it focussed on providing checklists, case studies and links to relevant websites for designing and teaching RE (DCSF 2010:4).

Several important changes had taken place since the 1994 and 2004 publications, which prompted this new guidance. The *Every Child Matters* agenda (HMSO 2003) and the *Children's Plan* (DCSF 2007) placed increased emphasis on personalisation and the development of the whole child. New types of schools came into existence, such as academies, and provision for children's early years had been extended. Following the first Jewish minority faith schools to open in the state sector, since 1997, Muslim, Sikh, Hindu and new Jewish voluntary-aided maintained schools were established. The curriculum was also less prescriptive, and schools had the flexibility to provide more coherent and integrated cross-curricular learning experiences to complement discrete subject teaching tailored to the needs of their pupils and community.

Thus, in practice, this meant that subjects such as RE, history or citizenship could be taught discretely but also together within a humanities framework. Some schools could choose to focus on intensive teaching of RE in particular years. Consequently, individual subjects might not have featured in the curriculum under their traditional names or indeed be taught always in discrete subject areas (DCSF 2010).

However, in RE, while schools were free to decide when and how subjects were taught and how much time was spent, they remained responsible for implementing the legally required syllabus or their individual one and for monitoring pupils' progress. Significantly, it positioned RE in the wider context of the rich heritage of culture and diversity of the UK. In an era of globalisation and an increasingly interdependent world, it is acknowledged that religion and belief for many people form a crucial part of their culture and identity (DCSF 2010).

Moreover, religion and beliefs became more visible in public life locally, nationally and internationally and the impact of religion on society and public life was constantly brought to public attention through extensive media coverage. The rapid pace of development in scientific and medical technologies and the environmental debate continued to present novel issues which raised religious, moral and social questions. The Internet was enabling learning and participation in public discussions of issues in revolutionary ways (DCSF 2010:5–6).

The period between 1993 and 2010 has been considered the 'golden age' with national developments and local and national bodies. However, the weaknesses of RE such as the confusion of its purposes and its statutory oddness were not resolved in those good years (Wintersgill and Brine 2016:264; cf. Castelli and Chater 2018:18). Moreover, the non-statutory status of all national RE documents has allowed variant practice and a lack of national coherence to become normal over time (Brine and Chater 2020).

Summary

Currently, the subject in primary schools is known as Religious Education. RE occupies a unique position within the curriculum of state schools in England. RE does not have a NC of its own. It is positioned outside of the NC, but part of the basic curriculum. It is a statutory subject supported by non-statutory guidance. All schools must make provision for RE for pupils aged 5–18. Parents have a right to withdraw their child from all or part of RE lessons and teachers likewise.

In maintained schools, the Local Agreed Syllabus is the statutory framework. In state-maintained schools without a religious character, RE must not be provided through any catechism or formulary, which is distinctive of a particular religious denomination. However, in state-maintained schools with a religious character, RE can be provided by the tenants of the designated faith. The RE in Free Schools and Academies will be determined by the school's funding agreement. There is no requirement in independent schools for RE *per se*. However, there are requirements in their standards for pupils to be taught about religions and belief systems. Special schools should provide RE as far as is practicable by following their locally agreed syllabus (LAS). RE must reflect the fact that the religious traditions in Great Britain are in the main Christian, whilst taking account of the teaching and practices of the other principal religions and non-religious traditions represented in Great Britain. RE is to be educational rather than indoctrinatory.

EXAMINING THE LEGAL REQUIREMENTS OF RE

The focus of this section is to explore the relationship of RE with the NC and explain the details of the structure and operative matters of SACRE. This discussion also covers some of the reasons for there to be an LAS, what you would expect to find in a typical one, visions and missions. It is often perceived that LAS is prepared in silos by people with self-interests. A critical section of how an LAS is produced will offer a nuanced alternative perspective. The closing section considers the status of RE in the different types of schools.

What is the status of RE?

Since 1944, all schools have had to teach RE to all pupils on roll except for those withdrawn from the subject at the request of their parents. Therefore, the teaching of RE includes school pupils in Reception classes as well as those in the sixth form (DCFS 2010).

Thus, it is a requirement of those responsible for running schools in England to ensure that all pupils receive their statutory entitlement to RE throughout all years of compulsory education unless withdrawn by their parents or they withdraw themselves, should they be aged 18 or over. This also means that all schools must teach RE at all key stages. It also makes RE a necessary part of the basic curriculum for every child. The teaching of RE contributes to delivering a 'broad and balanced' curriculum. However, schools are not obliged to provide RE to children who are under compulsory school age (DCSF 2010:10). Therefore, the compulsory requirement to teach RE does not apply to all nursery classes. Importantly, the law requires special schools to ensure that every pupil receives RE as far as is practically possible.

What is the nature of the RE that I have to teach?

In law and in practice, it is important to remember that the RE you teach and the syllabus you use should not seek to convert or urge a particular religion, belief or worldview on pupils in maintained schools. Significantly, the syllabus should not be produced in such a way as to proselytise or indoctrinate pupils in faith, worldviews, non-religious traditions or secular philosophies either. However, some schools with a religious character will prioritise learning about and from one religion. Nevertheless, all types of schools must recognise the diversity of the UK's population today and the importance of learning about its different religions and worldviews, including those with a significant local presence (REC 2013:12)

What is the relationship between RE and the National Curriculum?

Having discussed the status, nature and religious traditions and worldviews which can be taught in RE, the next section explains the crucial question of the relationship between RE and the NC, which is often confusing to many a trainee, as reflected by these reactions.

> It is standard practice to have a national curriculum for all the subjects. Therefore, I assumed that religious education also had a national curriculum.
> Since teachers need guidance so that they can teach. I thought there should be a NC for RE as well.

> There is one for all subjects so why not one for RE.
>
> No, I'm really shocked.

Moreover, the study by Dinham and Shaw (2015) found that one-third of parents in their study did not know that RE is not in the NC.

The NC states that all state schools are required to make provision for a daily act of Collective Worship and must teach RE to pupils at every Key Stage (DfE 2013:5). The appearance of these statements within the NC might create an impression among some student teachers that RE is *in* and *part* of the NC. Therefore, it is crucial for you to understand that whilst RE is a statutory subject across all Key Stages including in primary schools, it is not a subject *of* the NC. It is positioned outside the NC but exists as a constituent of the basic curriculum for all pupils, except for those withdrawn by their parents. Thus, RE must be taught alongside other curricula in operation in the school. In addition, unlike the NC subjects, RE is not subject to nationally prescribed purposes of study, aims and assessment arrangements, although it is subject to inspection.

RE is local unlike the National Curriculum

An LAS is a statutory syllabus for RE recommended by an ASC for adoption in a Local Authority. Thus, the NC operates at the national level while RE is administered at a local level. Each Local Authority has the responsibility for the production, adoption, implementation and review of their LAS, which sets out what pupils will be taught. A student reflected:

> It should stay local because different areas have different religions so it does not make sense to give everyone a general RE syllabus unlike history.

The Standing Advisory Council on RE (SACRE)

Every Local Authority must have a SACRE by law. A SACRE is a permanent body set up by a Local Authority. In essence, the role of a SACRE is two-fold: to advise the Local Authority on matters connected with acts of Collective Worship in community schools and on the RE to be given in accordance with an agreed syllabus. However, within its broader remits, it can also require the LA to review its current agreed syllabus. Concerning acts of Collective Worship, a SACRE must consider applications made by a head teacher that the requirement for Collective Worship in maintained, or community schools to be wholly or mainly of a broadly Christian character shall be removed and not apply to the Collective Worship provided for some or all the pupils or students at that particular school.

Moreover, within its broader role, a SACRE supports the effective provision of RE and Collective Worship in schools and monitor and review RE in their authority. Local authorities have the choice to decide what matters they wish to refer to their respective SACREs. Nevertheless, the 1988 ERA (HMSO 1989:8; Plater 2020:56) expected that the advice could include particular methods of teaching, the choice of teaching material and the provision of training for teachers. To support SACREs, the All-Party Parliamentary Group (APPG) recommended that LAs should ensure sufficient resources are made available to them so that SACREs provide high-quality RE support, monitor the quality of the provision and staffing of RE and develop networks to share good practice in RE (APPG 2013).

The Church of England has a stronghold on SACRE. It is given, as of Right, one committee in every SACRE. It has more direct political influence over the nature of RE in legislation than any group of professional religious educators (Copley 2008:3; Selway 2020). Despite the recommendations of the NNFRE (QCA 2004) that RE should address non-religious life stances, Humanists are not permitted to sit, as of Right, on Committee A (although they may be co-opted and sometimes are) (Conroy et al. 2013:58). An academy or group of academies can be represented through co-option onto the local SACRE or any SACRE if all parties are in agreement (DfE 2012). There are four committees of SACRE:

A   Christian denominations as such other religious and religious denominations as, in the authority's opinion, will appropriately reflect the principal religious traditions in the area.

B   The Church of England.

C   Teacher associations.

D   The Local Authority.

Role of SACRE

In the previous chapter, reference was regularly made to SACRE. In this section, details are provided about what it is, who is involved in it and what its role is. A SACRE exists to:

- determine the content for RE for their respective local maintained schools and have it reviewed every five years
- advise on matters of Collective Worship in maintained schools and RE
- advise on methods of teaching, choice of materials and training for teachers in RE
- assist with any complaints about RE or Collective Worship in schools
- publish an annual report on any action the SACRE has taken and any advice it has given
- consider requests from schools made by a head teacher following consultation with the governing body to allow some or all pupils to take part in Collective Worship that is not wholly or broadly Christian
- monitor the achievement, attainment and standards of RE in their local schools

What is an Agreed Syllabus Conference?

A further point for clarification is being included here. You may hear teachers and others declare that the Agreed Syllabus for RE is produced by a SACRE which is set up by each Local Authority. In as far as saying that a Local Authority has the legal responsibility for ensuring that an agreed syllabus is available, it would be correct to say so. However, there is a common misconception to address. Some think that a SACRE produces the syllabus. In reality, a SACRE appoints a committee from its members and others to produce the syllabus. This is called the ASC. It is this ASC that produces and recommends an agreed syllabus to the SACRE and then the SACRE recommends it to the local council (DCSF 2010:13).

For preparing an agreed syllabus for RE, every Local Authority must convene an ASC at least every 5 years to produce or revise an LAS. An ASC is a separate legal entity from a SACRE and, although common membership is permissible, it must be separately convened. The ASC must have the same four-committee structure as the SACRE but may draw in further expertise to carry out its task. However, unless and until the four committees and the full council of the local authority approve the syllabus, there can be no 'agreed' syllabus for schools in that region (Plater 2020:56).

The ASC produces and recommends an agreed syllabus for RE that meets fully the requirements of the 1988 ERA and is educationally sound. An agreed syllabus is deemed educationally sound if it meets the legislative requirements. It is noteworthy that only an ASC may recommend an agreed syllabus, and its recommendations must be unanimously agreed, otherwise the Secretary of State may be involved (DCSF 2010:13; Freathy and Parker 2015:8).

Each committee has a single vote no matter how many people belong to it. Any one group, therefore, holds a power of veto on all major decisions of the SACRE (Plater 2020:56).

A SACRE may also include co-opted representatives from another interested group or a religious educational specialist. However, co-opted members do not have voting rights. On any question to be decided by a SACRE, the groups each have a single vote. Decisions within a group about how a vote is to be cast do not require unanimity. A majority within each committee decides how the committee's single vote will be cast. This applies equally to the ASC, or to any sub-committee it may appoint (Northumberland 2016:12). That said, others contribute to and inform the deliberations that take place when creating a syllabus.

Why is there a locally agreed syllabus for RE?

LAS initially came into existence in the 1920s as a response to the problems encountered because of arguments for what could, and could not be taught (Watson and Thompson 2007:212). Nevertheless, it is the case that permissive legislation is likely to create diversity and, indeed, one of the main reasons for local determination of RE in England and Wales has been the need for it to be responsive to local situations. Agreed syllabuses have in the past allowed a certain degree of latitude to take account of the interest of both teachers and pupils (Watson and Thompson 2007:213).

You learnt earlier that the development of a syllabus for RE was controversially decentralised to Local Authorities by law (Copley 2008:134–146). In addition to this historical and legal basis, you might as well ask what factors are considered when syllabuses are prepared.

The Lancashire one, for example, parallels the four main purposes of the NC (Lancashire 2016:8–9). First, to establish an entitlement so that their syllabus secures for all pupils, irrespective of social background, culture, race, religion, gender, differences in ability and disabilities, entitlement to learning in RE. Second, to establish standards explicitly for all concerned. Third, to promote continuity and coherence so that it facilitates the transition of pupils between schools and phases of education. Fourth, to promote public understanding of, and confidence in, the work of RE in schools.

In addition to these educational aspirations, other factors are also taken into account including legal requirements, local and national factors, the age, aptitude, ability and experiences of pupils, whether they come from religious or secular backgrounds. Some take into account the views of the local community, including parents and educational experts. Moreover, some also consider matters related to quality, rigour, challenge, assessment, progression, support and resources. In others, pedagogical principles and theoretical perspectives also feature (Norfolk 2019) while the likes of Northumberland (2016) and others use the REC (2013) model to shape their content and units of work.

What will I find in a locally agreed syllabus?

Some LAS provide detailed material for the subject. This can be particularly useful for those who are non-specialists. It is therefore beneficial to be aware of the content of some of these syllabi to assist you to deliver high quality RE. Some exemplary content is shown in Table 1.1.

What are their visions and missions?

Unlike the NC, where there is one vision and mission for the whole country (except for Academies and Free Schools), each Local Authority has a different philosophical and educational standpoint in designing its syllabus. Moreover, the stronghold of these committees lies in and is represented by many religious groups, whom each conceptualise the teaching of RE in their way. For some, this perspective is informed by their religious traditions or otherwise. It is important to recognise this diversity.

Table 1.1 Exemplary content in a locally agreed syllabus

RE and assessment	Standing Advisory Council on RE	Subject content
RE in the EYFS	RE and spiritual, moral, social and cultural development	RE in different type of schools
Context for RE	Models of curriculum provision	SEND and RE
Withdrawal from RE	Legislative framework for RE	Inspection
RE in the school curriculum	KS1 RE Programme of Study	Glossary
Subject knowledge guidance	KS2 RE Programme of Study	Planning process
RE Attainment Targets	KS3 RE Programme of Study	Breadth of RE
Curriculum time	KS4 RE and for students aged 16-19	Mission statement
Long, medium and short term plans	Developing knowledge, skills and attitudes in RE	

To illustrate, consider the following aims:

■ To know about and understand a range of religious and non-religious worldviews by learning to see these through theological, philosophical and human/social science lenses.

■ To express ideas and insights about the nature, significance and impact of religious and non-religious worldviews through a multidisciplinary approach.

■ To gain and deploy skills rooted in theology, philosophy and the human/social sciences engaging critically with religious and non-religious worldviews (Norfolk 2019:5).

The Cornwall Agreed Syllabus Conference compared six English LAS and found that local authorities in stating their aims adopted a range of approaches.

In their earlier syllabuses, Cornwall themselves had established a personal and 'the whole child' aim, based on the Children's Act 2004 and Every Child Matters agenda: 'The aim of religious education is to help pupils to be healthy, to stay safe, to enjoy and achieve, to make a positive contribution and to achieve economic wellbeing' (Cornwall 2005:8).

Gillard (2001) examined twenty-three syllabuses (1973–1987) between the major Education Acts of 1944 and 1988. The aims shown in Table 1.2 were either explicitly stated or mentioned within the syllabus. He noted that although the words 'religion' and 'religious', appear the content usually refers to one or more religions.

Other local authorities had developed their aims around the ERA 1988. They defined it as promoting the spiritual, moral, social and cultural development of pupils and preparing them for the opportunities and responsibilities of adult life. The Birmingham syllabus, for instance, had stressed the SMSC development dimensions. RE emphasised personal education and transformation rather than the study of religious traditions *per se*, the latter was merely a means to realising the former overarching aim for the subject (BCC 2007:1). Perhaps this was a reflection of Grimmitt's focus on RE for human development (Grimmitt 1987). Moreover, Plater (2020:61) notes that the Cornwall study shows that other syllabuses tend to prioritise 'personal search' rather than personal transformation as the major purpose of RE, sometimes emphasising aspects of the study of religion as the means to this end, and sometimes identifying the promotion of SMSC development as the major emphasis. Following this analysis, Plater (2020) concludes that most agreed syllabi are very imprecise in stating their intentions for the subject, and, where this is done, there is little agreement between authorities. When the epistemological foundation of RE demonstrates such vagueness and confusion, Chater (2018:74) argues that the difficulties of compliance are magnified, since the law requires schools to teach RE but has nothing clear to say about why. Consequently, this vagueness invites scepticism about the value and viability of RE.

Table 1.2 Some aims of RE between 1944 and 1988

Aims	No of syllabuses
To explore, understand and/or respond to the attitudes, beliefs, experiences, key ideas and practices of religion (or of 'others')	23
To help pupils to form their own beliefs, commitments and judgements, and to find ultimate meaning and values	17
To appreciate Christianity and the Christian tradition	15
To explore world religions and to understand living in a multi-faith society	13
To foster reflection and search	11
To understand the distinctive nature and the source of religion	10
To appreciate the contribution of religion to moral, personal and social issues and practices	8
To contribute to the individual's educational development	3
To appreciate the nature of evidence and/or a balanced viewpoint in the study of religion	2
To help pupils to continue in their own beliefs	2

How do schools use a locally agreed syllabus?

Maintained schools must use their LAS and are inspected on it. However, this does not mean that schools do not have the freedom and flexibility in implementing and organising their syllabus. Some SACREs encourage schools to use models of delivery, which best suit the needs of pupils in their respective schools, whilst meeting the statutory requirements of the syllabus. In some cases, encouragement is also provided to schools to contribute to cross-curricular dimensions of the wider curriculum through RE. The idea of the syllabus permitting flexibility for certain material to be supplemented is enshrined in law even today (Watson and Thompson 2007:212).

How is a locally agreed syllabus produced?

Each Local Authority must produce its own syllabus as discussed above. You would expect, therefore, to be one for each of England's 150 or so local authorities (Plater 2020). However, in practice, you will notice that this is not always the case. All locally agreed syllabi result from some kind of collaborative work. In London, there is one syllabus for several boroughs. For example, after researching a range of syllabi, the ASC of London Borough of Hammersmith and Fulham schools decided to adopt, with minor changes, the Agreed Syllabus of the City of Westminster, which in turn was adopted from the Agreed Syllabus for Hampshire, Portsmouth and Southampton (Hammersmith and Fulham 2014). It is interesting to know that they took this action because the vision of the Tri-borough Children's Services programme was to combine services to tackle common problems, improve people's lives, achieve the best outcomes, protect their high-quality provision, improve effectiveness and reduce costs. This model also allowed close collaborations and joint training to take place, notwithstanding the fact that all these boroughs reflect a similar diversity (Hammersmith and Fulham 2014).

Similarly, the new *Manchester Agreed Syllabus for Religious Education 2016–2021* resulted from an association of five other Greater Manchester authorities, partnering with Tameside, Trafford, Stockport, Salford and colleagues from *RE Today* (RE Today 2016). Furthermore, the SACREs of Coventry and Warwickshire decided to work together and agree on a syllabus, which promoted good, effective and thought-provoking RE across both city and county. A syllabus that both builds bridges and engages with the aim of peace and reconciliation as pupils explore matters of faith, spirituality, religious community and moral issues (Coventry and Warwickshire 2017).

Other SACREs, to keep abreast of contemporary developments, integrate and make relevant changes whilst revising their Agreed Syllabus and use significant reports published since their last review. For example, they use reports such as *RE: The Truth Unmasked* (APPG 2013); *RE: Realising the Potential* (Ofsted 2013); the guidance on *Promoting Fundamental British Values as part of SMSC in Schools'* (DfE 2014); *A New Settlement: Religion & Belief in Schools* (Clarke and Woodhead 2015; Clarke and Woodhead 2018); *RE for Real* (Dinham and Shaw 2015); *Living with Difference* (Woolf Institute 2015) and Ofsted reports and frameworks.

Thus, you can observe cross-fertilisation among some syllabuses and the mutual interest and partnership work that exists between many Local Authorities. It also demonstrates that some SACREs ensure that their syllabi are not static but embrace innovation, research findings and incorporate current affairs and the wider social and political developments within and about the subject. That is not to suggest that differences within these authorities and across others are absent. Still, it is significant to recognise the input provided by 'external' people and the impact of other reports in the creation of a local syllabus.

Recently, concern has been raised that key players who support the subject have increasingly assumed control over the subject and moulded it to suit their vision and that opportunities for major reform are being used to reshape RE in a more Christocentric way by pushing for a narrowing of study that promotes more distinctively Christian ways of studying religion. Moreover, some SACREs are being used as a vehicle to disseminate syllabuses that are designed to suit the purposes of the Church of England rather than plural and predominantly non-religious society (Selway 2020:3).

Who contributes to a locally agreed syllabus?

It is a misconception to think that locally agreed syllabi are exclusively prepared by an ASC since the process involves many interested parties whose advice is sought and expertise solicited through consultation with academics, researchers and experts in the field of RE.

In some cases, valuable contributions to the review process and the development of the syllabus are taken from best practices among classroom practitioners and with extensive consultation with schools and faith communities. Some trial and test their content in classrooms before production (Hampshire, Portsmouth and Southampton 2016). Some schools provide examples of pupil work in RE which is included in the agreed syllabus. One SACRE petitioned teachers about what changes they would like to see when their agreed syllabus was revised (Northumberland 2016). Others use the expertise and experience of *RE Today Services* who are influential in developing many syllabi across the country. NATRE, county inspectors for RE and independent RE consultants also play their part.

Many of the syllabi are built on their previous ones, perhaps for continuity. Others incorporate new developments and content whilst retaining the core of the previous syllabus. However, this should not lead you to assume that they remain behind in addressing the concerns of the quality of RE and in keeping up to date with current thinking in pedagogies and wider developments in the education sector.

Other locally agreed syllabi are written in a way to be supportive of Academies and Free Schools so that they can fulfil the requirements of their Funding Agreements regarding the *A Curriculum Framework* for *RE in England* (REC 2013). Where such is the case, Academies and Free Schools are encouraged to adopt the LAS and take advantage of the resources, expertise and support that they provide (RE Today 2019).

Some ASCs feel that it was wise for them to use the *A Curriculum Framework for Religious Education in England* (REC 2013) to shape their statutory content so that the units of work in their existing agreed syllabus provide optional content to detail the statutory content (Northumberland 2016). However, some agreed syllabi continue to be rooted in the *Non-statutory National Framework for RE* (QCA 2004) and fulfil their legal requirements through it. In some cases, even the supplementary guidance for schools is given a thorough overhaul by removing out-of-date advice or enhancing the advice that is still relevant and fills any gaps that arise due to changes in government policy and/or refinements in the understanding of what constitutes best practice in RE (Northumberland 2016). The National Association of Standing Advisory Councils on Religious Education (NASACRE) provides support to local SACREs as well.

From the above analysis, it is evident that there is no single correct way of designing and delivering an LAS of RE. The crucial factor it seems is to ensure that outcomes of a local syllabus are met by the school which uses it. The quantity and quality of their content are non-uniform. Nevertheless, knowing this is particularly relevant to teachers, especially RE subject leaders, as these are resources, which can be utilised to understand the perspectives and thinking about RE, the varied pedagogies, and models of teaching used, the design of the RE curriculum, assessment practices and issues related to SEND. As a student teacher, this is equally relevant for your development and for accessing the valuable subject knowledge, concepts, skills and useful classroom-related information they contain such as curriculum plans, extensive support materials, including handbooks for primary and secondary schools and online resources.

Criticisms of the localised system for RE

The above discussion has made the unique and odd arrangements for RE clear for you. Unsurprisingly, this setup is criticised at several levels. Conroy et al. (2013:52) found that the deep localism manifested in England in the existence of SACREs is not replicated in any other subject. In RE, particular communities can directly influence curriculum content and pedagogy in a way that would not be considered appropriate elsewhere.

The structures that underpin the local determination of the RE curriculum have failed to keep pace with changes in the wider educational world. As a result, many local authorities are struggling to fulfil their responsibility to promote high-quality RE (Ofsted 2013:4). The system is reported to lack the capacity and effectiveness to provide improvement for RE (APPG 2013; Ofsted 2013), while many do provide effective models of curriculum planning (Ofsted 2013:13). Recently, it has been claimed that this system is collapsing as many and perhaps all local authority schools convert to academy status (Chater 2018:78).

Nevertheless, it is acknowledged that individual syllabuses can be good; however, the production of 151 versions of probably the same content, is phenomenally wasteful and introduces unfortunate variance in quality. Moreover, it is argued that it is educationally inappropriate to delegate 50% of the level of control to religious groups, who wish to represent themselves in a positive light (Chater 2018:78). The system underlines the anomalous nature of the subject and the exceptionalism accorded to RE and religious communities, even though the process and the products are sometimes wonderful and impressive, such special arrangements, it is claimed, diminish the status of the subject (Lawton 2018:28). Ofsted, in its final RE report, recommended that the DfE should review the current statutory arrangements for RE about the principle of local determination to ensure these keep pace with wider changes in education policy, and revise or strengthen these arrangements as appropriate (Ofsted 2013:7).

RE in different schools

You now need to consider the status of RE and the sources of its curriculum in the different types of schools. This is important as it enables you to understand the varied legal expectations placed on different schools and how these might influence the design and delivery of their RE curriculum.

Since 2000, there has been a gradual introduction of Academies and Free schools which can be 'sponsored' by businesses, individuals, churches or voluntary bodies, some contribute to the capital costs and even run the schools (West and Wolfe 2018). Since maintained schools must use an LAS and Academies and Free Schools are not controlled by a LA, what is the source of the RE curriculum for these and other schools?

The sources for the RE curricula taught in various schools across England may be categorised into three: An LAS for Local Authority schools, Academies and Free schools may choose their syllabus, and schools designated as faith/religious can either use the syllabus produced by their faith representative board or an LAS.

Community, foundation and voluntary-aided or voluntary-controlled schools without a religious character

These are schools under the control of a Local Authority. They are also known as Local Authority, state or community schools. These can be with or without a religious character.

Local authority maintained schools without a religious character must follow the LAS. The LA, the respective headteachers and governing bodies are required to ensure that RE is delivered in accordance with the agreed syllabus in all schools where the syllabus is legally binding.

Voluntary-aided schools with a religious character

The provision of RE in such VA schools will reflect the faith ethos and values, which are informed by their respective faith teachings, whilst allowing for the freedom of pupils to hold and express different beliefs. They may also admit pupils from varied faith backgrounds.

In these schools, RE is to be determined by the governors and in accordance with the provisions of the trust deed relating to the school or, where there is no provision in the trust deed, with the religion or denomination mentioned in the order designating the school as having a religious character. However, where parents prefer their children to receive RE in accordance with the LAS and they cannot reasonably or conveniently send their children to a school where the syllabus is in use, then the governing body must make arrangements for RE to be provided to the children within the school in accordance with the LAS, unless they are satisfied that there are special circumstances which would make it unreasonable to do so (Richmond 2020:52).

Foundation and voluntary-controlled schools with a religious character

Foundation schools and voluntary-controlled schools with a religious character must follow the LAS for all pupils. Parents may request the RE to be in accordance with the trust deed or according to the religious designation of the school.

RE in Academies and Free Schools

Academies are all-ability, state-funded schools. Some academies have a religious character (Richmond 2020:52). In law, Free Schools are Academies and are contractually required through the terms of their Funding Agreement with the Secretary of State to teach RE and provide Collective Worship. It is compulsory for them to provide every pupil with an RE curricular entitlement from Reception to Sixth Form except those whose parents exercise their right to withdrawal. The RE provision is based on what is set out in their Funding Agreement and there is no requirement on them to adopt the LAS of their local authority or that of another. However, they must adopt an RE syllabus (James and Stern 2019:26). They may use that of their local authority, or that of a different authority, devise it themselves or purchase a commercial one as long as their RE syllabus or curriculum meets their agreement. However, since many local syllabi tend to meet the needs of Academies and Free Schools, some have chosen to adopt them and, in so doing, a locally approved syllabus based on educationally sound principles for good RE becomes available in these schools just as it would in maintained schools.

For Academies without a religious character, this will be the LAS. In other words, it will be multi-faith and without any catechism or formulary distinctive to any particular religious denomination (DfE 2012). As for denominational academies with a religious character (Church of England or Roman Catholic, Muslim and most Jewish academies), this will be in line with the denominational syllabus. Some non-denominational academies with a religious designation (such as Christian) can use either the LAS or denominational syllabus, depending on the wishes of the sponsor and what is agreed by Ministers (DCSF 2010:15; Francis and Blaylock 2016; Richmond 2020:52). The APPG (2013:5) recommended that the DfE should require academies to use the LAS.

Recently, a parent complained about the failure of an academy to comply with its Funding Agreement with the DfE regarding the provision of RE which was being replaced by a combined life skills style programme. The complaint was upheld and the academy then offered RE on the curriculum as a distinct subject (NATRE 2020).

Private schools are not covered by any legislation on the curriculum (James and Stern 2019:26). Independent schools are entirely free of parliamentary legislation and may provide RE or not (Watson and Thompson 2007:212).

Responsibility of schools

This reflects a complex landscape of RE and ultimately shows the responsibility placed on schools to ensure that pupils' entitlement to RE is met. According to the *Religious Education in English schools: Non Statutory guidance 2010*, while schools are free to decide when and how RE is taught and how much time is spent on it, schools are responsible for implementing the LAS (whether the LAS or their individual one) and for monitoring pupil progress (DCSF 2010:2).

Inspection

The Office for Standards in Education (OFSTED) determines the effectiveness of the delivery of RE based on the LAS for local schools, even though RE is not subject to nationally prescribed purposes of study, aims, attainment targets and assessment arrangements. Where schools do not use an agreed syllabus, standards will be judged with the expectations set out in the RE Council's *Curriculum Framework for Religious Education in England* (REC 2013). It is to be noted that the continued changes in inspection arrangements mean that SACREs can no longer use inspection reports from individual schools as a basis for monitoring standards in RE. This places a greater responsibility on the agreed syllabuses to provide a clear benchmark for standards and achievement in RE (East Sussex 2017). The APPG recommended that Ofsted should require inspectors to report on non-compliance with statutory requirements and continue to monitor the quality of RE provision, through subject inspections (APPG 2013).

Summary

This section reiterates the non-proselytising nature of RE to be taught in local authority-maintained schools. It stressed that although RE is part of the basic curriculum, it is positioned outside the NC. Importantly, the syllabus for RE is determined at a local level. In doing so, you became aware of the responsibility and committee structure of the SACRE. A local RE syllabus is produced by an ASC for the adoption by the Standing Advisory Council on RE of a local authority. The chapter presented a rationale and criticism of this unique and odd arrangement as well. You have also discovered some of the contents found in an LAS. It made clear that the intentions, visions and missions of these LAS are ostensibly desperate with some similarities. It was highlighted that schools have some flexibility in using the material for RE as

---

BOX 1.3 VIGNETTE: A FLOURISHING COMMUNITY

I come from a Punjabi family. I have been raised as a Sikh. I have continued to follow the faith into my adult years. I attended multicultural schools in both primary and secondary school, which I thoroughly enjoyed. From a young age, teaching has always been something I wanted to do and that is why I opted to do a Primary Education Studies degree, which then led me to my PGCE. My sisters are all in the education sector and this has always inspired me. It is a demanding career but I think it is such a rewarding one also.

I chose RE as I have always had an interest in other religions and faiths as well as issues that are covered in RE which led me to take RE as a GCSE and A-level. I feel like from visiting various schools not much importance was put on RE even though in my eyes, living in the UK, it is one of the most important subjects. I think it is so vital to understand and accept various faiths. My main concern in teaching RE again is schools put it on the back burner. They will fit it into a timetable if they can and when rearranging lessons it is always the first that is dropped if lessons need to be cancelled. I want to be able to show and explain just how vital it is for our schools and children in our schools.

---

long as they fulfil the requirements of their LAS. You also discovered that there are many contributors including professionals in the development of an LAS. The landscape of RE becomes further complex when the syllabus requirements of RE in different types of schools are outlined. Ofsted inspection of academies will follow the same format as those of local authority-maintained schools. It is the responsibility of individual schools to ensure that they deliver the RE to which pupils are entitled (Box 1.3).

References

All Party Parliamentary Group (APPG) (2013) *RE: The Truth Unmasked: The Supply of and Support for Religious Education Teachers*. [Online] https://www.religiouseducationcouncil.org.uk/wp-content/uploads/2017/11/APPG_RE_The_Truth_Unmasked-FINAL-1.pdf (Accessed 05/12/2020).

Barnes, L. P. (2012) Entering the debate, in L. P. Barnes (Ed.) *Debates in Religious Education*, London: Routledge, pp. 1–9.

Birmingham City Council (BCC) (2007) *The Birmingham Agreed Syllabus for Religious Education*, Birmingham: Birmingham City Council http://www.faithmakesadifference.co.uk/

Brine, A., and Chater, M. (2020) How did we get here? The twin narratives, in M. Chater (Ed.) *Reforming RE*, Melton: John Catt, pp. 21–35.

Butler, R. A. (1944) *The Education Act 1944*, London: HMSO. [Online] https://www.legislation.gov.uk/ukpga/Geo6/7-8/31/enacted (Accessed 29/10/2020).

Castelli, M., and Chater, M. (2018) *We Need to Talk About Religious Education: Manifestos for the Future of RE*, London: Jessica Kingsley.

Chater, M., and Erricker, C. (2013) *Does Religious Education Have a Future? Pedagogical and Policy Prospects*, London: Routledge.

Chater, M. (2018) Why we need legislative change, and how we can get it, in M. Castelli and M. Chater (Eds.) *We Need to Talk About Religious Education: Manifestos for the Future of RE*, London: Jessica Kingsley, pp. 71–84.

Christopher, K. (2020) Don't panic, it's just change: A single educational aim for religion and world-views, in M. Chater (Ed.) *Reforming RE*, Melton: John Catt, pp. 83–90.

Clarke, C., and Woodhead, L. (2015) *A New Settlement: Religion & Belief in Schools*, Westminster Faith Debates.

Clarke, C., and Woodhead, L. (2018) *A New Settlement: Religion and Belief in Schools*, Westminster Faith Debates. [Online] http://faithdebates.org.uk/wp-content/uploads/2018/07/Clarke-Woodhead-A-New-Settlement-Revised.pdf (Accessed 15/11/2020).

Conroy, J. C., Lundie, D., Davis, R. A., Baumfeld, V., Barnes, L. P., Gallagher, T., Lowden, K., Bourque, N., and Wenell, K. J. (2013) *Does Religious Education Work? A Multi-Dimensional Investigation*, London: Bloomsbury.

Copley, T. (2008) *Teaching Religion: Sixty Years of Religious Education in England and Wales*, New Updated Edition, Exeter: University of Exeter Press.

Cornwall County Council (2005) *Agreed Syllabus for Religious Education 1995–2000*, Truro: Cornwall County Council.

Coventry and Warwickshire (2017) *Agreed Syllabus for Religious Education 2017–2022*. [Online] http://coventrycityofpeace.uk/wp-content/uploads/2017/11/Coventry-and-Warwickshire-Agreed-Syllabus-SACRE-2017-Extract.pdf (Accessed 14/11/2020).

Cox, E. (1966) *Changing Aims in Religious Education*, London: Routledge. [Online] eBook Published 2018 https://www.taylorfrancis.com/books/9780429032394

Cox, E. (1983) *Problems and Possibilities for Religious Education*, London: Hodder and Stoughton.

Cox, E. (1984) Agreed syllabuses, in J. M. Sutcliffe (Ed.) *A Dictionary of Religious Education*, London: SCM Press Ltd, pp. 18–20.

Cox, E., and Cairns, J. M. (1989) *Reforming Religious Education*, London: Bedford Way Papers/Kogan Page.

Cush, D. (2007) Should religious studies be part of the compulsory state school curriculum? *British Journal of Religious Education*, 29, (3), pp. 217–227.

DCSF (Department for Children, Schools and Families) (2007) *The Children's Plan: Building Brighter Futures*, Norwich: HMSO. Cm7280.

DCSF (Department for Children, Schools and Families) (2010) *Religious Education in English Schools: Non-Statutory Guidance 2010*, Nottingham: DCSF Publications. DCSF-00114-2010.

DfES (Department for Education and Science (1985) *Education for All: Final Report of the Committee of Enquiry into the Education of Children from Ethnic Minority Groups Under the Chairmanship of Lord Swann*, London: HMSO.

DES (Department for Science and Education) (1988) *Education Reform Act*, London: HMSO.

DfE (Department for Education) (1994) *Circular 1/94 Religious Education and Collective Worship*, London: DfE Publication Centre. [Online] https://assets.publishing.service.gov.uk/government/uploads/system/uploads/attachment_data/file/281929/Collective_worship_in_schools.pdf (Accessed 29/10/2020).

DfE (Department for Education) (2012) *Religious Education (RE) and Collective Worship in Academies and Free Schools*. [Online] https://www.gov.uk/government/publications/re-and-collective-worship-in-academies-and-free-schools/religious-education-re-and-collective-worship-in-academies-and-free-schools (Accessed 04/12/2020).

DfE (Department for Education) (2014) *Promoting Fundamental British Values as Part of SMSC in Schools: Departmental Advice for Maintained Schools*, Department for Education: Crown copyright. DFE-00679-2014.

DfE (Department for Education) (2013) *The National Curriculum in England Key Stages 1 and 2 Framework Document*, Crown Copyright. Reference: DFE-00178-2013.

DfEE (Department for Education and Employment) (1999) *The National Curriculum Handbook for Primary Teachers in England*, London: DfEE and QCA.

Dinham, M., and Shaw, M. (2015) *RE for Real*, Goldsmiths, UOL & Culham St. Gabriel's. [Online] https://www.gold.ac.uk/media/documents-by-section/departments/research-centres-and-units/research-units/faiths-and-civil-society/REforREal-web-b.pdf (Accessed 16/11/2020).

East Sussex (2017) *East Sussex RE Agreed Syllabus: Continuing the Journey*.

Editorial (1996) *British Journal of Religious Education*, 18, (3), pp. 130–132.

Erricker, C., Lowndes, J., and Bellchambers, E. (2011) *Primary Religious Education – A New Approach*, London: Routledge.

Forster, W. (1870) *The 1870 Elementary Education Act*, London: HMSO. [Online] http://www.educationengland.org.uk/documents/acts/1870-elementary-education-act.html (Accessed 28/10/2020).

Francis, D., and Blaylock, L. (Eds.) (2016) *Religious Education in Your Academy: Improving Religious Education in Academies and Free Schools*, Birmingham: RE Today Services.

Freathy, R. J. K., and Parker, S. G. (2015) Prospects and problems for religious education in England, 1967–1970: Curriculum reform in political context, *Journal of Beliefs & Values*, 36, (1), pp. 5–30.

Gates, B. (2005) Editorial, *British Journal of Religious Education*, 27, (2), pp. 99–102.

Gearon, L. (2013) *MasterClass in Religious Education: Transforming Teaching and Learning*, London: Bloomsbury.

Gillard, D. (2001) *Agreed Syllabuses 1944–1988: Changing Aims – Changing Content?* [Online] http://www.educationengland.org.uk/articles/10agreed.html (Accessed 15/11/2020).

Goldman, R. (1965) *Readiness for Religion*, London: Routledge and Kegan Paul.

Grimmitt, M. (1987) *Religious Education and Human Development*, Great Wakering: McCrimmon.

Grimmitt, M. (2000) (Ed.) *Pedagogies of Religious Education*, Great Wakering: McCrimmons.

Grosvenor, I. (1997) *Assimilating Identities: Racism and Educational Policy in Post 1945 Britain*, London: Lawrence & Wishat.

Hadow, H. (1931) *The Primary School*, London: HMSO. [Online] http://www.educationengland.org.uk/documents/hadow1931/hadow1931.html (Accessed 28/10/2020).

Hammersmith and Fulham (2014) *Living Difference*, Hampshire County Council/Portsmouth City Council/Southampton City Council. [Online] https://www.lbhf.gov.uk/sites/default/files/section_attachments/sacre_re_syllabus_final.pdf] (Accessed 14/11/2020).

Hampshire, Portsmouth and Southampton (2016) *Living Difference III*, Hampshire County Council/Portsmouth City Council/Southampton City Council/Isle of Wight Council.

HMSO (1938) *The Spens Report (1938) Secondary Education With Special Reference to Grammar Schools and Technical High Schools*, London: HMSO. [Online] http://www.educationengland.org.uk/documents/spens/spens1938.html (Accessed 27/10/2020).

HMSO (1989) *Education Reform Act 1988*, Volume 1/2. Reprint. [Online] https://www.legislation.gov.uk/ukpga/1988/40/pdfs/ukpga_19880040_en.pdf (Accessed 14/11/2020).

HMSO (2003) *Every Child Matters: Change for Children*, Norwich: HMSO. Cm5860.

Hull, J. M. (1989) Editorial: The content of religious Education and the 1988 Education Reform Act, *British Journal of Religious Education*, 11, (2), pp. 59–91.

Hull, J. M. (1990) Religious Education and Christian Values in the 1988 Education Reform Act, *Ecclesiastical Law Journal*, 2, (7), pp. 69–81.

Jackson, R. (2004) *Rethinking Religious Education and Plurality: Issues in Diversity and Pedagogy*, London, RoutledgeFalmer.

Jackson, R. (2013) Religious Education in England: The story to 2013, *Pedagogiek: Wetenschappelijk Forum Voor Opvoeding, Onderwijs En Vorming*, 33, (2), pp. 119–135.

James, M., and Stern, S. (2019) *Mastering Primary Religious Education*, London: Bloomsbury.

Lancashire (2016) 'SEARCHING FOR MEANING' Lancashire Agreed Syllabus For Religious Education (Revised 2016), Lancashire County Council: Lancashire SACRE.

Lawton, C. (2018) Time to abandon religious education: Ditching an out-of-Date solution to an out-of-Date problem, in M. Castelli and M. Chater (Eds.) We Need to Talk About Religious Education: Manifestos for the Future of RE, London: Jessica Kingsley, pp. 21–35.

Leonard, M. (1988) The 1988 Education Act, Oxford: Basil Blackwell.

Louden, L. M. R. (2010) The conscience clause in religious education and collective worship: Conscientious objection or curriculum choice? British Journal of Religious Education, 26, (3), pp. 273–284.

Loukes, H. (1961) Teenage Religion, London: SCM.

Lundie, D. (2012) Religious education in the United Kingdom and Ireland, in L. P. Barnes (Ed.) Debates in Religious Education, London: Routledge, pp. 22–51.

McCreery, E., Palmer, S., and Voiels, V. (2008) Teaching Religious Education, Exeter: Learning Matters.

Meredith, P. (1996) Farewell to the Education Act 1944, Education and the Law, 8, (3), pp. 189–190.

NATRE (2020) How a NATRE-Supported Parental Complaint Resulted in Improved Provision for RE at an Academy. [Online] https://www.natre.org.uk/uploads/Additional%20Documents/Academy%20Complaint%20timeline%202020%20-%20a%20case%20study.pdf (Accessed 30/11/2020).

Norfolk (2019) Norfolk Agreed Syllabus 2019: A Religious Education for the Future, Norfolk: Norfolk SACRE.

Northumberland (2016) Agreed Syllabus for Religious Education 2016, Northumberland SACRE: The Northumberland County Council.

Ofsted (2013) Religious Education: Realising the Potential, Manchester: Crown Copyright. Reference No: 130068. [Online] https://assets.publishing.service.gov.uk/government/uploads/system/uploads/attachment_data/file/413157/Religious_education_-_realising_the_potential.pdf (Accessed 05/12/2020).

Parker, S. G., and Freathy, R. (2011) Ethnic diversity, Christian hegemony and the emergence of multi-faith religious education in the 1970s, History of Education, 41, (3), pp. 381–404.

Parker, S. G., and Freathy, R. (2020) The Church of England and religious education, in T. Rodger, P. Williamson, and M. Grimley, (Eds.) The Church of England and British Politics Since 1900, Woodbridge: Boydell and Brewer.

Parker, S. G., Allen, S., and Freathy, R. (2020) The Church of England and the 1870 Elementary Education Act, British Journal of Educational Studies, 68, (5), pp. 541–565.

Plater, M. (2020) What is religious education for? Exploring SACRE member views, Religion & Education, 47, (1), pp. 55–76.

Plowden (1967) Children and Their Primary Schools Report of the Central Advisory Council for Education (England), London: HMSO.

QCA (2004) Religious Education: The Non-Statutory National Framework, London: Qualifications and Curriculum Authority. Reference: QCA/04/1336.

REC (Religious Education Council of England and Wales) (2013) A Curriculum Framework for Religious Education in England, London: The Religious Education Council of England and Wales.

RE Today (2016) Religious Literacy for All: RE Agreed Syllabus 2016–2021, Birmingham: RE Today Services 2016. [Online] file:///C:/Users/id105124/Downloads/Manchester_Agreed_Syllabus_abridged%20(3).pdf (Accessed 14/11/2020).

RE Today (2019) Derbyshire and Derby City: Agreed Syllabus for Religious Education 2020–2025, Birmingham: RE Today Services. [Online] https://schoolsnet.derbyshire.gov.uk/site-elements/documents/teaching-learning-and-school-governance/curriculum-and-assessment/derbyshire-and-derby-city-agreed-syllabus-2020-2025.pdf (Accessed 14/11/2020).

Richmond (2020) *Agreed Syllabus 2020 Religious Education in the London Borough of Richmond upon Thames*, London Borough of Richmond upon Thames.

SCAA (1994) *Analysis of SACRE Reports 1994*, London: School Curriculum and Assessment Authority.

SCAA (1994a) *Model Syllabuses for Religious Education, Model 1: Living Faiths Today*, London: School Curriculum and Assessment Authority.

SCAA (1994b) *Model Syllabuses for Religious Education, Model 2: Questions and Teachings*, London: School Curriculum and Assessment Authority.

Selway, C. (2020) *Understanding Christianity and the Study of Religions and Worldviews: How the Church of England Has Gained Control Religious Education*, London: National Secular Society.

Spens, W. (1938) *Secondary Education With Special Reference to Grammar Schools and Technical High Schools*, London: HMSO. [Online] http://www.educationengland.org.uk/documents/spens/spens1938.html (Accessed 28/10/2020).

Stern, J. (2018) *Teaching Religious Education Researchers in the Classroom*, London: Bloomsbury.

Thompson, P. (2004) *Whatever Happened to Religious Education?* Cambridge: The Lutterworth Press.

Thompson, P. (2007) Religious education from Spens to Swann, in M. Felderhof, P. Thompson and D. Torevell (Eds.) *Inspiring Faith in Schools: Studies in Religious Education*, Aldershot: Ashgate.

Watson, B., and Thompson, P. (2007) *The Effective Teaching of Religious Education*, Harlow: Longman. Second edition.

Watson, J. (2010) Including secular philosophies such as humanism in locally agreed syllabuses for religious education, *British Journal of Religious Education*, 32, (1), pp. 5–18.

Webster, M. (2010) *Creative Approaches to Teaching Primary RE*, London: Longman.

West, A., and Wolfe, D. (2018) *Academies, the School System in England and a Vision for the Future*, Clare Market Papers No. 23, London: LSE Academic Publishing. [Online] http://www.lse.ac.uk/social-policy/Assets/Documents/PDF/Research-reports/Academies-Vision-Report.pdf (Accessed 16/07/2021).

White, J. (2004) Should religious education be a compulsory school subject?, *British Journal of Religious Education*, 26, (2), pp. 151–164.

Wright, A. (2004) The justification of compulsory religious education: A response to Professor White, *British Journal of Religious Education*, 26, (2), pp. 165–174.

Wintersgill, B., and Brine, A. (2016) Government National Agencies for Inspection and Curriculum Development, in B. Gates (Ed.) *Religion and Nationhood: Insider and Outsider Perspective on Religious Education in England*, Tübingen: Mohr Siebeck, pp. 255–279.

Woolf Institute (2015) *Living With Difference: Community, Diversity and the Common Good*, Cambridge: The Woolf Institute.

2

Critiquing Religious Education post 2010

Introduction

The previous chapter enlightened you on the unique nature of Religious Education (RE) and how it is knotted in history and legislation. There have been several factors that have acted as major catalysts to spur the RE community into resolute action over the years. Bearing in mind that RE continues to enjoy a special protected status on the school curriculum as a compulsory subject, this chapter aims to engage you with the major publications, debates and initiatives related to RE from 2011 to 2020. The focus of this chapter is the recent re-invigorated enthusiasm and national activities following challenges and opportunities expressed about the subject. It brings to your attention the case for change and the proposed ways forward.

The period from 1994 to 2010 as you read in the previous chapter was a time when RE received attention and was active. Things were going well, although the underlying weaknesses were not attended to (Brine and Chater 2020:24). From 2010 onwards, several challenges were faced and calls for radical changes began to appear (Chater and Erricker 2013; Clarke and Woodhead 2015, 2018; CoRE 2018; Conroy, Lundie, Davis and Robert 2013; Dinham and Shaw 2015; Ofsted 2013; REC 2013a; Woolf Institute 2015). The overall effects of this have been to galvanise a unity of purpose amongst the RE community and to defend the subject (Parker, Freathy and Aldridge 2015). Lawton went further and argued that the subject in its current form could not survive as it had outgrown its legal, nominal and religious skin (p. 21) and suggested that the subject be known as Religious Studies because that has academic validity and should be the core of what goes on in these lessons (Lawton 2018:34).

Academies in the school system

Academies and Free schools, introduced in 2000, are directly funded by the government and are not run by the local authority. They have more control over how they do things than community schools and do not have to follow the NC. The subsequent expansion of the academies programme in 2010 led to a situation in which an increasing number of schools were not required to follow LAS for their RE teaching. Questions began to be raised about the need for SACREs. At the same time, the increase in free schools and academies led to more schools 'with a religious character' within the state system. For RE, this meant an increased diversity of approaches within state-funded schools (Dinham and Shaw 2015:2). In the same year, the funding for trainee teachers in RE was cut with the effect of increasing the proportion of non-specialist RE teachers, although the funding was reinstated in 2014, the bursaries were smaller than for the other three humanities subjects (Dinham and Shaw 2015:2). Recently, the government withdrew bursaries for secondary RE as the supply of people wanting to be teachers

DOI: 10.4324/9780429289743-4

rose because of the coronavirus for the 2021–22 academic year (NATRE 2020). Bursaries are important as they attract graduates to become RE teachers every year and they extend a career in RE teaching to people from a broader range of backgrounds such as criminology, history, law, philosophy, politics and sociology. They also indicate the position of the support from the DfE for the subject. Thus, the situation of RE worsened with the withering of local authorities under the pressure of academisation combined with under-resourcing (Woodhead 2018:8).

The 'new' National Curriculum

The Department for Education (DfE) after reviewing the NC in England published the new one in 2013 (DfE 2013). The objectives were many, including giving teachers greater professional freedom over the organisation and teaching of the curriculum and developing an NC that acts as a benchmark for all schools (DfE 2011). RE was not included as part of this important curriculum review and overhaul. Moreover, in another education policy, when the English Baccalaureate (EBacc) was introduced in 2010, which is a list of subjects used by the government to measure school performance in secondary schools, RE and other subjects were excluded from it, which led to a decline in RE provision in some schools (Ofsted 2013:4). Schools increasingly treated RE as a less significant subject and led to increased anxiety amongst RE teachers, who stood for its academic credibility in an attempt to persuade school leaders not to reduce the time given to it, or even to drop it all together (Cooling, Bowie and Panjwani 2020:15).

Nevertheless, the new NC stipulates that all state schools must teach RE and must publish their curriculum by subject and academic year online. RE continues to be part of the basic curriculum, although it is not prescribed in the NC (DfE 2013). Nevertheless, RE follows the NC's remit that every state-funded school must provide a balanced and broadly based curriculum that promotes the spiritual, moral, cultural, mental and physical development of pupils, and prepares pupils at the school for the opportunities, responsibilities and experiences of later life (DfE 2013:4).

A Curriculum Framework for RE

As the then government declined to review RE in 2013, the Religious Education Council of England and Wales (REC) voluntarily undertook a review of the subject in tandem with that of the NC to enable the RE community to adjust to the major changes that were being made to education in England at that time. To this end, it published *A Review of Religious Education in England*. The review provided a non-statutory NC framework for RE to complement the new NC programmes of study with an analysis of the wider context in which RE found itself (REC 2013a:6). Concurrently, it issued a parallel non-statutory curriculum *A Curriculum Framework for RE* (REC 2013b). This report is the only full national review of RE since 2004 (James and Stern 2019:26).

To begin with, it is important to emphasise that it is non-statutory guidance, and, as such, it does not hold any significance in law and practice, neither does it claim to be an exhaustive or final description of the place, value and scope of RE (REC 2013b:9). Nevertheless, being a curriculum document that was unanimously accepted by the main body representing religious and non-religious groups, it created much hope and excitement for the future of RE. However, once it was presented to the Government, its usefulness in providing high-quality RE was acknowledged, without any consequences for its implementation. The document had wide currency as it was based on extensive consultation and received much support that encouraged a coherent range of RE syllabuses. Subsequently, some SACREs used it to inform the revision of their syllabus (Surrey 2017:5). It is the curriculum, which *RE Today* adopted and used as a basis to develop several locally agreed syllabi across the country. In other words, despite not having any currency with the government, in practice, many local authorities adopted it via *RE Today* or directly.

The REC sees this document as out of date and therefore it does not represent their current purpose of RE. It was their stated position until 2018. However, with the publication of the

Commission on Religious Education (CoRE) Report in 2018, the Curriculum Framework on Religious Education (2013b) became redundant. This framework will be presented in Chapter 5. The CoRE report has shifted the debate significantly, towards an understanding that RE can no longer just focus on the study of a few specific religious traditions, with Humanism added in. The recommendation that the subject is renamed and reshaped to recognise a worldviews approach is now the central focus for the work of the REC. You will read about this later in this chapter.

RE: The Truth Unmasked

In the same year, the All Party Parliamentary Group on RE report, *RE: The Truth Unmasked* (APPG 2013), resulted from an inquiry carried out to investigate the supply of and support for teachers of RE. The report drew on over 400 sources of evidence and concluded that there were some serious issues, which needed to be addressed if schools were to provide high-quality RE for every young person. It was informed that there appeared to be fewer RE subject specialists, RE was often marginalised in schools and teachers undermined by the dismantling of the RE frameworks and support structures.

The main findings of the APPG inquiry included:

a   In over half of the 300 primary schools participating, some or all pupils were taught RE by someone other than their class teacher. In a quarter of these schools, RE was taught by teaching assistants. This was considered unacceptable and in many cases had a detrimental impact on the quality of RE.

b   About half of the primary teachers and trainee teachers lacked confidence in teaching RE.

c   About half of the subject leaders in primary schools lacked the expertise or experience to undertake their role effectively.

d   There was a wide variation in the extent of initial teacher training in RE and too many trainee teachers had little effective preparation for teaching the subject (APPG 2013:4).

They identified some contributory factors. There was a range of government policies, notably those relating to the EBacc and GCSE short courses which were contributing to the lowering of the status of RE in some schools leading to a reduction in the demand for specialist teachers. The reductions and changes in teacher training of time resulted in the closure of some outstanding university providers with a loss of opportunities for RE continued professional development (CPD). The combined effect of inadequate supply and inadequate access to support was that whatever their level of commitment, many teachers struggled to reach the levels of subject competence expected in the DfE's own teaching standards (APPG 2013:4). They recommended that the DfE ensures all teachers of RE meet the Teaching Standards and develop their confidence and expertise in teaching RE. Primary schools review the widespread practice of using staff other than teachers to teach RE and ITE training providers should improve the quality of RE training for primary trainees (APPG 2013:4).

RE: Realising the Potential

A previous Ofsted report on RE (Ofsted 2010) highlighted key barriers to better RE and made recommendations about how these should be overcome. In their 2013 survey, Ofsted found not enough that had been done since 2010. The *RE: Realising the Potential* report was based on evidence drawn from 185 schools visited between September 2009 and July 2012 (Ofsted 2013:4–5). It also drew on evidence from a telephone survey of a further 30 schools, examination results, other reports published by Ofsted, extended discussions with teachers, members of SACREs and other RE professionals, and wider surveys carried out by professional associations for RE. The sample of schools did not include voluntary aided schools or academies with a religious designation, for which separate inspection arrangements exist. Eight major concerns were discussed including:

- low standards
- weak teaching
- problems in developing a curriculum for RE
- confusion about the purpose of RE
- weak leadership and management
- weaknesses in examination provision at Key Stage 4
- gaps in training
- the impact of recent changes in education policy.

The report recommended that all schools should ensure that learning in RE has a stronger focus on deepening pupils' understanding of the nature, diversity and impact of religion and belief in the contemporary world. Primary schools, in particular, should raise the status of RE in the curriculum and strengthen the quality of subject leadership by improving the arrangements for developing teachers' subject expertise, sharing good practice and monitoring the quality of the curriculum and teaching (Ofsted 2013:7).

A New Settlement: Religion and Belief in Schools

This revised pamphlet follows their earlier publication (Clarke and Woodhead 2015), which resulted from assembling consultations and debates carried out by the Westminster Faith Debates, rather than research. The authors recognised that people were living through the single biggest change in the religious and cultural landscape of Britain for centuries, even millennia. It stressed that Britain was now diverse in a new way. The number identifying with non-Christian religions has been growing and the number who identify as Christian is falling, moreover, those who say they have 'no religion' (but are not necessarily secular) are now the majority (Clarke and Woodhead 2018:4). Therefore, they suggested that schools are equipped to help children handle these changes, changes that can otherwise be confusing, opaque and even dangerous. Good RE in schools supplies the tools to understand this and the best RE in schools today do. However, the picture is far too patchy and schools were being hindered (Clarke and Woodhead 2018:5). Nevertheless, their report seems to over-emphasise schools where RE is taken seriously rather than those with little concern for RE.

Clarke and Woodhead (2018:5) contended that the current legal relationship between religion, belief and schools is outdated in such a way that the law itself has become a barrier to schools' ability to help their children understand their situation and the world in which they are growing up. They proposed an urgent reform of the law that undergirds the way religion is handled in school.

They admitted that reforming anything to do with religion has been difficult in the past. Calls for change since the 1960s regarding the legal requirements concerning the statutory act of Collective Worship, RE and the basis of admission to faith schools have been dormant in law since 1944, except for small adjustments in 1988, which resulted from wider education reforms (Clarke and Woodhead 2018:6). Importantly, they stressed that over these 75 years, schools have changed almost beyond recognition while the map of religions and beliefs across the country has been transformed, the study of religion and theology in schools and HE has transformed, and new issues of community cohesion and contesting extremism have risen to the top of the political agenda. Politicians are cautious in considering a change in this area and fear taking steps that might create confusion and unnecessary conflict and whose social consequences could be unpredictable and damaging (Clarke and Woodhead 2018:6).

They inquired from a wide range of people in several different areas with a stake in the subject for their reaction to their proposals using a large number of face-to-face meetings, workshops and seminars and research. Following their earlier report (Clarke and Woodhead 2015), their revised conclusions and recommendations included:

- The name should be changed to 'Religion, Beliefs and Values', having previously suggested Religion and Moral Education (*vide* Clarke and Woodhead 2015:15).
- The nationally agreed 'Religion, Belief and Values' syllabus should be required in all state-funded schools with the option for schools with a religious character to complement the requirement with a further provision as required by their religious designation.
- Ofsted should ensure that all schools properly fulfil their duty to teach the nationally agreed curriculum.
- The legal requirement for RE at Key Stage 5, after the age of 16, should be removed.
- The right of parents to withdraw their children from the 'Religion, Belief and Values' part of the curriculum should be removed.
- Local Agreed Syllabus Conferences should be abolished.
- The local SACREs would be asked to assist in the local delivery and implementation of the new RE (or RBV) curriculum.

'RE for REal': The future of teaching and learning about religion and belief

This sociological project examined the future directions for teaching and learning in schools about religion and belief. The authors admit that the title puns on the RE name, and suggest that future teaching and learning needs to reflect the real religious landscape of today. The visual pun on *REal* is also intended as an abbreviation of 'RE alternative', to capture the possibility that RE as a subject could be rethought, as well as its relationship to possible alternative spaces for teaching and learning about religion and belief outside the RE space. It also maintained that RE was stuck in an outdated policy (Dinham and Shaw 2015:2; Dinham and Shaw 2020:51).

They carried out case study research with 19 self-selecting schools, which represented a geographical spread and a mix of rural and urban, although their age phase is unspecified. Some were Community schools and most had Academy status, including Church of England, ecumenical and schools with no religious character. Free schools were excluded to ensure a manageable range of variables in a highly complex school system. Thus, they achieved a total of 331 participants and 34 parents. Ten employers were interviewed to reflect a range of organisations within the public and private sectors. They used semi-structured interviews and focus groups to investigate their understandings of the purposes of RE, aspirations regarding content and their thoughts about the structures of teaching and learning of religion and belief.

Selected key findings showed that students were concerned that they hear many stereotypes in the media and in some of their learning. They wanted to know what is 'real'. Almost all want to learn about a wider range of religions and beliefs and were worried that many students learn about only one or two traditions. Students enjoyed learning about real 'lived' religion, especially through thinking about religion and belief controversies. Many thought that RE lacked status.

Selected key findings show that teachers were frustrated by how little time there was for RE, often resulting in teaching only one or two traditions. Specialist RE teachers emphasised RE as a humanities subject with an academic justification in its own right, while non-specialist RE teachers emphasised learning for cohesion and respect. Many saw RE as a key space for personal, spiritual and moral reflection in school. Eighty-six per cent of teachers in the study felt that RE should be an NC subject. Seventy-two per cent said it should be compulsory to at least 16.

Some parents wanted a name change. They thought that 'RE' puts young people off and almost all thought that this should include non-religious beliefs. Some employers felt that young people needed to learn about handling religion and belief diversity in ways that prepared them for workplace diversity.

Based on these findings, Dinham and Shaw (2015:1) recommended that:

- A statutory National Framework for Religion and Belief learning should be developed, and apply to all schools, balancing shared national approaches with school level determination.
- Since SACREs currently play a leading part in Religion and Belief learning, there is an urgent need for a review of their role, and the role of others in the forming of learning.
- The National Framework panel should be mandated to consider and make recommendations about (i) the purpose, (ii) content and (iii) the structures of teaching and learning. It should also consider the relationship between learning inside RE, outside in other subjects, and in the wider life of schools, especially about the Act of Worship, and the right to withdraw.
- Religion and Belief learning should be a compulsory part of the curriculum to age 16.
- Content should reflect the real religious landscape.
- There should be continued investment in training for subject-specialist RE teachers and non-specialist teachers of Religion and Belief.
- A review and a decision on the name.

The content for Religions and Belief learning should reflect the breadth of the real religious landscape and not focus solely on the traditions. Moreover, it should not over-emphasise instrumental concerns about cohesion and citizenship. Religions and Belief learning should be concerned with preparing students for the practical task of engagement with the rich variety of religion and belief encounters in everyday life (Dinham and Shaw 2020:63–64).

'Living with Difference': Commission on religion and belief in public life

The Woolf Institute convened an independent commission in 2015. Over two years, it undertook the first systematic review of the role of religion and belief in the UK. Although this was not directly related to RE in schools, it considered the state and role of RE in schools and made specific recommendations related to RE. Some of their findings are important for you to know as a teacher since the purpose was to consider the place and role of religion and belief in contemporary Britain. It also considered the significance of emerging trends and identities and made recommendations for public life and policy. Its premise was that in a rapidly changing diverse society everyone is affected, whatever their private views on religion and belief, by how public policy and public institutions respond to social change (Woolf Institute 2015:6).

They reported that over the past half-century, Britain's landscape in terms of religion and belief had been transformed beyond recognition. The number of people with non-religious beliefs and identities had increased. Almost a half of the population today describes itself as non-religious. There was a general decline in Christian affiliation, belief and practice. Thirty years ago, two-thirds of the population would have identified as Christians. Simultaneously, there has been a shift away from mainstream denominations and a growth in evangelical and Pentecostal churches. There was an increase in the diversity amongst people who have religious faith. Fifty years ago, Judaism was the largest non-Christian tradition in the UK. Now it is the fourth largest behind Islam, Hinduism and Sikhism. Faith traditions other than Christian have younger age profiles and are growing faster.

Furthermore, they noted that intra- and inter-faith disputes were inextricably linked to today's geopolitical crises globally. Many of these disputes are reflected in UK society, creating or exacerbating tensions between different communities. Therefore, twenty-first-century ethnoreligious issues and identities here in the UK and globally are reshaping society in ways inconceivable just a few decades ago, and how we respond to such changes will have a profound impact on public life (Woolf Institute 2015:6).

Given such concerns and the religion and belief landscape, there are many implications for public policy. Pertinent to schools, they recommended greater religion and belief literacy in every section of society, and at all levels. They noted that the potential for misunderstanding, stereotyping and oversimplification based on ignorance is huge. Therefore, the commission called on educational and professional bodies to draw up religion and belief literacy programmes and projects and celebrate best practices in the media (Woolf Institute 2015:8). All pupils in state-funded schools should have a statutory entitlement to a curriculum about religion, philosophy and ethics that is relevant to today's society and the broad framework of such a curriculum should be nationally agreed upon. The legal requirement for schools to hold acts of Collective Worship should be repealed, and replaced by a requirement to hold inclusive times for reflection (Woolf Institute 2015:8).

Furthermore, they argued that a national entitlement of content and outcomes can be flexibly applied at the level of the individual school, as is the case in Scotland. To them, this approach seemed far superior to the current approach in England and Wales where the variety of school, diocesan and local authority syllabuses, but with no underlying and unifying framework, creates a range of problems (Woolf Institute 2015:36). Importantly, they suggested that education about religion and belief must reflect not only the heritage of the UK, with its religious and non-religious traditions, but also the realities of present society. Crucially, it must take account of the ongoing social changes in religion and belief outlined in their report. They posited that if the curriculum was objective, fair and balanced, and did not contain elements of confessional instruction or indoctrination, then such teaching should be required in all schools and there would be no reason for a legal right to withdraw from learning about religion and belief (Woolf Institute 2015:36).

However, the report has been criticised on at least two grounds. For example, Barnes (2020) calls for evidence for the argument that 'objective' statutory, a national curriculum of the form Woolf Institute recommends, will remove the need for a parental right of withdrawal. Such assertions and conclusions need real attention to their justification or relevant evidence (Barnes 2020:190).

State of RE on the ground

Many challenges have been discussed concerning RE. Over the years, several reports indicated that the amount of training provided for primary teachers in RE has reduced over time (NATRE 2013, 2016, 2017, 2018). It is important to note that this has been the state in parallel with Ofsted reports, which have identified the need to improve provision (Ofsted 2007, 2010, 2013).

Related to the above issue is the status and treatment afforded to RE in some schools. Over the years, these reports have also demonstrated differences in the quality of RE in primary schools (Ofsted 2007, 2010, 2013; NATRE 2016, 2018). The problems include: 'breaches in school observation of the legal entitlement to RE, low status for RE as a subject in the curriculum, diminished time allocation within the busy primary timetable, underdeveloped systems of assessment and teachers' lack of experience and confidence due to lack of RE training and ongoing professional development' (Whitworth 2020:348). Moreover, some schools employ other teachers or Higher Level Teaching Assistants (HLTAs) to provide RE teaching in their schools. On the other hand, Whitworth (2020) highlights some good examples of practice across England. These include inspirational Agreed Syllabuses to dedicated organisations, local groups and teachers who promote the subject by outstanding teaching and resourcing. Among individual projects, Whitworth (2020) notes that the *Understanding Christianity* (CEM 2016), *RE-searchers* (Freathy et al. 2015) and *Primary 1000* (NATRE 2019) projects are making a considerable impact at the school level (Whitworth 2020).

Religion and Worldviews: the way forward

Following some of these high-profile reports, academic discussions, public and professional deliberations, it seemed appropriate for the main organisation representing the interests of RE to take a major initiative if the subject were to be fit for purpose. As a result of this reality, some radical rethinking took place. The REC established the CoRE comprising of 13 commissioners plus a chair, who were experts in their different fields and brought together a wealth of experience from teaching, school leadership, academia, journalism and law (Tharani et al. 2020:38). The Commission was fully independent and was not acting as representatives of any other groups. Following their interim report (CoRE 2016), their Final Report, *Religion and Worldviews: the way forward* was published in 2018. It sets out a National Plan for RE and called on the Government to adopt it. It is important to be clear that this was not a recommendation for developing a national syllabus, rather it was an attempt to address the need for a shared vision of RE nationally and would offer a baseline vision for all schools (Cooling 2021:6).

In addition to reviewing legal, educational and policy frameworks, the CoRE listened to evidence from a wide range of concerned parties. These included pupils, teachers, lecturers, advisers, parents and faith and belief communities and received over three thousand submissions, which convinced them that RE needed to be rejuvenated if it were to continue to make its important contribution due to the growing diversity of religions and beliefs that pupils today encounter, both in their locality and in the media. The second point related to the variable quality of RE experienced by pupils across the country and, finally, the fact that the legal arrangements around RE were no longer working as more schools were becoming academies (CoRE 2018). The new National Plan would ensure that learning remained academically rigorous and a knowledge-rich preparation for life in a world of great religion and belief diversity. It called for a paradigm shift (Cooling, Bowie and Panjwani 2020).

Of the 11 recommendations, the main points relevant to the discussions so far include:

1   Change the name to Religion and Worldviews.

2   A National Entitlement statement, describing pupil entitlement to curriculum content, which should be statutory for all publicly funded schools.

3   Non-statutory programmes of study for each of Key Stages 1–4 to be developed by a national professional body, at a similar level of detail as those for History and Geography in the NC.

4   Programmes of study should be reviewed whenever the NC is reviewed.

5   All Initial Teacher Education should enable teachers to teach Religion and Worldviews based on the National Entitlement.

6   The legislation regarding SACREs should be amended: the name of the body should be changed to Local Advisory Network for Religion and Worldviews (LANfRW), which must facilitate the implementation of the National Entitlement in all schools within the local authority boundaries by providing information about sources of support available. LANfRW must connect schools with local faith and belief communities and other groups that support the study of Religion and Worldviews in schools.

7   The LANfRW should be made up of members from five groups: teachers, school leaders and governors, ITE and/or CPD providers, school providers and other groups that support RE in schools.

8   Ofsted and faith-based inspections must report on whether schools are meeting the National Entitlement.

9   The DfE clarifies the right of withdrawal from Religion and Worldviews.

The CoRE recommended that the nature of the subject should be reconceptualised around the concept of 'worldview'. This has proven to be contentious. Some of their recommendations were well received by many within the RE community itself. There have also been some groups who criticised its proposals (Cooling, Bowie and Panjwani 2020). At the time of writing, they have not yet been taken forward by the government.

You read about the role played by faith communities in the captivity of RE in the previous Chapter 1. Grimmitt (2000b:13–15) placed this charge on the shoulders of politicians and religious groups, the former to control the subject at the local level, and the latter, to influence its content. That a 'National Plan', albeit recommended by independent commissioners, at the behest of the REC, has attracted criticisms among the competing RE community, and risks continuing the muddled intent, implementation and impact of RE and its future. Akin to the power devolved to local authorities, there appears to be an ideological debate underway in the 'current' crisis experienced by RE, which as you have read, is not recent but historical.

In critically reviewing the RE Commission's *Religion and Worldviews: The way forward* (CoRE 2018), Barnes (2020) reminds readers that the REC were the first to identify 'a crisis in RE'. It then commissioned a report to make recommendations on how to overcome the crisis. Thereafter, the Report recommended that the REC is given sole rights of appointing those who are to be given the responsibility for introducing the new proposed statutory national curriculum for RE of the form that the report recommends. Moreover, those appointed must approve of the approach taken to Religion and Worldviews that the Commission Report recommends. Barnes (2020), after analysing the steps taken by the REC, finds it impossible not to regard their position as ideological. Moreover, Barnes contends that the recommendations of the REC by nine experts, appointed by the REC itself, are self-serving and an attempt to gain power and control over the future direction and provision of RE (Barnes 2020:189).

However, Cooling (2021), in response, has accused Barnes of misrepresentation, misinterpretation and being unfair. Thus, the 'National Plan' has the potential to divide the community rather than unite. Unsurprisingly, Chater (2020:16) laments that the situation of RE and asserts that RE in most parts of the UK exists in a 'land of dreams': an imagined view of the UK and of religion that fails to reflect the realities of either. You could also reflect on the distinctions between 'religious' and 'secular'. Whilst welcoming the general thrust of the recommendations of CoRE (2018), Gearon et al. (2021) noted that some bodies representing secular humanism expressed reservations on the adoption of 'Religion and Worldviews' as the proposed name for the subject as it prioritised the religious over the secular.

Worldviews in Religious Education

The authors of the report *Worldviews in Religious Education* respond to the criticisms levied against the paradigm shift that underpins the proposed new National Plan on Religion and Worldview (CoRE 2018). They interpret and develop the idea of 'worldview' and explore its implications for the classroom. In essence, they argue that over the decades several significant shifts in the perceived purpose of RE have occurred, each responding to the changing social context in which schools exist (Cooling, Bowie and Panjwani 2020:9). In other words, adopting 'Religion and Worldviews' would be another significant paradigm change in thinking about the subject. You will read more about Worldviews in Chapter 4. They note three significant objections to CoRE's proposals, which are: that changing the focus to worldviews introduces additional non-religious subject matter diluting the proper attention that should be given to religions; that the concept of worldviews is confusing and unhelpful and that a focus on worldview means the true spiritual nature of the subject is lost.

In response to these objections, they argue that the worldview proposal should not be seen as a focus on the content to be taught. It is a way of framing how that content is introduced to the students to understand the worldviews being taught. The focus should not be so much on the institutional version as on the lived experience of adherents. The notion of personal worldview, with its emphasis on the heart as well as the head, needs to be central to this new approach to RE (Cooling, Bowie and Panjwani 2020:9–10).

Summary

This section has emphasised the main reports, which have had considerable influence in calling for reforms in RE. In so doing, the legal, structural, social and practical debates surrounding the subject have been featured. You have also considered some of the recommendations from these reports and reflected on the appeal to change the name of the subject, create a national entitlement, abolish or change the role of SACREs and review the right of withdrawal from RE. Simultaneously, as society becomes increasingly religiously plural, the case for moving RE forward, to improve the quality of its provision and to make it a respectable subject to be studied in its own right is evident and so is the need for investment, training and supporting schools and teachers.

The changed sociological realities such as the practice of religious faith in contemporary time are very different to the past. Some political concerns such as social cohesion impact the subject. Research projects and educational improvements in RE are some of the grounds for change initiatives. However, it is equally important to acknowledge that RE lives in a diverse environment in different surroundings. Only the future would tell what RE would look like in a standardised curriculum environment if at all it was to survive.

THE PARENTAL RIGHT TO WITHDRAW FROM RE

The law

The right of parents to withdraw their children, as shown in Box 2.1, from religious instruction in a community, foundation or voluntary school on conscience grounds was included in the Education Acts of 1870, 1944 and 1988 (Copley 2008:30; CoRE 2018:63). At this time, it was conceived as protecting the freedom of conscience of religious minorities specifically Christian, or those without religious faith from religious instruction which was of a Christian confessional nature (Louden 2004; Lundie and O'Siochru 2021).

Recently, this right is also protected by the European Convention on Human Rights, which states that parents have the right to educate their children in line with their religious and philosophical convictions (CoRE 2018:63).

Thus, legislation has retained the clause allowing parents to withdraw their children from all or any part of RE, this includes academies and free schools. Moreover, schools must not influence the parents' decision, although they may inform them about the content of the curriculum (DCSF 2010:28). Nevertheless, the right of withdrawal does not extend to other areas of the curriculum

---

BOX 2.1 THE ROOT OF THE WITHDRAWAL CLAUSE

This historical anomaly was originally provided on the basis that parents of Christian persuasions other than that of the Church of England could, according to conscience, be given the right of withdrawal. The clause remains, and is not infrequently used by Jehovah's Witness, Muslim, Pagan and Christian, as well as atheist parents, all for differing reasons. In some cases it is due to the fundamentalist and iconoclastic attitudes of parents, in some cases it is due to not wishing their child to learn about a specific religion such as Islam. In all cases it is due to the fundamental purpose and value of a properly taught RE not being understood, wilfully in many cases. At root it is about ignorance, wilful or not, and that is not so surprising. Present day RE and Collective Worship have completely different intentions, but they are both subject to compulsion and withdrawal. Logically, they are both, as a result, optional (Erricker, Lowndes and Bellchambers 2011:194).

---

when, as may happen on occasion, spontaneous questions on religious matters are raised by pupils or there are issues related to religion that arise in other subjects such as history or citizenship (DCSF 2010:28). More so, it is not meant to enable pupils to participate in other alternative activities or National Curriculum subjects (McCreery, Palmer and Voiels 2008:2). Sixth form students over the age of 18 may exercise the right for themselves, without reference to their parents. Every school should provide parents with information about the right of withdrawal (DCSF 2010:27–30).

The intention has always been to allow parents to be able to make arrangements for their own preferred RE. Hence, the RE provided must be sensitive to the rights of parents and pupils. It is not the place of teachers to belittle or deride the beliefs of parents and pupils and it is not appropriate that a teacher represents their views as unchallengeable right when it comes to their own religious or philosophical beliefs (Cornwall 2014:20). Moreover, teachers are expected to ensure that personal beliefs are not expressed in ways that exploit pupils' vulnerability or might lead them to break the law (DfE 2021).

Abolish the right to withdraw

The right of withdrawal is contested. It is argued that parents should not have a right to prevent their children from understanding the world in which they live and into which they will grow (Lawton 2018:30). For some, it is 'a ridiculous loophole', which is being misused as some are selective in withdrawing from particular religions (Myatt 2020:13). Clarke and Woodhead (2018:27) noted that some parents fear that their children will be exposed to faiths other than their own, or even just to broader discussion and teaching about religion than they find appropriate. In response, Clarke and Woodhead (2018:27) believe that RE is a normal academic subject like History, English and others and that the right to opt out is anachronistic, harking back to a time when it was confessional 'RI'. Thus, in their policy report, they recommended its abolition.

The Commission on RE found that there was widespread concern that some parents were using the right of withdrawal, especially partial withdrawal, to remove their children from any teaching on Islam as a result of racist or Islamophobic beliefs. In addition, school leaders reported that both full withdrawal and partial withdrawal were the result of racism, Islamophobia or political campaigns in fewer than 10% of cases. The withdrawal requests were based on some parents' conservative religious beliefs or their non-religious or secular beliefs and due to misunderstanding of the aims of RE (CoRE 2018:64). Three major stakeholders in schools, NAHT, NATRE and the Church of England, all called for an end to the right of withdrawal (CoRE 2018:64).

Lundie and O'Siochru (2021) questioned whether the provision to withdraw is still coherent or necessary for contemporary multi-faith RE. To this end, based on a survey of 450 head-teachers and RE coordinators, they found that 70.5% of participants in the survey believe that the right to withdraw is no longer required. It was reported that across all respondents, conservative religious beliefs remain the modal reason ascribed to parental requests for withdrawal. However, some participants who believed that the right to withdraw remains necessary were more likely to ascribe religious or secular motivations to parents who want to withdraw their child from RE. Conversely, participants who no longer saw a need for a withdrawal right were more likely to ascribe prejudiced beliefs or misunderstandings about the aims and purpose of RE to parents seeking such a withdrawal. In other words, the phenomenon is rather more complex than it might first suggest.

Respect the right to withdraw

Others favoured the preservation of the right. Some of these people emphasised that it should be retained in schools of a religious character. The NATRE primary survey in 2018 found that almost 16% of the schools surveyed said they had some parents using the right of withdrawal (NATRE and NAHT 2018). Some parents are concerned that multi-faith RE is as directive and confessional as the Christian religious instruction it supplanted (Lundie and O'Siochru 2021).

Consequently, the Commission on RE reluctantly recommended that the right of withdrawal be retained. Their main reason was that since schools have the freedom to design their curricula, it could not be guaranteed that every school curriculum nationally would be sufficiently 'objective, critical and pluralistic' to justify ending the right of withdrawal, particularly as so many of the challenges which have been brought have been successful (CoRE 2018:67). Nevertheless, the Commission sought legal clarification on several matters about this (CoRE 2018:18).

At this stage, you may want to reflect on your standpoint. In principle, do you think the right to withdraw should exist and whether this should be total or selective withdrawal and on what grounds, as some student teachers have done so? Consider these varied perspectives at five levels as shown in Tables 2.1–2.5.

Withdrawing from Religious Education

Table 2.1 Views on withdrawing from the subject	
No	Yes
Media portrays religion really negatively so we need religious education.	RE is personal and there can be offensive things, so they can withdraw. It is a controversial subject so it might go too far and cause arguments.
You are making RE more of a taboo by withdrawing compared with modern languages.	It is the beauty to allow or not to allow learning of religion in this country.
It is one of the biggest subjects, which shapes an individual and their identity, and it is opinions unlike other subjects with facts.	There is no harm in understanding other beliefs, it not about practicing, therefore, there should be no withdrawals, but if some doesn't want it, it can't be forced.
It is religious education and not religious instruction, which was over 50 years ago.	Yes, depends on the age and on the lesson.
Why treat it differently?	Let them with withdrawn as RE gives a wrong idea which is to be religious.

Teacher withdrawal

Table 2.2 Should teachers have the right to withdraw?	
No	Yes
Parents can as it is their right, but the classroom teachers should not withdraw because they are role models, and it falls under the professional values of the classroom teacher to be tolerant. They can have their opinions but not biased ones.	If children can, then teachers should also be able to.
As a teacher what attitude are you conveying to the children that you teach.	It is not in the national curriculum, therefore, you can withdraw from it.
I can't see why teachers should be allowed not to teach RE.	It is a matter of human rights and personal conscience.

Parents' withdrawal

Table 2.3 Should parents have the right to withdraw?

No	Yes
Is the child going to grow up and say, 'I wish I had learned it'. The parents are taking that away.	I disagree with learning RE, if they don't want it then fine. If they have no religion, then by teaching them we are imposing religion on them.
Parents would say I see maths as an abstract concept, so I don't want it – is ridiculous.	So long as they don't teach racist stuff, it is their right to bring up their children.
I don't think parents should have the right to withdraw their children because its crucial to gain an understanding of our religions in the world to diminish racism. I think RE needs to be arranged by the local communities and give themselves better control over the content that is relevant to them. RE needs to be a compulsory subject for the above reasons. It is a critical part of education to enable us to be understanding and respectful people.	Religion is such an individual personal thing whereas education fits with culture and religion so parents should have a driving force to avoid the influence of religions.

Pupil withdrawal

Table 2.4 Should pupils have the right to withdraw?

No	Yes
The child is being refused the right to learn about other religions and cultures. They might go out into society and be uneducated and oblivious to the world.	It is hard. I am not a religious person. I have seen children who do not belong to a religion being asked to do things belonging to other religions. So there should be withdrawal, otherwise, it's not fair.
No to withdrawal as it encourages them to develop their own identity.	They can withdraw as parents' educate will teach them religion.
They will be exposed to all sorts of information so they might as well get good knowledge in an unbiased way from the classroom teacher.	Parents can teach better than the classroom teacher who can be biased, therefore, they should be allowed to withdraw their children.
No – pupils will be exposed anyway. In society, they are already socialising. How will they understand people, if they leave RE.	There are 20 hours in a timetable. It is only one hour in which their child will be separated, concerns about socialisation are weak.

Withdrawing from selected religions

Table 2.5 Should the right to withdraw be selective?

No	Yes
You don't have to do anything. I had a child and she was fascinated and confused as well. She thought she had to be something and said she was Sikh. The class teacher was not clear. You don't have to be something or anything.	Jehovah's witness boys were removed from Easter and from religious education. In fact, any lesson with Christianity or Easter they did not go, but they participated in Sikhism as the child was left in the classroom. This pointed to the issue with Christianity.
It is not only one religion, in fact it is more than Christianity.	Why the uproar? It has always been there, so give them this right.
They should learn RE so that they can make a choice on what they can follow if they want to follow it when they are older.	RE is everything that I guess you stand for. Religious education is all about freedom and choice, so they should withdraw.

Teachers

The 1944 Act also protects teachers' right to withdraw from teaching the subject on grounds of conscience (with certain exceptions in Voluntary Aided schools) unless they have been specifically employed to teach, lead or manage RE (Education Reform Act 1988, S2 (1)(a)). An application to withdraw must be given in writing to the head and chair of governors. Pupils must not miss out on RE teaching because a teacher has withdrawn from teaching RE. The school must make alternative provisions for the pupils to be taught RE (Redbridge 2015).

Pupils

Historically, this right was first granted when RE was Religious Instruction and carried with it connotations of indoctrination and nurture into the Christian faith. However, currently, RE is significantly different as it is open, broad, critical and an educational enquiry of a range of religions and beliefs. Nevertheless, even today parents continue to have this right which must be respected when parents request to withdraw their child, to enable them to exercise their wish to provide their own RE (School Standards and Framework Act 1998 S71 (3)). In cases where RE is integrated in the curriculum, the school should discuss such arrangements with the parents and would need to assess and look at how the withdrawal can be best accommodated (Bristol 2016).

The process of requesting a withdrawal

The process for requesting a withdrawal from RE would usually involve the parent writing to the head-teacher regarding this matter. The request should make clear whether it is from the whole of the subject or specific parts. Parents do not have to provide a reason for their withdrawal and the school must comply with the request. Parents also should note that children may also encounter religions and beliefs in other parts of the curriculum such as in a history project or as part of a cross-curricular topic in art and design, a parent legally cannot request for withdrawal from this (DCSF 2010). Nevertheless, schools are duty-bound to promote community cohesion and this includes helping pupils understand ideas about identity and diversity, including within a religious context and a context of non-religious beliefs (Grimmitt 2010; Erricker, Lowndes and Bellchambers 2011).

Once a pupil is withdrawn, it is still the responsibility of the school to supervise them. However, this should not involve the provision of additional teaching or result in the school or LA incurring extra costs. In the situation where a pupil has been withdrawn, the law provides for alternative arrangements to be made for RE of the kind the parents want their child to receive (School Standards and Framework Act 1998, Section 71(3)). Parents would then be required to provide work of a religious, faith or belief-based nature as a substitute for the RE work (East Sussex 2017:7).

The alternative RE would usually be provided within the premises of the school in question, or by another local school in the locality, where this is reasonably convenient. However, should either approach be impracticable, an outside arrangement or external RE teaching suitable to the kind of RE the parent wants may be made for the pupil. For example, the pupil may be withdrawn from the school for a reasonable period to facilitate their attendance for this external RE as long as the withdrawal does not significantly impact their attendance. These arrangements are to be made by the parents; the school is not expected to make these arrangements. These outside arrangements for RE are permitted as long as the Local Authority is satisfied that any interference with the pupil's attendance at school as a consequence of such a withdrawal will affect only the start or end of a school session (Bristol 2016).

The school policy

All schools must have a policy expressing this right for parents and carers. They should also set out their RE provision and what parents should do should they intend to withdraw their child. Though not legally required, nevertheless, it is good practice to allow informed decisions to be made. Thus, in the first instance, a head-teacher could talk to parents to ensure that they know and fully understand the nature of RE, its aims, purposes and value and how it is taught.

Without any influence from the school, it may be useful to show them the policy and the syllabus as well (DCSF 2010). They may need to be reminded about the relevance of RE to all pupils and, importantly, that the school respects pupils' personal beliefs and the right to hold those beliefs. Schools, if they so wish, can request their SACRE for assistance or advice when talking to parents about this before honouring their rightful request. It is also good practice to review such requests annually with parents. As part of transparency and accountability, all schools are now required to publish their school curriculum by subject and academic year online, and this includes their RE policy on their school website (DfE 2014:5).

A useful checklist for managing the right of withdrawal might include the items in Box 2.2 (DCSF 2010:30).

Summary

This section has analysed the most contentious features of RE. It has discussed the right that parents have to withdraw their children fully or in part from RE lessons. You have considered both sides of the debate and the fresh calls to abolish and retain it.

PROVISION AND TIME FOR RE

Introduction

One of the most concerning and frequently raised issues that RE faces is related to the time allocated to it and the actual teaching of RE. It is mainly for this reason that a section has been devoted to the issue of provision and time for RE so that pupils' entitlement to RE becomes evident.

BOX 2.2 MANAGING THE RIGHT TO WITHDRAW FROM RE

■ Is the school careful to ensure that RE is of educational value to all pupils, whatever their belief background, thus reducing the likelihood of parental/carer requests for withdrawal?

■ Does the school ensure that the nature, objectives and content of RE are shared with parents?

■ Are parents or carers notified about plans for RE as part of the curriculum for the coming session for their child's class?

■ Does the school have a procedure in place for parents or carers who want to withdraw children from RE?

■ Does the organisation of the curriculum allow parents to exercise the right of withdrawal?

■ What practical implications arise from a request by parents to withdraw a child from RE and how might they be addressed?

■ Are all those who teach RE aware of the school's procedures?

Respondents to the APPGs enquiry said that some schools were failing to meet their statutory requirements about RE (APPG 2016:12). Recent research also indicated that RE in schools, which did not have a religious character, was less likely to be taught regularly (NATRE 2018). This suggests that beginner teachers were less likely to be given opportunities to teach or observe the subject (Whitworth 2020).

Legal requirements

The legal requirements for the provision of RE in maintained schools do not specify any particular time allocation. An Agreed Syllabus Conference (ASC) specifies what must be taught through the LAS, but is not required to specify the amount of curriculum time that must be allocated to RE by schools. Nevertheless, they may provide an estimate of how much time their syllabus would require to help schools to plan their timetable (DCSF 2010:13). Therefore, it is important to remember that the requirement is to devote sufficient time and resources to RE to enable schools to meet their legal obligations and to deliver an RE curriculum that is of high quality.

The issue of allocating a minimum time for RE has a history. The DfE (1994) suggested that when an ASC draws up an agreed syllabus they should assume that school leaders make reasonable time available for the study of RE. They should note the recommendations of Sir Ron Dearing's final report and assume that 36 hours per year will be devoted to KS1 and 45 hours in KS2 as in Table 2.6. The SCAA draft model syllabuses, it noted, also assumed around 40 hours per year (DfE 1994:16–17). Recently, *The State of the Nation* report (NATRE 2017:37) noted from the Dearing Report (1994:41) that schools devote at least 5% of curriculum time to RE (just one hour per week on average), most agreed syllabuses have either assumed or stipulated that this would be the time required to meet their outcomes. The report recognises that there were good reasons for this recommendation in 1994 which is also relevant in 2017, if not more so. It adds that the equivalent of an hour per week is not unreasonable given the legal expectation set out in the Education Act 1996 that RE should encompass Christianity and the other principal religions represented in Great Britain.

The issue of allocating time also relates to the requirement that a syllabus must reflect the fact that the religious traditions in Great Britain are, in the main, Christian while taking account of the teaching and practices of the other principal religions represented in Great Britain. To reflect this, syllabuses require the teaching of Christianity in KS1 and KS2, unlike other religions and worldviews. At the practical level, schools show this on their timetable over a term or through their MTP, where Christianity predominates at each Key Stage and features in no less than 50% of the RE taught, as can be seen in Chapters 4 and 8.

The Ofsted RE Research Review (2021) expressed disappointment at the interpretation of the legislation in percentage terms by some leaders, for example, by devoting 51% of RE to the study of Christianity and 49% to 'other religions'. It noted that for some time this approach does not guarantee a quality RE curriculum (Grimmitt 2000a). It also noted that such an approach can generate problems. It can unintentionally cause tensions by devoting more time to some religious or non-religious traditions. It can also prevent pupils from exploring the connections between traditions or even imply that there are no connections (Bowie 2019; Ofsted 2021).

Schools are expected to make their own decisions about how to divide curriculum time. They must ensure that sufficient time is given to RE so that pupils can meet the standards and

Table 2.6 Time for RE in the curriculum			
Reception	4–5 s	36 hours of RE	Integrated into learning, e.g. part of Personal, Social and Emotional Development, Understanding the World, etc.
Key Stage 1	5–7 s	36 hours of teaching per year	Equivalent to 50 minutes a week, or an RE week each term where 12+ hours of RE are taught
Key Stage 2	7–11 s	45 hours of teaching per year	Equivalent to an hour and 15 minutes a week, or a series of RE days where 45+ hours of RE are taught

expectations set out in their respective syllabus. For this reason, many schools have a clearly identifiable time for RE on their timetable. Since RE is a core subject of the curriculum for every pupil, the requirements of some agreed syllabi are not subject to the flexibility of the Foundation Subjects (Nottingham 2020), as the National Curriculum does not specify the amount of time to be devoted to each subject.

Nevertheless, the principles of good planning and delivery must apply to RE as they would to any other subject in school. Moreover, as noted above, RE is a component of the basic curriculum, which must be taught alongside other curricula and subjects. Hence, to ensure that the statutory programme of study in an agreed syllabus is covered in sufficient breadth, depth and rigour, many recommend and estimate the minimum hours, which need to be devoted for RE.

Having dedicated and sufficient time for RE ensures that all pupils receive their legal entitlement. In addition, it might also ensure that schools enable pupils to meet the expected standards as set out in a legally binding agreed syllabus, as discussed earlier. Furthermore, it supports a school effectively to deliver its plans. Moreover, it assists schools to sequence their curriculum so that progression across year groups and transitions between the Key Stages is achieved. Importantly, devoting an appropriate amount of time to RE facilitates the implementation of the intention of the curriculum, programmes of study or units of work to be in a suitably broad and balanced manner. This helps ensure that pupils receive a high quality, coherent and progressive experience of the subject.

However, while schools are free to decide when and how subjects are taught and how much time is spent on each subject, they remain responsible for implementing the legally required syllabus (whether the locally agreed syllabus or their individual one) and for monitoring pupils' progress (DCSF 2010:6).

Church aided schools tend to be advised to consult their diocese guidelines, as the time allocation for them will be greater. In some cases, the 5% may also be applied in non-denominational Academies and Free Schools that use an LAS. However, some maintained aided schools and denominational Academies and Free Schools tend to use 10% of curriculum time and supplement it with additional appropriate denominational material.

Most Agreed Syllabi specify the time, which must be devoted to RE per annum or per Key Stage, as shown in Table 2.6. They advise schools to allocate a minimum of 5% of curriculum time for RE learning and experiences in any one academic year across the Key Stages 1–4.

The lack of time allocated to RE has been noted to lower standards. Those responsible for RE in a school who do not plan to allocate sufficient curriculum time for RE are unlikely to be fully able to enable pupils to achieve the outcomes set out in a syllabus (Ofsted 2013). The APPG reported that even when RE is provided, often the time allocated for it is 'squeezed' in both primary and secondary schools due to a variety of factors. This lowers the status of the subjects and pupils are left with reduced opportunities to gain deep knowledge about, and engage critically with, different religions and beliefs, and may come to regard RE as being of trivial importance (APPG 2016:13).

Organising RE

At the practical level, it is useful to recognise that there is no single correct way of making appropriate provisions for RE as long as the outcomes are met since it is up to schools to decide how they plan their RE curriculum and its related experiences. Consequently do not be surprised to find many models in operation in schools. You should also be aware that these minimum time requirements include visits and RE curriculum days.

You will read in Chapter 8, some schools may teach RE as a weekly session. Others adopt a cross-curricular approach through blocked time, either weekly or fortnightly. However, in Lincolnshire (2018), it is recommended that approximately two-thirds of the time (over a year) is spent on its compulsory units and the reminder of the time on their additional units. Others suggest that the time can be allocated to RE creatively and flexibly over the school terms and that the subject can be planned in combination with other subjects, so long as the expected hours for RE are met (Pan-Berkshire 2018).

Others use this flexibly to enable more sustained work to take place, which they see as good practice. Sustained teaching is achieved through an RE themed day or an RE week, often complementing the regular program of timetabled lessons. However, this 'sustained teaching' usually does not replace the regular delivery so that depth and breadth are achieved. In all cases, the curriculum models and modes of delivery must ensure that there is a sequence by building on previous learning, coherence within the content and progression across the school year/s.

RE is different from assembly and Collective Worship

The curriculum time allocated for RE is distinct from the time spent in school assemblies and acts of Collective Worship (CW). Sometimes some schools make links between the CW and the topics of RE as they see this overlap as good practice, for many purposes. That said, it is important to know that the recommended time for teaching RE excludes the time required for CW and assemblies, as these may not necessarily be RE and, equally it is important to remember that RE is not the same as CW, both are different in law and practice.

Summary

The provision of RE in maintained schools is legally required, although the time to be allocated is unspecified. The allocation of a minimum time has a history, which relates to the requirement that a syllabus must reflect the fact that the religious traditions in Great Britain are, in the main, Christian while taking account of other principal religions represented in Great Britain. As such, schools are expected to make their own decisions about how to divide curriculum time. The interpretation of the legislation in percentage terms does not guarantee a quality RE curriculum and might generate problems (Box 2.3).

BOX 2.3 VIGNETTE: NATIONAL PLAN

I come from a Muslim British Bangladeshi household. My biggest educational achievement to date is my LLB (Hons) Law. I did not plan on going into teaching during my first degree as I thoroughly enjoyed Law. I soon learned from work experience that although I enjoyed learning the Law I did not want to go into the legal field. Teaching felt like the only right option. After discovering this, I felt teaching was something I was already involved in. I was tutoring my siblings and taught classes to children as well as adults as part of my self-employment. I was able to join an ITT course in my gap year to consolidate my research into teaching and to establish if it was the profession for me.

I chose to specialise in RE because I remember extensive amounts about the lessons I was taught in primary school. I found RE lessons fun and exciting. Going into practice in schools taught me there is a lot more that can be done in schools to promote the teaching of RE. I feel like I can help make a difference in the school I teach in. RE would give me the chance to be creative with lessons leaving room for cross-curricular activities incorporating subjects such as Art, i.e. making diva lamps when teaching about Diwali. I believe the learning of RE encourages respect and understanding for religions on the part of children in terms of beliefs and differing practices. I hope to take my positive experiences of RE into my specialism and make an impact on the way it is taught in the school I work in, for example, ensure it is taught as required by the local authority but make sure each lesson is memorable and fun.

I see challenges in the teaching of RE approaching soon if there is the change implemented as mentioned in the National Plan. The major change would be changing RE to RE

---

and Worldviews. This would mean teachers would need to allocate extra time in educating themselves on new content and carry out training to learn to teach the new content effectively. This is a difficult task with the current workload already being taken on by teachers.

I feel positive and confident about what I have already observed on my first placement in terms of teaching RE. I was able to teach RE myself during an observation. I felt the teacher placed importance upon RE even though it is not part of the national curriculum. I believe that is because RE helps develop moral understanding. Parents are also happy to engage in and support what children are taught in RE as this was demonstrated by the high attendance of parents at the Nativity play after the focus on Christianity that term.

References

All Party Parliamentary Group (APPG) (2013) *RE: The Truth Unmasked: The Supply of and Support for Religious Education Teachers*, London: REC. [Online] https://www.religiouseducationcouncil. org.uk/wp-content/uploads/2017/11/APPG_RE_The_Truth_Unmasked-FINAL-1.pdf (Accessed 05/12/2020).

APPG (2016) *Improving Religious Literacy: A Contribution to the Debate.* [Online] https://www.fionabruce. org.uk/sites/www.fionabruce.org.uk/files/2018-02/All-Party%20Parliamentary%20 Group%20on%20Religious%20Edcuation%20-%20Improving%20Religious%20 Literacy%20-%20A%20Contribution%20to%20the%20Debate.pdf (Accessed 19/12/2020).

Barnes, L. P. (2020) *Crisis, Controversy and the Future of Religious Education*, Oxon: Routledge.

Bowie, B. (2019) The implicit knowledge structure preferred by questions in English religious studies public exams, in G. Biesta and P. Hannam (Eds.) *Religion and Education: The Forgotten Dimensions of Religious Education*, Leiden: Brill, pp. 112–123.

Brine, A., and Chater, M. (2020) How did we get here? The twin narratives, in M. Chater (Ed.) *Reforming RE*, Woodbridge: John Catt, pp. 21–35.

Bristol (2016) *Awareness, Mystery, Value.* [Online] http://www.awarenessmysteryvalue.org/2016/a02-legal-framework-rights-responsibilities-withdrawal/ (Accessed 15/11/2020).

CEM (2016) *Understanding Christianity.* [Online] http://www.understandingchristianity.org.uk/ (Accessed 05/12/2020).

Chater, M., and Erricker, C. (2013) *Does Religious Education Have a Future? Pedagogical and Policy Prospects*, London: Routledge.

Chater, M. (2020) Preface, in M. Charter (Ed.) *Reforming RE*, Woodbridge: John Catt, pp. 15–16.

Clarke, C., and Woodhead, L. (2015) *A New Settlement: Religion & Belief in Schools*, Westminster Faith Debates.

Clarke, C., and Woodhead, L. (2018) *A New Settlement: Religion and Belief in Schools*, Westminster Faith Debates. [Online] http://faithdebates.org.uk/wp-content/uploads/2018/07/Clarke-Woodhead-A-New-Settlement-Revised.pdf (Accessed 15/11/2020).

Commission on Religious Education (CoRE) (2016) *Interim Report: Religious Education for All*, London: Religious Education Council.

Conroy, J., Lundie, C., Davis, D., and Robert, A. (2013) *Does Religious Education Work?* London: Bloomsbury.

Cooling, T. (2021) The commission on religious education – A response to L. Philip Barnes, *British Journal of Educational Studies*, 70, (1), pp. 103–118, DOI: 10.1080/00071005.2021.1954142

Cooling, T., Bowie, B., and Panjwani, F. (2020) *Worldviews in Religious Education*, London: Theos. [Online] https://www.theosthinktank.co.uk/research/2020/10/21/worldviews-in-religious-education (Accessed 16/07/2021).

Copley, T. (2008) *Teaching Religion: Sixty Years of Religious Education in England and Wales*, New Updated Edition, Exeter: University of Exeter Press.

CoRE (2018) *Religion and Worldviews: The Way Forward. A National Plan for RE*, London: Commission on Religious Education

Cornwall (2014) *Cornwall Agreed Syllabus for Religious Education 2014*, Cornwall SACRE: Cornwall Council.

DCSF (Department for Children, Schools and Families) (2010) *Religious Education in English Schools: Non-Statutory Guidance 2010*, Nottingham: DCSF Publications. DCSF-00114-2010.

Dearing, R. (1994) *The National Curriculum and Its Assessment: Final Report*, London: School Curriculum and Assessment Authority.

DfE (Department for Education) (1994) *Religious Education and Collective Worship*, London: Department for Education Schools. Circular 1/94.

DfE (Department for Education) (2011) *Review of the National Curriculum in England: Summary Report of the Call for Evidence*, Crown Copyright. [Online] https://assets.publishing.service.gov.uk/government/uploads/system/uploads/attachment_data/file/193519/NCR_-_Call_for_Evidence_Summary_Report.pdf (Accessed 15/11/2020).

DfE (Department for Education) (2013) *The National Curriculum in England Key Stages 1 and 2 Framework Document*, Crown Copyright. Reference: DFE-00178-2013. [Online] https://assets.publishing.service.gov.uk/government/uploads/system/uploads/attachment_data/file/425601/PRIMARY_national_curriculum.pdf (Accessed 19/09/2021).

DfE (Department for Education) (2014) *The National Curriculum in England Framework Document*. Crown copyright 2013. DFE-00177-2013. [Online] https://assets.publishing.service.gov.uk/government/uploads/system/uploads/attachment_data/file/381344/Master_final_national_curriculum_28_Nov.pdf (Accessed 19/09/2021).

DfE (Department for Education) (2021) *Teachers' Standards Guidance for School Leaders, School Staff and Governing Bodies*, Crown Copyright. Reference: DFE-00066-2011. [Online] https://assets.publishing.service.gov.uk/government/uploads/system/uploads/attachment_data/file/1007716/Teachers__Standards_2021_update.pdf (Accessed 19/09/2021).

Dinham, M., and Shaw, M. (2015) *RE for Real*, Goldsmiths, UOL & Culham St. Gabriel's. [Online] https://www.gold.ac.uk/media/documents-by-section/departments/research-centres-and-units/research-units/faiths-and-civil-society/REforREal-web-b.pdf (Accessed 16/11/2020).

Dinham, M., and Shaw, M. (2020) Landscapes, real and imagined: 'RE for Real', in M. Chater (Ed.) *Reforming RE*, Woodbridge: John Catt, pp. 51–64.

East Sussex (2017) *East Sussex RE Agreed Syllabus June 2017 Continuing the Journey*. [Online] https://czone.eastsussex.gov.uk/media/2423/east-sussex-agreed-syllabus-june-2017.pdf (Accessed 15/11/2020).

Erricker, C., Lowndes, J., and Bellchambers, E. (2011) *Primary Religious Education – A New Approach*, London: Routledge

Freathy, G., Freathy, R., Doney, J., Walshe, K., and Teece, G. (2015) *The RE-Searchers: A New Approach to Religious Education in Primary Schools*, Exeter: The University of Exeter. [Online] https://ore.exeter.ac.uk/repository/bitstream/handle/10871/18932/The%20RE-searchers%20A%20New%20Approach%20to%20RE%20in%20Primary%20Schools.pdf?sequence=1&isAllowed=y (Accessed 05/12/2020).

Gearon, l, Kuusisto, A., Matemba, Y., Benjamin, S., Du Preez, P., Koirikivi, P., and Shan Simmonds, S. (2021) Decolonising the religious education curriculum, *British Journal of Religious Education*, 43, (1), pp. 1–8.

Grimmitt, M. (2000a) *Pedagogies of Religious Education: Case Studies in the Research and Development of Good Pedagogic Practice in RE*, Great Wakering: McCrimmons.

Grimmitt, M. (2000b) Introduction: The captivity and liberation of Religious Education and the meaning and significance of pedagogy, in M. Grimmitt (Ed.) *Pedagogies of Religious Education*, Great Wakering: McCrimmons, pp. 7–23.

Grimmitt, M. (2010) (Ed.) *Religious Education and Social and Community Cohesion*, Great Wakering: McCrimmons.

James, M., and Stern, S. (2019) *Mastering Primary Religious Education*, London: Bloomsbury.

Lawton, C. (2018) Time to abandon Religious Education: Ditching an out-of-date solution to an out-of-date problem, in M. Castelli and M. Chater (Eds.) *We Need to Talk About Religious Education: Manifestos for the Future of RE*, London: Jessica Kingsley, pp. 21–35.

Lincolnshire (2018) *Lincolnshire Agreed Syllabus for Religious Education 2018–2023*, Lincolnshire: Lincolnshire County Council. [Online] https://www.lincolndiocesaneducation.com/_site/data/files/LAS/Lincolnshire-Agreed-Syllabus-for-Religious-Education-2018-2022-FINAL.pdf (Accessed 19/12/2020).

Louden, L. M. R. (2004) The conscience clause in religious education and collective worship: Conscientious objection or curriculum choice, *British Journal of Religious Education*, 26, (3), pp. 273–284.

Lundie, D., and O'Siochru, C. (2021) The right of withdrawal from religious education in England: School leaders' beliefs, experiences and understandings of policy and practice, *British Journal of Religious Education*, 43, (2), pp. 161–173.

McCreery, E., Palmer, S., and Voiels, V. (2008) *Teaching Religious Education*, Exeter: Learning Matters.

Myatt, M. (2020) Foreword: Reforming RE, in M. Chater (Ed.) *Reforming RE*, Woodbridge: John Catt, pp. 11–14.

NATRE (2013) *An Analysis of the Provision for RE in Primary Schools – Spring Term 2013*. [Online] https://www.religiouseducationcouncil.org.uk/wpcontent/uploads/2018/01/NATRE_Primary_RE_Survey_2013_1_2_fin.pdf (Accessed 05/12/2020).

NATRE (2016) *An Analysis of the Provision for RE in Primary Schools – Autumn 2016*. [Online] https://www.natre.org.uk/uploads/Free%20Resources/NATRE%20Primary%20Survey%202016%20final.pdf (Accessed 05/12/2020).

NATRE (2017) *The State of the Nation: A Report on Religious Education Provision Within Secondary Schools in England*. [Online] https://www.natre.org.uk/uploads/Free%20Resources/SOTN%202017%20Report%20web%20version%20FINAL.pdf (Accessed 05/12/2020).

NATRE (2018) *An Analysis of the Provision for RE in Primary Schools: Autumn Term 2018*. [Online] https://www.natre.org.uk/uploads/Free%20Resources/NATRE%20Primary%20Survey%202018%20final.pdf (Accessed 05/12/2020).

NATRE and NAHT (2018) *Guidance: Dealing With Withdrawal from RE*, London: NATRE.

NATRE (2019) *Primary RE 1000!* [Online] https://www.natre.org.uk/membership/primary-RE-1000. (Accessed on 05/12/2020).

NATRE (2020) *Removal of the Bursary for Those Training to be Secondary Teachers of RE*. [Online] https://www.natre.org.uk/news/latest-news/removal-of-the-bursary-for-those-training-to-be-secondary-teachers-of-re/ (Accessed 21/11/2020).

Nottingham (2020) *Religious Education for All the Agreed Syllabus for RE in Nottinghamshire 2015–2020*, http://www.nottinghamschools.org.uk/media/1170092/agreed-syllabus-15-20.pdf (Accessed 28/07/2021).

Ofsted (2007) *Making Sense of Religion*, Manchester: Crown Copyright. Reference no: 070045. [Online] http://www.educationengland.org.uk/documents/pdfs/2007-ofsted-religion.pdf (Accessed 15/11/2020).

Ofsted (2010) *Transforming Religious Education*, Manchester: Crown Copyright. Reference no: 090215. [Online] https://dera.ioe.ac.uk/1121/1/Transforming%20religious%20education.pdf (Accessed 05/12/2020).

Ofsted (2013) *Religious Education: Realising the Potential*, Manchester: Crown Copyright. Reference No: 130068. [Online] https://assets.publishing.service.gov.uk/government/uploads/system/uploads/attachment_data/file/413157/Religious_education_-_realising_the_potential.pdf (Accessed 05/12/2020).

Ofsted (2021) *Research Review Series: Religious Education*. [Online] https://www.gov.uk/government/publications/research-review-series-religious-education/research-review-series-religious-education#fnref:155 (Accessed 18/07/2021).

Pan-Berkshire (2018) *The Agreed Syllabus for Religious Education Pan-Berkshire 2018–2023*, https://wokingham.moderngov.co.uk/documents/s23390/Berkshire%20Syllabus%202018-2023.pdf (Accessed 28/07/2021).

Parker, S. G., Freathy, R., and Aldridge, D. (2015) The Future of Religious Education: Crisis, reform and iconoclasm, *Journal of Beliefs & Values*, 36, (1), pp. 1–4.

Redbridge (2015) *Agreed Syllabus for Religious Education 2015–2020*, RE Today Service and SACRE of the London Boroughs of Redbridge and Havering.

REC (Religious Education Council of England and Wales) (2013a) *A Review of Religious Education in England*, London: REC of England and Wales.

REC (Religious Education Council of England and Wales) (2013b) *A Curriculum Framework for Religious Education in England*. London: REC of England and Wales.

Surrey (2017) *The Agreed Syllabus for Religious Education in Surrey School 2017–2022*. [Online] https://www.cofeguildford.org.uk/docs/default-source/making-disciples/nurturing-education/education/sacre/sacre/agreed-syllabus/agreed-syllabus-for-religious-education-in-surrey-schools-2017-2022.pdf?sfvrsn=a33b2232_3 (Accessed 15/11/2020).

Tharani, A., Sarbicki, A., Guntrip, C., Cox, D., Freeman, K., and Hussain, D. (2020) The Commission on Religious Education, in M. Chater (Ed.) *Reforming RE*, Woodbridge: John Catt, pp. 37–50.

Whitworth, L. (2020) Do I know enough to teach RE? Responding to the commission on religious education's recommendation for primary initial teacher education, *Journal of Religious Education*, 68, pp. 345–357.

Woodhead, L. (2018) Foreword, in M. Castelli and M. Chater (Eds.) *We Need to Talk About Religious Education: Manifestos for the Future of RE*, London: Jessica Kingsley, pp. 7–10.

Woolf Institute (2015) *Living With Difference: Community, Diversity and the Common Good*, Cambridge: The Woolf Institute.

3

What is RE all about?

Introduction

Many lecturers including teachers in some schools sometimes have to justify the existence and the teaching of Religious Education (RE) in primary schools. Years ago, a session booklet was distributed during a first RE lecture to undergraduate trainees. On the cover of this booklet, in addition to the name of the institution, faculty and other related information, the session title read, 'What is RE all about'? During one of the years, a student inserted, in small writing, a response: 'Nothing mate J…'.

A few years later, in the autumn of 2018, in an RE session with a group of post-graduate students as part of their Foundation Subjects, students were given a set of RE-related images with questions to answer. Often, many students express their lack of knowledge regarding the specific responses to these varied images. One particular student may have found them particularly challenging, and, possibly, led them to make the following comment: 'Damn why do I have to teach his dreaded subject'.

These vignettes are shared to highlight the need for you to reflect and be clear about the rationale, place, value and role of RE in the education of pupils in the UK. RE is probably the most divisive subject in the school curriculum and it generates considerable discussion and elicits complex responses from a very wider audience like no other subject (Barnes 2012:1). As it raises profound ontological and epistemological questions, and potentially divides individuals and communities on the basis of worldviews, philosophies and/or ideologies (Freathy et al. 2017:425). Some have a clear view on whether it should or should not be taught, and whether the subject is taught, should be compulsory or not. Moreover, the current privileged status of RE has also been distrusted. It has been suggested that RE in the future will have to rely less on being a mandatory subject for all pupils by legislation, and much more on the intrinsic worth of the learning opportunities it offers (REC 2013a:54).

Given your readings of Chapter 1, you will recognise that RE has progressed from a subject, which was perceived as providing faith-based solutions to one that is basically about being curious and raising and exploring questions. Some of the different standpoints are represented in Box 3.1.

RE beyond the UK

Around the world, though, confessional RE is very common, institutionalised and accepted as the normal way to do RE (Stern 2018). Some promote confessional RE in the UK, for example, Thompson (2004a, 2004b, 2007), who argues that RE has been trapped by indifferentism and essentialism by shifting from the committed teaching of Christianity. The solution, she offers, is to recover the committed teaching of Christianity in a way that preserves an element of openness. Although it remains a minority approach in the UK, it has become more common in a wide range of schools with church foundations (Stern 2018:39).

 DOI: 10.4324/9780429289743-5

BOX 3.1 IDEOLOGICAL STANDPOINTS OF RE

On the question of ideology, the literature suggests that, in contemporary society, RE is underpinned by three contrasting ideological positions, which are at times set against each other in any attempt to reform, implement or evaluate the subject in public education. First, the pluralist position sees that all religious and non-religious beliefs alike are in some sense potentially valid. In this position different beliefs – which are compatible with post-Enlightenment critical thinking – are seen as moving to a more central and universal phase. Such a position, however, hardly appeals to orthodox religious adherents, essentially because it leaves out the distinctiveness of individual beliefs (Hobson and Edwards 1999). Second, the inclusivist position posits that while one dominant religion, say Christianity, is seen as the perfect means of attaining salvation, the other religions, too, can provide the means of gaining the right relationship with God and possibly even guaranteeing salvation (see also D'Costa 1986). Third, the exclusivist position assumes a conservative position on religious matters. Its proponents argue for 'education in faith' (i.e. commitment to a particular faith) as opposed to 'education in religion' (i.e. knowledge about various religious traditions). Christian proponents of this model, state that the saving acts and workings of God cannot be found in other religions (Hick and Hebblethwaite 1980) (cf. Matemba 2013:370).

It is important to recognise that across the globe RE varies in different countries in nature, purpose and name. In France and the US, the teaching of religion is banned in state schools. In Germany, children receive denominational teaching. In Australia, pupils are taught a social studies syllabus in which they not only learn about religion and society but also have a period of religious instruction given by teachers, usually volunteers, from their Christian denomination or another faith (McCreery, Palmer and Voiels 2008:1).

RE in every country is tied to the history of the country – whether that is the anticlerical French Revolution of 1789 or the separation of church and state in the US constitution (which still means that RE is rarely taught in state schools in France or the US) or the re-emergence of the power of the Orthodox Church in Russia in recent years which means that RE is now on the national curriculum of Russia. As you learnt in Chapter 1, in the UK, the Christian Church and state are closely connected, and this has meant that RE has been firmly established in the curriculum – but the nature of RE, and its relationship with Christianity, continues to be argued about and contested (James and Stern 2019:24–25; Selway 2020).

An international perspective on RE provided several benefits to some students. Consider the reflections in Box 3.2:

BOX 3.2 REFLECTIONS ON INTERNATIONAL PERSPECTIVES OF RE

1   It is apparent that in some countries RE is given considerable importance, whereas in others it is less so. It was also useful to recognise the diverse ways in which RE is conceptualised and taught internationally which enable me to position RE in England within this global dimension.

2   As a future leader, I discovered that in some countries the curriculum for RE was independent, whereas in others it was integrated with other parts of the curriculum, if not part of the school day. From the presentations on each country, it was evident that in many countries, over the years, RE had changed in terms of its emphasis, scope and content.

---

3   This was relevant for me as I could begin to see and question why and what for reasons RE in the UK should change or should not. I also learnt about the similarities and differences not only of the RE in the UK and other European countries, but also in different countries in other parts of the world, like Africa. I might go and teach abroad, so learning about RE in all these countries assisted me to know what to expect should I go and work in one of those countries. Most importantly, I engaged critically with the nature of RE provided in England with a view to improving it.

Should RE remain a compulsory subject?

A key debate related to whether RE should be a compulsory subject. White (2004) argued that both the compulsory status and RE as a separate entity should be abandoned as the justification for this was wanting and outdated. Some senior staff argued that organising timetables and resources would become more convenient should the compulsory status of RE be rescinded (Conroy et al. 2013:53). On the other hand, Cush (2007) and Wright (2004) argued that it was the best way to respond to religious plurality. In Box 3.3, Rudi Eliott Lockhart, former CEO of the REC, shared many reasons for it to remain so.

The importance of establishing the intent of RE

The multiplicity of the aim and purpose for RE in the English education system are natural and expected outcomes because other subjects are developed nationally whereas RE is determined locally. As you read earlier, RE must teach about Christianity and the other major religions of the UK and must be nondenominational except in the case of designated 'faith' schools. Other than this, no guidance was offered in educational law concerning its content, purpose or intention because this was to be determined by each local authority (Chater 2018; Plater 2020). As a

---

BOX 3.3 VIEWPOINT: RE SHOULD BE COMPULSORY

First, whether you're personally religious or not, religions and non-religious worldviews really matter. They are a key driver of politics, history, identity, art, literature, etc. Trying to understand humanity without looking at religion is daft.

What's more, they're often misunderstood, misrepresented, stereotyped and simplified in the media and wider society, so having a subject where pupils can learn about their complexity and diversity (both between and within), their fuzzy edges, their contested nature and the way they change over time and place really matters. If they don't do it in RE, they are not going to get a proper chance elsewhere.

Second, this country is very diverse. People have a huge range of religion and non-religion worldviews. If we let children leave school without some understanding of the religious diversity they're going to encounter (and what it means), we're not preparing them well.

Finally, RE is a subject where pupils can reflect on how their own beliefs shape the way they see and make sense of the world.

RE isn't about trying to make pupils more (or less) religious. It's about making sure they can engage with some stuff that really matters. It's about helping them to think critically, giving them the knowledge and skills to know when someone's trying to mislead them about religion. It's a key part of an academic curriculum, just like any number of other subjects. And it's right that it's compulsory in schools.

consequence, the aims of RE, depending on the sources used, fall into several categories, which can be determined by considering the statutory LAS. Chater (2018:72–73) has condensed these into five different aims:

- An academic study of religion in one tradition or group of traditions (theology).
- An academic study of religion in general (religious studies).
- An academic study of philosophical and ethical problems with reference to some religious and philosophical systems.
- An instrumentalist project to promote attitudes of respect, tolerance, community cohesion or British values.
- A personal development program to explore spirituality, personal beliefs, ethical issues and (sometimes) personal, social and health education.

RE is also well known for taking on board governmental, political and social agendas and, often, ends up becoming a 'Cinderella' subject. In other words, RE tries to appease everyone including the subjects of the NC. This has led some experts to judge that there is too much diversity, complexity and variation in articulating the aims of RE and a failure to clarify the relationship between the general aims of schooling, to which RE contributes, and the particular aims specific to RE (REC 2013a:51). This state is perceived to create an incoherent and scattergun curriculum that looks weak, desperate to chase relevance and unable to construct a progression pathway (Chater 2018). Moreover, the 'Does RE Work?' project found that divergence of aims and outcomes is harmful to the subject (Conroy et al. 2013). Although the confusion between the different aims of and rationales for the subject exists in many countries, Cush (2014) opines that it is preventing British RE from achieving its potential.

The lack of a clearly articulated purpose for RE has also been identified as a major cause of confusion for teachers, as seen in Box 3.4. Ofsted reported that RE was increasingly losing touch with the idea that RE should be primarily concerned with helping pupils to make sense of the world of religion and belief. Many primary teachers find it difficult to separate RE from the promotion of spiritual, moral, social and cultural development and, too often, teachers thought they could bring depth to the pupils' learning by inviting them to reflect on or write introspectively about their own experience rather than rigorously investigate and evaluate religion and belief (Ofsted 2013:14–15). Specific to RE, Dinham and Shaw (2015:3) note that there is also a lack of agreement over the balance between 'learning about' and 'learning

---

BOX 3.4 PROBLEMS WITH THE PURPOSE OF THE SUBJECT

Religious Educators from the teachers of under 5s to university professors are known nationwide for their inability to agree on the nature and purpose of the subject. There are a number of reasons for this, perhaps the most significant being the fact that RE is not a discipline in the way that most other subjects in the school curriculum can claim to be. School subjects such as English, mathematics, science, history and music can trace their origins to the academic disciplines that are taught in universities and share their name. There is no university discipline called Religious Education. Instead, RE as a school subject takes its knowledge base and its identity from a number of disciplines, more diverse than physics, chemistry and biology within science or human, physical and economic geography. RE draws primarily on theology, religious studies, Biblical studies, philosophy and sociology of religion. It also draws on history, anthropology, archaeology, psychology and the arts. These disciplines have their own distinctive approaches to study and research, which must be emulated at school level (Wintersgill 2017:45).

from' religion; between the 'intrinsic' and 'instrumental' aims of the subject. Consequently, the perceived inclusive purpose of RE has contributed to blurring the core purpose of the subject with other subjects, which are not in themselves religion or belief, resulting in RE in England being increasingly usurped. When boundaries with other subjects such as PHSE and citizenship are too weak and confused, RE becomes colonised (Chater 2018:73; Dinham and Shaw 2017:3; Gearon 2013). Significantly, it is seen as a contributing factor towards an ongoing poor quality of RE teaching in English schools (Conroy et al. 2013).

Unsurprisingly, the Commission on RE was tasked to consider the nature, purposes and scope of RE (CoRE 2018). From the viewpoint of pupils, the question persists: if you are not religious how is it useful? In addition, if you are religious, presumably school is not the place where you will get your education in religion; rather, it would be in your own religious community. Certainly, if RE is to be understood as educationally worthy it needs some defending (Erricker, Lowndes and Bellchambers 2011:7). Thus, the main purpose of RE should be to teach pupils the disciplinarian knowledge and skills associated with the communities of academic inquiry concerned with the study of religion(s) and worldview(s). For example, through theological and religious studies ('non-confessional' forms of theological studies promote the study of God, or the concept of God, in the context of studying theistic religions, and are open to scholars of all religious and non-religious persuasion) (Larkin, Freathy, Doney and Freathy 2020:5).

Wintersgill (2017:6) has offered some recent aims. A six-fold task for RE has been suggested by Watson and Thompson (2007:68–70). RE should aim to:

- Help pupils to challenge secularism in an open, non-dogmatic way.
- Teach pupils thinking skills understood as far more than just logical reasoning and problem-solving.
- Enable pupils to discuss what is meant by religion, and how that relates to religions, appreciating that this is an ongoing question.
- Inform pupils about a variety of religious and non-religious worldviews through depth of study.
- Invite pupils to practise critical affirmation rather than talk tolerance towards the beliefs and value-positions of others.
- Promote the spiritual development of pupils through access to holistic ways of learning and knowing.

Moreover, it is significant to recall that the aims of RE are not confined to knowing about the different religions, understanding the nature of religion, understanding and interpreting religion and acquiring the skills of analysis and insights from religious studies, though these are relevant in RE. Barnes (2015b:204) emphasises other aims that relate more explicitly to the educational, social and developmental roles of education. The moral purpose of education, he notes, is a common and constant theme in modern British educational legislation, such as the 1944 Education Act and the ERA 1988, which required the curriculum in a maintained school to promote the spiritual, moral, cultural, mental and physical development of pupils at the school and the society. This connection is also evident in RE publications such as (CoRE 2018; DCSF 2010; QCA 2004; REC 2013b) and the new NC (DfE 2013).

Barnes (2015b) further argues that even though the subject officially distances itself from moral education, it also advances the claim that post-confessional multi-faith RE challenges prejudice and intolerance. RE has always gone beyond the understanding of religion to include the social and moral aims of education (see Chapter 7). There are different ways of conceptualising and incorporating this material into classroom teaching to further liberal educational (social) aims; the Birmingham Agreed Syllabus of 2007 and 2022 provide one interesting, stimulating and educationally and philosophically sophisticated way of doing this (Felderhof and Thompson 2014; cf. Barnes 2015b:204; BCC 2022).

The value of RE

Before proceeding, it is important to reflect on the value that you attach to RE. You will be aware that the English education system places a higher premium on numeracy and literacy whilst at the same time the NC in its entirety is a statutory requirement for state schools. In practice, however, the accountability attached to each subject, the time and other related factors are variable. From a philosophical standpoint to assist you to examine your beliefs and values about each subject (why is one more valuable than another is?), it might be worthwhile to consider the value that you attach to each of the subjects. You could ask, to what extent is the value intrinsic to the subject (the value of the subject in itself), for example, in helping pupils to develop their own ideas? To what extent is the value extrinsic to the subject (the value of the subject for other purposes), for example, in helping qualify pupils for a job? Based on these questions, the activity in Table 3.1 from Stern (2018:5) offers a useful tool for analysis.

If all subjects in school in total had exactly a thousand units, how much would each subject be worth, and why? Try to complete five in pairs or threes. Once you have completed the values and the reasons for attributing those values, the responses can be discussed as a group. Try to experiment by changing one variable to see the impact that it might have on the other values. For example, if RE were to be abolished, which other subjects might increase the value to compensate for this loss, and how would that change? If RE were to become the study of a single religion, what value would it lose or gain? (Stern 2018:5).

What is not RE?

To reiterate an important purpose of RE which is that it is not about telling pupils what they should believe. Similarly, it is not about telling them that if they do not believe in a certain way they are not a part of a tradition. Moreover, RE is not about presenting religions and beliefs as a supermarket where pupils can simply pick and mix what they want to believe and do. RE is not about converting or proselytising. Religions are sophisticated and overly culturally embedded to permit that and teachers do pupils no favours by simply presenting religions as opinions that cannot be proved or simply adopted (Cornwall 2014). RE is not all opinions and there are right answers.

Table 3.1 The value of RE in the curriculum		
Subject	**Value**	**Why this value? (extrinsic and intrinsic)**
Art		
Computing		
Design and Technology		
Geography		
History		
Literacy		
Modern Foreign Languages		
Music		
Numeracy		
Religious Education		
Science		
Total value:	1,000 units	
Source: Stern, J. (2018:5) Teaching Religious Education: Researchers in the Classroom, Bloomsbury Academic, an imprint of Bloomsbury Publishing Plc.		

BOX 3.5 BIAS IN RE

If pupils are to see clearly that there is no hidden agenda to persuade them in their thinking, teaching must be objective in the sense that it is not informed by bias. This is not about apologising for, or watering down, traditions and truth claims or, indeed, the school's religious commitment (if that is relevant in terms of faith schools). It is about recognising that the school in the classroom, which is compulsory attendance, is a public area where respect for the individual's rights and privacy is paramount. The faith presumptions that characterise a voluntarily joint religious group do not apply in this context. We also need to distinguish between viewpoint and bias. A viewpoint is a consciously held opinion and, by implication, acknowledges the existence of other respectable views. However, bias can arise when teaching approaches have not been thought through so that they are influenced by unconscious ideas. If teachers do not adopt a conscious view, then education will be at the mercy of bias (Erricker, Lowndes and Bellchambers 2011:167).

What about remaining neutral?

This is an important question asked by the RE community, as evident in Box 3.5.

Conroy et al. (2013:140) suggest that a commitment to pluralism, as opposed to pretended neutrality is essential if RE were to mediate between an effective engagement with 'other people's beliefs' as well as pupils' own search for meaning. The claim of the neutralism of RE should also be questioned as it presents itself as a liberal Protestant endeavour and is therefore not unbiased (Barnes 2014; Grimmitt 2000; Revell 2012; Tharani 2020) and to note that at times only the 'sanitised' and 'the more benign and congenial aspects' of religion are presented in RE (Hand 2006:13). Jackson and Everington (2017:10) distinguish between 'impartiality' and 'neutrality'. Impartiality involves organising teaching and learning without discrimination as to ethnicity, religion, class or political opinions, with freedom of expression allowed within agreed limits. Neutrality, however, requires concealment of any personal commitment on the teacher's part, and any personal views of pupils are set to one side. They acknowledge that a neutral approach might be required in certain education and legal systems, and be entirely appropriate in such contexts.

The teaching of religion in RE

A primary purpose of RE is for pupils to acquire and develop knowledge and understanding of Christianity and the principal religions represented in Great Britain. To fulfil this purpose, you need to recognise that there are things to know and understand which pupils need to be considered religiously educated. There can be no content-less RE, skills are developed in RE relative to the content.

Teachers are also alerted to be careful not to 'secularise' the content of RE. For example, when teaching about Jesus' parables, the Cornwall syllabus (2014) suggests that they should not be seen simply as interesting stories but as stories, which have theological meaning that relates to concepts of God and humanity. Also, teachers of RE should be careful not to secularise their pupils by assuming that they have no belief or are born within a culture where religion is insignificant as a cultural force. Wright (2004:166) has argued that it is virtually impossible to make sense of the culture and politics of the present age without reference to organised religion. Michael Hand has argued that RE can be justified once a radical change in its content takes place. Rather than teach children about different religions, it should engage them in the examination of religious claims – about the existence of God, for instance, or whether there is an afterlife. These involve epistemologically distinctive forms of argumentation, to which all pupils should be exposed (Hand 2003).

To add to the complexity, some participants questioned the reductionist way in which religions have been represented in RE (Dinham and Shaw 2020:56). Previously Watson (2010) had found that some LAS included humanism as a compulsory subject and recommended secular worldviews through thematic or conceptual approaches. Advancing the case for the inclusion of humanism in RE, Aldridge (2015) maintains that a dialogic approach to RE is advanced in which subject matter emerges or transforms in the educational event. He demonstrates that RE, to be considered educational, must take seriously the possibility of the transformation of its subject matter. Approaches to RE that attempt to restrict in advance the contribution of Humanism or other non-religious standpoints do not take seriously the possibility of this transformation, and thus foreclose the possibilities for educational dialogue.

Barnes (2015a), on the other hand, argues that the inclusion of any non-religious philosophies should have a convincing educational argument to justify its inclusion in an RE curriculum and not just on recommendations by national bodies. He concluded that the case for the inclusion of non-religious worldviews in the content of RE is unconvincing on educational grounds and unnecessary given the secular nature of the school curriculum. Moreover, Felderhof responded to some prominent religious leaders, including the former archbishop of Canterbury, who pleaded for the inclusion of secular humanism within national Religious Studies (RS) exams. Felderhof's notes that his counter-arguments were related with honesty in education, with practical considerations, with legality, with philosophical and theological concerns, with educational and pedagogical imperatives. He contended that the presence of secular humanism in RE invariably leads to a secular and secularising study of religion, which is undesirable if RE in school is to serve its primary purpose of leading to the spiritual and moral development of pupils (Felderhof 2015).

The benefit and importance of RE

RE plays a very important role in the education of every pupil. Religion and belief are highly visible in public life and current affairs in many local, national and international spheres. In the absence of some knowledge of religion and belief systems, an informed understanding of the modern world would remain inadequate. RE strongly links with music, history, politics, social and cultural issues and global economics and matters of religion and belief have, directly and indirectly, affected all our lives and will continue to do so (REC 2009).

RE assists pupils to understand humanity. Religions concern themselves with existential, moral, ethical and social questions. They seek to address fundamental questions related to human existence and the value and purpose of life. RE is a space, which gives pupils to face questions. It is a time when pupils engage in their personal search for meaning. In RE they uncover the teachings of world religions and belief systems. They recognise how religion influences individuals, families and communities. Pupils observe the political and social impact of religious and secular ways of life. RE offers opportunities for constructing personal identity. RE considers religion and belief itself as a phenomenon consisting of both positive and negative features. RE is about engaging with the concept of religion and non-religious beliefs. RE is about the holistic and personal development of pupils. RE is about empowering pupils to negotiate a religiously plural society.

Relationships between religions and beliefs

Pupils should study how religions and beliefs relate and do not relate to each other. This will enable them to recognise both similarities and differences within and between religions and worldviews. Pupils should be encouraged to reflect on the significance of interfaith dialogue and where appropriate be involved in such initiatives for better community cohesion, reduction of religious prejudice and tolerance. Inter-faith dialogue has the potential to develop those attitudes, which are needed for harmonious living in a religiously plural society. Pupils explore why religious communities sometimes come into conflict and what areas of agreement and cooperation are there between religions in the fields of ethics, human rights and social matters. They consider the contributions religions make to reconciliation and the resolution of conflict (IFN 2001). But Byrne (2011) questioned the uncritical nature of some interfaith education initiatives, which encourage the continuation of cultural and theological bias and called for a more critical approach to differences of belief.

Beyond my own

RE has embraced more religious traditions in its collective and, over the years, has recognised the heterogeneity of these traditions. Therefore, through your teaching, pupils must become aware of the variety in belief and practice within individual religions and traditions. In other words, teachers should avoid giving the impression that all Christians worship in a Church on a Sunday in the morning. Equally, it is important that pupils become aware that not everyone believes in the existence of God, or is religious, and that some people are sceptics.

Related to the above, is the use of language. You may observe some LAS using the term Sikhs rather than Sikhism. The implication here, perhaps, is that the focus should be on Jews rather than Judaism; Hindus rather than Hinduism and so forth. In other words, RE should traverse beyond knowledge, concepts and understanding and embrace encounters with living faiths and people rather than relying on history and belief outlines.

RE is about enabling pupils to talk and share their own beliefs, viewpoints and ideas without embarrassment, ridicule or intimidation. Many pupils come from religious backgrounds. Others have no attachment to religious beliefs and practices. Thus, your curriculum and pedagogy should facilitate and ensure that all pupils' voices are heard and the RE curriculum is broad and balanced.

Beyond 'isms' and anti-racism

A function of post-Enlightenment 'scientific' study of religion has been to turn faith into isms and to impose names upon them (cf. Homan 2012:192). Some view this as a colonial legacy. Thus, some followers, in some religious communities, prefer to refer to their religious tradition on their terms. This is especially the case with the Dharmic traditions. Thus, preference would be given, for example, to Sanatana Dharma in place of Hinduism, Sikhi for Sikhism and Buddha Dharma for Buddhism. Moreover, it has been highlighted that talking about 'religions' in singular terms falls short of expressing the diversity within traditions (for example, 'Hinduisms' may be preferable to 'Hinduism' (Ofsted 2021).

It has been suggested that RE is yet to fully and directly address notions of colonialism in the curriculum or make an explicit effort to decolonise its curriculum. The subject's inclusive stance, for example, in Western countries has arguably led the way decades ahead of other subjects in the school or university curriculum (Gearon et al. 2021:1–8). Nevertheless, to this end, in wake of the global anti-colonial and anti-racism movement, NATRE (2021) produced some free anti-racist resources relevant to RE, and include units of work such as 'What can be done to reduce racism? What can religions do to play their part in a more just society?' The statement in Box 3.6 should assist you to think about your constructions of others.

BOX 3.6 DECONSTRUCTION IN RE

Our constructions are shaped and formed by colonial history. Therefore, we should help students explicitly examine their constructions. If you ask students and yourselves to imagine a Buddhist, in most cases, you will find that a man with a shaven head sitting in a meditation position is drawn. Where has this image come from? Where it is constructed from, how and why? This is a result of British colonial interaction with Sri Lanka. What is religion? We think it to be simple. Who says this is Christianity? Where did it come from? We can teach this to pupils (Anon).

Beyond the local

For some pupils religious diversity may not always be apparent, thus, they should learn about its wider contexts and understand it. RE should move them beyond their current life by including matters beyond their locality. The purpose of this kind of RE includes preparing them for life and work in a wider world: regionally, nationally and globally. Attending to such RE enables pupils to appreciate their own and others' beliefs and cultures and how these influences individuals, communities, societies and cultures. RE seeks both to develop pupils' awareness of themselves and others. It also helps pupils to gain a clearer understanding of the significance of religion in the world today. The Census data on religion is useful for contextualising the study of religion in RE. It can be used as a basis for discussion about the ways that people identify with particular religions and beliefs and so forth.

Beyond topical topics

Often the core knowledge, which is intended to be taught in RE, is expressed using topics or themes such as beliefs, leaders, places of worship, festivals and ceremonies, narratives, artefacts and rituals and practices. Attempts should be made to sidestep considering topics as ends in themselves. They should also be taught in an integrated manner rather than independent of each other. In other words, when studying festivals, for example, the religious doctrines and beliefs to which the festival gives meaning and expression, must be studied. Some sacred texts have a story to tell about their preservation and how they have been passed on (Mogra 2020). Hence, they are more than mere texts, but a witness to lived traditions and lives. Some artefacts are more than special objects and serve as aids to worship and prayer. They can be devotional utilities (Homan 2000). Instead of learning about artefacts in isolation, the interconnectedness between the belief, object and practice should be explored.

Beyond theology

Moreover, RE has a multidisciplinary nature (Hutton and Cox 2021). It involves drawing on theological perspectives, narratives, philosophical thinking, ethical standpoints, social phenomena and the associated disciplinary skills. The need for balanced curricula in RE is now emphasised as some teachers gave prominence to one disciplinary approach. Current initiatives propose the positioning of RE within strong academic traditions. RE has been enriched by exploring content through these different lenses and considering the world of religion and belief from different epistemological positions (CoRE 2018; Freathy and John 2019; Georgiou and Wright 2018, 2020).

A balanced disciplinary approach to designing an RE curriculum has the potential of providing more rigorous teaching and learning. The specialist, disciplinary and conceptual knowledge that materialises from this 'multifaceted matrix of RE' is clearly significant knowledge, as such, it can help to deal with the knowledge problem of RE (Kueh 2018:63; Kueh 2020). The human/social sciences is an umbrella term for a collection of subjects that explore what it means to be human including anthropology, human geography, history, law, linguistics, politics, psychology and sociology.

Beyond cognition

Hannam (2019) problematises current RE for its failure to take religion seriously as existential. Her alternative approach breaks away from the current dominant works of RE scholars like Andrew Wright, Clive Erricker and Robert Jackson. She offers the possibility of 'each unique child making her beginnings in the world of others' and of developing faith not conceptualised as belief in something but as a mode of existence, namely action that brings children to attend (pp. 115–118). For her, freedom and human existence are at the core of RE 'rather than epistemological conundrums about truth or kinds of more or less powerful knowledge' (p. 119). For Hannam, human beings are not merely cognitive 'understanders'. Therefore, teachers should 'increase the power of attention' (p. 125), which to her is faith; and not to consider the child as exclusively an understander of objects, but the subject who 'is brought to action and can become an actor in their own life' (p. 129). Thus, RE should recognise that all pupils are of special value. This means that all pupils should have their inner potential ignited. RE supports every pupil to reflect on their own identity as unique human beings. This can be achieved through reflecting on the purpose of life and understanding that there is a spiritual dimension to life. One of the criticisms of multi-faith RE is that it tends to ignore the existential dimension of living a religious life (Moulin 2011; Vestøl 2016). The primary reason why profound existential, epistemological, ethical and other such questions should be raised in non-denominational RE in schools without a religious affiliation is not because RE is deemed uniquely placed as a curriculum subject to provide answers to 'ultimate questions' but because pupils' answers will affect and be affected by their engagement with the subject matter. Thus, teachers need to develop pupils' critical awareness of their own beliefs, values and assumptions as learners in RE and focus on their thinking about and responses to what they are learning (Larkin, Freathy, Doney and Freathy 2020:44).

Essentialism and lived religions

There has been concern that the 'world religions approach' presented religions as essentialised and that it constructed religions along with the model of Protestant Christianity: with founders, sacred texts, specific places of worship, churchlike organisational structures and systems of doctrine. The study of religions at both university and school levels in the last 50 years has generally been framed within this paradigm. However, this model has been problematised both by academics and within classroom practices (Tharani 2020:10). Thus, RE has been called to be re-imagined. Dinham and Shaw (2015) note that cutting edge research in the sociology of religion suggests that RE will be strongest when it moves away from teaching the world religions as though 'they' are problematic, 'out there', exotic or other, or as historical traditions, either in the past or stuck there. They emphasise that research indicates that religion is contemporary, pervasive and real. It is lived. It is a fluid identity, as well as solid tradition, and it is contested internally in each individual's daily experience. How can we equip people to get to grips with the religion and belief, which turns out to be all around after all? In schools, what sort of teaching and learning about religion and belief can help? (Dinham and Shaw 2015:4).

McKain has defended essentialism. He suggests that many would agree with the concerns raised by the CoRE (2018) report that RE should go beyond studying six major world religions and cover the internal complexity of each one religion. It is assumed that to essentialise is to mislead students and dump down religions. However, McKain argues that to essentialise is to simplify to enable understanding. Students should be made aware of diversity but only after they have been taught the basics and the foundations. It is necessary, he proposes, to teach the basics first before introducing the complexity. As a subject community, he proposes further thinking about how to build and sequence knowledge in the study of religion and belief. For him, essentialism of the curriculum content is not the problem and it is not necessarily reductive (Orme, McKavanagh and McKain 2020:193–194).

Pupils should learn about themselves from religion for SMSC

RE affirms the important contribution that it makes to the education of all pupils growing up in contemporary British society. It seeks to contribute to a curriculum in schools, which the 1988 ERA expects to be balanced and broadly based. It focuses on the whole child as RE supports the two purposes of the curriculum, outlined in the NC (DfE 2013), and has a significant role in promoting the spiritual, moral, cultural, mental (SMSC) and physical development of pupils at the school and society, and prepare pupils for the opportunities, responsibilities and experiences of later life. To enable RE to inform the SMSC of pupils, the development of critical thinking is important. The time and space offered by RE are considered by pupils to be 'safe'; one wherein they are given an opportunity to explore ideas, debate and ask ultimate and/or controversial questions in a non-judgmental context. RE lessons offer a safe space for reflection, discussion, dialogue and debate. RE lessons provide opportunities for sensitive responses to be made to unforeseen events of a religious, moral or philosophical nature, whether local, national or global (REC 2013b).

A caveat

As noted above, RE contributes to SMSC development. RE also assists in the active promotion of 'British' values of mutual respect for and tolerance of those with different faiths and beliefs, and for those without faith (DfE 2021), and, in contributing to the minimising of violent extremism, community cohesion and countering hate crime. However, RE is not synonymous with these agendas and it is important that these should not overtake RE. Instead, RE ought to be at the heart of critiquing, questioning, deconstructing and decolonising such agendas.

What's in a name?

In the past, the subject was known as Religious Instruction, later Religious Education, and recently there have been calls to rename it as 'Religion and Beliefs' (Clarke and Woodhead 2018). From the study of Dinham and Shaw (2015), there were suggestions of 'Religious Awareness', 'Religious Literacy', 'Beliefs, Ethics and Values Education'. Moreover, the CoRE has recommended 'Religion and Worldviews' (R&W) (CoRE 2018) and Lawton (2018) proposes 'Religious Studies' as it conveys academic validity. These suggestions have provoked everyone to think about the name.

Advocates maintain:

- It reflects what schools are offering.
- The use of R&W will potentially attract more parents and pupils as it reflects all perspectives.
- Other subjects do not use the word 'education', so RE should not be the only one using it.
- It is all about the focus of the subject. By changing the name, it opens it up. We might have fewer withdrawals as it is not just religion but worldviews too.
- Change it to R&W because it is not just about religion, but the society and to grow up accepting and being aware of the changing society.

However, others have concerns:

- The inclusion of the word 'education' stresses that RE was about educating pupils and not indoctrinating them.
- Changing the name takes away from it what it stands for. RE allows pupils to recognise the way in which religion influences anything. By removing the religion, what will the subject be left with.
- Pupils are fascinated by religion. It's origin, key beliefs and how they shape life. It is academically rigorous, so removing religion would deprive them of an understanding of the world they are entitled to know.
- Why change when it is not broken. People know what it is. It is a generation. We don't change the name of science, history or geography.
- If you mix RE with worldviews, it is just like mixing history, geography and PSHE. All subjects will be bundled together and also with morals and ethics as well.

- Religious worldview is not RE so call it what you like.
- The name change is a red herring. It does not matter what you call the subject. The rationale behind the curriculum, what is taught, its coherence and its sequence is important not what its name is.

Regardless, others suggest the name change should not result in tokenistic changes; instead, the substantive changes in the curriculum and quality of provisions are more important.

RE and religious literacy

The concept of 'religious literacy', though controversial, has become popular among practitioners, scholars and policymakers in RE both as an aim for RE and as an organising principle for curriculum, pedagogy and assessment (APPG 2016; Biesta, Aldridge, Hannam and Whittle 2019; Clarke and Woodhead 2015; Conroy et al. 2013; Dinham and Shaw 2015; Woolf Institute 2015). Shaw (2020) presented religion and worldview literacy as a model with the potential to bridge perceived tensions between intrinsic and instrumental aims of RE and concerns around its knowledge-base. A characterisation of this kind of RE prompts a reflection on what would constitute a religiously literate person and what it means.

The term 'religious literacy' is a metaphor connected to the skills of being able to read, write and communicate (Dinham and Shaw 2017). In RE, James and Stern (2019:8) maintain that it is a teacher's role to create a learning environment where engagement with religious material is valued as pupils develop the ability to read and appreciate different kinds of religious texts and sources such as myths, figurative language, symbols, narratives, letters, poetry, art and art and drama. In other words, a religiously literal person understands that religions, although based on teachings that may not change, are internally diverse and movable in expression (James and Stern 2019:8–9). Moreover, Erricker, Lowndes and Bellchambers (2011:21) posit that religiously literate pupils will be discerning and critical about the value of religion, develop their emergent worldview and values and be constructively critical citizens within the social environment they will shape in the future to be confident and responsible citizens. It is also suggested that pupils who are religiously literate should be able to hold balanced and informed conversations about religion and belief (Dinham and Shaw 2015). They should be able to express human experiences of religion and belief. Theologically they talk about God, god, creation and the afterlife. They know and understand spiritual insights and secular worldviews. The potential consequences of poor religious literacy are depicted in Box 3.7.

BOX 3.7 AIMING BETTER FOR RE

The consequences of poor religious literacy can be significant. We can see the impact of this in a number of ways. On a public or institutional level, religious illiteracy can lead to media stories which perpetuate stereotypes, are inaccurate, or foster suspicion and government policies which damage relations between particular religious groups and the wider society. On a personal level, a lack of religious literacy can lead to overly simplistic assumptions about how beliefs, values and identities influence people's actions. They can also result in an inability to understand the meaning of symbols, rituals and language with religious roots, which continue to make up an important element of our national heritage and identity. At worst, a lack of religious literacy can lead to hatred and prejudice and the marginalisation of some groups (APPG 2016:4).

Religious literacy can be understood as composing four main elements:

- A basic level of knowledge about the particular beliefs, practices and traditions of the main religious traditions in Britain, and of the shape of our changing religious landscape today. This must be complemented by a conceptual understanding of what religious belief systems are, and how they may function in the lives of individuals.

- An awareness of how beliefs, inherited traditions and textual interpretations might manifest into the actions, practices and daily lives of individuals. Crucial to this is an understanding of the diversity within religious traditions, and an awareness of the way in which the same text, or religious principle, can be interpreted in different ways by different individuals.

- A critical awareness, meaning that an individual has the ability to recognise, analyse and critique religious stereotypes and engage effectively with, and take a nuanced approach towards, the questions raised by religion.

- A sophisticated ability to engage with religious groups in a way which promotes respect and plurality, and which enables effective communication about religion (APPG 2016:6).

The concept of religious literacy and its theoretical basis has been problematised (Biesta, Aldridge, Hannam and Whittle 2019) as it is a deeply political concept. Some question that for practical purposes how much religious literacy is needed to navigate the public sphere of life. There are also difficulties in bringing about religious literacy to the desired or necessary level of competence. Some want a level of literacy that allows for sophisticated and detailed discussions and opportunities for dialogue, meaning pupils could navigate, for example, the key differences and similarities between Sikhism and Islam. Others question how many 'religions' do pupils need to learn about to become religiously literate. If this is the case, then (Biesta, Aldridge, Hannam and Whittle 2019) question the need for the terminology of religious literacy, since it could be argued that it only serves to add a further complex layer. Nevertheless, in response to the question of whether religious literacy is a way forward for RE, they suggest that it depends first, on how one understands literacy. Second, religious literacy also depends upon how one wishes to understand religion itself; and for both literacy and religion, there is a significant variety of interpretations. Most importantly, regarding the future of RE and the possible role religious literacy might play in it, how the research question is responded to first and foremost depends on how one sees RE itself (Biesta, Aldridge, Hannam and Whittle 2019:30).

Brine has argued for the deconstruction of the content of RE and to re-integrate it into a new curriculum, to this; he (2020) contends that, arguably, a key mistake made in recent years has been the introduction of the concept of religious literacy. He asks if it would be better to think in terms of a functional literacy about religion and belief, and then look at ways to secure it within the curriculum, recognising it as part of a wider set of cultural and social literacy about the ways in which human beings go about creating meaning (Brine and Chater 2020:102).

The term 'literacy' tends to be reserved for the basic grasp of the material to secure competence but not excellence, as such, Lewis (2018:97) argues that this would be insufficient for achieving the larger goals for which religious literacy is usually proffered as the panacea, so expertise is needed not just literacy.

Concerns related to the teaching of RE

Students join ITE courses in a demanding context and one that contributes to a change in their identity. This is significant especially for career changers who have to develop a 'new work role identity' (Wilson and Deaney 2010). McCreery (2005) argued for the need to nurture trainees' initial enthusiasm and experiences in RE. She drew attention to the need to recognise that all trainees bring with them their own RE history. In addition to this, they also bring with them their feelings and emotions about RE. Revell (2005) suggested schools should enhance trainees' self-assurance in relation to RE. Conroy et al. (2013)'s study found that teachers were underconfident and undervalued. Therefore, you need to complete your training with positive attitudes and experiences in all subjects, including RE. Simultaneously, it is crucial to minimise your apprehensions regarding RE and to enhance your self-belief, optimism and confidence so that you respond to these challenges and meet these requirements successfully. Mogra (2014) found three major themes of concern. Subject knowledge was a concern for most trainees. The second relates to pedagogy and the third is linked to professional values.

Some anxieties are about subject knowledge:

> Lack of knowledge
> Confusing the religions
> Getting it wrong or using a wrong term
> The right language to use
> Lack of personal confidence

Looking closely at their anxieties, it becomes evident that some concerns relate to pedagogy:

> Teaching with sincerity
> Dealing with sensitive topics, e.g., death
> Making RE interesting, engaging and relevant
> Availability of appropriate resources
> Not separating an individual so that he/she stands out from the group
> What to do when there is a conflict of beliefs
> Providing too much information or missing out on key points

The third theme relates to concerns about professional values. Thus, some are worried about:

> The challenge of teaching without prejudice and withholding personal views
> Giving undue prominence to one religion
> Doing the subject justice when it is not a core subject, i.e., limited time
> Being sensitive and patronising
> Offending parents, children and religion
> The reluctance of parents towards other religions and RE
> Pressure from the governing body on the content in religion

Interestingly, trainees' concerns are not only related to subject knowledge, pedagogy or professional values. Children themselves are perceived to present challenges too. There is uncertainty about how to respond when, for instance:

> Children want to convert
> Children are requested to be excluded [by parents]
> Children ask challenging questions e.g., which God?
> They appear to know more than the teacher!

To address these concerns, trainees suggested that experience, research and cross-curricular links are helpful ways forward. The key ingredient to improve teaching RE is to be prepared, ask children where needed and know objectives well. It was also suggested that trainees remain detached, examine their assumptions and not get emotionally involved to avoid bias (Mogra 2014:8–9).

Placement in faith schools

In some faith-designated schools, the teaching of RE is delegated to members of their faith as the lesson might have catechism or a prayer before and/or after the lesson. In such a situation, it might be that you as a trainee teacher may ask to teach the lesson and opt out of the prayer element, which can be led by the class teacher or another adult. In this way, you will gain the experience of teaching in such a school and observe faith in practice in an educational setting.

The role of the RE teacher

Most teachers are concerned about all aspects of the education of all their pupils. This includes their spiritual, moral, social, cultural and personal development, all of which are at the heart of good RE. RE is concerned with enabling pupils to explore the meaning of life, the nature of faith and what it means to live life as a believer; it is not concerned with nurturing a particular faith.

Some teachers are happy to talk about their faith others have reservations. In any case, the privacy of the teacher must be respected and not everything is appropriate to share with all pupils (Cush 2014).

The teaching of RE does not require a teacher to belong to a faith community and be committed to a religious or non-religious perspective of life. However, it does require a recognition that such a view does exist. It also necessitates an acceptance that religion is significant to the many people across the globe, although not all, and, therefore, it is an important part of the curriculum and their education.

Summary

This section considered the nature of RE in the UK and beyond. It discussed the compulsory status, some names and highlighted the importance of the aims and purposes of RE. It considered the importance and value of the subject and examined several key features. It also highlighted the prospect of knowledge and critically discussed the concept of religious literacy. It shared some concerns expressed by trainee teachers to assist you to move forward with RE.

PURPOSES, AIMS AND FIELD OF ENQUIRY

Introduction

Following the above historical and 'theoretical' considerations, this section pays attention to the curriculum of RE and highlights the purpose and other aims of studying RE.

Curriculum design is the point at which teachers' understanding of RE's purpose impacts their week-to-week planning and teaching. Ofsted (2013:5) found this to be weak in RE and reported that the RE professional community could clarify the aims and purposes of RE and translate these into high-quality planning. They observed how RE was provided in many of the primary schools visited had the effect of isolating the subject from the rest of the curriculum. These factors were having a depressing effect on standards. For primary schools, they recommended an improvement in the quality of the curriculum to increase opportunities for pupils to work independently, make links with other subjects and tackle more challenging tasks (Ofsted 2013:7–8).

No matter what components are selected for the curriculum, the body of knowledge about one religion remains considerable, let alone the need to satisfy the main ones. Thus, some principles for selection would need to be established. There have been calls for the curriculum for RE to have sufficient depth, continuity and coherence to assist in raising standards and securing knowledge (Chater 2018:74). Pupils should encounter both implicit and explicit religious material. To provide depth they should know both about the significance of religious practice or belief and about the how, where, who, what, why and when. In other words, secure quality of learning is more desirable than a superficial and insecure quantity of learning. You should also aim to provide an academically rigorous and knowledge-rich curriculum in congruence with your school vision and values. In the current landscape, the intent, implementation and impact are to be clearly articulated.

RE in other parts of the world

Before considering the curriculum for RE in England, it would be instructive to become familiar with the relationship that RE has with state policies elsewhere, as illustrated in Box 3.8.

RE and the teachers' standards

Teachers make the education of their pupils their first concern. As they teach RE, they are accountable for achieving the highest possible standards in their work and conduct. They are expected to act with honesty and integrity as they teach RE. They forge positive professional relationships with parents and the wider community in the best interests of pupils. They uphold

---

BOX 3.8 STATE POLICIES ON RE

When it comes to curriculum policies by state education systems, there are three basic reactions. In countries that are committed to a strict separation of religion and state, such as the US, China or France, the secularist option is taken, where religion does not feature as a subject on the curriculum, either because it is considered that this is the fairest approach where there is a plurality of traditions, or because religion is suspect in the state ideology. RE in the sense of nurture is then a matter for the private sphere of the family and religious community. The second option, often taken where religion is an important component of the dominant construction of national identity, is for confessional RE, nurture in the faith tradition of heritage, to appear as a subject in the curriculum. This RE can either be offered only in the dominant tradition of the country, for example Orthodox Christianity in Greece, or – where plurality is recognised – there may be several options, for example in most German Länder until recently the choice was between Roman Catholic and Protestant traditions, or again in Finland between Lutheran RE, Orthodox RE or ethics for the non-committed. A similar situation is currently found in Indonesia, where the choice is between five officially recognised religious traditions: Islam, Roman Catholicism, Protestant Christianity, Hinduism and Buddhism. The third option, still very much a minority one, is the non-confessional multi-faith RE offered by the Agreed Syllabuses of England and Wales, and also found in Scotland, Norway, Sweden, South Africa and Namibia, and upper secondary years (16+) in Denmark and Finland. Obviously this three-fold division is an oversimplification, and there are lots of local variations and exceptions, such as the position of voluntary aided schools in England and Wales (these are state funded schools with a foundation in one particular religious tradition). Within these three basic positions, there are many diverse views on the aims and purposes, content and appropriate pedagogical methods (Cush 2007:219).

---

public trust in the profession and maintain high standards of ethics and behaviour, within and outside school by treating pupils with dignity, building relationships rooted in mutual respect, and, at all times, they observe proper boundaries appropriate to a teacher's professional position. They show tolerance of and respect for the rights of others and those with different faiths and beliefs. Teachers ensure that their personal beliefs are not expressed in ways, which exploit pupils' vulnerability in RE (DfE 2021). Based on qualitative research, Jackson and Everington (2017:19) concluded that in England many teachers, including those with strong personal commitments, are capable, in principle, of adopting an impartial approach. They also recognised that becoming and being an impartial teacher presents many challenges, which can be facilitated by training.

The non-statutory documents for RE

The NSNFRE (QCA 2004) was not designed to be a syllabus nor could it be used as such. It was a framework that needed to be detailed before it could be used to support the development of LAS. Likewise, *A Curriculum Framework for Religious Education in England*, chosen for this chapter, is a non-statutory national curriculum framework for RE, which was commended as a contribution to teachers' thinking, and to public understanding of RE's role and place in schools (REC 2013b:9).

The purposes of RE, as seen from the Religious Education Council's point of view, has been considered here as their expectations were ostensibly a reflection of the QCA (2004) document. It is important to stress that both were non-statutory, although they depicted the position of a government agency and influenced many agreed syllabi of the time as well as the recently proposed RE by the Commission on Religious Education (CoRE 2018).

As you read in the previous Chapter 1, many current agreed syllabuses have been produced with support from RE Today/NATRE, who had previously modelled their syllabuses on the one produced by the REC (2013b). Hence, it is being used here. Nevertheless, it is important to reiterate that, currently, it is a legal requirement for a local-authority-maintained school to use their locally agreed syllabus for teaching RE.

The vision and rationale for RE

It would be interesting to make some comparisons to understand the importance of establishing a vision and rationale for a subject and how and why they are influenced by policy, research and practice. The purpose that was envisioned by the Religious Education Council previously, which as you have learnt, is one only conception, among many, which appears in Box 3.9.

BOX 3.9 A MODEL PURPOSE OF RE

RE contributes dynamically to children and young people's education in schools by provoking challenging questions about meaning and purpose in life, beliefs about God, ultimate reality, issues of right and wrong and what it means to be human. In RE they learn about and from religions and worldviews in local, national and global contexts, to discover, explore and consider different answers to these questions. They learn to weigh up the value of wisdom from different sources, to develop and express their insights in response, and to agree or disagree respectfully. Teaching therefore should equip pupils with systematic knowledge and understanding of a range of religions and worldviews, enabling them to develop their ideas, values and identities. It should develop in pupils an

---

> aptitude for dialogue so that they can participate positively in our society with its diverse religions and worldviews. Pupils should gain and deploy the skills needed to understand, interpret and evaluate texts, sources of wisdom and authority and other evidence. They learn to articulate clearly and coherently their personal beliefs, ideas, values and experiences while respecting the right of others to differ (REC 2013b:11).

Compare these with the summative points from the new vision and current rationale presented by the CoRE (2018:26–31) as a basis for shifting practice and for a new paradigm.

- Young people need both to understand the worldviews of others and reflect on their own.
- Worldviews, whether personal or communal, are highly influential on the lives of individuals, groups and societies. Core knowledge both of the content of religious and non-religious worldviews and the conceptual structure of how worldviews operate, unlocks knowledge and understanding of important aspects of our cultural and intellectual life. Understanding worldviews enables young people to understand a wide range of human experience, from everyday behaviour to the arts, science, technology, literature, history and local and global social and political issues.
- The study of worldviews is a critical gateway to a number of other academic disciplines.
- Religious and non-religious worldviews continue to play a key role in public discourse locally, nationally and globally. They shape a wide range of contemporary debates, as well as practices from everyday interactions to actions on a national or global scale. It is very difficult to understand the significance of these debates or practices without a nuanced understanding of religious and non-religious worldviews and how they operate.
- The explicit, academic study of worldviews provides an opportunity to develop a range of specific and general transferable skills.
- Non-religious worldviews have increasingly been included as a legitimate area for study in RE, partly as a result of the increasing number of people holding non-religious worldviews.
- The existential questions that non-religious worldviews grapple with are the same as those that religious worldviews seek to respond to.

RE also has an important role to play in fostering social cohesion as it offers opportunities for encountering people of different beliefs, faith and lifestyles. However, claims that multi-faith RE contributes to social unity, or cultivates mutual respect or toleration in pupils has been questioned as having insufficient empirical support (Barnes 2014:19). Nevertheless, in addition to being religiously educated and literate, RE assists pupils to become skilled worldview navigators, able to handle the complexity of religious and non-theistic worldviews around them.

What can be the aims of RE

The aims of RE are contested and defined in various ways, as you have read. Teece (2011) suggests that this is part of the reason for the marginalisation of the subject. Be that as it may, the REC (2013b) had maintained that the curriculum for RE would aim to ensure that all pupils:

A   Know about and understand a range of religions and worldviews, so that they can:
- describe, explain and analyse beliefs and practices, recognising the diversity which exists within and between communities and amongst individuals;

O   identify, investigate and respond to questions posed, and responses offered by some of the sources of wisdom found in religions and worldviews;

O   appreciate and appraise the nature, significance and impact of different ways of life and ways of expressing meaning.

B   Express ideas and insights about the nature, significance and impact of religions and worldviews, so that they can:

O   explain reasonably their ideas about how beliefs, practices and forms of expression influence individuals and communities;

O   express with increasing discernment their personal reflections and critical responses to questions and teachings about identity, diversity, meaning and value, including ethical issues;

O   appreciate and appraise varied dimensions of religion or a worldview.

C   Gain and deploy the skills needed to engage seriously with religions and worldviews, so that they can:

O   find out about and investigate key concepts and questions of belonging, meaning, purpose and truth, responding creatively;

O   enquire into what enables different individuals and communities to live together respectfully for the well-being of all;

O   articulate beliefs, values and commitments clearly in order to explain why they may be important in their own and other people's lives.

These aims above encompass the 'learning about religion' and 'learning from religion'. You need to consider with your school how RE teaching addresses these aims (and others) and how pupils are supported to achieve the threefold aims.

Fields of enquiry of RE

Having established the aims, the next step to consider is what is known as the 'field of enquiry'. The field of enquiry of RE attempts to map and define the areas of content or information from which the subject matter for exploration and reflection in the classroom is to be drawn (Rudge 2000:94). The areas of enquiry feature as 'essential knowledge' as well (QCA 2004). Therefore, it might be helpful to consider these six areas of 'essential knowledge' as fields of enquiry (Erricker, Lowndes and Bellchambers 2011:192).

Two attainment targets

By the end of each key stage, pupils are expected to know, apply and understand the matters, skills and processes specified in the programme of study (REC 2013b:27). This should enable teachers to plan, assess and report on progress. Therefore, it is essential that both attainment targets feature in the planning and delivery of RE.

Attainment Target (AT1) is concerned with human experience, enquiry into the nature of religion, as well as the study of key beliefs, teachings, sources, practices and forms of expression. Attainment Target (AT2) is much more than just the personal response of pupils to their learning as it requires an increasing depth of knowledge and understanding as pupils develop their learning. It is also concerned with questions of identity and belonging, meaning, purpose, truth, values and commitments and communicating their responses (QCA 2004:34, REC 2013b:27). Good RE effectively balances learning about and learning from religion, faith, beliefs and worldviews.

In Tables 3.2–3.7, the six key areas of enquiry in RE are described. In addition, related disciplinary, pedagogical and curriculum content has been identified and illustrated to offer an overview of what RE is about. Some of these components feature in more detail later.

Attainment Target 1: Learning about religion and belief

Table 3.2 Beliefs, teachings and sources	
A. Beliefs, Teachings and Sources	(i) Interpreting teachings, sources, authorities and ways of life in order to understand religions and beliefs.
	(ii) Understanding and responding critically to beliefs and attitudes. Religious and non-religious ideas of the ultimate
Aspects for investigation	God, gods, gurus, teachers, philosophers, scriptures, key texts, philosophical works, enlightenment, truth, prophecy, the nature of evidence, soul, consciousness and life after death
Key question	How do religions, non-religious worldviews and philosophies understand and develop beliefs and teachings within their traditions?
Related disciplines	Metaphysics, epistemology and textual analysis
Key skills	Analysis, evaluation and interpretation
Key attitude	Commitment, curiosity, fairness, respect, self-awareness,
Key concepts	Authority, deity, enlightenment, God, life after death, revelation, salvation, soul, truth
Key disposition	Being curious, valuing knowledge, remembering roots, living by rules

Table 3.3 Practices and ways of life	
B. Practices and Ways of Life	(i) Exploring the impact of religions and beliefs on people's lives and behaviour
	(ii) Understanding and responding critically to beliefs and attitudes. Religious and non-religious practices and ways of life
	(iii) Recognising that there is diversity within and between religions and belief systems, that they change over time and are influenced by culture
Aspects for investigation	Worship, prayer, meditation, celebration and pilgrimage, as well as the religious artefacts, holy and special times and festivals associated with them
Key question	How do people practise and keep contact with their faith/philosophy?
Related discipline	Phenomenology
Key skills	Enquiry, investigation, synthesis
Key attitude	Commitment, curiosity, respect, self-awareness
Key concepts	Worship, belonging, celebration, charity, commitment, faith, meditation, morality, prayer, responsibility, ritual
Key disposition	Being loyal and steadfast, being fair and just, being merciful and forgiving, being regardful of suffering

Attainment Target 2: Learning from religion and belief

Table 3.4 Forms of expressing meaning

C. Forms of Expressing Meaning	(i) Appreciating that individuals and cultures express their beliefs, religion, doctrines and values through many different forms.
There are many different ways in which prophets, artists, poets, writers, architects, theologians, philosophers, composers, performers and story-tellers have attempted to express their beliefs and values.	
Aspects for investigation	Worship, music, pictures, symbols, metaphors, poetry, parables, stories, myths, jokes, sculpture, carving, dance, drama, buildings, creeds, prayers, meditations, rituals, calligraphy and philosophical writings. Aspects for investigation could focus on attitudes, behaviour and lifestyles of religious and non-religious people
Key question	How do people communicate their beliefs and values to others?
Related discipline	Language
Key skills	Expression and communication
Key attitude	Awe and wonder, commitment, self-understanding, open-mindedness
Key concepts	Analogy, devotion, imagery, metaphor, myth, parable, remembrance, sacredness, symbolism
Key disposition	Being courageous and confident, appreciating beauty, expressing joy, being thankful

Table 3.5 Identity, diversity and belonging

D. Identity, Diversity and Belonging	(i) Understanding how individuals develop a sense of identity and belonging through faith or belief
	(ii) Exploring the variety, difference and relationships that exist within and between religions, values and beliefs. Religious and non-religious ideas about human individuality and society
Aspects for investigation	Relationships, experiences, (local, national, global, virtual) communities, individuality, personality, feelings, preferences, faith, philosophy, causes of conflict, dialogue between faiths and philosophies
Key question	What do people say about human nature?
Related disciplines	Anthropology, psychology, sociology
Key skills	Analysis, evaluation and interpretation
Key attitude	Commitment, respect, self-understanding
Key concepts	Community(ies), conflict, conversion, dialogue, identity(ies), individuality, loyalty, religious experience, spiritual awareness, spiritual friendship, values
Key disposition	Remembering roots, creating unity and harmony

Table 3.6 Meaning, purpose and truth

E. Meaning, Purpose and Truth	(i) Exploring some of the ultimate and philosophical questions that confront humanity, and responding imaginatively and profoundly to them. The challenges and meanings of life's journey
	(ii) Understand the ways religions and beliefs impact on individual identity, on communities and societies
Aspects for investigation	Religious and non-religious views about suffering and sadness, life's wonders, its triumphs and tribulations, the place and role of human beings within the natural world, their rights, responsibilities and freedoms, the search for meaning, purpose and truth in philosophy, religion and science
Key question	How do people tackle the big questions of life?
Related discipline	Ontology
Key skills	Asking theological and philosophical questions, explaining,
Key attitude	Curiosity, fairness, self-awareness, open-mindedness
Key concepts	Change, creation, doubt, evil, good, justice, life and death, rights and responsibilities, suffering
Key disposition	Being reflective and self-critical, cultivating inclusion, identity and belonging

Table 3.7 Values and commitments

F. Values and Commitments	(i) Understanding how moral values and a sense of obligation can come from beliefs and experience
	(ii) Evaluating their own and others' values in order to make informed, rational and imaginative choices. Moral issues in today's world
Aspects for investigation	Religious and non-religious influences on values, commitments, laws, attitudes, behaviour and moral guidelines, and study of the sources of moral guidance which might influence decision making
Key question	How do I decide the best possible way of life for me? What is the best possible use of life?
Related discipline	Ethics
Key skills	Empathy, reflection, evaluation
Key attitude	Commitment, fairness, self-understanding, open-mindedness
Key concepts	Commitment, compassion, duty, generosity, love, right and wrong, wisdom, values
Key disposition	Caring for others, animals and the environment, being accountable and living with integrity

Current thinking in RE

The current thinking is reflected by the CoRE (2018:34–35) who noted that pupils, as an entitlement, must be taught:

1 About matters of central importance to the worldviews studied, how these can form coherent accounts for adherents, and how these matters are interpreted in different times, cultures and places.

2 About key concepts including 'religion', 'secularity', 'spirituality' and 'worldview', and that worldviews are complex, diverse and plural.

3   The ways in which patterns of belief, expression and belonging may change across and within worldviews, locally, nationally and globally, both historically and in contemporary times.

4   The ways in which worldviews develop in interaction with each other, have some shared beliefs and practices as well as differences, and that people may draw upon more than one tradition.

5   The role of religious and non-religious ritual and practices, foundational texts and of the arts, in both the formation and communication of experience, beliefs, values, identities and commitments.

6   How worldviews may offer responses to fundamental questions of meaning and purpose raised by human experience, and the different roles that worldviews play in providing people with ways of making sense of their lives.

7   The different roles played by worldviews in the lives of individuals and societies, including their influence on moral behaviour and social norms.

8   How worldviews have power and influence in societies and cultures, appealing to various sources of authority, including foundational texts.

9   The different ways in which religion and worldviews can be understood, interpreted and studied, including through a wide range of academic disciplines and through direct encounter and discussion with individuals and communities who hold these worldviews.

The CoRE (2018:35) also states that programmes of study must reflect the complex, diverse and plural nature of worldviews. To address this, they may draw from a range of religious, philosophical, spiritual and other approaches to life including different traditions within Christianity, Buddhism, Hinduism, Islam, Judaism and Sikhism, non-religious worldviews and concepts including Humanism, secularism, atheism and agnosticism, and other relevant worldviews within and beyond these traditions, including worldviews of local significance where appropriate.

Conceptions of curriculum

In recent years, there has been a renewed shift in emphasising the focus of educators on the design and principles of their curricula. Counsell (2018) for example, conceives a curriculum as narrative, as it underlines the importance of the journey: to take a shortcut would be to miss the point. It is also a reminder that curriculum is content structured over time (sic). Moreover, it points to the curriculum as continuous, not just a sequence or a chronology. Thus, for her, the term 'coverage', normally associated with curricula, has limited use.

Reflecting on her experience of creating a challenging and coherent curriculum for a school located in a deprived area, Thompson (2020) offers further principles which could be applied for RE as well. The curriculum has to be ambitious and flexible. It must be responsive to the context and the community and espouse social justice. It must continue to build on the richness that is already there and take it deeper and wider so that children soar higher than your own ambitions for them (Thompson 2020:57). In other words, the curriculum must not be an afterthought. Myatt (2018) suggests that educators should know what they are offering to their pupils and why and in what order.

Specific to RE is that new and completely different way of thinking about curriculum design offered by the Commission on Religious Education (CoRE 2018). Cooling (2021) notes that CoRE suggested that the focus should be on the way in which all humans make sense of their lives through a study of how religious and non-religious worldviews work in human life. In other words, he emphasises that curriculum design is not then primarily a matter of arguing about coverage and which worldviews to include, but is, rather, about using the principles outlined in the National Entitlement to plan pupils' learning about how worldviews work. As a result, for him, the selection of which traditions to study then becomes a professional judgment for teachers to make at the local level as appropriate to their own context and the educational needs of their pupils rather than being an attempt to balance the demands of various religious and non-religious communities (Cooling 2021).

Summary

This section has drawn attention to the importance of establishing the intent of the RE curriculum. You have become aware that, internationally, in some countries, religion does not feature as a subject on the curriculum. In others, the RE can either be offered only in the dominant tradition of the country or where plurality is recognised, there may be several options. A third category, a minority one, is the non-confessional multi-faith RE offered in England and Wales and a few other states. Within these three typologies, there are many different views on the aims and purposes, content and appropriate pedagogical methods.

The section has also highlighted that as a professional teacher you are expected to act with honesty and integrity as you teach RE. The aims and purposes of RE discussed above reflect that of the Religious Education Council of England and Wales. You will find other aims and purposes by other organisations, academics, local authorities and schools. The attainment targets were explained to show what pupils are expected to know, apply and understand the matters, skills and processes specified in a programme of study. The fields of enquiry were augmented with related disciplinary, pedagogical and curriculum content to enable you to visualise RE holistically and gain an insight into what RE is about. These are elucidated in the subsequent chapters (Box 3.10).

BOX 3.10 VIGNETTE: REPRESENTATION

My family has strong beliefs but not religious ones. We believe in looking after the planet, recycling and reusing, looking after and protecting the wildlife and have many activities that we do that support this.

None of my family is religious, my parents or grandparents. However, I was invited to go to church when I was little as my mother had always wanted me to be religious. She felt that having faith would be an amazing thing to feel. But although I was encouraged, I never developed faith, I did make some fantastic friends who were religious, including the vicar's sons and daughter, and spent many days at their house. I wanted to be like my mother but never found faith in me.

I have a degree in Fine Art but needed variety. After graduating, I work with children every day before I decided to return to university to become a teacher. I did not want to go into it as I did with art and found it was not for me. I enjoyed going into schools for performance prep with costumes or face paint. I was a playworker and enjoyed every aspect of this. I worked teaching EAL and loved the dynamic with one child. Teaching to me is all these aspects of being around children, interacting with them. Providing a space for learning but also fun and safety. After two years of teaching in this way, I pursued primary schools. My mother worked in a school as a TA, so I understood that it was not an easy job, and would be hard work, especially behaviour management.

RE was my favourite lesson in school. I am thoroughly invested in being a voice to keep it within schools and to have a prominent place within my future school. I think it is very important in creating an atmosphere for all children to be aware of different ways of life and to have a safe space for questions to be asked. I worked in a school where one teacher was the RE teacher. I have taught three RE lessons so far in year one, both online and in person. Negative experiences exist. The negative reaction to RE has been in the news with the current protests.

I have a very diverse group of friends with different religions, including Catholic, Atheist, Wicca, Muslim. I have not met anyone who truly believed it was not a worthwhile subject. The animosity towards it that I have seen is through a misunderstanding of it, rather than a hatred for the subject, and has been easily resolved through discussion.

I aim to help create a place where each religion is represented, in a classroom that is a safe space to ask questions without fear, and misconceptions to be addressed. The only fear I have is of pronunciation of names that I might not have heard used before, I struggle with reading myself. One concern with this would be teaching another member or staff how to teach their religion, as a non-religious person. Overall, I have fewer concerns with the RE but more with the 'Leading' aspect. Children loved it, teachers were engaged and RE display boards around the school.

References

Aldridge, D. (2015) *The case for humanism in religious education*, Journal of Beliefs and Values, 36, (1), pp. 92–103.

APPG (2016) *Improving Religious Literacy: A Contribution to the Debate*, All Party Parliamentary Group on Religious Education. [Online] https://nasacre.org.uk/file/nasacre/1-971-appg-on-re-improving-religious-literacy-full-report.pdf (Accessed 21/02/2021).

Barnes, L. P. (2012) Entering the debate, in L.P. Barnes (Ed.) *Debates in Religious Education*, London: Routledge, pp. 1–9.

Barnes, L. P. (2014) *Education, Religion and Diversity: Developing a New Model of Religious Education*, Abingdon: Routledge.

Barnes, L. P. (2015a) Humanism, non-religious worldviews and the future of religious education, *Journal of Beliefs and Values*, 36, (1), pp. 79–91.

Barnes, L. P. (2015b) Religious studies, religious education and the aims of education, *British Journal of Religious Education*, 37, (2), pp. 195–206.

BCC (2022) *The Birmingham Agreed Syllabus for Religious Education*, Birmingham: Birmingham City Council. [Online] https://www.birmingham.gov.uk/downloads/file/22257/birmingham_agreed_syllabus_for_religious_education (Accessed 30/3/2022).

Biesta, G., Aldridge, D., Hannam, P., and Whittle, S. (2019) *Religious Literacy: A Way Forward for Religious Education?* Oxford: Brunel University London & Hampshire Inspection and Advisory Service. [Online] https://www.reonline.org.uk/wp-content/uploads/2019/07/Religious-Literacy-Biesta-Aldridge-Hannam-Whittle-June-2019.pdf (Accessed on 21/02/2021).

Brine, A., and Chater (2020) A wholly educational rational for worldviews, in M. Chater (Ed.) *Reforming RE*, Melton: John Catt, pp. 95–113.

Byrne, C. (2011) Freirean critical pedagogy's challenge to interfaith education: What is interfaith? What is education? *British Journal of Religious Education*, 33, (1), pp. 47–60.

Chater, M. (2018) Why we need legislative change, and how we can get it, in M. Castelli and M. Chater (Eds.) *We Need to Talk About Religious Education: Manifestos for the Future of RE*, London: Jessica Kingsley, pp. 71–84.

Clarke, C., and Woodhead, L. (2015) *A New Settlement: Religion & Belief in Schools*, Westminster Faith Debates.

Clarke, C., and Woodhead, L. (2018) *A New Settlement: Religion and Belief in Schools*, Westminster Faith Debates. [Online] http://faithdebates.org.uk/wp-content/uploads/2018/07/Clarke-Woodhead-A-New-Settlement-Revised.pdf (Accessed 15/11/2020).

Conroy, J. C., Lundie, D., Davis, R. A., Baumfeld, V., Barnes, L. P., Gallagher, T., Lowden, K., Bourque, N., and Wenell, K. J. (2013) *Does Religious Education Work? A Multi-Dimensional Investigation*. London: Bloomsbury.

Cooling, T. (2021) The Commission on Religious Education – A response to L. Philip Barnes, *British Journal of Educational Studies*, 70, (1), pp. 103–118, DOI: 10.1080/00071005.2021.1954142

Cornwall (2014) *Cornwall Agreed Syllabus for Religious Education 2014*, Cornwall SACRE: Cornwall Council.

CoRE (Commission on Religious Education) (2018) *Religion and Worldviews: The Way Forward*, London: Religious Education Council.

Counsell, C. (2018) *Senior Curriculum Leadership 1: The Indirect Manifestation of Knowledge: (A) Curriculum as Narrative*. [Online] https://thedignityofthethingblog.wordpress.com/2018/04/07/senior-curriculum-leadership-1-the-indirect-manifestation-of-knowledge-a-curriculum-as-narrative/ (Accessed 01/08/2021).

Cush, D. (2007) Should religious studies be part of the compulsory state school curriculum? *British Journal of Religious Education*, 29, (3), pp. 217–227.

Cush, D. (2014) Autonomy, identity, community and society: Balancing the aims and purposes of religious education, *British Journal of Religious Education*, 36, (2), pp. 119–122.

D'Costa, G. (1986) *Theology and Religious Pluralism*, Oxford: Basil Blackwell.

DCSF (Department for Children, Schools and Families) (2010) *Religious Education in English Schools: Nonstatutory Guidance 2010*, Nottingham: DCSF Publications. DCSF-00114-2010.

DfE (Department for Education) (2021) *Teachers' Standards Guidance for School Leaders, School Staff and Governing Bodies*, Crown Copyright. Reference: DFE-00066-2011 [Online] https://assets.publishing.service.gov.uk/government/uploads/system/uploads/attachment_data/file/1007716/Teachers__Standards_2021_update.pdf (Accessed 19/09/2021).

DfE (Department for Education) (2013) *The National Curriculum in England Key Stages 1 and 2 Framework Document*, Crown Copyright. Reference: Reference: DFE-00178-2013.

Dinham, M., and Shaw, M. (2015) *RE for Real*, Goldsmiths, UOL & Culham St. Gabriel's. [Online] https://www.gold.ac.uk/media/documents-by-section/departments/research-centres-and-units/research-units/faiths-and-civil-society/REforREal-web-b.pdf (Accessed 16/11/2020).

Dinham, M., and Shaw, M. (2020) Landscapes, real and imagined: 'RE for Real', in M. Chater (Ed.) *Reforming RE*, Woodbridge: John Catt, pp. 51–64.

Dinham, M., and Shaw, M. (2017) Religious literacy through religious education: The future of teaching and learning about religion and belief, *Religions*, 8, 119, pp. 1–13 [Online] https://core.ac.uk/download/pdf/132195959.pdf (Accessed 21/02/2021).

Erricker, C., Lowndes, J., and Bellchambers, E. (2011) *Primary Religious Education – A New Approach*, London: Routledge.

Felderhof, M., and Thompson, P. (Eds.) (2014) *Teaching Virtue: The Contribution of Religious Education*, London: Bloomsbury.

Felderhof, M. (2015) Rejoinder: An opinion piece in response to the Religious leaders who have asked for secular humanism to be included in Religious Studies examinations, *Journal of Beliefs & Values*, 36, (1), pp. 124–129, DOI: 10.1080/13617672.2015.1027532

Freathy, R., and John, H. C. (2019) Worldviews and big ideas: A way forward for Religious Education? *Nordidactica – Journal of Humanities and Social Science Education*, 4, pp. 1–27.

Freathy, R., Doney, J., Freathy, G., Walshe, K., and Teece, G. (2017) Pedagogical Bricoleurs and Bricolage researchers: The case of Religious Education, *British Journal of Educational Studies*, 65, (4), pp. 425–443.

Gearon, L. (2013) *A Masterclass in Religious Education – Transforming Teaching and Learning*, London: Bloomsbury.

Gearon, L., Kuusisto, A., Matemba, Y., Benjamin, S., Du Preez, P., Koirikivi, P., and Shan Simmonds, S. (2021) Decolonising the religious education curriculum, *British Journal of Religious Education*, 43, (1), pp. 1–8.

Georgiou, G., and Wright, K. (2018) Re-dressing the balance, in M. Castelli, and M. Chater, *We Need to Talk About Religious Education*, London: Jessica Kingsley, pp. 101–113.

Georgiou, G., and Wright, K. (2020) Disciplinary, religion and worldviews: Making the case for theology, philosophy and human/social sciences, in M. Chater (Ed.) *Reforming RE*, Woodbridge: John Catt, pp. 149–164.

Grimmitt, M. (2000) *Pedagogies of Religious Education*, Great Wakering: McCrimmons.

Hand, M. (2003) Is compulsory religious education justified? in J. White (Ed.) *Rethinking the School Curriculum*, London: Routledge/Falmer.

Hand, M. (2006) *Is Religious Education Possible? A Philosophical Investigation*, London: Continuum.

Hannam, P. (2019) *Religious Education and the Public Sphere*, London: Routledge.

Hick, J., and Hebblethwaite, B., (1980) *Christianity and Other Religions: Selected Readings*, Philadelphia, PA: Fortress Press.

Hobson, P., and Edwards, J. (1999) *Religious Education in a Pluralist Society: The Key Philosophical Issues*, London: Woburn Press.

Homan, R. (2000) Don't let the Murti get dirty: The uses and abuses of religious 'Artefacts', *British Journal of Religious Education*, 23, (1), pp. 27–37.

Homan, R. (2012) Constructing religion, in L. P. Barnes (Ed.) *Debates in Religious Education*, London: Routledge, pp. 183–193.

Hutton, L., and Cox, D. (2021) *Making Every Lesson Count*, Carmarthen: Crown House.

IFN (The Inter Faith Network for the UK) (2001) *Inter-Faith Issues and the Religious Education Curriculum*, London: The Inter Faith Network for the UK.

Jackson, R., and Everington, J. (2017) Teaching inclusive religious education impartially: An English perspective, *British Journal of Religious Education*, 39, (1), pp. 7–24.

James, M., and Stern, S. (2019) *Mastering Primary Religious Education*, London: Bloomsbury.

Kueh, R. (2018) Religious Education and the 'Knowledge Problem', in M. Castelli and M. Chater (Eds.) *We Need to Talk About Religious Education*, London: Jessica Kingsley, pp. 53–69.

Kueh, R. (2020) Disciplinary hearing: Making the case for the discipline in Religion and Worldviews, in M. Chater (Ed.) *Reforming RE*, Woodbridge: John Catt, pp. 131–147.

Larkin, S., Freathy, R., Doney, J., and Freathy, G. (2020) *Metacognition, Worldviews and Religious Education: A Practical Guide for Teachers*, London: Routledge.

Lawton, C. (2018) Time to abandon Religious Education: Ditching an out-of-date solution to an out-of-date problem, in M. Castelli and M. Chater (Eds.) *We Need to Talk About Religious Education: Manifestos for the Future of RE*, London: Jessica Kingsley, pp. 21–35.

Lewis, A. (2018) The future of Catholic Religious Education in the context of proposed wider reform, in M. Castelli and M. Chater (Eds.) *We Need to Talk About Religious Education: Manifestos for the Future of RE*, London: Jessica Kingsley, pp. 85–99.

Matemba, Y. (2013) Spaces of contest for religious education reform in comparative perspectives: Scotland and Malawi as cases, *Compare: A Journal of Comparative and International Education*, 43, (3), pp. 366–386.

McCreery, E. (2005) Preparing primary school teachers to teach religious education, *British Journal of Religious Education*, 27, (3), pp. 265–277.

McCreery, E., Palmer, S., and Voiels, V. (2008) *Teaching Religious Education*, Exeter: Learning Matters.

Mogra, I. (2014) Responding to trainee teachers' feelings about Religious Education, *REsource*, 36, (2), pp. 7–10.

Mogra, I. (2020) *Understanding Islam: A Guide for Teachers*, London: SAGE.

Moulin, D. (2011) Giving voice to 'the silent minority': The experience of religious students in secondary school religious education lessons, *British Journal of Religious Education*, 33, (3), pp. 313–326.

Myatt, M. (2018) *Curriculum: Gallimaufry or Coherence*, Woodbridge: John Catt.

NATRE (2021) *Anti-Racist RE*. [Online] https://www.natre.org.uk/about-natre/projects/anti-racist-re/ (Accessed 17/07/2021).

Ofsted (2013) *Religious Education: Realising the Potential*, Manchester: Crown Copyright. Reference No: 130068. [Online] https://assets.publishing.service.gov.uk/government/uploads/system/uploads/attachment_data/file/413157/Religious_education_-_realising_the_potential.pdf (Accessed 05/12/2020).

Ofsted (2021) *Research Review Series: Religious Education*. [Online] https://www.gov.uk/government/publications/research-review-series-religious-education/research-review-series-religious-education#fnref:131 (Accessed 17/07/2021).

Orme, R., McKavanagh, S., and McKain, N. (2020) What should we teach our pupils? in M. Chater (Ed.) *Reforming RE*, Woodbridge: John Catt, pp. 179–195.

Plater, M. (2020) What is religious education for? Exploring SACRE Member views, *Religion & Education*, 47, (1), pp. 55–76.

QCA (2004) *Religious Education: The Non-Statutory National Framework*, London: Qualifications and Curriculum Authority. Reference: QCA/04/1336.

REC (2009) *Right Now, Everyone Has Something to Say About Religion. Religious Education Helps Make Sense of It*. [Online] http://religiouseducationcouncil.org.uk/media/file/recleaflet.pdf (Accessed 12/01/2021).

REC (Religious Education Council of England and Wales) (2013a) *A Review of Religious Education in England*. London: REC of England and Wales.

REC (Religious Education Council of England and Wales) (2013b) *A Curriculum Framework for Religious Education in England*. London: REC of England and Wales.

Revell, L. (2005) Student primary teachers and their experience of religious education in schools, *British Journal of Religious Education*, 27, (3), pp. 215–226.

Revell, L. (2012) *Islam and Education: The Manipulation and Misrepresentation of a Religion*, London: Trentham Books, Institute of Education Press.

Rudge, J. (2000) The Westhill Project: Religious Education as maturing pupils' patterns of beliefs and behaviour, in M. Grimmitt (Ed.) *Pedagogies of Religious Education*, Great Wakering: McCrimmons, pp. 88–111.

Selway, C. (2020) *Understanding Christianity and the Study of Religions and Worldviews: How the Church of England Has Gained Control Religious Education*, London: National Secular Society.

Shaw, M. (2020) Towards a religiously literate curriculum – Religion and worldview literacy as an educational model, *Journal of Beliefs & Values*, 41, (2), pp. 150–161.

Stern, J. (2018) *Teaching Religious Education: Researchers in the Classroom*, London: Bloomsbury. Second edition.

Teece, G. (2011) Too many competing imperatives? Does RE need to rediscover its identity? *Journal of Beliefs & Values*, 32, (2), pp. 161–172.

Tharani, A. (2020) *The Worldview Project: Discussion Papers*, London: Religious Education Council of England and Wales.

Thompson, P. (2004a) *Whatever Happened to Religious Education?* Cambridge: The Lutterworth Press.

Thompson, P. (2004b) Indifference and essentialism in religious education, *International Journal of Christianity & Education*, 8, (2), pp. 129–139.

Thompson, P. (2007) Religious education from Spens to Swann, in M. Felderhof, P. Thompson and D. Torevell (Eds.) *Inspiring Faith in Schools: Studies in Religious Education*, Aldershot: Ashgate.

Thompson, S. (2020) Creating a challenging and coherent curriculum for progress and pleasure, in C. Sealy (Ed.) *The researchEd Guide to the Curriculum*, Woodbridge: John Catt, pp. 49–58.

Vestøl, J. M. (2016) Textbook religion and lived religion: A comparison of the Christian faith as expressed in textbooks and by young church members, *Religious Education*, 111, (1), pp. 95–110.

Watson, J. (2010) Including secular philosophies such as humanism in locally agreed syllabuses for religious education, *British Journal of Religious Education*, 32, (1), pp. 5–18.

Watson, B., and Thompson, P. (2007) *The Effective Teaching of Religious Education*, Harlow: Longman. Second edition.

White, J. (2004) Should religious education be a compulsory school subject?, *British Journal of Religious Education*, 26, (2), pp. 151–164.

Wilson, E., and Deaney, R. (2010) Changing career and changing identity: How do teacher career changers exercise agency in identity construction? *Social Psychology of Education*, 23, (2), pp. 169–183.

Wintersgill, B. (Ed.) (2017) *Big Ideas for Religious Education*, Exeter: University of Exeter. [Online] http://socialsciences.exeter.ac.uk/media/universityofexeter/collegeofsocialsciencesandinternationalstudies/education/research/groupsandnetworks/reandspiritualitynetwork/Big_Ideas_for_RE_E-Book.pdf (Accessed 09/08/2021). With thanks to the copyright holders Barbara Wintersgill and University of Exeter 2017.

Woolf Institute (2015) *Living With Difference: Community, Diversity and the Common Good*, Cambridge: The Woolf Institute.

Wright, A. (2004) The justification of compulsory religious education: A response to professor white, *British Journal of Religious Education*, 26, (2), pp. 165–174.

The essentials of RE

Knowledge in RE

Introduction

It might surprise you to know that there was a time when schools in England did not have a defined curriculum, as the National Curriculum was first introduced in 1988. In other words, ostensibly, schools, by that overall teachers, decided what to teach as well as how to teach. In the case of Religious Education (RE), you have read its detailed history in Chapter 1 and became aware that 'the curriculum' for RE is a site of power struggle and contention, and remains as such, even though comparisons of Agreed Syllabuses reveal that most hold their content in common, despite the legal provisions for 'local determination' (Conroy et al. 2013:69). Other problems relate to subject knowledge, sequencing content, coherence and continuity (Wintersgill 2017:7). This section discusses the knowledge issue in RE.

A 'knowledge-rich' curriculum

There is an ongoing debate about the concept of a 'knowledge-rich curriculum' and 'powerful knowledge' and the use of direct instruction and memorisations. It is also referred to as a knowledge-led or knowledge-based curriculum (Sherrington 2017). The debate has been informed by discussions from cognitive science, such as the role of knowledge in underpinning reading and understanding (Willingham 2010). It has also been informed by a values-led philosophy based on empowerment through teaching 'powerful knowledge' (Young and Muller 2013; Young and Muller 2016). The significance lies in tackling education's knowledge question within an agenda for social justice (Rata 2016; Sherrington 2017:4). Moreover, Young (2020) maintains that this is not a tool telling teachers what knowledge to include or how to structure it in their teaching, which is the responsibility of teachers. However, Claxton (2021:39–52) has criticised ideas of Young and Hirsch and a 'narrow' conception of the knowledge delivered through didactic instruction, which matches the subjects and syllabuses of the traditional grammar school curriculum, and argues that knowledge and the curriculum, should take account of children's lifeworld, personal histories, current concerns, character development and be well-rounded education.

Counsell (2018) contends that curriculum is all about power. The decisions about what knowledge to teach are an exercise of power and therefore a weighty ethical responsibility, as what is chosen (and left out) to teach confers or denies power. She maintains that the suggestion that knowledge is less important than skills is to ignore how knowledge changes people, including our curiosity and capacity for new knowledge. Accordingly, there is a need for educators to be more coherent concerning the character of knowledge such as its structure, its origin, its status as a set of truth claims and the relationship of teachers and pupils to that knowledge.

DOI: 10.4324/9780429289743-7

RE is one of those subjects, as you will read in the section on the breadth of study where content choices are potentially infinite and selections must be made, not only between religious and non-religious traditions and between different religions but also within each religion. Thus, it is argued that RE is characterised, perhaps, by 'epistemological humility' where pupils (and teachers) recognise, through substantive knowledge and disciplinary knowledge, that there is more than what is taught to them and more than what teachers can teach, and that the results of one's study will be partial and flawed (Tharani 2020:16).

The prospects of knowledge in RE

The report *What Makes Great Teaching* (Coe, Aloisi, Higgins and Major 2014) found that the single biggest factor making a difference to student outcomes is teacher subject-knowledge. Rigour in RE consists of both a body of knowledge and a set of skills. One of the outcomes from recent initiatives and debates in RE has been the re-consideration and problematisation of the status of knowledge in RE (Hutton and Cox 2021).

Kueh (2020:131–132) thinks that the 'knowledge' problem plagues the R&W community, and notes that practitioners raise questions such as: does a turn to knowledge (as opposed to, say, generic skills-based level descriptors) mean a movement towards a reductive, fact-based curriculum, accompanied by naïve pedagogical application of direct instruction? He also remarks that, for others, framing the curriculum in terms of knowledge is assumed to be politically unpalatable: claims that all pupils need to know this or that particular body of knowledge is sometimes assumed to be championed by nationalistic ideologies or contested educational authorities. A third position is concerned about the more theoretical matters arising from a curriculum oriented towards knowledge. They lament that the rapid proliferation of interest in cognitive science becomes a lazy justification for the turn to knowledge. They also lament the fact that the relationship between knowledge and knower is under-theorised (Kueh 2020:131–132).

Quality curriculum: The Ofsted RE research review

Ofsted (2021) published its extensive review of RE which has far-reaching implications, not only for the way RE will be taught in schools but also on how its curriculum design will take place and what knowledge will be expected to feature in RE curricula.

It states that there is no single way of constructing and teaching a high-quality RE curriculum. Therefore, high-quality RE will consider the knowledge that pupils build through the RE curriculum because accurate knowledge about religion and non-religion can be beneficial for achieving different purposes and aims for RE. The curriculum is to have high expectations about scholarship in the curriculum to guard against pupils' misconceptions. What is taught and learned in RE is grounded in what is known about religion/non-religion from the academic study (scholarship). It will have carefully selected and well-sequenced substantive content and concepts. 'Ways of knowing' are appropriately taught alongside the substantive content and are not isolated from the content and concepts that pupils learn. It will consider when pupils should relate the content to their own personal knowledge (for example, prior assumptions). It will avoid covering excessive amounts of content superficially. A high-quality curriculum is ambitious and designed to give all learners the knowledge they need to succeed in life.

Types of knowledge in RE

The Review acknowledges its use of its own terms to define the types of knowledge due to a lack of established conventions within RE subject literature and recognises that different professionals and researchers use a range of terms.

The high-quality RE curriculum focuses on three forms of knowledge that are 'interconnected and sequenced'. This might be a fresh way of conceptualising and thinking about RE for many RE practitioners. It is also a way of grounding RE within its scholarly tradition, whilst also strengthening its identity and, perhaps, status. The three different types of subject-specific knowledge that pupils learn in RE are all-powerful and should not be confused with 'mere facts' (Ofsted 2021).

Substantive content and concepts in RE

Substantive knowledge is also known as 'contextual' or 'factual' knowledge'. Even the knowledge of abstract ideas can be classed as 'factual knowledge' where pupils acquire them as pieces of information without necessarily demonstrating any depth of understanding (Wintersgill, Cush and Francis 2019:4). By substantive, Kueh (2020:135–136) refers to that which has been traditionally understood as content. It is the 'stuff' that is referred to when pupils are taught. That substantive content might be framed factually, or systematically anchored around doctrines; or thematically (by finding commonalities between various lived traditions, such as festivals); or by means of provisional constructs (such as beliefs, practices or sources of wisdom, which arguably do not apply to non-Abrahamic worldviews). The nature of such knowledge is its (apparent) given-ness. It may well be said that such knowledge is contested between individuals, groups, communities or traditions, but even contestation has a sense of given-ness about it.

Ofsted (2021) offers further insight into the substantive knowledge of RE which includes the 'substance' of religious and non-religious traditions that pupils study in the curriculum. Substantive content includes different ways that people express religion and non-religion in their lives; knowledge about artefacts and texts associated with these, concepts that relate to religious and non-religious traditions and the very concepts of 'religion' and 'non-religion' and debates around these ideas. In a forthcoming section, you will read about the three well-established categories of concepts within RE. In other words, you need to be clear about what it is you want your pupils to learn, why and when you want them to learn it.

'Ways of knowing' in RE

Kueh (2020:137) advocates that, beyond the substantive knowledge, curriculum thinking needs to reflect on that which might bring shape, order and structure to the curriculum. Sophisticated curriculum thought must recognise that there will always be considerations associated with the substantive: some culturally contingent, others based on people's perspectives, others based on the provenance or jurisdiction of a curriculum. What is needed is something greater than each of these individual factors which does the job better and holds them all together. This is the disciplinary. A focus on this disciplinary dimension of the curriculum may offer fruitful insights into the nature of the discourse, which goes on within the religion and worldview classroom.

Disciplinary knowledge is generally developed in higher education and is sometimes known as 'procedural' or 'theoretical' knowledge. There is no agreed definition of disciplinary knowledge (Wintersgill, Cush and Francis 2019:4). The 'disciplinary knowledge' refers to the norms, concepts, theories, methods, approaches and general ways of going about things that distinguish a particular subject discipline. Disciplinary knowledge enables us to make sense of substantive knowledge. Kueh champions Michael Young's idea that disciplinary knowledge turns substantive knowledge into 'powerful knowledge', 'concepts that unlock a greater understanding of the world' (Kueh 2018:67).

Moreover, Ofsted (2021) explained that 'ways of knowing' is about being scholarly in the way that substantive content and concepts are approached. It refers to the different ways that pupils learn how it is possible to explore that substantive knowledge. With only substantive ('what to know') knowledge, the RE curriculum would be incomplete because pupils also need to learn 'how to know' in RE. At the primary and secondary levels, leaders and teachers might teach 'ways of knowing' by ensuring that pupils learn not only selected content, but also tools to explore that content.

Conversations and developments about the forms that this takes place are ongoing. One way that has become recently popular has been called the multi-disciplinary approach in RE. This 'way of knowing' suggests that RE should be approached through the disciplines of Theology, Philosophy & Social sciences (Georgiou and Wright 2020). Hutton and Cox (2021:6–9) prefer to call them the theology lens, philosophy lens and social sciences lens. In this case, the curriculum content is framed as if it were considered by, for example, theologians, philosophers or human/social scientists, as exemplified in Chapter 11. However, there is careful planning and implementation needed for these. These areas, cautions Brine, currently do not have a secure place within the school curriculum in their own right. Too often, this has the effect of making RE a proxy for these broader disciplines, undermining their own integrity (Brine and Chater 2020:103).

In other words, this is perhaps an attempt to remedy the dualism found in the UK where a tendency of divorcing pedagogy ('how') from curriculum content ('what') has existed. At the same time, it is attempting to address the serious criticism levied against RE for not having a discipline or suffering from disciplinary dissonance (Chater and Erricker 2013:46, passim 107).

'Personal knowledge' in RE

Ofsted (2021) offers a third dimension on 'personal knowledge'. This has been described by various educators as 'knower-knowledge', 'personal worldview', 'reflexivity' and 'positionality'. In other words, the Review states that when pupils study RE content, they do so 'from a position'. This position is their 'viewpoint' or perspective on the world, which is influenced by, for example, their values, and prior experiences and own sense of identity. Through the curriculum at the primary and secondary level, pupils build 'personal knowledge', which includes an awareness of the assumptions that they bring to discussions concerning religious and non-religious traditions. This form of knowledge is similar to academic reflections in higher education. It should be noted, however, that this is about pupils' understanding of how their opinion has been formed rather than just having an opinion about something.

Summary

This section has briefly discussed the knowledge in the curriculum debate. In the context of RE, it has taken account of recent proposals of the three types of knowledge. The substantive knowledge is the content and concepts of RE. The disciplinary knowledge in RE refers to the theories, approaches and 'ways of knowing'. The disciplinary knowledge enables pupils to make sense of substantive knowledge. Personal knowledge in RE is about how pupils know what they know and their positionality.

RE AND WORLDVIEWS

Introduction

A justification for teaching RE is that it prepares religiously literate pupils for life and work in a wider pluralistic world and contemporary Britain. Based on this instrumental objective, it is argued that, like the teaching of religious traditions, the exploration of secularist, humanists, atheistic and agnostic responses to human experience is also a worthwhile component of RE. Thus, this kind of RE, although contested, would be closer in representing and encompassing the broader questions around faith, belief, religion, spirituality, and reflects the lived reality of communities in the UK, in particular. Furthermore, over the years, RE has embraced the exploration of diversity *within* religious traditions, so that pupils understand the complex nature

---

BOX 4.1 KEY DEBATES IN RE

These academic debates have centred upon (i) the concern that teaching other religions alongside Christianity relativises truth claims (Christian ones in particular) (Barnes and Wright 2006); (ii) the confusion that an apparently objective presentation of a range of religions inculcates in children (Kay and Smith 2000; Thompson 2004); (iii) debates about how accurately teachers present world religions to children, including acknowledging their internal diversity and lived realities (Geaves 1998; Watson 2007); (iv) the extent to which the priority given to multi-faith RE, and the social purposes underpinning it, undermines and marginalises other legitimate aims for the subject, particularly that of religious nurture in the faith of the home (Thiessen 2007); (v) whether RE does, in fact, result in tolerance of religious pluralism in society (Felderhof 2007, 87–97) and (vi) the extent to which the influential phenomenological approach has secularised RE and society (Copley 2005), leading to calls for the revival of the teaching of Christianity and the reversal of the trends in world religions teaching begun in the 1960s (Parker and Freathy 2011:258; Thompson 2004).

---

of belonging and of faith traditions (Dinham and Shaw 2020; Francis, ap Siôn, McKenna and Penny 2017; Jackson 1997; Wintersgill, Cush and Francis 2019). This is about the nature and content dimension of the subject. However, in recent years, the term, 'worldviews' has the language of RE. First, however, a recap of the key controversies is necessary, as described in Box 4.1.

A new vocabulary

At least since the publication of the *Non-Statutory National Framework for RE* (QCA 2004:12), there has been a recommendation that all pupils, unless withdrawn, have an opportunity to study secular philosophies such as humanism. The QCA (2004:7) referred to world views [sic] a few times. It features about a hundred times in the *Curriculum Framework for Religious Education in England* (REC 2013). In a footnote, it is explained that the phrase 'religions and worldviews' [sic] is used in this document to refer to Christianity, other principal religions represented in Britain, smaller religious communities and non-religious worldviews such as Humanism. The phrase, they stress, is meant to be inclusive, and its precise meaning depends on the context in which it occurs, e.g. in terms of belief, practice or identity (REC 2013:11). Moreover, in the *Final Report Religion and Worldviews: The Way Forward*, which is a national plan for RE by the Commission on RE (CoRE 2018), it appears no less than 319 times. As you read earlier, out of several recommended new names for the subject, the CoRE preferred 'Religion and Worldviews'.

Consequently, since the publication of the *Final Report* there has been intense discussions, debates and controversy, not only about what it means and its intentions, but, significantly, the implications it has for curriculum design and classroom practice (Barnes 2020, 2021; Cooling 2019, 2021; Cooling, Bowie and Panjwani 2020; Flanagan 2021). There is anxiety that the introduction of worldviews may dilute RE. Others feel that it adds to an already overstretched curriculum and the teaching profession. However, others have welcomed a meaningful study of non-religious worldviews. As Flanagan (2020) observes, teaching worldviews raises questions of selection, such as, are all worldviews equally appropriate for pupils to study and consistent with the aims of education. Based on research undertaken with primary school teachers, she also revealed variations between teachers' worldview-consciousness and the impact of their worldviews on their teaching of RE (Brine and Chater 2020:98; Flanagan 2021). Thus, it is important that you engage with this concept.

A new vision for RE

The CoRE positioned the concept of worldview at the heart of its new vision for the subject to stimulate a debate about the content and paradigm of RE. This represents a significant shift from the current paradigm of focussing on Christianity, the five 'principal' religions and humanism. As reiterated above, this modification does not imply an expansion of content; as secular philosophies/nonreligious worldviews have featured on RE curricula for a long time. This vision acknowledges that the world is more than the six principal religions and humanism, as did the NNFRE when it stated that RE develops pupils' knowledge and understanding of Christianity, other principal religions, other religious traditions and other world views (QCA 2004:7). Moreover, it recognises that part of educational RE entails including pupils' development of beliefs, worldview, ways of living and learning.

The concept of 'worldview'

The English word 'worldview' is a translation of the German weltanschauung, which literally means a view of the world (Flanagan 2020). The CoRE defines worldview as a person's way of understanding, experiencing and responding to the world. It can be described as a philosophy of life or an approach to life. This includes how a person understands the nature of reality and their place in the world. A person's worldview is likely to influence and be influenced by their beliefs, values, behaviours, experiences, identities and commitments.

CoRE uses the term 'institutional worldview' to describe organised worldviews shared among particular groups and sometimes embedded in institutions. These include what they describe as religions as well as non-religious worldviews such as Humanism, Secularism or Atheism. They use the term 'personal worldview' for an individual's way of understanding and living in the world, which may or may not draw from one, or many, institutional worldviews (CoRE 2018:4). Thus, a worldview might be religious or secular or institutional or personal.

The worldviews to be included, according to CoRE, should be those which make ontological and epistemological claims (claims about the nature of reality and how we know things) as well as political and moral ones. They cite, Humanism, existentialism and Confucianism as examples of suitable non-religious worldviews for study in an age-appropriate way, while nationalism, global capitalism and Communism are examples of worldviews that would not be included in Religion and Worldviews (CoRE 2018:75).

The term 'worldviews' is employed across disciplinary boundaries, so Flanagan (2020) suggests that in the absence of an agreed definition it may obscure rather than clarify meaning. Consequently, the REC has initiated projects to develop an understanding of the ways that the concept of worldview might be used within RE and how its teaching can be supported in school. One of their projects embarked on seeking a shared set of understandings about the meaning of 'Worldviews' among REC member organisations, instead of pursuing a consensus on any one definition of the term (Cooling, Bowie and Panjwani 2020). There are two main outputs from the REC as part of their Worldview Project, discussed below.

Academic literature review

As the language of worldview was not particularly familiar to the British RE community, unlike the extensive discussion in the international academic literature, the REC commissioned an 'Academic literature review' to give academics, teachers, students and others access to that international literature. This Academic Review is a background resource to the Worldview Project (Benoit, Hutchings and Shillitoe 2020). Thereafter, Discussion Papers were produced through an innovative process designed to give expression to a wide range of opinions by involving thirteen leading academics and advisers working in a variety of fields relevant to RE (Tharani 2020). There is considerable discussion about whether 'worldview' denotes new subject content or a new approach to the subject. The discussions ranged over both, and it was almost impossible to separate the two (Tharani 2020:5). In other words, it is both about what is taught and how it is taught. The rest of this section draws from this to highlight some of the discussions and implications for teaching.

Why is a new concept needed?

An educational rationale has been proposed by Chater for the reconstitution of RE to be replaced by a new single-subject Religion and Worldviews. This would be manifestly different in its disciplinary identity. Its core identity would be secular but not secularist, in that it will not give preference to any religious body or secularism. Moreover, to minimise incoherence that plagues current RE, its quality would need to be defined in a single national curriculum document and enforced through inspection. It would also clarify the grammar of the subject which would be shaped by its constituent disciplines. The new subject would be more deeply ambitious by being responsible for securing knowledge and understanding of worldviews (Brine and Chater 2020:95–101).

Many of the academics were frustrated with the conceptualisation of 'religions' and non-religious worldviews in public and schools as unitary and monolithic. This was felt to be alienating some young people, who were given the impression that the content of the subject bears no relevance to their own life, thought or history. For such young people, the 'worldview' approach can function like a 'can opener' concept, re-opening the study of religious and non-religious worldviews and their interplay, at organised and personal levels and in-between, so that every young person can see themselves as having something to learn and to contribute. The paper stressed that this does not mean studying less religion – rather, it means studying religious and non-religious worldviews in different ways, leading to a wiser and more rigorous engagement with our own and others' worldviews (Tharani 2020:5–6).

Some helpful possible orientations

The team explored the range and variety of 'family resemblances' that might be covered by the term 'worldview'. A vast range of ideas and themes were covered, as described in Box 4.2.

Worldviews are more than non-religious worldviews

Chater and Donnellan (2020:126) argue that it is insufficient to merely present some arguments against the existence of a god and claim that non-religious worldviews have been covered. Humanism might lack the features normally associated with religions, such as rituals, holy texts, places of worship, but it makes up for that with its contribution to the history of ideas. It deepens the opportunities to explore rich concepts such as scepticism, empiricism, naturalism, autonomy, flourishing, human rights and evolution of morality.

As discussed above, Humanism is a worldview in the Commission's sense, in that it makes both ontological and epistemological claims (claims about the nature of reality and how we know things) as well as political and moral ones (CoRE 2018:75). According to Chater and Donnellan (2020:120–121), paganism and fundamentalism would qualify as a worldview. However, they posit that this is not the case for several other positions sometimes cited as non-religious worldviews, such as atheism, agnosticism and secularism, as these do not say anything about that person's approach to life. Secularism is not a worldview either. Often it is equated with atheism and sometimes anti-theism. Secularism is a political position that claims that the state should be neutral and its relationship with, and its attitude towards, religious and non-religious beliefs. Most humanists will be secularists and so will many religious people. This does not mean that concepts such as atheism, agnosticism and secularism would have no place in worldviews education (pp. 126–127). Atheism is the view that there is no God, its scope and ambition is unlike that of a worldview.

> ### BOX 4.2 MEANINGS OF 'WORLDVIEW'
>
> Worldview can include ideas about the cosmic order, the sacred, the transcendent and the nature of reality or realities. It may include classification systems and taxonomies. It may cover ideas about how we should live – the existential, the ethical and/or the political. It may denote the idea of orientation to the world or purpose in the world. It may include ideas about how an individual identifies with or belongs to a group or about who and what people are – the mind, brain, heart, soul and consciousness.
>
> Most of the academics favoured a much wider understanding including the experiential, the emotional, actions and sense of identity as well as beliefs and ideas. Cognition, beliefs, interpretation and perception were included, as were other mental states including desires and attachments. Worldviews can be expressed through mundane actions as well as propositionally or through the creative arts. Some of the group sought to emphasise the unconscious, unarticulated or 'taken for granted' aspects of worldview – unquestioned or unspoken, perhaps 'common sense' assumptions within a particular community, society, culture, time or place. Others emphasised the importance of wisdom and discernment as aspects of how worldviews are shaped.
>
> Worldview can refer both to the official teachings, ethical expectations, approved practices, definitions of membership or views on contemporary issues of organised institutions, and to the approach to life of an individual who may or may not identify with an organised group and for whom religious or philosophical traditions may be one of many influences upon them. Individuals and communities may perceive their worldviews as fixed, unchanging and uniquely and propositionally true, or fluid, flexible and changing. They may see them as having nothing in common with other perspectives or as having porous boundaries.
>
> The group emphasised the importance of power relationships and social and cultural situatedness in the development and expression of worldviews. Within this, for example, worldviews might belong to dominant or colonial groups, seeking to justify certain uses of power, or to marginalised groups seeking to resist or exercise power in a different way (Tharani 2020:6).

A radically different area of learning

A radical alternative vision by inverting the position of RE has been proposed by Brine who suggests that pupils should travel through the school curriculum from more generic to more specialist study. This generalised area of learning would encompass and prepare the ground for the later more specialist academic study of subjects like philosophy, anthropology, sociology, psychology, religious studies and theology (Brine and Chater 2020).

Thus, instead of constructing RE as a more complex multi-disciplinary subject, Brine advocates a modest study of religion and worldviews within a broader, more generic subject area of learning. The use of more generalised concepts drawn from wider cultural studies, philosophy and the human sciences would be made, rather than a specialised RE curriculum around complex theological and religious concepts. Such an integrated area of study would explore the diversity of ways in which humans have created meaning and embrace the insights of philosophy and human sciences, and would incorporate the study of religion and worldviews alongside other aspects of human cultural and social life. He claims that this model would resolve the persistent danger of privileging religion which offers it a special curriculum status and treats it differently from other forms of human life and expression. He offers a possible way forward for KS1–3:

> Foundation Stage and Key Stage 1: include the exploration of religion and non-religious worldviews within the broad area of 'knowledge and understanding of the world'.

Key Stage 2 and 3: incorporate the study of worldviews as themes within a new subject, which embraces cultural studies, philosophy and human sciences, possibly integrating aspects of citizenship and complementing the current humanities offer of history and geography

(Brine and Chater 2020:101–106)

Summary

In an increasingly complex world, this section has discussed the prominence that the concept of 'worldview' has recently gained in RE. It has shown that the term is loaded with controversy, both conceptually and practically, yet it is flexible and not narrowly defined. To drive the new vision for the subject, as advanced by the CoRE, the term was included as part of their new proposed name. Be that as it may, the section has highlighted that ultimately the CoRE wants to see a paradigm shift in what is taught in RE and how it is taught.

THE BREADTH OF STUDY IN RE

Introduction

The previous discussions have shown that the locally determined nature of RE is both a prospect and a problem. All pupils, unless withdrawn, have an entitlement to RE independent of their faith or non-religious background. This section addresses the question of representation and how the breadth of study is understood and implemented. It addresses the question of which religions, faith, beliefs and worldviews are recommended for teaching and when. This is important as it concerns, among other issues, quality of provision, continuity, coherence and progress.

The breadth of study in RE is defined as the context, activities and areas of study and range of experiences that pupils encounter at the different key stages (QCA 2004:11, fn. 5). The knowledge, skills and understanding in RE are developed through the breadth of study, which usually has three elements: religions and beliefs, themes, experiences and opportunities. The *Non-statutory National Framework for RE* suggested that when developing plans, it is important to balance the three elements of the breadth of study. For example, learning could focus on the discrete study of religion or another occasion the theme or experience could be the central element. It would also be possible to combine all three elements. For example, visiting a place of worship can enhance the theme of symbols as well as develop knowledge and understanding of the religion being studied (QCA 2004:11). Thus, an amalgamated characterisation is evident.

However, in the *Curriculum Framework for Religious Education in England,* the breadth of RE is explained from the legal perspective. The law, it recaps, requires that locally agreed RE syllabuses and RE syllabuses used in academies that are not designated with a religious character must reflect the fact that the religious traditions in Great Britain are in the main Christian while taking account of the teaching and practices of the other principal religions represented in Great Britain. For the REC, this means that from the ages of 5–19 pupils in schools learn about diverse religions and worldviews including Christianity and the other principal religions (REC 2013:12). On the other hand, their footnote states that good practice should enable pupils to study Christianity and at least one other example of religion or worldview through Key Stage 1 in a coherent way (REC 2013:15, fn.11), and through Key Stage 2 pupils should study Christianity and at least two other examples of religion or worldview in a coherent and progressive way (REC 2013:18, fn. 12). Thus, it seems that breadth is concerned with the number of religions or worldviews delivered coherently and progressively.

> We cannot learn everything; planning is as much about deciding what not to teach as it is about what to include.
>
> (Mary Myatt)

Using a locally agreed syllabus

You learnt that changes to the NC have ensured that schools know the knowledge expected of pupils at the end of each Key Stage. Locally Agreed Syllabi fulfil a similar role and explain the value and purposes of RE. They also specify for teachers what should be taught within each KS and age group. Moreover, they provide a framework for setting high standards of learning in RE for their local area to enable them to support their pupils to reach their potential.

Some of the syllabi do not prescribe the detail of what and when to teach. They tend to devolve these matters to their individual schools allowing them to plan, organise and teach to their individual needs and circumstances. In such cases, it would be the responsibility of the school to develop a scheme of work based on the programmes of study and the content in the syllabus to meet the needs of their pupils in light of the requirements set out in their syllabus. However, others provide a detailed scheme of work including long and medium plans, assessment guidance with supporting resources to enable teachers and schools to implement the syllabus. In the case of the latter, you can use a LAS, as a starting point for your planning, although you may need to supplement it with background knowledge, contextual understanding and be familiar with the local area. Such a combination will provide meaningful and relevant opportunities for the pupils to learn about and from religion and belief (Hill 2014:243).

Schools should consider the pupils they serve in deciding whether to go beyond the minimum entitlements to learning about religions and beliefs. The delineation of the issues of time and the content in many locally agreed syllabuses represents the minimum entitlement for pupils. This means schools have the freedom to plan to teach content from more than the minimum number of religions, without losing the importance of enabling pupils to study religions in-depth, progressively and sequentially. The appropriate implementation of a LAS aims to provide a coherent, continuous and progressive experience of RE for pupils from Reception to post-16 as they must identify what pupils should know and understand by the end of each year and how that contributes to what they will go on to study in the following years. The provision for RE in some of these syllabi is flexible. Therefore, in exercising flexibility, schools are expected to ensure that they meet the legal requirements of their syllabus and ensure that pupils' learning, progression and assessment are transparent and coherent and that teachers can report meaningfully on progression and attainment in RE.

Nevertheless, there are other challenges to be mindful of in trying to offer a broad and balanced curriculum as illustrated in Box 4.3.

How many and which traditions to teach?

Based on the ERA 1988, pupils must learn about Christianity and the other principal religions to provide breadth in RE, although some schools with a religious character will prioritise learning about and from one religion. However, all types of schools need to recognise the diversity of the UK and the importance of learning about its religions and worldviews (REC 2013:12).

The approach to address this requirement has been non-uniform. A statement like this is sometimes interpreted as a recommendation to teach all six religions in a key stage or across the primary phases. The inclusion and coverage of material from all six, whilst practically possible, raises questions of quality, depth and rigour. Learning from six religions across a key stage has been reported to be demanding. Therefore, it is important to reflect upon the preference given to greater depth over overstretched breadth and coverage. Some schools are encouraged

---

BOX 4.3 CHALLENGES TO A BROAD AND BALANCED RE

Most of the curriculum debates in our subject mainly operate at this substantive level. Whether we approach the curriculum as a discrete portion of subject matter being moved around a chessboard, or whether we talk about the broader themes that seem to sit above this content, as the recent Commission on RE has done, then we are still talking at the level of the substantive.

Yet there is still a dimension of curricular thoughts beyond this. Its absence becomes pronounced when debates about breadth and balance take place in the subject. To illustrate: one instinct of the curriculum designer is to expect to find breadth and balance at the substantive level. This impulsive is reasonable – so reasonable, in fact, that those who promulgate such a viewpoint find it difficult to understand why one might object to it. Surely (it might be said from a reasonable, liberal point of view, we must find a way of being inclusive of different worldviews – traditional religious ones; non-religious ones; institutional ones; non-institutional one; blended ones. Yet this simply begins a never-ending trap of looking for breadth and balance. From the vantage point of the null curriculum (the content that, as a result of your choices, is not included on the curriculum), there will always be somebody or someone who is perceived to be left out, or some dimension of depth that is sacrificed. The argument here could be made that in trying to do justice to the sum total of beliefs and worldviews, one runs the danger of doing justice to none of them (Kueh 2020:136).

---

to teach less but to teach in-depth with high quality. The previous Birmingham Agreed Syllabus (BCC 2007), for example, had determined not to require six religions to be covered, though more than six had featured as examples in their appendices. Instead, provision for the study of those religions that are deemed educationally and religiously relevant within the local context was to be made. It was thought that in many cases this would amount to fewer than six religions (Barnes 2008; Conroy et al. 2013:67; Stern 2018:85).

However, the new syllabus includes the nine religious traditions recorded to have significant representation within Birmingham: Bahá'í, Buddhism, Christianity, Hinduism, Islam, Jainism, Judaism, Rastafari and Sikhism, and established non-religious world views (NRWVs) such as Atheism, Humanism and Secularism. It also responds to the experience of the growing number of pupils whose families identify as 'nones' (BCC 2022:7). The 2022 syllabus differentiates between NRWVs and Nones.

Moreover, Barnes (2015) proposed that requiring pupils to study over ten different traditions of thought certainly suggests itself be a recipe for superficiality and confusion. The results of a survey of 2,879 pupils in Y9 in 22 schools in the maintained sector in England and Wales showed that pupils who had studied five or more religions were more likely to make mistakes than pupils who had studied between two and four religions (Kay and Smith 2000; Smith and Kay 2000). Whilst Barnes (2015:59) advocated the exposure of pupils to the seriousness and the diversity of religions, he questioned whether this needed a study of over ten religions.

Secure high-quality breadth

To secure effective practice, some LAS express concern about the resultant superficial learning that may take place by covering all or too many religions and beliefs in each key stage. They, therefore, place some restrictions in the implementation of their syllabus whilst keeping schools free to choose which religions other than Christianity to study at each key stage. Other LASs encourage schools to study the religions exemplified in their syllabus units so that all pupils gain an understanding of all six principal faiths up to KS3, as demonstrated in Table 4.1 (Buckinghamshire 2016:15).

Table 4.1 Exemplification of religions represented in a syllabus	
EYFS	In the EYFS, pupils follow the areas of learning as laid out in the EYFS curriculum and should choose material as appropriate.
Key Stage 1	Pupils should study Christianity plus one other religion in depth (Judaism recommended). This reflects best practice for younger pupils and the fact that the Key Stage lasts only 2 years.
Key Stage 2	Pupils should study Christianity plus two other religions in depth (Hinduism and Islam recommended).
Key Stage 3	Pupils should study Christianity and two other religions in depth (Buddhism and Sikhism recommended).

The recent review by Ofsted notes that high-quality RE prepares pupils to engage in a complex multi-religious and multi-secular world. To reach this goal, leaders and teachers might think about the overall conception of religion and non-religion that pupils build through the RE curriculum. To consider the overall concept of religion and non-religion that pupils build through the curriculum is perhaps more useful than thinking about the quantity and weighting of traditions to include (Ofsted 2021).

Pupil's voice

Teachers are also expected to consider the religious experience, beliefs and viewpoints of the pupils in the classroom and the school community when planning which religions to look at and in which order, as many pupils will come from backgrounds with no particular religious belief or affiliation (Census 2021).

Connecting religions

Pupils should also study how religions relate to each other so that they recognise both the similarities and differences within and between religions. Moreover, there is a movement across the country on Interfaith relations, pupils should be encouraged to reflect in RE on the significance of interfaith dialogue and the important contribution that religion and dialogue can make to community cohesion and combating of religious prejudice, discrimination and hate (Ipgrave 2013).

Local representation

Some schools deem it appropriate to teach about religions or beliefs of local significance that are not identified in their LAS or schemes of work to acknowledge their presence in the school community. Schools can add these and others at their discretion. However, this should be done in a way that avoids a tokenistic approach. For example, opportunities may be created for pupils to explore beliefs systems, traditions and secular philosophies such as the atheism, Bahá'í faith, local tradition of Buddhists, Druids, humanism, Jainism, Jehovah's Witnesses, Pagans, Quaker, Rastafari, Zoroastrianism or the followers of Sai Baba in Hinduism, independent Christian churches and New Religious Movements in an area (QCA 2004; REC 2013:13; Revell 2008). Another example is the inclusion of the traveller community, where this might be a significant part of the community.

To accommodate such an approach, Cornwall (2014:10), for example, requires that this teaching should be identified in the scheme of work as an addition to the time set aside for the delivery of the syllabus. It must also be for a specified amount of time. It may occur in an academic year where Christianity and one other religion are already being delivered and, where schools do this, they must be clear about two things. That the teaching of such a religious tradition is not detrimental to the programme of study and is at a level, which links attainment to the expectations of the syllabus; and that the school has a clear justification for doing so based on evidence from the school. Be that as it may, such an expansion would need careful consideration of time, curriculum space, relevance, appropriateness, representation, pragmatism, context and, indeed, subject knowledge, especially when many teachers of RE are not specialists and Ofsted raised concerns about this (Ofsted 2013).

Secondary phrase

Each key stage must build upon the previous one so that by the time pupils reach the end of the primary phase they should have had the breadth of study in RE, and, by the end of Key Stage 3, they should have had the opportunity to receive a broad and balanced RE. That said, some primary schools are advised to select their religions to study in consultation with their secondary counterparts to enable pupils across the age ranges to achieve continuity and progression.

Some syllabuses set the minimum number of religions to be covered by the end of KS4 to three such as Christianity, Islam and Judaism and highly recommend Buddhism. Despite such a requirement, they still prefer that pupils explore all six of the principal religions plus Humanism during their school careers as shown below (Bournemouth and Poole 2017).

What if a religion is not in a syllabus?

Should members of a religious community be represented in a school community, it would make sense to recognise and make pupils aware of that religion, even though it may not be identified in a LAS such as African indigenous and traditional religions (Matemba and Collet 2022). This could be treated as additional teaching beyond the syllabus requirements as discussed above. It is also important to be aware that sometimes there is an implied hierarchy of 'religions' – that Christianity is the archetypal religion and other religions are more or less worthy of study depending on how closely their features are matched to Christianity. Indigenous or sub-Saharan African religions are often not even considered as 'religions' or as worthy of study (Tharani 2020:10).

Comparing two models

The Bournemouth and Poole (2017:17) agreed syllabus recommends the pattern shown in Table 4.2.

Table 4.2 Exemplification of recommended religions across Key Stages 1–4				
Key Stage	**Year Groups**	**Ages**	**Religions and Worldviews**	
1	1–2	5–7	Christianity in every year group	Plus Islam and Judaism. Buddhism and Humanism are highly recommended. Other religions from: Hinduism, Sikhism and/or material from other religious traditions represented locally could also be included, e.g. the Bahá'í faith or Pagan traditions. At least 3× by the end of KS2.
2	3–6	7–11		
3	7–9	11–14		Plus Islam and Judaism. Buddhism and Humanism are highly recommended. Other religions from: Hinduism, Sikhism and/or material from other religious traditions represented locally could also be included, e.g. Bahá'í faith or Pagan traditions. At least 3× by the end of KS4
4	10–13	14–19		

BOX 4.4 EXEMPLIFICATION OF MANDATORY EXPECTATION OF RELIGIONS ACROSS KEY STAGES 1 AND 2

Primary Phase (Key Stages 1 and 2, Year groups Reception (F2) to Year 6, Ages 5–11)

It is a mandatory expectation of this syllabus that during the Primary Phase pupils will encounter: Christianity in both Key Stages plus Hinduism, Islam, Judaism and Sikhism.

(Buddhism and other religions and worldviews of local significance, e.g. Bahá'í, can be added at the school's discretion. Offering pupils an encounter with at least one non-religious worldview, e.g. Humanism during the Primary Phase would be beneficial, but this is not a mandatory expectation of the syllabus).

The recommendation is that Christianity is taught in every year group with one other religion alongside it. Which 'other' religion features in each year group is up to the school to decide, as long as by the end of Key Stage 2 the following five principal religions have been encountered: Christianity, Hinduism, Islam, Judaism and Sikhism (Pan-Berkshire 2018:10).

The Pan-Berkshire structure allocates specific religions to the primary phase and Key Stage 3 as core areas of study. Christianity is included as a core area of study in each key stage and recommended to be taught in every year group, as shown in Box 4.4.

Summary

This section has analysed the breadth of study in RE with a focus on which religions should be taught. Generally, pupils learn about Christianity and the five principal religions to provide breadth in RE. However, you have seen that there is scope to include other religious and non-religious traditions that provide a representation of western, eastern and African traditions, significant local beliefs and worldviews (Box 4.5).

BOX 4.5 VIGNETTE: NON-RELIGIOUS VIEWPOINTS

I am a Muslim. My family and I follow and practise the religion, Islam. My father is a priest and an Islamic teacher who is known as an 'Imam'. I have many friends from different religious backgrounds and we all respect each other's faiths and beliefs. My family, my friends and I believe it is compulsory to be educated about religious and non-religious viewpoints as part of being an understanding human. As a Muslim, I have to follow the five pillars of Islam, which are Shahadah, Salah, Zakat, Saum and Hajj.

I have wanted to become a teacher since a young age because I want to create a positive impact on children's lives and direct them to a promising future. Therefore, I studied for an undergraduate degree in education. Above all, I learnt that each child should be taught to believe in itself and respect others around them. I feel children can learn this through the provision of RE in schools. This is because I remember when I was taught RE in my child-hood, I was taught the importance of valuing diversity and respecting the similarities and differences of religions. However, as part of my current experiences in schools, I have realised that there is very little or no RE being taught, which is disappointing. The RE being taught in schools today consists of Humanistic values rather than core religions themselves.

If I were leading RE, I would take this as an issue because as a trainee teacher at this moment, I feel it is necessary for pupils to understand different religions and cultures as well as learn about humanistic values. This is because if pupils have a lack of

---

understanding towards a certain religious group, they may misjudge them and fail to accept them as part of society. This is a fundamental issue because pupils fail to understand that each religious group has their faiths and beliefs, which need to be respected and valued, and they need to be taught that it is not okay to be discriminative or perhaps racist towards a certain group. Another issue would be that some parents might disagree with their children being taught about a certain religious group.

I have therefore selected RE because I feel like children need to be taught this subject to explore wider opportunities of understanding religious and non-religious viewpoints. I feel it is significant to address misconceptions associated with religions. I feel RE should not be used to force a child to believe in a religion, but it should allow children to accept the beliefs of each religion. For example, if a child is not taught RE, they may not understand why certain religious people dress in a particular way, or why they need to pray at certain times of the day. This is an issue because children might question this amongst their peers in the classroom or their future work colleagues, which is highly disrespectful. I aspire to see children respect themselves as well as others around them in the future through RE and I hope to address any misconceptions.

References

Barnes, L. P. (2008) The 2007 Birmingham agreed syllabus for Religious Education: A new direction for statutory Religious Education in England and Wales, *Journal of Beliefs & Values*, 29, (1), pp. 75–83.

Barnes, L. P. (2015) Religious education educating for diversity, in L. P. Barnes, A. David and J. M. Halstead (Eds.) *Religious Education Educating for Diversity*, London: Bloomsbury, pp. 11–62.

Barnes, L. P. (2020) *Crisis, Controversy and the Future of Religious Education*, Abingdon: Routledge.

Barnes, L. P. (2021) The commission on religious education, worldviews and the future of religious education, *British Journal of Educational Studies, Online First*, pp. 1–16.

Barnes, L. P., and Wright, A. (2006) Romanticism, representations of religion and critical religious education, *British Journal of Religious Education*, 28, (1), pp. 65–77.

BCC (2007) *The Birmingham Agreed Syllabus for Religious Education*, Birmingham: Birmingham City Council.

BCC (2022) *The Birmingham Agreed Syllabus for Religious Education*, Birmingham: Birmingham City Council. https://www.birmingham.gov.uk/downloads/file/22257/birmingham_agreed_syllabus_for_religious_education (Accessed 30/3/2022).

Benoit, C., Hutchings, T., and Shillitoe, R. (2020) *Worldview: A Multidisciplinary Report*, London: Religious Education Council.

Bournemouth and Poole (2017) *The Bournemouth and Poole Agreed Syllabus for Religious Education 2017–2022*, Bournemouth: Bournemouth Borough Council.

Brine, A., and Chater (2020) A wholly educational rationale for worldviews, in M. Chater (Ed.) *Reforming RE*, Melton: John Catt, pp. 95–113.

Buckinghamshire (2016) *'Challenging RE 3': The Buckinghamshire Agreed Syllabus for Religious Education 2016–21*, Buckinghamshire County Council 2016.

Census (2021) *Religion*, [Online] https://www.ons.gov.uk/peoplepopulationandcommunity/culturalidentity/religion (Accessed 17/07/2022).

Chater, M., and Erricker, C. (2013) *Does Religious Education Have a Future? Pedagogical and Policy Prospects*, Abingdon: Routledge.

Chater, M., and Donnellan, L. (2020) What do we mean by worldviews? in M. Chater (Ed.) *Reforming RE*, Woodbridge: John Catt, pp. 115–130.

Claxton, G. (2021) *The Future of Teaching and the Myths That Hold It Back*, Abingdon: Routledge.

Coe, R., Aloisi, C., Higgins, S., and Major, L. E. (2014) *What Makes Great Teaching? Review of the Underpinning Research*, The Sutton Trust. [Online] https://www.suttontrust.com/wp-content/uploads/2014/10/What-Makes-Great-Teaching-REPORT.pdf (Accessed 09/08/2021).

Conroy, J. C., Lundie, D., Davis, R. A., Baumfeld, V., Barnes, L. P., Gallagher, T., Lowden, K., Bourque, N., and Wenell, K. J. (2013) *Does Religious Education Work? A Multi-Dimensional Investigation*. London: Bloomsbury.

Cooling, T. (2019) The return to worldview: Reflections from the UK, *International Journal of Christianity and Education*, 23, (1), pp. 3–9.

Cooling, T., Bowie, B., and Panjwani, F. (2020) *Worldviews in Religious Education*, London: Theos.

Cooling, T. (2021) Crisis, controversy and the future of religious education, *International Journal of Christianity and Education*, 25, (1), pp. 129–130.

Copley, T. (2005) *Indoctrination, Education and God*, London: SPCK.

CoRE (Commission on Religious Education) (2018) *Religion and Worldviews: The Way Forward*, London: Religious Education Council.

Cornwall (2014) *Cornwall Agreed Syllabus for Religious Education 2014*, Cornwall SACRE: Cornwall Council.

Counsell, C. (2018) Taking curriculum seriously, *Impact Journal of the Chartered College of Teaching*, September 2018 [Online] https://impact.chartered.college/article/taking-curriculum-seriously/ (Accessed 07/08/2021).

Dinham, M., and Shaw, M. (2020) Landscapes, real and imagined: 'RE for Real', in M. Chater (Ed.) *Reforming RE*, Woodbridge: John Catt, pp. 51–64.

Felderhof, M. (2007) Religious education, atheism and deception, in M. C. Felderhof, P. Thompson, and D. Torevell (Eds.) *Inspiring Faith in Schools*, Aldershot, UK: Ashgate, pp. 87–98.

Flanagan, R. (2020) Worldviews: Overarching concept, discrete body of knowledge or paradigmatic tool? *Journal of Religious Education*, 68, pp. 331–344.

Flanagan, R. (2021) Teachers' personal worldviews and RE in England: A way forward? *British Journal of Religious Education*, 43, (3), pp. 320–336.

Francis, L. J., ap Siôn, T., McKenna, U., and Penny, G. (2017) Does Religious Education as an examination subject work to promote community cohesion? An empirical enquiry among 14- to 15-year-old adolescents in England and Wales, *British Journal of Religious Education*, 39, (3), pp. 303–316.

Geaves, R. (1998) The borders between religions: A challenge to the world religions approach to religious education, *British Journal of Religious Education*, 21, (1), pp. 20–31.

Georgiou, G., and Wright, K. (2020) Disciplinarity, religion and worldviews: Making the case for theology, philosophy and human/social sciences, in M. Chater (Ed.) *Reforming RE*, Melton: John Catt, pp. 149–164.

Hill, E. (2014) Religious Education, in P. Smith and L. Dawes (Eds.) *Subject Teaching in Primary Education*, London: SAGE, pp. 232–247.

Hutton, L., and Cox, D. (2021) *Making Every Lesson Count*, Carmarthen: Crown House.

Ipgrave, J. (2013) The language of interfaith encounter among inner city primary school children, *Religion & Education*, 40, (1), pp. 35–49. DOI: 10.1080/15507394.2013.745361

Jackson, R. (1997) *Religious Education: An Interpretive Approach*, London: Hodder & Stoughton.

Kay, W. K., and Smith, D. L. (2000) Religious terms and attitudes in the classroom (part 1), *British Journal of Religious Education*, 22, (2), pp. 81–90. DOI: 10.1080/0141620000220203

Kueh, R. (2018) Religious Education and the 'Knowledge-Problem', in M. Castelli and M. Chater (Eds.) *We Need to Talk About Religious Education*, London: Jessica Kingsley, pp. 53–69.

Kueh, R. (2020) Disciplinary hearing: Making the case for the disciplinary in religion and world-views, in M. Chater (Ed.) *Reforming RE*, Melton: John Catt, pp. 131–147.

Matemba, Y., and Collet, B. A. (Eds.) (2022) *The Bloomsbury Handbook of Religious Education in the Global South*, London: Bloomsbury.

Ofsted (2013) *Religious Education: Realising the Potential*, Manchester: Crown Copyright. Reference No: 130068.

Ofsted (2021) *Research Review Series: Religious Education*, [Online] https://www.gov.uk/government/publications/research-review-series-religious-education/research-review-series-religious-education#fnref:131 (Accessed 17/07/2021).

Pan-Berkshire (2018) *The Agreed Syllabus for Religious Education Pan-Berkshire 2018–2023*, Pan-Berkshire: SACRE. [Online] https://wokingham.moderngov.co.uk/documents/s23390/Berkshire%20Syllabus%202018-2023.pdf (Accessed 02/08/2021).

Parker, S. G., and Freathy, R. J. K. (2011) Context, complexity and contestation: Birmingham's agreed syllabuses for Religious Education since the 1970s, *Journal of Beliefs & Values*, 32, (2), pp. 247–263.

QCA (2004) *Religious Education: The Non-Statutory National Framework*, London: Qualifications and Curriculum Authority. Reference: QCA/04/1336.

Rata, E. (2016) Pedagogical conceptual progression and the case for academic knowledge, *British Education Research Journal*, 42, (1), pp. 168–184.

REC (Religious Education Council of England and Wales) (2013) *A Curriculum Framework for Religious Education in England*. London: Religious Education Council.

Revell, L. (2008) Religious Education in England, *Numen*, 55, (2/3), pp. 218–240.

Sherrington, T. (2017) *The Learning Rainforest*, Melton: John Catt.

Smith, D. L., and Kay, W. K. (2000) Religious terms and attitudes in the classroom (Part 2), *British Journal of Religious Education*, 22, (3), pp. 181–191. DOI: 10.1080/0141620000220306

Stern, J. (2018) *Teaching Religious Education: Researchers in the Classroom*. London: Bloomsbury Academic. Second edition.

Tharani, A. (2020) *The Worldview Project: Discussion Papers*, London: Religious Education Council.

Thiessen, E. (2007) Religious education and committed openness, in M. C. Felderhof, P. Thompson, and D. Torevell (Eds.) *Inspiring Faith in Schools*, Aldershot, UK: Ashgate, pp. 35–46.

Thompson, P. (2004) *Whatever Happened to Religious Education?* Cambridge, UK: Lutterworth Press.

Watson, B. (2007) Secularism, schools and religious education, in M. C. Felderhof, P. Thompson, and D. Torevell (Eds.) *Inspiring Faith in Schools*, Aldershot, UK: Ashgate, pp. 3–15.

Willingham, D. (2010) *Why Don't Students Like School?* San Francisco, CA: Jossey Bass.

Wintersgill, B. (Ed.) (2017) *Big Ideas for Religious Education*, Exeter: University of Exeter. [Online] http://socialsciences.exeter.ac.uk/media/universityofexeter/collegeofsocialsciencesandinternationalstudies/education/research/groupsandnetworks/reandspiritualitynetwork/Big_Ideas_for_RE_E-Book.pdf (Accessed 09/08/2021).

Wintersgill, B., Cush, D., and Francis, D. (2019) *Putting Big Ideas into Practice in Religious Education*, [Online] https://www.reonline.org.uk/wp-content/uploads/2019/05/Putting-big-ideas-into-Practice.pdf (Accessed 09/08/2021).

Young, M., and Muller, J. (2013) On the powers of powerful knowledge, *Review of Education*, 1, (3), pp. 229–250.

Young, M., and Muller, J. (2016) *Curriculum and the Specialisation of Knowledge*, London: Routledge.

Young, M. (2020) From powerful knowledge to the powers of knowledge, in C. Sealy (Ed.), *The ResearchEd Guide to the Curriculum*, pp. 19–29.

RE in the Early Years, Key Stages 1 and 2

Introduction

This chapter traces the journey of RE for you from nursery to the end of key stage 2.

Religious Education in the nursery

To begin with, you need to revisit the law to ascertain and establish the RE entitlement for pupils. RE is a statutory requirement for all pupils registered on the school roll in maintained schools from the ages of 5 to 18 unless withdrawn by their parents. This legal requirement does not extend to children under compulsory school age in the nursery in maintained schools, as shown in Box 5.1. Nevertheless, it can be a valuable part of their overall educational experience at this age. This is evident from the fact that many nurseries offer some kind of provision of RE, consider the following:

BOX 5.1 CASE STUDY: RE IN A NURSERY

In our nursery, children learn about RE. This takes place through various episodes of learning, play based stations and experiential activities. These experiences are created as the foundation for future learning and build on pupils' current skills and prior experiences. We talk to children about their families, cultures, places, morals, lifestyle, beliefs, and explore the concepts of values. These are some of our themes and concepts. We take our children on visits to religious and significant places in our community. Visitors come to talk about their experiences to our staff and children.

The activities and experiences offered to children provide the building blocks for future development. Practitioners tend to begin with materials and content which are familiar to the children. Good teaching in the Early Years Foundation Stage (EYFS) will always build on children's interests, enthusiasms and current skills. Importantly, it takes account of their learning and development needs, and themes are developed accordingly. Practitioners give them plenty of hands-on activities and learning episodes, which are an important part of their learning, skills development and experiences at this early stage of development.

Nature of activities

The range of activities is wide in the nursery. For RE this may include:

- Making and eating festival food
- Developing a sense of belonging

DOI: 10.4324/9780429289743-8

- Articulating religious terminology
- Observing nature, growing plants
- Walking outdoors, in parks and streets
- Creative play, role-play, dance and drama
- Planting and growing to celebrate new life
- Listening to, singing and making religious music
- Hearing and talking about religious and secular stories
- Giving and collecting for charity, harvest, homelessness
- Imitating activities from home and cultural background
- Imagining a better world by making displays and 3D objects
- Thinking about fairness, kindness, goodness, similarities, differences
- Talking about the different ways in which people believe and behave
- Dressing up and acting out scenes from stories, celebrations or festivals
- Colour, paint, rub, sketch, manipulate, cut and paste values-based work
- Thinking about figures of authority in religious texts and our own lives
- Be quiet in a tent, whisper to friends, use torches to see lightness and darkness
- Exploring authentic religious artefacts, as well as 'soft toy' artefacts and books
- Talking and listening to each other about God, festivals, rituals, rites and beliefs
- Using dolls to explore religious practices of their own experience and new content
- Observe pictures, books and videos of places of worship and meet believers in class
- Enjoy events like celebrations, birth, weddings and wonder about the death of a pet

By using familiar concepts and carefully selected resources and themes, practitioners enable children to talk about their families, cultures and explore the human and religious concepts and shared values in a meaningful and appropriate manner. Thus, it is seen as good practice for all Foundation 1 and nursery settings to familiarise children with religious traditions and worldviews to acknowledge and celebrate each other's similarities and differences by developing an understanding of their own life experiences and those of others and thereby gain an awareness of communities. Moreover, the active promotion of 'British' values applies to all EYFS settings and, as such, by including selected elements of RE, children will learn respect for and tolerance of those with different faiths and beliefs from the nursery.

Religious Education in Reception

Based on the statutory requirement stated in Table 5.1, in practice, RE is the only compulsory subject in Reception. It also means that the curriculum offered to pupils in Reception classes must include RE. Hence, as discussed in Chapter 2 the recommended time allocation for RE in Reception for full-time pupils is 5% of curriculum time, which approximates to 36 hours over the course of the year to enable the requirements of the locally agreed syllabus (LAS) to be met. There will be a plethora of ways to organise and deliver. It also means that planning should identify RE to demonstrate that the requirement is being met and to enable parents to know what RE is being delivered. Moreover, it is a statutory requirement that learning and attainment in RE is reported to parents and carers upon at the end of the Reception year.

Value of RE

RE contributes to the spiritual, moral, social, cultural and personal development of pupils as they explore the world of religion and worldviews. An important element of spiritual development

Table 5.1 The status of RE		
Foundation Stage		**Key Stage 1**
Nursery	**Reception**	**Year 1 and upwards**
RE is non-statutory, but practitioners may choose to incorporate RE material into children's activities if they choose to.	RE is a compulsory part of the basic curriculum for all Reception age pupils, and should be taught according to the locally agreed syllabus, where applicable.	RE is a compulsory part of the basic curriculum for all Key Stage 1 pupils, and should be taught according to the locally agreed syllabus, where applicable.
Early Learning Goals outline what pupils should achieve by the end of reception year. The National Curriculum is not taught.		The National Curriculum is taught alongside RE.

is to enable pupils to reflect on that which matters most to them, to ponder upon their worth and that of the world around them. Another important element is for pupils to begin to recognise that spirituality, for many people, springs from their relationship with God.

RE in the Reception should help pupils to develop empathy, values and a capacity to make moral judgments and healthy choices. It should also help them to develop an understanding of their own culture and the culture of others. RE should also help pupils to understand religious and cultural diversity and to contribute to the preparation of pupils for adult life.

RE sits very firmly within the areas of personal, social and emotional development and understanding of the world. RE helps pupils to develop a positive sense of themselves, and others, and to learn how to form positive and respectful relationships. They begin to understand and value the differences of individuals and groups within their immediate community.

RE in Reception should contribute to pupils developing self-esteem and self-respect, developing respect for and knowledge about their own and other religions and worldviews, caring for others, thinking about right and wrong.

Curriculum

In Reception classes, RE should be taught in accordance with the LAS, where applicable, and it should be a discernible element of the curriculum, distinct from the EY Framework. You may discover that where Reception classes are integrated into Year 1 or KS1 classes, schools may follow the LAS programme of study for KS1 for pupils of Reception age, although some would derive their expectations from the EYFS profile. However, where mixed-age classes are taught incorporating KS1 and KS2, you may find that teachers may choose which religion other than Christianity to teach from the KS2 religions to be delivered. That said, RE in Reception is not dependent on what follows in Key Stage 1, but it does help in establishing a basis for future learning and teaching. The RE taught in this stage should be taught in a developmentally appropriate way. It should be well thought through, sequenced and progressive. It should adhere to the principles and commitments enshrined in the EYFS.

Topics that lend themselves to opportunities for RE work include those shown in Table 5.2.

Table 5.2 Topics for RE in Reception		
Myself	People who help us	Special times
My life	Friendship	Special places
My senses	Welcome	Special books
My special things	Belonging	Special people
Stories	Our community	The natural world
New life	Food	Happiness

Planning

EYFS planning often uses topics or themes to connect learning and exploration of the world of religion and beliefs in many ways. The concept of specialness and belonging in the context of religion is significant to many of the programmes and units of work for this stage. This makes learning exciting, engaging and responsive to pupils' interests and inquisitiveness. There should be specific planned programmes and activities for the term and year. However, you should be open and flexible to avail yourself of unplanned opportunities arising out of pupil's questions, comments and interests and impromptu events.

The content is commonly organised around topics or themes such as special people, special places, special books, special occasions, festivals and celebrations, special artefacts and objects, people who help us, our natural world, new life, our homes and our community, stories from across the world. Pupils are given opportunities to begin to use a range of technical terms from religious traditions. They may use all their senses in exploring religions and beliefs, practices, behaviours and forms of expression. They may reflect on their feelings and experiences. They may use their imagination and curiosity to develop their appreciation and wonder of the world, which they inhabit. These rich opportunities in RE are important steps towards preparing them for Key Stage 1.

Pedagogy

Pupils should begin with familiar experiences and these should then be widened to take them into new and less familiar areas. It is often said that in Reception there should be 'little but often' in providing pupils with learning in RE. Learning does not easily fit into fixed boxes, rather child-centred approaches are encouraged to follow where the pupil's interest and curiosity leads. When practitioners lead the activity these should be for 10–15 minutes, thereafter, pupils then engage in an activity or activities connected with what has been explored with the teacher. The most effective pedagogy brings to gather teaching and freely chosen instructive play activities. The use of sustained shared thinking makes for most progress and the use of open-ended questioning and modelling have been linked with better cognitive achievement (Sylva, Melhuish, Siraj-Blatchford and Taggart 2004). Care should be taken to use language, activities and materials appropriate and suitable to everyone. Practitioners will do this through talking, asking, playing, exploring, active learning, creating and thinking and by supplementing videos, posters, artefacts, costumes, 'soft toys', persona dolls, visitors and visits to their learning activities. To provide intellectual challenge, it is important for practitioners to intervene during children free-play. This guided play is a pedagogy that balances between direct teaching and free play (Weisberg, Hirsh-Pasek and Golinkoff 2013).

Learning experiences

At the EYFS, pupils are more likely to learn when they are provided with opportunities to:

- talk about their feelings
- develop empathy for others
- produce festive food and music
- create patterns, designs, models
- perform dances, dress up, role play
- know and use religious terms accurately
- share their own beliefs, ideas and values
- partake in times of quietness and stillness
- reflect on their own and others' experiences
- use all five senses – smell, taste, see, touch and hear

- be curious about texts, artefacts, rituals, rites, celebrations, festivals
- listening to, talking about, retelling, reflecting on appropriate stories
- encounter worldviews through visitors from non-faith communities
- imagine, appreciate, be in awe and wonder at the beauty of the world
- ask questions which are philosophical in nature and have them taken seriously
- use technology for exploring religious beliefs and phenomena locally, nationally and globally
- experience religion and observe places of worship and talk to visitors from faith communities.

Provisions should aim to balance cognitive, emotional and social skills as positive lifetime outcomes are dependent on such an approach (OECD 2015).

The contribution of RE to the ELGs

The REC recommends that pupils should encounter religions and worldviews through special people, books, times, places and objects and by visiting places of worship. They should listen to and talk about stories. Pupils can be introduced to subject-specific words and use all their senses to explore beliefs, practices and forms of expression. They ask questions and reflect on their feelings and experiences. They use their imagination and curiosity to develop their appreciation of and wonder at the world in which they live. RE is a legal requirement for all pupils on the school roll, including all those in the reception year (REC 2013:13).

The New Early Years Framework

A new framework for all Early Years' providers in England has become mandatory. In it, the level of development children should be expected to have attained by the end of the EYFS is defined by the early learning goals (ELGs). Some of these are selected to show how RE can contribute to their development. However, the ELGs should not be used as a curriculum or in any way to limit the wide variety of rich experiences that are crucial to child development (DfE 2021:11).

It is suggested that practitioners must consider the individual needs, interests and development of each child in their care, and must use this information to plan a challenging and enjoyable experience for each child in all areas of learning and development (DfE 2021:15). As for children whose home language is not English, providers must take reasonable steps to provide opportunities for children to develop and use their home language in play and learning, supporting their language development at home (DfE 2021:16).

Pedagogically, the new framework does not prescribe a particular teaching approach. Nevertheless, it reiterates that play is essential for children's development, building their confidence as they learn to explore, relate to others, set their own goals and solve problems (DfE 2021:16). In planning and guiding what children learn, practitioners must reflect on the different rates at which children are developing and adjust their practice appropriately. Three characteristics of effective teaching and learning are as follows:

- Playing and exploring – children investigate and experience things, and 'have a go'.
- Active learning – children concentrate and keep on trying if they encounter difficulties, and enjoy achievements.
- Creating and thinking critically – children have and develop their own ideas, make links between ideas, and develop strategies for doing things (DfE 2021:16).

Tables 5.3–5.14 show suggested teaching approaches and content to support the early learning goals.

Table 5.3 Supporting listening, attention and understanding ELG through RE

Communication and language: Listening, attention and understanding ELG

Children at the expected level of development will	Teaching approach	Suggested content
Listen attentively and respond to what they hear with relevant questions, comments and actions when being read to and during whole class discussions and small group interactions.	Read a story. Use a prop or puppet. Use hot sitting to respond to living with faith in the UK. Watch a video to facilitate comments. Use a poster to talk, question, clarify thinking and express feelings. Use mimes and dramatic depictions.	Stories on Jesus, Muhammad, Guru Nanak and others. BBC Religions of the World – a collection of animated films. Talking Pictures: A picture pack from RE Today. Use local pictures of special places. Story of Esther. Invite a faith leader in class.
Make comments about what they have heard and ask questions to clarify their understanding.	Use prompt cards with 'who', 'how', 'when'' 'where' and 'why' questions about their own experiences and to respond to different stimuli and resources.	Stories: Noah's Ark, Jonah and Whale, Feeding of the 5000, Guru Nanak and the Cobra, Yusuf in the Well, Moses and the parting of the sea, King Sagar and the Ganga.
Hold conversation when engaged in back-and-forth exchanges with their teacher and peers.	Use circle time to make children highly active participants, adult to child and small group instruction.	Place multiple artefacts on each table and allow talk. Invite visitors to talk about their belief and in living in the UK focus on 'back and forth' interactions.

Table 5.4 Supporting speaking ELG through RE

Communication and language: Speaking ELG

Children at the expected level of development will	Teaching approach	Suggested content
Participate in small group, class and one-to-one discussions, offering their own ideas, using recently introduced vocabulary.	Teach how to say some words. Use think, pair, share. Display a wide range of RE related vocabulary and point to it during teaching. Use Apps/iPad.	Discuss how objects, symbols and actions are used in mandir, synagogues, gurdwara which show what people believe in. Build vocabulary in and for appropriate topics.
Offer explanations for why things might happen, making use of recently introduced vocabulary from stories, non-fiction, rhymes and poems when appropriate.	Use questioning to develop children's confidence in their own beliefs and practices. Ask them to explain and reason. Use questions that have no right or wrong answer and require sharing and discussion of ideas.	Religious festivals: Explore when, how and why they are celebrated. Share stories about them. Show and share food commonly eaten. Create a class rhyme on a festival. Write a class poem about a festival.
Express their ideas and feelings about their experiences using full sentences, including use of past, present and future tenses and making use of conjunctions, with modelling and support from their teacher.	Use interviews. Use discussion and art. Explore the past and present through experiences, books and recounts. Compose a sentence orally before writing it. Say out loud what you expect them to write about.	Talk about people who help us, e.g. faith leaders. Observe the world and space. Invite adults to come to share their life experiences. Explore birth and wedding ceremonies. Talk about what they do at home.

Table 5.5 Supporting self-regulation ELG through RE

Personal, social and emotional development: Self-regulation: ELG		
Children at the expected level of development will	**Teaching approach**	**Suggested content**
Show an understanding of their own feelings and those of others, and begin to regulate their behaviour accordingly.	Create a conscience alley. Use a puppet. Use freeze frames to show actions of caring and uncaring. Use persona dolls to explore feelings and actions.	Bilal: A slave set free to call Muslims to pray. Joseph and his brothers. The Good Samaritan. Talk: to care or not to care for animals.

Table 5.6 Supporting managing self ELG through RE

Personal, social and emotional development: Managing self ELG		
Children at the expected level of development will	**Teaching approach**	**Suggested content**
Be confident to try new activities and show independence, resilience and perseverance in the face of challenge.	Use treasure hunting. Try some ideas from: Crab and Whale: a new way to experience mindfulness for kids and Breathe Like a Bear: 30 Mindful Moments for Kids to Feel Calm and Focused Anytime.	Hide some pictures, words, artefacts from different religious and non-religious traditions and pupils find them. Narrate and discuss David and Goliath.
Explain the reasons for rules, know right from wrong and try to behave accordingly.	Use role-play to demonstrate acceptable and unacceptable behaviour. Use and discuss scenarios to identify the wrong and right behaviour. Discuss emotions as part of the consequences. Circle time on why rules are needed to behave. Exploring actions and consequences in Hindu teachings.	Discuss rules at home, school and elsewhere. Narrate the boy who cried wolf. Talk about the purpose of sacred books. Read a Hindu story (Sharavan, King Shibli, Sadhu's Blessings).
Manage their own basic hygiene and personal needs, including dressing, going to the toilet and understanding the importance of healthy food choices.	Use cooking and baking. Talk about healthy and unhealthy food choices. Talk about hygiene. Use re-enactments.	Make and share kheer as part of Wesak celebrations. Explore langar, halal, kosher and vegetarian diets. Teach about hygiene in Sikh, Hindu, Muslim, Jewish tradition.

Table 5.7 Supporting building relationships ELG through RE

Personal, social and emotional development: ELG: Building relationships

Children at the expected level of development will	Teaching approach	Suggested content
Work and play cooperatively and take turns with others.	Explore examples of cooperation between different people. Make flags with a message and hang in class.	Read: Ammalli – A True Friend. Read: Rebuilding the Wall in Jerusalem. Each child makes their own flag.
Form positive attachments to adults and friendships with peers.	Discuss: how do they belong to the same school/class? Wear masks: how do they belong to different groups? Role-play or video: How a baby is welcomed after they are born into their family.	Teach about belonging in different religions, school communities. Read the Proud Helper (Bahá'í).
Show sensitivity to their own and to others' needs.	Use circle time: what does it mean to be a true friend? Hot-seating: how they would like to be treated and how they should treat others. Use puppet: know some children don't always enjoy the same things. Use QR code to show the work of a charity.	The Crying Camel and Muslim beliefs about creation. Investigate the Hindu festival of Raksha Bandhan. Make a collection for charity/foodbank. Write or draw a picture to say thank you.

Table 5.8 Supporting gross motor skills ELG through RE

Physical development: Gross motor skills ELG

Children at the expected level of development will	Teaching approach	Suggested content
Negotiate space and obstacles safely, with consideration for themselves and others.	Use recipes. Use play opportunities. Use cooking. Use role-play.	Cook and share some delicious sweets, snacks and savoury for Diwali, Holi, Vaisakhi and Eid and sweet honey cake at Rosh Hashanah, crispy potato latkes at Hanukkah.
Move energetically, such as running, jumping, dancing, hopping, skipping and climbing.	Select as appropriate	Hindu, Sikh and Jewish dance, Holi celebration, Worship dance or liturgical dance in Christianity. Read to inspire Fauja Singh Keeps Going.

Table 5.9 Supporting fine motor skills ELG through RE

Physical development: Fine motor skills ELG

Children at the expected level of development will	Teaching approach	Suggested content
Use a range of small tools, including scissors, paint brushes and cutlery.	Use a range of art, draft, design, calligraphy, papier-mâché, play doh, painting, drawing, colouring, cutting, pasting and doodling.	Rangoli patterns, diwas, stained glass windows, candle flames. Make models of places of worship. Offer a 'feely bag' to be curious about artefacts.
Begin to show accuracy and care when drawing.	Use group work and independent tasks. Use the playground. Use natural material to make.	A dharma wheel, a bodhi leaf, a lotus flower, a Buddhist flag. Using chalk to write words and draw.

Table 5.10 Supporting past and present ELG through RE

Understanding the world: Past and present ELG

Children at the expected level of development will	Teaching approach	Suggested content
Talk about the lives of the people around them and their roles in society.	Interview visitors. Circle time using artefacts from other religions. Use drama. Use Venn diagrams. Use discussion.	Talk about Me and My family; Me and My toys. Talk to real people who help us, e.g. fire-fighters and police. Talk to faith leaders. Study and role-play religious clothing.
Know some similarities and differences between things in the past and now, drawing on their experiences and what has been read in class.	Use photographs. Use video. Read books. Use assorted resources. Use persona dolls.	Study the past and present of religious celebrations, places of worship, sites of pilgrimage, texts, writing, statutes, artefacts and clothing.
Understand the past through settings, characters and events encountered in books read in class and storytelling.	Use a visualiser. Use stories. Use images. Use drama.	Life of Guru Nanak, Jesus, Muhammad, Buddha, Moses, Adam and Eve. Recall significant events in their own experience.

Table 5.11 Supporting people, culture and communities ELG through RE

Understanding the world: People, culture and communities ELG

Children at the expected level of development will	Teaching approach	Suggested content
Describe their immediate environment using knowledge from observation, discussion, stories, non-fiction texts and maps.	Use a local map. Use visits. Use images. Use videos. Use visitors.	Investigate, talk and share experiences and feelings about My Home, Special Places, Places of Worship, My Special Things, My Special People and My Special Book.
Know some similarities and differences between different religious and cultural communities in this country, drawing on their experiences and what has been read in class.	Use group work. Use Venn diagrams. Use a visualiser. Use pie-charts. Use adults in school. Use an interview.	Explore the local community. Explore the Census of religion and belief in the local area. Shabbat, Sunday and Friday and how they are marked as significant. Compare the mandir and gurdwara. Contrast a synagogue and a mosque. Adults in school share their cultural and religious experiences.
Explain some similarities and differences between life in this country and life in other countries, drawing on knowledge from stories, non-fiction texts and – when appropriate – maps.	Use group work. Use a national map. Use puppets. Use stories. Use images. Use videos. Use books.	Living in Makkah, Amritsar, Jerusalem and London. Make food from different cultures. Observe art from different cultures. Make buildings from different cultures. Study clothing from different cultures. Experience languages from different cultures.

Table 5.12 Supporting the natural world ELG through RE

Understanding the world: ELG: The natural world

Children at the expected level of development will	Teaching approach	Suggested content
Explore the natural world around them, making observations and drawing pictures of animals and plants.	Use nature to walk around the woodland, grassland, habitats, allotment or playground. Use seasonal items. Use logs for insects. Use videos.	Show animation of creation stories from Christian, Jewish, Sikh, Hindu and Muslim traditions. Explore their differences on how and when creation happened and the role of God in each story. Muhammad and the Cat. Talk about teachings from different religions on the environment and caring for living things. Explore Hindu positions on animals and rivers. Discuss ahimsa in Buddhism.
Know some similarities and differences between the natural world around them and contrasting environments, drawing on their experiences and what has been read in class.	Use pictures. Use books. Use visualisers. Use videos. Use the Internet. Use recycling fabric and other material. Use papier-mâché.	Visit local places of worship. Make domes, minaret, stupa and spire. Create their own films of their school, playgroup and local area. Create their own imaginary world. Create their own imaginary animals.
Understand some important processes and changes in the natural world around them, including the seasons and changing states of matter.	Use observations and real objects. Use pictures and images. Use drawings and paintings for expressing themselves.	Study Spring and Autumn. Talk about life and death. Talk about birth and growing up. Talk about youth and being aged. Talk about health and illness. Talk about happiness and sadness. Study infant baptism and adult baptism.

Table 5.13 Supporting creating with materials ELG through RE

Expressive arts and design: Creating with materials ELG

Children at the expected level of development will	Teaching approach	Suggested content
Safely use and explore a variety of materials, tools and techniques, experimenting with colour, design, texture, form and function. Share their creations, explaining the process they have used. Make use of props and materials when role playing characters in narratives and stories.	Use modelling, explanation, examples. Use adult-led activities. Use a range of media and materials. Use constructive play.	Draw an image of the Buddha. Design Buddhist prayer flags. Decorate candles and prayer wheels. Design Buddha under the bodhi tree. Colour a Buddhist shrine. Dress up as Buddhist monks. Make a lotus flower and a lantern for Wesak. Make a kite for Vaisakhi. Make the Nishan Sahib, Vaisakhi cards, Khanda and models of 5Ks. Create a 3D seder plate. Make a Sukkah in the corner. Make a menorah using felt. Make hand puppets of ten plagues. Create and design a diva. Create a 3D Kaaba using Lego. Design silhouette mosques. Use paper plates to create an Islamic mosaic art gallery of names of Allah and the Prophets. Design and make a prayer mat.

Table 5.14 Supporting being imaginative and expressive ELG through RE

Expressive arts and design: Being imaginative and expressive ELG		
Children at the expected level of development will	**Teaching approach**	**Suggested content**
Invent, adapt and recount narratives and stories with peers and their teacher.	Use performing. Use acting. Use drama. Use role play. Use imaginative play.	Stories of Nativity, Purim, Khalsa, Hijrah, Exodus, Ganesh and the Emperor's seed and Ling. Play in dens and tents.
Sing a range of well-known nursery rhymes and songs. Perform songs, rhymes, poems and stories with others, and – when appropriate – try to move in time with music.	Use listening. Use vocalisation. Use singing. Use performance. Use religious terminology, e.g. hymns, ragas, chants, bells, tilawat, shabad and kirtan.	All Things Bright And Beautiful. Allah Made Everything (Zain Bhikha) Hanukkah songs for children. Hymns in Christianity. Explore use of music in celebrations and festivals. Listen to sounds and music in different religions, e.g. mool mantar. Sounds, songs and music from around the world, expressing ideas and feelings through dance, movement and music.
Children can start to compose simple rhythmic tunes to respond to religious stories or events.	Use composition	Compose simple songs inspired by religions. Compose sound and music to express moods, e.g. joy, sorrow, devotion, celebration, prayer. Muhammad arrival in Madinah (Tala al Badru 'Alayna). Gayatri mantra (Hindu).

Summary

This section has offered the opportunity available to make provision for RE in nursery, though it is not a legal requirement, as it provides children with a wealth of experiences for their emotional, personal and social growth. It has suggested the nature and type of activities, which can be used. It then discussed the contribution that RE can make toward Early Learning Goals as outlined in the New Early Years Framework.

RE in Key Stages 1 and 2

RE in Key Stage 1

Key Stage 1 should build on children's growing awareness of religion and religious life which they experienced in the Foundation Stage. In Key Stage 1, it is recommended that pupils should develop their knowledge and understanding of religions and worldviews, recognising their local, national and global contexts. They should use basic subject-specific vocabulary. They should raise questions and begin to express their own views in response to the material they learn about and in response to questions about their ideas (REC 2013:15). The new position of the REC was analysed in Chapter 2. However, according to the REC's (2013) earlier version, as illustrated in Table 5.15, more specifically pupils should be taught to:

Table 5.15 Non-statutory RE requirements in Key Stage 1

Requirements	Examples and notes
Note: as this is not a statutory document, these are not legal requirements as in the national curriculum.	Note: the examples from religions and worldviews given below do not constitute a syllabus but illustrate what is meant in the first column.
A1. Recall and name different beliefs and practices, including festivals, worship, rituals and ways of life, in order to find out about the meanings behind them.	• Pupils enact stories and celebrations from Easter, Diwali or Eid-ul-Fitr, finding out about what the stories told at the festivals mean, e.g. through welcoming visitors to talk about their festivals • Pupils experience thanking and being thanked, praising and being praised and notice some ways Christians or Jewish people believe they can thank and praise God • Linking to English and computing, pupils recount a visit to a local church using digital photographs and find out about the meanings of symbols for God that they saw there.
A2. Retell and suggest meanings to some religious and moral stories, exploring and discussing sacred writings and sources of wisdom and recognising the traditions from which they come.	• Pupils choose their favourite 'wise sayings' from different sources or key leaders and talk about what makes these sayings wise, and what difference it would make if people followed them • Pupils retell (for example through drama) two different stories about Jesus considering what they mean. They compare the stories and think about what Christians today could learn from the stories • Linking to English, pupils respond to stories from Hindu, Muslim or Jewish sources by identifying the values which different characters in the stories showed, and recognising the religions from which the stories come • Pupils ask and answer 'who', 'where', 'how' and 'why' questions about religious stories and stories from nonreligious worldviews.
A3. Recognise some different symbols and actions which express a community's way of life, appreciating some similarities between communities.	• Pupils choose to find out about the symbols of two different religious traditions, looking for similarities between the ways they use common symbols such as light, water, trees or rock • Pupils discover how and why Muslims wash, bow and pray in a daily pattern, noticing similarities to another religion or worldview • Pupils select examples of religious artefacts from Christianity or Judaism that interest them, raising lists of questions about them and finding out what they mean and how they are used in festivals and worship • Pupils hear three moral stories, for example from Christians, Hindus and humanists, and think about whether they are saying the same things about how people should behave.
B1. Ask and respond to questions about what individuals and communities do, and why, so that pupils can identify what difference belonging to a community might make.	• Pupils find out about what people with different religions and worldviews do to celebrate the fruitfulness of the earth (e.g. in Harvest festivals, and in generosity to those in need), responding to questions about being generous • Pupils discuss reasons why some people go to mosques, synagogues or churches often, but other people never go to holy buildings, and why some people pray every day, but others not at all • Linking to PSHE, pupils make lists of the different groups to which they belong and consider the ways these contribute to human happiness.

(Continued)

Table 5.15 Non-statutory RE requirements in Key Stage 1 *(Continued)*

Requirements	Examples and notes
B2. Observe and recount different ways of expressing identity and belonging, responding sensitively for themselves.	• Pupils learn about the daily life of a Muslim or Jewish child (e.g. from a teacher's use of persona dolls), and make an illustrated list of signs of belonging including using special food, clothing, prayer, scripture, family life, worship and festivities. Pupils make a list of the ways they show how they belong as well • Pupils express creatively (e.g. in art, poetry or drama) their own ideas about the questions: Who am I? Where do I belong? • Pupils watch a short film about the Hindu creation story and talk about different stages of the cycle of life.
B3. Notice and respond sensitively to some similarities between different religions and worldviews.	• Pupils use a set of photos or a list of religious items they have encountered in Key Stage 1 RE to sort and order, saying which items are connected to a particular religion and which are connected to more than one religion • Linking to English, pupils use key words (e.g. holy, sacred, scripture, festival, symbol, humanist) to present ideas or write about two different religions or worldviews about which they have learned.
C1. Explore questions about belonging, meaning and truth so that they can express their own ideas and opinions in response using words, music, art or poetry.	• Pupils work in groups to use art, music and poetry to respond to ideas about God from different religions and worldviews, expressing ideas of their own and commenting on some ideas of others • Pupils ask and answer a range of 'how' and 'why' questions about how people practise their religion • Linking to 'Philosophy for Children', pupils think about and respond to 'big questions' in a classroom enquiry using a story of Adam and Eve or a video clip of children asking questions about God as a stimulus.
C2. Find out about and respond with ideas to examples of co-operation between people who are different.	• Pupils discuss stories of co-operation from different traditions and sources and make a 'Recipe for living together happily' or a 'Class charter for more kindness and less fighting' • Linking to English and PSHE pupils could play some collaborative games, and talk about how the games put the teaching of the 'Golden Rule' into action • Pupils notice and talk about the fact that people come from different religions, responding to the questions – 'How can we tell? How can we live together when we are all so different?'
C3. Find out about questions of right and wrong and begin to express their ideas and opinions in response.	• Pupils respond to a quiet reflection or a guided visualisation by choosing one value they think the world needs more of today from a list of values, and by illustrating their choice in different media • Linking to English, pupils could ask questions about goodness, and write sentences that say what happens when people are kind, thankful, fair or generous, and what happens when people are unkind, ungrateful, unfair or mean • Pupils look at how different people have expressed their ideas about God, and think and talk about their own ideas about God.

RE in Key Stage 2

In Key Stage 2, it is recommended that pupils should extend their knowledge and understanding of religions and worldviews, recognising their local, national and global contexts. They should be introduced to an extended range of sources and subject-specific vocabulary. They should be encouraged to be curious and to ask increasingly challenging questions about religion, beliefs, values and human life. Pupils should learn to express their own ideas in response to the material they engage with, identifying relevant information, selecting examples and giving reasons to support their ideas and views (REC 2013:17). According to the REC (2013), as illustrated in Table 5.16, more specifically pupils should be taught to:

Table 5.16 Non-statutory RE requirements in Key Stage 2

Requirements	Examples and notes
Note: as this is not a statutory document, these are not legal requirements as in the national curriculum.	Note: the examples from religions and worldviews given below do not constitute a syllabus but illustrate what is meant in the first column
A1. Describe and make connections between different features of the religions and worldviews they study, discovering more about celebrations, worship, pilgrimages and the rituals which mark important points in life, in order to reflect on their significance.	• Pupils make some connections between Hajj for Muslims and pilgrimage to Lourdes, Iona or 'the Holy Land' for Christians, describing the motives people have for making spiritual journeys • Pupils describe spiritual ways of celebrating different festivals, and reflect on the reasons why some people value such celebrations very highly, but others not at all • Pupils compare how Christians, Muslims, Hindus or humanists celebrate a marriage and express and argue for ideas of their own about partnership, in discussions or in writing.
A2. Describe and understand links between stories and other aspects of the communities they are investigating, responding thoughtfully to a range of sources of wisdom and to beliefs and teachings that arise from them in different communities.	• Linking to English, pupils consider how some texts from the Torah (e.g. the Shema), the Bible (e.g. 1 Corinthians 13) and the Qur'an (e.g. The 1st Surah, the Opening) are seen as sources of wisdom in different traditions. They respond to the ideas found in the texts with ideas of their own • Pupils investigate aspects of community life such as weekly worship, charitable giving or beliefs about prayer, showing their understanding and expressing ideas of their own • Pupils compare the texts in the Christian gospels that tell the stories of shepherds and wise men at Jesus' birth, exploring how they are remembered and celebrated in a range of Christmas festivities.
A3. Explore and describe a range of beliefs, symbols and actions so that they can understand different ways of life and ways of expressing meaning.	• Pupils pursue an enquiry into beliefs about worship, relating the meanings of symbols and actions used in worship such as bowing down, making music together, sharing food or speaking to God (e.g. in prayer) to events and teachings from a religion they study • Pupils consider how the meanings of a parable of Jesus are expressed in poetry, video, stained glass and drama. • Pupils describe the impact of Hindu teaching about harmlessness (ahimsa) on questions about what people eat and how people treat animals. They express their own ideas.
B1. Observe and understand varied examples of religions and worldviews so that they can explain, with reasons, their meanings and significance to individuals and communities.	• Linking to History and Design Technology pupils consider how the architecture of churches, mosques, mandirs or gurdwaras expresses a community's way of life, values and beliefs • Pupils develop their understanding of beliefs about life after death in two religions and humanism through seeking answers to their own questions and articulating reasons for their own ideas and responses • Pupils use their detailed understanding of religious practice such as the Five Pillars of Islam and worship of a deity in a Hindu family and a mandir to describe the significance of being part of a religion.

(Continued)

Table 5.16 Non-statutory RE requirements in Key Stage 2 *(Continued)*

Requirements	Examples and notes
B2. Understand the challenges of commitment to a community of faith or belief, suggesting why belonging to a community may be valuable, both in the diverse communities being studied and in their own lives.	• Pupils explore the lives of key leaders from Buddhist and Christian contemporary life, describing the challenges they have faced and the commitments by which they have lived • Pupils find out about how celebrating Diwali brings the Hindu or Sikh community together, and expresses commitment to values of interdependence and generosity • Linking to the expressive arts, pupils develop their own imaginative and creative ways of expressing some of their own commitments such as working hard at sport or music, caring for animals and the environment, loving their family or serving God.
B3. Observe and consider different dimensions of religion, so that they can explore and show understanding of similarities and differences within and between different religions and worldviews.	• Pupils use their thinking about stories of Moses and Jesus to explore how Jews and Christians today celebrate key events from their history (e.g. in Passover and Lent) • Pupils list and describe similarities and differences in the ways different traditions express what 'belonging' means to them • Linking to English, pupils find out about different forms of prayer and meditation in different religions and worldviews, and write some prayers or meditations suited to particular occasions and traditions. This is one point, among many, where RE can provide key opportunities for pupils' spiritual development. Note: different dimensions of religion or worldview include, for example, narratives, beliefs, ethics and social life
C1. Discuss and present thoughtfully their own and others' views on challenging questions about belonging, meaning, purpose and truth, applying ideas of their own in different forms including (e.g.) reasoning, music, art and poetry.	• Pupils discuss different perspectives on questions about the beginnings of life on Earth, so that they can describe different ways science and religions treat questions of origins • Linking with the expressive arts curriculum, pupils create works of art or music which express their understanding of what it means to belong to a religion or worldview • Pupils discuss and debate reasons why different people have different ideas about the divine, e.g. whether God is real and what God is like. Note: pupils are not required to express personal beliefs in any coercive way in RE; good RE encourages an open hearted and broad-minded approach to different beliefs.
C2. Consider and apply ideas about ways in which diverse communities can live together for the well-being of all, responding thoughtfully to ideas about community, values and respect.	• Pupils discover and explore what Jewish people, humanists and Christians teach about how people can live together for the well-being of all • Pupils discuss and apply ideas from different religious codes for living (e.g. Commandments, Precepts or Rules), to compile a charter of their own moral values, applying their ideas to issues of respect for all • Linking to Mathematics and Geography, pupils use local and national census statistics to develop accurate understanding of the religious plurality of their locality and of Britain today. Note: This work offers valuable opportunities for engagement with religions with a significant local presence: pupils may learn about the contributions of, for example, Jains, Zoroastrians or members of the Bahá'í faith to inter faith work. These communities can also be studied elsewhere in the RE curriculum.

(Continued)

Table 5.16 Non-statutory RE requirements in Key Stage 2 *(Continued)*

Requirements	Examples and notes
C3. Discuss and apply their own and others' ideas about ethical questions, including ideas about what is right and wrong and what is just and fair, and express their own ideas clearly in response.	• Pupils apply their own ideas about justice and fairness to the work of three development charities such as Christian Aid, Islamic Relief and Oxfam • Pupils write persuasively about the reasons why people who have a particular religious background or non-religious worldview try to help people who are vulnerable (e.g. victims of natural disasters or prejudice, people who live with disabilities or people affected by war) • Linking to Citizenship Education, pupils consider the Ten Commandments (Jewish) and the Five Precepts (Buddhist), expressing their ideas about right and wrong in the light of their learning. Note: this is one point, among many, where RE can provide key opportunities for pupils' moral development.

Summary

As you will surmise thus far, there are many 'powers' at play in the terrain of RE. It has been suggested that a teacher, who understands how forces outside the classroom, politics, philosophy, educational change and cultural change affect RE, is in a position to teach their subject more effectively and with greater clarity (Buchanan 2005; Revell 2008:237). The important thing, therefore, is that teachers do not let the structures which are in place to support the teaching become a clamp tying them down at every turn. These structures include a non-statutory national framework, Diocesan policy, scheme of work, agreed syllabus, attainment targets, reporting procedures, targets, grades, curriculum reviewers, teacher, pupil and self-assessment (Watson and Thompson 2007:214). Whilst some of these have been addressed to an extent, funding, high expectations of teachers, Ofsted and the expectation to tackle societal problems continue to impact schools and teachers (Box 5.2).

BOX 5.2 VIGNETTE: CURRICULUM

I am a British Bangladeshi Muslim. Raised in a liberal family with relatives from different faiths and cultures. I studied BA Economics and Finance. I have always dreamed of being a teacher but leaned more towards teaching Economics at secondary school, as I was inspired by my Economics teacher.

School experience days at a primary school in Birmingham tempted me to pursue a career in primary education rather than secondary as I enjoyed the broad and rich curriculum. For me, teaching means impacting a child's life in their early stages of development in a positive way. Which then gives them the tools to succeed in adulthood through their career, relationships with those around them and their mental and physical health.

RE interests me, as there are many misconceptions around the subject. Some believe it may be outdated to teach children about religions as we live in a secular country. I think it is important as it teaches children to grow into adults who are open to learning about matters they may disagree with but also respect.

RE isn't a subject I remember being taught vastly in primary school. We had an external adult teach us about the New Testimony and Christian based nursery rhymes. Not many other religions were taught apart from Christianity and Islam (as the school was predominately Muslim). RE is very important to my family and friends around me. I am lucky to have people around me who would like to learn new things and meet new people.

I am hoping to achieve confidence in leading a subject such as RE which may be overlooked by teachers, parents and children. Bringing a love for inclusion of all faiths and cultures, as I believe that RE is a subject that gives children the tools to engage in conversation with their peers and learn more about each other's beliefs. I fear battling stereotypes. As a leader, I am concerned about the lack of confidence teachers may have when teaching RE. During SBT1, I taught RE during the last week before Christmas. It was taught over a full day.

References

Buchanan, M. (2005) Pedagogical drift: The evolution of new approaches and paradigms in religious education, *Religious Education*, 100, (1), pp.20–37.

DfE (2021) *Statutory Framework for the Early Years Foundation Stage: Setting the Standards for Learning, Development and Care for Children from Birth to Five*, London: Crown copyright. [Online] https://assets.publishing.service.gov.uk/government/uploads/system/uploads/attachment_data/file/974907/EYFS_framework_-_March_2021.pdf (Accessed 30/7/2021).

OECD (Organisation for Economic Cooperation and Development) (2015) *Skills for Social Progress: The Power of Social and Emotional Skills*, Paris: OECD.

Revell, L. (2008) Religious Education in England, *NUMEN*, 55, (2–3), pp.218–240.

REC (Religious Education Council of England and Wales) (2013) *A Curriculum Framework for Religious Education in England*. London: REC of England and Wales. [Online] https://www.religiouseducationcouncil.org.uk/wp-content/uploads/2017/09/RE_Review_Summary.pdf (Accessed 19/09/2021).

Sylva, K., Melhuish, E., Siraj-Blatchford, I., and Taggart, B. (2004) *The Effective Provision of Pre-School Education (EPPE) Project: Findings from Pre-School to End of Key Stage 1*, London: Institute of Education.

Watson, B., and Thompson, P. (2007) *The Effective Teaching of Religious Education*, Harlow: Longman. Second edition.

Weisberg, D. S., Hirsh-Pasek, K., and Golinkoff, R. M. (2013) Guided play: Where curricular goals meet playful pedagogy, *Mind, Brain and Education*, 7, (2), pp.104–112.Religious Education in the nursery

Toenco our staff and children.

The development of concepts, attitudes and skills in RE

Introduction

Pupils should have access to the central concepts underpinning religions and beliefs. Pupils need to master these key concepts and ideas of Religious Education (RE) to gain a secure understanding of the areas of knowledge and understanding that they are being taught. They should be planned for and assessments should focus on pupils' understanding of these main concepts and areas.

The development of concepts

You will undoubtedly have encountered the term concept, both in RE and in educational discourse in general. It is understood in multiple ways and used for a variety of purposes. James and Stern (2019:11–12) think that a concept is a 'big idea', or an idea that is at the centre of a whole set of ideas, or at the centre of a 'theory' – a network of connected ideas. Concepts are the essence of that which shapes the understanding and behaviour of something. In RE, these relate to how humans understand or make sense of life and the world. The exploration of the concepts of religion and belief and their roles in the spiritual, moral and cultural lives of people in a diverse society helps individuals develop moral awareness and social understanding (DCSF 2010:7). Based on a range of research studies, Stern (2018:81) concluded that focussing on concepts is beneficial for all pupils including SEND and gifted and talented.

Each concept is capable of being explored at different levels and depths. Concepts do not exist in silos. Nevertheless, each concept is distinctive whilst it can relate to other concepts. For example, identity; purpose; value. Concepts tend to be deep, sophisticated and can be expressed in different ways. They are found in art and design, symbols, drama and dance, rites and rituals, history, language and music as well. Therefore, conceptual clarity is important to maintain the integrity and minimise potential confusion. Teece (2015:25) suggests that the key to assisting pupils to understand anything is to enable them to understand concepts. They play an important role in building conceptual bridges between the pupils' experience, humanity, religion and particular religious contexts.

For Watson and Thompson (2007) imagination is intimately connected with the development of religious concepts. However, they express concern that inadequate concepts may cause people to misinterpret religious people's behaviour and commitment, to take literally what may have been intended metaphorically or symbolically, and not even to see the *possibility* [sic] of the truth of religious concepts. Therefore, they suggest that effective RE must be concerned with the building-up of concepts, which are worthy of a person's total development, emotional, experiential and intellectual, and which fairly represent what is at the heart of all great religious traditions. They further claim that only on this basis can people make the informed choice of what is the hallmark of an educated person (Watson and Thompson 2007:116).

To this end, Erricker, Lowndes and Bellchambers (2011:65–66; 78–86) devised three categories for their enquiry methodology. The pedagogy of conceptual enquire will be exemplified in Chapter 10 as a method for you to use in your teaching. In this section, the three categories, which also feature in Teece (2015) and, transiently in James and Stern (2019), are presented below so that you can begin to think about developing conceptual understanding in the classroom in similar lines to developing skills and attitudes in RE. All three types of concepts contain some that are simpler and others that are more complex; this is particularly true of those falling under universal human concepts (Erricker, Lowndes and Bellchambers 2011:65). Prescott (2015:39) refers to them as universal concepts, universal religious concepts and specific religious concepts. There may be some overlap with them, perhaps with distinct interpretations as well.

Category A: Discerned from shared human experience

In a broader sense, these types of concepts focus on those that are generic within human experience and important in the classification of human experience, as exemplified in Table 6.1. They are common to religious and non-religious experiences. Therefore, whilst wide-ranging, it has been suggested there should be some systematic way of relating them to pupil's development and experience and to link them explicitly to religious practices. Since younger pupils lack the ability to think in a more sophisticated fashion but can respond to terms within their own vocabulary and experience, so the concepts used have to be readily accessible to them. Belonging, celebration and special(ness) are the most obvious concepts to introduce with pupils in Foundation Stage and Year 1. Here they link their own vocabulary, narratives and concerns to those that are most transparent within religious behaviour. As they progress, further concepts of a more complex kind can be introduced, such as authority, and, then, in upper primary the likes of freedom and justice (Erricker, Lowndes and Bellchambers 2011:65–66). These types are not in themselves religious but are very helpful in enabling pupils to make links amongst religions, worldviews and the types of questions referred to in the purpose of the study of RE (REC 2013). They might be referred to as 'spiritual' as they can help us make sense of our shared human experience (Teece 2015:25).

Category B: Derived from the study of religions

These types fall under general religious concepts and are commonly used for the study of religion, as exemplified in Table 6.2. They are common to many religions and are identifiable by their use of figurative language: symbolism, ritual, sacred, myth and worship. These are the basis for religious literacy (Erricker, Lowndes and Bellchambers 2011:66). They can help pupils make sense of religion in a general way. For example, it is important that pupils begin to understand something about the nature of religious language and communication. All religions communicate essential truths in non-literal ways. Therefore, a concept like myth is important in this sense. It is also important because, like a number of concepts in this category, it has been devalued and reduced in its meaning in many Western societies (Teece 2015:25).

Table 6.1 Concepts discerned from shared human experience	
Concepts derived from our share human experience	Authority, belief, belonging, care, celebrations, change, commitment, community, creation, custom, devotion, difference, duty, environmentalism, equality, festival, freedom, forgiveness, good and evil, growth, guidance, hope, identity, justice, leadership, love, loyalty, mystery, pattern, peace, persecution, prejudice, power, purity, remembrance, relationship, responsibility, ritual, rule, sacrifice, secularity, service, special place, special time, spirituality, suffering, teacher, truth, unity, wholeness, wisdom, wonder, worldview

Table 6.2 Concepts derived from the study of religions	
Concepts common to many religions and that are used in the study of religion	Belief, blessing, creation, devotion, discipleship, faith, fasting, God, god, holy, initiation, pilgrimage, prayer, prophethood, ritual, religion, religious tradition, revelation, rites of passage, sacred, salvation, scripture, symbolism, martyrdom, myth, worldview, worship

Category C: Emerging from specific religions

These types of concepts belong within a specific religious tradition and are important for believers, as exemplified in Table 6.3. They relate to key beliefs and values of the tradition but also provide the lens through which a follower views the world. Those chosen below reflect what might be called the spirituality or religiousness of the tradition. Alternatively, in other words, they are concepts that are essential if one is to understand something of how a Christian, Buddhist, Hindu, etc. sees the world (Teece 2015:25). They are the basis of worldview analysis or understanding how a particular tradition makes sense of the world and how different branches of a tradition interpret those concepts to give a distinctive cast to its worldview. They have to be ones that underpin the beliefs and practices of the religion in question and not one that describes the practice itself. Erricker, Lowndes and Bellchambers (2011:66) emphasise that it is the 'why' behind the 'what' of practice and behaviour that is sought. Thus, resurrection is a key concept in Christianity but prayer is not. Torah is a key concept in Judaism but Passover is not. Dharma is a key concept in Hinduism but prasad is not. Sewa is a key concept in Sikhism but langar is not.

Examples of concepts

These are selected examples of key concepts (lenses) particular to specific religions and humanism through which the believers and people see the world.

Table 6.3 Concepts emerging from specific religions						
Sikh	**Christian**	**Jewish**	**Hindu**	**Muslim**	**Buddhist**	**Humanism**
Akhand Path	Agape	Brit	Ahimsa	Akhirah	Anatta	Agnosticism
Amrit	Atonement	Covenant	Atman	Akhlaq	Anicca	Atheism
Annad	Church	Elokim	Avatar	Allah	Bhavana	Compassion
Bani/shabad	Discipleship	Halakhah	Bhakti	Din	Buddha	Empathy
Gurmukh	Faith	Israel	Brahma	Ibadah	Dhamma	Evolution
Guru	Forgiveness	Kashrut	Brahman	Iman	(dharma)	Happiness
Haumai	Grace	Kedusha	Brahmin	Islam	Dukkha	Human co-operation.
Ik Onkar	God the Father	Mitzvah	Darshan	Jihad	Kamma	Humanist Ceremonies.
Jivan Mukhti	Holy Spirit	Mashiach	Dharma	Muslim	(karma)	Meaning in worldly life
Jot	Incarnation	(messiah)	Guna	Nabi	Karuna	without afterlife.
Khalsa	Jesus the	Rabbi	Jati	Qadar	Metta	Moral values as
Langar	Christ	Redemption	Karma	Qur'an	Nibbana	human conceptions.
Manmukh	Love	Shabbat	Maya	Rasul	(nirvana)	Rationalism
Maya	Mother of God	Shalom	Moksha	Risalah	Prajna	Responsibility
Mukti	Redemption	Shekinah	Murti	Shari'ah	Sangha	Rights
Nadar	Repentance	Synagogue	Samsara	Shirk	Sila	Scepticism
Nam Simran	Resurrection	Tenakh	Shakti	Sunnah	Tanha	Science and world
Niguna	Salvation	Teshuvah	Shiva	Tawbah	Upaya	knowledge.
Panth	Sacrament	Torah	Smriti	Tawhid		Secularism
Sewa	Sin	Tzedekah	Sruti	Ummah		The human heritage.
Sikh	Trinity	Tzelem	Varna			The human spirit.
		Zion	Vishnu			Toleration
			Yoga			Universe as a natural
						phenomenon.
						Value of life.

Planning for conceptual development

As you plan for effective lessons, you may break tasks down into constituent components when first setting up an independent practice. You should also plan to use modelling, explanations and scaffolds, and acknowledge that novices need more structure early in a domain. To promote good progress, you should build on pupils' prior knowledge by sequencing lessons so that pupils secure foundational knowledge before encountering more complex content, whilst at the same time, you should identify possible misconceptions and plan how to prevent these forming, especially when similar concepts feature in religious and non-religious traditions (DfE 2019).

As you teach, you should encourage pupils to share their emerging understanding and points of confusion so that misconceptions can be addressed. Then links should be made to what pupils already know to what is being taught, for example, by explaining how the new concept builds on what is already known about a similar or different concept. Sometimes you may need to make use of expositions. This can be done by using a concrete representation of abstract ideas, for example, by using analogies, metaphors, examples and non-examples. It is also effective to combine a verbal explanation with a relevant graphical representation of the same concept, where appropriate (DfE 2019).

In terms of designing a curriculum, disciplinary knowledge and sequencing are essential. Teachers should plan a cohesive and sequential curriculum, which is both knowledge rich (having conceptual depth) and has coherence. The lists above can be useful for improving your subject knowledge as you teach particular traditions on an ongoing basis. There are many more concepts. Therefore, you can keep adding to these over time to personalise your inventory. The more these concepts are rooted and related to the experiences and the lives of pupils and their communities the more engaging and deeper understanding might occur. Since each concept attempts to convey an underlying idea to understanding how religion works, pupils should be enabled to make links between actions and beliefs. In addition, questions may consist of one or more concepts, such as; 'Is God Merciful?' involves the concepts of 'God' and 'mercy'. The question 'What are 5Ks for?' involves the concepts of identity, symbolism and community. Therefore, concepts offer opportunities to help pupils understand, interpret human experience and make sense of the world.

In the classroom

Give pupils a selection of concepts and ask them to categorise them into those (i) we know, (ii) we like to know more and (iii) we don't know. Thereafter design tasks to focus on learning those in the final category to ensure high-level content and prompt progress in learning. Importantly, it creates a safe environment where pupils are encouraged to express their need to learn, and thereby expressing humility.

At the start of a topic or religious tradition, retrieve and create a class or personalised glossary of current concepts known to them and continue adding to it as the lessons progress.

Ask pupils to investigate some concepts by completing Table 6.4.

Consider the following activities, designed with students, which are based ostensibly on concepts derived from shared human experience. Dual coding which is the combination of

Table 6.4 An activity to investigate concepts	
Concept	**Torah**
Religion	
Symbol /image	
Write a sentence	
Write its importance	
Influence on life	
(add your own feature here)	

pictures and words can also be used here, which reduces chances of cognitive overload (Watson and Bradley 2021). You could use graphic organisers, diagrams, sketch notes, posters, drawings, displays, slides, infographics, walkthrus and icons (Caviglioli 2019).

Commitment

This is the state or quality of being dedicated to a cause. An active learning activity to show what commitment means could involve, for example, planting a flower or vegetable. Pupils can visually see the effects of commitment and dedication to their cause (in this case, planting a flower). It takes a lot of time and actions (watering, sunlight, care, nurture). There is also a need to take precautions to make the plant grow. This allows pupils to understand religiously how all faiths require commitment (religious actions, e.g. prayer, fasting, charity, kindness) to achieve the ultimate reward of abiding by religion. Some people come with sincere commitment and intention. This concept can be visually represented through pupils growing plants as they will also be committed to making their plants grow. The result of a blossomed flower will be the reward for their commitment. A parallel can be drawn with the concept of rewards given in the Hereafter, for example.

Mystery

This activity teaches the concept of 'mystery' by having a simple group talk. During the talk, each pupil will have the chance to discuss their beliefs about religion and God (whether or not they believe in God and their personal beliefs). They may also be asked if they have any unanswered questions about the world/life. They can talk about what is mysterious to them and why. They close their eyes and visualise the daytime and night sky and think about its mysterious nature.

Love

For some people, their thinking process involves love and respect, which are incorporated in this activity. It is also an important concept as teachers develop self-esteem, which is similar to self-love. Pupils create a fact file about themselves answering questions. These include what is your favourite place to visit? What religious beliefs (if any), do you and your family follow? Where were you born? Pupils then share these facts to learn more about one another and become more confident in themselves.

Authority

Using role-play pupils act out the scene of King Herod to show authority whereby he wanted all the baby boys killed. They could dramatise the story of Pharaoh.

Identity

To help pupils understand the concept of identity, first explain the meaning of identity so that they have a basic understanding. Then ask them to draw a picture of themselves in the middle of a page. Thereafter, they mind-map different aspects of their identity around their picture. They could include aspects such as the colour of their hair, eyes, faith and ethnicity and so on. They can then compare their picture with their peers talking about similarities and differences. This will allow them to identify how they have different identities.

Creation

Using the creation story, invite pupils to role-play each of the six days. Then invite the pupils to talk about what is happening whilst they are in role about the first day when the light was created and so forth. There could be an empty tent in the classroom and then the pupils could turn torches to remove darkness and discuss this.

Leadership

This activity would be more appropriate for pupils in Year 5 or 6 as it could be complex. Split the pupils into groups. Give them materials to make an object. The object can be anything they choose but it has to meet the set criteria. For example, the object has to be able to move so they could build a car with wheels perhaps. Pupils decide a leader. Pupils work together but some are to take a leadership role. It is important that those who lead consider their peers' ideas. It is important to teach the pupils to have respect when doing a project. They then list the characteristics of a leader.

Celebrations

Discuss the shared human concept of celebrations by first asking them to define and then provide a definition of celebration and compare it with their ideas. Proceed to ask for examples of celebrations. Ask for any personal events they celebrate. Inform them that they will research a specific celebration (this is more suitable for KS2). Each table is allocated a specific celebration such as Eid, Vaisakhi or Christmas. Each group presents their research and shares their knowledge.

Change

Pupils draw a basic outline of a person on a piece of A4 paper. They then switch their drawing with the pupil sitting next to them. The teacher will say comments like 'I don't like your shoes' and the pupils will crumple up the drawing. Then they will switch their drawings back and as the teacher says kind comments, they will straighten their drawing. The teacher will ask whether the wrinkles have come out of the paper because they complimented the drawing. This leads to a discussion around the deeper meaning words can hold, and that people need to change the way they talk to others, to be kind, supportive and not upset others. Then the pupils will discuss ways in which they can change the way they treat others based on a few fictional dilemmas.

Community

To help pupils understand the concept of community, start the session by explaining and defining the concept of community. After this, ask pupils to create a mind-map with themselves in the middle and all the communities they are a part of branching out, e.g. their religious community, the school community, etc. They could use colour and draw pictures to show different communities. To study belief, teachers or students cut out key beliefs from two religions and the pupils have to match up the similar ones. This allows pupils to begin to understand different religious communities and how they compare to each other.

Belonging

Invite pupils to sit in a circle to discuss where they feel that they belong. Reiterate that the circle is a 'safe place'. They can bring out ideas such as school, extra-curricular activity clubs, families, etc. then discuss the school uniform as a symbol of 'belonging'. Relate this to symbols of religion and their roles. Talk about how symbols create a sense of belonging for many people. Invite pupils to express their sense of belonging and how it makes them feel using a writing or drawing task.

Loyalty

Begin with a brief discussion about what 'loyalty' means to the pupils. Then set them on a task to fill out a storyboard about a time they felt they were being loyal to a friend, family member or a time that a friend or family member was loyal to them. Pupils incorporate their thoughts and feelings in their storyboards. Once the task is completed the teacher chooses pupils to read out and present their storyboards and ask why they felt the need to be loyal towards that person or how it made them feel when someone else was loyal towards them (depending on what their storyboard is about). As a whole class, they write an acrostic poem on loyalty.

Justice

An active learning activity. Pupils play a game such as building a tower. Give some pupils resources such as paper and sellotape and the other Lego, for example. The pupils who are given the paper will evidently start to struggle and it gives the pupils with the Lego a clear advantage. This should show the pupils that they have not been treated equally. Then discuss how often justice is linked to finding fairness and being treated equally. Follow on with asking them to share their definitions of justice. Then explore 'Why is justice important?' and using post-it notes display their ideas. Read and discuss a faith-based story on justice.

Remembrance

This is aimed at KS2. Firstly, spend 15 minutes, in the beginning, outlining what remembrance means and why it is important. Introduce three important remembrance events which are recognised worldwide and their key features and moments. For example, Remembrance Sunday, Armistice Day and World Day of Remembrance for Road Traffic Victims and others. Create a group of five pupils and give them ten minutes to research one of these events. Give them a further 15 minutes to create, draw, model or perform a key symbol of remembrance for their event with a short 5-minute presentation. Invite them to explain why these symbols are important worldwide. Invite them to highlight how and why these symbols give meaning to people and why Remembrance Day is an important concept globally.

Forgiveness

Ask pupils their reaction to a time when they may have upset someone. Then ask pupils if they apologised to the person whom they upset. How did they forgive and why? Introduce the concept of forgiveness to link with the idea that apologising is one way of seeking forgiveness and learn about forgiveness in one or more religions exploring why, when, how and who. Discuss why for some people apologies are challenging.

Kindness

Set a task for the whole class to carry out an act of kindness during the day. At the end of the day, ask each pupil to share what they did and why. List these so that everyone can see them. Invite them to reflect upon some of these, asking them about their importance and the impact, if any, this has made upon them and on others.

Summary

Concepts are the 'big' or 'core' ideas that underpin scholarly thinking in RE. This section has discussed the three main categories of concepts and exemplified them. The learning activities should be designed in ways, which facilitate the acquisition of substantive, disciplinary and personal knowledge. They should offer opportunities to consider meta-concepts and religious reasoning. Pupils should also learn that religious scholars and communities debate these concepts and their origins.

THE DEVELOPMENT OF ATTITUDES IN RE

Introduction

In the previous sections, you learnt that growth in knowledge, flourishing in understanding and acquisition of skills are essential in RE. However, schooling also encourages and embeds various attitudes, qualities and dispositions. The promotion of attitudes and dispositions should be accomplished

---

BOX 6.1 THE NEED TO DEVELOP ATTITUDES

Another aspect of plurality is that there is no consensus on the aims and purposes of education: some stress skills and qualifications for employment and economic success, others the initiation of each new generation into the cultural heritage of their ancestors, others the fulfilment of individual human potential and still others that children need to know the truth about reality and correct behaviour based on a particular religious or ideological worldview. Nevertheless all would agree to some extent that education should help children and young people cope with the world they find themselves in, and this world is one in which religious beliefs and practices need to be comprehended (Cush 2007:218).

---

through all areas of school life, its ethos and formal and informal curricula such as care, fairness, kindness. Inevitably, the fostering of attitudes overlaps with other formal and informal curricula.

They should be considered at the beginning of the medium-term planning stage so that the intent of the curriculum shows that every child is learning and personal development is being maximised. These plans will also demonstrate how the curriculum aims to enable all pupils to reach their true potential, fulfil all the requirements of the syllabus for RE and promote pupils' awareness of their spiritual development and moral education.

RE is a valuable subject that can enhance the overall curriculum through developing key skills and personal reflection. Still, concerning RE, there are certain attitudes and characters which are fundamental to RE, in the sense that they are prerequisites for participating fully in the study of religions and learning from that experience (Cornwall 2014:14). RE fosters and deepens the development of positive attitudes to pupils' learning and the learning of the beliefs and values of their peers and others. This is argued in Box 6.1.

Silence and talk

It is argued that communication, verbal and non-verbal, is a fundamental skill that needs to be practiced, and to do it well, pupils need to have common experiences so that they can understand their own and other's perspectives (Webster 2010:17). Therefore, it is the role of the teacher to direct pupils in RE towards communicating their innermost thoughts to make sense of the outer reality (Webster 2010:17). Moreover, communication is the only tool that a child can use to publicly express their internal thoughts and help them create their own sense of self and identity, which is a key aim of RE (QCA 2004:9).

In addition, individual time for pupils is also an important feature in RE. It is suggested that learners have the time to themselves to reflect as all learning is not through talk; instead, sometimes pupils need quietness and stillness to focus on themselves, on the material presented to them and the conversations they have. Thus, learning in RE is also about becoming self-aware (Larkin, Freathy, Doney and Freathy 2020:24). Moreover, after distinguishing between stillness and quiet, Watson and Thompson (2007) observe that the activist nature of society makes it particularly important to help pupils experience some silence. The very difficulties involved in this indicate quite how necessary and important an educational task it is (Watson and Thompson 2007:187). By inviting pupils to study their awareness, teachers will be asking pupils to make a careful investigation of an ordinary aspect of their own nature (Hay 2000).

Attitudes in RE

It is important to distinguish between attitudes and skills. Kay (2007:107) concluded that to apply the term 'skill' to what is entirely an emotional quality (empathy) appears to be entirely misplaced. James and Stern (2019:12) explain that an attitude is a disposition to think or act in a particular way in relation to oneself and other individuals or groups or to events. The following fundamental attitudes are critical for good learning in RE and need to be consistently cultivated across all age phases (Lincolnshire 2018:8). The *Non-Statutory National Framework for RE* included the development of some of these and many Locally Agreed Syllabi have incorporated them as well (QCA 2004). Some parents in the study of Dinham and Shaw (2015) emphasised attitudes – respect and tolerance – rather than knowledge, as being the main point of learning about religion and belief. There are a plethora, however, the commonly found ones in the literature on RE include self-awareness, self-understanding, respect, open-mindedness, awe and wonder, curiosity and fairness.

The fostering of positive attitudes has the potential to contribute towards pupils' moral and ethical standpoints as they explore a range of questions and issues in an informed, analytical and balanced way. It helps pupils consider matters of significance to humans at a deeper level. Simultaneously, recognition should be made of the potential to hinder the processes of learning that negative attitudes may have in engaging enthusiastically with matters in RE.

Self-awareness

In RE, Box 6.2 shows the activities and it means the following:

- Willing to contribute to a diverse society for the well-being of all.
- Recognising their uniqueness as human beings and affirming their self-worth.
- Becoming increasingly sensitive to the impact of their ideas and behaviour upon others.
- Developing a realistic and positive sense of their own religious, moral and spiritual ideas and a mature sense of self-worth.
- Enabling pupils to feel confident about their own beliefs and identity and to share them without fear of embarrassment or ridicule.
- Drawing meaning from significant experiences in their own and others' lives and religious questions and answers.

BOX 6.2 ACTIVITIES FOR DEVELOPING SELF-AWARENESS THROUGH RE

- Using a concentric circle, pupils record various aspects of their identity, faith, language, ethnicity, school, locality and nationality.
- Engage pupils to talk about envy, sadness and anger and illustrate them, and then, as a class, explore solutions to address, how to respond to them, what religions teach about these.
- Engage pupils to talk about kind-heartedness, happiness and calmness and illustrate them, and then, as a class, explore their importance and how to develop or enhance them further.
- Talk about and expose pupils to atmospheres of holiness, sacredness, prayer, worship and meditation.
- Invite pupils to share insights of their own into being an atheist, a Jain, a Sikh and a Bahá'í.
- Pupils write a letter to an alien explaining who they are and are not.
- Invite pupils to be still and to listen to themselves and be mindful of their own bodies.
- Study a few metaphors. Ask pupils to investigate how they affect people's perceptions and actions.

BOX 6.3 ACTIVITIES FOR DEVELOPING SELF-UNDERSTANDING THROUGH RE

■ Organise a non-uniform day and invite pupils to wear religious and cultural clothing.

■ In circle time, involve pupils to notice, share and value spiritual responses from their peers and others.

■ Organise pupils with protected time to talk in-depth with a peer from a religion or worldview they do not belong to.

■ Pupils create finger puppets to express various beliefs, feelings and emotions.

■ Involve pupils in local and global issues such as interfaith work, a peace protest, response to local or international disaster and an environmental crisis.

■ On a paper, cut in the shape of a tick, pupils record the importance and relevance of their beliefs and practices; religious or otherwise such as fasting, charity and reading.

Self-understanding

Lessons in RE should enable pupils to be involved in the activities of Box 6.3 and in the following:

■ Develop an appreciation of the identity of others.

■ Recognise and acknowledge bias and prejudice in themselves.

■ Express deeply held beliefs, thoughts, feelings and experiences.

■ Discern the personal relevance of religious and other questions.

■ Deepen an awareness of the role of belief and tradition in shaping identity and culture.

■ Recognise personal, intellectual and moral integrity when considering their own religious, moral and spiritual ideas.

Respect

RE gives opportunities for pupils to be involved in the following and in the activities of Box 6.4:

■ Discern between what is worthy of respect and what is not.

■ Avoid ridiculing beliefs and practices of others and their own.

■ Be sensitive to the feelings, ideas, needs and concerns of others.

■ Respect those who have different beliefs and customs to one's own.

■ Recognise the right to hold different beliefs, views and practices of their own.

■ Recognise that people's religious or other convictions are often deeply held and felt.

■ Be ready to look at and value the positive potentialities of diversity and difference for the common good.

■ Appreciate that some beliefs and practices are not inclusive and consider the issues that this raises for individuals and society.

Open mindedness

In the context of RE, Box 6.5 shows the activities for this and it involves pupils as follows:

■ Willing to go beyond superficial impressions.

■ Knowing that beliefs are different from knowledge.

BOX 6.4 ACTIVITIES FOR DEVELOPING RESPECT THROUGH RE

- Create visually powerful posters to display a range of RE topics in class and around school.
- Organise a food festival, pupils and teachers bring and share 'religious' and cultural foods.
- Make a message box and invite pupils to anonymously post a list of things worthy and unworthy of respect. Read anonymously and discuss.
- Pupils write an acrostic poem on respect and display these.
- Using census data as a table. Ask pupils to interpret and talk on the diverse nature of society.
- Theme day – each day children learn about different religions in a more focused way.
- Discuss respect, its meaning, importance and how to express it.
- Study a prayer or letter to identify religious and personal views and language.
- Use re-enactments. One pair disrespects another. Explore feelings, reason and what religions and others teach about respect.
- Write a poem on respecting religion and beliefs.

- Willing to gain new understandings and being prepared to re-consider existing views.
- Recognising that people hold different opinions and they are many opinions on a single matter.
- Being open to varied interpretations of meanings of language, text, practices, rites and rituals.
- Developing attitudes that distinguish between such things as superstition or prejudice and such things as conviction and faith.
- Developing the ability to argue respectfully, reasonably and evidently about religious, moral and spiritual questions, without abuse or belittling.

Awe and wonder

RE provides opportunities for pupils to be involved in the following and in Box 6.6.

- Develop imagination.
- Recognise that knowledge is limited.

BOX 6.5 ACTIVITIES FOR DEVELOPING OPEN-MINDEDNESS THROUGH RE

- Pupils watch religious ceremonies and discern the meanings, values and beliefs being exhibited.
- Present a controversial issue to discuss and explore the various viewpoints about it.
- When using images which show religious practices challenge stereotypes and use them to break generalisation, when pupils react with 'They are so poor' and 'Why are they dirty'.
- To develop open-mindedness and deeper understanding use conscience alley.
- In addition to visitors, explore the everyday life of children and adults in school and their events to identify differences in what they do, what their family does, how things are done differently, why families expect dress, worship and food to be in a certain way.
- Use the story of the Ugly Duckling to rethink ideas of ugliness and beauty.

> ### BOX 6.6 ACTIVITIES FOR DEVELOPING AWE AND WONDER THROUGH RE
>
> - Study and visit places of worship to reflect and capture the architecture.
> - Create a small garden. Use 3D material for the story of creation.
> - Divide the class into six groups for six days of creation. Each produces artwork, poetry, songs and clay to appreciate the world. Each shares their work at the end and displays it.
> - Adam and Eve story – show a video and explore how they felt when they were the first people on earth and the kind of earth they inherited.
> - Pupils close their eyes to visualise and create a mental image of the future. They then discuss and record the values and qualities associated with that.
> - A film is created by pupils who act as news presenters to describe a religious or national event, positive and negative.
> - A gallery of images is created by pupils based on pictures taken of the natural world, animals and insects following the study of precepts in Buddha Dharma.

- Explore the nature of religious practice and teachings.
- Develop a sense of awe, wonder, delight and reverence.
- Wonder at the ugliness that religious beliefs can bring out.
- Appreciate the sense of wonder at the world in which they live.
- Appreciate the beauty, order, shape, pattern, the mystery of the world.
- Wonder at the ugliness and tensions that religious beliefs can bring out.
- Value insight, imagination, curiosity, observation and intuition as ways of perceiving reality.

Curiosity

Pupils in RE lesson should be involved in the activities of Box 6.7 and in the following:

- Develop curiosity and inquisitiveness.
- Recognise that knowledge is bounded by mystery.
- Explore new avenues of enquiry and investigation.
- Be willing to look carefully at 'the other' and be open to learning from it.
- Follow mysterious and profound lines of thinking through to see where they lead.
- Develop their interest in and capacity to respond to questions of meaning and purpose.

Commitment

In learning RE, this includes the activities of Box 6.8 to develop the following:

- A willingness to develop values and commitments.
- A willingness to develop a positive approach to life.
- The ability to learn, whilst living with certainty and uncertainty.
- The capacity to challenge and be challenged, in a respectful way.
- A willingness to examine ideas, questions and disputes about religious and spiritual questions.
- Understanding the importance of commitment to a set of beliefs and values by which to live one's life.

BOX 6.7 ACTIVITIES FOR DEVELOPING CURIOSITY THROUGH RE

■ Use drama for expressing values and morals based on beliefs and life experiences.

■ Use role-play for acting. Allocate characters and give them scenarios to explore and experiment with emotions based on moral and religious stories.

■ Use circle time where pupils talk about their experience and the class to ask questions.

■ Use religious drawings and paintings to show imagination, curiosity and reflection.

■ Use freeze frames to guess the unknown behind an action to develop their imagination.

■ Use puppet theatres for alternative modes of thinking, perspectives and asking new questions.

■ Use research of books on religious topics; artefacts, images and talk about deeper meanings.

■ Use quizzes to search for answers and develop questions to think about what happens in the world and the reason for things happening.

■ Use quotes from different sacred texts and interpret these and draw out relevance for current times.

Fairness

In the context of RE, they participate in the activities of Box 6.9 and this means the following:

■ Careful consideration of other views.

■ Readiness to look beyond surface impressions.

■ Being open to points of view different from one's own.

■ Willing to consider evidence, experience and argument.

■ Listening to the views of others without prejudging one's response.

■ Developing the courage to pursue fairness and challenge unfairness.

■ Developing the skills of listening and a willingness to learn from others.

■ Distinguishing between opinions and beliefs in connection with issues of conviction and faith.

BOX 6.8 ACTIVITIES FOR DEVELOPING COMMITMENT THROUGH RE

■ Use the Shema, Al-Fatihah, Lord's Prayer, Mool Mantra, Gayatri Mantar for commitment, beliefs and values. Use group discussions and textual analysis to explore its importance in life, daily use, meaning for their respective believers and how these can make humans better.

■ Use the story of Abraham to illustrate commitment and identify his other qualities.

■ Use the story of the hare and the tortoise for developing a positive mind-set.

■ Use an image of a stick person. Invite pupils to write around it about who and what they are committed to and then to give reasons.

■ Use the story of Jonah to discuss talents, facing challenges and repentance, sin.

■ Using a scale of 1–10, pupils rate themselves on commitment to class or school rules.

BOX 6.9 ACTIVITIES FOR DEVELOPING FAIRNESS THROUGH RE

- Use discussion on whether they think ever telling on a friend is wrong or right. Pupils justify their stance to show the 'without prejudice' aspect.

- Use an image. In pairs, one describes it to their partner who draws it and they reverse roles. They ought to conclude that although it is the same picture, they have a different view of it.

- Use parables to examine meanings and phrases, pupils to understand that not everything is literal.

- Use debate on a specific topic related to pupil life and experience. Pupils listen to and present evidence, their experiences and the reason for their position.

- Use group discussion and give the statements to examine, 'Is it fair that...', giving reasons.

- Use thought showers to examine and discuss fairness and unfairness, their meaning, limitations, advantages and applications.

- Read and discuss religious and moral stories and teachings on fairness, revenge, greed, theft.

Well-being

This might have a broader interpretation (Pett 2012), and in RE it could involve pupils in the activities of Box 6.10 and as follows:

- Being fascinated with the world.
- Exploring meanings and sources of happiness.

BOX 6.10 ACTIVITIES FOR DEVELOPING WELL-BEING THROUGH RE

- In groups, pupils define and discuss sources of happiness. They draw a cartoon character exemplifying happiness.

- Study the teachings of religious people who have responded to challenges in positive ways.

- Create graffiti walls to express a range of emotions.

- Discuss the benefits people derive from communal participation.

- Explore the benefits of voluntary service.

- Use picture books to learn about living in the wider world, health and well-being.

- Play a board game on needs and wants.

- Explore hygiene in different religious teachings.

- Explore religious and civic rules on drugs, alcohol, smoking and harmful substances.

- Listen to music in unison.

- Explore means of solace and calmness, e.g. candle light, flower, eyes closed, quietness.

- Create a poster of individual beliefs and symbols of positive and negative values for a display drawing on religious and other sources.

■ Pondering over words of wisdom, wise sayings and insights.

■ Exploring a deeper understanding of well-being: spiritual, emotional and cognitive.

■ Being resilient, resistant and responsive to challenges, suffering and hardships in life.

■ Thinking about healthy choices and lifestyles as taught by religious traditions and others.

Feedback on attitudes

Some locally agreed syllabi (LAS) recommend that teachers give feedback to pupils on the attitudes presented in their RE learning (Bristol 2020). They offer the following examples: Do they grow in *confidence* about their own beliefs and identity? Do they *reflect* on what they are learning and use *empathy* and *imagination*? Do they look *beyond surface impressions* and search for *meaning in life*? Do they *listen carefully* to the views of others and consider *evidence* and *argument*? Do they recognise the *needs and concerns of others*? Do they appreciate that people's beliefs are often *deeply felt*? Do they develop a balanced sense of *self-worth and value*?

Summary

These attitudes endorse the position that RE can play an important role in fostering the personal development of pupils. In line with promoting tolerance and an overall positive outlook, you may well have to consider developing their understanding of others' negative aspects for them to appreciate good relationships so that pupils are well rounded. RE can play a key role in developing and assisting pupils to become independent enquirers, team workers, self-managers and effective participants.

THE DEVELOPMENT OF SKILLS IN RE

Introduction

This section explores the status and various key skills to be developed in RE and some activities for you to consider for your teaching. It is intended to encourage you to create opportunities to make your pupils religiously informative, sensitive and critical. It begins with a discussion on thinking skills which is then followed by five principles to support you in planning for skills. Thereafter a justification and some benefits are offered. It ends with an exposition of essential skills and suggested activities.

Skills development in RE

The importance of skills development in RE is evident from both non-statutory guidance issued for the subject. The NNFRE explains that learning about religion includes enquiry into, and investigation of, the nature of religion, its beliefs, teachings and ways of life, sources, practices and forms of expression. It includes the skills of interpretation, analysis and explanation. Pupils learn to communicate their knowledge and understanding using specialist vocabulary. It also includes identifying and developing an understanding of ultimate questions and ethical issues (QCA 2004:11). Learning about and from religions and beliefs, through the distinct knowledge, understanding and skills contained in RE within a broad-based curriculum, is essential to achieving these aims (DCSF 2010:7). 'Skills' usually refers to those specific competencies required for the successful completion of particular activities (Pring 2001:114).

The REC and the CoRE also emphasise skill development. Pupils should gain and deploy the skills needed to understand, interpret and evaluate texts, sources of wisdom and authority and other evidence. They should learn to articulate clearly and coherently their personal beliefs, ideas, values and experiences whilst respecting the right of others to differ (REC 2013:11). Pupils must be taught the different ways in which religion and worldviews can be understood, interpreted and studied, including through a wide range of academic disciplines and through direct encounters and discussion with individuals and communities who hold these worldviews (CoRE 2018:13).

To achieve these aims, Larkin, Freathy, Doney and Freathy (2020:5–6) believe that the main purpose of RE should be to teach pupils the disciplinary knowledge and skills associated with the communities of academic inquiry concerned with the study of religion(s) and worldviews, of which there will be several. In the context of RE, this complexity is borne out in the plethora of possible pedagogical approaches, each reflecting different assumptions about the nature of religions and worldviews, what we can do about them and how we should study them. Following the CoRE Report, they suggest that these are tangible at the levels of disciplinary skills and transferable skills.

Disciplinary skills, including qualitative and quantitative research skills (at age-appropriate levels), philosophical enquiry, hermeneutical approaches to texts and approaches for understanding the arts, rituals, practices and other forms of expression (CoRE 2018:77).

Transferable skills: analysing a range of primary and secondary sources, understanding symbolic language, using technical terminology effectively, interpreting meaning and significance, empathy, respectful critique of beliefs and positions, recognising bias and stereotype and representing views other than one's own with accuracy (CoRE 2018:29).

Problematising thinking skills

Thinking is an act of broadening and deepening understanding of the validity and utility of the 'knowledge claims' that are presented to people. Registering things without actively engaging with them in this way is called remembering (Claxton 2021:54). In addition to memorisation and remembering, thinking skills in RE has also been the subject of much debate (Kay 2007; Pike 2006; Pike 2008; Watson and Thompson 2007; Wright and Wright 2012). It is argued that RE should aim to teach pupils thinking skills understood as far more than just logical reasoning and problem-solving. Watson and Thompson (2007:69) make three relevant points about this position. They advocate an RE which can hold up its head intellectually in the modern secularist world and encourage RE teachers not to be afraid of challenge and debate. More so, RE needs to show and challenge the notion that the mind and emotions are in separate compartments. RE needs to show that the assumptions upon which this dichotomy is based are challengeable and unnecessary (Watson and Thompson 2007:69). Third, they suggest that there is an urgent need to make thinking skills an integral part of RE right from the beginning, from Key Stage 1 upwards. Faulty thinking, they advocate, needs exposing and pupils need help to think straight. It should promote openness without loss of integrity. In particular, it should develop the capacity to discern authentic religion from its many subterfuges (Watson and Thompson 2007:69). Following a critique of skills-centred approaches to teaching and learning in RE, Wright and Wright (2012:223) propose that the cultivation of a set of pedagogical virtues namely attentiveness, intelligence, reasonableness and responsibility ought to take priority over the cultivation of specific thinking skills.

However, the NNFRE notes that RE provides opportunities to promote thinking skills (QCA 2004:16). To be reflective pupils need space, yet in contemporary busy classrooms, it is difficult to get any physical or emotional space to help mental clarity (Webster 2010:17). In practice, many schemes of work and curriculum maps focus on key questions such as 'Who am I?' and 'Where do I belong?' amongst others. Thus, developing the skills of thinking involves confidence, reasoning, memory, logic and creativity. Thinking skills acquired in RE are valuable in preparing children for the future (Webster 2010:18). When planning a lesson, McCreery, Palmer and Voiels (2008:60) suggest that you should ask yourself when the pupils are going to have an opportunity to think and what sort of thinking they will be doing. You will find their

---

BOX 6.11 REFLECTIVE THINKING

There are many other reasons for giving careful thought to developing children's capacity for reflective thinking.

1   Such an emphasis in RE relates to the questions pupils actually ask. They are interested in metaphysical questions. RE is one of the few opportunities in the school timetable where such questions can be pursued in some depth.

2   Truth per se matters; beliefs and values based on falsehood or mere prejudice are unstable and likely to cause damage and hurt. Reflective thinking in RE can help to guard delusion and prejudice.

3   Such work would help to protect pupils from indoctrination from whatever source, religious or secular.

4   Such work will also help pupils approach the diversity of religious beliefs in an open and non-dogmatic way without succumbing to the relativism which tends to regard different beliefs as just a matter of opinion (Watson and Thompson 2007:130).

---

chapter on *Developing thinking skills in RE* informative and practically useful in planning for Foundation, Key 1 and 2 activities. They offer examples with specific RE content for each of the different skills. In Box 6.11, Watson and Thompson (2007:130) offer some reasons for giving careful thought to developing children's capacity for reflecting thinking.

Planning principles for skills

One of the main purposes of RE should be to enable pupils to develop the motivation, understanding and skills to make enquiring into religious questions a lifetime activity. Five principles have been derived from the *Big Ideas for Religious Education* and have been related to skills development planning in RE (Wintersgill 2017:5).

Most syllabuses require teachers to put together a scheme of work drawing on several lists of items such as a list of knowledge, skills and understanding, breadth of study, content in terms of religions/non-religious worldviews and themes or topics they must include. The assumption is that teachers would make connections between these different items (Wintersgill 2017:12). Hence, skills should be seen by teachers as part of a whole rather than in isolation.

Moreover, it is noted that the content is often expressed alongside skills or processes. For example, 'recognise' some different symbols or 'interpret' ways that the history of religions and worldviews influences individuals. In these, as in other instances, Wintersgill (2017:12) suggests that it is important for specific skills and processes not to be attached to a particular area of content (in this case, symbols or history). In other words, cross-fertilisation should be attempted so that pupils 'recognise' and 'interpret' symbols as well as the ways history and culture have influenced individuals. *Big Ideas* mark a separation of subject knowledge from learning processes, leaving teachers to decide how to juxtapose these elements.

A third principle to consider is that skills and processes should only be applied where a task or content naturally presents itself (Wintersgill 2017:40, fn.). This means that there should be a deliberate identification of particular skills in a given activity for pupils to acquire and develop, rather than a scattergun approach.

The essential question for a teacher to ask is, 'what knowledge and skills do I expect all students in this group to acquire?' (Wintersgill 2017:42). The implication here is that you need to base your decision-making more on what needs to be provided to allow your pupils to make further progress, rather than waiting to discover what your pupils are unable to do.

Finally, the questions, skills and processes used to carry out an enquiry in RE will depend on the discipline(s) reflected. Thus, when pupils are engaged in an enquiry into an aspect of RE that derives from theology and Biblical studies, they need to deploy the skills of literary analysis, hermeneutics, language skills, historiography and critical thinking. When they engage in enquiries into religious communities today, pupils will draw on skills and processes used in the sociology of religion such as interviewing, observation, data analysis and interpretation. However, Wintersgill (2017:45) offers a caution maintaining that if students try to apply, for example, sociological or ethnographic approaches to a philosophical enquiry, the result is likely to be confusion and failure to achieve the learning objectives. It is also necessary to distinguish between the skills needed to study religion and the skills arising from a study of religion (Kay 2007:107).

Status of skills in RE

One of the primary purposes of RE is for pupils to acquire knowledge and understanding of the principal religions and non-religious worldviews. To successfully realise this purpose, teachers need to recognise that there is a body of knowledge and understanding which pupils need to be taught to be considered religiously educated. However, the foundation of the significant contribution that RE can make to pupils' overall personal and academic development lies also in the development of certain key skills and attitudes that are at the heart of the process of teaching and learning to understand people's beliefs and ways of life. Vygotsky (1978) argued that learning takes place through the interaction pupils have with their peers, teachers and other experts. Thus, good communication and listening skills are vital for authentic collaboration which work towards a common goal. Social metacognition refers to our understanding of how others are thinking and feeling. It enables us to understand that people may think differently about something even though they are observing or reading about the same event. Social metacognition also enables us to put ourselves in the shoes of others and see the world through their eyes (Larkin, Freathy, Doney and Freathy 2020:24).

A factor that influences the progress of pupils in RE is the extent to which provisions are made and opportunities given by teachers to develop a wide range of skills that enable them to understand and engage with the content and concepts being taught. It is argued that RE should be content-driven and, simultaneously, focus on the acquisition and promotion of key skills. These skills are promoted in RE relative to the content. It is through the interface of the knowledge, skills, attitudes and dispositions that RE can become a stronger basis of spiritual, moral, social and cultural education of pupils and their personal development. Holt (2017) has argued that pupils can learn from each other. Therefore, due care and attention should be given to the planning and the development of activities that require pupils to use such skills with increased maturity and complexity over the years.

All curricula operating in the primary school promote skills. Some are related specifically to certain subjects, and many others are more generic, which are transferable and support the overall learning by pupils. Therefore, the capacity for creative and critical thinking is essential for effective lifelong learning (Hollander 2015:51). However, the difference within RE is the context, the concepts to be developed, and the enquiry methodology required (Erricker, Lowndes and Bellchambers 2011:164).

Reflection in RE advocates either a radical constructivist or social constructivist model of learning as it encourages discussion with others about the personal understanding of the world. It is important to distinguish between thinking and reflecting, however, as reflecting can be seen as another word for thinking and it is easy to confuse the two. It is suggested that reflection is the method of slowing down the thinking process so that a child isn't an activist immediately reacting to a question or opinion (Honey and Mumford 1986) but first deliberates on what they know; considers what they understand and then ruminates on what they need to do next to help them discover more and learn from the original stimulus. Each stage encourages thinking, but is a stepping-stone within the process, hence the value of the skill of reflection in RE is that it allows children occasion and freedom to create more considerate responses to events that happen within the school and the wider global community (Webster 2010:17–18).

You should realise that there are no specific skills unique to RE. Thus, it is useful to adopt a cross-fertilisation stance in creating opportunities for the application of various skills across the curricula you design and teach. They are not exclusive to RE nor a prerogative of RE. Nevertheless, in the process of studying and exploring religions, beliefs and values, RE strives to develop the ability of pupils in a set of common skills and processes which are prominent in the literature in RE and commonly found in most LASs. McCreery, Palmer and Voiels (2008:60–65) and Rivett (2007:54–55) offer content-specific activities for developing these skills.

They should be reflected in learning activities and experiences across all age phases which should be considered at the design stage of your plans for the work for pupils growing up in modern Britain. The development of higher-order thinking should be planned to be progressive and age-appropriate. The use of technology is prevalent in twenty-first-century pedagogy which offers many skills and benefits for pupils in RE. Technology should be deployed to enable pupils to engage seriously with religions and non-religious worldviews (REC 2013:11–12).

Pupils should be given the opportunities to build on and consolidate these skills to achieve progression in RE. Progress will be shown through processes and areas of knowledge, understanding and evaluation that they have developed across the age phases. Progression depends on regular opportunities for pupils to engage in and develop these skills. In terms of assessment, it is suggested that the focus should be on whether pupils have understood the key areas of knowledge and skills rather than whether they have reached a particular level (Wintersgill 2017). There are many sources for these and commonly found activities in the literature are presented.

Life skills in RE

The skills of investigation tend to involve

- Identifying key concepts.
- Developing a sense of curiosity.
- Observing, listening, reading and thinking.
- Approaching those sources in a critical manner.
- Asking relevant and deep questions in a sensitive manner.
- Knowing what may constitute evidence for understanding religions.
- Knowing how to use different types of sources to gather information.

In the classroom

Pupils engage in the activities of Box 6.12.

The skills of enquiry tend to involve an ability to

- Be curious in seeking after the truth.
- Live with ambiguities and paradoxes.
- Desire to search for the meaning of life.
- Improve ideas by asking further questions.
- Plan what research is needed and how to find it.
- Identify relevant questions and draw conclusions.
- Be prepared to reconsider existing views critically.
- Develop a personal interest in ultimate or metaphysical questions.

BOX 6.12 ACTIVITIES TO USE FOR SKILLS OF INVESTIGATION

- Pupils prepare and select questions for a postal/online interview with a humanist/faith visitor.
- Pupils survey a religious phenomenon, such as, how many places of worship there are, what peers in their class believe or value about a faith or social issue.
- In a given sacred text, pupils identify and highlight key information.
- For a festival, pupils gather, select and organise information using a range of sources, e.g. multimedia presentation or art work.
- Pupils watch, listen and make notes from a presentation or film on a ceremony.
- Using a thought shower, pupils note questions they want answered on a particular pilgrimage.
- Pupils use sacred texts, religious believers and works of art to explore religion and worldviews.
- Pupils are given selected materials on a topic, they list questions and find answers to them from the sources.
- Pupils investigate beliefs about God or life after death in different traditions.
- Pupils use research sources, websites and texts (encyclopaedia, books) to select information.
- Pupils email a believer and atheist to ask about particular beliefs and practices.
- Pupils question a visitor to the classroom about their religious beliefs and practices.

In the classroom

Pupils participate in the activities of Box 6.13.

Thinking skills in RE

The skills of reflection tend to involve the ability to

- Ponder upon ultimate questions.
- Deliberate on religious beliefs and practices.
- Contemplate carefully about religious and spiritual matters.
- Reflect on one's own feelings, thoughts, relationships, experiences, ultimate questions.
- Reflect on others' feelings, thoughts, relationships, experiences, beliefs, values, practices.
- Reflect on the reasoning behind their own beliefs and values and the reasoning behind those of others.
- Use stillness to think with clarity and care about significant events, emotions, places, artefacts and sounds.

In the classroom

Pupils complete the activities of Box 6.14.

BOX 6.13 ACTIVITIES TO USE FOR SKILLS OF ENQUIRY

- Present an artefact to the class. In groups, ask them to design and carry out research on it.
- Present a research question and let them find out: What is the importance of the Shema to Jews?
- Inform the pupil about a visit to the Gurdwara. In groups, they identify key questions and collate them.
- Introducing a controversial issue. Use the Six Hats of De Bono thinking process to explore the issue.
- In any given lesson use a variety of activities and structure the discussions such as pair and share, jigsaw and snowball discussion.
- Use a learning wall or mind map to record what they would like to know more about in a new topic.
- Research the importance of the environment and natural world from religious and other views.
- Pupils use the question 'Does God exist?' to enquire from different perspectives.
- In circle time, pupils discuss the question, 'Do we act freely?'

The skills of discernment tend to involve

- Developing insight(s) into personal experience and religions.
- Enlightening the significance of religious beliefs and practices.
- Developing insight into people, motives, actions and consequences.
- Considering how individuals might learn from the religions they study for themselves.

BOX 6.14 ACTIVITIES TO USE FOR SKILLS OF REFLECTION

- Invite pupils to narrate about a visit to a place of worship in terms of emotions and feelings only.
- Invite pupils to use silence to deepen their thinking and reflections in a place of worship or garden.
- In circle time, allow pupils to relate life's deeper experiences to beliefs and values.
- In role play, provide opportunities for pupils to step into the experiences of those they disagree with sensitively.
- Based on a contemporary issue or a hypothetical crisis or dilemma, ask pupils what might a religious leader do in such a situation.
- In a place of worship, invite pupils to ponder how the place makes them feel. They reflect on the kind of atmosphere they think is created within the place. Invite pupils to think about what makes it important for believers.
- Use an appropriate stimulus to engage pupils in stilling or guided visualisation.
- Following the examination of quotes from famous people or sacred texts, invite pupils to add their own quote to the 'wall of wisdom' to register their insights and wisdom.

BOX 6.15 ACTIVITIES TO USE FOR SKILLS OF DISCERNMENT

■ Use natural habitats within the school grounds to develop a sense of awe, wonder and imagination.

■ Use places in the local area to provide opportunities for pupils to use their senses in a way which evokes a sense of spirituality.

■ Design activities for pupils to respond genuinely to what they find amazing and mysterious.

■ Provide opportunities to pupils to explore sacred and special spaces such as parks, labyrinth, spiritual trail, sensory garden, clouds, sky, snow fall, drizzle and rain, full moon, crescent and eclipses.

■ Use artwork or photographs to capture the beauty of the earth and the natural world.

■ Provide an opportunity for pupils to consider whether religion does more harm than good and justify their views.

■ Invite pupils to personally evaluate the contribution of religious figures they are studying.

■ In a place of worship, explore the soundscape and whether it is an important part there.

■ Find out the role of the sound in a place of worship, how would they describe the kind of music used, its purpose and emotions it evokes for believers in that tradition.

■ Give pupils a selection of value statements and ask them to order them using a hierarchy and justify the order.

■ Design a task to explore questions of ultimate meaning including the purpose of life, what happens after humans die and is there life after death.

■ Exploring the positive and negative aspects of religious and secular beliefs and ways of life.

■ Making discerning judgements about the personal value of religious beliefs and practices.

In the classroom

Pupils carry out the activities of Box 6.15.

The skills of interpretation tend to include the ability to

■ Interpret religious language.

■ Suggest meanings of religious texts.

■ Make sense of religious terminology.

■ Draw meaning from stories, artefacts, works of art, poetry and symbols.

■ Consider texts in a variety of ways including literally, allegorically, devotionally, theologically.

In the classroom

Pupils complete the activities of Box 6.16.

BOX 6.16 ACTIVITIES TO USE FOR SKILLS OF INTERPRETATION

■ Use artefacts and works of art as a starting point to stimulate response, enquiry and interpretation.

■ Provide pupils with opportunities to interpret religious language by beginning with their own experiences and using extracts from sacred texts and quotations.

■ On the carpet, read prayers to the class and talk about the language, meaning and what they say about the person's beliefs, feelings and relationship with God or people.

■ Design a drama or role play to explore the meanings of teachings from parables and metaphors.

■ Use puppet or persona doll to teach and explain religious language and concepts inviting pupils to explore their meaning for believers and the feelings or ideas being expressed.

■ On the wall, to explore a range of artefacts, works of art, signs and symbols, connected to religions, display some standard questions such as (What do you think it is? What could it be used for? Does it remind you of any other religious artefact? Why do you think it is special? What does it mean? How is it used? Who uses it?).

■ Use images and posters to explore what pupils think is happening in them, what they would like to ask about the image, what they think is the most important element of the photo, what questions they would like to ask.

■ Display a Hindu murti and ask pupils to talk about it from the viewpoint of a Hindu.

■ Display a Bible and ask pupils to talk about it from their own point of view.

■ Using a scatter diagram, invite pupils to record the symbolic language used to speak of God and ask them for their interpretation.

■ Pupils discuss why some people believe God does/does not answer their prayers and how they know.

■ Provide pupils with opportunities to consider the atheists and theists ideas, outlooks and positions in textual form.

Learning skills in RE

The skills of analysis tend to include

■ Drawing out essential ideas.

■ Being able to sort out component parts.

■ Distinguishing between opinion, belief and fact.

■ Recognise bias, caricature, prejudice and stereotyping.

■ Distinguishing between the features of different religions.

■ Being critical of sources, drawing conclusions and making inferences.

■ Recognising similarities, differences and distinctiveness of religious ways of life.

In the classroom

Pupils get involved in the activities of Box 6.17.

> **BOX 6.17 ACTIVITIES TO USE FOR SKILLS OF ANALYSIS**
>
> ■ Pupils identify and discuss similarities and differences between the ways beliefs are expressed.
>
> ■ In lessons, pupils use reasoning, examples and experiences to support their ideas and opinions.
>
> ■ In lessons, pupils explain and interpret beliefs and values in increasingly sophisticated ways.
>
> ■ In lessons, pupils offer balanced analysis of problems, perspectives and worldviews.
>
> ■ Use role play and freeze-frame to interpret the meaning of a faith or moral story.
>
> ■ Pupils sort out pictures of religious artefacts and symbols matching them to the correct faith, practice, books or festival.
>
> ■ Design activities for pupils to name, identify and explain key beliefs from given information.
>
> ■ Design activities for pupils to identify the odd one out from the beliefs, practices and rituals within a religion and justify their responses.
>
> ■ Design activities for pupils to categorise phrases or quotations in their respective faith and belief traditions.

The skills of synthesis tend to involve

■ Making links between religion and human experience.

■ Linking significant features of religion in a coherent pattern.

■ Connecting different aspects of life into a meaningful whole.

■ Connecting ideas and different aspects of religions, including the pupil's own experience.

In the classroom

Pupils explore and engage in the activities of Box 6.18.

The skills of evaluation tend to include

■ Looking at different viewpoints before making up one's mind.

■ Drawing balanced conclusions based on evidence and dialogue.

■ Justifying a viewpoint relating to ultimate questions and religious issues.

■ An ability to debate issues of religious significance with reference to evidence, experience and argument.

■ Drawing conclusions with reference to experience and individual belief based on reasoned arguments, evidence, experience and dialogue.

■ Weighing respective claims of self-interest, consideration for others, religious teachings and individual conscience.

In the classroom

Pupils participate in the activities of Box 6.19.

BOX 6.18 ACTIVITIES TO USE FOR SKILLS OF SYNTHESIS

- Ask pupils to show pictorially the relationship between Tawḥīd and the five pillars in Islam.

- Use ideas like 'holy books' or 'sacred buildings' to show things from more than one religion.

- List and talk about similarities and differences between Christmas, Diwali and New Year.

- Use different disciplines to understand and interpret marriage customs or funeral rites.

- Use a festival story and ask pupils for links between the story and practices from the religion.

- In a given topic or issue in RE use the P4C method to think about it.

- Use Venn diagram to draw conclusions between similar beliefs in Judaism, Christianity and Islam.

- Use a graphic organiser to compare and contrast a mandir and a church.

- Design opportunities for pupils to think and talk sensitively about religious issues, spiritual topics and values to recognise the significance of special moments, people, places and artefacts.

- In circle time, talk about whether or not all of our knowledge comes from sensory experiences.

- In circle time, talk about whether there are limits to human knowledge.

BOX 6.19 ACTIVITIES TO USE FOR SKILLS OF EVALUATION

- Share their own responses to questions about being a Jew, Sikh, Christian or a Muslim.

- Present several statements on a range of religious and social issues and ask pupils to respond to them on a scale of 1–10.

- Talk about Abraham, Jesus or Prophet Muhammad (pbut) with respect and in a well-informed way.

- Following the study of religious and other leaders, invite pupils to draw conclusions about the impact of these leaders and give reasons to support them.

- Conduct different types of debates which have self-interest and consideration of others.

- Provide a selection of statements of belief and ask pupils to give their personal responses to them.

- Invite pupils to talk about how they would handle an ethical dilemma by encouraging them to refer to a variety of sources of information.

- Use sorting or ranking activities such as diamond ranking statements to record pupils' thinking about a question or issue.

- Use questions such as what might a Buddhist or Humanist think in a given situation?

Social skills in RE

The skills of collaboration tend to include the ability to

■ Negotiate a win–win solution.

■ Contribute to and accept consensus.

■ Achieve the objectives of the group.

■ Work together and learn from each other.

■ Work effectively with others on a common task.

■ Take action with respect to the needs and contributions of others.

In the classroom

Pupils communicate through the activities of Box 6.20.

The skills of expression tend to include

■ Explaining concepts, rituals and practices.

■ An ability to articulate ideas, beliefs and values.

■ Discussing and sharing profoundly held beliefs and values.

■ Responding to religious issues and other questions through a variety of media.

■ An ability to respond to religious ideas, beliefs and questions through a variety of media.

■ Identifying and articulating matters of deep conviction and concern by a variety of means – not only through words.

In the classroom

Pupils engage in the activities of Box 6.21.

The skills of application tend to include

■ Recognising the rights and responsibilities of the individual.

■ Applying one's own beliefs and values to other people's life.

■ Identifying key religious values and their interplay with secular values.

BOX 6.20 ACTIVITIES TO USE FOR SKILLS OF COLLABORATION

■ In pairs, pupils design and explain what religious words such as Ramadan, Easter, Vaisakhi refer to and mean.

■ In groups, pupils describe how a festival is celebrated and its significance to celebrants.

■ As a class, pupils present their perspective on a religious phenomenon being debated.

■ Pupils justify their points of view with increasing sophistication using both religious and personal perspectives on a controversial matter.

■ As a table group, they design their own symbols for their table or for something representing a religious belief, teaching, place or practice.

BOX 6.21 ACTIVITIES TO USE FOR SKILLS OF EXPRESSION

■   Use music, drama, role play, dance and mime to explain the significance of stories to a faith tradition.

■   Use interactive displays, charts, diagrams, video, PowerPoint as visual representations of learning.

■   Use debate, presentation, chat show or new broadcasts to develop oral responses.

■   Compose letters, newspaper reports, reflective diaries, poetry, narrative stories or interviews.

■   Create games such as snakes and ladders on good and bad deeds, karma or knowledge based questions on religions.

■   Use collage for words, images, symbols, right and wrong, good and evil, light and darkness.

■   Applying one's beliefs and values to situations and concepts in their personal life.

■   Applying what has been learnt from/about a religion or belief system to new and relevant situations.

■   Making connections between religion, the individual, local community, national and international life and events.

In the classroom

Pupils work through the activities of Box 6.22.

BOX 6.22 ACTIVITIES TO USE FOR SKILLS OF APPLICATION

■   Show visual resources of synagogues, ask pupils to suggest what goes on inside the building.

■   Pupils talk about the similarities and differences between sacred places and personal special places.

■   Ask pupils to respond to dietary rules in religious traditions and link this learning to their own diet.

■   Ask pupils to make a set of rules for themselves, their class, their community and the world.

■   Pupils discuss and design a symbol for themselves and one collectively for their class.

■   Pupils write stories for acting and to show the meaning of a faith story as a contemporary re-telling.

■   Pupils listen to different viewpoints and reach a conclusion on a chosen issue or matter.

■   Present a dilemma or a statement of problem, invite pupils to respond themselves and to think how different religious traditions would respond to the issue.

■   Encourage pupils to communicate their feelings in a reflective poem or prayer for a prayer tree or wall.

■   Provide opportunities for pupils to appreciate and recognise the significance of special moments.

Empathy in RE

In RE this includes fostering and developing pupils' abilities to

- Listen with care and respect and engage with content and people.
- Evaluate the coherence of beliefs and lifestyles.
- Develop the capacity to deepen understanding of beliefs and practices.
- Develop the capacity to identify feelings of forgiveness, joy, compassion.
- Develop the power of imagination to identify feelings such as love, sorrow, sadness.
- See the world through the eyes of others and appreciate issues from their point of view.
- Consider and wonder on the thoughts, feelings, experiences, attitudes, beliefs and values of others.
- Appreciate how religion functions in the lives of individuals and communities.

In the classroom

Pupils participate in the activities of Box 6.23.

Logic problems

McCreery, Palmer and Voiels (2008:65) suggest that the capacity to think logically is essential in the study of all areas of disciplines and can be begun at Key Stage 2. Simple logic problems can be incorporated into RE to convey basic understanding or conversely religious subject matter can be included in logic problems. When introducing logic problems to children it is probably better to start with examples from immediate experience before moving on to explicitly religious ones. They provide an example as shown in Box 6.24.

BOX 6.23 ACTIVITIES TO USE FOR EMPATHY

- Invite pupils to respond to a religious story through an active learning method.
- Ask pupils to record the varied emotions experienced by a character in a religious or moral story using cartoons, speech bubbles or thought showers.
- Use moral dilemmas and ask pupils to use a line graph or bar graph to plot feelings.
- Pupils use a religious narrative to write about it from the point of view of different characters.
- Provide opportunities for pupils to contribute or participate in class councils.
- Use a Venn diagram to record that which makes them happy, sad and indifferent.
- Pupils write shape poems about feelings, their own and that of others.
- Following a lesson on creation, pupils pretend they are a fish, an animal, flower or tree and write a letter to humans about themselves.
- Pupils research teachings from different religions about supporting the poor and needy.

BOX 6.24 CASE STUDY: LOGIC PROBLEMS

The apostle Paul, the founder of organised Christianity, celebrated Jewish Passover when he was a child.

Which religion came first, Judaism or Christianity?

Muslims believe that the Qur'an was first revealed to Muhammad. The Qur'an speaks about events several centuries earlier, in the life of Jesus.

Who lived first, Muhammad or Jesus?

Also, discussions of fallacies (false arguments) can revise religious knowledge and extend understanding and challenge stereotyping. Children may find these difficult but at least it starts them talking and thinking. For example, ask the children what the problem is with these arguments:

> Sikhs wear Turbans.
> Amar wears a turban.
> Therefore Amar is a Sikh.
> (Other people than Sikhs wear turbans).
> Michelle is a Christian.
> Michelle is nasty about people.
> Therefore Christians are nasty about people.
> (Michelle's nastiness is nothing to do with her being Christian).
> All Jewish men wear kappas.
> David does not wear a kappa.
> Therefore David is not a Jew.
> (The argument is sound but the first statement/premise is false).

Source: McCreery, Palmer and Voiels (2008:65) Teaching Religious Education, Exeter: Learning Matters.

Summary

This section explored the importance of skills development in RE. It discussed the contested nature of developing thinking skills in RE. To link theory to practice, it suggested some planning principles to support you with preparing for the classroom. The section also highlighted the status of skills in RE and identified and explained life skills, thinking skills, learning skills, social skills and empathy. Within each of these broad categories, it offered ideas on how to plan RE activities for these skills so that pupils become religiously mindful, informative and critical. The activities will also provide pupils with the opportunity to engage with the knowledge learnt and reflect on what that knowledge means to the wider community and how they may, if at all, relate it to themselves (Box 6.25).

BOX 6.25 VIGNETTE: VALUES

My family is very value-orientated. As a family, we have a very close bond with one another, we respect and value each other and tend to do most things together. My background is that I am Pakistani and my culture derives from there. My primary school experience was very negative; I struggled throughout these academic years and was very relieved when I left. This experience left me with a bitter taste towards education and educators. However,

---

moving to my secondary school I had an excellent experience in terms of the teaching, the teachers and the environment. I knew I had a very strong support system behind me and would not be embarrassed if I struggled with anything. I also went on to study in my school's sixth form and although I failed maths numerous times during this, my teachers never gave up on me. The support I received from all my teachers was immense and I finally passed maths. This experience defined the type of teacher I wanted to be.

I have always had the idea of wanting to go into either teaching children or interior designing. Having completed secondary school and comparing the experiences I had in both schools, I was determined that I want to be a primary teacher that gives her children the best level and quality of teaching. From my own experience, I also knew that giving children the best possible experience in school was vital. I wanted to be a teacher that children remembered and were inspired by. I did not want children to think back on their negative experiences. A teacher to me means someone who is there to support children to succeed and who has a positive impact on the lives of the children so that they remember us as well as what we teach them in the future.

My family and my RE in school have formed my ideas of the subject. I feel as though my wider knowledge of RE is weak. A general conception in my community and amongst my family, when talking about RE, is that it only covers Islam. This is not the case as there is a much broader RE. It covers aspects of Islam as well as other religions. I chose RE as a specialism to gain a deeper understanding that I needed to become conscious of other religions. By studying RE, I wish to understand the different cultural beliefs and opinions of individuals today. This will also give me a chance to reflect on my religious background.

I am concerned that I may say something during my teaching, which is incorrect and can cause conflict or I will be in a situation where I am unable to address misunderstandings. I am hoping I can secure my wider knowledge in this subject to be able to address my concerns. In my placement, my mentor and class teacher do not differentiate between RE and any subject, it is given importance.

References

Bristol (2020) *Awareness, Mystery, Value,* [Online] http://www.awarenessmysteryvalue. org/?s=attitudes (Accessed 28/02/2021).

Caviglioli, O. (2019) *Dual Coding With Teachers,* Melton: John Catt.

Claxton, G. (2021) *The Future of Teaching and the Myths That Hold It Back,* Abingdon: Routledge.

CoRE (Commission on Religious Education) (2018) *Religion and Worldviews: The Way Forward,* London: Religious Education Council.

Cornwall (2014) *Cornwall Agreed Syllabus for Religious Education 2014,* Cornwall SACRE: Cornwall Council.

Cush, D. (2007) Should religious studies be part of the compulsory state school curriculum? *British Journal of Religious Education,* 29, (3), pp. 217–227.

DCSF (Department for Children, Schools and Families) (2010) *Religious Education in English Schools: Non-Statutory Guidance 2010,* Nottingham: DCSF Publications.

DfE (2019) *ITT Core Content Framework,* London: Crown Copyright.

Dinham, M., and Shaw, M. (2015) *RE for Real,* Goldsmiths, UOL & Culham St. Gabriel's. [Online] https://www.gold.ac.uk/media/documents-by-section/departments/research-centres-and-units/research-units/faiths-and-civil-society/REforREal-web-b.pdf (Accessed 16/11/2020).

Erricker, C., Lowndes, J., and Bellchambers, E. (2011) *Primary Religious Education – A New Approach*, London: Routledge.

Hay, D. (2000) The religious experience and education project: Experiential learning in religious education, in M. Grimmitt (Ed.) *Pedagogies of Religious Education*, Great Wakering: McCrimmons, pp. 70–87.

Hollander, P. (2015) Creative skills and strategies: The TASC model, in S. Elton-Chalcraft (Ed.) *Teaching Religious Education Creatively*, Abingdon: Routledge, pp. 51–63.

Holt, J. (2017) *How Children Learn*, London: Hachette UK.

Honey, P., and Mumford, A. (1986) *Using Your Learning Styles*, London: Peter Honey.

James, M., and Stern, S. (2019) *Mastering Primary Religious Education*, London: Bloomsbury.

Kay, W. K. (2007) 'Can "skills" help RE?', in M. Felderhof, P. Thompson and D. Torevell (Eds.) *Inspiring Faith in Schools: Studies in RE*, Aldershot: Ashgate, pp. 99–110.

Larkin, S., Freathy, R., Doney, J., and Freathy, G. (2020) *Metacognition, Worldviews and Religious Education: A Practical Guide for Teachers*, Abingdon: Routledge.

Lincolnshire (2018) *Lincolnshire Agreed Syllabus for Religious Education 2018–2023*, Lincolnshire SACRE: Lincolnshire County Council.

McCreery, E., Palmer, S., and Voiels, V. (2008) *Teaching Religious Education*, Exeter: Learning Matters.

Pett, S. (2012) The contribution of religious education to the well-being of pupils, *Research Papers in Education*, 27, (4), pp. 435–448.

Pike, M. (2006) From beliefs to skills: The secularization of literacy and the moral education of citizens, *Journal of Beliefs and Values*, 27, (3), pp. 281–289.

Pike, M. (2008) Faith in citizenship? On teaching children to believe in liberal democracy, *British Journal of Religious Education*, 30, (2), pp. 113–122.

Prescott, G. (2015) Creative thinking and dialogue, in S. Elton-Chalcraft (Ed.) *Teaching Religious Education Creatively*, Abingdon: Routledge, pp. 35–50.

Pring (2001) Education as a moral practice, *Journal of Moral Education*, 30, (2), pp. 101–112.

QCA (2004) *Religious Education: The Non-Statutory National Framework*, London: Qualifications and Curriculum Authority. Reference: QCA/04/1336.

REC (2013) *A Curriculum Framework for Religious Education in England*. London: REC of England and Wales.

Rivett, R. (Ed.) (2007) *A Teacher's Handbook of Religious Education*, Birmingham: RE Today Services. Third edition.

Stern, J. (2018) *Teaching Religious Education: Researchers in the Classroom*, London: Bloomsbury Academic. Second edition.

Teece, G. (2015) Creative learning about and from religion: Principles underpinning effective RE planning and religious understanding, in S. Elton-Chalcraft (Ed.) *Teaching Religious Education Creatively*, Abingdon: Routledge, pp. 18–31.

Vygotsky, L. S. (1978) *Mind in Society: The Development of Higher Psychological Processes*, Mass.: Harvard University Press.

Watson, B., and Thompson, P. (2007) *The Effective Teaching of Religious Education*, Harlow: Longman. Second edition.

Watson, E., and Bradley, B. (2021) *The Science of Learning: 99 Studies That Everyone Should Know*, Abingdon: Routledge. Second edition.

Webster, M. (2010) *Creative Approaches to Teaching Primary RE*, London: Longman.

Wintersgill, B. (2017) (Ed.) *Big Ideas for Religious Education*, Exeter: The University of Exeter.

Wright, E., and Wright, A. (2012) Thinking skills, in L. P. Barnes (Ed.) *Debates in Religious Education*, London: Routledge, pp. 223–234.

The development of dispositions in RE and SMSC

Introduction

Religious Education (RE) is also concerned with contributing to children's spiritual, moral, social, cultural and personal development. RE plays an important role in preparing pupils for adult life, employment and lifelong learning. It helps pupils become successful learners, confident individuals and responsible citizens. It gives them the knowledge, skills and understanding to discern and value truth and goodness, strengthening their capacity for making moral judgements and for evaluating different types of commitment to make positive and healthy choices (DCSF 2010:7). Religion and beliefs inform human values and are reflected in what they say and how they behave (DCSF 2010). The Commission on RE (CoRE 2018:77) suggested that the Religion and Worldviews curriculum should enable young people to develop wider transferable skills and dispositions. This section focuses on fostering dispositions in RE.

The Birmingham model

Before considering the dispositions, it might be worth reflecting on the nature and significance of the Birmingham Agreed Syllabus (BCC 2007), as it had been described as departing 'from received wisdom in statutory religious education' (Barnes 2008:79) and, with its predecessor syllabi, sought to respond to religious pluralism in the context of RE, amid wider educational, religious and political debates about the subject (Parker and Freathy 2011:250).

It is noted that the BCC (2007) was developed in opposition to some aspects of the 'ruling model' of RE (Barnes 2009) and that its aim was that children should have 'their feelings deepened' and they should be required to develop particular dispositions. Significantly, the BCC (2007) reversed and re-worded the attainment targets of the Non-Statutory National Framework for RE (NSNFRE) (QCA 2004). It chose 'learning from faith and learning about religious traditions' (Parker and Freathy 2011:258).

However, the new one presents four dimensions of learning: (1) Learning from Experience; (2) Learning about Religious Traditions and Non-Religious Worldviews; (3) Learning from Faith and Non-Religious Worldviews and (4) Learning to Discern. The dimensions will assist pupils in developing skills to consider issues, not only from their own perspective but also from an analytical viewpoint (BCC 2022:7).

Previously, it had also adopted a different approach to any existing syllabus of the time and was heralded as a breakthrough in statutory RE (Barnes 2008:75). It had broken the mould of their own previous syllabuses as well as that of other Agreed Syllabuses developed in the preceding 30 years (Parker and Freathy 2011:258). Moreover, the strong linkage between children's moral education and their RE, which had often been deliberately disassociated from the 1960s

DOI: 10.4324/9780429289743-10

onwards, and the aim of fostering the conative, dispositional domain, marked BCC (2007) out as distinctive and divergent from existing trends (Parker and Freathy 2011:258).

The syllabus required, in pursuing its two attainment targets, the 'development of pupil dispositions, using and deploying the resources found within Christianity and the traditions of other religions' (BCC 2007:4). Parker and Freathy (2011) reveal that, in contrast to their 1975 syllabus, the BCC (2007) did not mention the possibility that children might learn their values from non-religious stances for living. Thus, although BCC (2007) sought to represent agreed notions of what is true across religious traditions, unlike BCC 1975 and the NSNFRE, it did not consider secular worldviews as a valuable focus for learning (Parker and Freathy 2011:259). However, this is now no longer the case as the syllabus acknowledges a complete spectrum of beliefs and views (BCC 2022:7).

Barnes (2008:77) pointed out that the syllabus was evidence of 'local democracy' and of community and religious leaders alongside educators and educational administrators reaching agreement at the local level on the content of RE to be taught in schools (Parker and Freathy 2011:259). The BCC (2007) was more determinedly nurturing, or in its own terms 'cultivating' than any Agreed Syllabus for some time. Furthermore, at face value, what it required of RE by way of shaping the pupils' moral outlooks, given the limited curriculum time and resources for the subject, appeared highly ambitious (Parker and Freathy 2011:259).

The 24 dispositions

In other words, the Birmingham syllabus of 2007 resorted to religious and faith traditions to develop children's virtues and dispositions. The 24 dispositions of pupils were to be developed using what it termed 'the treasury of faith' which are drawn from the beliefs, expressions and practical actions of religious traditions so that pupils should grow intellectually, affectively/emotionally and practically (BCC 2007:5).

The current syllabus has retained the centrality of dispositions. In other words, rather than starting studies from the perspective of a religion or worldview, in Birmingham the dispositions are the starting point, enabling a universal viewpoint to be shared and understood before extending study to points of agreement, and distinctiveness, through four dimensions of learning (BCC 2022:7).

In this new syllabus pupils' learning of RE is guided by encouraging 24 dispositions as illustrated in Table 7.1. The dispositions derive from a number of sources including the Cardinal Virtues from the Classical tradition, Theological Virtues and Religious Practice. They are equally applicable to, and inclusive of, the religious, those who have an established non-religious world view and those classing themselves as 'nones' (BCC 2022:7). This was the starting point in 2007 as well. However, the Non-religious traditions are the addition.

The Birmingham Agreed Syllabus is particularly appropriate for a twenty-first century education where quality is defined in terms of an education which is cohesive rather than fragmented, developing children holistically to become happy, confident, ambitious and discerning. Understanding and living out the dispositions has positive effects on children's wellbeing and mental health (BCC 2022:7).

Planning the curriculum

In developing these dispositions, it requires that Christianity must be used and taught in the main at each key Stage. The religious tradition/s of pupils in the classroom must be used and taught. The religious traditions, which will *broaden* and *deepen* the curriculum should also be used and taught. The content of each religious tradition as correlated to the dispositions has been provided and each of the dispositions is associated with a range of religious traditions such as the Bahá'í faith, Buddhism, Christianity, Hinduism, Islam, Jainism, Judaism,

Table 7.1 Dispositions in Birmingham

Disposition	**Universal** (How the disposition is understood by the general population, including the non-religious and those who don't identify with the religious or nonreligious.)	**Religious** (How the disposition is understood by people who practice a faith)	**Considerations** (How the disposition may be evaluated)
4. Being thankful	Being conscious that individuals are not self-sufficient but are dependent upon others and the resources of the natural world.	Being aware of God's gifts in creation and expressing gratitude, growing an appreciative heart.	When is mere thankfulness insufficient? E.g. if we are just glad for the good things we have and don't give any thought to those without.
7. Responding to suffering	Recognising the pain of self and others, nurturing the will to help and maintaining one's solidarity with and empathy for others.	As the reality of suffering is part of the human condition many followers recognise God being alongside them as they face it. Many followers feel that God can transform pain and suffering, giving the strength that helps them, and gets them through, so that they learn from the process.	Are there any circumstances when we can take the suffering of others too much to heart? Do people ever respond to the suffering of others in a way that has negative consequences for their own friends and family? Is it possible to embrace suffering for a perceived greater good, but one which is not accepted by wider society?
10. Living by rules	Recognising authority and the needs of shared life.	Human beings were created to live in accordance with divine rules as received by particular faith communities. Religious traditions have codes about how people should live in obedience to these divine laws. Ignoring these laws is seen as disobedience and seen to impair the relationship with the divine.	Should we follow the rules of a community even if they can be shown to be wrong? What about times when the claims of justice are stronger than the rules of the tradition? When do laws challenge religious people? Do people ever apply laws regardless of the consequences? Is it possible for people to follow the letter of the law while ignoring the spirit of the law? How can our conscience be informed by teachings in sacred texts?
24. Being attentive to the sacred, as well as the precious	In the midst of everyday life, having the ability to observe and focus on things that really matter, which one would consider sacred or precious. This is helped by making time for reflection and by learning to be mindful, i.e. clearly aware of the present moment without being clouded by a distracted or preoccupied mind.	Being attentive to the spiritual part of one's being, and living in a way that constantly recognises God's presence in the world. This awareness can be nurtured day by day, through prayer and silent meditation, through reading, singing or listening to sacred teachings, as well as through the experience of serving others selflessly and engaging in creative activity.	Can this lead to a misunderstanding? When should silence be ended and speaking begin again? Do people ever concentrate too much on the sacred and not enough on taking responsibility for the care of others?

Source: Birmingham City Council (2022).

BOX 7.1 VIEWPOINT: THE NEED TO DEVELOP DISPOSITIONS

Religious educators have developed strategies that attempt to minimise the significance of religious differences and weaken the boundaries between religions; attempts are made to remove the 'hard edges' of disagreement. Apart from being hopelessly unrealistic, this approach fails to appreciate the nature of diversity and the way in which diversity and differences can become a source of division in society. Religious differences are not the cause of bigotry and intolerance; religious differences become the occasion for the human manifestation of bigotry and intolerance. What our earlier analysis showed is that any difference can come to elicit negative attitudes and behaviour in some people in certain circumstances, though ethnic, religious and racial differences frequently attract negative attitudes and behaviour because they are particularly visible markers of identity, by which individuals and communities are distinguished. The solution for schools and education, however, is not to seek to convincing pupils that the differences between them are unimportant or insignificant, but to aim to develop in them the personal resources and dispositions of character to come to respect those with whom they differ. Respecting others and tolerating their beliefs and values are necessary social values in a pluralistic society where the reality and the challenge of diversity and difference are genuinely acknowledged. British religious education has failed to take diversity seriously. (Barnes 2015a:57).

Source: Barnes L.P. (2015) Part One Religious Education: Teaching for Diversity, Bloomsbury Academic, an imprint of Bloomsbury Publishing Plc.

Rastafari and Sikhism and established non-religious world views such as Atheism, Humanism and Secularism. It responds to the experience of the growing number of pupils whose families identify as 'nones'. In Box 7.1, an argument is made for developing in pupils dispositions to respect those with whom they differ.

The website offers the teacher planning tools comprising content overviews and key questions identify appropriate content from religious traditions and non-religious worldviews. The syllabus has listed the 24 dispositions and

- Defines them in universal terms. For example, the disposition 'Living By Rules' recognises the need for authority and the needs of shared life as communities within a moral code.

- Explores them in religious and non-religious terms. For example, in the same disposition, religious traditions and non-religious worldviews have codes about how people should live in accordance with laws. Ignoring laws impairs the relationship with the divine or, for those with a non-religious worldview, with other human beings. The exploration is therefore an interpretation of a disposition that those who follow a particular religious tradition or non-religious worldview would recognise, to a greater or lesser degree. The way that the disposition is understood or lived out within a particular religious tradition or non-religious worldview is explored in the Teacher Planning Tools: Content Overviews.

- Encourages considerations. Testing the boundaries of the dispositions takes us in a new direction and helps to define possible areas of critique and discernment.

In the classroom

These are some activities to support the development of some of the dispositions.

Creating inclusion and identity and belonging

Tree of life

■ Draw hands together to symbolise the unity between everyone, no matter what they believe. Hangs these on a tree.

■ On a hand shape, they write what a Muslim does, e.g. reads Qur'an, what Christian does, etc. and then every pupil sticks their hand on the tree.

■ Invite pupils to reflect: 'We all do better when we work together. Our differences matter but our similarities matter more'.

Creating unity and harmony

The mighty pebble

■ Starter thought: discuss as a class what unity and harmony mean to the pupils and then explore what it means in a/their religion.

■ Starter activity: pupils work together to move a small pebble from one end of the room to another. They have to work as a team and all participate at the same time.

■ Tell the story of Prophet Muhammad (pbuh) and the Black stone.

■ Repeat activity: see if they can work together better this time.

■ Plenary: has the pupil's perception changed now? What have they leant?

Being reflective and self-critical

Circle time

■ Pupils say something positive about the person sitting next to them, allowing them to reflect on themselves, celebrate their peers and create positive attitudes. Invite them to think about: 'A cheerful heart is a good medicine, but a crushed spirit dries up the bones' (Proverbs 17:22).

Teddy time

■ A pupil holds a teddy bear. Pupils discuss how, when, why and where it could be bullied. Individually they write about how teddy might be feeling, what it could do and why bullying is wrong. Read a poem from Cloud Busting.

Listing time

■ List pupils' answers to what is good or what is bad. From this list, they choose what good they have done why they did it. They list the bad they have done and how they would change it. Read the story of Guru Nanak, Bhai Lalo and Malik Bhago to show change of character.

Quiet time

■ Pupils spend 1–3 minutes in silence. They listen to the world around them. Reflect on what makes them feel peaceful, what happiness is and what gives them happiness.

■ Read the Happy Monk story from the Jataka Tales to the class.

Living by rules

- Read the story of Adam and Eve and identify rules in the extract.
- Discuss why God gave rules? Explore why people have rules? Explore why their class has rules.

Being temperate, self-disciplined and seeking contentment

- Explore stories on greed, e.g. Scrooge on not being satisfied.
- Explore being happy with who you are, e.g. the Ugly Duckling.
- Explore contentment, e.g. the Hindu story of the Saint and the mouse.
- Explore appreciating what one has, e.g. the story of two brothers, Jacob and Esau.
- Read and talk about the story of Guru Nanak & The Brahman's Pure Food.
- Teach about the eightfold noble path.
- Discuss Buddhist vows for laypeople – the five precepts.
- Explain and examine the duty of fasting in Islam.

Being open, honest and truthful

- Read the story of The Boy Who Cried Wolf, explain and identify the moral of the story.
- Share and discuss quotes on honesty from several religions, invite pupils to write their phrases.
- Create a circle time to ask pupils if there has ever been a time when someone else has been dishonest with them and what happened.
- Ask pupils to interpret: 'The Holy One, blessed be He, hates a person which says one thing with his mouth and another in his heart' (Judaism).

Being accountable and living with integrity

- Discuss and reflect on what it means to be accountable and what it means to have integrity.
- Think about personal life as well as school, discuss when they are accountable, to whom and what for.
- Discuss how some religions have the idea of being accountable for one's actions and living with integrity.
- Use the story of Joseph to think about integrity.
- Discuss how a belief in Judgement Day influences being accountable and living with integrity.

Summary

RE contributes to and plays an important role in fostering dispositions. Pupils develop dispositions and explore how religions impact the decisions made by individuals and the lifestyles they adopt. Pupils understand that religious and non-religious traditions desire that their respective followers live by certain values, characters and dispositions.

SPIRITUAL, MORAL, SOCIAL AND CULTURAL DEVELOPMENT

Introduction

This section examines the important contribution that RE can make to the spiritual, moral, social and cultural (SMSC) development of pupils. It begins by emphasising the need to present RE as a distinct academic subject and to be clear about its aim and purposes with the intent of securing the quality contribution of RE. Then a discussion about the relationship between RE and moral education follows with the intent of highlighting an area of debate about the aim of RE so that you can consider your position. Thereafter, suggestions for pupils' SMSC and personal development, 'fundamental British values' and the meaning of living in contemporary Britain is considered.

Being clear with RE

This section begins by highlighting some curriculum problems in RE and then discusses how RE can contribute to the SMSC of pupils. RE also has the potential of making important contributions to other aspects of the school curricula such as RH(S)E (relationship, health and (sex) education), the humanities and other issues such as education for safeguarding, child protection, intercultural development, sustainable development, 'fundamental British values', citizenship, anti-racist education, character and political education. It offers opportunities for personal development. In doing so, the religion and worldview perspective and these contributions need to be made well defined. Moreover, a clear distinction needs to be made between RE as a distinct academic subject and such initiatives. None of these is RE. However, some have the potential to be mistaken for RE and confused with it (Chater 2020:77).

It has been reported that weaknesses in the curriculum limited the effectiveness of RE and that RE was sometimes confused with the school's wider contribution to pupils' SMSC development. Moreover, some schools continued to confuse RE with other subjects or aspects of other curricula. Ofsted (2013) observed that it was not uncommon, for example, to find schools presenting evidence in RE portfolios about pupils 'learning from' religion that included work from the personal, social and health education (PSHE) programme, charity activities, visits to old people's homes, Christmas pantomimes or literacy work on topics such as 'feelings'. While these were worthwhile activities, they were not evidence of 'learning from' religion (Ofsted 2013:13).

Thus, RE must not be treated as a reactionary subject to assorted issues that originate from different eras in history or in current times. To achieve coherence within RE, pupils should get to know the knowledge and teachings from religious traditions that have something to say directly about these issues. Of course, that is not to suggest that RE should shy away from contemporary and controversial issues, far from such a proposition, RE should be at the heart of these debates and lived experiences. Otherwise, as Chater (2020:78) laments, the consequences may be that the subject might wander over disciplinary boundaries: traversing through spirituality, passing by character education, resting a while in storytelling or mindfulness workshops, moving on through personal development and perhaps ending in sociology. He suggests that disciplinary clarity should be the guiding principle rather than sentiments and that teachers should be observant of distinctive intellectual approaches or else pupils might be confused.

RE and opinions

Student teachers are often heard expressing enjoyment and praising RE for being 'all about opinions'. There is a place for having an opinion about something, at the same time, it is significant to remember that RE is not all about opinions. There is a body of knowledge and facts to know and understand.

RE is not about telling pupils what they should believe; likewise, it is not about telling them that if they don't believe in a certain way, they aren't a part of a tradition. What is clear, though, is that RE is not about presenting religions and beliefs as a supermarket where pupils can simply pick and mix what they want to believe and do. Religions are too complex and too culturally embedded to allow that and teachers do pupils no favours by simply presenting religions as opinions that cannot be proved or simply adopted (Cornwall 2014:14).

Moral education and religious education

Among some RE educators, there is concern about the deficiency of moral education in RE. Parker and Freathy (2011:258) discussed the 'disassociation' of RE from moral education. As such, Barnes (2015b) suggested that by divorcing RE from moral education, the former lost much of its relevance to the interests and lifeworld of pupils. Furthermore, he contends that RE, for the most part, does not make any significant contribution to the moral development of pupils or to the realisation of the moral and social aims of education (Barnes 2015b:201). Even though the moral purpose of education is a common and constant theme in modern British educational legislation of 1944 and 1988, as you read in Chapter 1. For Lawton (2018) moral development is the business of every teacher, otherwise there may be a total failure for everyone.

The rise of this situation is attributed to the source of RE. One of the effects of adopting an influential approach to religious studies by religious educators was that RE became re-orientated around exclusively religious content and diminished its role in providing moral education and contributing to the moral development of pupils. This, for Barnes, was one of the origins of the contemporary 'crisis' in RE, i.e. divorcing from moral education, under the influence of religious studies and the importation of a phenomenological methodology and interpretation of religion into RE (Barnes 2015b:202).

The new National Curriculum (DfE 2013) reiterates the statutory and enduring relationship between the SMSC and schooling. This was the case within the NNFRE (DCSF 2010; QCA 2004; REC 2013) albeit as non-statutory guides. These show that RE is relevant and contributes towards the realisation of the moral and social aims of education. According to Barnes (2015b) although the subject officially distances itself from moral education; it also advances the claim that post-confessional multi-faith RE challenges prejudice and intolerance. In other words, the aims of RE have always extended beyond that of facilitating an understanding of religion to include contributing to the social and moral aims of education – to prepare pupils to live amidst moral and religious diversity; to help them to develop self-respect, to make wise moral choices and to equip them to contribute positively to society (Barnes 2015b:204).

Practically, the natural and obvious place for religious educators to look to 're-moralise' RE is to the moral content of the different religions: each of the religions has a vision of the good both for the individual and for society; each of the religions has a historically evolving body of moral teachings, and each of the religions has made important responses to contemporary moral issues. There are different ways of conceptualising and incorporating this material into classroom teaching (Barnes 2015b:204; Felderhof and Thompson 2014).

Homan (2012) highlights the analysis of Ashraf (1992) that the evacuation of moral content is the consequence of a secular agenda. Ashraf (1992) affirmed a 'religious sensibility' by which is meant 'that element in human nature that makes human beings aware of the transcendent selfless norms of Justice, Truth and all such values that pull the heart away from selfishness towards selflessness'. The prevailing secular regard for religion for its intellectual rather than its spiritual content inhibits teachers from connecting with or stimulating the religious sensibilities of the pupils. By that measure, Ashraf argues, RE is defective. The implication is that moral standards are offered for information rather than with anything as strong as a recommendation. Moreover, he is indignant that because they are atheists and agnostics about we should 'bow down' to them and teach religion in a secular manner (Ashraf 1992:90; cf. Homan 2012:191).

Spiritual, moral, social and cultural development

Schooling has always been concerned with the wider development of the whole person. The new National Curriculum reiterated this as one of the purposes of education, thereby showing the significance of SMSC: Every state-funded school must offer a curriculum, which promotes the spiritual, moral, cultural, mental and physical development of pupils at the school and of society (DfE 2013). Thus, it is the responsibility of the whole school, including all staff, all subjects and all the curricula operative within a school to fulfil this role, although RE offers major and distinctive opportunities to promote SMSC development.

Ofsted takes the inspection of provision for SMSC very seriously. A school with serious weaknesses will have one or more of the key judgments graded inadequate and/or have important weaknesses in the provision for pupils' SMSC development (Ofsted 2019:33). The notion of developing not just academic and practical skills in the emerging generation but also self-knowledge, moral courage, a capacity for imaginative sympathy for others and so on has long been a desired outcome of education. It is about the sort of person an education system hopes to create (RE Today 2020:102).

RE lessons should offer a secure, structured and positive space for reflection and conversations. Pupils should engage in discussion, dialogue and debate which enables them to make their reasoning clear and which supports their cognitive and linguistic development. Pupils will see the relevance of RE teaching especially when lessons allow for prompt and sensitive responses to be made to unforeseen events of a religious, moral or philosophical nature, whether local, national or global (REC 2013). The development of critical thinking in RE is important to enabling RE to inform the SMSC lives of pupils and such thinking needs to challenge pupils in their search for truth and the purpose and meaning of life.

There are contested and different interpretations of SMSC development and various models (Eaude 2008, 2016; Hand 2003, Hay and Nye 2006; Nye 2009; Stern 2011; Watson 2007; Wright 2000).

Spiritual development through RE

Defining spirituality and how schools might educate in this aspect of schooling had been fraught with difficulties. Fraser-Pearce (2021) has argued that spirituality concerns connectivity, or relationship, with the transcendent. However, a distinction is made between relational education, which concerns a wide range of relationships, and spiritual education as a subspecies of relational education, which specifically concerns the relationship with the transcendent (Fraser-Pearce 2021). In the educational context, spiritual development is not the same as religious development within the faith context. The 'spiritual' should not be confused with 'religious' as well. Spiritual development refers to the aspects of the child's spirit which are enhanced by school life and learning and may describe the 'spirit' of determination, sharing or open-mindedness. Spiritual development describes the ideal spirit of the school (RE Today 2020:103). Spiritual development is broadly defined as the non-physical aspects of human life and existence. For some, it is linked with belief in the soul and expressed in religious beliefs and practices, for others it is not so (Surrey 2017). A practical account of how spiritual education as a subspecies of relational education might be realised in schools appears in Pearce (2019). Table 7.2 offers a plan for spiritual development.

Moral development through RE

All teachers are in some sense moral educators (Orchard 2021), as such, a conception of this kind invites teachers to keep moral development as part of their every work. From the student perspective, Baker (2020:922) drawing on data from the Millennium Cohort Study, studied the moral attitudes of UK youth and concluded that morality is clearly important for understanding

Table 7.2 Spiritual development through RE
Provision for the spiritual development of pupils includes developing the following: • Ability to be reflective about their own beliefs (religious or otherwise) and perspective on life.   • Knowledge of, and respect for, different people's faiths, feelings and values.   • Sense of enjoyment and fascination in learning about themselves, others and the world around them.   • Use of imagination and creativity in their learning.   • Willingness to reflect on their experiences (Ofsted 2019:59–60).

RE provides opportunities to promote spiritual development through the following:	RE can support this by promoting the following:
• Discussing and reflecting on questions surrounding faith, belief, ethics and morality. • Learning about and reflecting on important beliefs, practices and experiences which are axiomatic to religious and other traditions and practices. • Considering how beliefs and concepts are expressed culturally and creatively through the arts and human and natural sciences. • Considering how religions and other world views perceive the human value and relations which each other, the natural world and with God. • Enabling students to develop their self-knowledge, self-esteem and self-confidence. • Developing their own views and ideas on religious, philosophical and ethical issues (Surrey 2017).	• Self-awareness: offering opportunities for pupils to reflect on their own views and how they have been formed, as well as the views of others. • Curiosity: encouraging pupils' capacity for critical questioning, such as by keeping big questions in a 'question box' or as part of a wall display, and allowing time and space where these questions can be addressed to show that they are important. • Collaboration: utilising lesson techniques which engender group collaboration and communication such as Community of Enquiry/P4C, circle time, debates, Socratic Circles or group investigations. • Reflection: providing a space to reflect on pupils' own values and views, as well as those of others, and to consider the impact of these values. • Resilience: promoting a spirit of open enquiry into emotive or complicated questions, in order to learn how to cope with difficult ideas when they arise in the future. • Response: exploring ways in which pupils can express their responses to demanding or controversial issues. • Values: promoting an ethos of fairness and mutual respect in the classroom and compassion and generosity in pupils through exploring inspiring examples of these qualities in others. • Appreciation: encouraging pupils' ability to respond with wonder and excitement by exploring some of the marvels and mysteries of the natural world, of human ingenuity, and examples of the capacity of humans to love, create, organise and overcome adversity (RE Today 2020:103).

| How do some schools develop spiritual learning? Collective Worship, gardening, outdoor learning, singing, visiting places of worship, forgiveness, studying artists' religious themes. To experience awe, wonder, sadness, joy through stories, celebrations, rituals and different expressions of religion and worldviews. Reflecting on my sense of self (Who am I?), unique potential (what is special about me?), fundamental questions (Why and how am I here?). Considering questions about God. Exploring spiritual practices such as worship, meditation, yoga, mindfulness, prayer, recitals and considering the impact of these on believers. Each class uses a 'just a minute' (JAM) in a day to stop and think what matters to them and to be with their inner self. |

the emergence of social order, culture, identities, learning, institutions and decision-making. Moral development is about exploring and developing pupils' moral outlook and understanding of right and wrong and acting appropriately on this knowledge (Surrey 2017). It is also about learning to navigate the fact of moral diversity in the world (RE Today 2020:103). The evolutionary improvement of human beings both individually and socially underpins both education and moral development (Conroy 2021). Thus, moral reasoning and development can encourage the development of social capital and be mindful of communal interests. Table 7.3 offers a plan for moral development.

Table 7.3 Moral development through RE

Provision for the moral development of pupils includes developing the following:

- Ability to recognise the difference between right and wrong and to readily apply this understanding in their own lives, and to recognise legal boundaries and, in doing so, respect the civil and criminal law of England.
- Understanding of the consequences of their behaviour and actions.
- Interest in investigating and offering reasoned views about moral and ethical issues and ability to understand and appreciate the viewpoints of others on these issues (Ofsted 2019:60).

RE provides opportunities to promote moral development through the following:	RE is extremely well-suited to exploring social and personal morality in significant ways:

<ul><li>Considering what is of ultimate value to pupils and believers through studying the key beliefs and teachings from religion and philosophy about values and ethical codes of practice.</li><li>Exploring the influence of family, friends and media on moral choices and how society is influenced by beliefs, teachings, sacred texts and guidance from religious leaders.</li><li>Thinking about matters of ethical and moral concern.</li><li>Studying issues that promote respect of race, religion and belief.</li><li>Distinguishing between what is right and wrong and respecting the civil and criminal law of the UK.</li><li>Considering the importance of rights and responsibilities and developing social awareness (Surrey 2017).</li></ul>	1 Valuing others: in exploring the views of others, young people are well prepared in RE to appreciate the uniqueness of all humans and their moral value, and to act in the world and towards others accordingly.
	     In the classroom: offer activities, which enable teamwork and trust and require empathy. Welcome speakers or visit places of worship to learn from people of different backgrounds; explore case studies centring on forgiveness, generosity and other beneficial social moral values; use puppets, toys or persona dolls with younger children to develop their sense of moral connection with others.
	2 Moral character development: RE offers a safe space where pupils can learn from their mistakes, appreciate ideas of right and wrong, continue to strive after setbacks, take the initiative, act responsibly and demonstrate resilience. RE should present pupils with the challenge of responding in real and concrete ways to some of the moral questions they face.
	     In the classroom: encourage your pupils to take part in whole-school endeavours to enlarge their characters. Involve them in establishing appropriate moral codes for the classroom, school and the wider community. Suggest participation on the school council or the school play, in sport, music and debates, to contribute to charity events or take part in mentoring or 'buddy' schemes.
	3 Moral diversity: activities in RE lessons should help pupils feel confident when taking part in debates about moral issues. Debates and discussions should prepare pupils for the fact that there will always be disagreement on matters of morality and their right of expression is balanced by a responsibility to listen to the views of others.
	     In the classroom: choose age-appropriate topics which allow exploration of different moral outlooks such as religious texts about right and wrong, codes for living, treatment of animals and the environment, gender roles in religion, religious views of homosexuality and so on (RE Today 2020:103).

How do some schools develop moral learning? School rules, charity work, civic law and religious law. Showing concern for others through shared experience. Religion and bullying. Studying artists' work on ethical issues. By exploring the ten commandments and the sayings of religious leaders and others. Enquiring the importance of service to others in religious traditions. Exploring religious responses to evil and suffering. Promoting racial and religious respect and community cohesion. Asking about war, peace, hate, reconciliation, sin, salvation, exploitation and environment. Using the National Curriculum to enhance ethical issues of truth, justice and trust and developing a sense of conscience and personal integrity.

Social development through RE

Social development refers to the ways young people are shaped in schools with an eye on the sort of society that people wish to create in the future. Developing children socially means giving them the opportunities to explore and understand social situations and contexts they may encounter in school or outside (RE Today 2020:104). It is to do with how the individual relates and responds to others and with exploring how a sense of belonging is expressed in a variety of ways by different groups or communities (Surrey 2017). Goldberg et al. (2019:774) carried out a meta-analysis of 45 studies that sought to determine the effectiveness of interventions adopting a whole school approach to enhancing children and young people's social and emotional development. They concluded that a growing body of research suggests that for optimal impact, social and emotional skill development needs to be embedded within a whole school, multi-modal approach. This approach, they suggested, typically involves coordinated action between curriculum, teaching and learning; the school ethos and environment; and family and community partnerships. Table 7.4 offers a plan for social development.

Cultural development through RE

There are two meanings associated with 'cultural' development, and RE embodies both. First, the term refers to the pupils' own home culture and background, whether religious or not and second, the term describes our national culture. Schooling should prepare all young people to participate in Britain's wider cultural life, whatever their background (RE Today 2020:104). Developmental psychologists have highlighted the importance of the school as a context for academic and socio-emotional development (Schachner 2019). Schools should provide opportunities to adjust and prepare for life in an increasingly multicultural society and a globalised world. They can use contact-based intervention, knowledge and learning-based interventions, cooperative learning techniques, identity affirmation interventions, fostering multilingualism and teachers as promoters of a positive diversity climate (Schachner 2019:8–10). Table 7.5 offers a plan for cultural development.

Personal development through RE

RE is not only about gaining knowledge and understanding about religions and beliefs. RE has an important contribution to make to the personal development of pupils. RE helps pupils to develop their understanding of the world and how to live, in the light of their learning, developing understanding, skills and attitudes. Ofsted inspectors will use a range of evidence to evaluate personal development, including how the RE curriculum contributes to pupils' personal development and how well leaders develop pupils' character through the education that they provide (Ofsted 2019). RE has the potential to develop their confidence and make the most of their abilities to develop a healthy, safer lifestyle and good relationships. It offers opportunities for self-understanding including developing a sense of self-worth and value.

RE and 'British values'

Schools must also actively promote 'fundamental British values' (FBV) and prepare pupils for life in modern Britain. The definition of 'FBV' is contested for a variety of reasons (Eaude 2018; Elton-Chalcraft et al. 2017; Mogra 2021). The government in the controversial 2011 Prevent Strategy (HM Government 2011) set them up. These values, derived outside educational discourse and found within the security agenda, are tolerance and mutual respect between those of different faiths and beliefs, democracy, the rule of law and individual liberty. RE contributes to

Table 7.4 Social development through RE

Provision for the social development of pupils includes developing the following:

- Use of a range of social skills in different contexts, for example working and socialising with other pupils, including those from different religious, ethnic and socio-economic backgrounds.
- Willingness to participate in a variety of communities and social settings, including by volunteering, cooperating well with others and being able to resolve conflicts effectively.
- Acceptance of and engagement with the fundamental British values of democracy, the rule of law, individual liberty and mutual respect and tolerance of those with different faiths and beliefs. They will develop and demonstrate skills and attitudes that will allow them to participate fully in and contribute positively to life in modern Britain (Ofsted 2019:60).

RE provides opportunities to promote social development through the following:	In the RE classroom, such social situations may include exploring the following:
<ul><li>Considering how religious and other beliefs lead to particular actions and concern.</li><li>Addressing issues relating to democratic processes, promoting respect for the basis on which the law is made and applied across the UK, while exploring potential tensions with religious laws.</li><li>Investigating social issues from religious and non-religious perspectives recognising diversity within and between difference as well as the common ground between religions and beliefs.</li><li>Expressing pupils' personal views on a range of contemporary social issues while developing a capacity to consider respectfully the views of others on a range of contemporary social issues (Surrey 2017).</li></ul>	<ul><li>Shared values: opportunities to consider values which are or should be part of society, such as those associated with right and wrong, treatment of others or diversity.</li><li>Idealised concepts: topics which require reflection on the abstract concepts our society is built on, such as justice, fairness, honesty and truth, and specific examples of how they affect our common life, such as in relation to how people treat each other in the classroom and school, issues of poverty and wealth, crime and punishment.</li><li>Moral sources: a chance to reflect on *where* ideas about how we should behave come from, whether religious or non-religious texts, teachings or traditions, in order to more fully understand social and behavioural norms.</li><li>Influences: opportunities to explore and reflect on the great influence on individuals of family, friends, the media and wider society, in order to understand how our behaviour is affected for good or ill.</li><li>Social insight: a chance to acquire insight into significant social and political issues which affect individuals, groups and the nation, such as how churches and gurdwaras may contribute practically to needs in their local communities, or how some religious and non-religious charities fight to change government policies where they are unjust.</li><li>Role models: teachers should model the sort of behaviour we expect of our children and young people, and RE should explore role models, from the famous like Desmond Tutu, to the many local examples in the school and its community.</li><li>Experiential learning: pupils should have opportunities to embody for themselves expected behavioural and social norms, whether through class discussions, group work and ongoing behaviour expectations, or through special events such as school visits or drama workshops (RE Today 2020:104).</li></ul>

How do some schools develop social learning? Collective Worship, school council, sports, choir singing in the community, sports and other celebratory events, religion on crime and drugs, sense of belonging, conflict resolution, inter-faith activities, considering respect for difference, considering the social impact of religion, enquiring about faith-based charities. Activities to learn about the responsibilities and rights of being a member of various family, local, national and global communities. Activities to develop social skills, qualities, attitudes and characteristics such that they can play a full and fulfilling part in their community and society as, for example, family members, citizens, learners and workers. It is also about examining the consequences of anti-social behaviour.

Table 7.5 Cultural development through RE
Provision for the cultural development of pupils includes developing the following: • Understanding and appreciation of the wide range of cultural influences that have shaped their own heritage and that of others. • Understanding and appreciation of the range of different cultures in the school and further afield as an essential element of their preparation for life in modern Britain. • Ability to recognise, and value, the things we share in common across cultural, religious, ethnic and socio-economic communities. • Knowledge of Britain's democratic parliamentary system and its central role in shaping our history and values, and in continuing to develop Britain. • Willingness to participate in and respond positively to artistic, musical, sporting and cultural opportunities. • Interest in exploring, improving understanding of and showing respect for different faiths and cultural diversity and the extent to which they understand, accept and respect diversity. This is shown by their respect and attitudes towards different religious, ethnic and socio-economic groups in the local, national and global communities (Ofsted 2019:60–61).

RE provides opportunities to promote cultural development through the following:	Cultural development could be evident in RE in two major ways:

• Encountering people of faith from different religions, beliefs and cultures.
• Considering cultural diversity within the same religious or non-religious tradition.
• Promoting tolerance, racial and interfaith harmony and respect for all, combating prejudice and discrimination.
• Contributing positively to community cohesion and interfaith cooperation (Surrey 2017).
	1 Own culture: RE is the perfect subject in which to explore Britain's rich diversity of religious, ethnic and geographical cultures. Although all children share Britain's common life, cultural diversity is part of that life and no child should feel their cultural background is a barrier to participation. Some common RE activities which promote children's understanding of communities and cultural groups, including their own, could include:
	    In the classroom: explore food, festivals, music, art, architecture and other forms of religious and cultural expression. Where possible, visit areas with a strong cultural flavour to observe shops, cafes, people and houses. Some parents may be willing to come and talk about their home culture, or send personal artefacts to school with their children such as books, photos or clothes. Students who belong to a particular cultural group should be encouraged to share their experiences in class discussion, give a talk or even an assembly.
	2 Wider culture: schooling is a preparation for adult life in terms of behaviour and expectations as well as in achieving qualifications. This wider cultural education prepares children for adulthood.
	    In the classroom: cultural education is found whenever children make sense of the world around them and explore why we act the way we do. Provide opportunities for participation in classroom and whole-school events, including art, music, drama, sport, activism and serving others; explore what it is like to encounter difficulties in learning and relationships, and be open about the sorts of behaviours that are expected (RE Today 2020:104).

How do some schools develop cultural learning? Learning foreign language, using key terms in RE, class assemblies, celebrating festivals, visitors, being curious and exploring similarities and differences in a multi-cultural and multi-faith Britain, investigating UK saints and leaders, enquiring and engaging with sacred text, artefacts and devotional utilities other sources from different cultures and religious backgrounds.

supporting these values. However, it is important not to equate the two. RE is a subject in its own right, while the promotion of FBV is one part of the SMSC. Therefore, all subjects including RE should offer opportunities for promoting these. Schools need to promote them through the school ethos as part of their SMSC development. If schools teach about religious law, particular care should be taken to explore the relationship between state and religious law. Pupils should be made aware of the difference between the law of the land and religious law (DfE 2014).

Summary

Concerning modern life in Britain and RE, one of the criticisms made was that RE attempts to cover too much. However, this does not mean that the teaching of RE should not avail itself of the opportunities that it can make to important and genuine issues affecting contemporary life in Britain. On the contrary, one of the ways of showing pupils what it means to live life as a believer can be done by bringing religious teachings to bear on these everyday matters. It then helps pupils learn about these key areas of RE including beliefs, identities, values and commitments, which influence some people, which can be supplemented with non-religious perspectives. It brings to the fore important matters related to dialogue, interfaith, inter-theological understanding and radicalisation in religious and secular communities. While these are a useful addition to pupils' knowledge acquisition and wider understanding, RE should not suffer or be replaced because of them (Box 7.2).

BOX 7.2 VIGNETTE: SENSITIVITY

RE has always played an important role in my community. There have always been different kinds of events where different religions and cultures come together. This got me interested in why different people do things and why it is important for them. As far as my education is concerned, both my primary and secondary schools were Church of England faith schools, promoting the respect, and understanding of different religions and cultures. I explored, as Deputy Head Girl, the school's Christian ethos including the respect of all pupils no matter their religious background.

My attitude to teaching has always been that teachers deserve the utmost respect for the hard work and dedication they give daily. I have always admired what teachers stand for and the work they do. I studied Early Childhood Studies where my respect for the EYFS heightened. I explored the hard work that early years staff do and that just because the pupils are younger does not mean that the early stage of life is less important. It is more important than I realised.

I was prompted into teaching by the idea that I can make a difference and that by being there for the children I can help them achieve things they never dreamt was possible. For me, teaching means to not only be there for pupils to educate them but to be their point of call and assist them through this stage of their life.

I was motivated to select RE as I have a passion for understanding and respecting the different religions and cultures in our world and I want to go into my ECT feeling prepared to help the pupils develop this amount of respect and understanding for their peers and their world. My religion has always played a big part in who I am, therefore, I want to help develop RE in schools so the cultures and regions of the diverse classrooms can be celebrated and contribute to everyday school life.

My experience of RE has been interesting as there seemed to be less pressure around the subject so my confidence to explore my beliefs and understanding of others was

---

promoted. I enjoyed the fact that RE was less formal than the core subjects which meant that I felt comfortable in dealing with the more sensitive topics. However, I noticed that other religions were just skipped over, and I only remember covering Christianity plus two other religions. I feel that as teachers we should promote the equality of all religions and help pupils to respect them and not just think they are different.

The perception of RE from a lot of my friends is that it was not covered much apart from Christianity so they do not understand much about other religions. I also find that there is the agnostic belief as my friends are often confused and have questions but do not have the confidence or the opportunity to explore this. For example, if God is real why does He let so much evil and hate into our world? As a teacher, that question would be difficult to answer which in turn highlights the importance of schools needing support in the teaching of RE.

I am hoping to achieve a safe and comfortable environment where pupils can explore their beliefs by asking questions and sharing experiences in which they go through. I want to promote respect for RE in schools so that it is not seen, as the bottom subject that no one cares about. I fear answering difficult questions especially in religions that are not my own. I worry about misunderstanding a topic and it is coming across wrong where it appears to offend or confuse the pupils. I feel that this is what puts many teachers in RE and that the pressures of school will make me do the same. I am concerned about leading RE as I do not know all the religions, as well as I, know Christianity and I feel that an RE lead should have at least the basic knowledge of these religions to help assist teachers in leading the subjects across the whole school.

During SBT1, it was good to see that the school respected the unique child and promoted the different beliefs of their pupils. The pupils in my class enjoyed RE and they liked asking questions and understanding their peers. For example, a group of pupils were talking to a pupil who was a Jehovah Witness. They wanted to understand why she did not come to the assembly and celebrate Christmas as they did. It was really good to see the respect they had for her comments and that they did not just think she was wrong because her beliefs were different to the ones of their own.

References

Ashraf, S. A. (1992) The religious approach to religious education: The methodology of awakening and the disciplining the religious sensibilities, in B. Watson (Ed.) *Priorities in Religious Education: A Model for the 1990s and Beyond*, London: Falmer, pp. 83–94.

Baker, W. (2020) The moral attitudes of UK youth: Bringing morality back to the sociology of education, *British Journal of Sociology of Education*, 41, (7), pp. 911–926.

Barnes, L. P. (2008) The 2007 Birmingham Agreed Syllabus for Religious Education: A new direction for statutory Religious Education in England and Wales, *Journal of Beliefs & Values*, 29, (1), pp. 75–83.

Barnes, L. P. (2009) *Religious Education: Taking Religious Difference Seriously*, London: Philosophy of Education Society of Great Britain.

Barnes, L. P. (2015a) Part one religious education: Teaching for diversity, in M. Halsted (Ed.) *Religious Education: Educating for Diversity*, London: Bloomsbury, pp. 11–62.

Barnes, L. P. (2015b) Religious studies, religious education and the aims of education, *British Journal of Religious Education*, 37, (2), pp. 195–206.

BCC (Birmingham City Council) (2007) *The Birmingham Agreed Syllabus for Religious Education 2007*, Birmingham, UK: Birmingham City Council.

BCC (2022) *The Birmingham Agreed Syllabus for Religious Education*, Birmingham: Birmingham City Council. https://www.birmingham.gov.uk/downloads/file/22257/birmingham_agreed_syllabus_for_religious_education (Accessed 30/3/2022).

Chater, M. (2020) The seven deadly sins of RE, in M. Chater (Ed.) *Reforming RE*, Woodbridge: John Catt, pp. 65–82.

Conroy, J. C. (2021) Chaos or coherence? Future directions for moral education, *Journal of Moral Education*, 50, (1), pp. 1–12.

CoRE (Commission on Religious Education) (2018) *Religion and Worldviews: The Way Forward*, London: Religious Education Council.

Cornwall (2014) *Cornwall Agreed Syllabus for Religious Education 2014*, Truro: Cornwall Council.

DCSF (Department for Children, Schools and Families) (2010) *Religious Education in English Schools: Non-Statutory Guidance 2010*, Nottingham: DCSF Publications. DCSF-00114-2010.

DfE (2013) *The National Curriculum in England Key Stages 1 and 2 Framework Document*, Department for Education: Crown copyright. DFE-00178-2013.

DfE (2014) *Promoting Fundamental British Values as Part of SMSC in Schools: Departmental Advice for Maintained Schools*, Department for Education: Crown copyright. DFE-00679-2014.

Eaude, T. (2018) Fundamental British values? Possible implications for children's spirituality, *International Journal of Children's Spirituality*, 23, (1), pp. 67–80.

Eaude, T. (2016) *New Perspectives on Young Children's Moral Education: Developing Character Through a Virtue Ethics Approach*, London: Bloomsbury.

Eaude, T. (2008) *Children's Spiritual, Moral, Social and Cultural Development: Primary and Early Years*, Exeter: Learning Matters.

Elton-Chalcraft, S., Lander, V., Revell, L., Warner, D., and Whitworth, L. (2017) To promote, or not to promote fundamental British values? Teachers' standards, diversity and teacher education, *British Educational Research Journal*, 43, (1), pp. 29–48.

Felderhof, M., and Thompson, P. (Eds.) (2014) *Teaching Virtue: The Contribution of Religious Education*, London: Bloomsbury.

Fraser-Pearce, J. (2021) Spiritual education as a subspecies of relational education? *British Journal of Religious Education*, DOI: 10.1080/01416200.2021.1877613

Goldberg, J. M., Sklad, M., Elfrink, T. R., Schreurs, K. M. G., Bohlmeijer, E. T., and Clarke, A. M. (2019) Effectiveness of interventions adopting a whole school approach to enhancing social and emotional development: A meta-analysis, *European Journal of Psychology of Education*, 34, pp. 755–782. [Online] https://doi.org/10.1007/s10212-018-0406-9 (Accessed 28/07/2021).

Hand, M. (2003) The meaning of spiritual education, *Oxford Review of Education*, 29, (3), pp. 391–401.

Hay, D., and Nye, R. (2006) *The Spirit of the Child*, London: Jessica Kingsley Publishers.

HM Government (2011) *Prevent Strategy*, London: HMSO. Cm8092.

Homan, R. (2012) Constructing religion, in L. P. Barnes (Ed.) *Debates in Religious Education*, Abingdon: Routledge, pp. 183–183.

Lawton, C. (2018) Time to abandon Religious Education: Ditching an out-of-date solution to an out-of-date problem, in M. Castelli and M. Chater (Eds.) *We Need to Talk About Religious Education: Manifestos for the Future of RE*, London: Jessica Kingsley, pp. 21–35.

Mogra, I. (2021) Fundamental British values: Are they fundamental? in V. Bower (Ed.) *Debates in Primary Education*, Abingdon: Routledge, pp. 46–61.

Nye, R. (2009) *Children's Spirituality: What It Is and Why It Matters*, London, Church House Publishing.

Ofsted (2013) *Religious Education: Realising the Potential*, Manchester: Crown Copyright. Reference No: 130068. [Online] https://assets.publishing.service.gov.uk/government/uploads/system/uploads/attachment_data/file/413157/Religious_education_-_realising_the_potential.pdf (Accessed 05/12/2020).

Ofsted (2019) *School Inspection Handbook*, Manchester: Crown Copy copyright. Reference no: 190017.

Orchard (2021) Moral education and the challenge of pre-service professional formation for teachers, *Journal of Moral Education*, 50, (1), pp. 104–113.

Parker, S. G., and Freathy, R. J. K. (2011) Context, complexity and contestation: Birmingham's Agreed Syllabuses for Religious Education since the 1970s, *Journal of Beliefs & Values*, 32, (2), pp. 247–263.

Pearce, J. (2019) From Anthroposophy to non-confessional preparation for spirituality? Could common schools learn from spiritual education in Steiner schools? *British Journal of Religious Education*, 41, (3), pp. 299–314.

QCA (2004) *Religious Education: The Non-Statutory National Framework*, London: QCA.

RE Today (2020) *Derbyshire and Derby City: Agreed Syllabus for Religious Education 2020–2025*, Derbyshire: Derbyshire County Council and Birmingham: RE Today Services.

REC (Religious Education Council of England and Wales) (2013) *A Curriculum Framework for Religious Education in England*. London: REC of England and Wales.

Schachner, M. K. (2019) From equality and inclusion to cultural pluralism – Evolution and effects of cultural diversity perspectives in schools, *European Journal of Developmental Psychology*, 16, (1), pp. 1–17.

Stern, J. (2011) *The Spirit of the School*, London: Bloomsbury.

Surrey (2017) *The Agreed Syllabus for Religious Education in Surrey Schools 2017–2022*, Surrey SACRE.

Watson, J. (2007) Can children and young people learn from atheism for spiritual development? A response to the national framework for religious education, *British Journal of Religious Education*, 30, (1), pp. 49–58.

Wright, A. (2000) *Spirituality and Education*, London: RoutledgeFalmer.

Planning for RE

ORGANISING THE CURRICULUM

Introduction

An interesting observation is that no curriculum subject, other than Religious Education (RE) uses the word 'syllabus' which focuses entirely on the prescription of content, but prefers instead the more multi-layered word 'curriculum' (Erricker 2010:27). Nevertheless, there are several ways of organising the teaching and delivery of RE. Much of this depends on how the individual school thinks about learning and teaching and what it ultimately wants the children to achieve and become. Often external factors drive the decisions made regarding the planning. Teaching RE as a separate subject in the curriculum or integrating it with other curriculum subjects is a contentious matter. As far as the subject is concerned, it aims to promote, through an encounter with its curriculum, pupil's search for values, meaning and purpose. Therefore, whatever form of organisation of the subject is applied, with other areas of the curriculum or on its own, it must ensure that the distinctive subject matter of Christianity, other religions, beliefs and worldviews are covered with high quality.

To begin, some important features from the Core Content Framework, which you need to learn to demonstrate good curriculum knowledge, are highlighted below so that they are at the forefront while you consider matters about organising and planning RE (DfE 2019). You need to learn that:

- ■ A school's curriculum enables it to set out its vision for the knowledge, skills and values that its pupils will learn. [What is your vision for RE?]

- ■ Ensuring pupils master foundational concepts and knowledge before moving on is likely to build pupils' confidence and help them succeed. [Are you familiar with the three types of concepts in RE?]

- ■ Anticipating common misconceptions within particular subjects is also an important aspect of curricular knowledge. [How will you identify misconceptions before and after teaching?]

- ■ Explicitly teaching pupils the knowledge and skills they need to succeed within particular subject areas is beneficial. [What activities can you use explicitly to teach them?]

- ■ For pupils to think critically, they must have a secure understanding of knowledge within the subject area they are being asked to think critically about. [How can you ensure that your pupils have a secure knowledge base?]

DOI: 10.4324/9780429289743-11

■ In all subject areas, pupils learn new ideas by linking those ideas to existing knowledge, organising this knowledge into increasingly complex mental models (or 'schemata'). [How will you sequence and make your teaching coherent to facilitate this process?].

Religious Education in English schools: Non-statutory guidance (DCSF 2010:31) encourages schools to weigh the advantages of regular coherent provision, say every week, against those of a more flexible provision when more time can be allocated in one week, term or year than in another. This flexibility can be applied, it stresses, as long as the programme of study required by the agreed syllabus is covered. Moreover, schools need to ensure that their RE provision includes a distinct body of knowledge and enables all pupils to make effective progress in achieving the RE learning outcomes. Planning for RE should also ensure all pupils have a high quality, coherent and progressive experience of the subject.

The case study in Box 8.1 shows the provision of breadth and depth in an agreed syllabus (DCSF 2010:24). As you read through, you may want to begin to identify your preferred approach and note your justifications. These could be discussed with your peers. For each approach, consider its implications for your teaching and any challenges you envisage.

A study using a questionnaire with teachers in 22 secondary schools explored whether a systematic, thematic or mixed approach to world religions was used. It found that confusion

---

BOX 8.1 CASE STUDY: BREADTH AND DEPTH IN AN AGREED SYLLABUS

Case study: How an Agreed Syllabus Conference (ASC) might handle breadth and balance within an integrated curriculum.

Systematic study that looks at one or more religion and nonreligious view in detail, by exploring some of its key concepts, such as beliefs, teaching and sources, or values and commitments. For example, a major unit in Year 5 on Christianity could include a study of how Christian worship and practice reflects the life and teachings of Jesus; or in a Year 9 unit comparing Judaism and Humanism, examples could focus on the beliefs, teachings and sources that motivate them to take social action to improve the world.

Thematic study that looks at a question, concept or issue and explores it in relation to one or more religions or beliefs, by enquiring into how and why the questions are answered. For example, a Year 4 unit on practices and ways of life could investigate how and why some people observe religious occasions at home, including Christian ways of marking Lent and Muslim ways of marking the month of Ramadan. A Year 8 unit on environmental campaigners could look at the religious and non-religious values and commitments that lead some people to take action against roads, runways or the treatment of animals. A Year 11 unit on fair trade, just war or ending life could explore the beliefs and commitments of Buddhists and Bahá'ís.

Cross-curricular study that uses key concepts or processes from two or more subjects to engage pupils in a challenging exploration. For example, a Year 6 unit could use the investigation processes in science and RE to generate questions about the concept of truth in relation to different accounts of the origin of the universe. A Year 7 unit could address the historical concept of causation, the citizenship concept of rights and the RE concept of identity to investigate migration, with specific reference to the Jain and Zoroastrian communities and the particular culture and values they have contributed to British society.

By offering a balance of all three, RE syllabuses can promote pupils' understanding of the different impacts that religion and belief have on individuals and communities and enhance pupils' awareness of the kinds of questions raised by religion and ethics and how different religions answer them.

---

was shown to be significantly linked with the mixed approach regardless of how many religions pupils had studied (Kay and Smith 2000).

Some prefer that RE should be taught systematically. In dealing with one religion at a time, teaching systematically seeks to build a holistic picture of one religion at a time and can be used more frequently in upper key stages (James and Stern 2019:30). This involves an emphasis on the content of the religion being taught which can lead to a coherent understanding of what that means to a religion. In addition, it shows dedicated time allowance for the religions being studied and affords a balance to be achieved between religions (Rivett 2007:3). When delivering RE as a discrete subject, perhaps weekly or as a focus topic, day or week, the themes are better drawn from the RE syllabus.

Alternatively, a thematic approach emphasises concepts across and between religions and often it is directly related to children's own experiences. It deals with cross-religious material and studies religions through themes such as holy books, places of worship and initiation rites. It usually stresses similarities between religions and can be used more frequently in lower key stages (James and Stern 2019:30).

In some schools, a rolling programme of units is offered which allows them to meet the needs of mixed-age classes. The units are planned in such a way that the expectations for each unit are matched to the different ages and abilities. For example, a mixed Year 4 and 5 are taught in a series of RE units over a two-year cycle ensuring that the learning intentions and activities are progressively and sequentially planned for the age, capacities and abilities of the pupils.

The way a school classifies their RE curriculum may be another indication of the extent to which a school prioritises RE. Fancourt (2016), drawing on educational work by Bernstein, considers that RE is strongly classified where it is typically treated as a discrete subject and weakly classified where it might be part of a more thematic curriculum (Ofsted 2021). Although it is possible for pupils to know more and to remember more of the RE curriculum in both classifications of RE, problems can emerge when RE is too weakly classified. Sometimes, this can lead to erosion in the curriculum. Some examples of RE being too weakly classified might be: at primary, a key stage 2 topic approach that provides pupils with a rich historical and geographical knowledge, but has relatively little RE content (Ofsted 2021).

Discrete teaching approaches

Teaching as a single discrete subject makes it possible to focus on a well-structured enquiry which, among other things, facilitates independent thinking, learning and develops in-depth knowledge and understanding in RE. Dinham and Shaw (2015) reported that some teachers, parents and pupils preferred RE as a separate subject. This approach may assist in addressing concerns often raised when RE is seen as a 'Cinderella' subject that wants to please and involve all the other subjects and contribute to local, national and global issues (Larkin, Freathy, Doney and Freathy 2020). Chapter 11 will show links between RE and other curriculum areas. Discrete teaching is often referred to as subject-based teaching and, in practice, this might often mean that schools would dedicate one lesson a week on the timetable for RE, a double lesson once in a fortnight, or delivered in blocks of time at different points in the year. Based on some internal observation of religious studies, Cush (2007:223) concluded that a discrete academic subject dealing with religious traditions and spiritual or secular alternatives was the most effective way of addressing religious plurality in education.

Advantages

- There is a stable curriculum content for RE.
- There is consistent delivery of RE.
- There is a specific time for RE.

> **BOX 8.2 REFLECTION: RE AS A DISCRETE CURRICULUM SUBJECT**
>
> First, it would mean a loss of specific curriculum space for pupils to engage with the religion and non-religion worldviews they will encounter in UK society. To try to cover this within other subjects risks only cursory attention on the complex range of worldviews and scant chance for critical reflection. This isn't fair on religious and non-religions worldviews, and isn't fair on the other subjects which already have heaps of content to cover.
>
> Second, RE provides a place for pupils to reflect on how their own religion and beliefs shape the way they see and make sense of the world. Other subjects could cover elements of this, but they're not necessarily compulsory subjects (so some pupils would miss out) and you'd risk losing the focus on religions (and Non-Religious World Views) by merging this content with other subject content.
>
> Third, religion and non-religion worldviews are so frequently misunderstood, misrepresented, stereotyped and simplified in media and wider society, and yet are so important for understanding people, politics, society, etc. that to lose the place in the curriculum where pupils can learn about their complexity and diversity (both between and within), their fuzzy edges, their contested nature and the way they change over time and location would be a huge loss. It's great when other subjects cover elements of this but it's not realistic to think they could cover it all in appropriate depth.

- The progress can be steady.
- Pupils know what they are getting.
- Teachers have a grasp of where things are.
- The monitoring of progress can be regular.
- It allows for peripatetic teaching of RE by specialists across the school (Pett 2015).

Limitations

- The peripatetic model can potentially de-skill teachers in RE.
- The peripatetic model may give a negative message to children and parents when taught by one person.
- There is potential for RE to be swallowed and taken out easily by something else.
- Deeper learning might be affected with such short burst lessons (Pett 2015:18).

A discussion took place on Twitter on the potential consequences of RE losing its discrete curriculum status. Some expressed the view that nothing much would be lost. However, Rudi Eliott Lockhart, then CEO of REC, expressed serious concerns, as reflected in Box 8.2.

Cross-curricular approaches

Cross-curricular approaches are valued by many teachers. This approach to organising learning is viewed as motivating and enjoyable and has the capability to build meaning, relevance to the curriculum and raise standards (Barnes 2015b). Nevertheless, Alexander (2010) recognised that cross-curricular approaches can sometimes be counterproductive if the teachers do not possess sufficient subject knowledge when delivering the lessons. Some teachers and schools affirm this approach because religious faith and beliefs often permeate other areas of the NC and EYFS curricula. It has been noted that RE topics also lend themselves to a cross-curricular approach (McCreery, Palmer and Voiels 2008:97). Still, some foundation subjects work stronger while others require rigorous thought, planning, creativity and preparation to make the links appropriate.

This approach provides deeper knowledge, understanding and enables the acquisition of practical skills through the content of different subjects. The links between subject information are said to help pupils learn more effectively and efficiently (Rowley and Cooper 2013). It is also suggested that it makes learning more creative and inclusive especially with well-organised and flexible lessons that are accessible to pupils (Desailly 2015). Moreover, Lucas and Spencer (2017) suggest that cross-curricular approach facilitates the child's ability to think more imaginatively rather than limiting their thinking. Be that as it may, these benefits should not be confined to result exclusively from cross-curricular approaches.

The decision to link cross-curricular themes or topics with RE should be based on an educationally valid RE rationale. Therefore, it is important to make strong rather than tenuous links. RE could form a substantive part of an approach or a smaller aspect of the theme or topic. However should they be made, they should develop pupils' knowledge and understanding through effective planning and clear learning objectives from RE, whereas, for the other subjects, their specific outcomes should be derived from the NC. Moreover, these should be referenced accordingly in planning documents. Crucially, though, granted that RE contributes to other subjects, it should, nevertheless, be remembered that RE must not be defined by or confined to the outcomes of the NC. You must first clarify the aims and rationale for RE so that you can justify a compulsory subject on its right before throwing the net wider. If RE is being integrated into a cross-curricular learning approach, the theme or topic can be taken from any source, including the pupils.

The cross-curricular approach should not be confused with the thematic approach to teaching. There are subtle differences between these in educational literature (Webster 2010:21, 103; Webster and Misra 2015:7). A cross-curricular approach involves two subjects being taught simultaneously and they drive the lesson. For example, the objective of observational drawing in Art is taught at the same time as the objective of the features of a place of worship in RE. Both objectives are taught in tandem (Webster 2010:21). Therefore, when implementing this approach, you should plan objectives for both subjects and build in assessment opportunities for both (Webster, 2015; Webster and Misra 2015:8).

Advantages

Some of the benefits of such an approach in RE include the following:

- Children understand that religion is an integral part of life not something distinct from the rest of life.
- Children see the connections between different subject areas.
- Children will learn to see that different subject area bring different sets of questions, and different responses to the same topic.
- It is an economic use of curriculum time when time is short (McCreery, Palmer and Voiels 2008:17).
- It reflects the holistic way a child views the world.

Limitations

There are some limitations in adopting this approach such as the following:

- Children end up with a mishmash of information from various religions and can become confused.

- Key aspects of religion and key skills in studying religion are overlooked because they don't fit in with the topic covered.
- The same content could be returned repeatedly.
- Sudden reference to an aspect of religion does not make sense to children because they have no context for it. For example, stating that some Sikhs wear a turban in a topic on hats, can be meaningless if they have not come across the term Sikh before (McCreery, Palmer and Voiels 2008:17).
- It may water down the subject identity of the discipline (Barnes 2012).

Ways forward

Nevertheless, it is suggested that good planning can make it possible to have the best of both approaches. Teachers should plan discrete units of work to introduce pupils to religion but they should draw on examples from religions the pupils have studied before in cross-curricular topics (McCreery, Palmer and Voiels 2008:18).

- So cross-curricular planning requires planning objectives for both subjects.
- It should include opportunities for assessment in both subjects.
- It requires you to monitor your preferences so that they do not influence one subject over the other.
- In cross-curricular approaches, usually two or sometimes three subjects are used simultaneously, but not more are taught (Barnes 2015a; Webster 2010:21).

Thematic or topic-based approaches

Some schools give preference to a theme or topic approach to their planning, often this is called a thematic approach or topic-based work.

In thematic teaching, three or more subjects can be taught with similar themes, yet the objectives of only one of the subjects will be developed and taught within the lesson (Webster 2010:21–22). For example, the theme 'Our Locality' could involve a visit to a place of worship for RE and look at how faith is expressed in a sacred building but does not require a local study or any specific geographical skill (Webster 2010:21–22). Moreover, Webster and Misra (2015:7) emphasise that in thematic teaching you would plan, teach and assess for one subject while linking to others.

In a later work, Webster and Misra (2015:7) provide a useful analogy to help distinguish between cross-curricular and thematic approaches. A cross-curricular approach is like a tandem bicycle. Two seats are moving the bike (the lesson) forward. Thematic teaching is like a single bicycle, but one that is connected to buggies (the subjects that link).

RE, like other subjects, is afforded space in the thematic plan and links with other subjects as a series of lessons. In the case of RE, a thematic teaching plan would include the following:

- A relevant focus for RE.
- It would specify a fixed period for RE.
- It would identify outcomes to be addressed for RE.

In terms of delivery, the theme could be organised into 2/3 weeks or longer. In some cases, this might be for half a term. This would mean that pupils learn RE for five hours a week and relate their study to History and Geography, for example (Pett 2015). This approach affords opportunities for deeper exposure and continuous experience of RE. It also consolidates learning in RE. However, its potential might be limited should the themes not link strongly with RE. Moreover, there may also be limited opportunities to provide sufficient depth in such planning.

Ways forward

For good quality RE, a 'bolt on' approach should be avoided and you must move away from a 'tick box' attitude. RE is not a bedfellow for every subject or initiative of the school, and so it does not have to be linked to every subject. Providing RE teaching through topics ensure that there is sustained learning. In your selection and sequencing of RE topics ensure you have a clear rationale. The topic should also have a clear structure with coherence.

In all approaches, the diverse experiences, interests and strengths that pupils bring must be used and made relevant in RE. Some pupils are committed within their faith communities, others will have limited contact and some will have no participation at all. Quality teaching takes account of these varied religious backgrounds and quality plans to meet the needs of individuals, acknowledges family backgrounds and respects the beliefs and practices in the communities.

RE focus approaches

As schools have the flexibility to complement discrete subject teaching with cross-curricular approaches, it means that you should be driven by the needs of your pupils and school to tailor the learning experiences you design and offer them. In practice, your RE could be taught discretely at some points during the year, but at other times, it could be linked with other subjects, particularly when carrying out a sustained enquiry to provide a coherent, in-depth and sequential design and delivery. For example, you could plan RE for merged timetable days, or as part of weekly work or as monthly or termly projects. The themes for these are better drawn from the subject specific content of RE. You may wish to consider the strengths and constraints of this approach.

Big RE days

These Big RE days could be discrete, cross-curricular or thematic. Some schools immerse their pupils in RE for a whole day. This whole day is then followed up by related lessons in subsequent weeks (Pett 2015). The limitation is that planning for a whole day of activities can be demanding and the provision of resources to support many activities can be a challenge. Though it can be demanding of teachers, it helps the school focus and develops the subject (Moss 2015:75). A whole day of RE can enhance the importance of the subject and offers the subject extra specialness. These whole days can supplement regular RE provision. For example, pupils can spend a Whole Day learning about a leader, a sacred text or a sacred space. Pupils can spend a Whole Day investigating a faith-based charity (Blaylock, Moss, Pett 2013; Pett 2015).

With careful planning and clear intentions, a whole day of RE can be useful. However, you need to be alert that it can also produce sporadic results and minimum achievement by all in all aspects of learning. Pupil recall and evidence surface learning. You may need to approach this critically and question the effectiveness of a whole day approach, and whether it might have far too much information as cognitive load theory pays attention to pupils learning through long-term and working memory (Kirschner 2002; Sherringdon 2019; Sweller, Van Merrienboer and Paas 1998).

The delivery of a RE by dropdown days needs careful thinking for all pupils, but more so for the development of pupils with special educational needs and disability who develop their understanding at a slower pace and need regular reinforcement of concepts.

Big RE weeks

These Big RE weeks could be cross-curricular or thematic. This offers many benefits. It allows a considerable part of the RE curriculum to be delivered. It allows for clear progression within the area of study. It allows for Assessment for Learning. It is possible to deliver several Big RE weeks in a year. However, there are some challenges including a full week of RE would be insufficient especially when there are about 39 weeks in a school year. For example, the class can use the Whole Week learning about Easter Week, Diwali or Hanukkah. This 'RE week' or 'RE day' should then be followed up with bridging lessons over some weeks. Though these can be demanding, nevertheless, they are good for bringing all teachers or year group teachers to plan RE for the whole school, phase or years to develop the subject and enhance its profile. The success for this depends on the clarity about the RE learning that is planned (Moss 2015:75).

Issues-based

The issue-based approach is seen by Rivett (2007) as one which combines elements from both the thematic and systematic approaches. It aims to develop conceptual understanding through themes and, at the same time, gives an overview of each religion being studied. It can be based on fundamental questions of human experience that makes it more relevant to the personal development of the individual. For example, Is there a God? Is the Bible true? Why is there suffering? What do I believe?

Summary

In deciding on any particular model of curriculum organisation and delivery, it is important to make provision for the parental right of withdrawal (DCSF 2010:31). If RE is being integrated into a cross-curricular learning approach, the RE content must be identified. RE may form a substantive part of such learning or a smaller aspect of that theme or topic. In all cases, pupils should recognise and be able to articulate the learning and progress in RE that has taken place. All approaches should ensure that they meet the learning needs of all pupils. As a teacher, you will need to be able to demonstrate their learning in RE for reporting purposes. In all approaches, it is important to ensure that the quality of provision is high and that the curriculum for RE is broad and balanced and they address the expectations of the MTP (Medium-Term Plan) and LTP (Long-Term Plan) of the school.

PLANNING THE CURRICULUM

Introduction

Thus far, Chapter 3 established the aims and purposes of teaching RE and its fields of enquiry. Chapter 5 outlined the expectations of its curriculum. The focus of this part is to bring these two together and prepare for their implementation in schools and classrooms. The process through which this takes place is known as planning or curriculum mapping. Before venturing on the minutiae of the various components of planning, it is important that you reflect and analyse some principles for implementation in RE. A reflection about the learning culture and mindset in any classroom would be useful before considering planning in detail.

Growth culture

Pupils should believe that they can be better and be motivated to persevere in the face of challenges and setbacks. To develop this, a culture of excellence needs to be created, where the right environment which helps pupils to work hard, learn and improve is set and has to be seen as a philosophy rather than an intervention (Watson and Bradley 2021). In a growth culture, pupils are encouraged to compare themselves to themselves. The environment is one of high expectations, both of what teachers think pupils can achieve but also what pupils think they can achieve. Finally, it is about creating an environment that treads the line between celebrating success without sitting back while also learning from the mistakes without dwelling on them.

Principles of planning

As discussed earlier, covering all or too many religions and beliefs does not seem an effective practice. Therefore, you will find that some schools use three or four religions across the key stages as depth is more important than overstretching breadth. These approaches place importance on quality over quantity, curriculum over coverage, secure knowledge over superficiality. Continuity and sequence to develop a coherent understanding of what is being studied. Moreover, it is useful for pupils to be aware of relatedness. This is the idea that religions are not seen as entirely exclusive; rather there may be a relationship between one religion and another, which is accounted for when choosing the religions and beliefs to study.

Internationally, there is renewed attention being given to curriculum principles and curriculum practice. The ideas bring together theory, research, policy and practice to provide you with a practical guide to a coherent curriculum design. Myatt (2018) offers a relatable analogy stressing the strangeness of some practices in some schools. She invites teachers to imagine a restaurant owner who guarantees the completion of their paperwork, training of their front of house staff, and then continues to assume that all is well, without verifying the quality of the ingredients being used by the chef, which will oblige the customers to return. She argues for the need to understand cognitive science for designing a coherent curriculum reminding readers, from Willingham (2009), that people are hard-wired for stories. Children form long-term memories more easily from narratives than from disjointed facts; therefore, a curriculum should create an overarching narrative for the pupils. It should keep multiple strands all spinning at once (Myatt 2018:33). Teachers should have a clear picture of the overall provision map for RE across the year and provide coherence and tell the story. Pupils need to know how each unit fits into the wider whole so that they can learn a particular by locating it in the general. Pupils should be able to make sense and see the why of their learning. Myatt (2018:19) stresses that all pupils 'ought to be able to tell us what they are learning about and why it is important. If they can't, we haven't taught them properly'. This is a key principle for a coherent curriculum.

Seven curriculum design principles

Brine and Chater (2020) have applied the seven curriculum design test devised by Dylan Wiliam to RE to lay the groundwork for teaching about worldviews, whether a new curriculum or a single subject.

A well-designed subject should *balance* between knowledge and skills and strike balance over the increasingly broad range of religions and beliefs to be studied. The pathway to *rigorous* RE lies through immersion in disciplines that represent one or more powerful and distinct ways of thinking about the world. The lack of disciplinary clarity is the most significant challenge in RE. *Coherence* enables the young mind to construct mental models. A mental model of the subject gives the learner an overall sense of how all the disparate pieces of content hold together. The different mental models should be able to build on and challenge each other. The curriculum should be vertically integrated (*progressive*). From the start of KS1 to the end of A levels, the pupil is on a journey within the holding encasement of a recognised subject. Content will change, become more complex but there should be a clear sense of a progression pathway based on the content. There should be a spiral revisiting of content at higher levels of intellectual demand. Content should be *appropriately* matched to the age and aptitude of learners. In RE, the unmanageable breadth of content and the pressure to include an in-depth study of a range of beliefs with considerable conceptual differences makes matching the level of content a complex task. *Focused* in most subjects including RE, there is simply too much eligible knowledge clamouring for curriculum time. The only way to improve a curriculum is to leave out important material to spend more time on more important material (Wiliam 2013:36). *Relevant* content need not be directly relevant to pupils, but its teaching must be connectable to young minds and their experience. We need young minds to experience the subject, not simply its contact (Brine and Chater 2020:106–108).

The need for quality planning

The quality of RE teaching in English schools is mixed. Ofsted reported that the teaching of RE in primary schools was not good enough for several reasons. This included poor and fragmented curriculum planning. They also found that how RE was provided had the effect of isolating the subject from the rest of the curriculum (Ofsted 2013:5–6). This suggests that in RE pupils, if you so decided, should be given opportunities to work with the outcomes of other subjects in a coherent and progressive way.

The starting points for RE

One of the purposes of RE is to assist pupils to make sense of the world and the world introduced to them by their educators. In the world of religion, you need to be aware of some of the basic issues, which might affect you, and the discussion you have when teaching RE. Personal beliefs, the background of pupils, being sensitive in your approach and cross-curricular planning are considered below.

The first one, which McCreery, Palmer and Voiels (2008:15) highlight, is to know where you, as a teacher, are starting from. They suggest that it is important to know yourself when you study religion and when you teach others to study religion. They maintain that everyone has experiences of religion, positive or negative, whether or not they belong to a faith community. They also note that everyone has beliefs, fears and hopes; for some this may include belief in God but not for others. Thus, they argue that such experiences and beliefs will inevitably shape the way the teaching of explicitly religious content in RE is approached by teachers. A strong conviction or even an unquestioned assumption in the truth of one's faith position may lead teachers unintentionally to promote their faith position and/or to subtly dismiss or disparage the beliefs and practices of others as superstitions.

In some sections of British society, there is scepticism about RE in school. On rare occasions, an odd student teacher has expressed exasperation when invited to reflect on the importance of teaching RE, whereas the vast majority welcome it enthusiastically as evident from these quotations.

> Do I have to be religious to teach RE?
> Why do I have to teach this damn RE!
> What is RE about? Nothing mate.

Such questions and comments prompt the consideration of a second practical issue emphasised by McCreery, Palmer and Voiels (2008:15) who state that teachers of RE do not need to believe in the existence of God to teach RE. RE, they assert, is a subject where pupils learn what different people believe about God and explore their own beliefs. To allay such concerns, they suggest that you need to search for a way of teaching about religion that is honest to your own beliefs. An atheist can teach that Islam teaches that there is one God, without believing that God exists. Some student teachers express concerns about their pupils asking teachers questions, which are personal in nature and often related to their own beliefs. For example, some trainees enquire about what they should do if a pupil asks:

> Do you have a religion?
> Do you believe in God?
> Are you Christian?

In some schools, perhaps more so in multicultural and multi-faith schools, out of curiosity some pupils are eager to know more about their teachers. Since teachers are looked upon as a figure of authority, some professionals have expressed concern about teachers unwittingly imposing a view on pupils. Based on their experience, McCreery, Palmer and Voiels (2008) suggest that the best way of answering is, to be honest, and, if possible, to return the question to the pupil. Nevertheless, they propose that you should acknowledge your own beliefs and simultaneously acknowledge other viewpoints and ask the pupils for their ideas as well. A further connected issue is to remember that not every religious item is a matter of personal faith. Hence, McCreery, Palmer and Voiels (2008:15) suggest that you need to learn to differentiate between items that are factual, in the sense that they are uncontested by the majority of people and are open to historical enquiry, and those items which are matters of faith and belief.

In Chapter 3 you read that some student teachers were anxious about some of their pupils knowing more about religion or a topic than themselves. Such a phenomenon is worthy of celebration as this means that some pupils belonging to faith traditions or none are potentially a rich resource for you and your class. Third, regarding the religious background of your pupils, McCreery, Palmer and Voiels (2008) remind teachers of the need to be tactful and sensitive in their approach. They recommend the need to be careful about asking pupils directly about their faith unless they have strong evidence to indicate they are happy with this. It is equally important to remember that just because a child belongs to faith it does not necessarily mean that they know everything about that faith. Moreover, it is beneficial to recognise that whatever a child conveys may be a representation of one perspective from that tradition. Furthermore, teachers should also be alert to the possibility that the child may not want to share their experiences, for a variety of reasons. Therefore, it is suggested that teachers leave the space open for the pupil to come forward to share their experiences and beliefs (McCreery, Palmer and Voiels 2008:16). You should not be surprised to see this happen as pupils usually do so. You need to be prepared for the conviction of the pupils in your classrooms, which might have an impact on the discussion that takes place. Some pupils from particular faith backgrounds come to school with a strong, and maybe to you, shocking antipathy to the study of religions or convictions about their own (McCreery, Palmer and Voiels 2008:16). So, one of the main features of successful planning in RE is the depth of the teacher's subject knowledge (Hill 2014:243).

The fourth issue relates to the continuous controversy in RE and in other subjects as to whether RE should be introduced to pupils as a discrete subject or whether it should be part of a cross-curricular or thematic program connected with other subjects like history, geography, design technology and art and design. This has been discussed earlier.

Planning in RE should be underpinned by certain concepts, as reflected in Box 8.3. Mary Myatt (2020) justifies:

Big Ideas for Religious Education

Planning in RE needs to pay particular attention to the important ideas in RE. Every syllabus will have its own description of these. They are applied to every age group and James and Stern (2019:172) caution that if these are ignored or any other equivalent list then you are not planning RE but planning a set of more-or-less RE activities.

> **BOX 8.3 THE SIGNIFICANCE OF CONCEPTS IN PLANNING**
>
> Concepts and big ideas are like 'holding baskets' – they are the cradle for a lot of information; they help to make sense of disparate knowledge and potentially unconnected facts. Through anchoring the subject's planning in concepts, we provide a route through for pupils to get to grips with the foundations of key beliefs and practices in religions and world views. The insight into the foundational importance of concepts is supported by cognitive science, for example Willingham's (2009) conclusion: 'Students can't learn everything, so what should they know? Cognitive science leads to the rather obvious conclusion that students must learn the concepts that come up again and again – the unifying ideas of each discipline'.
>
> What follows from this is that if I am planning a unit in Christianity about the birth of Jesus, this will be underpinned by the concept of incarnation. Incarnation is a fundamental element of Christian theology, namely that the divine became human in the form of a baby. Very young children can grasp this, if it is taught explicitly. It then means that the gospel accounts of the birth of Jesus, the nativity plays and the festivities that take place in primary schools, are underpinned by the idea that this is important for Christians because they believe that God became human through the birth of baby Jesus. Unless that conceptual understanding is in place, it is just a random list of things that children experience without making the deeper connections.
>
> Similarly, if I am planning to teach about the langar in Sikhism, this needs to be understood in terms of the concept of sewa. Without the building of the concept, then it is just understood as a free meal provided at a gurdwara.

There are two publications of interest, which delineate Big Ideas in RE. *Big Ideas for RE* discussed, among other features, the characteristics of Big Ideas (Wintersgill 2017). This was followed by a sequel demonstrating how Big Ideas might be put into practice for the selection and organisation of subject knowledge and assessment. It is intended for anyone who designs syllabuses, schemes of learning and units of work in RE (Wintersgill, Cush and Francis 2019:2). The revised Big Idea narratives are:

Big Idea 1: Continuity, change and diversity

Religions/worldviews involve interconnected patterns of beliefs, practices and values. They are also highly diverse and change in response to new situations and challenges. These patterns of diversity and change can be the cause of debate, tension and conflict or result in new, creative developments.

Big Idea 2: Words and beyond

People often find it difficult to express their deepest beliefs, feelings, emotions and religious experiences using everyday language. Instead, they may use a variety of different approaches including figurative language and a range of literary genres. In addition, people sometimes use non-verbal forms of communication such as art, music, drama and dance that seek to explain or illustrate religious or non-religious ideas or experiences. There are different ways of interpreting both verbal and non-verbal forms of expression, often depending on a person's view of the origin or inspiration behind them. The use of some non-verbal forms of communication is highly controversial within some religious groups, particularly their use in worship or ritual.

Big Idea 3: A good life

Many people, whether religious or not, strive to live according to what they understand as a good life. Religious and non-religious communities often share an understanding as to the sort of characteristics and behaviours a good person will seek to achieve, as well as dealing with what is, or is not acceptable moral behaviour. The ideal is usually presented in the lives and character of exemplary members. There are points of agreement and disagreement over the interpretation and application of moral principles both across and within different religions/worldviews.

Big Idea 4: Making sense of life's experiences

Many people have deeply felt experiences, which they may refer to as being 'religious' or 'spiritual' or simply part of what it means to be human. These experiences can take place in both religious and non-religious contexts and may produce a heightened sense of awareness and mystery, or of identity, purpose and belonging. The experience is sometimes so powerful that it transforms people's lives. As a result, people may change their beliefs and allegiances and on rare occasions, the experience of a single person has led to the formation of a new religion/worldview.

Big Idea 5: Influence and power

Religious and non-religious communities interact with wider society and cultures. These communities affect societies by shaping their traditions, laws, political systems, festivals, values, rituals and arts. The patterns of influence vary significantly in different societies and at different points in time. Some societies are influenced predominantly by one religion/worldview, others by several or many. Religions/worldviews often appeal to a highly respected authority or vision, and this can have significant impacts on societies and cultures, whether positive or negative.

Big Idea 6: The big picture

Religions/worldviews provide comprehensive accounts of how and why the world is as it is. These accounts are sometimes called 'grand narratives'. They seek to answer the big questions about the universe and the nature of humanity. These narratives are usually based on approaches to life, texts or traditions, which are taken to be authoritative. People interpret and understand these texts and traditions in different ways.

Planning

This section encourages you to think about the multiple components of planning, with the ultimate aim of promoting your autonomy. You are invited to consider whether knowing about the nature of RE and having the knowledge of its curriculum is sufficient. You will have an opportunity to reflect on the factors which are required for successful planning and teaching. You will also consider the importance of planning through which a teacher is enabled to transfer and interpret the nature of RE, its disciplines and its content into effective planning sequences and engaging experiences in RE.

Importance of planning

Planning is intended to provide a clear focus and purpose for learning and teaching. It supports teachers when reflecting on their practice and enables them to maximise the time available to them. Systematic planning has been recognised as being important for effective teaching.

It is often said that quality teaching and learning require quality planning, in turn, this often depends upon how well pupil learning is assessed.

Another significant principle to emphasise is that planning should be conceived as a process, rather than a product. Of course, the document is a 'product' (if there is to be one); however, the implementation and execution of what is on a paper are dependent on the interaction taking place during teaching. As such, the planning is not static as teachers continuously review, respond and think ahead while they are in the midst of their lesson with their pupils.

Effective planning is essential for classroom management (Fautley and Savage 2013) and good classroom management creates an atmosphere for pupils to engage better with learning which in turn affords more time for learning and ensures that less time is lost on behaviour management. Significantly, many student teachers testify that carefully prepared plans have the potential to raise their confidence in RE teaching. Importantly, it supports teachers when they reflect on their practice.

Planning cycle

Planning in educational literature is usually presented as a cyclical process. Familiarity with the planning cycle provides some direction and time for reflection for future learning. It has been mentioned to assist you in revisiting the planning process and, importantly, to emphasise that RE lessons should be given detailed thought. You should avoid taking excessive recourse to quick-fix solutions such as worksheets or some easily accessible materials available online. You need to recognise and identify the key features and benefits of good planning in RE. Significantly you should keep in mind the aims and purposes of RE at all stages of the planning process and ensure that the sequence of learning and progress is considered at the very outset.

Planning backwards

Another model is known as planning backwards. This suggests that teachers must begin by identifying the outcomes and results which they intend to observe. Thereafter, they should determine the evidence they would expect from their pupils. In other words, to establish how they will know what they want their pupils to know. Finally, to plan and decide the teaching method/s and learning experiences that will achieve the desired impact.

Planning for the environment

There are many characteristics of good teaching including the need for clear planning, preparation, classroom management, environment and knowledge and understanding of internal and external factors (Wiliam 2013). You should move beyond the tendency of looking at planning from the viewpoint of documents and of positioning the learning environment as a segment of behaviour management. Planning is about relationships. You should reflect on positioning your relationship with the pupils, the ethos of your classroom and its physical environment within the segment of planning as they are integrated as they flow with the flow of the planning cycle.

The Teachers' Standards expects you to establish a safe and stimulating environment for pupils, rooted in mutual respect (DfE 2021). This environment should be complemented with features, which take account of and promote the spiritual, moral, social and cultural development of pupils. The celebration, in your classroom environment, of images, texts and artefacts, and, occasionally, music from religious traditions and cultural groups will assist pupils to understand their lives in relation to those around them (Hill 2014:239).

Beyond the physical environment, you need to be aware, as noted above, of your pupils' religious and cultural backgrounds, extrinsic and intrinsic motivators, the context of socialisation, their preferences to learning activities, their self-image and their expectations.

School planning and the locally agreed syllabus

Before venturing to detail the three layers of planning in school, it is important to recap the relationship between locally agreed syllabi (LAS) and school planning. Some are detailed with LTP, MTP and STP (Short-Term Plan), others are less, and devolve MTP and STP to their schools. In essence, a LAS is the long-term mega planning document for an authority. A LAS establishes the aims, objectives and basis for planning learning in RE for maintained schools across an authority or more. A LAS specifies broadly what must be taught, while affording teachers the opportunity to exercise their professional judgement to determine the detail, sequence, pedagogy and resources to be used. They also tend to specify and exemplify the principles, steps of progression and models of assessment. This gives teachers a coherent structure for planning and makes clear what pupils will achieve and the progress they will make. In turn, this enables effective reporting and target setting. Some LAS apply a pedagogical approach or an enquiry approach, although this is not necessary.

Other LAS offer pedagogical models. They prefer their syllabus to be delivered using a pedagogical approach (Cumbria 2017; Hampshire 2016; Norfolk 2019; Wedell 2010). Nevertheless, a LAS is not intended to be a detailed scheme of work to be fully delivered by all teachers to all pupils in a school. It is the role of the RE subject leader, alongside teachers and senior managers, to use the LAS to design and plan an appropriate curriculum and learning experiences for their respective schools. The concern of the LAS would be that schools ensured that their programme of study is delivered and requirements are met. Nevertheless, conceptually and practically, some schools consider their LAS as their long-term plan for RE. In such cases, subject leaders use their professional judgement to plan 'Learning Structures' (Schemes of Work) appropriate to their pupils' learning needs, experiences and the school's curriculum maps to inform their MTP for RE. This would need to be supplemented with some background knowledge, contextual understanding and familiarity with the local area. Such a combination will provide meaningful and relevant opportunities for the pupils to learn RE (about and from religion and belief) (Hill 2014:243). In turn, from this MTP, class teachers are then able to plan lessons (STP) for their classes, which build on their pupils' prior learning and ensure that they design appropriate learning experiences and opportunities in the classroom for all pupils.

Stages in planning

Planning is usually undertaken at three levels within different contexts. LTP provides an overview for teaching for all the years in a pupil's education in school for RE. In some instances, this might include the whole school curricula outlines which set the topics for study within each year group as reflected in a local syllabus or programme for RE. MTP provides the details of the program for a particular year. These tend to include relevant activities, resources and assessment opportunities. The third level is known as STP (lesson or session plan) which has greater detail because of the pupils being taught.

Long-term planning

The key features of a LTP are that it should be sequential, coherent, provide continuity and progression within the whole school. It shows what units or topics are to be taught throughout each year group, as such, the responsibility of this usually lies with the RE subject leader. LTP must identify what pupils should know and understand by the end of each year and how that contributes to what they will go on to learn. A LTP is a useful mechanism to ensure that pupils are not learning Christmas, Eid, Diwali and other recurring events in similar and repetitive ways every year without additional depth and sophistication. A LTP might also demonstrate the term during which certain themes, big questions or topics are delivered across key stages. Some LTPs also map out transitional matters between year groups. Others will record when, where and for whom external visits and visitors will be organised. In essence, a LTP for RE reflects the vision, mission, values, ethos and needs of a particular school and its pupils. It also reveals the intent, implementation and impact of RE. Some LTPs may include transitional arrangements to show continuity, progression and sequences from one year to another or from one topic such as festivals during the different years.

An overview of an LTP

Schools often refer to their LTP or MTP as a scheme of work. Compare the two schemes of work shown in Tables 8.1 and 8.2, and consider the titles of the units, the position of the topic in relation to the age of the pupils, sequence, continuity, progression and the representation of religious and non-religious traditions (CIST 2004).

Mid-term planning

There are many models of MTP. Ostensibly, the MTP operates at the year group or phase level and demonstrates how each unit or topic will be taught in a term or half a term. In the main, the responsibility for producing this lies with teachers in consultation with the RE subject leader. Herein lie opportunities for teachers to embed their critical thinking, innovation and creativity. The planning format and the extent of the detail will depend on individual schools; some create their own whereas others use published layouts or those offered by a LAS. The MTP sets out what is expected to be delivered through the lessons to enable the intended learning to be met. They also determine the age-related expectations and the most appropriate content for pupils. The MTP also outlines the duration in terms of weeks or number of anticipated lessons, resources, key questions and notes for teachers.

Teachers should plan to use a variety of strategies to deliver their MTP. The RE subject leader should ensure this is reflected across the school and it might be a useful exercise, based on an

Table 8.1 RE-based topics

Map of learning – RE-based topics					
Stage	**Autumn term**		**Spring term**		**Summer term**
FS	Who am I? Where do I belong?		My community. Who are you? People who give and care		Who is God? Where and what are the signs of God
KS1 Y1	Friends and families	Who was Jesus?	Are rules needed?	The Bible	The Church	Living as a Christian
KS1 Y2	Our earth and the natural world	What are festivals for?	Stories and parables from the Bible	The Easter story	Rites of passages in life	
KS2 Y3	What is it like to be Jewish?		Who was Jesus?		Disciples of Jesus	
KS2 Y4	Harvest	Christians and the Creation story?	Good and bad/ right and wrong	Christian hope and love	Hindu Dharma	
KS2 Y5	Rosh Hashanah and Yom Kippur	Repentance and forgiveness	Festival of Pesach	The festival of Easter	Who is the Holy Spirit?	The Worldwide Church
KS2 Y6	Diwali – festival of light	Jesus – the light of the world	Christian worship and prayer	Hindu worship and prayer	What is it like to be a Hindu?	Pilgrimage – Christian

Table 8.2 Theme-based RE						
Map of learning – Theme-based RE						
	Key Stage 1		**Key Stage 2**			
	Year 1	**Year 2**	**Year 3**	**Year 4**	**Year 5**	**Year 6**
Autumn 1	Unit 1.1 Ourselves	Unit 2.1 Our Family	Unit 3.1 Rites and rituals	Unit 4.1 Faith in Action	Unit 5.1 Communities	Unit 6.1 The journey of life
Autumn 2	Unit 1.2 Giving	Unit 2.2 Light and dark	Unit 3.2 Remembering	Unit 4.2 Light	Unit 5.2 Peace	Unit 6.2 celebrations
Spring 1	Unit 1.3 Stories	Unit 2.3 Leaders	Unit 3.3 Heroes and heroines	Unit 4.3 Leaders	Unit 5.3 Preachers and teachers	Unit 6.3 Justice and freedom
Spring 2	Unit 1.4 Special times	Unit 2.4 Beginnings and Endings	Unit 3.4 Fasting and Food	Unit 4.4 Festivals	Unit 5.4 Worship and devotion	Unit 6.4 Hope
Summer 1	Unit 1.5 Living in our world	Unit 2.5 Prayer, promises and poems	Unit 3.5 Sacred Books	Unit 4.5 Belief	Unit 5.5 Earth, water and fire	Unit 6.5 Stories and songs
Summer 2	Unit 1.6 Worship	Unit 2.6 Inside sacred places	Unit 3.6 Sacred journeys	Unit 4.6 Our world and the environment	Unit 5.6 Pilgrimage and Journeys	Unit 6.6 Sacred Places

analysis of all MTPs, to track the various strategies being deployed by all the teachers. This provides an overview and helps to show the extent to which pupils are experiencing a wide range of learning and pedagogical approaches. In some schools, you may notice that some MTP are a detailed scheme of work to be delivered by teachers to pupils. In such cases, individual STPs may not be prepared.

Short-term planning

STP is sometimes referred to as lesson plans, lesson overviews or weekly plans. During your school-based training, you are most likely to be required to provide a lesson plan to the person carrying out a formal observation of your lesson. In some schools, as part of your continuous professional development, senior managers may also expect you to provide them with a plan, sometimes ahead of your lesson, as they quality assure and monitor teaching in their school.

A lesson plan is important as it enables you to think through carefully each episode and process involved in teaching your lesson. It is more than a physical form. It is part of a continuous process of learning, which reflects teachers' thought procedures of how they deliver and guide pupils' learning (Robinson, Bingle and Howard 2013). Planning your teaching will assist you in rationalising the decisions you will have made about your teaching.

In many schools, lesson plans are prepared, whereas, in others, MTPs suffice as they detail the requirements of what and how lessons are to be delivered. Nevertheless, you need to be clear about learning being progressive. To enable progression at least two lessons with sequential learning is required as it ensures that activities are planned in the correct order to support outcomes to be attained and for children to understand how they have achieved the objectives (Barnes 2015c).

Having said that, you need to adopt a flexible approach to your plans to accommodate for the unexpected. Remember the plan is a means to an end and not an end in itself. Therefore, as a teacher, you should not be held back from responding to the impromptu questions and natural curiosity of pupils (Grigg and Hughes 2013:24). You must be prepared not only for teaching spontaneously but also to be led, in a reasonably different direction following the inquisitiveness of your pupils. It is you, the autonomous, reflective and decision-making person, who uses your experience, initiative, innovation and creativity to interpret the specific requirements of the RE curriculum and turn it into sequential and coherent lessons for your pupils. Your lesson should balance between internal and external rewards (Hewitt and Wright 2019).

Moreover, over-planning can be an issue for teaching challenging classes (Fautley and Savage 2013). Teachers can become over-reliant on planning, failing to adapt teaching to the current situation. Therefore, professional judgements need to be made on how the lesson should be delivered. Timings may need to be adjusted, or more explanation may be needed (Fautley and Savage 2013).

You may find it helpful to note what you will do during a lesson and with whom so that you do not inadvertently give an impression that you are supporting and working in isolation. Thus you need to minimise this perception and work with all pupils, when necessary. Related to this is the role of supporting adults. An issue with teaching assistance is that their understanding of their role, and the perception of differentiation, as well as of RE itself, may not match the teacher's (Fancourt 2012:220). Therefore, a conversation about intent, implementation and impact should be had at the planning stage.

Plans should be simple and not over complicated. A lesson plan indicates the consideration that you have given to their previous learning, content, subject vocabulary, key questions, the process of learning and how to learn, pupils' experiences and learning needs, anticipated pupil responses, progress and intervention, time management, organisation of pupils, assessment, deployment of adults, resources and the next step. You may also want to take account of the disciplines which might inform your lesson and how they could be applied.

As a developing teacher, you will have to recognise that they are different formats used by schools. They should not burden themselves with excessive detail. These formats in themselves are less of a concern. Nevertheless, examine each of the features below and reflect on the purpose and impact it can have upon pupils' learning and the quality of your teaching. You should also compare and contrast the models when you receive them and evaluate the strengths and limitations of each different template.

To plan and teach well-structured lessons, the Core Content Framework expects you to know that effective teachers introduce new material in steps, explicitly linking new ideas to what has been previously studied and learned. Paired and group activities can increase pupil success, but to work together effectively pupils need guidance, support and practice. You should also know that how pupils are grouped is also important; care should be taken to monitor the impact of groupings on pupil attainment, behaviour and motivation. Where prior knowledge is weak, pupils are more likely to develop misconceptions, particularly if new ideas are introduced too quickly (DfE 2019).

Prior learning

- Do you need to revisit prior learning?
- What is the purpose of your recap and retrieval?

Key questions

- What is the Big Question?
- What are the subsidiary questions?
- How do the subsidiary questions relate to the Big Question?

Subject vocabulary/concept

- Which ones are new?
- Which ones are for consolidation?

Learning objectives

- ■ Do they consist of knowledge, understanding, skills and attitudes?
- ■ Are they expressed in child-friendly language?
- ■ Do you plan to discuss and explain them to the class?
- ■ Think about the extra educational value in requiring pupils to copy them verbatim.
- ■ Are they linked to or derived from the MTP?
- ■ Will you adapt these to meet the learning needs of all pupils?
- ■ Do they reflect ambitious intentions?
- ■ Are you equipped with strong knowledge which your learners need?
- ■ Are they communicated meaningfully or mechanistically?

Assessment

- ■ Have you given thought to assessment at an early stage in the planning process?
- ■ Does this describe pupil activity or the action you will undertake for the assessment?
- ■ Does it have features of assessment for learning?
- ■ Is it diagnostic in nature?
- ■ Does it take many forms – verbal, written, visual?
- ■ Will adults, pupils, or both carry it out?
- ■ Is the intent reflected in assessment results?

Success criteria

- ■ Make these explicit and explain to them so that they know how to achieve
- ■ Use these to give formative feedback and feedforward so that they know what they have achieved and what they need to do to progress further in RE

Introduction

- ■ Is it captivating and motivational?
- ■ Is this short and sharp?

Main activity

- ■ Is the pace appropriate? as an undeveloped pace can result in pupils switching off or struggling
- ■ Are the activities challenging? as too difficult or too easy task may discourage them
- ■ What specific action will be taken for those pupils whose first language is not English to support them to fully access the RE curriculum?
- ■ What specific action will be taken for those pupils with SEND to support them to fully access the RE curriculum?
- ■ If learning is effective, pupils will have achieved regardless of their barriers, what will you do to minimise the effect of barriers to learning?
- ■ Is there a clear knowledge teaching?
- ■ Is there a sequence in your lessons?
- ■ Do the tasks build their understanding progressively?
- ■ Are you going to offer high-quality materials?

- Are they sufficient or too many?
- Is there repetition to embed information in the long-term memory?
- Is discussion included?
- How are pupils to be grouped?

Plenary

- Do you need one?
- What is the purpose?
- How long will you have it for?

Teaching resources

- How will these enhance your teaching and support all pupils' learning?

Summary

This section emphasised the importance and need for planning. It highlighted some principles, which will provide affordance to high-quality planning. Some planning models were illustrated to make you aware of what some schools might be using and their rationale was considered. Some essential features of lesson planning were presented to support you in considering your formats (Box 8.4).

BOX 8.4 VIGNETTE: PLANNING

My parents are originally from Bangladesh. However, since I was born in the UK, I believe I have conformed to British culture. The faith I practice is Islam and have always tried to practice it. My personal educational experience had been a ride with some stages of struggles on the way, also with some strong support systems around. I have a degree in Education Studies but social studies have always interested me too.

I have always been interested in teaching but could never decide until the placement year of my undergraduate degree. My dad had been a primary school teacher in Bangladesh. I believe one thing about teaching I valued most is that time is given to learners to teach and support their development. My placement experiences made a great contribution towards helping me decide teaching as my future career ambition, which I feel I enjoyed the most. I engaged with SEND pupils from which I began to question how and why teaching must be accessible to all pupils. It also allowed me to recognise the role and demands of a teacher more closely.

My teaching philosophy is built on a simple but strong belief that all children are unique individuals and can be stimulated in different educational environments to grow physically, mentally, emotionally and socially. Although my RE knowledge hadn't always been great, I've always had an enthusiasm for RE. Following the question of what is RE's place in the curriculum, I realised that RE is marginalised when in fact it tries to deliver an inclusive education for pupils through concepts of differences, acceptance and morality.

I have planned for an RE lesson and contributed to many RE discussions in my placements to understand the importance of teaching RE. I feel it affects me more. Now I feel that I must contribute as a leading RE specialist.

I feel RE is all around, my family and friends believe RE is important to respect and understand other pupils' practices and faith. RE allows unity and humanity in the community that demonstrates a most diverse society around the UK. I am hoping that children will get what they are entitled to which is receiving information in RE which is still an important subject study. I am hoping to gain a better understanding of why RE is marginalised in our schools and curriculum when it is mandatory in law. I fear challenging parent perception who may want to opt-out in teaching their child RE in believing that it is indoctrination. My concerns have been, how much of the complexity in RE will challenge other pupils' ideas and whether it could create a conflict in teaching RE at schools.

At my placement, RE was mostly taught through cross-curricular connections. It mostly involved the Christian faith when in fact the majority of the school were from other religions. This was obvious as learners demonstrated practising their faith in Sikhism by wearing a turban covering the hair (kesh).

References

Alexander, R. (2010) *Children, Their World, Their Education: Final Report and Recommendations of the Cambridge Primary Review*, Abingdon: Routledge.

Barnes, J. (2015a) *Cross-Curricular Learning 3–14*, London: SAGE. Third edition.

Barnes, J. (2015b) An introduction to cross-curricular learning, in P. Driscoll, A. Lambirth, and J. Roden, (Eds.) *The Primary Curriculum: A Creative Approach*. London: SAGE, pp. 260–283. Second edition.

Barnes, L. P. (Ed.) (2012) *Debates in Religious Education*, London: Routledge.

Barnes, R. (2015c) *Teaching Art to Young Children*, Routledge: London. Third edition.

Blaylock, L., Moss, F., and Pett, S. (2013) *Big RE: Enriching RE Through an RE Day or an RE Week*, Birmingham: RE Today Services. [Online] https://shop.retoday.org.uk/pdfs/9781905893874. pdf (Accessed 27/02/2021).

Brine, A., and Chater, M. (2020) A wholly educational rationale for worldviews, in M. Chater (Ed.) *Reforming RE*, Melton: John Catt, pp. 95–113.

CIST (2004) http://www.cist.org.uk/pv/pm/pp1001.htm (Accessed 27/02/2021).

Cumbria (2017) *Cumbria Agreed Syllabus for Religious Education Revised 2017*, Cumbria SACRE: Cumbria County Council.

Cush, D. (2007) Should religious studies be part of the compulsory state school curriculum? *British Journal of Religious Education*, 29, (3), pp. 217–227.

DCSF (Department for Children, Schools and Families) (2010) *Religious Education in English Schools: Nonstatutory Guidance 2010*, Nottingham: DCSF Publications. DCSF-00114-2010.

DfE (Department for Education) (2021) *Teachers' Standards Guidance for School Leaders, School Staff and Governing Bodies*, Crown Copyright. Reference: DFE-00066-2011 [Online] https:// assets.publishing.service.gov.uk/government/uploads/system/uploads/attachment_data/ file/1007716/Teachers__Standards_2021_update.pdf (Accessed 19/09/2021).

DfE (2019) *ITT Core Content Framework*, London: Crown Copyright. Reference: DfE-00230-2019.

Desailly, J. (2015) *Creativity in the Primary Classroom*, London: SAGE.

Dinham, M., and Shaw, M. (2015) *RE for Real*, Goldsmiths, UOL & Culham St. Gabriel's. [Online] https://www.gold.ac.uk/media/documents-by-section/departments/research-centres-and-units/research-units/faiths-and-civil-society/REforREal-web-b.pdf (Accessed 16/11/2020).

Erricker, C. (2010) *Religious Education: A Conceptual an Interdisciplinary Approach for Secondary Level*, London: Routledge.

Fancourt, N. (2012) Differentiation, in L. P. Barnes (Ed.) *Debates in Religious Education*, Abingdon: Routledge, pp. 213–222.

Fancourt, N. (2016) The classification and framing of religious dialogues in two English schools, *British Journal of Religious Education*, 38, (3), pp. 325–340.

Fautley, M., and Savage, J. (2013) *Lesson Planning for Effective Learning*, Maidenhead: McGraw-Hill Education.

Grigg, R., and Hughes, S. (2013) *Teaching Primary Humanities*, Harlow: Pearson.

Hampshire (2016) *Living With Difference: The Agreed Syllabus for Hampshire, Portsmouth, Southampton and the Isle of Wight*, HPSI SACRE: Hampshire, Portsmouth, Southampton and the Isle of Wight County Council.

Hewitt, D., and Wright, B. (2019) *Engaging, Motivating and Empowering*, London: SAGE.

Hill, E. (2014) Religious Education, in P. Smith and L. Dawes (Eds.) *Subject Teaching in Primary Education*, London: SAGE, pp. 232–247.

James, M., and Stern, S. (2019) *Mastering Primary Religious Education*, London: Bloomsbury.

Kay, W., and Smith, D. L. (2000) Religious terms and attitudes in the classroom (Part 1), *British Journal of Religious Education*, 22, (2), pp. 81–90.

Kirschner, P. A. (2002) Cognitive load theory: Implications of cognitive load theory on the design of learning, *Learning and Instruction*, 12, (1), pp. 1–10.

Larkin, S., Freathy, R., Doney, J., and Freathy, G. (2020) *Metacognition, Worldviews and Religious Education: A Practical Guide for Teachers*, London: Routledge.

Lucas, B., and Spencer, E. (2017) *Teaching Creative Thinking: Developing Learners Who Generate Ideas and can Think Critically*, Carmarthen: Crown House.

McCreery, E., Palmer, S., and Voiels, V. (2008) *Teaching Religious Education*, Exeter: Learning Matters.

Moss, F. (2015) Engaging children creatively: Effective planning for developing inquiry, in S. Elton-Chalcraft (Ed.) *Teaching Religious Education Creatively*, Abingdon: Routledge, pp. 64–77.

Myatt, M. (2018) *The Curriculum: Gallimaufry to Coherence*, Melton: John Catt.

Myatt, M. (2020) *Curriculum Design for Religious Education in a Post-Commission World*, [Online] https://www.marymyatt.com/blog/curriculum-design-in-a-post-commission-world, (Accessed 27/02/2021).

Norfolk (2019) *Norfolk Agreed Syllabus 2019 A Religious Education for the Future*, Norfolk SACRE.

Ofsted (2013) *Religious Education: Realising the Potential*, Manchester: Crown Copyright. Reference No: 130068.

Ofsted (2021) *Research Review Series: Religious Education*, [Online] https://www.gov.uk/government/publications/research-review-series-religious-education/research-review-series-religious-education#fnref:155 (Accessed 18/07/2021).

Pett, S. (Ed.) (2015) *Religious Education: The Teacher's Guide*, Birmingham: RE Today Services.

Rivett, R. (Ed.) (2007) *A Teacher's Handbook of Religious Education*, Birmingham: RE Today Services. Third edition.

Robinson, C., Bingle, B., and Howard, C. (2013) *Primary School Placements: A Critical Guide to Outstanding Teaching*, Northwich: Critical Publishing.

Rowley, C., and Cooper, H. (2013) *Cross-Curricular Approaches to Teaching and Learning*, London: SAGE.

Sherringdon, T. (2019) *Rosenshine's Principles in Action*, Woodbridge: John Catt.

Sweller, J., Van Merrienboer, J. J., and Paas, F. G. (1998) Cognitive architecture and instructional design, *Educational Psychology Review*, 10, (3), pp. 251–296.

Watson, E., and Bradley, B. (2021) *The Science of Learning: 99 Studies That Everyone Should Know*, Abingdon: Routledge. Second edition.

Webster, M. (2010) *Creative Approaches to Teaching Primary RE*, London: Longman.

Webster, M. (2015) Religious Education, in M. Webster and S. Misra (Eds.) *Teaching the Primary Foundation Subjects*, Maidenhead: Open University Press, pp.127–142.

Webster, M., and Misra, S. (Eds.) (2015) *Teaching the Primary Foundation Subjects*, Maidenhead: Open University Press, pp. 1–9.

Wedell, K. (2010) Evaluating the impact of the Hampshire agreed syllabus: 'Living Difference' on teaching and learning in religious education, *British Journal of Religious Education*, 32, (2), pp. 147–161.

Wiliam, D. (2013) *Redesigning Schooling 3: Principled Curriculum Design*, London: Specialist Schools and Academies Trust. [Online] http://www.tauntonteachingalliance.co.uk/wp-content/uploads/2016/09/Dylan-Wiliam-Principled-curriculum-design.pdf (Accessed 27/02/2021).

Willingham, D. (2009) *Why Don't Students Like School?* San Francisco: Jossey-Bass.

Wintersgill, B. (Ed.) (2017) *Big Ideas for Religious Education*, Exeter: University of Exeter. [Online] http://socialsciences.exeter.ac.uk/media/universityofexeter/collegeofsocialsciencesandinternationalstudies/education/research/groupsandnetworks/reandspiritualitynetwork/Big_Ideas_for_RE_E-Book.pdf (Accessed 09/08/2021).

Wintersgill, B., Cush, D., and Francis, D. (2019) *Putting Big Ideas into Practice in Religious Education*, [Online] https://www.reonline.org.uk/wp-content/uploads/2019/05/Putting-big-ideas-into-Practice.pdf (Accessed 09/08/2021).

PART

Making it happen

9

Learning about learning

Introduction

This section considers a basic understanding of some theories and processes of learning summarised from Pritchard (2018). To find out more about the implications that some major theories may have on your teaching, you may find the critical perspectives and links to practice discussed by Aubrey and Riley (2019) useful. Bates (2019) offers succinct summaries of over 130 theories and models from different schools of thought. You will find more at https://infed. org/mobi/category/thinkers-and-innovators/ and in the *Science of Learning*, Watson and Busch (2021) have translated 99 of the most influential studies on the topic of learning into accessible overviews.

The Teachers' Standards define the minimum level of practice expected of trainees for the award of qualified teacher status. However, they make no direct reference to learning theory. Nevertheless, some familiarity with theory and research is implicit. Teachers must demonstrate knowledge and understanding of how pupils learn and how this impacts teaching, teachers should be able to promote a love of learning and children's intellectual curiosity and have a secure understanding of how a range of factors can inhibit pupils' ability to learn (DfE 2021). Thus, you need to know and learn about the learning process. Knowing about how learning takes place is important for developing curricula and activities and for selecting teaching methods and strategies. This will potentially contribute to successful and high-quality learning to take place in classrooms (Pritchard 2018:17).

Experience has shown that some students use theory, pedagogy, methods and strategies interchangeably, as though they all mean the same. Strategies are not the same as theories. The theory is something that can explain what is observed, upon which strategies – what is actually done in the classroom to achieve particular learning outcomes – are based (Pritchard 2018:17). Trainee teachers learn about a range of approaches and strategies to use and adopt in their teaching. However to approach your teaching without considering the underlying theory would be to leave the job only half completed and leaves you with little understanding of the reasons for such approaches (Pritchard 2018:18).

Given the changing educational landscape, becoming familiar with theories, which inform the design of curricula and teaching methods, has become more important. Aubrey and Riley (2019:1) argue that current education is being ideologically driven and promotes a traditional view of teaching and learning, which is focused on the acquisition of knowledge and skills needed to compete in the global market, rather than for personal fulfilment and development. They caution against a return to the more traditional, didactic and examination-focused approaches contrary to many theorists. If theories, which are based on empirical evidence and substantial observations of practice, are discounted in education, there is a risk of adopting formulaic and step-by-step approaches to teaching (Aubrey and Riley 2019:2). The *ITT Core Content Framework* expects ITT curricula to integrate additional analysis and critique of theory, research and expert practice (DfE 2019).

Theories of learning

In essence, behaviourism is a school of thought which focuses on motivation. It considers learning to be a matter of stimulus and response. Knowledge is transferred from teachers to pupils, who are seen as passive participants. Positive and negative reinforcement can be motivators for pupils. In response to the right stimulus, teachers give the information. Teachers use this behaviour to show pupils how they should react and respond. It is done in a repetitive way to keep reminding pupils of the behaviour and expectations that teachers desire. Repetition and positive reinforcement go together.

Constructivists theorise that pupils actively construct their knowledge by using their previous knowledge as a basis to build on new information. Learning is seen as unique to an individuals' experience. Pupils' background, previous knowledge, beliefs and experiences influence how they can learn. They also learn how to learn, as they learn. Learning is an active process and a social activity, which uses discussions, group interaction, reading and activities. Teachers provide contextual knowledge, rather than isolated facts. Learning and knowledge are personal, as each pupil will have their own experiences to draw from. In addition to experiences and actions, the mind is engaged for successful learning. Intrinsic motivation is key to learning.

The humanism school of thought argues that education should focus on the needs of the individual learner and that what is important are the aspects of personal and emotional growth (Aubrey and Riley 2019:3). Another school has provided theories related to brain-based learning or information processing theory which focuses on the anatomy of the brain and its capacity to cope with complex human reactions such as intelligence, thinking and learning (Bates 2019:72).

Confucius (Kong Zi) (551–479 BC)

Collinson, Plant and Wilkinson (2000:218) note that Confucius believed passionately in the pursuit of knowledge. Education was a matter of acquiring moral knowledge. This was not simply knowledge that certain actions and attitudes were good; it was also knowledge acquired in practice and through experience; by being good and by doing good. One learned from the example of one's teacher and then taught others by being an example for them. Such education began in a person's early years and continued throughout life. *Ren* or benevolence is the most important single attribute of what he called 'the gentleman'. This is the person who loves learning so much that in eager pursuit of it he 'forgets his food' and 'does not perceive that old age is coming on' (Collinson, Plant and Wilkinson 2000:219).

Knowledge and learning help to develop a moral acumen so that one can see how to deploy one's generosity towards a true good. Knowledge, learning and experience help a person to recognise what is unalterable in life and to distinguish it from what may be changed by endeavour. He practised a system of education that was open to all and in which the actual practice of what a person had learned was the test of genuine ability. It did not suffice merely to adopt the ways of 'a gentleman'; one must retain and practise them by ruling well, by guiding others and establishing correct rites by one's example (Collinson, Plant and Wilkinson 2000:220–221).

Confucius did not engage in elaborate metaphysical speculation; nor did he advance any theory about the nature or possibility of human knowledge. Yet he was sensitive to the limits of what the human intellect might claim to know and was reluctant to make claims that were not securely grounded in what would commonly count as experiential knowledge. A man once spoke to him rashly. To him, he said, 'Where a gentleman is ignorant, one would expect him not to offer any opinion'. He remarked to a follower: 'Shall I tell you what it is to know?

To say you know when you know, and to say you do not when you do not, that is knowledge' (Collinson, Plant and Wilkinson 2000:222).

Abu Hamid Muhammad ibn Muhammad Al-Ghazali (1058–1111)

To him, rational knowledge was attained exclusively by the intellect and religious knowledge was received from the prophets. Both were important for the purification of the mind and soul. However, the ultimate aim of knowledge was the purification of the soul (Al Zeera 2001:77). Through reason, the soul had the potential to know the essence of things and knowledge of God (Jackson 2006:88).

Theoretical knowledge assisted in the comprehension of the transcendental world. Practical knowledge complimented theoretical knowledge and its active function lies in human conduct. To him, theoretical knowledge of scriptures was insufficient. Thus, education should habituate children to practice acts of devotion as well.

Parents were duty-bound to educate children in good conduct. Al-Ghazali saw them as bright as jewels and as soft as candles free from any impressions. They were soft like clay in which every seed could grow. Therefore, with good training of character, children could follow the truth in adulthood and gain happiness, but a lack of proper education would spoil them.

He emphasised the preparation of lessons by teachers and the need for a thorough knowledge of what they were to teach. Lessons were to be developed in collaboration with pupils. He advanced the idea that new knowledge should be related to prior knowledge. He dissuaded teachers from presenting complex material in the beginning and encouraged them to proceed from the simple to the complex. He reasoned that if complex matters were introduced very early, pupils could be confused and lose interest in the subject. Teachers should have love and sympathy for their pupils and should embody good manners so that pupils may emulate their example. Al-Ghazali encouraged teachers to have full knowledge of the abilities, capacities, interests of their pupils, and plan accordingly (Alavi 1988:39–48).

John Locke (1632–1704)

Concerning education, he addressed the nature of human understanding, how the human mind collects, organises, classifies information from the senses and ultimately makes judgements based on what has been collected, organised and classified. Locke emphasised the crucial role played by the experience of the senses, rather than what he called speculation. He set out the idea that at birth the human mind is complete and likened it to a blank writing slate, a tabula rasa, ready to be written upon as experience presents itself to the learner. Simple notions, he suggests, are added to and built upon, simple ideas are expanded and combined to create a more complex understanding. He separated experience into two categories: his ideas of sensation – seeing, hearing and feeling; and, ideas of reflection: thinking, questioning and believing (Bates 2019:14). Locke proposed an approach modelled on the rigorous scientific method of experimental science, a time when rote and direct instruction were the order of the day (Pritchard 2018:140). According to Locke, the goal of education is to create a person who obeys reason rather than passion and Locke believed firmly in nurture as the major driving force in child development. Locke considered that learning should be enjoyable, and language and communication to be a critical element (Pritchard 2018:141).

Jean-Jacques Rousseau (1712–1778)

Rousseau suggested a more natural and authentic alternative to the didactic style of education. Teach your scholar to observe the phenomena of nature; you will soon rouse his curiosity, but if you would have it grow, do not be in too great a hurry to satisfy this curiosity. Put the problems before him and let him solve them himself. Let him know nothing because you have told him, but because he has learnt it for himself. Rousseau emphasised how allowing free expression and a focus on the environment instead of acting to repress curiosity will produce a well-balanced, free-thinking and educated child. A child's education should focus on the child's interests. Rousseau viewed education as to how the natural makeup of individuals could be extended not only to improve the individual but also to improve society. This would be brought about by the manner in which individuals engaged with each other. The aim of developing the character of individuals, for both their own sake and for the sake of society, was the most basic aim of all and should not be minimised by the transmission and reception of factual information which dominated education in his time. Teachers were to guide learners in such a way that they come to understand the difference between right and wrong. This understanding should come about not because of being punished, but through coming to understand the consequences of actions (Pritchard 2018:142). Pupils should be able to learn what they want to learn, pupils should be able to learn when they want to, and at the speed, they want to. Teaching should be based on discovery and guidance and enriched by the covert direction of the teacher (Bates 2019:16).

Johann Pestalozzi (1746–1827)

To him, education should be broken into its basic elements to have the fullest understanding of what it really is. He stressed that every aspect of the child's life contributes to the formation of the child's personality, character and reason, and is based on what the child learns. He valued individual differences, sense perception and, what he termed, the child's self-activity. Pestalozzi suggested a four-sphere concept of life. The three 'exterior' spheres: home and family, vocational and individual self-determination and state and nation. These spheres recognised the family, the utility of individuality and the applicability of the parent-child relationship to society as a whole in the development of a child's character, the child's attitude towards learning and the child's sense of duty. The last sphere, the inner sense, refers to the view that education, having provided a means of fulfilling basic needs, leads to a feeling of inner peace and a firm belief in God. From him, we now consider the following:

- Taking account of the interests and needs of pupils.
- A child-centred rather than teacher-centred approach.
- Active rather than passive participation.
- Giving children direct experiences of the world and use of natural objects as part of their schooling.
- Use of the senses in training pupils in observation and judgement.
- Cooperation between the school and the home.
- All-round education – an education of 'the head, the heart and the hands, but which is led by the heart', should form a central element of the curriculum.
- Cross-curricular learning.
- Authority based on love, not fear (positivity rather than negativity, respect and mutual trust).
- Education emphasises how things are taught as well as what is taught (Pritchard 2018:143–145).

Friedrich Froebel (1782–1852)

Froebel was best known for the 'kindergarten system' and for education through informal and naturalistic means. His philosophy consists of four basic components: free self-activity, creativity, social participation and motor expression. In his first kindergarten, education was based on 'play and activity' and the nurturing of creativity through the systematic deployment of a sequence of gifts (such things as coloured balls, mosaic tiles, geometrical blocks and much more). His goals were to teach children how to learn, observe, reason, express and create through play while employing philosophies of unity and interconnectedness. The kindergarten has three essential elements: creative play, singing and dancing and observing and nurturing plants to stimulate an interest in the natural world (Pritchard 2018:145). Parents are the first educators. There should be close links between home and school. The main goal is to teach children socially, academically, emotionally, physically and spiritually (Bates 2019:208).

John Dewey (1859–1952)

Dewey's concern with interaction, reflection, experience and interest in community and democracy were brought together to form a highly compelling approach to education. He did consider that children should, in some measure, direct their learning, but he also believed strongly that children need a clear structure and guidance to allow them to control their learning. Dewey saw the role of education as being far more important than the acquisition of factual knowledge. It should have a broad social purpose and prepare learners to become effective members of society. The teacher is not in the school to impose certain ideas or to form certain habits in the child but is there as a member of the community to select the influences, which shall affect the child and to assist them in properly responding to these influences (Pritchard 2018:146). The teacher becomes a partner in the learning process, guiding learners to independently discover meaning within a subject context. He held some of the tenets of the child-centred movement, but he was not a fully-fledged free-educator. He believed that learning should include constructive occupations and games should be built into the curriculum so that learners are more engaged. Game-like activities and practical tasks break down the artificial gap between school and life outside of school (Pritchard 2018:146). He placed importance on reflection for both teachers and learners (Aubrey and Riley 2019:8).

Rudolf Steiner (1861–1925)

Steiner believed that the fundamental aim of education should be to develop every child's potential. His approach provides children with the ability to think clearly, with sensitivity and with a strong will. It assumes the interdependence of physical, emotional, social, spiritual and cognitive development. Steiner believed that children flourish and learn best in a calm, peaceful, predictable, familiar and unhurried learning environment that emphasises sensory experiences and feelings. He also believed that young children need to experience the relevance of their world before they are expected to separate themselves from it and begin to analyse and understand it in a detached, meaningful way. Learning, he suggests, becomes meaningful in relation to its relevance to the life of the child and learning should be integrated into the child's experience of daily living. For this reason, the learning experience of children under the age of seven in Steiner schools is not subject-based but almost completely integrated. However, Steiner's approach goes further than simply teaching a short cross-curricular topic each half term. It is an approach to the total curriculum. There is an early and significant emphasis on art, the use of the natural world and the links between art and science. Children are introduced to reading, writing and mathematics at a later age than is traditional in the UK. Singing is a part of daily routine and children are encouraged to play a musical instrument. The story is the main approach. Children revisit and retell the stories to improve both memory and the spoken word. At a later stage, after recall and expression have developed, the process of writing is introduced. Individualisation, creativity, independence and imagination are at the heart of the Steiner curriculum and the use of technology at young ages is discouraged (Bates 2019:242; Pritchard 2018:147–149).

Maria Montessori (1870–1952)

Unlike Rousseau's blank slate, Montessori believed that children were born with a unique potential for learning. The role of education was to reveal this potential fully. She believed that those with responsibility for educating children should pay attention to preparing a natural and life-supporting environment, observing the child moving and engaging within this environment and adapting the environment to allow the child to work towards fulfilling their potential mentally, emotionally, physically and spiritually.

The method emphasises the individual nature of learning, independence of the child and children are seen as inherently curious and driven to learn. The method does not emphasise knowledge acquisition for its own sake. She believed that adults expect children to be disciplined, and at the same time be receptive to the information presented to them by teachers. She wanted to allow children to make discoveries about their world through a practical approach, rather than the information being passed down from above. What the child experiences and internalises depends largely on the setting in which they find themselves and what types of information and experiences might be provided.

Children are ready to learn different types of skills at different specific points in their development. The age at which each sensitive period occurs will vary from child to child. Teachers must be aware of when the right time is to introduce new ideas to individual children; this, in turn, requires close observation and intimate knowledge of the child's development. Montessori believed that classrooms should have readily available, plentiful and well-organised learning materials. The environment should be appealing, pleasing and attractive and include items that the teacher wants the child to experience. Montessori wanted children to be responsible for their education and in this way develop skills for later life. The teacher is less prominent and is there to be a guide for the child's independent learning. The teacher is an active observer and an assessor who makes decisions about when children have reached particular sensitive periods when new concepts might be introduced (Aubrey and Riley 2019:8; Pritchard 2018:148–150).

David Ausubel (1918–2008)

He proposed meaningful learning in opposition to rote learning. To learn meaningfully, the learner must relate new knowledge to what they already know. It places behaviourism in direct opposition to constructivism. However, Ausubel developed the notion further by devising what he called an advance organiser as a way to help learners to connect their existing ideas with new knowledge. He suggested that new concepts can be incorporated into more inclusive concepts to be internalised. These more inclusive concepts are advanced organisers. They can be verbal phrases or schematic diagrams, which outline an idea and its relation to others. The advance organiser provides a framework upon which to attach new information.

Ausubel's key concept is the cognitive structure. He sees this as the total of all the knowledge that we have acquired and the relationships between the facts, principles and concepts that make up that knowledge. This is learning that is related to experiences with events or objects and is usually the result of a positive commitment to relate new knowledge to prior learning. In contrast, he describes rote learning as arbitrary, verbatim, with the non-substantive incorporation of new knowledge into a cognitive structure. Rote learning requires little or no effort in the process of integration with existing concepts into a cognitive structure. It is not generally related to experience with events or objects and requires little or no commitment to relate new knowledge to prior learning. The role of the teacher is to clarify the aim of the lesson, present the organiser, relate the organiser explicitly to prior knowledge and make the organisation of the new material explicit (Pritchard 2018:150–151). Understanding and meaning are both vital for learning to take place, which must be organised and structured (Bates 2019:54).

Jerome Bruner (1915–2016)

Bruner recognised the importance of interest, motivation, culture and the environment in learning. The idea of a spiral curriculum considers that knowledge is refreshable and needs revisiting to further develop (Aubrey and Riley 2019:120). It reinforces understanding, gives greater depth and adds vigour. Unlike Piaget's sequential and predetermined stage, Bruner suggested three ways to develop experiences into learning. The *enactive mode* relates to where children do things for themselves through action and play. The *iconic mode* happens when children can comprehend images, pictures and numbers. The *symbolic mode* is where children can understand abstraction, language and reason. He stressed that the acquisition of these modes was not a sequential process, but relied on being developed with others.

Bruner's notion of discovery learning argued that behaviour modification was achieved through the learner participating actively in the process rather than being spoon-fed. Practitioners were not to impart information by rote learning but instead to facilitate the learning process by designing sessions that help the individual to discover the relationship between bits of information. A critical aspect of discovery learning is that learners should be given the essential information they need to solve the problem, but not organising it for them (Bates 2019:56).

Len Vygotsky (1896–1934)

Vygotsky believed that knowledge and thought are constructed through social interaction with family, friends, teachers and peers. He referred to the people that we learn from as Most Knowledgeable Others (MKOs) and the process of learning through social interaction as being in the Zone of Proximal Development (ZPD). He suggested that when learners were in the ZPD, they develop an understanding of a subject that may have been beyond their previous level of comprehension. He also developed the concept of scaffolding to describe the teacher's role in engaging with pupils and supporting their development while they were in the ZPD. He maintained that scaffolding could be used by teachers to help people safely take risks and reach a higher level of understanding than would be possible by the individual's efforts alone (Bates 2019:48). He considered play as vital for intellectual development (Aubrey and Riley 2019:59).

Albert Bandura (1925–2021)

Bandura suggested that behaviour modification using rewards and sanctions was too simplistic (Aubrey and Riley 2019:132). He proposed that people identify with, and imitate specific individuals with characters they deem desirable. Bandura thought that individuals were more likely to model those people that they can identify with. Self-efficacy is the confidence that an individual has in themselves to produce desired results. Self-regulation is the ability that a person has to regulate their behaviour, emotion and thoughts in responses to particular situations. He argued that behaviourism alone could not account for all learning. So, in his social learning theory, he proposed that behaviours are learnt through observing and imitation, and later, his social cognitive theory, took account of thought processes, like attention and memory, which he proposed were key to learning (Aubrey and Riley 2019:145).

The science of learning

Attention span

The extent of an individual's ability to stay focused for sustained periods is variable and shorter than is often assumed. 'Transient attention' refers to a short-term response to a stimulus that holds the individual's attention on a very temporary basis. A passing stimulus can take away attention from a task for a short period.

'Selective sustained attention' is needed if tasks are to be completed. Older children can pay attention and stay on task for longer than younger children. We can stay focused for longer when we are doing something that we find enjoyable, interesting or that is in some way intrinsically motivating. Remaining focused is also enhanced when tasks in question are easily carried out and if the task incorporates something that is being learnt for the first time. The negative effects on attention span are tiredness, hunger, local distractions and emotional stress (Pritchard 2018:154).

Cognitive flexibility theory

Cognitive flexibility theory was devised in response to the way that learners have been perceived to deal with information from multiple perspectives. The theory emphasises the importance of knowledge being constructed by the learner. Learners need to be allowed to develop their representations of information to learn effectively. When learning situations provide multiple representations from various types and sources and when the sources are interconnected at a sophisticated level, construction, rather than the transmission of knowledge leading to understanding, will proceed smoothly.

The integration of ideas and factual content rather than compartmentalisation, which is sometimes seen in formal learning situations, is encouraged. The theory suggests that the learner is better able to understand a complicated set of ideas if they are presented with multiple representations of the same information in different contexts. By experiencing the same concepts in a variety of forms, from a variety of media, it is considered that the learner will develop a greater number of neural connections and, in so doing, construct a stronger base of understanding. In this time of great accessibility to very large and technologically mediated sources of information and activity, the scope for presenting multiple representations of new ideas is large. Paying attention to these possibilities for a variety of representations has the potential to help in the planning and delivering of successful learning experiences (Pritchard 2018:155).

Cognitive load

The basic idea of cognitive load theory is that the capacity in working memory is limited and it is notoriously hard (maybe impossible) to realistically measure it (Watson and Busch 2021). This means that if a task requires too much capacity, learning will not proceed easily. The remedy to plan learning tasks is to make the best use of working memory capacity and to avoid what has been called cognitive overload. A distinction is made between long-term memory and short-term memory. Long-term memory is that part of memory where vast amounts of information are held, more or less permanently. Short-term memory is where small amounts of information are held, but only, for a very short period. More recently, the term 'short-term memory' has been replaced by the use of 'working memory' to stress that this component of memory is responsible for the processing of information, rather than being a temporary repository.

Looked at simplistically, we could characterise this as 'not giving them too much to think about at a time' and, in a way, this is accurate. Cognitive load is expected and without it, no work can progress. A problem arises when the load exceeds the capacity of the person processing it. For this reason, we can see that what overloads the mind of the beginner may not overload the mind of the notional expert in the subject. Teachers, in terms of cognitive load theory, should carefully consider the nature of the learning task and ensure that extraneous cognitive load, at least, is kept to a minimum (Pritchard 2018:156).

Dual coding theory

Paivio's theory presupposes that human cognition has two sub-systems, one for accessing and processing language and one for doing the same with non-verbal signals. Humans can deal simultaneously with language and with non-verbal events. The aspect of human cognition which deals with language is capable of symbolising functions for and interpreting the meaning of non-verbal objects, events and behaviour. 'Imagens' for mental images and 'logogens' for verbal entities are described by Paivio as 'chunks'. It is the chunks that are then processed and combined to present a coherent mental representation of the perceived reality. Dual coding theory suggests that presenting new material (facts, concepts) in a dual format allows for a greater prospect of understanding and that memory in the form of recall and recognition is made more reliable when information is presented in both visual and verbal form (Pritchard 2018:158).

Mindsets

Having high expectations that all learners can improve is central to good teaching (Watson and Busch 2021). Dweck proposes that the intelligence of a learner with a fixed mindset appears to be limited. In this frame of mind, challenges are avoided and attempting new aspects of work in question is considered pointless. Conversely, a growth mindset sees intelligence as capable of development. It was through efforts and perseverance that anyone could improve their ability, rather than results. Challenges are relished and the learner has a belief that improvement is possible. With a growth mindset, a lack of success and subsequent feedback is considered as positive and provides support for working towards improvement. With a fixed mindset, failing and receiving feedback is seen as negative. An individual can have different mindsets in different areas of activity. Individuals are not necessarily aware of their place on the mindset continuum. Mindsets can be affected by environmental events. When praise is used, for example, saying, 'Well done', children are far more likely to develop a fixed mindset. With a subtle change in wording, for example, 'Well done, you've worked very hard', they are more likely to develop a growth mindset (Aubrey and Riley 2019:262; Pritchard 2018:161–162). Learners need to be intrinsically motivated to want them to work (Bates 2019).

Spacing and interleaving

Ebbinghaus identified what is referred to as a 'Forgetting Curve'. He showed that newly acquired information is quickly forgotten if it is not in some way refreshed or reviewed after a short period. To increase retention to a fairly high degree, learners going back over the newly experienced content at short intervals seems to reinvigorate the systems for remembering and being able to recall to the extent that almost full recall is possible after quite some time from the initial learning event (Pritchard 2018:163).

Spacing

Spacing refers to the idea that to learn we need to practise or, in the terms of Ebbinghaus, 'review' newly learnt material in one way or another. Learning will benefit from repetition. Sometimes practice is scheduled to be over one or perhaps two extended periods (massed practice). Sometimes practice is taken in shorter bursts spread out over time (spaced practice) (Pritchard 2018:164). Spacing is more effective than cramming (Watson and Busch 2021).

Interleaving

The theory suggests that interleaving requires learners to constantly retrieve from memory. This continued recall allows learners to both install items more firmly into long-term memory and to be more agile when it comes to retrieving them. This calls into question the traditional system of lessons being of a certain length and in regular order.

If a learner is told that a list of words will be tested after having been studied for some time and then later told that it will not be tested, it is forgotten to a much greater extent, when it is subsequently tested, compared to other lists which the learner had been told would certainly be tested. This points to the importance of stressing at the stage of learning the purpose of the learning and possibly of referring to the future utility of the learning, if not stressing that it is being learnt simply for the sake of a test (Pritchard 2018:165–166).

The Zeigarnik effect

Zeigarnik theorised that, because our brains are essentially goal-focused, unfinished tasks would persist in memory for longer than the completed tasks. This has implications for practical learning contexts. It is suggested that a break in the learning activities – a recap or a short contrasting activity – has the potential to enhance the learning outcome. A 'cliffhanger' end to a television serial means that viewers are more likely to remember what is happening and be keen to watch the next episode. Zeigarnik discovered that people are likely to remember incomplete tasks better than they might remember completed tasks if the following conditions are met: the interruption comes in the middle or towards the end of the piece of work and there is a strategy in place for completing the task; the interruption is not expected; the learner actually aspires to complete the task (Pritchard 2018:166)

Summary

This section has offered a selection of the common theories as a basis to explain how learning takes place. These have influenced discourse in education research and practice. It is important to acknowledge that they all have limitations, as learning is a complex phenomenon. Nevertheless, they help in making more informed decisions about the design and delivery of learning. You need to know the substantive knowledge for Religious Education (RE) and understand how pupils learn. In addition to these, you need to know how to teach the subject content for learning to take place. This means you also need to learn how to sequence this logically and progressively so that it makes meaning to pupils. Pedagogical subject knowledge consists of knowing a range of teaching strategies and skills, planning and sequencing lesson and use appropriate assessment tools for the specific subject content.

CLASSICAL PEDAGOGIES

Introduction

In the earlier chapter you examined the significance of planning and evaluated some models. Having analysed learning theories, this section and the next chapter introduce you to the pedagogies of RE and other teaching methods. The UK has seen the emergence of a range of pedagogies of RE (Gearon 2013; Grimmitt 2000c:104). Some of these were developed following research and each contributed towards understanding the nature of RE in the UK and to the development of ways of learning and teaching appropriately to meet the demands of the subject and needs of pupils. These pedagogies also revealed the different ways in which the two main ideas of 'learning about RE' and 'learning from RE' were interpreted.

In RE there are some recurring themes in the debate about learning and teaching. First, there are questions about the nature of the subject; what should its curriculum constitute of and its compulsory status. Then, there is debate about its aim and purposes; whether it is about nurturing or understanding. The third concerns the process of learning and teaching, and finally, the role of the child. As you have read in the earlier chapter, the first two have been attended to by policymakers. The latter two are left to the discretion of the professional teacher. Atwal (2019) asserts that the greatest influence on the quality of pupil's learning experiences in schools is the quality of teaching. That said, the current expectation is that you should learn that explicitly teaching pupils the knowledge and skills they need to succeed within particular subject areas is beneficial (DfE 2019). Nevertheless, how this is done is debatable, and, as such, is at the heart of these two chapters.

To begin with, issues of teacher identity are raised and then the significance of pedagogy is discussed which is followed by an examination of the overview of some well-established pedagogies. The key characteristics are presented with examples of how they can operate in the classroom. The process of putting into action some of these pedagogies is then illustrated. Before ending the chapter, a pedagogical fantasy is shared to emphasise the need for teachers to experiment and inquire about their practices. Overall, the intent is to show the rigour expected in the development of pedagogies and the role of research and the significance of rooting these in the classroom.

You the teacher

Teaching is not a neutral activity and teacher identity is complex. It is influenced by a host of factors including socio-culture environments, policies, theories, life-world and experiences of the pupils you teach, your own beliefs, values, experiences and about what the purpose of education is, what should be taught and not, and how it should be taught. Your conceptualisation of what it means to be a teacher, whether it is a competent craftsperson or a professional scholar (Stone 2021), or both, play a role too.

One of the branches of philosophy is epistemology, which is concerned with the different ways of knowing, and thinking about what the most valid ways of knowing are. The concern for teachers is to reflect on how they can move beyond their personal opinions and folk pedagogy to something that has validity, rigour and is wise. Some things teachers know because they are based on a reason other than experience. Then teachers learn from research and experienced others. Importantly, teachers know based on their everyday empirical knowledge through observations and interactions with pupils. Thus, through these, teachers develop their own 'self', pedagogy and philosophy of education. Harris and Lowe (2018) maintain that teachers might find themselves in agreement with the current prevailing ideology of education or at times find themselves teaching in ways which they fundamentally believe to be misinformed. Thus, they suggest, following Pollard, that a reflective teacher should be open-minded enough to constructively critique their own beliefs, as well as those of others (Harris and Lowe 2018:74). Effective teaching demands engagement with a broad range of knowledge bases, which Stone (2021:42) argues are much more powerful when they are research-informed. Whilst acknowledging that teachers need to be competent, and their work needs to draw on evidence of 'what works', however, teachers need to be able to make wise educational judgments (Biesta 2012) to develop the capacity to be critical of policy, practice and research. You are invited to look at 'what works' style research and go beyond this to ensure you have a broad spectrum to draw from.

Pedagogy and methodology

There are many delineations and understandings of the term pedagogy. It is seen by some as the 'art of knowing' as a teacher how to conduct intentional and systematic intervention to influence the development of the learner (Baumfield 2012:205). Pedagogy in Greek means the process by which a pupil is led to learning. This has informed the role of the teacher as being someone holding the pupils and walking with them from the unknown to the known. In other words, pedagogy is the knowledge of how pupils develop and learn, and the practices enacted to serve that process.

Pedagogy is more than the process which leads a learner to learn. Chater and Erricker (2013:46) explain that it is a complex set of forces acting on every teacher, whether they know it or not. These forces include the curriculum, the surrounding culture and the lifeworld of the children and the depth of the teacher's understanding of these. Children do not differ only in age and 'ability', which explains why teaching is complicated and contingent (Claxton 2021:xx).

Similarly, Baumfield (2012:206) following Alexander (2001) stressed that the role of pedagogy should not be seen as simply the act of teaching, but also as the theories, beliefs, policies and controversies that inform and shape it. This can help teachers to understand that different purposes will be served by different types of processes and call for different types of interactions, which in turn, will yield different types of understanding (vide Grimmitt 1981:42). In other words, contemporary demands of the teacher require a secure rationale for the purpose, design and delivery of the curriculum and of pedagogies that drive professional judgment. It is not about liking one over another, but it is to know how to best approach learning in RE (Baumfield 2012:208). In the context of RE, Grimmitt (2000b:16) supplies a working definition of pedagogy as being a theory of teaching and learning encompassing aims, curriculum content and methodology … or a science of teaching and learning embodying both curriculum and methodology. The term methodology has been understood in multiple ways. In RE it refers to a system of teaching strategies, methods and learning activities.

This implies being reflective, receptive and responsive. One way to do so is to adopt an inquiry stance in teaching which enables you to go beyond 'folk pedagogy' to gain insights into the beliefs about learning that are implicit in current practice and subject them to critical appraisal (Baumfield 2012:209). To make teaching progressive and professional activity, pedagogy needs to retain a close relationship with practice but which can also provide a basis for the development of theory (Baumfield 2012:210). She suggests that teachers must scrutinise simplistic and reductive uses of the term pedagogy particularly by policy advisers that separate it from interaction with the wider social cultural contexts so that it becomes a means simply to select effective teaching methods. The need to have a clear view about the pedagogies being used is seen as contributing to the quality of learning and research emphasises the need to offer the opportunity to engage learners in a variety of pedagogical tasks (Jackson et al. 2010).

Classical pedagogies of RE

Several researchers tried to provide distinctive and informed approaches to teaching RE, which Erricker, Lowndes and Bellchambers (2011:29–33) eventually called the great and the good in RE. Further details of the pedagogies offered below including responses by project initiators to criticism levelled against their pedagogies are found in Grimmitt (2000a) and thoughtful discussion also appears in Aldridge (2012:200–203), Stern (2018:69–71), AMV (2016) and Baumfield (2012:210–212).

Religion in the service of the child

John Hull (d. 1935–2015) initiated this project and, although it provided a pedagogical procedure and structure for teachers to follow, it was not presented as a coherent approach to RE

Table 9.1 The Gift approach

The teaching strategy consists of four steps, sometimes all four steps might be present in one short lesson or the first two steps only, while the remaining happen in another. The steps could be seen as four perspectives to be adopted at different points during teaching.

1 *Engagement*
    This does not require a long experiential introduction to present religious content as the religious material spoke for itself directly to the children. This is the opening moments when the attention of the child is attracted to the numen. Children guess what is under a beautiful black velvet cloth as it is slowly lifted. The length and the character of the engagement period is usually dependent upon the degree to which the numen might be unfamiliar to the children, or might come out of a very different context.

2 *Exploration*
    This is the time when the children are encouraged to approach the numen, to observe it, to listen to it, or whatever. It is during this period that the children come close to the material through the entering device.

3 *Contextualisation*
    Children passed through the first two stages without necessarily realising that the material comes from a religious tradition. They study Ganesha without being told a word about Hinduism. They learn about Bernadette of Lourdes without hearing a word about Christianity. At the contextualisation stage, the numen is placed back into the context of the tradition which venerates it. Now we learn about Aideen, who worships in the church of our Lady of Lourdes, lights a candle before her, and still in her wheelchair, travels on pilgrimage to Lourdes.

4 *Reflection*
    This is the time when the gifts are made articulate. Bilal was the first Muslim to call people to prayer. What would you use to call everyone if you could get up to a high place with a microphone? Jonah was called to Nineveh. What do you think you might be called to do one day? What are you been called to do today?

---

pedagogy and curriculum design, even though a set of books were published to support it (Grimmitt, Grove, Hull and Spencer 1991; Hull 1996). This methodology, shown in Table 9.1, focused pupils' initial attention on religious items, images or sounds that pupils would engage with and learn from. These examples of religious material were referred to as 'numena'. From being a 'religious stuff', numen came to mean a religious element charged with the sacred beauty of faith and thus offering to the child something of the numinous (Hull 2000:115). The team saw the 'numen' as a gift to the child and that engaging with it would, in some way, develop their own spiritual insight and growth; that child would learn from religion. However, when the stimuli are removed from the context of the religious community into an educational concept, questions arise about the purpose in this new context. Erricker, Lowndes and Bellchambers (2011:25–26) contend that if it was for pupils' curiosity and the questions that might be raised about their significance to religious adherents, then it would seem educationally sound. However, if the numen were expected to stimulate similar responses to those of its adherence, then there may be an underlying nurturing element. It is, therefore, important to make a distinction as to whether the use of the 'numen' is meant to have a spiritual nurturing function or it is simply enriching pupils' understanding of the world views of others (Erricker, Lowndes and Bellchambers 2011:25–26; Hull 2000:112–129).

Religious experience and education project

Hammond (2015) explained that research into religious experience by Hay and Nye (1998) showed that a dominant secular culture was continuing to marginalise personal religious experience and a religious view of the world. Thus, the exercises in *New Methods in Religious Education* (Hammond et al. 1990) were designed to reinstate this marginalised dimension by providing a means for pupils whereby the validity of these experiences could be acknowledged and the relatedness to the lives of religious people explored. The methods of experiential RE are designed to encourage pupils to reflect on their own interior life as a means of better understanding the nature of religion. It utilises symbols, stories and practised structured silence. However, it had faced criticism of being subjective, too preoccupied with inner experience and promoting privatised religions (Hammond 2015:113–114).

David Hay led this project which originated from an interpretation of the Darwinian thesis that religious or spiritual experience was an innate part of being human. The pedagogy and material focused on awakening sensitivities to religious and spiritual experiences to enable pupils to relate to and reflect on the spiritual or religious experiences of others. It was assisting students to have empathy with the personal world of believers (Hay 2000:73). The team suggested that the most significant feature of being religious is the experiential dimension. Therefore, teachers should design and provide opportunities for experiential learning to awaken pupils' awareness of the religious experiences of believers.

This approach was well-received as it establishes the importance of encouraging pupils to be reflective and search their inner selves and reasons for their feelings, beliefs and responses to life. However, although these draw on religious material and practices, the strategies were not designed to represent religion as such but drew on religious material of a spiritual kind to develop pupils spiritually. Having noted this, thereafter, Erricker, Lowndes and Bellchambers (2011:32) highlight that there is a significant difference in the purpose of RE if its principal aim is promoting the spiritual development of pupils by drawing selectively on enriching religious practices and writings for that purpose, as opposed to the study of religions in a more critically informed fashion. The approach offered classroom activities of six types: Getting started, Raising awareness, Embodying awareness, Framing awareness, Extending awareness and Endings (Hay 2000:78).

The Warwick project

This project focussed mainly on ethnography and RE. It aims to avoid stereotyping by recognising that individuals from a particular religious background may present their religion in ways that are in some respects different from generalised accounts given, for example, in textbooks (Jackson 2014). They produced materials through which pupils engaged with the actions, objects and technical terms through storybooks about 'real' children from different ethnic and religious backgrounds around 'key ideas' for Key Stages 1–3. These general concepts suggested areas where bridges can be made from pupils' experience of life to the experience of the children introduced in the story (Jackson 2000:138). Taking account of the inner plurality of beliefs and practices within religions is important and recognises the importance of enabling pupils to develop a constructive critical stance within RE (Jackson 2000:136). It involves pupils in a process of comparison and contrast between one's own worldview and that of the people being studied (Jackson 2000:144).

The interpretive approach concentrates on three sets of issues, summarised below, related to learning about religions: how religions are represented to learners (*representation*); how religious language and symbols are interpreted (*interpretation*) and how learners respond to their learning about religions (*reflexivity*). Teachers can work creatively with these three general principles, devising their own particular strategies.

Representation

Regarding the representation of religions, the interpretive approach uses three inter-related 'levels'. The individual level is where everyone is unique. It is at this level that the human face of religion is best appreciated and the personal stories are heard which break stereotypes. A 'group' level might be a denominational group, or some combination of these with other kinds of groups, such as ethnic groups. The third, broadest level, is the religion or 'religious tradition'. Thus 'Christianity' encompasses all its different denominational and cultural manifestations.

In using these levels there is no intention to fragment religions. It is the relationship of individuals, groups and tradition, used together, that can provide insight into religion as lived and practised by people, including the religious lives of pupils.

Interpretation

The key is to attempt genuinely to understand as far as possible the meaning of the religious language of another person. This is not done by suppressing one's own current understanding in trying to empathise with someone else. Rather, it attempts to use one's current understanding as a starting point in making an imaginative leap, to make sense of what another is explaining, even if the learner's world view is very different from that of the person, group or tradition being studied.

Reflexivity

The interpretive approach is concerned with trying to understand the meaning of religious language, symbols and ways of living, but it also anticipates discussion of questions of truth and the relationship of meaning and truth (e.g. when you make a certain claim to truth, what exactly do you mean?). Reflexivity includes (a) opportunities for pupils to reflect on their own current understandings and values in relation to what they have learned and (b) the provision of opportunities for distanced, constructive criticism of the material studied.

The two different aspects of reflexivity – coming close to the material to empathise and distancing oneself from the material to apply critical faculties, can be divided into a range of possible activities:

1   Self-awareness: becoming more aware of one's own current views and prejudices, and learning how to examine and challenge these (through considering what influences might have shaped them).

2   Values associated with other religions: discussing and recording values from the individuals/ groups/religion studied which are rooted in the religious tradition, and comparing and contrasting them with one's own values, which overlap with one's own, but are not identical.

3   Learning from others' values: considering how the personal values from the individuals/ groups/tradition studied are relevant to/might contribute to social values, such as citizenship.

4   Similarities and differences to one's own beliefs and values: considering how the beliefs of individuals, in the context of their groups and tradition, are different from/similar to/ overlap with one's own beliefs.

5   Improving study methods: reflecting on the methods of study used and suggesting ways of improving them to get a better and deeper understanding of others (Jackson 2014:35–39).

The Stapleford project

This was set up by Trevor Cooling with a focus on providing an approach to teach about Christianity through investigating concepts exclusively dealing with Christian material. It developed a concept-led approach informed by the work of Jerome Bruner and Margaret Donaldson. It argued for RE to go to the heart of the subject, rather than continually scratching at the surface as the way to promote excellence in learning. Drawing on this insight, it identified the importance of identifying key concepts that are central to RE and communicating these ideas rather than conveying information that was to be learnt (Cooling 2000:156). The pedagogical strategy for the classroom is known as *Concept Cracking*, see below.

Human development project

To use Grimmitt, in contrast to instructional approaches, this approach draws on a constructivist approach to learning and offers a three-staged pedagogical strategy. First, pupils are engaged in an enquiry into and reflection upon their own *experience* to *prepare* them conceptually and linguistically for an encounter with the item of religious content. Second, pupils are confronted with the item of religious content *directly*, but without explanation and instruction, so that it becomes the stimulus for them to construct their own meaning and understanding by using observation, formulating hypotheses, drawing on their own experiences and that represented in the group. In the third stage, pupils are provided with additional or *supplementary* information about the content (i.e. as listed earlier) which enables the constructions to become more complex and embrace alternative perspectives (Grimmitt 2000d:216–217). Stern explains that this pedagogy is guided by the need for RE to enable human development as it draws from psychology, social science disciplines and philosophy and questions of meaning to establish a creative tension. The place of religion as a distinctive human discourse, in flux and flexible, is defended even in those relatively secular cultures like those of the UK (Stern 2018:67).

The children and worldviews project

This narrative project was essentially concerned with children's experiences and the way pupils learn in RE. It developed because it was convinced that RE tends to be overly concerned with the acquisition of knowledge about religious beliefs and practices with insufficient emphasis given to the experiences of children themselves and the way children make sense of that experience (Erricker and Erricker 2000:188). Their research suggested that effective learning takes place when children are encouraged to be reflexive about and articulate responses to their experiences in life when they are enabled to share their 'narratives' in an environment that is respectful, safe and free from criticism or ridicule. For them, good RE happens when it is child-centred and child-driven and when it deals with concepts that are of interest to children and that resonate with their lives. However, the project was criticised for resisting the value of RE and for proposing a form of values education in its place (Erricker, Lowndes and Bellchambers 2011:32).

The Westhill project

This project also emphasised concepts in the teaching of RE and identified them into broad categories: those concepts relating to shared human experience and those relating to traditional belief systems. These concepts were built into the field of inquiry that was selected as appropriate for different age groups. The field of enquiry of RE was used to define the areas of content from which the subject matter for the classroom was to be drawn. The content may be drawn from three broad areas (Rudge 2000:94–97).

1   *Traditional belief systems* is a generic term referring to the major religions by highlighting certain features for educational purposes. The focus was on the generational tradition which continues to influence peoples' lives in many ways. These beliefs are presented as focal points of educational exploration. They are also systematic, not in a monolithic way, in communicating a point of identity for those who follow their beliefs and belong to their group. They argued that it was impossible to represent the wholeness of the traditions, therefore, the educational enterprise does require teachers to select those areas of exploration which focus on the educational value.

2   *Shared human experience* refers to experiences of life common to most human beings simply because of the shared humanity. The value of these experiences for RE is to be found in the issues and questions they raise since it was not simply about any common human experience, rather it was those experiences that have significance for people because they raise profound issues and questions about the human condition, such as questions about the purpose of life, its meaning and value, people's sense of identity, issues about personal and cosmic origins and destiny, and the authority for belief. These are summarised in the question, 'what does it mean to be human?' In the project, these were classified as the natural world, relationships, rules and issues, stages of life, celebrations, lifestyles and suffering.

3   *Individual patterns of belief* refers to the varied, shared and complex experiences, beliefs and values that pupils and teachers bring with them into the classroom depending on the makeup of the class.

In Figure 9.1, adapted from Rudge (2000:95), the outer circles represent the observable phenomena associated with each of the areas of exploration. In the traditional belief systems, they represent all the actions, words, symbols, stories and observances associated with the followers of that tradition. In the shared human experience, it represents the experiences associated with dramatic moments in life, the practical lens through which ultimate

Interrelationships within the field of enquiry

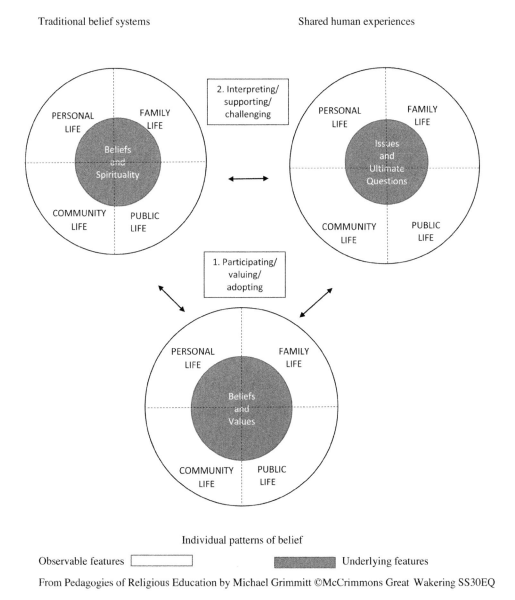

Individual patterns of belief

Observable features ☐   ▒▒▒▒ Underlying features

From Pedagogies of Religious Education by Michael Grimmitt ©McCrimmons Great Wakering SS30EQ

Figure 9.1 The Westhill project.

questions and issues are focused. For individual patterns of belief, it represents the actions and observable behaviour of individuals, which provide a window into their world of beliefs and values. For the purposes of RE, the model also suggests that teachers need to take account of four contexts for observing and defining the appropriate content. These are the context of the individual, family, community and public behaviour. The model also represents the dynamic relationship observable between the three areas. This dynamic relationship is itself an important part of the field of enquiry.

Spiritual education and religious literacy

Andrew Wright developed a critical realist pedagogy that recognised the importance of demonstrating diversity within religion, with a particular focus on Christianity. Five key pedagogical principles were identified.

First, critical RE seeks to do justice to the horizon of religion, meaning not only should pupils learn more than Christianity but the tensions within specific religious traditions as well. It reflects religious and secular perspectives on religion and accepts the ambiguous, controversial and conflicting nature of theological truth claims (Wright 2000:177). Second, critical RE must do justice to the horizon of the pupil, meaning that children come into school with an already developing worldview and challenges the assumption that pupils should learn to be neutral and unbiased in their approach to religious traditions other than their own. Third, critical RE seeks to equip pupils to recognise and respond appropriately to power structures inherent in religious and educational discourse, meaning it provides pupils with the skills, knowledge and wisdom to be able to explore their own ideology and the various ideologies presented by religious and secular traditions. Fourth, critical RE enables a critical dialogue between the horizon of the child and the horizon of the religion, and fifth, it develops in pupils a religious literacy rooted in attentiveness, intelligence, reasonableness and responsibility.

Interestingly these pedagogical principles do not demand any one specific teaching methodology and are rooted in a spiral rather than linear models of learning (Wright 2000:177–179; 180). Erricker, Lowndes and Bellchambers (2011:31) note that some of these pedagogies focused mainly on religious material and how to enable pupils to access them to make sense of it in relation to their own life experiences. However, other pedagogies mainly concern the spiritual development and experiences of the child as a way of accessing and making sense of religious material.

Following a historical and critical of the theories of Jackson, Wright and Erricker, Hannam (2019:33–59) concludes that they conceptualise religion in different ways, as a result there is no agreement between them on what should be done about representation of religions in classrooms. She contends that knowledge for all three is positioned at the centre of religion education which, to her, risks obscuring the child, who is the educational subject.

In the classroom

Table 9.2 summarises the key ideas of six approaches and what they could be used for with pupils. It also suggests some planning prompts to bring these together. To show these in action, the specific classroom examples are presented from Moss (2015:68).

Ways forward

It is important to highlight that considering Grimmitt's (2000b:16) working definition of pedagogy, the above approaches may be better designated as 'methodologies', since not all are 'pedagogies', as not all encompass aims, curriculum content and methodology. Nevertheless, there is some overlap and distinctive features between them and no one approach adequately covers

Table 9.2 Six pedagogies in the classroom

1 *Phenomenological approach* organises religion into myths, doctrines, beliefs, rituals, experiential, social and material dimensions of religion.	It can be used to: Assist pupils understand the phenomena of religion. Help pupils know and understand specific beliefs and teachings. Develop pupils' ability to give accounts of the impact of some religious teachings upon believers.
The teacher can plan the study of religious practices, investigations of the meaning of symbols, significance of stories, role of art and use of architecture and music in religions, explore regulations on food and clothing and lived-dimensions of religions to understand their meaning and significance to members of the faith community.	Example: A teacher plans to introduce a class to the Muslim religion for the first time, and uses a selection of artefacts from the mosque. Pupils are asked to develop their understanding of what Muslims do, and what they say and think about their actions. Pupils select 10 artefacts, images and texts to sum up all they have learned about the Muslim faith so far.
2 *Experiential approach* begins with either human experience of everyday life or with human experience of religion as recognised through its 'experiential' dimension.	It can be used to: Help pupils make sense of their own experience in the light of their learning about and from the religious experience of faith communities. It recognises that pupils have spiritual capacities of their own.
The teacher, to develop spiritual capacities within their pupils through RE, may plan to use ice-breaking exercise, stilling and listening, life history, questions of personal identity, metaphors, imaginative use of symbols, trust and cooperation and experiential work to open their creative imagination.	Example: A teacher wants to enable spiritual development through RE so they use stilling, guided story and creative imagination to explore religious and spiritual experiences, questions and beliefs increasingly deeply in the classroom. After a guided story on Pesach which focused on Jewish concepts of freedom, tradition and community, pupils express their own spiritual ideas about concepts like these and concepts of love, sacrifice, submission or thankfulness in sculptures and poems.
3 *Ethnographic / interpretative approach* shows the complexity of religious and cultural interactions. It invites teachers to be aware of the beliefs and values embedded in the experiences of pupils. It emphasises that understanding is increased through examining the relationship between individuals, groups and the wider religions. There is also a focus on trying to interpret religious language and symbols.	It can be used to: Encourage pupils to relate to a way of life that is different from their own. Listen to the voices of those who follow the tradition being studied. Provide opportunities for pupils to actively interpret religious meaning making, not just passively receiving information about a tradition. Enable pupils to encounter with the experiences, views, beliefs, perspectives and ways of life of followers of different faith communities and they use this to reflect on their own world-view and experiences.
The teacher plans to introduce authentic material from religious traditions and helps pupils to connect it with their own personal knowledge and experience. The teacher uses real accounts of how followers of religions practise their faith in contemporary times. These learning methods aim to enable pupils to draw meaning from these encounters with religion for themselves, thus they become researchers in their lessons.	Example: Starting work on Hindu Dharma, a teacher begins with four rather contradictory accounts of how Diwali is practised in a UK city and in India today. Emphasising religion as it is lived (not merely history, texts or beliefs); pupils become enquirers themselves into the varieties of religion and belief. The key skill of making sense or interpreting gradually extends pupils' awareness of living communities of faith.
4 *Conceptual learning* is where pupils understand the meaning of Christianity for believers, like the phenomenological approach, but differs in that this will only be achieved	It can be used to: Encourage pupils to consider religious content in ways that reflect and are consistent with the religious community's interpretation of that material. Provide opportunities

(Continued)

Table 9.2 Six pedagogies in the classroom (*Continued*)

if more attention is given to exploring the theological concepts, which are the source of meaningfulness and significance for Christians.	for pupils to ask their own questions about what life would be like if everyone followed the example of leaders of religion and beliefs. Relate values and 'truth claims' to their own experiences. Explore the concepts of the religions and reflect on the insights these shed on different ways of understanding and making sense of life.
The teacher plans lessons which are rich in key concepts that are taken from religions and from religious studies as a discipline to enable pupils to be increasingly reasonable about religions. The teacher applies the *Concept Cracking* approach to: Unpack concepts, then Selects a couple of concepts as focus for the lesson, then Engages with the pupils' world of experience and finally Relates it to the religious concept. (U S E R)	Example: In the unit about Christian beliefs about God, pupils learn three concepts: Incarnation, Trinity and Resurrection. They enquire into the ways these concepts make sense of the Christmas and Easter narratives, and how these festivals are celebrated. They develop understanding of beliefs, and think about how beliefs can be tested by argument or experience, moving towards analysing truth claims from religion for themselves.
5 *The Ultimate questions approach or Human development approach* involves pupils in learning about religion and religions. It uses enquiry to encourage interaction of thought and experience. It makes a link between the life-world of the content being studied. It uses critical reflection of one's own knowledge to contrast with alternative cultural perspectives.	It can be used to: Encourage pupils to develop their own patterns of belief and behaviour through exploring religious beliefs and practices and related human experiences. Provide opportunities for pupils to develop spiritually, morally, socially and culturally.
The teacher plans lessons which use 'big questions' to explore meaning, value, purpose, identity and truth to explore the impact of religion on life, to construct meaning and to challenge the learners to deepen their own ideas. They study religious responses to the questions that life presents to humans. The teacher asks questions and offers practical and group work.	Example: Pupils begin a unit of work by raising all the questions they would like to ask of God / the creator / the Supreme Being / the ultimate brain. With stimulus from religious texts and practices, the class uses a 'Philosophy for Pupils' (P4C) method. A 'community of enquiry' activity explores the pupils' own questions. Afterwards, the class develops pieces of personal work using their own and religious ideas about the ultimate questions explored.
6 *The Children and Worldviews Project approach* stresses the reflexive character of engagement. Uses a narrative pedagogy in that all 'knowledge' is relative principle. It is about the relationship between the aims of RE and their relevance to the learning experience of the child.	It can be used to: Encourage pupils to develop their natural capacities for individual storying and constructing meaning. Challenge pupils to develop their own world views by relating their own experiences and reflecting on their own patterns of belief and behaviour.
Teachers plan and attend to the means which enable articulation of meaning. They attend to the security and negotiations to enable speaking. They attend to the cognitive, spiritual and emotional degree of freedom and independence needed. They attend to the balance of authority and authoritative statements.	Example: After teaching about commitment and values, pupils begin with their own commitments, and generalise from these. Exploring the ways their everyday commitments can be structured into a view of what matters, a view of the world, is more important than gathering understanding of religion, as the aim of RE is to clarify the learner's vision of life.

all aspects of learning in RE. Some are informed by theory, textbooks and empirical research. Therefore, you are encouraged to examine them and may well develop your own preferences. It is also important to identify which approach/es are best suited to achieving the particular purposes of RE in your teaching, to be clear about these and have a rationale for your decision. It is also wise to use a variety of approaches over time. Consider this popular pedagogical imaginary.

A pedagogical fantasy

Teachers researching what happens in their classroom as they teach RE can experiment with different methods as suggested by Blaylock's who playfully demonstrates 'Six ways around Easter: A pedagogical fantasy' in Table 9.3. However, it does not exemplify confessional RE, despite its popularity in many countries (Stern 2018:66). The descriptions can be used as a diagnostic tool for the pedagogical priorities in an RE scheme or school planning (Aldridge 2012:198).

These approaches are available at the disposal of the teacher. However, it is important to be reflective and aware of teacher bias and the ontological and epistemological basis that informs pedagogy and curriculum design. Erricker (2013:75) has argued that phenomenological and ethnographic/anthropological approaches to RE are inadequate as they fail to allow for a full range of evaluative judgments to be made about religious forms and because they promote representations of religions that mirrors the liberalism of those approaches.

Table 9.3 A pedagogical fantasy
Six ways around Easter: A pedagogical fantasy
At the start of term, the new RE teacher Miss X noticed in her syllabus that she was to teach the 11-year-olds about the Festival and stories of Easter, the beliefs associated with the celebration, and the impact of these beliefs in the Christian community. She had just been trained by some phenomenologists (as in Smart 1983), and so planned two lessons on the phenomenon of Easter. Using artefacts – a variety of crosses, some icons, some 'He is Risen' badges, hot crossed buns and a video of the Easter celebrations in an Orthodox and an Evangelical setting – she taught them about the festival, its terminology and its diversity. After two lessons, Miss X read Michael Grimmitt's book on RE and human development (Grimmitt 1987) and realised she had been neglecting pupils' learning from religion. She planned some fresh activities: pupils were asked some provocative questions. What if you were in charge of the Easter celebrations for the two churches nearest school? What music would you choose for Good Friday and Easter day? What does the idea of 'life out of death' or 'resurrection' or 'life after death' mean to you? Can you explain an occasion when hope seemed hopeless, but you held on anyway? More good work emerged as pupils related the festival to their own experiences. After these two lessons, she went on a course with Trevor Cooling and learned the methods of 'concept cracking' (as in Cooling 1994[b sic]). Inspired by the new pedagogy of the conceptual analysis of truth claims, she planned two lessons of Biblical study in which the claims of the resurrection were presented to the class. They responded to the challenge – some who thought it would be impossible discussed their view with others who thought it a miracle. Some Christian children in the class stayed at the end to say how affirming they had found the exploration of their own faith. During half term, she checked her notes from college and remembered all about the deconstruction of religion for postmodern young people (as in Erricker and Erricker 2000). The next two lessons were used to dissect how the Easter festival is sometimes used to keep people in their place – a heavenly reward for a life of drudgery. One child asked, 'So, Miss, is religion just a way of keeping people in their place?' She knew she was getting somewhere when a group of boys announced they didn't believe in Easter, and wouldn't be bothering to wait till Sunday before eating the chocolate. There was another course on interpretive approaches to RE (as in Jackson 1997), and Miss X was edified. She decided to plan a couple more lessons, the first on the diversity of Easter as Christian children describe it (she used accounts from 13-year-old Catholics, Methodists and Quakers, from Bristol, Birmingham and Nigeria). Then she asked pupils to write interpreter's notes on the *Hallelujah chorus*, making sense of its origin, use today, and impact within and beyond the Christian community. As the term wore on, Miss X was visited by the local adviser, who was signed up to spiritual and experiential approach to RE (as in Hammond et al. 1990). She realised what was missing in the terms' lessons and used a guided fantasy based upon the appearance of Jesus to two disciples travelling to Emmaus. Pupils finished the term creating works of art inspired by the work on a choice of themes: 'Back from the Dead' or 'My Hope for the Future' (Stern 2018:69).
Source: RE Today Services (Blaylock 2004).

DIRECT INSTRUCTION

Direct Instruction should not be confused with didactic and teacher led instruction taking place from the front of the class with pupils having a passive role. Instead pupils are involved in thinking and actively participating. It is a specific programme with scripts, focused resources and teaching sequences planned to the most detail. It emphasises the teacher being in complete control of the learning process. It uses examples and non-examples to clarify the knowledge and learning. Direct Instruction manages cognitive workload; it avoids split attention and redundant information. It makes heavy use of retrieval, spacing and frequently uses dual coding. It has been argued that the absence of direct instruction means an absence of the best ability to teach (Boulton 2019:26).

Summary

There are many pedagogies and methodologies for teaching RE, each has its starting point in some assumptions about the nature of religion and belief in the world and in knowing, teaching and learning, and each has its strengths and weaknesses. It is expected you will be in a continuous search for methods to improve your teaching and so provide high-quality RE for your pupils. Simultaneously, it means you should reflect and acknowledge your assumptions and expectations so that you can become a better teacher.

References

Alavi, Z. (1988) *Muslim Educational Thought in the Middle Ages*, New Delhi: Atlantic Publishers & Distributors.

Aldridge, D. (2012) Schemes of work and lesson planning, in L. P. Barnes (Ed (Ed.) *Debates in Religious Education*, London: Routledge, pp. 194–204.

Alexander, R. J. (2001) *Culture and Pedagogy: International Comparisons in Primary Education*, London: Blackwell.

Al Zeera, Z. (2001) *Wholeness and Holiness in Education: An Islamic Perspective*, Richmond: The International Institute of Islamic Thought.

AMV (2016) *Appropriate Methodologies for Awareness, Mystery and Value*, [Online] http://www.aware-nessmysteryvalue.org/2016/f03-guidance-methodology-pedagogy/ (Accessed 25/07/2021).

Atwal, K. (2019) *The Thinking School: Developing a Dynamic Learning Community*, Melton: John Catt.

Aubrey, K., and Riley, A. (2019) *Understanding & Using Educational Theories*, London: SAGE.

Bates, B. (2019) *Learning Theories Simplified*, London: SAGE. Second edition.

Baumfield, V. (2012) Pedagogy, in L.P. Barnes (Ed.) *Debates in Religious Education*, London: Routledge, pp. 205–212.

Biesta, G. (2012) The future of teacher education: Evidence, competence or wisdom? *Research on Steiner Education (Rose)*, 3, (1), pp. 8–21.

Blaylock, L. (2004) Six schools of thought in RE, *Resources*, 27:1, pp. 13–16.

Boulton, K (2019) What was project follow through? in A. Boxer, (Ed.) *The ResearchED Guide to Explicit & Direct Instruction*, Melton: John Catt, pp. 15–28.

Chater, M., and Erricker, C. (2013) *Does Religious Education Have a Future?* Abingdon: Routledge.

Claxton, G. (2021) *The Future of Teaching and the Myths That Hold It Back*, Abingdon: Routledge.

Cooling, T. (1994) *Concept Cracking: Exploring Christian Beliefs in School*, Stapleford: The Stapleford Centre.

Cooling, T. (2000) The Stapleford Project: Theology as the basis for Religious Education, in M. H. Grimmitt (Ed.) *Pedagogies of Religious Education*, Great Wakering: McCrimmons, pp. 153–169.

Collinson, D., Plant, K., and Wilkinson, R. (2000) *Fifty Eastern Thinkers*, London: Routledge.

DfE (Department for Education) (2021) *Teachers' Standards Guidance for School Leaders, School Staff and Governing Bodies*, Crown Copyright. Reference: DFE-00066-2011 [Online] https://assets.publishing.service.gov.uk/government/uploads/system/uploads/attachment_data/file/1007716/Teachers__Standards_2021_update.pdf (Accessed 19/09/2021).

DfE (2019) *ITT Core Content Framework*, London: Crown copyright. Ref: DfE-00230-2019. [Online] https://assets.publishing.service.gov.uk/government/uploads/system/uploads/attachment_data/file/974307/ITT_core_content_framework_.pdf (Accessed 28/08/2021).

Erricker, C., and Erricker, J. (2000) The Children and Worldviews Project: A narrative pedagogy of Religious Education, in M. H. Grimmitt (Ed.) *Pedagogies of Religious Education*, Great Wakering: McCrimmons, pp. 153–169.

Erricker, C., Lowndes, J., and Bellchambers, E. (2011) *Primary Religious Education – A New Approach*, Abingdon: Routledge.

Erricker, C. (2013) Phenomenology and anthropology: The advocacy of religion as an approach to RE, in M. Chater and C. Erricker (Eds.) *Does Religious Education Have a Future? Pedagogical and Policy Prospects*, Abingdon: Routledge, pp. 58–73.

Gearon, L. (2013) *MasterClass in Religious Education: Transforming Teaching and Learning*, London: Bloomsbury.

Grimmitt, M. (1981) When is 'commitment' a problem in Religious Education? *British Journal of Education Studies*, 29, (1), pp. 42–53.

Grimmitt, M. (1987) *Religious Education and Human Development*, Great Wakering: McCrimmon.

Grimmitt, M., Grove, J., Hull, J. M., and Spencer, L. (1991) *A Gift to the Child: Religious Education in the Primary School*, Hemel Hempstead: Simon and Schuster.

Grimmitt, M. (2000a) *Pedagogies of Religious Education*, Great Wakering: McCrimmon.

Grimmitt, M. (2000b) The captivity and liberation of Religious Education and the meaning and significance of pedagogy, in M. Grimmitt (Ed.) *Pedagogies of Religious Education*, Great Wakering: McCrimmon, pp. 7–23.

Grimmitt, M. (2000c) Contemporary pedagogies of Religious Education: What are they? in M. Grimmitt (Ed.) *Pedagogies of Religious Education*, Great Wakering: McCrimmon, pp. 24–52.

Grimmitt, M. (2000d) Constructivist Pedagogies of Religious Education Project: Rethinking knowledge, teaching and learning in Religious Education, in M. Grimmitt (Ed.) *Pedagogies of Religious Education*, Great Wakering: McCrimmon, pp. 207–226.

Hannam, P. (2019) *Religious Education and the Public Sphere*, London: Routledge.

Harris, K., and Lowe, S. (2018) Short-, medium- and long-term planning, in H. Cooper and S. Elton-Chalcraft (Eds.), *Professional Studies in Primary Education*, London: SAGE. Third edition, pp. 66–94.

Hammond, J. (2015) Developing experiential RE creatively, in S. Elton-Chalcraft (Ed.) *Teaching Religious Education Creatively*, Abingdon: Routledge, pp. 113–122.

Hammond, J., Hay, D., Moxon, J., Netto, B., Raban, K., and Williams, C. (1990) *New Methods in Religious Teaching: An Experiential Approach*. Essex: Oliver and Boyd.

Hay, D., and Nye, R. (1998) *The Spirit of the Child*, London: HarperCollins.

Hay, D. (2000) Religious Experience and Education Project: Experiential learning in Religious Education, in M. H. Grimmitt (Ed.) *Pedagogies of Religious Education*, Great Wakering: McCrimmons, pp. 70–87.

Hull, J. H. (1996) A gift to the child: A new pedagogy for teaching religion to young children, *Religious Education*, 91, (2), pp.172–188.

Hull, J. M. (2000) Religion in the Service of the Child Project: The gift approach to Religious Education, in M. H. Grimmitt (Ed.) *Pedagogies of Religious Education*, Great Wakering: McCrimmons, pp. 112–129.

Jackson, R. (1997) *Religious Education: An Interpretative Approach*, London: Hodder.

Jackson, R. (2000) The Warwick Religious Education Project: The interpretive approach to Religious Education, in M. H. Grimmitt (Ed.) *Pedagogies of Religious Education*, Great Wakering: McCrimmons, pp. 130–152.

Jackson, R. (2006) *Fifty Key Figures in Islam*, Abingdon: Routledge.

Jackson, R., Ipgrave, J., Hayward, M., Hopkins, P., Fancourt, N., Robbins, M., Francis, L. J., and McKenna, U. (2010) *Materials Used to Teach About World Religions in Schools in England*, London: Department for Children, Schools and Families. Research Report DCSF-RR197.

Jackson, R. (2014) *Signposts – Policy and Practice for Teaching About Religions and non-Religious World Views in Intercultural Education*, Strasbourg: Council of Europe.

Moss, F. (2015) Engaging children creatively: Effective planning for developing enquiry, in S. Elton-Chalcraft (Ed.) *Teaching Religious Education Creatively*, Abingdon: Routledge, pp. 64–77.

Pritchard, A. (2018) *Ways of Learning: Learning Theories for the Classroom*, Abingdon: Routledge. Fourth edition.

Rudge, J. (2000) The Westhill Project: Religious Education as maturing pupils' patterns of belief and behaviour, in M. H. Grimmitt (Ed.) *Pedagogies of Religious Education*, Great Wakering: McCrimmons, pp. 88–111.

Stern, J. (2018) *Teaching Religious Education: Researchers in the Classroom*, London: Bloomsbury. Second edition.

Stone, P. (2021) Reconceptualizing teacher identity, in V. Bower (Ed.) *Debates in Primary Education*, Abingdon: Routledge, pp. 35–45.

Watson, E., and Busch, B. (2021) *The Science of Learning: 99 Studies That Every Teacher Needs to Know*, Abingdon: Routledge. Second edition.

Wright, A. (2000) The Spiritual Education Project: Cultivating spiritual and religious literacy through a critical pedagogy of Religious Education, in M. H. Grimmitt (Ed.) *Pedagogies of Religious Education*, Great Wakering: McCrimmons, pp. 170–187.

10

Contemporary pedagogies

Introduction

Teaching is multi-dimensional, contextual and complicated, as a teacher you need to have a wide repertoire of teaching strategies at your disposal. Having debunked the scientific rationale for the idea that direct instruction is the only valid way of teaching, Claxton (2021:141) asserts that there is no one best way to teach. There are different ways of teaching. Moreover, since there are multiple aims of education, different ways of teaching may impact these different design outcomes differently. Different desired outcomes develop on different time scales. Direct instruction and discovery learning have their place and so does the importance of ascertaining pupils pre-existing knowledge and experience and teaching them accordingly.

The ten Principles of Instruction advocated by Rosenshine (2012) are becoming increasingly applied in education. These are founded on three distinct research areas of cognitive science, classroom practices and cognitive support. Some of these have relevance in teaching Religious Education (RE) and, as such, they are presented for your consideration. These are: begin a lesson with a short review of previous learning, present new material in small steps with student practice, ask a large number of questions and check the responses of all students, provide models, guide student practice, check for student understanding, obtain a high success rate, provide scaffolding for difficult tasks, require and monitor independent practice and finally, engage students in weekly and monthly review (Sherrington 2019). These principles should be seen as a framework or guide and be supplemented with other principles and practices, rather than a checklist or requirement.

Independent learners

As pupils progress through schooling life, it is important that they become increasingly independent learners and seekers of wisdom. To build their ability to do this, they need to manage their motivations, thoughts and emotions, and the strategy of scaffolding is helpful (Watson and Bradley 2021). Scaffolding entails teachers creating a support structure in place, and then reducing the amount incrementally as the pupil progresses. It is important to remember that learning is not linear and that some failure is probably good for them in the long term (Watson and Bradley 2021). The amount of support that needs to be offered can vary from one day to the next. There is evidence to suggest decreasing support too quickly can do more harm than good. Scaffolding is also about teaching pupils to manage their thoughts and feelings. Therefore, effective scaffolding needs to be well thought out and gradually reduced.

DOI: 10.4324/9780429289743-14

THE RE-SEARCHERS APPROACH

Introduction

The RE-searchers approach encourages pupils to think about the significance and effectiveness of different methodologies and methods of inquiry in RE. It aims to initiate pupils into the communities of academic inquiry concerned with theological and religious studies and assumes that religions are complex, diverse, multi-faceted, evolving and multi-dimensional phenomena. It recognises that there are multiple methodologies and methods for generating knowledge and understanding of religion(s) derived from many disciplinary perspectives including theological, philosophical, archaeological, literary, psychological, sociological, cultural and anthropological (Freathy and Freathy 2013a:161; Freathy and Freathy 2013b). Importantly, it advocates a multi-methodological and multi-perspectival pedagogy which, it suggests, is necessary to avoid favouring one particular approach over others and privileging one interpretation over another. It posits that otherwise pupils are not given the freedom to see religions from alternative viewpoints (Freathy et al. 2017). Accordingly, a critical, dialogic and inquiry-based RE encourages pupils to be autonomous and self-regulating learners. RE, they advance, should provide open-ended inquiries in which pupils evaluate their methods as they co-construct knowledge in collaboration with their teachers and peers.

The introduction of this new approach chimes with the recommendation that pupils must be taught: 'the different ways in which religion and worldviews can be understood, interpreted and studied' (CoRE 2018:13). The RE-searchers approach helps pupils with learning about religion(s) and learning how to learn about religion(s) by creating a balance between:

   i   subject content and issues of representation;

   ii   learning processes and research methods; and

   iii   personal evaluation, self-reflection and reflexivity (Freathy et al. 2015:8).

Accessibility to pupils

The RE-searcher approach currently uses four key characters who adopt different research methodologies. To make it accessible, they have personified the methods as cartoon characters. Individually, they are called Debate-it-all Derek, Ask-it-all Ava, Have-a-go Hugo and See-the-story Suzie, collectively known as the 'RE-searchers', as shown in Figure 10.1.

Each character holds different assumptions about religion(s) and advocates different research methods. For example, questioning and arguing, interviewing and empathising, participating and experiencing and narrating and exploring interpretations. Once acquainted with these characters and their respective characteristics as researchers, pupils can then undertake learning activities associated with each of them in pursuit of different understandings of religion(s).

The characters

Planning an enquiry

There are multiple ways to plan units of work using the RE-searchers approach. A unit of work, on single or multiple topics, can be used to develop the ability of pupils to research in the style of one of the RE-searcher characters. This is a 'boot camp' model of RE-searchers'

Ask-it-all Ava (*Interviewer/Empathiser*)	
	Ava likes talking to religious people about what they believe and do. She listens carefully to those she interviews in order to learn how people's backgrounds, families, communities and traditions shape their lives. She compares these answers with her own, those of other believers and those of religious traditions in general.
Debate-it-all Derek (*Philosopher/Critic*)	
	Derek is interested in what is true and what is right. He asks himself and others Big Questions such as: 'Is there a God?', 'What happens after we die?' and 'What is good and evil?' He likes to think on his own and with others about where religions agree and disagree to decide which views he agrees with (if any) and always seeks to give good reasons and provide evidence for his beliefs.
Have-a-go Hugo (*Experiencer/Participant*)	
	Hugo likes to take part in religious activities. He does this in order to try to understand religious people and to see what it feels like to join in. He believes that feelings are more important than beliefs when trying to understand religious people. He is interested in what people feel to be true in their hearts rather than what they believe to be true in their heads. He wants to know or imagine what it feels like to be religious and to be able to sympathise with those that are.
See-the-story Suzie (*Narrator/Interpreter*)	
	Suzie likes to compare stories and different versions of the same story. She likes to develop her own interpretation of these stories and explore her own responses and reactions. Suzie likes to engage with the characters, the story-line and different interpretations of the same story. She suggests ways in which religious people's lives might be affected by the way they understand the religious stories.

Figure 10.1 The 'RE-searchers'.

Source: Freathy, G., Freathy, R., and University of Exeter (2016).

RE. Alternatively, units of work can combine RE-searcher inquiries in order to offer a multi-methodological approach to engaging with a single topic. The Carrol diagram in Table 10.1 demonstrates the resulting four different types of RE-searchers' units (Freathy and Freathy 2016:24).

Table 10.1 Four different types of RE-searchers' units		
	Single Focus	**Multiple Foci**
Single RE-searcher	**TYPE A** A unit of this nature allows pupils to explore the complexity of a particular topic in depth using one or more activities associated with a single RE-searcher character.	**TYPE B** This type of unit allows pupils to develop their skills as a particular RE-searcher whilst ensuring broad curriculum coverage. One or more activity associated with a particular RE-searcher is chosen and matched to a range of learning foci over the course of a unit.
Multiple RE-searchers used	**TYPE C** A unit of this type permits pupils to explore the complexity of one focus in death, whilst also evaluating the effectiveness of each of the RE-searchers' approaches. A sequence of enquiries is conducted utilising a number of RE-searcher characters to explore a single focus.	**TYPE D** A unit of this kind utilises multiple RE-searcher characters and looks at a range of foci associated with the topic. This is the most challenging form of enquiry to plan. However, it does allow for the most appropriate matching of curriculum coverage with RE-searcher style/activity to optimise learning experience for all and best illustrate typical enquiries for each RE-searcher.
Source: Freathy, G., Freathy, R., and University of Exeter (2016).		

The basic inquiry cycle

The RE-searchers approach is an inquiry-based approach to RE where knowledge about the focus of the study is constructed collaboratively. As such pupils should be as far as possible involved in the following process:

The basic inquiry cycle of Figure 10.2 could be adopted with or without the use of RE-searcher characters. In fact, at the beginning of a unit, some teachers prefer to run a full inquiry cycle with pupils without reference to the RE-searcher characters. Commonly this inquiry lasts one lesson and allows pupils to engage with a range of sources of information in the manner they see fit and without their research style being predetermined by a designated RE-searcher character chosen by the teacher. Giving pupils a context (e.g. being 'curators in a museum') and a client (e.g. the 'director of the museum') is a great way to motivate pupils and make this learning more meaningful for them. They call this 'free-style' approach,

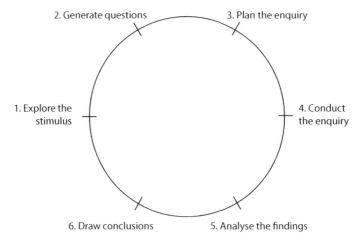

Figure 10.2 The basic inquiry cycle.

Source: Freathy, G., Freathy, R., and University of Exeter (2016).

'FREe-search'! The quality of this approach will be affected by the motivation of the pupils, the range and quality of the resources available and the extent to which they are well-matched to the abilities of the pupils in the class. Pupils will need to be well-trained at using the resources and working collaboratively to make such an approach effective (Freathy and Freathy 2016:25).

Their concern with FREe-search (inquiries which do not deploy the RE-searcher characters) is that insufficient attention might be given to the methodologies and methods by which the inquiry is being undertaken. In the RE-searchers approach, methodologies and methods matter, and thus need to be taught explicitly, as one might teach a 'practical lesson' in science, or a 'source work' lesson in history (Freathy and Freathy 2016:25). A range of strategies for introducing the characters at an age appropriate level (e.g. Freathy et al. 2015:17); engaging pupils in the evaluation of the characters' values and research preferences, alongside the fidelity of pupil *performance* when 'role-playing' characters are described in the literature. Videos (Freathy et al. 2015:98), puppets, cartoon strips and a range of classroom aide memoirs (Freathy and Freathy 2014:50) have been used to support these ends, alongside a range of interactive role-play and warm-up activities (Freathy et al. 2017:35–75).

Inquiry in action

Each step of the inquiry process is explained below:

1   Choosing a stimulus which benefits from being:
    ○   Real – in the sense of non-fictional, they should pertain to real people, organisations and events in the world.
    ○   Relevant – often a successful stimulus aligns with the interests and concerns of pupils and is appropriate to their age and current preoccupations. They should neither be too abstract nor mundane, too disturbing nor too bland.
    ○   Ripe – arising from contemporary events and current trends and appetising for all!
    ○   Religious – sufficiently linked with the designated religious topic so as to ensure the questions arising from the stimulus require deeper and broader subject content understanding in order to explore, solve, discuss, etc.

2   Generating questions by supporting children as they formulate inquiry questions. Teachers may challenge pupils to generate a wide range of questions with or without generic or RE-searcher specific 'question stems' to help them.

3   Planning the inquiry. Although teachers may opt to permit pupils to conduct 'FREe-search' (where pupils pursue answers to their own questions), the RE-searchers approach is designed to move pupils beyond what they can already do and to introduce discipline-specific research methodologies. As such, teachers should not be afraid of determining which of the questions surfaced in the last session will be pursued or the RE-searcher character that will be used to pursue the answer. It is during this phase that, commonly, the RE-searcher characters are explicitly taught to enable pupils to plan inquiries in-keeping with corresponding research questions.

4   Conducting an inquiry. During an inquiry pupils should carry out their plans to discover answers to the question selected previously. Pupils should act in accordance with the RE-searcher character identified at the planning stage.

5   Analyse the findings. Having completed their inquiry pupils must collate the information they have found and check that they know what it means.

6   Draw conclusions. Pupils should be invited to consider the extent to which the information they have gathered from their inquiry has or has not answered their question(s). Pupils should be invited to draw conclusions about what has been learnt, what has not been learnt

and the merits of the enquiry approach taken as a way of developing their knowledge and understanding about the topic. Pupils should be invited to reflect on their performance 'in role' as the RE-searcher character and any reasons they can think of as to why this approach has or has not suited them.

This is an inquiry cycle and can be repeated over and over again with different questions, methods and foci (Freathy and Freathy 2016:26–29).

Summary

The RE-searchers approach reconceives pupils and teachers as co-researchers to tackle the problems pertaining to representing the complex, diverse, multi-faceted and evolving nature of religion(s). It adopts a multi-methodological and multi-perspectival pedagogy and seeks to avoid favouring one methodology or one interpretative framework over others. The methodologies, methods and other interpretative lenses become objects of study in their own right.

USING DE BONO'S THINKING HATS

Introduction

Many different strategies have evolved to enhance pupils' thinking skills. The use of a community of inquiry tends to be considered a valuable method for building thinking skills (Desailly 2015:5). The popular method of De Bono's 'Thinking hats' is designed to promote creative thinking. Importantly for RE, it facilitates and enhances 'real' thinking to make the process of thinking productive and focussed. It allows pupils to think more clearly and objectively. Each hat is a different style of thinking, and, as such, it partly influenced the work of RE-searchers, where, as you read, they developed four cartoon characters each with very different research strengths and interests, but all committed to theological and religious studies (Freathy et al. 2015:101).

The six 'thinking hats' are separated into six different roles and each role is identified with a symbolic colour. The approach helps to redirect ideas by consciously switching from one hat (thinking) to the other, as an attempt to enhance clarity and depth especially when there are many factors to think about. However, it is suggested that each hat must be used for a limited time only and to be mindful that some will feel that using the hats is uncomfortable or against their better judgement. The black hat is the most valuable of all the hats and the most used, as it points to the difficulties, dangers and potential problems (De Bono 2000:xii).

In a group inquiry, it involves each group member being responsible for a certain type of thinking rather than ranging from one type to another.

- ■ White – facts, data and information. What do we already know?
- ■ Yellow – looking at the bright side, being optimistic, positive, adding value. What are the benefits?
- ■ Red – expressing intuition, emotions, reactions, opinions. What do we feel?
- ■ Blue – managing and process controlling, looking at the bigger picture. What are our aims?
- ■ Green – exploring other alternatives, creativity, solutions. What new ideas have we got?
- ■ Black – being realistic, practical, weaknesses, being cautious, finding where things might go wrong, discovering difficulties. What are the problems?

In the classroom

In RE, plan for it to be used in a structured way to facilitate each pupil to develop devices for thinking about particular issues. To apply this approach pupils will need to have had the approach modelled and to have discussed how each group member is required to think within their own sphere for the duration of the discussion and not to take on someone else's way of thinking (Desailly 2015). Once they are used to a hat they should be allowed to use different hats on different occasions. They discuss and then think about which ones feel most comfortable to them personally and why. You may provide actual hats to them or coloured cards with examples of prompt questions, as shown in Table 10.2. It is important to keep in mind that allowing pupils to discover key ideas for themselves without full guidance from the teacher has been criticised (Boxer 2019). Therefore, monitor carefully the knowledge acquisition of the pupils and use teacher led instruction as well.

Table 10.2 De Bono's 'Thinking hats'

	Should Eid be a national holiday?	Should we have competition for harvest festival	Should veganism be compulsory
White	Every year we get certain days off for Christmas and Easter. Those celebrating Eid with their families struggle because days have to be booked off and sometimes it is not approved.	The children are organising a harvest festival and require everyone to bring in charity donations and food.	There are very few vegans.
Yellow	Allows people to have time to celebrate. Respectful of others and their beliefs. Teaches more people about Eid.	Yes. The competition will motivate children to bring in food, which will help the needy. Make it friendly so that no child feels left out.	The health benefits are many. Protects rainforests.
Red	It should be. I think it is important to be inclusive. I don't know if everyone would agree.	Yes. A good idea because pupils will be doing something good. Good especially if they have financial issues.	Damages the whole meat industry. Overgrowth of vegetation. It is expensive.
Blue	If we were to have it, how could the date be set?	Get as much as possible, no competition. Do a class contribution as usual.	What do we know about veganism? How can we make it more popular?
Green	Schools can get involved in Eid exploring cultural differences, process of Eid and its importance. Raise money for charity – tackling issues in the community, for example, homelessness – giving back. Those celebrating have a day off.	We could have a competition on who brings the most donations in each class? Maybe we could do it as a year group this time.	grow your own food knowledge (expenses) – grow your own food (expensive). Do people follow it? Why? (Is it religion?) Deforestation anyway, for animal feeding.
Black	There is no fixed day. It isn't the largest religion in the UK, therefore, some people may be unhappy with this. Which Eid would be the national holiday? both? We need to talk about other religions, as people would think it's unfair.	Can everyone afford to donate? Also some people don't agree with the harvest festival itself.	Are the health benefits real? Should it become a religion? What are the ethical implications for choice?

Summary

This is another way of exploring real-life issues in RE. It can provide, with careful planning and organisation, many opportunities for clear thinking, adoption of a standpoint and deeper investigations of contemporary issues.

USING ENQUIRY IN RE

Introduction

Pupils are curious and tend to enquire. It is this inquisitive disposition that has the potential of furthering the relevance of RE. Thus, the use of questions in teaching RE is essential, albeit with appropriate sensitivity and with an effective presentation in a secure environment. An enquiry-based approach to RE is an environment in which learning is driven by a process of enquiry owned by the pupils (Wintersgill 2017:44). Pupils suggest and identify the main issues, questions and concepts to be investigated and how they will learn. Enquiry is a process involving an open-ended key evaluative question that the pupils seek to answer (Erricker, Lowndes and Bellchambers 2011:60). Pupils are actively engaged and encouraged to go deeper and critically analyse the subject matter at hand. Sometimes these are related to a real problem, which may be presented in the form of a scenario, a case study or a project. They acquire relevant knowledge by examining the available resources. The teacher sets up the focus of the enquiry, ensures that the necessary resources are available, and facilitates and monitors their learning (Wintersgill 2017:44). It is the pupils who form the '*why*' and the '*what*' of the learning process and the teacher shapes it towards the *how, when* and *so what*? (Webster 2010:19).

Delivering high-quality enquiry

The skills of enquiry are seen as a key to improving teaching in RE (Ofsted 2013). A weakness in primary RE was the poor approach to enquiry. For example, pupils rarely developed their skills of enquiry into religion: to ask more pertinent and challenging questions; to gather, interpret and analyse information and to draw conclusions and evaluate issues using good reasoning (Ofsted 2013:9). In addition, when teachers used an enquiry approach, they did not intervene to ensure that the pupils maintained a focus on the key questions driving the enquiry (Ofsted 2013:10). Moreover, enquiries were not sustained after having identified questions at the start, teachers rarely extended these into a genuine investigation (Ofsted 2013:9). Often, pupils were given insufficient time to process their findings and extend their enquiry: teachers provided opportunities for gathering and summarising factual information but then moved the pupils quickly to a superficial summary instead of extending and deepening their understanding of the material (Ofsted 2013:10). Some teachers were limiting enquiries by directing pupils to a 'happy end' by signalling to them that they wanted a positive 'right answer' about the value of religion, limiting the opportunity to explore more controversial possibilities. There was also too much focus on the product of the enquiry rather than the process (Ofsted 2013:10–11). The importance of critical enquiry is also endorsed by the Commission on RE who considered scholarly and academic practices, together with teachers who promote scholarly accuracy and critical enquiry, to be part of high-quality RE (CoRE 2018:35). Recent criticism calls for teachers to teach new knowledge directly if they want pupils to learn new ideas and build on previous knowledge (Boxer 2019). This means that when using the enquire method teachers should ensure that by the end pupils have acquire the intended substantive knowledge of the query or topic at hand.

As you implement the enquiry method, you should communicate a belief in the academic potential of all pupils by setting tasks that stretch pupils, but which are achievable, within a challenging curriculum. Planning should connect new content with pupils' existing knowledge and/or provide additional pre-teaching if pupils lack critical knowledge. It is through assessments that you can check for prior knowledge and pre-existing misconceptions. Then, use intentional and consistent language that promotes challenge and aspiration and make use of well-designed resources (DfE 2019).

Subject to the type of enquiry undertaken, Eaude (2019:114) notes that it can be unsettling for teachers as pupils may ask questions for which they may not be very knowledgeable and be taken into unfamiliar territories, such as where God came from. Nevertheless, he suggests that current, complex and contested enquiries are more relevant and meaningful and help pupils see that it is happening now. This embeds their learning and enables them to apply it in future contexts. Teaching with purpose about the real world can empower pupils.

How to prepare enquiry questions?

There are many ways of designing an enquiry and many forms of enquiries. In fact, the term 'enquiry' is used to cover a wide variety of learning activities that require students to create hypotheses, plan and execute investigations, solve problems, think creatively and critically and make connections (Wintersgill 2017:45). Ofsted (2013:23) commends a straightforward model, which starts by asking questions, then carrying out the investigation, followed by drawing conclusions, evaluation, reflection and expression.

However, Hutton and Cox (2021:150–151) think that enquiry questions are not the same as the pedagogical tools called 'cycles of enquiry' which can be pupil led and often guide the structure of a lesson or a series of lessons. Enquiry questions can be the basis of a cycle of inquiry, but it is not always the case. They propose that curriculum design can be based around enquiry questions. They advocate the use of enquiry questions for curriculum design rather than a pedagogical tool. This would mean that pupils, over a series of lessons, would build their substantive knowledge and understanding to be able to answer a question. They suggest that several enquiry questions could be used over the course of a topic.

A question might include an underlying concept, for example, what are crosses used for, which uncovers the concept of symbolism or a question might be based on a concept, such as, Is God kind? The importance of conceptual development and the three main categories were elucidated in Chapter 6. Thus, conceptual enquiry is where the big ideas and religions and worldviews become the focus of learning. This is considered helpful in avoiding a fragmented approach to teaching in RE. In developing pupils' knowledge and understanding, wise teachers adopt a pedagogy of conceptual enquiry rather than one based on the acquisition of propositional RE knowledge (James and Stern 2019:12). In Chapter 8, you learnt that there is more than one way to organise planning for learning in RE: thematic, systematic or cross-curricular approaches. So, a third way is to set up an enquiry into a theme across different religions and beliefs or aspects of one religion or belief.

Some schools use it to help them produce a balanced scheme of work that enables pupils to develop an understanding of the differing or specific disciplinary dimensions in the study of religion. For example, the title of a unit of work may consist of both theological and phenomenological questions, such as, what do Muslims believe and how do they show this in their lives. Teachers and pupils would then be expected to develop additional enquiry questions within this unit of work to ensure both types of disciplinary questions are addressed. They could also identify ethical questions, such as, how and why do Muslims care for others and why should people care for others. In addition, they could raise philosophical questions within this or other units of work, such as questions about miracles and life after death. These 'big questions' provide a context for carrying out an investigation (Ofsted 2013:24). Furthermore, enquiry can also be taught through challenges such as a statement where the pupils prove or disprove it through debate, discussion and research or through clearly design activities that scaffold the pupils to one answer or religious truths, which in turn inspires further learning and questions (Webster 2010:19).

Effective enquiry in RE

In the most effective RE teaching, an enquiry is placed at the heart of learning, which:

- Is not age-limited – effective enquiry is found at all ages.
- Involves sustained learning – in which pupils set up the enquiry, carry it out, evaluate their learning and revisit the questions set.
- Starts by engaging pupils in their learning – making sure they can see the relevance and importance of the enquiry and how it relates to their own concerns.
- Allows pupils time to gather information and draw conclusions before asking them to reflect on or apply their learning – the focus on 'learning from' usually comes later as they ask the key question – so what?
- Enables pupils to reconsider their initial thinking and extend their enquiry as they begin to see new levels of possibility – if pupils have identified key questions at the outset, they reconsider these, add more or re-prioritise them.
- Allows pupils to use their creativity and imagination – ensuring that experiential learning and opportunities to foster spiritual and creative development are built into the process of enquiry.
- Emphasises 'impersonal evaluation' – asking pupils to give well-founded reasons and justify their conclusions or views rather than simply expressing their personal feelings or responses to the enquiry (Ofsted 2013:23–24).

The recent Ofsted RE Research Review (Ofsted 2021) has emphasised the accuracy of teachers questioning, especially 'enquiry' (sic) questions. It was observed, following the work of Panjwani and Revell (2018), that imprecise questions sometimes encourage pupils to use weak generalisations or unsustainable stereotypes (for example, 'what's the difference between Islam and Christianity?'). Instead, rich and precise questions, which emphasise 'social actors' and their uses of traditions, promote the use of accurate representations (for example, 'how have different Muslims understood Islam's relationship with Christianity?').

Drawing on and enhancing skills

Enquiry-based learning enables pupils to draw on and develop their skills as they investigate issues in RE. The cycle of enquiry provides the opportunity to:

- Generate and refine questions.
- Develop lines of enquiry using a range of methods and sources.
- Research complex issues and explore a range of viewpoints.
- Gather, compare and synthesise information, interpreting, analysing and evaluating findings.
- Develop knowledge and understanding of religion and belief and the impact these have on individuals and communities today.
- Use critical thinking and reasoning to draw conclusions.
- Reflect on their ideas, beliefs, values, experiences and feelings concerning what they have learnt through the enquiry.

In the classroom

There are some variations in the steps and terminologies used for the enquiry approach, as shown in Table 10.3. It is expected that pupils would become less teacher-reliant and more independent in using these steps as they progress.

Table 10.3 The enquiry approach

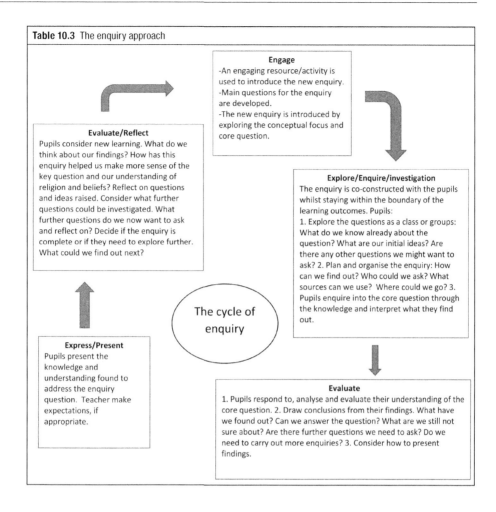

Engage
-An engaging resource/activity is used to introduce the new enquiry.
-Main questions for the enquiry are developed.
-The new enquiry is introduced by exploring the conceptual focus and core question.

Evaluate/Reflect
Pupils consider new learning. What do we think about our findings? How has this enquiry helped us make more sense of the key question and our understanding of religion and beliefs? Reflect on questions and ideas raised. Consider what further questions could be investigated. What further questions do we now want to ask and reflect on? Decide if the enquiry is complete or if they need to explore further. What could we find out next?

Explore/Enquire/investigation
The enquiry is co-constructed with the pupils whilst staying within the boundary of the learning outcomes. Pupils:
1. Explore the questions as a class or groups: What do we know already about the question? What are our initial ideas? Are there any other questions we might want to ask? 2. Plan and organise the enquiry: How can we find out? Who could we ask? What sources can we use? Where could we go? 3. Pupils enquire into the core question through the knowledge and interpret what they find out.

The cycle of enquiry

Express/Present
Pupils present the knowledge and understanding found to address the enquiry question. Teacher make expectations, if appropriate.

Evaluate
1. Pupils respond to, analyse and evaluate their understanding of the core question. 2. Draw conclusions from their findings. What have we found out? Can we answer the question? What are we still not sure about? Are there further questions we need to ask? Do we need to carry out more enquiries? 3. Consider how to present findings.

Summary

The enquiry approach is useful as it offers quality learning. The questions and the process are key to its successful use.

USING THE CASE STUDY METHOD IN RE

Introduction

Pupils in your class will reason differently. Some may adopt reasoning which might be deductive, inductive, critical or counterfactual. The use of case studies can be an effective classroom method for reasoning. It is commonly applied in law, business, medicine and the social sciences. Its use can be powerful in RE especially when you want pupils to examine something real and an issue affecting contemporary situations.

A strength of teaching through case studies is that it gives focus to the subject content and skills as the case is explored (Monk and Silman 2011:63). Pupils actively engage in working out principles from the case, which develops their problem solving, analysis, inductive reasoning and decision-making skills. It may also assist them in coping with uncertainties. Moreover, it has been found to have the potential to move pupils beyond the recall of knowledge and facilitates interdisciplinary learning as they relate RE specific domain knowledge to individual knowledge and grapple with real societal issues.

In the classroom

The kind of case to use will depend on your learning intentions. You can create and present cases in various formats; whichever style you use, it is important to make them accessible for all pupils. You may use text, newspaper cutting or a video. Organisationally, pupils can work in table groups or individually. You can provide them with a set of questions or keep it open-ended.

The process might involve identifying the central question or problem to explore first. Preference should be given to something relevant to their lives and what is accessible. It should be sufficiently complex to yield multiple perspectives, layers of meaning and diverse solutions. It is useful to provide the context to keep the exploration confined and to set the scene. Sometimes it is more productive to have a clear structure, time frame, set of questions and definitions to enhance the quality of the process. Sometimes you can keep it open-ended by allowing pupils to follow their lines of enquiry. Whatever method you adopt, some pupils may require scaffolding depending on their needs.

An alternative way to explore the case would be to invite pupils to interview each other after having studied the case, or you, as a reporter, could interview a small group to extend their learning and, simultaneously, assess their progress and evaluate their learning process.

A third model involves organising a forum where 8–10 pupils have a structure or unstructured discussion, perhaps in the Socratic or fishbowl format. A volunteer from each forum then reports to the rest of the class. The teacher then collects the points from each group and then conducts a whole class discussion, like a discussant at a conference.

To dig deeper into the concept within the case study, providing pupils with some related reading material tends to be highly effective and provide further challenge.

Sometimes it is tempting to use current events reported by the media in RE lessons. Before substituting a previously planned curriculum, it is important to ask about its relevance to RE lessons and the extent to which it adds to the already cohesive and sequential scheme.

Topics for case studies

You can find a dilemma faced by a key figure from among the stories of prophets and faith leaders. Extract a paragraph or page as historical material and convert it into a case study. You can add an appropriate illustration if needed. Thereafter create some questions, dilemmas and issues for the pupils to explore. For example, Abraham's sacrifice, Jonah fleeing or the challenge of Noah at the drowning of everything.

You can use newspaper cutting, which reports an issue affecting religion and religious behaviour. This can vary from food, wearing symbols, animals, clothing, festivals, holidays and construction of places of worship or issues faced by people at the workplace where their faith and work are not always compatible.

You can also use case studies based on pollution, environmental concerns, violence, peace and racism. For example, you create a case study based on the teachings of Sikhi about pollution. Pupils can then debate and discussed the case.

Summary

There are different types of case studies. These can be selected to deliver lessons that help to achieve the intention of RE successfully.

USING PHILOSOPHY FOR CHILDREN IN RE

Introduction

Philosophy for Children (P4C) and its associated teaching methodology, the Community of Inquiry (CoI) have become well-established internationally. It is a pedagogical approach to assist pupils to look at the world around them in a different way, said to have been developed by Matthew Lipman in 1970 (Lipman, Sharp and Oscanyan 1980). It has been influenced by Vygotsky, Piaget, Dewey as well as the tradition of Socratic dialogue (McDowell 2020). The need for teachers to create a classroom community where enquiry and natural discovery is encouraged has been highlighted. The self-reported benefits suggest that P4C can be a useful approach to address disruption, bullying and other anti-social behaviours (Siddiqui, Gorard and See 2017).

The P4C approach focuses on self-determined learning, questions rather than answers and participation rather than judgement, communities of learners rather than a hierarchy of knowledge so that the way for active free learning is opened (Kizel 2016:1). This approach helps pupils to listen to their minds, body, spirit and emotions which embed the subject matter that they have an interest in learning about (Ricci and Pritscher 2015). In other words, the agenda should be driven by the learners. The P4C approach relates to aspects of a constructivist theory developed by John Dewey, whereby pupils learn best through experiences, reflecting on them and by asking questions to gain new knowledge through researching their questions to find solutions.

There is disagreement theoretically and in practice about what P4C means. P4C is also presented as a community of philosophical inquiry (CPI) which can equip pupils with tools to become more critical and to develop a more social and global consciousness so that they can take, as adults, the role of constructing democratic societies (Echeverria and Hannam 2017). International perspectives suggest that at its core, in addition to improving critical thinking and exposing pupils to an important academic tradition, is a method of transforming education that centres on inquiry by moving beyond the arguments of child-centred and teacher-centred education. It helps pupils to think naturally rather than technically (Naji and Hashim 2017).

Nevertheless, in running regular P4C sessions, a teacher builds a learning environment that develops four types of thinking. *Caring thinking* demonstrates care about the subject and each other and involves showing respect for people and views. *Collaborative thinking* involves listening to and building on each other's ideas, but not necessarily agreeing with each other. *Creative thinking* is introducing new ideas and new ways of thinking about things. *Critical thinking* involves clarifying, challenging and evaluating ideas (Prescott 2015:43), to develop higher-order thinking skills, concept understanding and universal values.

Schools and P4C

There are different ways in which schools implement P4C. Some use it as a formal and systematic approach to develop critical thinking skills by introducing it in reception and run it through to year 6. In others, it is facilitated weekly in KS2, fortnightly in KS1 and in EYFS twice every half term. Other schools introduce P4C across the whole school, and where all teachers complete the training and are certified for this status. Since it is a means of opening up pupil's learning through enquiry and the exploration of ideas, you may see in such schools that it adopts an integrated approach into their day-to-day curriculum with the intent of creating enquiring classrooms. It would then feature in creative writing, enquiries in science and other activities like the school council.

Teachers talk about P4C as having an impact on personal, listening and reasoning skills, fostering independence and emotional and social development. Pupils learn to think before they speak and justify what they say. Some teachers also mention that it has a positive impact on behaviour in the playground. Moreover, it is thought to empower pupils to think in a philosophical way which enriches them as learners and as individuals.

Using P4C in the teaching of RE

Philosophy can establish connections between different religious, philosophical or secular positions. To do so, Jørgensen (2009:14) suggests that philosophy should play an independent role in RE and should not be mistaken for philosophy of religion. Pupils are involved in reflecting on and enquiring into philosophical ideas, and because the philosophy of religion is a major school of philosophy, RE is a natural context in which to use P4C (Prescott 2015:37). In RE, there is individual and collective recognition between all to decide on the points to be made based on the key question. This helps to promote positive peer relationships and mutual respect. It promotes self-esteem as they develop a perception of themselves as capable of intelligent thought (Thwaites 2005:7). The effects of the practice of P4C on pupils' affective engagement in RE was explored by Lancaster-Thomas (2017) in a secondary school. The practice of P4C has been linked to the development of caring and collaborative thinking and the study considered that relationship. The findings suggested that P4C can foster affective engagement in many pupils, particularly for those pupils finding emotional expression and interpersonal interactions challenging. It was recommended that implementing a P4C program must be executed carefully and with the mindfulness that it may not have the same potential or usefulness for all pupils universally.

In another primary study, data from questionnaires and semi-structured interviews suggested a considerable change in the pupil's perception and enjoyment of RE as a result of using P4C. In turn, their greater participation resulted in RE lessons becoming more vibrant and exciting and the role of the teacher was reported to have shifted from the distributor of knowledge to the facilitator of the enquiry in which pupils make sense of their worldview. It allowed pupils to attain higher levels of thinking within 'learning about religions' than using more traditional didactic teaching methods (Thwaites 2005:5–7). Recently, McDowell (2020) investigated how P4C in RE creates effective dialogue and found a clear improvement in pupil's religious literacy, thinking and communication skills.

Over the years, the prevalence of philosophy in schools has been an impressive development, nevertheless, Watson and Thompson (2007) raise the concern that it focuses on problem-solving so that even when extended into thinking about values and beliefs, it tends to see this as largely problem-solving. From one point of view, this is right, however, they argue that because of the context of our society, generally the impression of relativism is very easily conveyed. That is, it is for pupils to conjure up their own values. As a result, the notion of the existence of a moral and spiritual order which we need to relate to, rather than negotiating values for ourselves, is normally quite weakly presented, if at all (Watson and Thompson 2007:131). Some teachers might be sceptical in using it and may perceive it as 'a challenge of faith' (McDowell 2020).

Organising P4C in RE

In this pedagogy, the classroom is set up sometimes as a circle and the dialogue is managed through a process called Community of Inquiry (Echeverria and Hannam 2017). This reflective approach to discussion involves asking pupils various questions to encourage them to think about their morals, natural curiosity, ways of thinking, thoughtfulness. Pupils are said to flourish as the medium is ostensibly oral. The agenda is set by the pupils who tend to ask philosophical questions. Thinking time is built into the process deliberately. Pupils explore the ideas without the fear of being right or wrong, whilst they learn that their ideas and those of others have value and that there are no 'right' answers since all reflections and thoughts are given a hearing (James and Stern 2019:121). A safe and secure environment is established where disagreement is accepted and normal. Pupils are allowed to change their minds and viewpoints. The role of the teacher as a guide rather than authority is emphasised. The teacher problematises concepts, content, questions and responses to help pupils to internalise their understanding of the concepts deeply. It is important to consider that when discussing controversial issues, it is the idea that should be challenged not the individual. Some pupils take criticism of the ideas they express as an *ad hominem* attack. This is not always easy and RE teachers need to help their pupils navigate this terrain (McKain 2018:179).

The procedures

RE is energised through the use of P4C. Prescott (2015:37) offers some helpful suggestions for the successful use of P4C. It can often be confused with circle time, as both require pupils to sit in a circle. Therefore the distinction is that P4C requires pupils to talk and think together as a group, [sic] a process facilitated by sitting in a circle. It can be a lengthy process, thus, the more pupils get used to it the better. Sometimes a full enquiry process could be run, whereas, at others, some parts of it or it could be run into a second session.

Traditionally it has ten steps (McDowell 2020), although it is flexible. It can be cyclical and acts as a framework rather than a rigid plan. P4C is generally introduced as follows:

1   Preparation – this could be an activity or game which bonds the groups or community together. To warm up they try to match pairs that have things in common.

2   Sit in a circle and agree to a set of ground rules.

3   Present the stimulus and share immediate reactions – this could be a film, artwork, text, story, image, prayer, poetry, artefact or music to provoke their thinking.

4   Individual thinking time – to focus and identify key ideas, concepts, issues.

5   Generation of philosophical questions – pupils raise open-ended and philosophical questions, they or the teacher records their words/thoughts/concepts generated from the stimulus.

6   Airing of questions – sharing and sorting questions by the community.

7   The teacher explains that the questions now belong to everyone and that no one group 'owns' them.

8   Democratic selection of questions – pupils vote for the questions and the most popular is selected.

9   First words – pupils share their initial thoughts and build on or challenge the ideas expressed.

10 Final thoughts – pupils reflect and express some of their final thoughts and detect any changes in their thinking through the enquiry.

11 Review and evaluation – final reflections on one's own or others' thinking, the process and their involvement.

In the classroom

Set high expectations for all by creating a culture of respect and trust that supports all pupils to succeed, for example, by modelling the types of courteous behaviour expected of pupils in the exchange that take place during P4C (DfE 2019). Moreover, to stimulate pupil thinking and check for understanding, you should plan activities around what you want pupils to think hard about and also include a range of types of questions in class discussions to extend and challenge pupils, for example, by modelling new vocabulary or asking pupils to justify answers. You should also provide appropriate wait time between question and response where more developed responses are required (DfE 2019).

In some infant classes, the session may be less formal and often as a response to everyday issues, such as charity, friendships or kindness. Pupils are introduced to a stimulus and then encouraged to 'wonder' about it and develop their understanding of the concepts within the stimulus. Thereafter, teachers guide pupils through discussion, reflection and encourage them to think about 'small' and 'big' questions.

Using stimuli

Using a powerful stimulus, pupils could begin by asking, for example, what a picture is saying. Thereafter, they use the grid shown in Table 10.4 to discuss or record their ideas.

Sentence stems

Some teachers emphasise the use of sentence stems during P4C. It is also good practice to address pupils and their ideas by their first name. For example, when agreeing with a pupil, a teacher could begin with 'I agree with [name] because…'. '[Pupil]'s idea is interesting. To extend it, I think … could be used'. The repetitive reference to the pupil's name is considered to project feelings of pride, recognition and celebration, regardless of disagreeing or agreeing with their opinion and thoughts. However, this might not be so in every instance with every pupil.

Question stems

This process can support pupils to think more deeply by generating questions about all aspects of life through the lenses of religion, belief, faith and non-faith, including within their own lives. The use of question stems is also evident in some classrooms.

- What is … (e.g. What is God's intention for the world?)
- What makes … (e.g. What makes some places sacred?)
- Would you be … (e.g. Would you be the same person if you were born elsewhere?)
- How do we know what … (e.g. How do we know what lies are?)
- What if … (e.g. What if people didn't care for others?)

Table 10.4 In-depth exploration of stimuli		
Write 2–3 questions which can be found in the stimulus and there is no argument about the answer.	Examine closely	
Write 2–3 questions which might need to be researched and where there is no argument about the answer.	Research further	
Write 2–3 questions where there could be many possible ideas and we need to look for evidence in the stimulus.	Solve it	
Write 2–3 questions where we leave the stimulus behind and think about the big ideas within it.	Think and look beyond	

- Always or never (e.g. Should we always obey the religious/civic law?)
- What if ... (e.g. What if honesty did not exist?)
- Is it possible ... (e.g. Is it possible to come alive again after death?)
- Can ... (e.g. Can suffering be a good thing?)
- When ... (e.g. When is happiness a bad emotion?)
- Who ... (e.g. Who decides what is best for humans?)
- Why do we say ... (e.g. Why do we say 'cheaters never prosper'?)
- If God is ... (e.g. If God is everywhere, why to go to a place of worship?).

P4C in action

Box 10.1 shows philosophy for children is used as a whole-school approach.

Summary

P4C is well-known internationally and can be an additional pedagogy for RE. You may want to read further on it at www.sapere.org.uk and wwwp4c.com. It has very useful materials for introducing thinking skills and Socratic inquiry. A teacher's guide is also available https://p4c.com/about-p4c/teachers-guide/.

BOX 10.1 CASE STUDY: P4C IN PRACTICE

Intent

We use the P4C approach to teaching and learning. This helps develop pupils into effective, critical and creative thinkers. They take responsibility for their own learning. This is done in a sensitive and collaborative way. Pupil develops attitudes, skills and dispositions which enable them to contribute as responsible citizens. This supports the school's culture, ethos and values where the school and classroom listens and respects children and they do the same with each other.

Implementation

P4C is delivered as stand-alone sessions. A stimulus is shared in the classroom, for example, a drawing, story, film or photograph. Pupils then have thinking time to devise their questions. Thereafter, together the class selects one question to enquire into it further. We link P4C to a particular topic or curriculum subject such as English, history, PSHE or RE. Importantly, we take the opportunity to make links with lived experiences and issues of personal concern. These can include friendship, environment, caring, death, growing up, bullying. We also include philosophical issues such as identity, free will, truth, right and wrong, justice.

Impact

Overall, pupils become confident communicators. They show respect and sensitivity towards their peers. P4C creates an environment where a pupil's thinking and questioning can flourish. It helps to enhance the quality of learning as a whole.

USING ACTIVE LEARNING FOR RE

Introduction

Teachers are well aware of the significance of using a range of teaching styles for their teaching. The Cambridge Review recommended that teachers work towards a pedagogy of repertoire rather than a recipe, and principle than a prescription (Alexander 2010). This section offers some ideas to use as well as stimuli to develop others to extend the repertoire of your active learning strategies.

Active learning engages and challenges pupil's learning and thinking when using real-life and imaginary situations. Active learning is the process when pupils take ownership of their learning. They 'actively' engage in learning rather than passively receive information. In an active classroom environment, the teacher is a facilitator, supporting pupils as they learn and develop their skills, attitudes and dispositions by working independently and with others through solving problems, negotiating, assessing evidence and making informed decisions. Often it uses play, quizzes, role-play, presentations, experiments, drama, discussions, visits and performances so that the responsibility of learning is placed on the pupils (Rivett 2013). Vygotsky (1986) argued that social interaction and language were at the core of learning. Thus, the social element of learning is significant in active learning. *The Experiential Approach* discussed in Chapter 9 ostensibly takes an active learning approach that follows six steps to develop an awareness of religious understanding (Hammond 2015; Hay 2000).

Kolb's learning cycle shows that learning begins with a concrete experience and proceeds with reflection and modification resulting from that experience. Thus, opportunities for reflection should be incorporated within active learning experiences (Kolb 1984). Monk and Silman (2011) emphasise that it does not have to involve physical activity, but encompasses reflection, both independently and with peer and teacher involvement. Some active learning methods are particularly useful for promoting reflection, analysis, synthesis and evaluation. If pupils are to be motivated and empowered their learning experiences must be active rather than passive, with pupils constructing meaning for themselves (Hewitt and Wright 2019). Simply put, it is learning by doing and experiential learning.

Three-dimensional work

Pupils can make and display the items illustrated in Table 10.5 using a range of materials and resources.

However, there are certain factors such as preparation time, space, seating arrangements, resources, risk and shyness to be considered when planning such activities. Active learning might not be effective for all pupils. Importantly, RE teaching should go over and beyond active learning and the needs of all pupils including those with SEND. The adoption of an active learning pedagogy plans and prepares for this. Stephen, Martlew and Ellis (2010) suggest that pupil's levels of engagement will somewhat differ, as some may be disengaged and some would be intermittently engaged. Thus, the needs of all learners should be considered.

Table 10.5 Three-dimensional work

Create	Name	Religion
Cube	Kaabah	Islam
Candelabrum	Hanukkah	Judaism
Dance stick	Dandia	Hinduism
Windom	Stain glass	Christianity
Flag	Nishan Sahib	Sikhism

Active learning does not preclude cognitive work and includes talking, thinking and questioning. Through 'active learning' pupils can have an element of excitement and can be more engaged in their learning, making their learning experience enjoyable, memorable and motivational. It also increases pupils' cognitive development, critical thinking and higher-order abilities as they offer a diversity of experiences. Classroom dynamics may limit active learning if they are not considered carefully such as the profile of the class, e.g. size, interests, abilities, specific needs, prior experienced and pupils anticipated responses.

In the classroom

For setting high expectations, create a positive environment where making mistakes and learning from them and the need for effort and perseverance are part of the daily routine. To promote good progress, it is suggested that you reduce distractions that take attention away from what is being taught and break complex material into smaller steps. You can increase the likelihood of material being retained by planning regular review and practice of key ideas and concepts over time through structured talk activities and balancing exposition, repetition, practice and retrieval of critical knowledge and skills (DfE 2019).

- Artefacts – make them three-dimensional using play-doh or clay.
- Collage – invite pupils in groups to represent their views on a religious or human concept in a creative way using magazines, newspapers, sticky shapes, paper and card, based on stories in religions.
- Discussion about their viewpoint and those of believers on a faith-based current topic.
- Drama performances and talk about how they see events in a story, exploring good and bad.
- Freeze frames – ask pupils to pose as a still image representing a scene of a significant moment in a story for a believer and each scene will discuss and recognise the issues and needs of others.
- Hot sitting is used to show quick thinking and make them realise their own bias.
- Jeopardy – give pupils answers to questions on a topic, invite them to develop questions to match the answers about festivals.
- Poster – pupils make of faith leaders, beliefs, symbols and practices to display in the lower classrooms.
- Re-enactments help pupils reflect on the situation by changing the person involved and then asking how someone might have felt.
- Role-play scenario with cards of a religious issue. Set pupils in groups. Give each one a card. Let them have an open discussion and express their viewpoints. Give all the pupils a card, which says the scenarios. Card 1 ABC, Card 2 DEF, Card 3 neutral and Card 4 XYZ to disagree with Card ABC. This creates a debate and helps pupils understand that everyone has a different view.
- Storyboarding and cartoons use for story telling especially in lower years.
- Moral problems and situations for highlighting pupils' positions such as where and what they base their moral judgment upon.
- Performance as an assembly to the whole community.
- Video pupils answer questions and use recall and memory.
- Writing a diary entry to showcase their emotions, experiences, reflections and feelings.
- Zone of relevance – pupils have to think through given statements to consider their relevance about the question and place it at an appropriate place within the circular zone of relevance.

Role-play

Role-play can mean different things to different people and there are variants of it. It is an approach that can help learners to experience a new attitude, increase their sense of empathy and helps to follow procedures based on facts (Sotto 2007). In role-play, the role can be allocated or self-created. In both cases, it is important to make it easier for pupils and adults to step out of the role.

Summary

This section has drawn attention to the use of active learning strategies in RE. You have seen that active learning is both the cognitive engagement and physical involvement of pupils in the learning process. High ambitions should be held for all pupils and you should adapt teaching responsively by providing targeted support to pupils who struggle to increase their success.

USING GODLY PLAY IN RE

Introduction

In some primary schools, especially Christian, the use of Godly Play may be evident. Some teachers question the use of Godly Play in RE in maintained schools. This is another creative and imaginative method, which has the potential to be added to the repertoire of teaching approaches, whilst ensuring that it avoids dogmatism and faith nurture.

The method has been developed over many decades and has been well-tested and researched. It was designed as a method mainly for children aged 2–12 in parish faith communities by Berryman (1991) who based it on the tradition of Maria Montessori (d. 1870–1952) and others in RE (Berryman 2013). However, Hyde (2011:342) examined his works and revealed some anomalies in his approach to RE when compared with the Montessori method, especially his focus on play as opposed to work, as well as creativity and the creative process, as opposed to Montessori's grounding of the imagination in reality. These anomalies raise questions about the extent to which Berryman is, in fact, a true Montessorian. Nevertheless, it is significant to recognise that Godly Play is a distinct method applied for Christian nurture, formation and spiritual growth. It is well-known as an engaging pedagogy for strengthening Christian faith and heritage and is an indirect preparation for the Christian children to be involved directly in the worship of the congregation (Berryman 2009). Therefore its use, presence and place in formal educational settings outside of parish faith communities have been questioned and critiqued (Grajczonek and Truasheim 2017:174). It relies on the assumption that play is important for learning.

The story is the bedrock of this method. It tends to use various story types such as sacred, parables and liturgy. Pupils explore faith and beliefs through Bible-based stories by using appropriate resources such as banners, symbols, artefacts, 3D wooden saint figures, felt birds and animals, natural everyday material like stone and sand objects, and also plaques, illuminated manuscripts, underlay, cloth, booklets as well as words. The main focus is wondering questions and open-ended response time to encourage them to make meaning for themselves and spiritual development. Pupils enhance their religious vocabulary and have an opportunity for spiritual experience through wonder, creativity and play (Hyde 2014). The technique invites them into stories and to connect the stories with their personal experience. The method values process and considers discovery, openness, community and relationships as important. However, applying Godly Play rigidly in its own format by excluding other pedagogies might significantly limit young children's fullest engagement with, as well as their deep knowledge and understanding of, the biblical stories. Thus, in early years educational settings, Grajczonek and Truasheim (2017:183–184) caution against an uninformed and 'critique-less' implementation of Godly Play.

Principles

There are some principles to be mindful of:

- The narrative says only what needs to be said.
- It emphasises simplicity and the essence of the story rather than exciting explanations.
- The gestures and silence from the storyteller are important as well as the words.

Some of the common stories used include creation, the Exodus, the Ten Commandments, Advent, the circle of the Church's Year, Easter, Parables, the Good Shepherd, the Good Samaritan and the Sower, Moses and Abraham.

Reflections

Some student teachers, following visits to the Salvation Army, reported some benefits:

It is good for reflection and makes use of open space.

The pace tends to be slow, so I have to think about that and the learning happening.

You do get a sense of communal feeling and pupils to learn about each other's thoughts and beliefs in more personal ways.

I think this is a good example of using theological and sometimes social perspectives.

We were let free to wonder in a safe space to think deeper without thinking about what others might say.

You need to know the stories well and be familiar with the context and artefacts of religion and be creative, but it is not about entertaining pupils.

I was unsure about it, as it seemed to show Christian approaches to God through liturgical action.

In the classroom

The lesson follows a set format, akin to being involved in worship. Like a congregation, in the preliminary stage, the environment is set up and pupils gather in a circle around the resources that will tell the story, mostly from the Bible. They then gather and enter into the story as the storyteller, having taken a designated place in the circle, unfolds the designated script of a story using the objects in the circle. Slowly, the storyteller takes plenty of time by focussing on the materials and draws out the implications with the children. In the time of reflection, the storyteller asks wondering questions about the story (O'Shea 2018). For example:

- *I wonder which is your favourite part of the story?*
- *I wonder which is the most important part of the story?*
- *I wonder if we could leave anything out and still have the story we need?*
- *I wonder where you are in the story?*
- *I wonder which part of the story is about you?*

Thereafter, there is some scope for artistic responses centred on the story when pupils are given some time to explore their ideas through creative work. Pupils can leave the circle to create a personal response after they have had individual thinking time. They may select from a range of materials including cardboard, clay, papier-mâché, wood, construction materials, collage, junk, poetry and music. During the plenary session, pupils share their thoughts. At the sending out stage, pupils are sent out to whatever the event may be next either playtime, dinnertime or home.

A criticism levied towards this approach relates to its prescribed use of the wondering phases as part of the classroom pedagogy. It is considered rather contrived and artificial (McCreery 1994). In addition, the prescriptive nature, structure and guidelines embedded in Godly Play with its focus on faith formation may be rendered an inappropriate religion programme when implemented in educational settings. As such, Grajczonek and Truasheim (2017:174) suggest that consideration should be given to contemporary early childhood educational theory and practice and to evaluate the extent to which Godly Play reflects this theory and practice.

Summary

The use of Godly Play, which is a story-telling approach, can be used in RE to achieve educational aims and purposes.

USING QUESTIONS TO QUESTION IN RE

Introduction

The use of questions is probably the most powerful and most frequently used strategy in RE. This seeming straightforward strategy erupts, excites and engages pupils as soon as teachers declare the question or present a statement. However, it is important to pause and observe. Who answers? Who engages? Who is reflecting? Who is thinking? Who is conversing? It is likely to be the confident, the articulate, the more secure or even the 'usual ones'. Therefore, it is important to monitor your practice and ensure that everyone joins in some way so that no one is disadvantaged in their participation. Sometimes it requires targeting questions to specific individuals (Erricker, Lowndes and Bellchambers 2011:160).

You need to learn that questioning is an essential tool for teachers; questions can be used for many purposes, including checking pupils' prior knowledge, assess understanding and break down problems. Retrieval practice, for example, forces pupils to generate answers to questions. It has been proven to be one of the most effective learning strategies (Watson and Bradley 2021). You should learn how to provide appropriate wait time between question and response where more developed responses are required (DfE 2019).

The most frequent oral form of expression that humans use is asking questions which is a natural way of learning. It has been characterised as the lifeblood for RE (Moss 2015:67). Therefore, it is important to allow time for pupils to internalise the questions you present, think about them and conjure answers. Be mindful, however, of answering the question yourself and the question being perceived as intimidating.

RE has both personal and academic aspects to it. The personal dimension can sometimes be intense and sensitive which necessitates a learning environment that is not only safe and secure but is also attentive to inner matters. RE is concerned with the exploration of beliefs, faith, expressions, motivations and lived realities of humans. As such, it deals with matters of faith, psychology, spirituality and personal sentiments. All pupils have these inner aspects in themselves. Some may express these, whereas others may not; for reasons best known to them. The use of questioning in RE requires additional care. As a teacher, you should be cognisant of the potential of questions being perceived by pupils as an affront to their faith and as a challenge to their self-hood (McKain 2018). You may hear teachers say that asking the right questions, in the right way, at the right time, is the single most important thing a teacher can do in a lesson. Simultaneously, asking the wrong questions, at the wrong time, or to the wrong person and in the wrong way, can have demoralising effects.

In the classroom

You should plan activities around what you want pupils to think hard about and include a range of types of questions in class discussions to extend and challenge pupils. It is important to provide appropriate wait time between question and response where more developed responses are required. You should make use of well-designed resources to stimulate curiosity and plan to connect new content with pupils' existing knowledge or provide additional pre-teaching if pupils lack critical knowledge. For your lessons, you should use assessments to check for prior knowledge and pre-existing misconceptions. You may need to consider modelling effectively by narrating thought processes to make explicit how experts think, for example, asking questions aloud that pupils should consider when working independently and drawing pupils' attention to links with prior knowledge. To stimulate pupil thinking and to check their understanding, you should consider the factors that will support effective collaborative or paired work. You should also prompt pupils to elaborate when responding to questioning to check that a correct answer stems from secure understanding. At times you may also need to reframe questions to provide greater scaffolding or greater stretch (DfE 2019).

The ethos of the class should be non-threatening and mutually respectful. Some prompts to think about include: Is your classroom a questioning one? Are your RE questions rooted in a multi-disciplinary approach? Who is responsible for the questions? Do your questions aim for higher-order thinking and advance their cognitive stakes? Do you question engagement leading to the higher challenge? Who is controlling the question and learning process? Have you prepared more than one answer, where applicable? Are your outcomes and impact thought through?

There are myriad ways of presenting questions to pupils. Presenting from the front of the classroom is just one.

- Quizzes – short recap quizzes at the start of each lesson to review prior knowledge.
- Choral response – in addition to the quizzes, use choral responses where pupils call out collectively the correct answer.
- Mini-homily – organise mini-lectures by mixing pupils and tables where pupils 'lecture' for one minute on a given question.
- No hands up – everyone is expected to answer, sometimes the teacher selects, sometimes pupils choose, sometimes use a lolly stick.
- In the hot seat – pupils have a rota to sit in the hot seat to ask and answer questions.
- WhatsApp a friend – pupils pretend to use WhatsApp across the class to share an answer, both pupils contribute the answers.
- I want to know box – have a class box with questions devised by the pupils. On Friday draw out some to discuss as a class.
- I want to ask the box – have a class box with questions in it devised by the teacher. On Friday, draw out some to discuss as a class.
- My big question – collect questions devised by pupils and teachers over time on a given topic to be answered by faith leaders or visitors.
- What is the question – provide answers on strips and reverse the process by asking them to devise the question for the answers.

- Think-pair-share – pupils share ideas with a partner and respond to a set question.
- Detective – when pupils work in groups, go around and ask questions to tables based on what you hear them discuss.
- Devil's advocate – as appropriate, use it to ensure pupils recognise alternative viewpoints.
- Dragons Den – pupils must answer a range of questions about how to visit a place of worship.
- Retrieval practice – encourage pupils to come up with answers to questions.
- Interleaving – vary the type of problems which pupils answer within a topic.
- Pre-questions – asking questions about the material or issue before teaching it.
- Elaborative interrogation – getting pupils to ask 'why is this the case?' or 'why is this true for X but not for Y?'

Questions that matter

Moreover, in addition to using pupils' experiences, your curriculum should be beyond the life-world of your pupils. For RE to be life-changing and transformative it needs to consider national and international questions. High-quality RE invites the asking of profound personal and communal questions that dig deep into life's meanings and purposes. RE explores these questions and the range of answers that different religions and beliefs have to offer. The following enquiry questions cover the main dimensions in the study of religion and fields of enquiry that are appropriate for school-age pupils. Each type of enquiry question is distinctive but relates to the other enquiry questions. These are exemplified in Bristol, Kensington and Chelsea, Sunderland and other syllabi and identified by some student teachers.

Phenomenological questions

These are questions that focus on how the beliefs of a religion are expressed in practice and ways in which the beliefs make a difference to the lives of individuals and communities, e.g. How do Buddhists express their beliefs? How do Christians celebrate Easter? How and why do people use rituals in their lives? How are the arts used to express spirituality and belief?

Personal questions

How can I be happy? How can I best manage my relationships? What skills do I need to succeed in life? What emotional resources do I need to maintain a healthy lifestyle? We can get insights from religions and philosophies studied in RE and get practice in 'skills for life', such as empathy, sensitivity, humility and in thinking and communicating well.

Theological questions

These are questions about the particular beliefs of faith traditions (and secular world views), e.g. What do Christians believe about God? Why is Jesus special to Christians? What do religions believe about life after death? What do humanists say about life after death?

Philosophical questions

These are ultimate questions of meaning, purpose and truth, e.g. questions about the meaning of life, suffering, life after death, the existence of God and the validity of religious belief. They are the sort of questions that all humans may ask, whatever their religious or non-religious beliefs are, e.g. Why do people suffer? Is death the end? Do miracles happen? What is the meaning of life? Where are we going? What is 'true'? What is 'best'? What is our origin?

Political, social and psychological questions

How can we best understand the relationships between people? Why do religion and belief feature in the news so much? What do religious and belief groups say about various contemporary issues? How can we best understand the religious practices and festivals celebrated by our neighbours? What motivates people? Why are our public institutions set up in the way they are? How do/should people behave when in positions of power? How do/should people react when others have power over them? Without knowledge of religions and beliefs, our understanding of these big questions will be incomplete.

Cultural and historical questions

Where do we come from? Why are people different and why do they have different tastes and preferences? What is to be gained from a diverse society? How can we understand the history and traditional cultures of Britain and other countries without a knowledge and understanding of the religious and philosophical traditions which helped to form them?

Moral and ethical questions

RE focuses on ultimate questions in the light of the many moral and ethical dilemmas humans face in life, ranging from the personal to the global. These are questions about people's values and actions and how many moral decisions are made as a result of beliefs. Ethical questions may focus on particular moral issues and the religious and non-religious responses to these, e.g. How and why do religious people care for others? Why should people with religious faith care for the environment? How do people make moral decisions? Should religious people take part in wars? What is it to lead a good life? How do we know? Whom should we trust? How can we decide? Religious and philosophical principles and insights can help guide us when faced with moral dilemmas.

Sociological questions

These are questions about the impact of religion on society and the role of religion in communities, both locally and globally. These could include questions about how religions and beliefs affect people's sense of identity and belonging, questions about the diversity of beliefs, interfaith harmony and conflict, and the role of religion in politics, e.g. What does it mean to live in a religiously diverse country? How can religious beliefs affect identity? What issues does this raise? Do religions bring conflict or harmony? To what extent is the portrayal of religions in the media accurate?

Artistic, musical and literary questions

Many great artists, composers, musicians and writers had deep religious and/or philosophical motivation and inspiration for their work. Many use religious themes and employ references to religious literature and thought in their work. How can we understand the insights they are communicating without knowledge of some key religious ideas and stories?

Questions of origin

Where am I from? Where is my family from? Where did Adam and Eve come from? Are we related to Adam and Eve? Who created the big bang? How did we originate? What was before life? What do creation stories teach? Are we an accident or a plan? Did we begin with love, or was it random? Do holy books tell us nothing or something about the start of it all? What can science tell us? What can science not tell us?

Questions of meaning

What is the meaning of life? Is meaning in life or at the end of life? Does everyone experience meaninglessness? Why do we feel we need meaning/plan? Do we all have the same meaning in life? Who determines my meaning of life? Are some people more important in life than others? What meanings have I found in my experience? Why do humans disagree about life's meanings? Does life have to have a meaning?

Questions of purpose

Does everything have to have a point? Is play pointless, and fun because of that? What is fate? How much is meant to be? How much can we control? What's the point of making an effort? Are there purposes in life beyond games and shopping? What are they and why?

Questions of truth

What do we mean by truth? How do you know something is true? Can there be more than one truth? Who decides what is true? Where do you find the truth? Is it necessary to know what the truth is? Is it necessary to search for the truth? What evidence is there for God or atheism? Why do people disagree so much about God and life after death? Does reason tell us the truth or does experience? Can you feel the truth? Can you think the truth? Can you learn the truth? Is doubt inevitable and knowledge impossible? Should we always question what people tell us?

Questions of identity

Who am I? What makes the self unique – if it is unique? Who has made me? Genes or environment, nature or nurture? Am I more than my parents made me or am I less? Can I choose who to be? Am I important or significant? Why and how? Do I have free will?

Questions of belonging

What groups do I belong to? Why do people need me? Do I need other people? Would it make a difference if I wasn't there? Can an individual make sense of life without the group? Can a community make sense of life? Why and how might they need me? Can I be a human by myself?

Questions of value

What matters most to you? Why? Who influences your values? Is there something more valuable than money? What brings value to your life? Where do your values come from?

What are my values? Who influences them? Do I practice my values, or am I hypocritical? Why is it so hard to do what I mean to do? Can I use my values to judge others, or should we not judge each other? Why are some different values so common across the world?

Questions of commitment

What is a commitment? Why do we have commitments? Is commitment necessary, if so when? Who am I committed to? What are my commitments? How can we commit to each other? How do my commitments affect others and affect me? How do others' commitments affect me? Why won't some people commit? Is commitment necessary all the time? What will I live for? What would I die for? Why do other people's commitments look fanatical and extreme? Who has influenced my commitments?

Questions of destiny

Where are we heading? What happens when we die? What will we know at the end of life, but not before? Is death destiny or disaster or neither? If Heaven, Paradise, Moksha and Nirvana are all 'made up', why do humans keep making these ideas up? Why do so many believe in them? What if someone came back from the dead, would we believe what they told us?

Summary

The sensitive and effective use of questioning in RE is an important strategy. Questions should be developed based on multiple disciplinary approaches and focus on understanding, meaning and interpretation.

USING THE *HALAQAH* IN RE

Introduction

The *halaqah* is probably the most ancient method. In this section, ideas are inspired from the Muslim tradition. Halaqah (pl. halaqāt) in Arabic means a circle. In other words, a learning circle where pupils learn 'around' their teacher or text. It is usually a small group setting, although it can take the form of a larger gathering, depending on the duration, structure, topic, text, subject, purpose, teacher and location. It is also known as a *majlis*, lit., a sitting or gathering. Ostensibly it is an oral pedagogy also used by the Prophet Muhammad (peace be upon him) as he taught the early Muslims both in Makkah and Madinah (Boyle 2004). His companions tended to sit around him. It was the primary mode of organising learning at that time.

Currently, the legacy of this historical teaching method has been preserved and it remains a feature in the experience of many Muslims across the world. Overall they can be formal and informal. They can be of mixed age and multigenerational grouping for males and females. Contemporary expressions of the halaqah are eclectic. Some are organised in mosques, whereas others are held in homes, community settings, offices, formal educational institutions, in mosques, under trees, on holidays and virtually on the Internet. Some sit on the floor, others may use desks. The curriculum would be subject to the needs of the participants or a text chosen by a teacher, which means students can choose to attend or not and move between teachers and texts. Within the learning circle, collaborative groups may be created to facilitate discussions, peer tutoring and support systems. Students question and discuss the text, their peers and teachers. In other words, there may be less of a distinction between formal and informal learning. However, in faith-based situations, they nurture the religious, spiritual, social, moral, theological, eschatological, emotional and intellectual needs of Muslims.

In some Shakhsiyah Schools in the UK, character education is central to their school life. For this, the *halaqah* method provides them with a daily dialogic space that acts as the core of a thematic curriculum (Ahmed 2019). The curriculum incorporates the study of Islam, other religions, PSHE, citizenship and other subjects. As pupils engage within the *halaqah*, they develop a sense of agency, criticality, openness and reflexivity about themselves, their faith, their learning within and outside school, others' beliefs and views, wider society and contemporary issues. In the model of Ahmed (2020) the worldview employed in their *halaqah* is that of Islam; however, it is often about other ways of thinking and almost always concerning the specific contexts of children's lives in multicultural twenty-first-century Britain (Ahmed 2020). In their classrooms, since a *halaqah* is at the core of a thematic curriculum, ideas discussed therein are developed elsewhere. Ahmed exemplifies this. In the theme Ancient Egypt, pupils learn historical enquiry skills by examining objects from the era; they explore the Qur'anic and Jewish narratives of Musa (Moses) with Pharaoh. They look at what it means to be a refugee in the contemporary world and relate that to the family of Yusuf (Joseph) seeking refuge in Ancient Egypt and the people of Musa fleeing Egypt centuries later.

In primary schools for RE, the *halaqah* perhaps can take the form of circle time and the process might involve dialogic pedagogy, the Socratic method and 'Philosophy for Children'. The collaborative feature would enable metacognition, and through dialogue with others, pupils come to know about themselves. Collaboration can be part of a task; it does not have to be the whole task though. These tasks should require decision making as when pupils have to make a real decision, they begin to reflect on how they are making them and hence on their thinking (Larkin, Freathy, Doney and Freathy 2020:23). The RE *halaqah* can also be a forum, a forum that provides room for pupils to consider issues that may be bothering them or an opportunity to voice their thoughts (Webster 2010:17).

Summary

The *halaqah* method has the potential of helping with deeper learning and understanding. To make learning be retained and improve the memory, evidence suggests that pupils should teach the material to somebody else, which helps them learn the material more deeply and organise their knowledge (Watson and Bradley 2021).

USING VISITS AND VISITORS: RE IN THE REAL WORLD

Introduction

In Chapter 2, you read about the importance of providing pupils with the opportunity of encountering lived religions based on research (Dinham and Shaw 2020). When pupils encounter lived religion in a learner-active way, for example, by exploring buildings, artefacts and practices, they are introduced to diversity across and within religions, whether in face-to-face interaction or by virtual means. Students in the study of Unstad and Fjørtoft (2021) revealed that encountering the insider view enhanced and expanded their knowledge about the particular religion and familiarised them with the different epistemologies, overarching concepts and ways of representing information associated with RE. They, therefore, proposed that a greater awareness of the many academic traditions that inform RE could provide students with disciplinary relevant strategies.

Visits

There are many parts of the world where the classroom continues to occupy the 'outside' and is beyond the confines of physical structures and spaces. For many years, the concept of learning outside the classroom has been a popular initiative in the UK context. Using the 'real world' is considered a cherished way of making learning more accessible and concrete for pupils, no matter their age, aptitude, interest or ability. Learning in this mode can significantly enrich pupils' educational experiences. Education is about offering pupils authentic experiences through which they can begin to understand themselves and their relationship with the world around them (Rowe and Humphries 2012). Therefore, pupils should encounter religions and world-views through special people and by visiting places of worship (REC 2013). It has been found that learners are more likely to remember knowledge that is stored in a positive emotional context (Waite 2011), which means visits should offer an element of emotional attachment, joy and curiosity so that pupils are more likely to retain information.

To promote good progress, it is suggested that you build on pupils' prior knowledge by sequencing lessons so that pupils secure foundational knowledge before encountering more complex content and by identifying possible misconceptions and plan how to prevent these from forming. It is also important to encourage pupils to share their emerging understanding and points of confusion so that misconceptions can be addressed (DfE 2019).

Conceptual clarity

The concept of 'sacred' places or places of 'worship' has different connotations. As such, it is useful first, to allow pupils to think of the meaning of a 'sacred', 'special' space and a 'place of worship'. Expect them to think of religious places, natural landscapes, cemeteries, stadia, monuments, parks, gardens, bedrooms, rivers or caves. Places that are considered sacred tend to be demarcated from ordinary and mundane spaces. Smart included such places among the 'material' dimension of religion (Smart 1998). For him, the material dimension of religion encompassed sites, such as the Ganges, Jerusalem, chapels and Cathedrals.

Pupils can discuss: Is a sacred space always a sacred space? Are makeshift sacred spaces the same as permanent sacred spaces? How does a place become sacred? Can the whole earth be sacred? Will humans make sacred spaces on the moon?

Curriculum clarity

Visits and meetings can be valuable experiences because they are genuine and organic and enable the pupils to learn about differences in the ways that religious and non-religious people live (Salter 2020).

However, the recent Ofsted RE Research Review noted that sometimes teachers can be unclear about the curriculum object when pupils meet faith practitioners. Thus, the curriculum object may be any number of things, such as the following:

- To learn about the experiences of faith practitioners (i.e. testimonies that could be used as case studies).
- To learn how knowledge about religion might be gained through interviews (i.e. aspects of disciplinary 'ways of knowing').
- For pupils to recognise their own assumptions as they listen to an individual from a faith community (i.e. 'personal knowledge').
- To apply previously learned generalisations about religion that can be 'tested' through an encounter with 'lived' faith practitioners (i.e. using the internal dynamics and internal plurality of religious traditions to illustrate that religious traditions are not simply one thing) (Ofsted 2021).

Where to visit

Any visit to a religious place must be undertaken with attention to the curriculum intent to maximise its impact on pupils. It must enhance whatever happens in the classroom. Visits can be made to a Buddhist pagoda, vihara, monasteries, local church, chapel, cathedral, abbeys, gurdwara, kingdom hall, mandir, meeting house, mosque or synagogue and others. Some schools organise day trips on an annual basis to cities where multi-faith opportunities are accessible, and, at times, such visits would encompass visiting local shops and community centres to meet and learn about different faith-based organisations and their services. Occasionally, some schools take their pupils to special exhibitions arranged by religious communities or to open day events organised for the whole community. Museums sometimes also hold exhibitions based on religious traditions displaying their history, arts, artefacts, manuscripts, clothing and other items. In other words, visits for RE take varied forms and give pupils opportunities to know and understand different worldviews. This would be one way of developing disciplinary literacy in RE as it combines outsider perspectives with insider perspectives on religious phenomena (Unstad and Fjørtoft 2021).

Religious and belief groups can enrich your RE curriculum by hosting your pupils. You should seek out these and value them as opportunities to make RE learning real as it gives pupils occasions of meeting people directly, to experience a new religious environment, and converse with individuals who can offer answers to their thoughts and questions. They can go on a trail as well. In this way, visits contribute to pupils' spiritual and cultural development.

Mindful visits

To set high expectations you should seek opportunities to engage parents and carers in the education of their children (DfE 2019). There are certain things to be mindful of when visiting places of worship. Pupils should be briefed on the etiquettes and expected behaviours. Parents should understand the intent and impact of the visit. Parental rights to withdraw their child from a visit should be respected. Always carry out a risk assessment and ensure accessibility for all. Have a shared understanding of the purpose of the visit with the host and ensure they are aware of the age of the pupils.

Classroom matters

One of the important tasks is to let pupils gain a deeper understanding of how these spaces are used by worshippers for worship. Pupils' attention should be drawn to the focal point in these places, such as a statue that commands interest and plays a pivotal role for the community concerned. Pupils should be invited to talk about something which surprised them as an unexpected feature. They should observe the natural, water features and ponder over their use and how, if any, there is harmony with nature. In many places, there are repeated patterns, pupils should note these and reflect on the impact and purpose of repetition. There are decorative and intricate features in most sacred places, pupils should explore the feelings these evoke and the meanings they convey. Pupils should have an opportunity to locate a 'mysterious' piece or intriguing structures and talk about it. It would be important to encourage pupils to imagine a space of their own. They can design one to show how sacred buildings will look in years to come.

Greater depth

Pupils should be able to discern the main external and internal features of some sacred places of worship and recognise, through comparisons, some of these features will differ from one 'denomination' to another as they express different emphasis in history, belief, practice and ritual. As an outdoor location, pupils might also learn about the location of some buildings, like churches being at the centre of a village or in the countryside and their construction. Pupils will be intrigued to learn how and why their local places of worship are named as they are and understand the history of the community. In exploring these features, where appropriate, in addition to local and national sites, pupils should learn of religious places of global significance. In promoting progress, it is suggested that teachers avoid overloading working memory by taking into account pupils' prior knowledge when planning how much new information to introduce (DfE 2019).

Multidisciplinary visits to multi-faith spaces

There exists a cornucopia of devotional material from which to reap high-quality sources for learning in RE. Pupils should be invited to engage hermeneutically in explaining what they see and what sense they make of the place as a whole. They should ask socio-historical questions about the places they encounter. Pupils should also engage in thinking through the architecture in terms of spirituality, symbols and how it supports their ritual. Where applicable, you could ask pupils, why animals are cast in the role of gods or why they feature where they feature and why not in other places. Pupils should be encouraged to reflect on the use of art and architecture as an expression of religious identity and their atmosphere. With a historical perspective, they may explore the significance of these places and what they reveal about how people used to live in the past, what was important to them and how society was organised. Geographically, they should discuss the orientation of some of these places, the features and fixtures within them and how different spaces are used for a variety of purposes and why they are religiously important. Pupils should explore the commonalities and differences between the architectural features of sacred spaces and geographically diverse locations, both inside and outside, and how they have changed or remained the same over time. By adopting an ethnographic approach as they encounter these places, pupils can gather nuanced insights and understand the beliefs of adherents, their life, devotions and their experiences within them by interviewing, drawing and taking pictures. They understand how some people organise their day in sync with the events at their place of worship. They should uncover how and why people worship together and how and why special events are celebrated in these places. Theologically and intellectually, they can examine how these sites are sources of academic and scholarly activity and means of connecting with the self, holiness and God. From the humanitarian dimension, they learn how people of faith work to assist their local communities and those that have a greater need abroad. An example of using a three disciplinary approach is shown in Table 11.1 in Chapter 11.

The participant observation method

This activity uses the methodology of participant observation, which invites pupils to develop their sense and embodiment of a situation and place. It is about immersing themselves in the ethos, values and culture of the sacred space. The participant observation can be carried out intentionally or incidentally. During the visits invite pupils to partake in activities, where appropriate, in and around the place of worship. It might be useful for them to record their observations in more detail than they would normally do. For example, think about the walls, floor, ceiling, pillars, displays, windows and other halls.

They should be interested in the host. Here again, there is much to learn. What are they wearing? Can they observe any symbols? What greetings did they use? Were any gestures made? How do they behave in different parts of the place? How do they handle their artefacts? What were they not doing?

Visual language method

It is quite common for pupils to take recording equipment with them. Most places will give their permission but still ask. Explore the sacred place through these lens. Ask them to take photographs of items that they consider to be symbolic and which they think makes the place unique. To allow closer visualisation try to avoid features that can be available elsewhere.

Sounds in spaces

Pupils may have the opportunity of using their hearing senses or aids. If there is such an opportunity consider: What is the source of the sound? What types of sounds can they hear? Who is making the sound? Is it communal or both? In what direction, if any, is the sound coming from? Can they categorise the sounds? Are they human sounds? Are sounds made by instruments? What language is the sound made in? What does the sound tell them about the place they are studying? These investigations will give them a deeper understanding of the place.

Sacred space and mundane space

How is the sacred space and the 'mundane' space demarcated and why? What 'barriers' exist? How is the space organised? How are the congregants organised? How is the size allocated? What are the different rooms called? What are they used for? Are they accessible to anyone? How do adherents behave in each of these spaces?

Imaginative drawing

This activity encourages imagination. It also develops their listening and questioning skills. They will sit back-to-back with a friend. Their partner describes the features to them and they draw them.

Visitors in schools

It is common for schools to invite visitors to supplement their RE. It is important that any visitor coming into school understands the nature of RE and how to present their material engagingly and interestingly. You need to make them aware of the significance of presenting their content in a meaningful and age-appropriate level of understanding. The visitor should add value to your curriculum, which means you need to make their 'content' fit into your plans.

Outdoor RE

The teacher can work in a fundamentally different way with pupils when learning is taken outside. It can become a fantastic cross-curriculum vehicle for learning across the curriculum where children may pose their problems and find their solutions and use a multidisciplinary approach to learning. Given this range of possibilities, it is important to be clear about what precisely you expect pupils to learn from the encounter and, importantly, how that links to RE curriculum goals. Otherwise, meeting faith practitioners and being outdoors may be enjoyable for pupils but is unlikely to lead to curriculum impact (Ofsted 2021). Reynolds (2018) has suggested that it is important to maintain a focal point otherwise their concentration may be disrupted outdoors by external factors and that some children will need confidence in their environment for them to be able to engage in learning, as, in unfamiliar surroundings, some children may feel vulnerable and thus unlikely to engage happily. The venues for outdoor learning are many and include natural areas such as allotments, forests, parks, woodlands, gardens and others, which provide pupils with numerous opportunities for both informal and formal learning experiences. Some of these informal and embodied learning experiences can make important contributions to a pupil's emotional, cognitive, social and physical development (van Dijk-Wesselius, van den Berg, Maas and Hovinga 2020). Pupils ask big questions about creation or reflect which aid their spiritual, moral and cultural development as well.

A sense of awe and wonder

In a natural environment, pupils can be encouraged to consider the nature of the world humans and all living things inhabit and explore the varied meanings of 'spiritual'. The teacher should invite pupils to consider their relationship with nature and develop respect for it. They can be provoked to think about the limitlessness of the universe and the frailty of humans. Teachings about the environment can be drawn from a range of religious traditions so that pupils can consider how they view it and the responsibility laid on their followers. Pupils need to understand that they are part of the environment and which they embody so that they understand what it means to be human and the relationship between belief, practice and action.

Gardens of peace

Many schools have gardens which support several subjects of their curricula. In the context of RE, these can be used as a 'contemplation space'. In some schools, like one where I taught, one of our younger colleague had suddenly passed away during the Easter break. The school decided to honour them by planting a willow tree, a bench and put up a plaque in the quad area. Later, this became an area for quiet reflection, mediation and a symbol of loss and friendship.

Cemeteries

Many churches have churchyards, which are often used as graveyards. Pupils can learn why these were established and who used them. They can study the headstones and other memorials and why cemeteries were introduced. They study the tombs of saints and others. Beyond this, pupils can then look at and learn from cemeteries in other religions and traditions. These sites reveal much about the celebration of life, beliefs and practices related to angels, afterlife, heaven, God, hope, mercy and love and how scripture is used for the deceased. Pupils learn about the different burial and mourning customs. When dealing with this, it is important to be aware of their age appropriateness and sensitivity to pupils. It might be that virtual exploration of cemeteries takes place.

Environmental RE

There is a renewed concern about the environment and the debate has returned to the public arena. RE, with appropriate planning, can contribute to further the understanding of environmental concerns from the viewpoint of a religious tradition by examining what each teaches about these issues. This organisation focuses on religion and the environment. https://reepinfo.org/

Summary

For some pupils, visiting a place of worship during their schooling can be a lifetime experience. It is a life-enriching experience, provides empathy, makes it memorable and pupils develop mature attitudes. There are many opportunities of using the outdoors as a classroom and you should avail yourself of these sites.

USING STORY-TELLING IN RE

Introduction

The use of stories is a common and powerful strategy for RE. They should be used creatively and in an age-appropriate manner.

Humans and stories

The first dimension is to consider both the external and internal nature of the stories being used in RE. There is a time and place factor. For some people, stories began with creation; giving RE its first story. Stories are written and narrated. However, stories are internal too. They are within people. It is difficult to separate the story of who we are from our being and ourselves. In RE, both are learnt, crafted and mastered by educators and learners.

The second dimension is to invite you to think about the relationship between stories and religions in three ways. First, you will discover when you look deeply into religious traditions that most, if not all, have a story of how the religion or philosophy began. Thus, the story of revelation shows how Islam began, then of Sikhi and Buddhism. Second, each religious tradition has a sacred text and all of them have stories, which serve a range of purposes. Third, Jesus, Muhammad (peace be upon them), Guru Nanak, Buddha told stories to convey their doctrines, beliefs, practice and teachings. Thus, there is a very strong relation between stories and religious traditions.

The third dimension is to consider the relationship between education and story. Every classroom has stories. The second point is to look at the curriculum and observe that many subjects use stories to convey their substantive and disciplinary knowledge. Third, stories are part of learners' lives. Unsurprisingly, pupils seem to be attached to them.

Hull (1982) proposed that storytelling was one of the oldest arts of the religious educator. Stories are versatile which allow the beliefs and imagination of all pupils to be valued and to contribute to their personal development. They can incorporate controversial issues making RE real, relevant and empowering. Stories assist in addressing misunderstandings, misconceptions, stereotyping and generalising. They encourage empathy and possess a unique cognitive potential, which can add a new dimension to understanding many other areas (Arthur 1988).

Students were asked what makes a story religious and what a religious story is. Consider their responses. It is about angels. It conveys beliefs. It is about religious festivals and religious rituals. It is from a religious text. It consists of a religious event, e.g. baptism. It is about a sacred place. It has a subliminal message. It is radical. It is about reincarnation. It is from and about significant religious figures. It is about a higher being. It is symbolic or metaphorical. It has certain groups of people in it doing some religious deeds. It is historical, passed down, traditional. It contains teaching about God and/or is from God. It is about a miracle. It is about sacrifice. It is about the afterlife.

Summary

Stories are an important source for RE, personal and SMSC development. Storytelling is a popular pedagogy in RE. However, they should be used in a child-friendly yet challenging manner, with sensitivity to the pupil, the text and the tradition.

RE THROUGH COMPUTING AND DESIGN AND TECHNOLOGY

Introduction

You would be expected to teach good practice in internet use and to direct pupils to specific sites to avoid time-wasting 'surfing' and to have strategies to prevent pupils from copying from the internet (Wintersgill, Cush and Francis 2019). Conservation about authentic and unreliable information and educational, polemical and proselytising can be had so that pupils become more perceptive about the varied purposes for which information is available.

It is worth reminding yourself that these should be used as tools and media to support and develop their understanding of the concept being taught and enhance the teaching of RE.

In other words, you will need to provide opportunities for pupils to create work that has academic purpose and meaning. Technology is part of life and learning for most pupils. All pupils including those with SEND benefit from technology in various ways. Computer-based materials tend to break down the skills and content into manageable and achievable steps. This learning can happen in their 'own world', their own pace with less pressure from the rest. Mistakes are seldom exposed and instant feedback is received. However, it is important to remember that the computer is a machine and cannot replace human personal interaction. A child with a visual impairment might use a screen reading software that reads aloud the text. Voice dictation software can be used to support their writing and capture their thoughts and interactions. Features such as text to speech and speech to text make a huge difference to them. The appropriate selection and use of integrating technology within RE lessons help meet the needs of all pupils.

Virtual multi-faith walks and trails

Pupils have an excellent opportunity to learn about their local and national religious and faith communities, especially their place of worship, which are a hub for them. Virtual faith trails in the absence of physical ones can be undertaken using online maps, which enable pupils to visit individually or as groups different places of worship and interest. Pupils can experience the richness and internal diversity of religious communities. The example below can be adapted and used with other sites.

Virtual synagogue

1   Visit the https://www.bpsjudaism.com website, read and note some information.
2   Create a profile of the synagogue. Here are a few suggestions:
3   When was it consecrated? What does this mean? What does it involve? Why was there a need to consecrate it?
4   What services does it offer to the Jewish community?
5   Does it promote inter-faith dialogue? When? How? Why?
6   Has it always been located here? Where was the synagogue situated before? Why did it re-locate?
7   Choose some pictures both from the inside and outside and write about them.
8   How often are prayers/services held?
9   Ask some questions related to the history of the synagogue.
10 What else is it used for? How is it different to an orthodox synagogue?

Live events

Some religious events and pilgrimages are broadcast live. With careful planning, they could be shown to the class. Some of these are live-streamed on YouTube and other platforms.

Films

Films are an excellent addition to support your lessons. There are some resources around sacred texts and the daily life of a believer on many sites. You may want to explore some newly available ones from the British Library's Discovering Sacred Texts and the BBC such as 'My life, my religion' and 'A day in the life of…'. These are good as they give accounts of life experiences. It is important, nevertheless, to be mindful of avoiding stereotypes from such depictions.

TrueTube

TrueTube is a free website for schools. It provides short films and lesson plans for RE and other subjects. It was originally set up to encourage young people to make films dealing with the issues they cared about. Over time, the library grew and now teachers use these downloadable films in the classroom. The Holy Cribs has lesson plans and useful tours of the holy building and other topics.

Design and technology

In design and technology, pupils should be taught knowledge, understanding and skills needed to engage in the process of designing and making creatively (DfE 2013). Pupils could first learn about the material dimension of religions such as building, places, space, texts, artefacts, voice, food and clothing. Following this knowledge acquisition, they could be briefed to create a model of whatever they are learning about or invent something of their own and justify it.

The IWB or iPads can be used to show and search sacred places from around the world to explore how they will construct theirs. Alternatively, everyday material can be given to pupils to be creative, innovative and traditional. They should be engaged in discussing the materials to use and explain their decisions. Thereafter, pupils can evaluate their ideas and products against the design criteria (DfE 2013) and RE related learning.

Healthy suhoor or iftar bar

Following a lesson exploring examples and non-examples of halal and kosher diet or after a lesson learning about the suhoor (pre-dawn meal) and iftar (breaking of the fast) in the context of Ramadan, pupils can prepare a snack bar. This recipe makes 5–10 bars. It can be adapted to your needs.

Ingredients:100–250 g dates; 40–80 g sliced pistachios, 15–25 grams of oats, 1 tablespoon honey, 1–2 tablespoon water, 50–90 g desiccated coconut. Equipment: bowls, spoon, scale. Method: (1) Take the seeds out of the dates, place them in the bowl and use the spoon to mix them until they are together. (2) Weigh the ingredients as required. (3) Add the pistachios, oats, honey, water and the desiccated coconut to the dates. (4) Using a spoon, mix the mixture until thoroughly mixed and then tip it onto a clean surface or a tray. (5) Make the mixture into rectangular bars to suit your size. (6) Fill another bowl with the rest of the coconut, and then roll the bars around in it one at a time until they are evenly coated. Be mindful of allergies.

Education robotics

Education robotics (ER) refers to a learning approach that requires pupils to program robots such as bee bots through play and hands-on activities. Di Lieto et al. (2020) state that ER can improve cognitive and learning abilities. Pupils could program the bee bot based on a route from their school to various sacred places of people of different religions and beliefs. Pupils sequence a set of instructions and program the bee bot according to this.

Scratch

Pupils can use Scratch to program their own and traditional interactive stories, visits, contemporary issues, moral dilemmas and animations to share their creations with others in the online community. It is designed and developed by a non-profit organisation and is provided free of charge.

Summary

In using computing and design and technology it is crucial to ensure that the necessary foundational content knowledge of RE is taught first in these lessons. You should also be aware of reducing distractions that take attention away from the RE that is being taught, perhaps, by keeping the computing, technical and design matters of a task to a minimum so that greater attention is focused on the content and concepts of RE.

USING PERSONA DOLLS IN RE

Introduction

There are many educational reasons for adopting the use of Persona Dolls in your RE teaching. It provides opportunities to appreciate similarities and differences, empathy, clarifies misunderstandings and misconceptions, invite a problem-solving approach and other social and personal benefits (Ebrahim and Francis 2008), inter-faith dialogue (Siôn 2014) and is used in different contexts (Bozalek and Smith 2010; Logue, Bennett-Armistead and Kim 2011; Papouli 2019).

Knowing a Persona Doll

To begin with, the guidance suggests that it is important to distinguish a Persona Doll from a play doll and a puppet. Persona Dolls are unlike play dolls, which are often found in play-areas in a class. They are a 'child visitor' and usually visit the pupils during circle time. Importantly, they have a purpose in coming to the pupils, often to tell a story. Persona Dolls are friends with whom the pupils in the setting can bond. They facilitate the exploration of various big questions in RE, enable the examination of important social questions in a non-threatening pedagogy.

Another important feature of Persona Dolls is that it is not puppetry and the user does not become a ventriloquist. In other words, it is meant to have its voice. The user speaks on behalf of the Dolls to the class. It could be made from inflexible plastic or soft-bodied rag dolls, without a face (Webster 2010:53). Some prefer it to be a child-sized soft-bodied doll, which can sit on the user's lap, resembling a pupil seated. Some use larger Dolls. For RE, varieties of soft and rigid bodied Persona Dolls are available in a range of religious traditions. The Persona Doll is treated with respect by all just as any visitor to the setting would.

Developing a life story for the Dolls

Practitioners suggest, as illustrated in Table 10.6, that before the Persona Dolls visit the class, the adult will need to create a life story or a life history script which they must adhere to (Hammond 2015:171; Vickery 2011). It is stressed that if any new information about the Dolls is used it must be added to their Persona file. Consequently, Persona Dolls would not reside in the home corner or resource box. Pupils become friends of the Dolls. They care for it, respond respectfully, thoughtfully and empathetically. Pupils share their happiness and sadness. Pupils offer support when they are sad, annoyed or scared. Persona Dolls can also join pupils and celebrate positive events such as birthdays, weddings, festivals and the arrival of a new baby. They are an ideal context for exploring scapegoating of stereotyping (Hammond 2015:173).

A template to create a Persona Doll

Table 10.6 Creating a life story	
Name	
Age	
Appearance	
Favourite foods	
Pets	
Favourite toy	
Favourite activities	
Type of house resident live in	
Family background	
Religion	
Language	
Other significant details	

Pedagogy to introduce the Persona Dolls

It is common for the Persona Doll to visit the pupils whilst they are seated in a circle and quickly become part of the setting. Thereafter, the Doll sits on the user's lap and the user listens to the Doll and informs the pupils what the Doll has said. The user provides a few facts about the Doll (name, residence) and encourages the pupils to ask more questions. The pupils quickly accept them as friends and identify with them. This encourages the pupils to make friends with the Doll on every visit.

Welcoming Persona Dolls in RE

Some schools may not have easy access to members of a faith community so the Persona Doll visits to explain about its faith or non-religious background. In such a situation:

■ The Persona Doll visits the pupils as a new friend and talks about their favourite items such as toys, food or pet for a few visits before introducing the aspects of the faith that you want to teach the pupils about.

■ If there are parents/carers from that faith and, if possible, the local faith community can be asked to contribute ideas or lend resources, artefacts for the Persona Doll to bring to the setting.

■ As the pupils will have met and made friends with the Doll before, they will show a natural curiosity for the stories and artefacts they will want to learn more from their friends.

Resident Persona Dolls in RE

The Persona Doll can help to convey some important messages about the UK, especially when it is introduced in contexts where pupils are all from the same religious, ethnic or cultural groups to promote multi-faith and multi-cultural understanding. They can learn that:

- British society is multi-faith with a wide range of different religions and non-religious traditions.
- There are many positive features about living in a diverse society.
- There are some negative features about living in a diverse society.
- The way an individual or their family live is only one possible way of living.
- Individuals can choose some things for themselves and some things will always remain part of their religion, culture or heritage.

The use of Persona Doll in RE lessons can assist pupils to understand and accentuate empathy with different religions and non-religious perspectives, including death and anger (Webster 2010:53).

In the classroom

The Persona Doll could tell a story, talk about a religious artefact or special object, show the use of traditional dress, share special food which is consumed during important occasions and explain a celebration or festival. It can talk about a visit to a place of worship and to stimulate a discussion about an incident that has happened in the school (the situation described by the Dolls would be similar, but not identical, to the actual event).

God and Creation in EYFS

One of the topics in EYFS can be 'God and Creation'. Pupils learn about the importance of God to Christians, Muslims or Jews, for example. They learn about this from the point of view of a Persona Doll. They learn about God as the creator, perhaps using the creation stories. Thereafter, they can explore the idea of creation in a variety of ways using different media including painting, play-doh, collage, fabrics, Lego and other everyday material.

Persona Dolls are good for exploring a concept or practice in different religions and for sharing life experiences openly (Jesuvadian and Wright 2011). For example, pupils can learn about the characteristics of places of worship. They can then accompany the Doll on a 'Special Place Trail' to search for spaces in and around to decide their suitability for worship or prayer. They look for quietness, size, brightness and access. They use phrases such as 'I wonder if...' They can then explain how their identified space can be used and what for?

In the EYFS, in particular, RE requires a multi-sensory approach. Pupils are provided with opportunities to learn and understand themselves and others. They develop their abilities to express themselves. Pupils also develop a growing sense of their community and their place within this. Through the Persona Dolls, they can encounter all these religious and non-religious people and ideas.

Activities based on an ethnographic approach can be used to assist pupils to relate stories, celebrations, religious festivals and artefacts to particular pupils in a particular faith and non-faith communities. Pupils with the Persona Dolls can talk about the life of a living faith leader, a layperson or a child from different traditions. This brings RE close to a living tradition, minimises misunderstanding and provides some concrete distinction. Visitors can be helped in demonstrating the use of artefacts and pronunciations of terms. The ethnographic approach provides opportunities for pupils to identify with the life of 'real people', who could be similar in some respects and also be different in other respects, in terms of their faith, festival, naming and wedding ceremonies, religious stories and practices and cultural experiences (Warner and Elton-Chalcraft 2018).

Summary

The use of Persona Dolls affords a unique pedagogy to add to your teaching. Training, resources and support material is widely available to enhance your RE teaching.

USING PARDES IN RE

Introduction

There is an interesting traditional method to learn from the Jewish community to use in RE. Its purpose is to extract wisdom and meaning from primary texts. Each line of the Torah or liturgy is studied by applying the *pardes* method. The four-dimensional hermeneutical model is represented by the acronym called *PaRDeS*, which takes its name from the sound of the first letter of each dimension. Each letter represents a layer of Torah interpretation (Ninan 2017:38–39). In Hebrew, *pardes* means orchard or paradise offering a helpful image of the Bible as a fruitful orchard, with truths to be picked from (Bjoraker 2018; Feurer 2021).

- ■ P'shat – the simple, explicit: what does it say, who said it, who did something to whom, how and what the result was. The aim is to find out the authorial intent and authentic meaning. To find the literal meaning first even in symbols, allegory, figurative language.

- ■ Remez – the meaning, the hint: looking at the language, metaphors of the text, makes links within the text and beyond, reading between the lines subjectively for deeper meaning within the text, considers motives of actors.

- ■ D'rash – what is the story, the homily: looks at the unknowns, completes the dialogue and difficulties in the text which readers fill by using their imagination and creativity to develop meanings, looks at the text as a whole, readers try to know themselves in relation to others.

- ■ S'ad – the secret, what is the hidden meaning: looks are the secret, what is not said, the unknown meanings within the text, which assist readers to relate to it today, influences the contemporary world, relies only upon the readers' inner subjective understanding.

Summary

This method of understanding scripture, although with its origins in the Jewish community, can be used with stories and texts in other religious traditions for a deeper level of understanding and to engage with sources through multiple dimensions.

USING SACRED UTILITIES AND ARTEFACTS IN RE

Introduction

The sacred utilities, 'artefacts', found in religious traditions are an offering to teachers to serve RE. They are a means to develop the knowledge and understanding of traditions, and of recognising differences and similarities within and across traditions and worldviews. They may act as powerful stimuli to give insight into religious practice and belief. They afford opportunities to acquire the appropriate language and talk about them sensitively. Teachers can model reverence in learning in context and break down religious barriers of misunderstanding. For pupils, not only does it aid retention, but it offers exposure to the unfamiliar, an exploration of their sacred and symbolic purposes and an understanding of the numinous significance for those who use them.

A religious sacred utility and a cultural artefact is an object that can have religious, cultural or personal significance. All religious traditions have objects that are used in worship, festivals, rites of passage as part of their beliefs and practices. They can be a visible connection to its history and identity. It can be a communal symbol of key principles, a sign of commitment and belonging.

More than an 'artefact'

The use of 'artefacts' creates awe and wonder (McCreery, Palmer and Voiels 2008). Many teachers justify its use in terms of engaging pupils, i.e. in terms of their kinaesthetic appeal rather than as an encounter with the sacred. In the early years, there is a focus on resources that provide sensory experiences, 'artefacts' the pupils can observe and touch, recipes for festival-related cooking and eating and music to listen to. At another level there may be tensions between a primary school pedagogy of concrete, 'hands-on' learning and the particular nature of religious 'artefacts' which often have sacred significance (Jackson et al. 2010:149). Hence, it is important to be mindful that the 'artefact' is 'no mere attention-seeker' but an embodiment of human religious meaning (Hull 1998:79).

In Box 10.2, Homan (2012) has invited a critical view of the use of 'artefacts' and cautioned against the 'material' and 'physical objects' approach to using devotional objects in RE lessons by taking them away from their sacred import and spiritual domain. Thus, when providing hands-on experiences, it is important that the effect of dislocating these apparatuses of devotion are not deprived of the spiritual value with which they are properly invested (Homan 2012:189).

In the section on classical pedagogy, you read about the *Gift to the Child* approach, wherein the sacred and spiritual value is discovered by pupils by a taboo on touching or even going close and by avoidance of affected rituals of reference (Hull 2000). To highlight their spiritual worth and not to regard them merely for their ritual functions, Homan (2000:29) argues that the definition of devotional objects as 'artefacts' misrepresents their significance. For example, in the sacramental traditions of the Christian faith, many would not touch a chalice with their hands, yet a facsimile may be passed around the classroom, and the Guru Granth Sahib, when seen as an 'artefact', is to ground its understanding in terms of human craft and not in the divine visitation, which is the basis of regarding them in RE. The *Gift* approach honours the object of faith within a non-confessional pedagogy, and the *numina* allow connection with the original meaning and significance. Otherwise, Homan argues that the plundering of the means

---

BOX 10.2 VIEWPOINT: PROBLEMS WITH USING ARTEFACTS

The seductive capacity of 'artefacts' for teachers has four aspects. First there is a learning theory – not always appropriate in respect of religion – that pupils need to touch and feel. Second, they are educational suppliers who assemble kits with instructions. Third, the acquisition of some kind of subject specific hardware gives teachers of RE a sense of parity with other elements of the curriculum. And fourth, the notional authenticity (albeit some are manufactured specifically for the education market) gives non-specialists confidence that they are doing the right thing (Homan 2012:189).

of devotion is to disconnect. It is to render the spiritual and mystical as the concrete. That is not to represent religion but to misrepresent it (Homan 2012:190). In other words, it is not by licence but by restraint and exclusion that the notion of the holy comes to be understood (Homan 2000:36). It is also important to recognise that the exclusive use of physical objects in RE might neglect those faith traditions that have little to offer by way of 'artefacts'. For example, the 'light within' which is the quest of Quakers is not conveyed by physical apparatuses (Homan 2000:34).

This account should encourage you to use sacred utilities and 'artefacts' by first researching about them, what you can use and how you must use them. For example, the notion of the touchy-feely bag and the practices surrounding it have been critiqued to represent a corruption of the innovation of the 'mystery bag' as part of the *Gift to the Child* project. The word mystery allows the fabric of the bag to be understood as a veil, not as a barrier to be conquered; the object is to engage the content, and need not be to celebrate pupil skills of detection (Homan 2000:32).

Guidance to consider

The opportunities for using sacred utilities are many. Logan (1997) offers some guidelines such as:

- Try to keep the objects on a table, not on the floor.
- Don't allow pupils to play with the artefacts.
- The artefacts are often part of a person's religious adherence and in some cases are treated reverently in themselves.
- For some pupils and their parents, using the artefacts and reciting the appropriate words/prayers, etc. could be construed as an act of worship. This can offend.
- Be humble! Sometimes a pupil may tell you off for using it incorrectly. It is an invaluable part of the learning process for teachers and pupils to learn from each other!
- Make sure both you and the pupils appropriately handle the artefacts.
- Make sure you, as a teacher, are familiar with the artefact and any particular ways of using it.
- Remember that integrity is the keyword. This includes yours as well as the pupils. Don't try anything that you feel uncomfortable with. Having said that, the best way to learn to use artefacts is to use them and learn with the pupils!

To this may be added, the need to recognise that not all religious groups have such sacred objects. To be aware that some pupils, and their parents, feel compromised by having to handle sacred objects from a faith other than their own. Therefore, you will approach such a situation sensitively. Moreover, sometimes, you may not want to use them as your pupils act too immaturely and would not handle them appropriately; hence, you will change your teaching method by presenting them in a dignified manner. Some pupils face challenges to adorn their religious artefact as evident from Box 10.3. Furthermore, you will consider that not everyone within a religion practises in the same manner and with the same artefacts. Thereby, avoid creating stereotypes, for example, by saying 'All Muslims would…'

The case study offers time for reflection. As a class teacher, what questions might you want to ask your Sikh students and/or their parents about their religious needs; are there other religious groups and the special needs that students of each faith might have; how might you alter your curriculum or teaching method to accommodate their needs; how could you, as a practitioner, mitigate or respond to religious and cultural tensions.

BOX 10.3 CASE STUDY: EMBODYING ARTEFACTS

A Sikh teenager, Sarika Singh aged 14, was suspended from school for declining to remove a religious bangle in 2007. Her parents considered a legal challenge against the girls' comprehensive school in South Wales. She was taught in isolation for nine weeks before being excluded. The headmistress maintained that the code of conduct permitted only two items of jewellery, a watch and a pair of plain metal stud earrings. All visible religious symbols were banned by the bans, including Christian crosses and Muslim headscarves. However, Miss Singh won the backing of the Valleys Race Equality Council and her parents considered a challenge in the High Court. The kara (metal bangle) is one of five religious attire which all Sikhs are expected to adorn themselves with. It is a reminder to do good work with the hands. Miss Singh, who was suspended for five days, began wearing it two years earlier after a family visit to India. The school took action only in September. Her mother, Sanita Singh, said: 'Sarika told us, "I don't go to school any more, I go to prison"'. The school's governing body, said: 'We made our decision only after prolonged research into the previous stated cases across the UK, interrogation of the law, including human rights and race relations legislation'. Sarika had eventually won her case.

In the classroom

To increase the likelihood of material being retained, it is suggested that there is regular review and practice of key ideas and concepts. You should make good use of expositions by using these artefacts as a concrete representation of abstract ideas and concepts. Moreover, you should also reframe your questions to provide greater scaffolding or greater stretch and monitor pupil work during lessons, including checking for misconceptions (DfE 2019).

There are some strategies that evidence suggests makes learning better retained and improves pupils' memory which can be applied when teaching with and about artefacts. Space out learning by doing little and often is better than a lot all at once. Interleaving is varying the type of problems pupils answer within a topic. Pre-questions which is asking questions about the material before teaching it. Elaborative interrogation getting pupils to ask 'why is this the case?' or 'why is this true for X but not for Y?' (Watson and Bradley (2021).

Layers of evaluation

As their knowledge becomes more secure, to increase the challenge, you may want to rehearse and retrieve learning about and from artefacts based on these four layers. Logan (1997) maintains that understanding the faith of others is often very difficult by the very nature that teachers are outsiders to that belief and experience. 'Artefacts' can give us glimpses into the faith of others. They can help piece together a picture of faith, albeit partially for the teachers, and, similarly, pupils can only be taken so far along the continuum from outsiders to insiders. A key question faced by teachers relates to how they can help pupils gain an understanding of the faith community in the classroom. Logan (1997) identified five layers to help in this process.

The first is the observational level. This involves treating the object as a phenomenon in its own right. Pupils are encouraged to ask questions about the superficial features of the 'artefacts', such as, what are the different features of the 'artefact'? What does it look like? What is it made of? Pupils use the senses to explore.

Second, pupils begin to give a context to the 'artefacts' through investigation and research, such as, What is it called? What is it used for? Who uses it?

Third, there is the contextual level, such as, Where does this belong? How does this fit into the life, worship and faith of the believer? When and where is this used? How would it be treated by the members of the faith who use it? How does the way it is treated reflect the beliefs of the people whose 'artefact' it is? What might it make a believer think about?

The fourth reflective level approaches the meaning and significance of the object for the believer and encourages pupils to make comparable links with their own experience/beliefs. How should we treat it? What symbols, if any, are incorporated into it? What does it symbolise? What beliefs does it express? What does it make you think about?

The final level is the devotional level. This only is accessible for believers themselves, as the 'artefact' is used in worship and devotional life. It is at this point that a person moves from the experience of an outsider to that of an insider. This point becomes the responsibility of the individual and the faith community and it is not appropriate for teachers to take pupils into that realm of experience.

Philosophical enquiry

Select appropriate items suitable for a philosophical enquiry and invite pupils to think about the 'force' religious artefacts contain; what could that 'force' be and how can it be accessed. Thereafter, discuss these questions: Should only religious people use religious artefacts? How should we treat items which some people think are sacred/holy/special? Do you think people should 'try' using an item, which is not part of their faith or worldview, as a focus for meditation? What makes an item sacred and who decides that? When does an item become sacred?

In the activities below, pupils should be encouraged to observe, describe, deduce, interpret, compare, explain, evaluate and contextualise.

Matching activity

These simple activities are intended to develop pupils' ability to locate aspects of faith correctly. There are many variations, for example, artefacts may be linked with pictures of other features of faith or with each other where they both are linked within a service or with specific prayers. Some of the possibilities include artefacts matched with a place of worship, with a prayer, with sound, with a sacred text, extract or with a symbol (Gateshill and Thompson 1992).

Developing language

Pupils should acquire the technical language of the faiths from which the items emanate, cross, mezuzah and chauri, for example. Pupils discuss several items in groups. Some record the words used to describe the items. In class, the discussions, keywords and phrases are supplemented by the teacher. The teacher shows one item at a time and the whole class calls out its name in unison. Alternatively, give pupils a set of words and ask them to find their meaning using a dictionary.

Questioning

Pupils take turns to describe an item to their class or group without using names and the rest have to guess what religion the item relates to. Ask the pupils to identify the questions which can be answered from the item itself and those which require other information.

Classification

A collection of artefacts from different faiths are presented. Pupils classify the artefacts by faith. Some artefacts of a similar kind, e.g. rosary beads, subha (Muslim prayer beads) and mala (Sikh prayer beads). The key question would be how a group of items helps us to understand the beliefs/practices of faith and invite explanations on their use.

Interpretation

Begin with observation and description and ask what does the item inform us, what can we learn from the item about, what is the maker trying to tell us, what makes you think that, how has the maker tried to represent the idea of faith, holiness, truth, sanctity and/or obedience.

Lived-experience

Invite visitors to share their experience of using sacred utilities in their tradition, alternatively invite pupils to reflect upon the story and consider the meaning and relevance of 'artefact' to people today.

Narrative and display

After making a display, there are many possible endings. Involve the pupils in creative writing about each item or as a collective. The whole class jointly writes a story with the teacher as the scribe. Pupils write their labels to place next to an item.

Dialogue and display

Alternatively, pupils write a conversation about what might a believer do and say about the display. They could write dialogue about what was happening in the display. This is better done as a group or in pairs. The teacher could scribe for children needing support.

Research

In a table of six, allocate an 'artefact' to each pupil. They carry out their research on it. Then each pupil teaches the rest of their table group. As a group, they then identify further questions which they would like answered. Teaching material to somebody else helps pupils learn the material more deeply and organise their knowledge (Watson and Bradley 2021).

For more challenging work there are particular concepts and vocabulary which may need exploring with some artefacts, including devotion, icon, iconography, idol, idolatry, memorial, reverence and veneration.

Summary

The section discussed the sensitive use of sacred and devotional utilities and 'artefacts'. It suggested that they should be employed as a way into the beliefs and practices of the religions to which they are related and pupils should be encouraged to understand the special meanings which they have for believers by retaining their sacredness and mystical relevance.

References

Ahmed, F. (2019) The potential of *halaqah* to be a transformative Islamic dialogic pedagogy, in N. Mercer, R. Wegerif and L. Major (Eds.) *The Routledge International Handbook of Research on Dialogic Education*, Abingdon: Routledge, pp. 647–659.

Ahmed, F. (2020) Educating for personhood – Personalised character education for young British Muslims, *Impact Journal of the Chartered College of Teaching*, November 2020. [Online] https://impact.chartered.college/article/educating-for-personhood-personalised-character-education-young-british-muslims/ (Accessed 28/08/2021).

Alexander, R. (2010) *Children Their World, Their Education, Final Report and Recommendations of the Cambridge Primary Review*, London: Routledge.

Arthur, C. J. (1988) Some arguments for the use of stories in Religious Education, *British Journal of Religious Education*, 10, (3), pp. 122–127.

Berryman, J. (1991) *Godly Play: An Imaginative Approach to Religious Education*, Minneapolis, MN: Augsburg.

Berryman, J. (2009) *Teaching Godly Play: How to Mentor the Spiritual Development of Children*, Denver, CO: Morehouse.

Berryman, J. (2013) *The Spiritual Guidance of Children: Montessori, Godly Play, and the Future*, Harrisburg, PA: Morehouse.

Bjoraker, B. (2018) *The Place of Story and Storytelling in Messianic Jewish Ministry: Rediscovering the Lost Treasures of Hebraic Narrative*, [Online] https://www.kesherjournal.com/article/the-place-of-story-and-storytelling-in-messianic-jewish-ministry-rediscovering-the-lost-treasures-of-hebraic-narrative/ (Accessed 06/02/21).

Boxer, A. (2019) Introduction, in A. Boxer (Ed.) *The ResearchED Guide to Explicit & Direct Instruction*, Melton: John Catt, pp. 9–14.

Boyle, H. N. (2004) *Quranic Schools: Agents of Preservation and Change*, Abingdon: RoutledgeFarmer.

Bozalek, V., and Smith, C. (2010) Using Persona Dolls as an anti-oppressive technique in the South African Social Work Curriculum, *Social Work*, 46, (3), pp. 283–298.

Claxton, G. (2021) *The Future of Teaching and the Myths That Hold It Back*, Abingdon: Routledge.

CoRE (Commission on Religious Education) (2018) *Religion and Worldviews: The Way Forward. A National Plan for RE (Final Report)*, London: Religious Education Council of England & Wales.

De Bono, E. (2000) *Six Thinking Hats*, London: Penguin. Revised and updated.

DfE (2013) *The National Curriculum in England Key Stages 1 and 2 Framework Document*, London: Crown Copyright. [Online] https://assets.publishing.service.gov.uk/government/uploads/system/uploads/attachment_data/file/425601/PRIMARY_national_curriculum.pdf

DfE (2019) *ITT Core Content Framework*, London: Crown Copyright. Reference: DfE-00230-2019.

Desailly, J. (2015) *Creativity in the Primary Classroom*, London: SAGE. Second edition.

Di Lieto, M. C., Pecini, C., Castro, E., Inguaggiato, E., Cecchi, F., Dario, P., Cioni, G., and Sgandurra, G. (2020) Empowering executive functions in 5- and 6-year-old typically developing children through educational robotics: An RCT study, *Frontiers in Psychology*, 10, 3084, pp. 1–10. DOI: 10.3389/fpsyg.2019.03084

Dinham, M., and Shaw, M. (2020) Landscapes, real and imagined: 'RE for Real', in M. Chater (Ed.) *Reforming RE*, Woodbridge: John Catt, pp. 51–64.

Eaude, T. (2019) Learning to enquire: The role of the humanities, in S. Ogier (Ed.) *A Broad and Balanced Curriculum in Primary Schools: Educating the Whole Child*, London: Learning Matters, pp. 105–117.

Ebrahim, H., and Francis, D. (2008) You said, 'Black girl': Doing difference in early childhood, *Africa Education Review*, 5, (2), pp. 274–287.

Echeverria, E., and Hannam, P. (2017) The community of philosophy of inquiry (P4C): A pedagogical proposal for advancing democracy, in M. R. Gregory, J. Haynes and K. Murris (Eds.) *The Routledge International Handbook of Philosophy for Children*, London: Routledge, pp. 3–10.

Erricker, C., Lowndes, J., and Bellchambers, E. (2011) *Primary Religious Education – A New Approach*, Abingdon: Routledge.

Feurer, M. (2021) *Pardes: History as Spirit in Action*, [Online] https://prizmah.org/pardes-history-spirit-action (Accessed 20/09/2021).

Freathy, R., and Freathy, G. (2013a) Initiating children into hermeneutical discourses in religious education: A response to Rachel Cope and Julian Stern, *Journal for the Study of Spirituality*, 3, (2), pp. 156–167.

Freathy, R., and Freathy, G. (2013b) RE-searchers: A dialogic approach to RE in primary schools, *Resource*, 36, (1), pp. 4–7.

Freathy, R., and Freathy, G. (2014) The RE-searchers: Promoting methodologically oriented RE in primary schools, *RE Today*, 31, (3), pp. 50–51.

Freathy, G., Freathy, R., Doney, J., Walshe, K., and Teece, G. (2015) *A New Approach to Religious Education in Primary Schools*, Exeter: The University of Exeter.

Freathy, G., and Freathy, R. (2016) *A New Approach to Religious Education in Primary Schools: A Quick Start Guide With Exemplar Units of Work and Activities*, Exeter: The University of Exeter.

Freathy, R., Doney, J., Freathy, G., Walshe, K., and Teece, G. (2017) Pedagogical Bricoleurs and Bricolage researchers: The case of Religious Education, *British Journal of Educational Studies*, 65, (4), pp. 425–443.

Gateshill, P., and Thompson, J. (1992) *Religious Artefacts in the Classroom*, London: Hodder & Stoughton.

Grajczonek, J., and Truasheim, M. (2017) Implementing Godly Play in educational settings: A cautionary tale, *British Journal of Religious Education*, 39, (2), pp. 172–186.

Hammond, J. (2015) A creative approach to community cohesion, in S. Elton-Chalcraft (Ed.) *Teaching Religious Education Creatively*, Abingdon: Routledge, pp. 166–175.

Hay, D. (2000) Religious experience and education project: experiential learning in religious education, in M. H. Grimmitt (Ed.) *Pedagogies of Religious Education*, Great Wakering: McCrimmons, pp. 70–87.

Hewitt, D., and Wright, B. (2019) *Engaging, Motivating and Empowering*, London: SAGE.

Homan, R. (2000) Don't let the Murti get dirty: The uses and abuses of religious 'Artefacts', *British Journal of Religious Education*, 23, (1), pp. 27–37.

Homan, R. (2012) Constructing religion, in L. P. Barnes (Ed.) *Debates in Religious Education*, London: Routledge, pp. 183–193.

Hull, J. (1982) Editorial, *British Journal of Religious Education*, 4, (3), pp. 114–167.

Hull, J. (1998) *Utopian Whispers: Moral, Religious and Spiritual Values in Schools*, Norwich: Religious and Moral Education Press.

Hull, J. M. (2000) Religion in the Service of the Child Project: The gift approach to religious education, in M. H. Grimmitt (Ed.) *Pedagogies of Religious Education*, Great Wakering: McCrimmons, pp. 112–129.

Hutton, L., and Cox, D. (2021) *Making Every Lesson Count*, Carmarthen: Crown House.

Hyde, B. (2011) Montessori and Jerome W. Berryman: Work, play, religious education and the art of using the Christian language system, *British Journal of Religious Education*, 33, (3), pp. 341–353.

Hyde, B. (2014) *Jerome W. Berryman: The Spiritual Guidance of Children: Montessori, Godly Play, and the Future*, New York/Singapore: Morehouse/Springer Singapore.

Jackson, R., Ipgrave, J., Hayward, M., Hopkins, P., Fancourt, N., Robbins, M., Francis, L. J., and McKenna, U. (2010) *Materials Used to Teach About World Religions in Schools in England*, London: Department for Children, Schools and Families.

James, M., and Stern, S. (2019) *Mastering Primary Religious Education*, London: Bloomsbury.

Jesuvadian, M. K., and Wright, S. (2011) Doll tales: Foregrounding children's voices in research, *Early Child Development and Care*, 181, (3), pp. 277–285.

Jørgensen, H. V. (2009) Philosophy with Children in Religious Education – A brief history, in G. Y. Iversen, M. Mitchell, G. Pollard and G (Eds.) *Hovering Over the Face of the Deep: Philosophy, Theology and Children*, Münster: Waxmann, p. 13.

Kizel, A. (2016) Philosophy with children as an educational platform for self-determined learning, *Cogent Education*, 3, (1), pp. 1–11.

Kolb, D. A. (1984) *Experiential Learning: Experience as the Source of Learning and Development*, Upper Saddle River, NJ: Prentice-Hall.

Lancaster-Thomas, A. (2017) How effective is philosophy for children in contributing to the affective engagement of pupils in the context of secondary religious education? *Journal of Philosophy in Schools*, 4, (1), pp. 102–122.

Larkin, S., Freathy, R., Doney, J., and Freathy, G. (2020) *Metacognition, Worldviews and Religious Education: A Practical Guide for Teachers*, London: Routledge.

Lipman, M., Sharp, A. M., and Oscanyan, F. S. (1980) *Philosophy in the Classroom*, Philadelphia, PA: Temple University Press.

Logan, J. (1997) *Artefacts for an Occasion*, Middlesex: BFSS National RE Centre.

Logue, M. E., Bennett-Armistead, V. S., and Kim, S., (2011) The Persona Doll Project: Promoting Diversity Awareness Among Preservice Teachers Through Storytelling, *Child Development and Family Relations Faculty Scholarship*. [Online] https://digitalcommons.library.umaine.edu/chf_facpub/1 (Accessed 01/05/2021).

McCreery, E. (1994) Towards an understanding of the notion of the spiritual in education, *Early Child Development and Care*, 100, (1), pp. 93–99.

McCreery, E., Palmer, S., and Voiels, V. (2008) *Teaching Religious Education*, Exeter: Learning Matters.

McDowell, K. (2020) *How Does Philosophy for Children (P4C) in Religious Education Create Effective Dialogue?* The Farmington Institute, Oxford: Harris Manchester College. Report PS099.

McKain, N. (2018) Religious Education as a safe space for discussing unsafe ideas, in M. Castellai and M. Chater (Eds.) *We Need to Talk About Religious Education*, London: Jessica Kingsley, pp. 169–183.

Monk, J., and Silman, C. (2011) *Active Learning in Primary Classrooms: A Case Study Approach*, Harlow: Longman.

Moss, F. (2015) Engaging children creatively: Effective planning for developing enquiry, in S. Elton-Chalcraft (Ed.) *Teaching Religious Education Creatively*, Abingdon: Routledge, pp. 64–77.

Naji, S., and Hashim, R. (Eds.) (2017) *History, Theory and Practice of Philosophy for Children: International Perspectives*, Abingdon: Routledge.

Ninan, M. M. (2017) *An Introduction to Christian Caballah*, Normal, IL: Global Publishers.

Ofsted (2013) *Religious Education: Realising the Potential*, Manchester: Crown Copyright. Reference No: 130068. [Online] https://assets.publishing.service.gov.uk/government/uploads/system/uploads/attachment_data/file/413157/Religious_education_-_realising_the_potential.pdf (Accessed 05/12/2020).

Ofsted (2021) *Research Review Series: Religious Education*, [Online] https://www.gov.uk/government/publications/research-review-series-religious-education/research-review-series-religious-education#fnref:155 (Accessed 18/07/2021).

O'Shea, G. (2018) A comparison of Catechesis of the Good Shepherd and Godly Play, *British Journal of Religious Education*, 40, (3), pp. 308–316.

Panjwani, F., and Revell, L. (2018) Religious education and hermeneutics: The case of teaching about Islam, *British Journal of Religious Education*, 40, (3), pp. 268–276.

Papouli, E. (2019) Diversity dolls: A creative teaching method for encouraging social work students to develop empathy and understanding for vulnerable populations, *Social Work Education*, 38, (2), pp. 241–260.

Prescott, G. (2015) Creative thinking and dialogue: P4C and the community of enquiry, in S. Elton-Chalcraft and Sally (Eds.) *Teaching Religious Education Creatively*, Abingdon: Routledge, pp. 35–50.

Ricci, C., and Pritscher, C. P. (2015) *Holistic Pedagogy*, New York: Springer. http://dx.doi.org/10.1007/978-3-319-14944-8

Rivett, R. (2013) *More than 101 Great Ideas*, Birmingham: REToday.

REC (Religious Education Council of England and Wales) (2013) *A Curriculum Framework for Religious Education in England*, London: REC of England and Wales.

Reynolds, O. (2018) A critical analysis of outdoor learning experiences and the impact on pupil development and conceptual understanding, *The STeP Journal: Student Teacher Perspectives*, 5, (1), pp. 22–29.

Rosenshine, B. (2012) Principles of instruction: Research-based strategies that all teaches should know, *American Educator*, 36, (1), pp. 12–39.

Rowe, S., and Humphries, S. (2012) *The Coombes Approach Learning Through an Experiential and Outdoor Curriculum*, London: Continuum.

Salter, E. (2020) Welcome to my church: Faith-practitioners and the representation of religious traditions in secular RE, *Journal of Religious Education*, 68, (3), pp. 289–303.

Sherrington, T. (2019) *Rosenshine's Principles in Action*, Woodbridge: John Catt.

Siddiqui, N., Gorard, S., and See, B. H. (2017) *Non-Cognitive Impacts of Philosophy for Children, Project Report*. School of Education, Durham University, Durham. [Online] http://dro.dur.ac.uk/20880/1/20880.pdf?DDD34+DDD29+czwc58+d700tmt) (Accessed 24/01/2021).

Siôn, T. (2014) Religious Education, interfaith dialogue and community cohesion in Wales: An empirical investigation of the contribution made by the Standing Advisory Councils on Religious Education, *Contemporary Wales*, 27, (1), pp. 148–166.

Smart, N. (1998) *The World's Religions*, Cambridge: Cambridge University Press. Second edition.

Sotto, E. (2007) *When Teaching Becomes Learning, A Theory and Practice of Teaching*, London: Continuum.

Stephen, C., Martlew, J., and Ellis, J. (2010) Taking Active Learning into the Primary School: A matter of new practices? *International Journal of Early Years Education*, 18, (4), pp. 315–329.

Thwaites, H. (2005) Can 'philosophy for children' improve teaching and learning within attainment target 2 of religious education? *Education 3–13*, 33, (3), pp. 4–8.

Unstad, and Fjørtoft (2021) Disciplinary literacy in religious education: The role and relevance of reading, *British Journal of Religious Education*, 43, (4), pp. 434–442.

van Dijk-Wesselius, J., van den Berg, A., Maas, J., and Hovinga, D. (2020) Green schoolyards as outdoor learning environments: Barriers and solutions as experienced by primary school teachers, *Frontiers in Psychology*, 09 January 2020 [Online] https://doi.org/10.3389/fpsyg.2019.02919 (Accessed 23/07/2021).

Vickery, S. (2011) *Persona Dolls in Religious Education*, Gloucester: Jumping Fish Publications. [see also https://www.gloucester.anglican.org/wp-content/uploads/2017/08/An-introduction-to-using-Persona-Dollss.pdf]

Vygotsky, L. (1986) *Thought and Language*, Cambridge, MA: MIT Press.

Waite, S. (2011) Teaching and learning outside the classroom: Personal values, alternative pedagogies and standards, *Education 3–13*, 39, (1), pp. 65–82.

Warner, D., and Elton-Chalcraft, S. (2018) Race, culture and ethnicity teaching in post-European Times, in H. Cooper and S. Elton-Chalcraft (Eds.), *Professional Studies in Primary Education*, London: SAGE. Third edition, pp. 318–338.

Watson, B., and Thompson, P. (2007) *The Effective Teaching of Religious Education*, Harlow: Longman. Second edition.

Watson, E., and Bradley, B. (2021) *The Science of Learning: 99 Studies That Everyone Should Know*, Abingdon: Routledge. Second edition.

Webster, M. (2010) *Creative Approaches to Teaching Primary RE*, London: Longman.

Wintersgill, B. (2017) (Ed.) *Big Ideas for Religious Education*, Exeter: University of Exeter.

Wintersgill, B., Cush, D., and Francis, D. (2019) *Putting Big Ideas into Practice in Religious Education*. [Online] http://www.reonline.org.uk/knowing/bigideas-into-practice/ (Accessed 27/02/2021).

Multidisciplinary pedagogies

THEOLOGY, PHILOSOPHY AND HUMAN/SOCIAL SCIENCES IN RE

Introduction

Religious education is considered a multidisciplinary subject. Currently, the Religious Education (RE) communites are searching searching for a framework that would bring cohesion to the subject by exploring the role of the disciplines of theology, philosophy and human/social sciences, in particular. Kueh (2020:142) has proposed the historical-critical discipline as the fourth one. One of the reasons for this search is an attempt to address the problematic combination of several disciplines in competition with each other (Chater and Erricker 2013). Moreover, the lack of agreement as to the domain of the subject also contributes to the contested nature of the subject in the UK. It has been some time since the question as to whether RE is a subject, a discipline or a field of knowledge has been raised in the wider debate regarding the status and function of disciplinary knowledge in contemporary education (Baumfield 2005). Freathy et al. (2017) advocate an approach which is not neutral and value-free, but committed to providing pupils with the knowledge, skills, attributes and values associated with the communities of academic enquiry concerned especially for theology and religious studies.

The social sciences encompass several disciplines such as anthropology, archaeology, critical pedagogy, economics, ethnic and race studies, gender studies, geography, history, law, linguistics, performing arts, philosophy, political science, psychology, sociology, theology and others. Hutton and Cox (2021:7) suggest that the three disciplines provide teachers and students with the specific lens to teach and study religion and worldviews. In other words, they contend that the same subject content can be studied from three different perspectives. However, it would require an understanding of the conventions and shared discourse and language used in the different fields of theology, philosophy and the social sciences.

Disciplines provide different ways of understanding the world; they employ different methods and the bodies of knowledge are distinct. Georgiou and Wright (2020:150) further explain that theology provides a lens through which to primarily explore religion and worldviews ontologically, i.e. to consider core existence. One might ask questions relating to authority, reliability, internal consistency and the coherence of the text. The human and social sciences enable us to explore religion and worldviews through a phenomenological lens. These disciplines explore questions raised by the lived experience of religion and worldviews now and throughout history. One might ask questions relating to the nature of religion itself, to the diversity of the lived experience of religion and worldviews, and the symbolic relationship between individuals and groups about religion and worldviews. Philosophy as a discipline involves exploring

DOI: 10.4324/9780429289743-15

Table 11.1 Example of using a three disciplinary approach

Places of worship		
Theological perspective	**Philosophical perspective**	**Social science perspective**
What do places of worship say about God? What do places of worship offer to their respective religion? How does a place of worship reflect its religions' beliefs? How are places of worship built in the image of God? How often do believers attend their places of worship? How do the beliefs of the community affect how they use the place? Does worship always have to be congregational? Do you need to go to a place of worship to practice the religion? Why is a place similar in some respects and not in all respects? Why does the religion need a place of worship? Why do you need a dress code to enter some places of worship? Why are some places of worship built in specific directions?	What do believers think about their place? Why do believers decide to attend a place of worship? What can we learn from other places of worship? What can you learn in a place of worship that you can't learn in a sacred text? What can believers gain in a place that they can't gain elsewhere? How do places of worship enlighten other people about their religion? Why do people need a sacred place?	What is the importance of having a place of worship? What effect does a place have on people's lives or practices? How is a placed used? How do mosques bring Muslims together? How do mosques bring communities together? How do places of worship allow people to express their religion? Does everyone use it in the same manner? How do places of worship allow people to have an open conversation about religion? How do you become a religious leader, i.e. Rabbi, priest, Imam? What does the design of the place say about its local culture? Who designs a place of worship? Who decides where a place of worship should be? Should a Prime Minister be allowed to prevent congregational prayer?

religion and worldviews epistemologically, logically and ethically. They acknowledge that this understanding of philosophy reflects their own westernised worldview and that philosophy can be interpreted differently (Georgiou and Wright 2020:152–155). Some trainees attempted this as shown in Table 11.1. It has been suggested that an RE, which balances these three disciplines, is stronger than the one which experiences multidisciplinary chaos (Chater and Erricker 2013).

In practical terms, they propose that the different disciplinary lenses can consider different types of questions to ask when studying religion and beliefs. For example, theological lens questions about belief: what it is, what it has come from, how it has changed over time and how it is applied in different contexts. Philosophical lens questions the nature of reality, existence and knowledge. The social sciences lens questions the way that religion and beliefs are lived and the impact they can have at an individual, communal and societal level. In addition, taking a balanced view of the disciplines helps to create a challenging curriculum and gives pupils the tools they need for future study. This means that it is also essential that teachers understand their own lens as they may have an unconscious bias towards one or more of the disciplines (Hutton and Cox 2021:8). A balanced disciplinary approach to designing an RE curriculum helps to provide more rigorous and coherent teaching and learning and it gives academic legitimacy to a subject. The knowledge that materialises from this multifaceted matrix is significant (Kueh 2018:63).

Moreover, they note that pupils will have their own lens which they will have developed from their life experience and learning. They should understand that when studying religion no one is entirely neutral in their approach, because everyone views the world from their own perspective (Hutton and Cox 2021:9).

However, it is important to distinguish between lens and disciplines. Hutton and Cox (2021:9–10) explain that a pupil's lens is not their opinion or an aspect of belief or practice; rather it is an understanding of what has formed their opinion or perspective. For example, pupils may hold the opinion that abortion is wrong. This in itself is not a lens. The lens is about recognising that this viewpoint has been formed through so many things: the way they have been brought up, conversations with others, personal experiences and the impact of other beliefs will all have helped to form their view. Therefore, in the classroom talking about our lens alongside the disciplinarian lenses helps pupils understand the plurality and complexity of religious and non-religious beliefs. Consideration of the disciplinary offers possibilities for both curriculum and pupils. Kueh (2020:147) thinks that for such pupils, acts may become acts of transformation on many different levels including memory transformation, worldview transformation, existential transformation, character transformation and transformation as they form new identities as learners.

Summary

Taking a multidisciplinary approach to RE would offer opportunities to pupils to see the subject in a multifaceted, complex and connected way. The use of theology, philosophy and social science disciplines is useful in providing structure, coherence and rigour to the RE curriculum. It would offer pupils various perspectives and methods to help with their learning.

ARTISTIC RE

Introduction

One of the ways through which religions have impressed their messages and ideas upon people is through visual stimuli – works of art in the broadest sense. Thus, art can be considered a classical and historical pedagogy. This means that there is some beautiful work in a wide range of media at the disposal of the teacher of RE to draw upon. The guiding question is to help pupils know and understand how art, architecture, music, poetry and dance express religious beliefs, practices and thoughts. Similarly, other 'subject' areas are to be used in the service of RE. This is an attempt to ensure that the quality of RE, its content and concepts is not trivialised. Pupils should come out from a lesson with unambiguous learning in RE.

RE through art and design

The National Curriculum states that as pupils progress they should think critically and develop a more rigorous understanding of art and design. They should know how art and design shape and reflect history and contribute to the creativity, culture and wealth of the nation (DfE 2013c). Unsurprisingly, it has been proposed that cross-curricular approaches facilitate pupil's ability to think more imaginatively which can then increase their courage and self-esteem (Janes 2014; Lucas and Spencer 2017). In other words, such a combination has the potential to enhance their inner-creativity, thinking and learning processes. Moreover, the teaching of RE through creative approaches, such as using art, drama, dance and music follows in the tradition of these being used in religious worship, expression and the uplifting of the spirit in connection with the divine, which are commonly found in the religions that pupils will be studying (Webster 2010:23).

Webster (2010:27) also suggests that art is a fantastic vehicle for learning about and learning from religion. She notes that there has been a long-standing strong relationship between religion and art since it is a sophisticated way of communicating religious messages (Jensen 2000). Furthermore, she observes that, historically, religious leaders preached their doctrine mainly through oral tradition and different art forms. In the Christian tradition, for example, story-telling, drawings, stained-glass windows and mosaics, dramatic narratives were used to spread the word (Goldburg 2004). This seems to have been the case elsewhere too. In the vast continent of Africa, Hackett (1988) has shown that artistic works play an important role, especially in some areas where oral traditions dominate, for the communication of beliefs about the relationship between the human, spiritual and natural worlds. In her work, she sought a greater understanding of the philosophical and religious aspects of African art and challenged western perceptions of what is 'important' in terms of artistic representation.

Religion and arts

Hence, it could be argued that religions and the arts, in the broadest sense, are inherently linked. The arts play many roles in religion and religions, in turn, use art in different ways for varied purposes. It is used to instruct, convey symbolism, represent moral behaviour and its consequences, inspire faith, induce devotion, express experiences and so forth. These beliefs and practices are communicated verbally and physically. Religious art embodies and symbolises the meanings and essence of faith traditions and provides windows into their central beliefs and practices. For instance, by exploring the cross or the crescent or reflecting on a seated Buddha or working with Islamic geometric patterns which decorate mosques or statues of the dancing Siva, pupils can come to understand more of the insights and motivations of the believers (Hammond 2015:116).

Whatever the religion, each piece is likely to contain a message about the fundamental belief systems of the faith and how to practice it. Traditionally, the purpose was to reinforce and teach the doctrine of the faith (Nes 2006). However, in contemporary society, most people can read and write so the use of art for such teaching has reduced. Consequently, Webster (2010) contends that today's art seems to be more in tune with the expression of an artist's faith and/or interpretation of the religious story.

Art has been considered a universal language, which allows humans the ability to express themselves in various ways. Importantly, at a time when the world is increasingly becoming more visual, there is considerable opportunity for teachers to tap into the rich religious and cultural art forms to enhance RE and offer pupils the media through which they can understand and appreciate religions and worldviews better. Ogier (2017:10) explains that through art and design pupils can express their thoughts visually and act as a safety net by creating an outlet for their misconception and fear. Thus, the arts are a powerful media through which faiths and beliefs can be taught and linked to emotional literacy. Your role in RE is to direct pupils towards communicating their innermost thoughts as a way to make sense of the outer reality (Webster 2010:17).

Ofsted has consistently remarked upon the effectiveness of using art and drama as a means of encouraging pupils to express ideas in RE (Ofsted 2007) and, where teaching was good and outstanding, it involved sustained learning and linking of RE to other areas subjects, notably English, art, drama and music (Ofsted 2010:17). Nevertheless, in so doing, RE content must drive a topic, rather than always trying to fit in with the other subjects (Ofsted 2013:12). The arts can provide some pupils with an effective method through which to express difficult concepts and ideas, nevertheless, Miller (2003:209) cautions against distorting the arts in the name of creativity. In other words, the intentions of RE should be explicit before you teach in this way otherwise both might suffer.

Learning in RE

Thinking is a cognitive process and links to communication. It requires pupils to communicate in some form what they know and understand. Thinking skills can be taught, but in RE, this is mainly related to deciding how the pupils can communicate what they know and understand to you, themselves or another one. It can be related to reflection tasks, but not always (Webster 2015:130–132). Therefore, aesthetically and emotionally, pupils should:

1   Describe the function of works of art and how they show important beliefs.

2   Explain symbolic meanings in the art, architecture, calligraphy, music, poetry by using religious concepts and language.

3   Identify similarities and differences in the way beliefs and values are reflected through arts within and between religions.

4   Create and express their values, beliefs and ideas that are important to them.

5   Study the art, architecture, buildings, music, calligraphy, poetry used by religions to represent beliefs, ideals and ideas.

Pupils can communicate what they know and understand about a concept in written or non-written form. In an enquiry, pupils are encouraged to ask big questions that do not have a set answer. For some, this can be challenging as some pupils prefer to have a fixed answer. However, in RE, in some topics and issues, there are many answers and it is up to the individual, based on evidence and argument, to decide which they feel is the correct one for them. Some teachers find using 'I wonder…' as a good way to encourage big questions as this raises the question without it suggesting that an answer is expected. Reflection is considered to be an internal personal process. Therefore, pupils must be provided with regular opportunities to reflect.

Seeking RE concepts in the arts

The various works of art can be linked to RE concepts by asking pupils which concepts are represented in various pictures, images, sculptures, drawings, calligraphy and other art forms. Pupils could identify beauty, reverence, humility, hope, fear, worship, love, hatred, eternity, life and others. Importantly, after they ascertain the concepts, you should discuss their meanings and significance with them.

You can encourage pupils to speculate and share their ideas through 'think-pair-share' and then hear them all as a class. It would be interesting to find out their thoughts on whether artists worship as they produce their work and if they express their beliefs in their work.

Planning using Big Questions

One of the popular ways of organising a series of lessons is to use Big Questions, such as, 'how do people express their faith or their spiritual ideas through the arts', to engage pupils with spiritual values through the arts. Pupils would then think for themselves about questions concerning the history, artist, functions, meanings, beliefs and spirituality associated with the work being studied. They would consider what can be learned from these expressions of faith by referring to their own experiences, beliefs and values. This approach can be applied across the age ranges. It can be used for sustained 'RE through Arts' project work for a longer period than usual. Alternatively, as part of a sequence of work, you can invite an artist, calligrapher, craftsperson, poet, sculpture or singer to school.

In the classroom using nature

Pupils should have opportunities to analyse, investigate and respond to a range of natural objects such as leaves, wood, insects, birds, pets and shells in the context of the natural world or creation stories. They can visualise and describe personal and sacred spaces and special people and extraordinary things. They can discuss and draw scenes or characters from religious stories or nature. They can bring and share the religious art they possess, if any, such as building, cards, calligraphy, icons, illuminated manuscripts and offer personal responses and individual interpretations or reactions. They can sequence a set of images as a narrative to document a festival or celebration. It is also suggested that they can draw on their thoughts and ideas as a starting point for visual work by making personal drawings based on experiences of hope, fear, sadness or happiness. They can observe first-hand examples of religious art by visiting places of worship, museums, galleries and record their visits through a series of drawings, for example. They explore and make religious symbols. You can show them the 'Tree Cathedral', which is a cathedral grown in Milton Keynes and discuss what this natural 'green' place of worship means and why people love it, at https://www.theparkstrust.com/events/discovery-stroll-newlands-tree-cathedral and explore the eco-mosque at https://cambridgecentralmosque.org/

Religion and beliefs in architecture

Let the pupils in your class wonder and be in awe with some of the monumental, beautiful and grand architecture evidenced in religious traditions. Teach them that the La Sagrada Família in Barcelona is a giant Basilica still under construction since 1882. Invite them to estimate the size of the largest Hindu mandir, and research some of the largest ones. At the same time, ask them to ponder over the simplicity of the Kaabah in Makkah.

Pulpits, altars, fonts, takhts, palkis, arks and bemas are useful examples that come in different sizes and shapes, some simple and others highly decorated and which convey emotional-spatial-spiritual characteristics of sacred places. These different facets serve a distinct purpose and can relate to the belief system of that faith or society of the time (Webster 2010:31). In mosque architecture, for example, the minbar had a high place because it was more effective for communication. Moreover, its verticality and loftiness symbolised the 'ascension towards God' which is the function of prayer and ritual speech (Jones 2012). It is usually located to the right of the mihrāb. The minbar and the mihrāb form an integrated whole, 'a [sacred] centre in a centre', as both ritual elements orient the preacher and the audience ultimately towards God (Jones 2012:57).

In the classroom

Across the world and in the UK, religious architecture in the form of structures and buildings is a prominent phenomenon. These are probably the most influential and noticeable spaces in their respective communities. Pupils can use GoogleEarth© to study these. They can also compare and experience the great interior images of churches, cathedrals, temples, pagodas, gurdwaras and synagogues (Hammond 2015). There are many sites to use for the study of such impressive religious architecture. This one is a list of 25 awe-inspiring edifices following a historical time-line. https://www.onlineschoolscenter.com/25-impressive-examples-religious-architecture/

Enquiries can be set to investigate, what it means to make a building 'for the glory of God', and 'mosques belong to Allah' and 'door to the Guru'. In class, ask each table group to study one globally significant religious building and write about why that place matters in that religion. Alternatively, each table could look at different globally significant places within one religion and share their findings with the class. Invite them to comment on what they find impressive and why.

These questions could be used to plan a sequence of lessons on architecture and buildings.

- What does it mean to make a building 'for God'?
- Do people need a sacred building to worship in?
- Why does Britain have so many churches?
- What makes a place special?
- What is a sacred place?
- Are all places sacred?
- What does a synagogue look like?
- Does a sacred place always remain sacred?
- Why does Britain have mandirs, gurdwaras and mosques?
- Why do religious communities value their holy buildings so much?
- How do people express their beliefs through and in special buildings?
- Should religious communities build huge buildings for worship or give generously in charity?

'Light upon light'

Light as a universal symbol is found in many religious traditions and non-religious settings. Often, it takes the form of a candle or diva light. It has symbolic and metaphorical meanings and is habitually contrasted with darkness. Light tends to be associated with the concepts of celebration, divinity, guidance, happiness, hope, life, prosperity and purity. On the other hand, darkness is frequently depicted as being bad, chaotic, death, evil, fear, loneliness, mystery and the unknown. As a teacher, it is important to be mindful of the possibility of conveying the idea that 'black is bad' to pupils and of the potential influence that this might have on their perceptions of blackness.

Light has a symbolic role related to sacred and religious beliefs. It is found in religious buildings, sacred texts, cemeteries, shrines, homes, workplaces and memorials. Antonakaki (2007) asserts that it plays a part in the creation of worshipping and aesthetic forms of religion and is an influential factor in both the spiritual relation between the believers and the religion and in the spatial relationship between the believers and the building. Spatial structures construct the religious environment whilst light re-construct the religious experience (Antonakaki 2007:1).

In the classroom

Various activities could be designed to explore light, its use and its symbolism in religion and society. Pupils can write their phrases about light. They can interpret the meanings of phrases such as: 'You are the light of the world. A city set on a hill cannot be hidden' (Christian); 'Allah is the Light of the heavens and the earth' (Muslim); 'If you light a lamp for somebody, it will also brighten your path' (Buddhist) and 'There is only one air, earth and only one light of the God in each being' (Sikhi).

Shrines and tombs

Shrines are interesting structural and spatial features found in many religious traditions and non-religious settings. In some cases, you will find them within the place of worship or in the home. In your travels, you might catch a glimpse of a portable one before an aeroplane takes off. It is common in some countries to find them at crossroads or by a road, or at the burial sites of saints, martyrs or religious figureheads. These provide opportunities to learn about their communal purposes, if any, the relics, images, icons, funerary art and mausoleum. The reasons for visiting these sites will differ in different traditions, which pupils should understand. At the same time, within a particular religion, pupils should also encounter alternative viewpoints which might shun shrine and tomb visitations.

Statues and sculptures

In Christianity, statuary and sculptures presented the fundamental beliefs of the Christian faith when the majority of Christians could not read or write, and so, these were necessary for any illiterate person to learn about the religion (Jensen 2000). It has been suggested that having them in some churches reminds some Christians that saints and Christ are close to their thoughts. They feature predominantly in the Catholic Church as reminders of faith, devotion, events, beliefs and prominent individuals in church history. In Hinduism, colourful paintings and statues are used as part of daily worship and each god holds items that are an emblem for their characteristics (Webster 2010). In Buddha Dharma, Buddharūpa is the term used for a statue. There are many ways of representing the Buddha and they differ according to the artistic style, the canons of the different traditions and the cultural and geographical location in which they are made. However, some features are common to most statues, which pupils could identify.

In the classroom

Pupils can be shown images and describe what they observe and study the inscriptions, if any, and explain why they think they were written and what they say. Pupils can also design their tombstone and write a message, which they would like to leave behind for themselves. Pupils can take a virtual of a shrine to see what it looks like, how people visit it, what is found there, why they visit it and the rituals performed there. Pupils can be given a profile sheet to complete for a saint or significant leader. Some people see stones as symbols of strength, so pupils can be provided with these, asked to decorate them and write a word that can help them personally to be strong.

Expression of religion through visual art

Religions have defined and contributed hugely to the visual culture around the world and this contribution is important for understanding many of the key works of art. There are many different ways visual artists explore their ideas about the world to help them with their personal journey in making sense of the world. Pupils can learn from such a process within RE lessons and use it to explore some difficult concepts related to religions (Webster 2010:34). The multi-dimensional aspect of religion, as discussed above and previously, needs to be reflected in your RE lessons. Consider the ideas in Box 11.1.

Pictures and photographs

There are different ways of using pictures and the methods you choose will depend on the intent, age and experience of the pupils. To learn through a picture requires attributing some importance to it, for example, by mounting it. Practitioners use different kinds of pictures in RE including pictures of people engaged in religious activities, religious artefacts and religious places, imaginative representations of religious experience and significant figures. That said, the latter kind of images are the ones to be more mindful of.

In Islam, there is a prohibition on the representation of Allah, thus, recourse is usually made to alternative forms of art. In some Jewish traditions, the portrayal of God is discouraged. So, perhaps, it would be important to raise questions about the legitimacy of representing the Divine in human form. The prohibition on making of idols in the Ten Commandments because of the ever-present danger of worshipping what is created rather than the Creator lies behind both Muslim and Jewish nervousness about figurative art (Watson and Thompson 2007:125). In Buddhism, there is a wide variety of images of the Buddha, Bodhisattvas, deities, spirits, heavenly beings and also pictures of kings of wisdom. In Sikhi, you will find portraits of the Gurus depicted in natural, communal and spiritual scenes to inspire and lift the soul. In Hinduism and Christianity, representational art is plentiful.

BOX 11.1 VIEWPOINT: THE POWER OF VISUAL IMAGES

The world is full of visual images: signs, posters, advertisements, newspapers, magazines and films are seen on a daily basis. Children learn quickly to 'read' information or interpret the image presented. They begin to unpack the meaning behind the image. Advertisements are a prime example of visual imagery that conveys meaning. By using such and such the user will acquire the lifestyle, looks, status, be envied and so on. They rely upon you being able to picture yourself in the given situation. Critical thinking applied to such imagery questions the assumptions, it asks the pertinent questions and it identifies the implications. All these are vital skills in beginning to understand how the process of belief begins, what it means to be human, social persuasion and the society to which we belong (Erricker, Lowndes and Bellchambers 2011:48).

In the classroom

The exploration of photographs and objects with younger children is particularly useful as it provides opportunities to develop their oral communication skills and shared thinking (Siraj-Blatchford and Mayo 2012). Thus, the teacher is in a good position to model deep talk and analytical thinking about the pictures.

Pupils can create an art exhibition of high-quality images of work that they have produced in a given topic, for example, as a category of leaders. Pupils can be given the different stages and events in the life of a leader and, once completed, the 'whole life' can be put together in chronological order as a display. Another activity would involve reading a religious story that inspired an artist and investigating the artist and how their work came to be created, the features and the messages within it. Pupils can be involved in producing an album; the top half of someone or something is drawn and in the bottom half a text to accompany the picture. The album is then taken to a reception class for a 'show and tell' session about the leader, practice or issue.

Imagery

Erricker, Lowndes and Bellchambers (2011:48) suggest that imagery is easily remembered and provides a focus, motivates thoughts, stimulates or inspires a reaction. It may encourage empathy, feelings and emotions and also encourage research and inquiry. The use of visual arts in teaching RE can, thus, be a means of expressing and deepening the understanding and religious awareness of pupils and their teachers (Miller 2003:200). Art is commonly created as a way to express an aspect of a person's faith, and so, it is interesting to explore such art with pupils as they can then consider how they use art to express or to help integrate how they feel (Webster 2010:29).

A study of pictures, photographs and images requires the development of certain skills, which can sometimes be developed in stages, although commonly pupils will use these skills concurrently. Thus, pupils should learn to observe closely, describe in detail, understand, explain, interpret, compare and analyse so that they reflect the religious beliefs, concepts, stories and behaviours within them. In the experience of Connor (2018:8) pupils with autism can be very easily distracted by too many visual stimuli. Therefore, they may need provisions made for them that are personalised, consistent and given tablets or iPads (Cohen and Gerhardt 2014).

You also should be alert to the need for a balanced representation of faiths and belief systems, their followers and their practice. Homan (2012:191) noted that the exclusive use of positive images disaffects some teachers and some regard positive images as a distortion from real RE. Therefore, the complexity of religions, their followers and their behaviours should be presented through pictures and over simplification for the sake of keeping things easy should be questioned.

Nevertheless, importantly, Cooling (1994) emphasises that pictures should help pupils grasp the centrality of the message or belief in religions and belief systems. Teachers should avoid an overly descriptive approach to religion that concentrates on giving information about religions at the expense of exploring their meaning for believers and of showing its relevance to modern children. Pupils, he suggests, should not leave the lesson with a feeling that religion is very peculiar.

Stained glasses

Today and historically, the most common art form available to the general public could be stained-glass windows which were built into structures of sacred spaces and which also contained iconographic motifs. Most Christian religious buildings have stained-glass windows within them that present the message of the faith (Webster 2010:27). In Judaism, there is an opportunity for pupils to learn about the history of the image in the stained-glass windows, the reasons for including scenes from stories, the passages from scripture, and the natural objects from the Holy Land. Some sanctuaries will have twelve windows, which according to some people, represent the twelve tribes. In Hindu Dharma, there are images of Brahma, Vishnu, Shiva and others. Pupils can make their own or use those available in colouring books. Some of the world most beautiful ones can be found here: https://www.cntraveler.com/galleries/2015-11-11/the-worlds-most-spectacular-stained-glass

Adverts

Advertisements are a complicated and potentially tricky concept to use with children because they need to have a grasp of language and be able to consider somebody else's viewpoint to be able to debate the issues that the adverts raise. They can be used with upper KS2 for debate about how to be religiously sensitive; the influence of the media on religion and discussion on whether adverts promote tolerance or respect of religions (Webster 2010:33).

In the classroom, pupils could discuss whether these images or any religious explicit image, should be used to sell a product. Pupils can look at the imagery and symbols within an advert and understand that art is wider than a picture or sculpture. The media can be a very powerful tool to turn someone onto or against religion (Badr 2004). Consequently, they should be viewed and interpreted with caution because of the possibility of prejudice and/or questionable agendas when the items were created (Webster 2010:33).

Personal expressions of faith

People express their personal faith and beliefs through a variety of other forms of practical and useful art (Webster 2010:40). A mezuzah in Judaism is one way of expressing personal faith. Many different types of these exist, some of which are very ornate and decorated with scripture, calligraphy or pattern. Islamic art is also a personal expression of faith. It is believed that it is a visual representation of the divine nature of Allah and the beauty of all that God has created. Much of Islamic art is symmetrical as it is believed by some to be an expression of the infinite nature of God with no obvious beginning or end (Webster 2010).

In the classroom, ask pupils to make their mezuzah with their codes. There are many styles of calligraphy that can be explored with pupils to write their names and messages and create their pieces.

Paintings

The use of painting is common in schools. There are some useful artists whose work can be used in RE for inspiration and study including those by Yasmin Kathrada and Sikhi art offers some excellent work on Sikh art, Hindu art and fantasy art as seen here https://www.sikhiart.com/

In the classroom, pupils make, paint and decorate tiles based on themes of justice, oppression, freedom, hate and hope in the style of a particular artist using material from religious traditions. Pupils and teachers can explore the *Discovering Sacred Texts* of the British Library, which provides access to the richness of the texts from Buddhism, Christianity, Hinduism, Islam, Judaism, Sikhism and the Bahá'í Faith, Jainism and Zoroastrianism from here https://www.bl.uk/sacred-texts#

Spirited arts

The National Association of Teachers of RE (NATRE) holds regular competitions for schools across the country. These provide pupils with an opportunity to be creative and imaginative in RE. The project combines spiritual ideas and skills. Teachers incorporate these competitions into their RE lessons and many schools have a unit of work or a special learning 'RE through the arts week'.

These have been running since 2004 and many of the poems and artwork produced by pupils are showcased as wonderful galleries for you to use and inspire your pupils. In 2021, entries were invited for Art (painting, drawing, sketching), poetry, photography, dance, music, drama and sculpture at https://www.natre.org.uk/about-natre/projects/spirited-arts/spirited-arts-2021/

Summary

This section began by discussing the importance of teaching RE through the arts in the broadest sense. The aim was to highlight some of these and share strategies that have proved to be useful and successful so that you can reflect on, adapt and apply them in your teaching. The section is concluded with some principles.

You should give attention to both contents and the quality of the works used as these have an impact on the representation of religions and the learning experiences of pupils. You will also have opportunities through these to assess pupil's knowledge and understanding in RE.

It is important not to assume that pupils will automatically question a resource and extract the necessary information from it. Graphicacy will need to be developed gradually using modelling, scaffolding, explaining and exemplifying. Pupils, especially younger ones, need guidance to see 'a picture' as being part of the 'bigger picture' of the religion being studied. Hence, you should facilitate that connection.

Art and design are used as a means for spiritual expression and uplifting. To be able to express their feelings, pupils will first need the vocabulary to be able to communicate this. For some pupils, this can be challenging. Therefore, ensure that you offer a rich language and vocabulary environment in your classroom.

When selecting pieces of art for RE, one of the challenges you might face, as a teacher, is that you will not be starting with a blank slate. Someone has already expressed their worldview in the resource at your disposal. Therefore, you need to be aware of their and your own ontological and epistemological standpoints in the selection process, which might influence the worldview being conveyed to the class.

The role of art and design in different religious traditions differs it might be so even within a religion. Therefore, you need to be aware that in some traditions the 'arts' play an important devotional role, whereas, in others, it might be absent, restricted or conditional. The use of resources from authentic sources of information enhances the appeal and accuracy of the subject content of RE as well as the power and beauty of the works of art.

DRAMATICAL RE

Introduction

There is an apparent relationship between the 'secular' drama and 'ritual' drama in religion. In the religious tradition, you will notice dramatisation of festivals, miracle and morality plays, and some African traditional religions abound with theatrical elements (Mogra 2022). Nevertheless, there are some religions, which may censure certain elements, as they are considered blasphemous or objectionable. Second, it is also important to be mindful that drama might discourage some pupils from taking part by feeling foolish and shy. Third, after a drama, pupils should not be left thinking, for example, that Diwali is about fireworks and Christmas is an annual play. Indeed, they are helpful, although they should not replace a well-planned RE curriculum which deals with the big questions and key concepts of religion. Fourth, you need to learn that paired and group activities can increase pupil success, but to work together effectively pupils need guidance, support and practice. Fifth, that pupils with SEND are likely to require additional or adapted support and so identifying effective strategies is essential (DfE 2019). Hence, as a teacher, you will need to be mindful of these factors in RE lessons, as all pupils are expected to be enabled to participate in and gain knowledge, skills and understanding associated with the artistic practice of drama (DfE 2013b:14).

Mantle of the Expert

Mantle of the Expert is a drama approach that gives greater responsibility to pupils in their learning. It involves the creation of a fictional world where pupils assume the roles of experts in a real-life situation in a designated scenario. It is based on the principle that treating pupils as responsible experts increases their engagement and confidence. It promotes creativity, improves teamwork, communication skills, critical thought and decision-making (Taylor 2016).

The key elements include:

- Pupils – the team of experts.
- The client – who sets up a fictional enterprise.
- The Commission – set by the client(s) engaging pupils in specific tasks by giving a real sense of tension (Heathcote and Bolton 1995).

A collective imagination and fantasy through problem-solving are set for the class. Pupils are contracted for an enterprise, whereby, as a team of 'experts', they use imaginative role-play to explore the issue. Usually, an imaginary client, such as a faith leader, commissions the team. For example, as a team of architects, they are to design a new peace room in the school. Pupils then get involved in mimed activities, improvisation, research, consultation, costing, survey and design. The focus should be on the enquiry process, although it can lead to real outcomes such as 3D replicas or 2D rooms.

The participants are always aware that fiction is something that can start and stop when they or the teacher decides (MoE 2021). The teacher's role is to guide the drama, stepping in and out of the role as necessary, providing resources and guiding the process to enable reflection and decision-making. Importantly, it is not about creating simulations, but contexts where pupils fully understand that they are not experts. They can intellectually move from inside to outside the fiction (Taylor 2016).

In the classroom

You should apply high expectations to all groups, and ensure all pupils have access to a rich curriculum. It is suggested that you can provide an opportunity for all pupils to experience success by adapting lessons, whilst maintaining high expectations for all so that all pupils have the opportunity to meet expectations. You should also balance the input of new content so that pupils master important concepts. Moreover, you should make effective use of teaching assistants and other adults in the classroom (DfE 2019).

Pupils have a contract from a fictional client to build a Buddhist pagoda. They become Buddhist monks, nuns and laypersons. They prepare documents, as architects they design, as archaeologists they excavate, as builders they construct, as bankers they pay, as hosts they write invitations for the opening ceremony, as Buddhists, they create the shrine, order and position the artefacts, flowers and ornaments and make different Buddha statues. Thus, pupils learn about real-life companies, have a deadline and meet client expectations. The following could also be used:

- Hajj – pupils prepare a hajj package for a Muslim family of five.
- Baptism – a local church commissions baptism for a newly arrived Christian orthodox from Greece.

■ Food – a hotelier orders food to serve Hindu and Jewish customers for lunch.

■ Vaisakhi celebration – pupils plan an authentic Sikhi event for the Prime Minister.

In all these scenarios, the client ensures that the challenge is high and pupils are given clear feedback. The teacher can use the client to ensure that learning outcomes are explicit and appropriate.

Drama-based pedagogy

The drama-based pedagogy (DBP) is an approach that is an embodied way of learning through kinaesthetic, social and collaborative processes. The activity involves pupils using their background knowledge to role-play the life of a religious person, disciple or character from a moral story. They work in pairs to use dialogue, image work and role-play (Dobson and Stephenson 2020). The use of the DBP allows pupils to have meaningful communication, and thereby develops many social skills, empathy and metacognition.

In the classroom

Drama provides opportunities for pupils to take on various roles in the context of RE stories. These include The Pharisee and the Tax Collector or The Parable of the Sower. They can hot seat characters from the story of Joseph and his Brothers. Pupils can use freeze-frame for representing symbols and images, for example, symbolic actions to represent peace or forgiveness. Pupils use drama to begin to explore their own and others' feelings about issues, for example, imagined eyewitness accounts of Moses crossing the sea, the sacrifice of Abraham, the Sikh story of the milk and the jasmine flower, the Hindu story of King Janaka and the monk.

THEATRICAL RE

Introduction

Phillips (2003) stressed that 'Theatre of Learning' is a process, not a place. The process was developed over many years to make RE make sense. It uses circle work and experiential learning techniques in a multi-sensory setting with music, artefacts and displays to motivate, engage, improve behaviour and written work, but most important of all, these techniques have the potential of changing the way young people see themselves and others. Over time, she found that the methods developed pupils emotionally, spiritually, as well as academically (Phillips 2006). It was the growing awareness of a pupil's own inner selves and the change to their attitudes and values, which became the most important aspect of this work. In Vygotsky's terms, children's learning is a social affair; they obtain knowledge and an understanding of the world through engaging with others (Vygotsky 1978).

Principles

The method uses:

1   Circle work built on mutual trust and respect.

2   A multi-sensory learning environment in which literacy is never the starting point. This means that it cannot provide a barrier to learning. Every pupil takes part equally in the experiences and the discussions that follow.

3   Religion neutral exercises, which parallel the aspect of the religion being studied and develop the pupil's own spirituality. They are religion-neutral because they are not directed towards a divine being and are tradition neutral, for example.

4   Participatory symbols, which enable pupils to understand that ritual and liturgy are very powerful and enable believers to feel changed. Symbolic actions enable people to understand something at a much deeper level than if they are simply described.

5   A concrete platform created to teach abstract concepts using a multi-sensory environment, combined with exercises involving the imagination to enable pupils to remember, understand and think about ideas that might otherwise be difficult to access.

6   Hitting the spiritual target in which all lessons are planned to develop the universal spirituality that is common to all human beings, whether they belong to a religious tradition or not.

7   Re-enactment where these techniques are all combined and expressed. Working in this way develops pupil's own spirituality, enables them to understand and empathise with the spirituality of others – and makes RE make sense.

In the classroom

A theatre of learning – the Guru Granth Sahib

To give a sense of the reverence with which the Guru Granth Sahib is held within the Sikh community and to understand how and why Sikhs honour it, the classroom can be set up as a 'theatre of learning'. The first step would be to decorate a side of the class with pictures of Gurus, the Nishan Sahib, bunting with triangular flags with the Khanda in the middle (pupils make this in advance), Ik Onkar and other images showing Sikhs worshipping and paying their respects. Colourful flickering lights and red, yellow or gold tinsel are placed on the window or wall. Then spread white cloth covering the area including where pupils will sit. Some tinsel could be placed around a cushion. Plastic food, fruit, bags of rice and flour and bottles of oil are placed on one side of a desk. Then prepare a raised platform using a desk from the nursery covering it with a decorated shiny red and gold cloth. Place a cushion on the desk and place a large book on it. Make a box for the donations using cardboard and colour it. Any other container could be wrapped with paper and placed near the cushion but slightly to one side. Place the Chaur Sahib on the right-hand side. Inform the pupils that they are going to learn about something that is honoured by Sikhs and is treated like a human by them. The class has been prepared like a theatre to view the Guru Granth Sahib in a Gurdwara.

Inform the class that no one is refused from entering the Gurdwara to see the holy book. However, before entering the Gurdwara a person should not have consumed tobacco or other intoxicants. Inform the pupils that some bathe before coming to the Gurdwara. They will remove their footwear and cover their heads and wash their feet if they are dirty or soiled. Whenever the Guru Granth is brought in, every Sikh stands to show respect. They will sit on the carpet, boys on one side and girls on the other. Show them how Sikhs respect their sacred book: walking respectfully towards it, clasping the hands together close to the chest and bowing the head slightly. Explain that some Sikhs place their forehead onto the floor and offer money or gifts.

Thereafter, having had a glimpse of the congregation in a whisper Sikhs say, 'Waheguru ji ka Khalsa, Waheguru ji ki Fateh'. Show them how the Guru Granth Sahib is unwrapped, opened, read and how the chauri is flagged. Inform the class that it contains teachings of the Gurus, hymns, songs and prayers. To conclude, share with the pupils some prashad in the form of a sweet representing the tradition of giving a blessing from the Guru to the congregants. It is received whilst seated with the hands cupped and raised as a mark of humility. When they leave, they move a few steps back or sideways to avoid a direct turn to avoid implying rudeness. Finally, show them a video of the Guru Granth Sahib being put to bed in a Sach Khand (Mogra 2018:68–70).

Summary

This section has highlighted the useful contribution that dramatical and theatrical pedagogies make to learning and has discussed some factors, which you need to be aware of in RE.

GEOGRAPHICAL RE

Introduction

The title of this section might perplex you at first sight and you might as well wonder what religion has got to do with geography and vice versa. However, an instructive chapter by (Park 2005) shows that many interesting questions about how religion develops, spreads and impacts people's lives are rooted in geographical factors and they can be studied from a geographical perspective. Park (2005) discussed the important points of contact between the two disciplines. For example, spatial variations in religion within and between countries, and the global pattern of religion, are interesting in their own right because they illustrate cultural diversity. These patterns generally reflect the interplay of many different factors, and they provide interesting opportunities for the study of the diffusion of ideas and the movement of people and the dynamics of human populations. Park (2005) concludes that this interest extends beyond people and their belief systems because it embraces themes such as sacred space and sacred directions. Religious beliefs also fuel religious practices which have spatial expressions, such as pilgrimage and visits to sacred places. There are multiple ways of reading a landscape and the perspective adopted strongly influences what is seen and how it is interpreted (Park 1994:199).

Population and spatial patterns

Pupils, at an age-appropriate level, can study religious diversity as it is globally distributed and the national patterns of religion in particular countries. Religion and demography can be linked to lessons in mathematics where pupils can explore population dynamics and the impact of religion on people. Spatial patterns have traditionally captured the geographical imagination, and the study of the distribution of religion at different scales is doubtless what most of the disciplines expect geographers to be engaged in (Park 1994:56). So, pupils can examine the links between geography and religion. They can also explore 'cradle lands' of the main religions, like Palestine, western Arabia, Northern India, Punjab and the diffusion of these religions to other parts of the world.

Pilgrimage and movement

The notion of sacred space is one of the more prominent geographical dimensions of religious expression. Most religions designate certain places as sacred or holy. This designation often encourages believers to visit those places in pilgrimage and put responsibilities on religious authorities to protect them for the benefit of future generations (Park 1994:245).

Many RE schemes and syllabi give ideas of using concepts in geography for examining similar concepts in RE.

Pilgrimage is considered one of the most geographically significant forms of religious behaviour, whether it is driven by cultural, nationalistic, religious-spiritual or personal reasons (Scriven 2014). Pilgrimage is understood as a distinct journey and has a lasting appeal for people. In its traditional religious-spiritual form, it attracts millions of believers annually to take up some form of the journey inspired by faith, devotion and invocation: three to five million Muslims make the Hajj, approximately five million Catholic pilgrims go to Lourdes in France, and 28 million Hindu pilgrims travel to the River Ganges (Scriven 2014:249).

It is suggested that pupils should have opportunities to explore the theme of life as a journey, including the emotional, physical, social, moral and spiritual changes that take place. The curriculum plan can include the theme of a journey through the year by studying key religious festivals. Pupils can explore some of the reasons for and effects of people movement, for example, the story of the Exodus, or stories of people who had to move to other places or countries because of religious persecution such as the Pilgrim Fathers, the Huguenots or Jewish people. In contemporary times, they look at how migration and other factors including conversion and growth change the demography.

Landscape features

These are the most obvious visible signs of the imprint of religion on an area. Landscape features serve some function in worship. They are domestic altars, yards and roadside shrines, chapels, church and temple architecture. Parishes are amongst the oldest spatial divisions in English landscape history. Then there are landscapes of death in different cultures and religions and how the dead are disposed of in different ways. This gives rise to sites of cremation scattering the ashes. Then burials give location and selection of cemeteries and cemetery architecture (Park 1994).

Locational awareness

In visiting places of worship, pupils have an opportunity of developing their locational awareness through first-hand observations of the physical and built environment of local religious buildings. Learning about significant local, national and global places will develop their knowledge of the national monuments, sites and religious places and their sense of belonging. They study St Paul's Cathedral in London, The Church of St Martin, as an ancient Church of England parish church, in Canterbury, England. They research and locate the cities where the first mosque, mandir, gurdwara, synagogue and Buddhist centres were established in the UK.

Pupils will know and understand the locational origins of the main faith traditions globally. They will know the names of the cities where some faith leaders like Abraham, Guru Nanak, Siddharta Gautama, Jesus and Muhammad and others were born and had spent their life, in so doing they will encounter the names of cities, countries and continents. They create city profiles and learn that the Dharmic traditions of Hindu, Jain, Buddhist and Sikh originated in what is today known as India. Pupils can find these places on maps, globes and determine the directions of these places from their location. Pupils can explore the local geographical and cultural influence on the style of buildings, artefacts, food, clothing and symbols.

Sacred directions

In addition to space, pupils should explore sacred directions and orientations, such as the reverence for the east in ancient religions based on sun worship. In Judaism, the north was unfavourable unlike the direction of Jerusalem. In Islam, the first qiblah was Jerusalem and then Makkah. Pupils can investigate the orientations of churches, mosques and synagogues (Park 2005). To these can be added rituals of burials as well.

Change over time

Pupils examine past and present images to observe changes over time within living memory. The use of technology has altered these religious places in many ways. Making links with history would appear to be apt, as pupils review how in previous centuries, the main options for travel were by land or sea, often long and perilous, nevertheless, these pilgrimages were still undertaken as a reflection of faith and commitment. Pupils can compare changes and the impact of modernisation on the sites of pilgrimage.

Holy grounds and conflict

Perhaps at Key Stage 2, pupils can extend their geographical understanding beyond Europe by studying places in other continents and civilisations. They can consider how people decided what is sacred in a place, why these locations were determined for pilgrimage and what the similarities and differences are between some of these holy sites. Equally, pupils should also know and understand that sacred spaces are sometimes contested and, in some cases, can be and are sites of conflict. Some of the holy spaces are the focus of historical disputes and communal violence and/or the hubs of resistance for oppressed groups.

Special attributes are ascribed to sacred spaces making them distinct from other comparable non-sacred locations. At times, notes Hassner (2009), such attributes are not demonstrable in any physical sense and are tied to their associated doctrines and institutions of faith. These are sites of infinite beauty and, at the same time, some have a history of violence and conflict, both localised and international (Hassner 2009). Pupils can learn about the contestation of space. Today, Jerusalem remains one of the main issues in the Israeli-Palestinian occupation. They can learn about the Promised Land and Jerusalem as holy to Judaism, Christianity and Islam. The case of Babri masjid and the storming of the Harmindar Sahib (Golden Temple) outraged Sikhs, accusing the troops of desecrating the faith's holiest shrine.

Nature, rivers and mountains

Park (1994:246) notes that different dimensions of the natural world are designated as sacred in different religions and they are respected in honour of their assumed holiness.

Water has a role in rituals and is seen as a natural symbol of purification, possessing the power to heal, and is associated with myths and stories in many religions. For example, some in the Orthodox Church celebrate the Feast of Theophany, which is the remembrance of the baptism of Jesus, which usually has a service by the river or canal and where the priest blesses the waters by saying prayers and throwing the cross seven times. The other ways of baptism include immersing, pouring and a sprinkling of water.

Water is a major theme in the Qur'an. The word 'water' occurs over 60 times, 'rivers' over 50 and 'the sea' over 40, whilst 'fountain', 'springs', 'rain', 'hail', 'clouds' and 'wind' occur less frequently. However, the Qur'an is not a scientific text; it treats the theme of water not only as an essential element but also of profound significance and far-reaching effect in the life and thinking of individual Muslims and Islamic society and civilisation (Abdel-Haleem 1989:34).

Holy grounds and sacred spaces hold diverse meanings and conceptions. Pupils can learn about burial grounds, tombs and shrines as having religious and spiritual significance. Moreover, in Hinduism, for instance, they discover that a mandir is god's home on earth, and, within it, the holiest section is the inner shrine called a garbhargriha, with a statue to the god or goddess. The Ganges River is also a sacred place for Hindus to go on pilgrimage and bathe in sacred waters. Some Hindus prefer to have their ashes scattered in the Ganges after cremation.

Mount Kailash is believed to be sacred in Hindu, Sikh and Buddhist traditions. In the Hindu faith, it is the abode for the deities Shiva and Parvati. Mountains have been sites of revelation, for example, Moses is said to have received the Ten Commandments on Mount Sinai and Muhammad received the first revelation in the Cave Hira housed in Mount Nur. The Black Stone is believed to have come from Heaven. Passing through the Grotto at Lourdes is a place of prayer, hope and healing. Kilimanjaro means 'mountain of the evil spirit'. Pupils explore stories, names, rituals and locations associated with them.

My special place

A special space is not often at a distance, pupils can learn about special places within their own homes and of others. Sikhs might have a dedicated room, many Hindus worship at a home shrine, Muslims may earmark a space and direction for salat (daily prayers). For the Shi'a, a prayer stone (turbah/mohr) moulded from clay from a holy Shi'a city illustrates the importance of the earth as a sacred tableau (Haider 2011). For Muslims, the entire earth is a place of prayer. Pupils learn about the rituals, rites and practices carried out in these places and their inner significance. In doing so, the curriculum and their learning can become coherent and systematic.

Summary

Geographical RE allows components of religious education to be studied through the discipline of geography. Some of the prominent geographical dimensions of religious expression have been included in this section such as sacred space, sacred sites and sacred directions.

HISTORICAL RE

Introduction

British history, as you may know, is closely linked to its politics, religion, literature and architecture. As you travel in the land, you will notice some of these illusions, imagery, symbols and structures are woven into the fabric of British society. You should recognise how these internal features affect RE as well as your worldview and perspectives. In other words, you should know that RE, including the current 'liberal', 'pluralistic' and 'multi faith' contemporary conception of learning about other religions and non-religious traditions, is not about pushing a particular RE, just as it is not about indoctrinating pupils into a religious, secular or humanist tradition. As an RE teacher, you have read at the beginning the theology, politics and history of RE and their structural influences on RE. You, therefore, need to understand the bias that may be brought to influence the nature, curriculum and delivery of RE.

Homan (2012:192–193) highlights the competing constructions in RE and the mismatch of what we may observe and what we may teach. He notes that the delivery is partly constrained by the trained habits of the teacher. It is also subject to the appetite of those who bear down upon education with their prescriptions. At times curriculum content is chosen not for its authority and authenticity but the convenience of an educational agenda. As a result, some of the difficult components of the curriculum, like religious conflict and other sensations are left to the tabloid press to investigate and judge.

Political RE

At an appropriate age, it would be fascinating to discuss with pupils the idea of whether or not politics and religion should be separated. Some will be aware of the controversial role of politics in wars and sanctions that have taken place in some parts of the world. At the same time, religion continues to play some role in world politics, both internationally and locally in some countries. Such that international political factors now shape the role of religion in education (Gearon 2013).

There is growing recognition that religion and politics were never separate spheres of human thought and action. In the modern world, as in earlier times, religion and politics continue to combine in important ways to shape the public arena in which the many issues about the human predicament are debated and acted upon (Moyser 2005:423).

Pupils can also explore the notion of the ultimate source of political authority, whether or not that should be revelation or reason. They can explore how individuals navigate religious and civic laws, if and when they conflict. They can discuss the similarities and differences between laws made through democratic processes and laws from sacred scriptures. Some of these questions might appear unproblematic in RE. However, McKain (2018:175–176) imagines, what if a Muslim or Christian student says that their faith matter more to them than the rule of law. What would the teacher do, he asks. Then he concludes that the idea that an RE classroom can be considered a safe space is not as straightforward as it might appear.

Pupils can understand what a theocracy is and what is a democracy and the role of religion in societies, which operate under these systems. They can learn that the term 'theocracy' has its roots in Greek to mean 'the rule of God'. They can look at historical examples of theocracy, for example, in ancient Egypt and China or Tibet in the recent past as headed by the Dalai Lama or modern ones such as the Vatican government and Iran. They can discuss whether these can co-exist.

Histories in Religious Education

Pupils should be involved in the discipline practised by historians to make sense of the past and to study people and their actions. Teachers use chronology to facilitate pupil's understanding of the historical development of religion, for example. The perception of time is an integral part of history education as it helps pupils build their identity and extend their perceptions of the world as a whole (Sole 2019). It has been suggested that the Piagetian model of cognitive development, which proposed that children are unable to think in the abstract and handle complexity, could be a barrier to controversial history teaching (Wrenn et al. 2007:16). Thus, Clarke (2020) suggests that developing chronological understanding is important for younger pupils to enable them to make better sense of their daily lives as well as talk about past and future events with understanding.

History of RE

Pupils can learn about the history of the subject of RE itself and discover what children were taught and how they were taught, say before 1960 and after 1988. They can reflect on the nature of their own RE, which is multi-faith and educational unlike the indoctrinatory and Christian formation type and how they learn, which is exploratory, rather than the didactic approach of the past, and decide their preferred model. They can then be invited to imagine the future of RE.

Timeline of religions

Pupils can take a glimpse of the timeline of the development of religions in general from ancient times. They can also then look at timelines of the development of individual religions, like Islam and Sikhi to highlight important historical dates, figures and events chronologically as a framework for understanding and organising the historical period of these religions. When studying specific religions they explore when events happened, what happened at that time and how things developed or changed to gain insights into the context of current beliefs and practice. They can write logs or chronicles of events and build up class timelines incrementally for the religion or key person being studied.

History of religious material

Pupils should be invited to think historically about places, texts, artefacts and ask questions such as how old something is, who in the past might have used it, who decided its significance and why, what beliefs they held and convey, and compare historical and modern versions. This experience must provide sufficient cognitive demands on pupils, especially when using worksheets, for example.

In the case of Islam, for instance, pupils can learn how the history of Makkah and Madinah and the history of the early Muslim community continues to influence their life and thought. For the Sikhs, their beliefs, rituals, practices, symbols and names are intertwined with the history of Sikhi and the biographies of the Gurus. Pupils compile personal life timelines for themselves or for key historical characters such as, 'Guru Nanak: This is Your Life'.

Changes over time

Pupils should have opportunities to investigate their own and others' personal history. They can write their autobiography by including significant events such as birth, Naam Karan, aqiqah, baptism, first communion and confirmation, varna, upanayana, Bar and Bat Mitzvah and others.

In the previous section, you read about encouraging pupils to identify the causes and consequences of changes over time, including how places of worship and sites of pilgrimage have changed over the years. In addition to this, pupils can identify similarities and differences between ways of life, past and present, for example, between life in biblical times, of Makkah and Babylon times and religions in ancient Persian, Egypt and Greece and current manifestations. Pupils can sequence pictures or artefacts according to periods.

To bring a secure understanding of the constant influence of religion on its adherents and its relevance to the contemporary world, pupils should also be encouraged to study local personalities, their achievements and contribution to the richness of religions and of addressing social issues in their area and nationally.

The religious landscape of Britain

Pupils can explore changes that have taken place in the religious landscape of Britain over the years. In a plural society, there is a need for children both to understand the views and beliefs of those who are different from them including humanists and other atheists who have beliefs and values, just not religious ones (Rodell 2020:34).

A window into historical Britain

English Heritage (2011) guide provides a historical overview of the various churches and buildings of other faiths. There are research reports based on the scoping survey of Hindu, Jain, Bahá'í and Zoroastrian faith buildings in England which can be used to extract relevant data found here https://research.historicengland.org.uk/Report.aspx?i=16739

There is useful information, images and podcasts on England's extraordinary history of faith and belief at https://historicengland.org.uk/get-involved/100-places/faith-belief/#Section8Text. Another website provides information on religious architecture as well found here https://heritagecalling.com

Stonehenge

The Stonehenge and Avebury World Heritage Site has a history spanning 4,500 years, which has many different meanings to people today. It is a wonder of the world, a spiritual place and a source of inspiration. The Stone Circle is a masterpiece of engineering, and building it would have taken huge effort from hundreds of well-organised people using only simple tools and technologies. It is an iconic symbol of Britain.

Churches

There is plenty of history to uncover from the 42,000 churches, chapels and meeting houses in the UK. They are a network of public buildings which sustain many local communities.

1701 – Synagogue

The Bevis Marks Synagogue in Aldgate, in London, is Britain's oldest synagogue opened in 1701 and is affiliated with London's historic Spanish and Portuguese Jewish community. It is the only synagogue in Europe that has held regular services continuously for more than 300 years. Images of 10 of England's most beautiful Synagogues are accessible from here. https://heritage-calling.com/2015/08/07/top-synagogues/

1872 – Buddhists

The first Buddhist temple and meditation centre was erected in 1872 in Wimbledon, London. Japanese Pure Land Buddhists (1840–1907) established the first Buddhist 'mission' in the West in 1889 in central London. The mission, however, was short-lived, as its Irish founder emigrated to Japan three years later. Theravada influences grew in England during the early twentieth century who founded London's Buddhist Society in 1924 and the Theravada London Buddhist Vihara in Chiswick in 1926 (see https://www.bbc.co.uk/religion/religions/buddhism/history/britishbuddhism_1.shtml).

1889 – Mosques

The first mosques in Britain probably dates from the late nineteenth century, though there had been a Muslim community in the country since the sixteenth century. The first recorded mosque was a Georgian terrace in Liverpool opened by Abdullah William Quilliam, a British convert to Islam. The first purpose-built mosque is in Woking. At the same time, Bengali, Somali and Yemeni sailors living in England began to convert pubs and houses into places of worship in the towns and cities they had settled in. These included South Shields, Liverpool, east London and Cardiff. You will find five buildings that reveal the fascinating history and variety of mosques in England here https://heritagecalling.com/2016/02/05/5-magnificent-english-mosques/and more at https://historicengland.org.uk/listing/what-is-designation/heritage-highlights/where-was-britains-first-recorded-mosque/

1908 – Gurdwara

Despite the early arrival of the Maharajah of Patiala, the first Sikh Gurdwara was not established until 1911, at Putney in London and was partly funded by him. Most early British Sikhs have their origins in immigration either from Punjab or from East Africa. The first recorded Sikh settler in Britain was Maharajah Duleep Singh, who was the last ruler of the Sikh kingdom of Punjab. The Maharajah was dethroned after six years' rule, and exiled to Britain in 1849 at the age of 14, after the Anglo-Sikh wars. There is a statue of the Maharajah at Butten Island, Thetford, Norfolk, where he lived in Britain. The statue was unveiled by the Prince of Wales in 1999. The aptly named *Central Gurdwara* of London is the oldest Sikh institution in Europe, tracing its origins back to 1908 (see https://heritagecalling.com/2022/07/14/a-brief-history-of-gurdwaras-in-england/).

Summary

Studying religion in the UK from a historical perspective is valuable as it promotes self-respect. It encourages an understanding of history and culture and helps understanding global affairs and movements. It provides opportunities to help challenge stereotypes. It can encourage pupils to value themselves and the communities within which they live.

RELIGIOUS EDUCATION THROUGH ENGLISH

Introduction

RE explores issues concerned with belief, life and its ultimate meaning and value. These may feature in English, art, history and geography as well. The national curriculum (NC) in England provides pupils with an introduction to the essential knowledge that they need to be educated citizens. It is just one element in the education of every child which promotes their spiritual, moral, cultural, mental and physical development and prepares them for later life (DfE 2013a:6). RE has a strong connection with English. The *ITT Core Content Framework* expects you to know that every teacher can improve pupils' literacy by explicitly teaching reading, writing and oral language skills specific to individual disciplines (DfE 2019). Thus, you need to learn how to apply high expectations to all groups and ensure all pupils have access to a rich curriculum and discuss with expert colleagues how to help pupils master important concepts in RE.

Language and literacy

The NC states that high-quality education in English teaches pupils to speak and write fluently so that they can communicate their ideas and emotions to others. Pupils, through reading in particular, have an opportunity to develop culturally, emotionally, intellectually, socially and spiritually. Literature plays a key role in such developments. Reading also enables them to acquire knowledge and to build on their existing knowledge. Moreover, teachers are to develop pupils' spoken language and vocabulary as integral aspects of the teaching of every subject. English is both a subject in its own right and the medium for teaching to provide pupils with access to the whole curriculum (DfE 2013b:10). In all, the skills of language are essential to enable pupils to participate fully as members of society (DfE 2013b:13). All these elements of language can be used to serve the purposes of RE and should feature in the overall design and delivery of the RE curriculum so that they can communicate with depth, reason and precision. RE can help pupils be enthusiastic about the power and beauty of language. Writing can be multimedia, multimodal as well as textual. In addition to digital technology, they can be screen-based texts and stills to engage with multiple modes of communication. The recent Ofsted Review (2021) stressed that high-quality RE curricula equip pupils with subject components (for example, language, vocabulary and concepts).

Scaffolded dialogue

It is tempting to enter a monologue when teaching due to the pressures of time and the eagerness to cover the content. In some cases, this might lead to an interaction where the teacher waits for the right answer. Sinclair and Coulthard (1992) identified that the most common type of teacher-pupil interaction was the pattern of Initiation-Response-Feedback (IRF). This is where teachers look for the 'correct' answer to their question and once it is given will move on to another question or aspect of the lesson (Reynolds, Smith and Vallely 2021). There are five aspects of teaching talk identified by Alexander (2008) noting that the most learning took place during the discussion and scaffolded dialogue.

- Rote (teacher-class): The drilling of facts, ideas and routines through constant repetition.
- Recitation (teacher-class or teacher-group): The accumulation of knowledge and understanding through questions designed to test or stimulate recall of what had been previously encountered, or cue pupils to work out the answer from clues provided in the question.
- Instruction/exposition (teacher-class, teacher-group or teacher-individual): Telling pupils what to do, and/or imparting information, and/or explaining facts, principles or procedures.
- Discussion (teacher-class, teacher-group or pupil-pupil): The exchange of ideas to share information and solve problems.
- Scaffolded dialogue (teacher-class, teacher-group, teacher-individual or pupil-pupil): Achieving common understanding through structured and cumulative questioning and discussion which guide and prompt, reduce choices, minimise risk and error and expedite 'handover' of concepts and principles. There may, or may not, be a right answer but justification and explanation are sought. Pupils' thinking is challenged and so understanding is enhanced. The teacher is likely to share several exchanges with a particular child several times to move the thinking on (Reynolds, Smith and Vallely 2021).

Spoken language and oracy

Oracy (debates, dialogues, discussions, expositions, listening, questioning, expressing, whispering) nourish every aspect of RE. For instance, these could become especially prominent at the start of an inquiry. Spoken language is important for pupils' development across the whole curriculum – cognitively, socially and linguistically (DfE 2013b:13). Therefore, you need to learn to model and require high-quality oral language and recognise that spoken language underpins the development of reading and writing and you need to learn that high-quality classroom talk can support pupils to articulate key ideas, consolidate understanding and extend their vocabulary (DfE 2019). Thus, pupils in RE as well should be taught to:

- Speak clearly and convey ideas confidently.
- Justify ideas with reasons.
- Ask questions to check understanding.
- Negotiate, evaluate and build on the ideas of others.
- Give well-structured descriptions and explanations.
- Develop their understanding through speculating, hypothesising and exploring ideas (DfE 2013b:10).

In excellent RE, pupils ask and listen to perspectives from faith leaders, for example. They convey their thinking and articulate their beliefs, values and commitments clearly to explain why they may be important. Pupils evaluate religious and non-religious viewpoints and arguments carefully. They justify reasonably their ideas about how beliefs, practices and forms of expression influence individuals and communities. They articulate their personal reflections and critical responses to questions about identity, diversity and ethical issues (REC 2013). The power of reading aloud to pupils is a joyful activity in a class. In contemplative RE, pupils listen to personal and religious stories, children's stories, dramatic stories, stories using props and video and puppetry stories. Pupils read aloud books on RE and retell religious stories to the whole class and in assemblies. They read poetry and hymns aloud on Sikh Gurus, Rosh Hashanah, hijab and sayings by the Buddha on compassion, joy and anger.

Reading and writing

The NC states that teachers should develop pupils' reading and writing in all subjects to support their acquisition of knowledge, promote wider reading, promote accurate spelling and include narratives, explanations, descriptions, comparisons, summaries and evaluations in writing (DfE 2013b:10).

Therefore, you should learn how to use the concrete representation of abstract ideas by making use of analogies, metaphors, examples and non-examples in RE (DfE 2019). In groundbreaking RE, they read about 'Amazing Muslims who have changed the world'. Pupils read short biographies of the ten Gurus. A rich RE environment in a class will have traditional or 'folk' tales including myths, legends, fables and fairy tales many of which originate in oral traditions in most cultures to provide culturally diverse resources for pupils to read (Mogra 2022). These stories pass on traditional knowledge or cultural beliefs. Pupils read about life's important issues. They learn to read about characters who represent the archetypical opposites of good and evil, hero and villain, strong and weak or wise and foolish. They read fables to learn lessons about life. They reflect on how ideas, values and emotions are explored and portrayed. In thoughtful RE, pupils read a variety of styles of prayer including spontaneous, responsive, formal, informal, petitions, thanking and praising prayers. Therefore, you should discuss and analyse with expert colleagues how to teach different forms of writing and how to support younger pupils to become fluent readers and to write fluently (DfE 2019).

High-quality RE teaching provides opportunities to improve pupils' skills in English. Schools should ensure pupils can see themselves in their curriculum. They read, interpret and make inferences from sacred texts, stories and sayings from different religions and consider their meanings. They examine how and why some texts have been influential over time, like the Torah, Bible and Qur'an. Pupils can compare texts, appreciating their style, identifying themes, linguistic features and identifying concepts in the Mool Mantra and Gayatri Mantar. They read poems silently. They critically evaluate the presentation of religions and their adherents in contemporary print and digital media. Pupils perceive and appreciate the use of similes, parables and metaphors used in religious communication. They decipher and apply their growing knowledge of root words (etymology) and read reference books and create glossaries for the RE books they have read using correct spellings.

In engaging RE, pupils write for different purposes. They write explanatory texts on rites of passages and list instructions for making a menorah. They write to persuade an end to religious hatred and banning religious slaughter. They write a postcard about Vaisakhi. They write letters to friends on how they mark a festival. They create brochures following a visit to a mandir. Pupils convert the Christian creation story into a play script. They compose free verses and structural poems about heritage, identity, belonging, faith, morals, values, God, humanity, nature and spirituality. This approach gives writing a meaningful context and a real-life application. Pupils consider environmental issues by writing a balanced argument based on religious and non-religious views. They write biographies of faith leaders, send a piece to the local newspapers about a festival marked in school, blog about their fundraising event and RE work for their school website and their local radio.

They compose narrative poems such as ballads, which tell stories. Pupils compose their own wise words and add them to the cumulative human heritage. They write a fantasy to fuel their imagination and use imagery to help them describe places and things their readers have never seen such as paradise or their ideal world. They write contemporary fiction and recounts, often reflecting their own experiences, including stories at school, home, in the community or media which they know themselves, hear or recognise such as Islamophobia, anti-Semitism and faith-based bullying. They write real events and dilemmas with suspense or choices of right/wrong course of action to explore their role of faith and its expression in contemporary Britain. In their extended writing, citing evidence, they synthesise and distinguish between beliefs, facts and opinions and differing views and beliefs. Pupils read first-hand accounts of activists to see faith in action.

Vocabulary development

Pupils' command of vocabulary is key to their progress in RE. The quality and variety of language that pupils hear and speak in RE are vital for developing their vocabulary and grammar and their understanding of reading and writing in RE. The *ITT Core Content Framework* expects you to learn how to teach unfamiliar vocabulary explicitly and plan for pupils to be repeatedly exposed to common vocabulary in what is taught (DfE 2019). Pupils should have access to the words of the academic disciplines and subject-specific domains. They are the keys to scholarship and intellectual curiosity and pupils should access them in classroom conversations.

In discussing, suitable procedures, methods and strategies in RE, the Ofsted RE Research Review (2021) suggests that teaching activities should be well matched to pupils' prior knowledge and that when teachers use textual sources and longer reading extracts (such as sacred literature, religious narratives or scholarship), they need to consider whether these are accessible to pupils. Pupils will require sufficient vocabulary knowledge to make sense of the text. Teachers may act on this, for instance, by teaching pupils subject-specific vocabulary before they encounter it in content.

It might be that you begin by pre-teaching them the essential vocabulary before the actual lesson. You might also display these as a regular point of reference for the class and build on them as the sequence of lessons unfolds. Moreover, you might use low-stakes multiple-choice quizzes to have pupils recall vocabulary.

In vocabulary rich RE, pupils acquire specialist vocabulary and concepts which they use accurately and consistently. They feel empowered as they use these words and, simultaneously, recognise the limitations of language. However, they learn more than simple definitions and their recollection by focussing on the core idea and its relationship with other concepts and how they are distinct in different religions. They practice terms in pairs to complete RE tasks. Pupils learn from flashcards as an effective way of stimulating their vocabulary in engaging ways. As they talk, they fluently use and write accurately with growing confidence to show their understanding. They draw from a range of books, including faith narratives, moral stories, myths and legends, and retell them orally. As they advance and gain confidence in using them, it enables them to recognise misconceptions that individual pupils may have had and correct their misunderstandings. When they make relevant comments on their learning in RE, they courageously articulate as best as they can unfamiliar and new words from languages other than English. For progression in RE, teachers monitor their pronunciation, accurate usage and comprehension. They do not overlook the assessment of RE outcomes as they SPAG pupils RE work.

Summary

All forms and genres of literacy should be used effectively to engage and connect pupils to RE in a pedagogically appropriate way for all age groups.

MATHEMATICAL RE

Introduction

You may think there is little if any, connection between religions and mathematics. However, aspects from religions can be seen through the lens of mathematical concepts which helps with expositions and retrieval of important knowledge. Mathematical concepts in religions relate to seasons, festivals, astronomy, calendar and other practices. Some information can be reduced to smaller data to enhance retention. Therefore, tasks that support pupils to learn key ideas securely can include quizzes and summaries of information (DfE 2019). Some key concepts are discussed below.

Key mathematical concepts in religions

A pattern is a repeated design or recurring sequence. These are visible in nature and many other religious practices. For example, rangoli patterns are a practical and creative way to uncover symmetry, reflection and tessellation. The spiritual benefits, the experiences of devotees and how, when, where and why they are used should be discussed.

Shape and space are the properties of physical materials and the results of how they are located and positioned. Some examples of these were discussed in the Geographical RE section. In addition, shape and space should also be explored as a way of understanding the world and the place of humans and living things in the physical world. At the same time, pupils should have an opportunity to have a sense that there is more to life than material things. They should learn how space helps people to come together as a religious and spiritual community.

Geometry is concerned with issues of shape, size, relative position of figures and the properties of space. In some traditions, there is a belief in sacred geometry where certain shapes, symbols and digits have a spiritual meaning and these are used to energise the mind and get closer to the Ultimate. The concept of sacred geometry also influences art and architecture in some traditions and offers a focus for contemplation. The circle, for some, is a symbol of God, unity and infinity. The equilateral triangle is seen as a Christian symbol of the Trinity. The Star of David is a hexagram, made up of two equilateral triangles. For some Hindus, the dot represents the soul and the circle represents the Hindu universe because they believe the world to be timeless, cyclical and infinite.

In Buddhism, there is the flower of life which is shaped through evenly-spaced overlapping circles. You will observe this interlocking design which demonstrates the interconnectedness of all living things and how everyone is linked to one another. Another mystical diagram is the Sri Yantra (Queen of Yantras). This tends to feature nine interlocking triangles. In the centre, there is a single dot, which symbolises the place from which all creation emerges. The Sri Yantra represents the female and male energies of the universe. It also represents how these forces join to form the entire cosmos. Many believe that it holds the secret to enlightenment. Thus, spiritual awakening is found by following its patterns.

Statistics is about the collection, organisation, analysis, presentation and interpretation of data as exemplified below. You can involve them in calculating percentages of tithing, dasvanth, zakat and tzedakah, for example. A few examples of numbers are given for consideration.

Numbers

There are five elements in Daoism, five precepts in Buddhism, five pillars in Islam, five kakar and five beloved ones in Sikhi. You may also find five sacred principles (pancha maha yagnas) of Sanatana Dharma, as well their four purposes of life (dharma, artha, kama, moksha).

Some people consider 13 to be unlucky, especially when it coincides with a Friday, then it is an unlucky day. This belief impacts their avoidance of some actions, such as marrying, travelling or purchasing something important.

The number six offers six days of creation. There are six points on a Star of David. There are six symbolic foods on the Seder plate. The Wheel of Becoming (Bhavachakra) is a picture representing the Buddhist view of the universe. The Wheel is divided into five or six states.

Looking at seven, it is believed that the Buddha, as a baby, took seven steps at birth and seven lotus blossoms bloomed from each spot the babe's feet had touched the earth. On the seventh day following the birth of a child, some Muslims prefer to perform the aqiqah, shave the hair and give a name to the baby, and circumcise a boy. A Muslim performs seven circuits of the Kaabah. Muslim pilgrims collect 49–70 pebbles from Muzdalifah, and pelt seven on day one and twenty-one (7×3) on the subsequent two days at the pillars at Mina. In Hindu tradition, the wedding ritual is completed only after the couple takes seven steps around a holy fire and recite seven vows to seal their marriage. It is believed that the souls are joined for seven lifetimes. Some Christian denominations are known as the Seventh-day Adventist Church and the Seventh Day Baptists, for observing the seventh-day Sabbath. In Judaism and Christianity, God is believed to have rested on the seventh day. The Shiva is the mourning period lasting seven days in Judaism. Passover is traditionally celebrated in Israel for seven days and eight days amongst many Jews elsewhere. Shavuot (Feast of Weeks) recalls the revelation of the Torah on Mt. Sinai. It is believed that it took Moses and the Israelites seven weeks of trekking through the desert to reach it. Sukkot (the Feast of Tabernacles) is celebrated in the seventh month.

There is the 8-fold path of Buddhism and ten offers the Ten Gurus in Sikhi. Generally, it is the Ten Commandments in Judaism and Christianity. You may find ten disciplines in Hindu Dharma, which are divided into five political goals (yamas) and five personal goals (niyamas). The holiest day, Yom Kippur (Day of Atonement), of the year in Judaism falls 10 days after the new year. In Islam, the tenth Muharram is important.

Probably the most feared number is 666. There is more than one reference to 666 in the Bible, one of which is to the beast and is often associated with the devil. However, in China it has positive connotations, meaning excellent.

Time

Time is another prominent feature in many religious and non-religious traditions. In some religions, time is cyclical, linear or never-ending. Certain months, for example, Ramadan, in Islam hold religious significance. In others, you will see that weeks have importance, as in Christianity. Furthermore, as shown above, some days are holy and blessed. You will also find that certain nights are held in higher esteem than others are, for instance, the Maha Shivaratri is celebrated at night. During the day and night, in some religions, there are also precious times and moments. In Islam, time is a blessing from the Creator, although God exists beyond time. Thus, time becomes sacred in religions. It is because of these beliefs which some religions hold about these times that their life events and lived experiences materialise in festivals, rituals, ceremonies, pilgrimages and their prayers rotate and operate within them.

Emotion graphs

When you teach stories wherein there is emotion involved, for example, the stories of Moses, Job, Bilal, Jonah and Guru Gobind; you can use an emotion graph by exploring how the character felt at certain points in their life or story. Pupils then create a bar chart illustrating the different emotions at certain moments.

Data analysis

There are many opportunities in RE where the phenomenon of religion and social information related to beliefs can be studied by using mathematical information and calculating, and interpreting and presenting findings. In RE pupils can order events in time, like biographical information and key historical events. Pupils can design and conduct their survey and interpret their results and present their findings as graphs and charts to draw conclusions and ask further questions about issues relating to religion. You can use a pie chart to demonstrate the main world religions and other belief systems in percentages and then show these on a world map with the number of followers of each religion.

Census data

In addition to the https://faithsurvey.co.uk/, the census data is an invaluable resource to use in RE when considering statistics about religions and non-religions. Pupils can be given data of their city with a set of questions to interrogate the data or design their questions. They can explore the data nationally and regionally. They could predict what might happen at the next census. The use of pie charts and their discussion is useful to tackle misconceptions.

Pupils can learn that London is the 'most religious' region. The least religious (i.e. the highest 'no religion') local authority area is Norwich in England, whilst the most religious (i.e. lowest 'no religion') is the London borough of Newham (Rodell 2020).

Methodologically, pupils can interrogate the terms used by surveys such as 'other' or related terms and consider the extent to which they reflect religious beliefs, religious practice or religious identity and cultural affiliation.

Jane Yates (Cumbria SACRE) provides an interesting set of questions to think about the Census as seen in Table 11.2, based on the work of Georgiou and Wright (2020).

On the Let's Count website, there is access to past census data on local areas and a free chart-generation tool. This allows you to create colourful pie charts and bar charts https://letscount.org.uk/en/about-lets-count/

Summary

This section has shown the use of the mathematical lens to explore and learn some important information about religions. Along with knowing these facts, as shown in the subsection on numbers, pupils should also understand the significance and impact of these on people and religions. Pupils can store this information in their memories to help them understand the life-world of believers.

Table 11.2 Examining the Census Data

Exploratory questions (disciplinary knowledge)	Explanatory questions (substantive knowledge)
Theology – 'thinking about and thinking through believing'. Does it matter if you state your religion on the census but never go to that place of worship? Do you need to pray to be religious?	What is the census? Who completes the census and how often? When was the first census? Do all countries complete the census? Why is the census going digital? What questions on the census relate to religion and worldviews? Why do Humanist UK think the census is controversial?
Philosophy – 'thinking about and thinking through thinking. Who decides if someone is religious or not? Should everyone complete the census? Does it matter? Should we ask if people are religious?	
Social or human – 'thinking about and thinking through living'. Is completing the census easier for some people than others? How is the census helping people? E.g. Welsh and Jewish communities, fire brigade. Why might events alongside the census be important? E.g. religious or community groups.	
Source: Jane Yates, Cumbria SACRE and Georgiou and Wright (2020).	

MULTI-SENSORY RE

Introduction

Religious traditions are sometimes explained in terms of beliefs, mystical experiences and eschatological ways as in God, deities, nirvana, angels, moksha, afterlife, heaven and hell. However, though these are important metaphysical constituents, they are not the only ones. The other elements relate to their actual and lived forms. Thus, how people engage with the world of belief and faith through their physical senses is a key question to explore in RE.

Sensory learning is related to allowing pupils to get to the essence of lived experiences of religion. Hammond (2015:114) discusses the importance of exposing the inner elements in lessons so that pupils understand aspects of human experience that religions address, and from which they could better understand what the faiths are about. He contends that the methods of experiential RE also bring pupils to a deeper awareness of their own inner life and enables them to come to a real understanding of the nature of religions. It is also about bringing a valid understanding of the religious dimension of human experience in an increasingly secular society.

Learning in RE can present barriers for some pupils with special and complex needs. Some pupils will have difficulty understanding abstract concepts such as spirituality, belief, opinion, friendship, justice, cooperation, conflict and empathy (TDA 2009). A pupil, for example, with severe language delay may not fully comprehend the intricate concepts underpinning a Hindu puja offering. However, they can smell the incense, feel the water on their skin and hear the bell (McCreery, Palmer and Voiels 2008:24). Thus, they suggest that teachers should use as many senses as possible and, rather than talking about food, pupils should be given the chance to taste it, whilst observing health and safety matters. Learning about worship in some religious traditions provide many opportunities for inviting pupils to see how worship can be very sensory. Simultaneously, teachers can provide a sensory experience to their pupils to learn in RE.

In the classroom

In the Orthodox Church, worship is considerably sensory. Both art and music are used to deepen the spiritual experience of worshippers. Singing and chanting create a reverent atmosphere, although instruments are not used during services. It might involve lighting candles which are a visible sign of prayer to God and gazing at them. Kissing the icons and artefacts. Smelling the incense which is burned to represent prayers rising to God in heaven. To enhance joy and solemnness, and to encourage full participation, their services are sung or chanted. They also touch the Gospel with the forehead. In observing these pupils are provided with very concrete examples of some abstract ideas and gain a better understanding of beliefs and practices and that these are often woven through culture, local contexts and denominational standpoints.

Jewish home in class

You can set up a Jewish home in a tent in your classroom. Place the following labelled artefacts selectively on different days: challah board, challah bread, challah cover, chanukiah, dreidel, havdalah candlesticks, kiddush cup, kosher food, kippah, matzah cover, menorah, mezuzah (placed at the entrance), seder plate, siddur (prayer books), Shabbat candle and candle holders, shofar, Star of David, tallit, tefillin, Torah scroll, tzedakah box and a yad.

Allow one group to visit in a day to record what they found. Thereafter, each group reports back on the objects that they found to the class. In the following week, in one lesson, the whole class finds information about these artefacts in more detail. You can provide some questions to guide them, whilst retaining an open-ended study.

Table 11.3 Examining artefacts

Religion	Hearing	Touching	Smelling	Seeing	Tasting
Islam	Call to prayer	Hat/hijab	Perfume	Prayer mat	Dates
Hinduism	bells, gongs, conch shell,	lighted wicks	incense	water, flowers, deities	Prashad
Christianity					
Judaism					
Buddhism					
Sikhism					
Vegan					
Vegetarian					

Complete the table

Pupils can be given the challenge to complete a table focusing on one religion or a topic across several traditions to investigate the use of senses as shown in Table 11.3.

Experiences

Based on an RE theme or question, pupils could be taken out into the playground, a local park or a new place for a sensual experience. They should write about this sensual experience based on the sense whilst they are there. On return to the class, they review the accounts of their peers and comment on them. Alternatively, the children could use talk exclusively for this.

Vision

Pupils could be shown and appropriate tasks designed by using images of faith leaders. These could be contemporary as well as historical ones such as images of Jesus, Guru Nanak, Buddha and others. They observe holy icons, murtis, stained-glass windows and the heat and light at ceremonies. Paintings, statues, verses from the scriptures, abstract and floral geometric patterns, and sculptures help pupils learn about the conception of deities and God in some religions. In the empty space of the Kaabah there is a reminder of the most significant Muslim belief about the un-representable Allah (Hammond 2015:118).

Hearing

Pupils should be provided with experiences of listening, which exist in religions. They can listen to recitations of the Qur'an, chanting of prayers, readings, creeds, mantras, poems, songs, hymns, carols and in the liturgical prayer services of many religions. These play a primary role in some religious practices, both individually and collectively during various occasions and events. Pupils can therefore experience these and explore the purposes of 'sound' and 'music' when it is used, why and by whom and its spiritual and emotional impact and other benefits that it proffers.

Smell

Pupils should use their olfactory sense in RE. This might present some challenges. However, with some creativity and innovation, the overall pupil experience can be enhanced through smelling and narrating. Teachers can bring objects which give a smell, like perfume, a Shabbat spice box, incense and scented candles. Pupils can then learn about the use of these before prayer, meditation and for other occasions, like festivals.

Taste

There are many tasty things that pupils could make and bake in RE lessons. Teachers will need to be sensitive and respectful of pupils who may have reservations in tasting and making some food items. Pancakes and hot cross buns have been traditionally popular in school. Pupils could taste bread, bitter herbs, rice, sweet meals, challah loaf, matzah, kara prashad and charoset and other festival foods and explore dietary regulation in religious and secular contexts.

Touch

Teachers often ask pupils to look closer. When analysing images pupils should be invited to comment on how touch contributes to a sense of community and what forms and styles these take place in. They should explain how, when, where and what touch is used for in rituals and rites and acts of worship in general. Pupils can be invited to explain why people kiss sacred objects and use beads. They could touch natural materials and wonder at their beauty and creation. Pupils can handle some religious artefacts and symbols such as the mezuzah, tallit, menorah or Star of David. Conversely, they investigate why certain things are not touched or entered except in a ritually pure state, like the Qur'an.

Silence

In teaching through all the senses, teachers should also attend to the role of silence. Silence features in human activities including religious practices. Pupils should observe where, when, why and how it features in religions.

Through the process of stilling exercise I can begin to set aside distractions, the clamour of all the deeds done and the demands of others, and just be still, aware of and present to myself. All I have to do is do nothing. Let go of the business of hiding or justifying; just be still and wait. In this state of openness and apparent positivity I can come to an awareness of myself and gain insights available only within the silence (Hammond 2015:115).

Summary

The sensory approach to RE is very powerful as the human external sensation is based on the sensory system and organs. Most humans use these for most of time for most of the day. Pupils can experience these beyond a cognitive experience. The use of senses is very effective for memory; often things that pupils touch, feel, see and taste are remembered longer than merely being told about them. It is important to use the experiences in an educational manner rather than as used in religious settings.

MUSICAL RE

Introduction

There is sound in the natural world and sound created by humans. These communicate beliefs, feelings, emotions, thoughts and silence. It crosses religions and cultures and contributes to the spiritual and well-being of humans. Responses to music are non-uniform, and often this depends on pupils' experiences, location, time, culture, beliefs and personal preferences, some may be averse to some kind of 'music'.

In RE, pupils can use their imagination in music to represent their ideas, thoughts and feelings and respond in a variety of ways to what they hear or be silent. They can explore questions about belonging, meaning and truth so that they can express their ideas and opinions in response to these through using music. Pupils can use music to respond to ideas about God from different religions and worldviews, express ideas of their own and comment on some ideas of others. In the context of sound and music, pupils ask and answer a range of 'how' and 'why' questions about how people practise their religion or lifestyle. They explore and describe a range of beliefs, symbols and actions so that they can understand different ways of life and ways of expressing meaning through music. They can enquire into beliefs about worship, relating the meanings of symbols, sounds and actions used in worship; or for speaking to God (e.g. in prayer), or in events and teachings from religions they study (REC 2013). Pupils learn how participating musically in communal activities and individual worship promotes religious identity, a sense of belonging and fellowship. Thus, the use of religious music has the strong potential of allowing pupils access to authentic elements of religion and other traditions. It can do so in a way that affords profound reactions from pupils (Stern 2004; cf. Stern 2018:81–82). Through such encounters, pupils can experience the way music is used in religion. That said, pupils should not be invited to worship through music in a faith that is not their own, but to gain an understanding of the role, place and use of 'music' in faith and non-faith contexts.

The use of music in RE can provide wider benefits. You should know that teachers are key role models, who can influence the attitudes, values and behaviours of their pupils and that building effective relationship is easier when pupils believe that their feelings will be considered and understood, for which music can play a part. Teachers can make valuable contributions to the wider life of the school in a broad range of ways through incorporating music in RE (DfE 2019).

It is important to use quality material and to be clear about the concepts to be learnt. If good recordings of such sounds cannot be found, a short discussion may be necessary so that pupils do not end up making inappropriate judgements (Hunt 2018:28). In the context of SEND teaching, to maximise the potential impact of music in RE, Hunt (2018:26–27) suggests that key concepts ought to be extracted from contemporary music as that is important in the lives of many young people. He maintains that some of it provide comments on relevant moral, spiritual and religious issues. The inclusion of music in RE enables pupils with SEND and high prior attainers to participate and discuss lyrics and be involved in the composition and performance of short musical works (Mercier and Long 2015:82).

Sacred sound and music in religious traditions

Most religions have an affinity with music and use it as an expression of faith. Beck (2009) explored six religions through music and showed the centrality of musical activity in belief and practice. Some of these chants, hymns and verses are committed to memory and passed down through generations and continue to influence religious lives. Music promotes reflection, aids meditation and, importantly, it is the medium through which many sacred scriptures are recited or intoned, which had led Mercier and Long (2015:91) to argue that we cannot make sense of religion without engaging with music and the visual arts. Webster (2010) offers activities, resources and case studies of schools and teachers to support and creatively connect RE with music. Hollander and Houston's book (2009) *RE and Music Education: Singing from the Same Song Sheet?* provides teachers with imaginative and creative ideas on using music in RE. NATRE (2021) provides a range of resources for developing subject knowledge and classroom practice from different religions. As part of her Farmington Scholarship in RE, Parrott (2009) dealt with the history of music and its importance in some religions. Summaries of key points are presented to support subject knowledge in this area of learning.

Music in Judaism

Jewish music is diverse and ancient. Sometimes it is religious in nature and other times it is secular. The rhythm and sound of the music vary greatly depending on the origins of the Jewish composers. The earliest music used in Synagogues was based on a system used in the Temple in Jerusalem. The orchestra consisted of twelve instruments, including a harp, drums and cymbals, and a choir of twelve male singers. There are many references to music in the Bible – David playing the lyre, the Psalms, the Song of Solomon, Joshua's trumpet and dancing, singing and playing instruments. After the destruction of the Temple, music was initially banned, though later, restrictions were relaxed and liturgical poems were introduced. Some of the music was based on phrases from the Bible which recalled songs from the Temple itself. Today music remains a fundamental part of Jewish worship.

In a traditional Synagogue, the majority of the service is chanted or sung out loud, and the Torah reading is also chanted. Different melodies are used for the prayers and Torah readings on weekdays, Shabbat and holidays – these form a calendar in song. Some Jewish music is used for services and large gatherings, some are sung in the home around Shabbat. Some Jewish music uses instruments, but in traditional communities songs for Shabbat and holidays are from voices alone, as it is forbidden to play instruments at those times. Different Jewish communities also bring songs reflecting their heritage. Some congregations prefer traditional music whilst some use popular new melodies. Other religious music includes melodies utilised to heighten devotional fervour.

Music in Christianity

There is a vast quantity of classical and popular music composed in every book of the Bible (Mercier and Long 2015). Parrott (2009) notes that music is an important part of Christian worship, thanksgiving and celebration. It shows how worshippers feel towards God and unites the congregation so that God is worshipped with one voice. A wide variety of music is used including hymns, psalms, choral music, gospel songs, contemporary music and instrumental music, played for meditation and reflection. Christian music is one to express personal or communal beliefs regarding Christian life and faith. Most Christian worship involves singing accompanied by instruments. Psalms are songs of praise to God and in them are many references to music and the playing of instruments to the glory of God. The Catholic Church developed the 'Canticle' where passages of the Bible were sung at specified times in worship and these are still part of the Roman Catholic liturgy today.

Over time, religious music expanded. Composers borrowed melodies from secular and popular songs, writing religious words to them so that hymns, anthems and the chorus for both Protestant and Catholic churches were 'born'. Later, religious music transformed to suit a changing and evolving congregation. Liturgies were simplified and often translated into a country's language instead of Latin. Music was simplified and composers set religious texts to folk melodies to encourage congregations to join in the singing. In the latter half of the twentieth-century contemporary Christian music was born. From the folk-rock of the seventies with its guitars and drums to the Christian rap group of the twenty-first century, music continues to evolve, preserving the message of the Church whilst meeting the needs of an ever-changing world.

Sounds in Islam

Muslims see the universe as a symphonic orchestra full of sound, rhythm, tones, beats and form synchronised for perfect melodious harmony in unison, precisely and perfectly composed, directed and conducted by its Creator, Allah, with many sounds, movements, rhythms and beats in specific arrangements in the various forms of nature.

The necessity of reciting the Qur'an beautifully resulted in the birth of the art of 'music' modes and styles. Rules of solemn recitation – cantillation were made based on poetic musical language and its renditions. These became the model for both experts in Qur'anic recitation and a huge genre in poetry.

The issue of 'music' is contested amongst Islamic scholars (Harris 2006; Mercier and Long 2015). Parrott (2009) notes: Many scholars have been generally inclined to condemn all forms of music, with the singular exception of ad-duff (tambourine) at weddings, quite a few have taken a more positive approach of considering music containing sensual, pagan or unethical themes or subliminal messages as being categorically forbidden. The latter view seems to be more consistent with the general nature of Islam, which is undoubtedly a complete way of life that caters to all of the genuine human instincts and needs within permissible limits. Thus, it is to say that all music in Islam does not seem to agree with the balanced approach of Islam to issues of human life and experience. Whilst everyone agrees that all forms of music that contain pagan, sensual themes or subliminal messages are forbidden, a group of scholars considers all forms of music free of such themes and messages as permissible. Nevertheless, certain instruments are specifically proscribed. There is a view on the consensus of audio arts being impermissible. Some have noted the historical contribution of Muslims to the theory and use of music making some cultural and folks ones controversial and the vocalisation of rituals like adhan, tilawat, talbiya, takbir, zikr and nasheed as uncontroverted.

Music in Sikhi

Music plays an important part in Sikh worship. Guru Nanak emphasised the singing of divine music and believed that singing hymns shaped an individual's character as well as enhanced physical and spiritual well-being (Mercier and Long 2015:95). Sikhs believe that God's truth is revealed through the Guru Granth Sahib which is written in poetry, arranged in stanzas named shabads. It contains hymns that praise God, reveals his nature and gives guidance on living a good life. Each hymn is found on the same page in every copy and there are no spaces between the words so that nothing can be added to them. People have to be taught to read it and not everyone has that skill. Many people recite these hymns daily in their devotions at home. Each hymn has its traditional tune. The singing is called kirtan which plays a major part in the worship. The music notation is named Raag. The musicians are named ragis, who usually play tabla drums and harmoniums. The singing is accompanied by cymbals, sometimes other instruments are added, such as the sitar or the violin.

Children can be involved in playing percussion instruments. Both men and women play the instruments and sing simultaneously, though the other worshippers do not usually join in the singing. The musicians sit to the right of the Guru Granth Sahib facing the worshippers. The singer sits in the middle, playing the harmonium as he or she sings. Sikh worship aims to give praise to God. Only sounds that are made by the voice-box are allowed therefore clapping and whistling are not allowed. The second type of music is 'man-made' poems set to music. These can be sung in services but do not command the same respect as the shabads from the Guru Granth Sahib and are regarded as 'weak music'.

Dance and music in Hindu Dharma

Worship may be through words, music, dance or silence. Indian classical music is part of worship. They use kirtan (chanting of the mantras with instruments and dance) and bajan (devotional song) during worship in the temple. They use Raga, which is a seven-note scale, and Tala, which is a rhythmic pattern of beats accompanied by tabla drums, harmoniums and percussion instruments. An important element of Hindu worship is Bhajari, which means adoration and indicates worship with love. This often refers to devotional singing or the hymns themselves.

In Hindu tradition, the world was created by Shiva, whose aspects include Lord of the Dance, therefore, dance often forms part of the worship in a temple, along with music and songs of praise (bhajan and kirtan). Worshippers dance spontaneously or it is danced by classical dance troupes. Their dances recount stories from the spiritual epics. Each hand gesture (mudra), movement or facial expression will have a special meaning known to the audience. This sort of dance is a form of worship in its own right, to recount stories about the gods.

The Bharatanatyam is a narrative form of dance. Before the dance begins, the earth on which it is performed has to be sanctified. As dance is akin to trampling on the earth, the dancer seeks permission of mother earth to trample on her. The dancers touch the ground and bow to it at the beginning and the end of the dance to make connections between spirituality, the environment and the dance they perform. By doing this they learn to respect the earth. The dancers dance barefoot using hands and body gestures, put to music, to tell a story. The traditional stories, which are based on nature and human emotion, are drawn from Mahabharata and the Ramayana.

The Gita is a special chapter in the Mahabharata representing the 'Song of the Lord'; this is an elaborate moral code that shows the 'how and why' of doing good deeds containing numerous love poems narrated through the dance. 'Sringara' (love) is the dominant theme – love for people and the environment. The costumes of the dancers are made in colours to represent the earth; red, brown, yellow and green.

The voice in Buddha Dharma

In the introduction to the musical practices of Buddhism, Powell (2021) offers practice from several countries.

The Three Jewels, as a statement of Buddhist belief, is chanted frequently as part of the early ritual services. Theravada chanting is generally conservative and limited to a few basic notes. The principal chanter is followed line by line in response by the other monks. Chanting of the Vedic Three Refuges is normally preceded by a short drum sequence. Theravada Buddhists regard music as a type of sensual luxury, and they approach it with great caution. The risk is that one might focus on the musical quality rather than on the teachings within the chant. The voice, however, is revered as essential for the performance of Buddhist rituals in Mahayana and Theravada traditions. In Theravada Buddhism, music has a little actual liturgical function but helps preserve the Pali Canon. The Buddha's First Sermon is regularly chanted as a unison chant without call and response. Theravada chant is either didactic or for warding off evil spirits and not to invoke the presence of deity. The drums and horana have a place to inaugurate auspicious moments. Theravada Buddhism relies primarily on the non-musical chanting of scriptures in the Pali language and chanting does not follow a melody. Instead, because the words are considered of paramount importance, this type of chant is sung in a monotone.

In populist Mahayana Buddhism, sutras come to treat music in a more positive light. Buddhist services are essentially readings of doctrine, not occasions for worship in the Western sense. Their chant texts include words attributed to the Buddha himself, commentaries, statements of vows and faith, dedications, mantras (recitation formulas) and hymns of praise. The Lotus Sutra, based on the sermons of the Buddha, and other texts specific to their cultures or translations of texts are used as recitations which itself is an act of worship.

Instrumental music most often serves to demarcate aspects of Buddhist rituals. Mahayana Buddhism uses a wide variety of wind as well as percussion instruments. These wind instruments include horns, double-reed oboe-type instruments, end-blown flutes and conches. Circular breathing – the act of inhaling through the nose whilst expelling air through the lips – can in itself be a meditative practice that leads to tremendous focus and breath control. Drums are very common in Mahayana Buddhist ritual performance practice. The act of proclaiming the Buddhist teaching is traditionally known as 'sounding the drum of the Dharma', and the drum appears frequently in Buddhist iconography.

Music and movement see the use of instrumental music in worship in clockwise circulation around a stupa, or funerary or reliquary building. In walking around a stupa, the worshippers not only honour the Buddha and his teachings but physically enact the movement of the sun around the cosmic mountain, as it is represented by the stupa. Despite the early proscriptions regarding music, both vocal and instrumental music retain a position of importance within Buddhist traditions.

Sounds to welcome and call to devotion

Hindu gods and goddesses are depicted playing or holding musical instruments. The three gods of Hindu trinity – Brahma, Vishnu and Shiva, who play the hand cymbals, conch and damaru (drum) respectively – symbolise the Nada-Brahman, the sacred sound represented by the symbol Om, which generates the universe. Teachers can explore Vishnu's avatar, Krishna, depicted playing the flute and invite pupils to critically reflect on the meaning and significance of different objects and instruments held in the hands of the gods (Mercier and Long 2015:95).

The most common use for church bells was to call people to worship. Bells are now most commonly rung before a service or mass, marking a funeral or wedding and for marking times of prayer. In medieval times people relied on the bells to schedule their day as services were many. Bells often commemorate special occasions such as the coronation of a new monarch, to welcome a new vicar of the parish or to welcome a new baby.

The sound of the shofar is greatly symbolic to the Jews. It reminds Jewish people today of God, Judgment Day, the future Resurrection of the Dead and some events in the Hebrew Bible such as creation, sacrifice and Mount Sinai (Mercier and Long 2015:96–97). It is blown at synagogue services particularly at Rosh Hashanah, marking the beginning of the New Year and signifies the need to wake up and repent. It is also blown on Yom Kippur, the Day of Atonement. It is considered to be a commandment to hear the shofar blown. The shofar is the bent horn of a ram or another kosher animal. It was used in ancient Israel to announce the New Moon and gather people. Its purpose is to rouse the Divine in the listener. It must be an instrument in its natural form and be naturally hollow to remind people to be honest to God and the sound produced by human breath which is breathed into human beings by God. The sound it produces symbolises the lives it calls Jews to lead. The curve in the horn symbolises the different directions human lives take and mirrors the contrition of the people repenting as they bend before the Lord. It is blown on the left side of the body symbolising that the message comes from the heart.

The 'Adhan' is the Islamic call to prayer, recited by the 'muaddhin' usually from a minaret five times daily. The purpose is to inform people of the approaching time of prayer. It also brings to the mind of everyone the substance of Islamic beliefs, its spiritual teachings and the importance and benefit of prayer. Often a recorded adhan is used. In some mosques, the minaret is not used as it would disturb the neighbours, instead, it is given from inside and relayed via a transmission to homes. The Islamic call to prayer and the art of reciting the Qur'an have influenced artistic expression in Muslim culture. Islamic worship incorporates 'music' into worship, but not in the same sense as Christian choral or organ music, for example. Recitation of the Qur'an beautifies the words through tone, rhythm and the shaping of words. The living Qur'an is not only the written word – it is first of all the recited word of Allah, sounded with perfection and beauty. The sound produced is not regarded as 'music' as understood in Western art music terms. Therefore, teachers are to be mindful of the language used in explanations about Islamic recitation of the Qur'an and the call to prayer (Mercier and Long 2015).

Celebrations

'Music' is used in most faiths in festivals, acts of celebration and rites of passage to express worship, thanksgiving and joy. Many songs have been written for children and adults in the many traditions, some for use in worship or to explain the reasons for particular celebrations.

Some songs have been written to explain Islamic values and celebrations, though these are not used in worship. Some special events are marked by ceremonies to seek God's blessing where hymns are sung. For example, the marriage hymn (Lavan), specially written for weddings by Guru Ram Das has four verses each explaining a different aspect of marriage. They are read one at a time and then sung whilst the bride and groom walk in a clockwise direction around the Guru Granth Sahib.

This is a useful RE Jukebox: https://open.spotify.com/playlist/0WbIxTgvGhPMJIX3l8f08 t?si=qATvF2tNRdqnPXuxNHXjGA

Summary

Sacred sound and music play an important role in society. It is useful to study them, their uses and purposes and explore the similarities and differences. Pupils should have opportunities to work creatively with sound. They can choose sounds to add mood and atmosphere to parts of a story in RE. They can sing, use and perform with simple instruments by listening to, joining in and remembering a range of religious songs, hymns and choruses. They can take part in singing as a class, group or individual. They can listen to a variety of religious music and respond to their own and others' music-making and the beat using appropriate actions, for example, nodding head, tapping foot, clapping hands, marching. Pupils can also respond imaginatively through movement, drama or dance to a wider range of religious sound and music. They can be invited to think and talk about the simple features of music and how they are used in religious music from different styles and cultures, for example, loud and quiet, high and low, fast and slow in music associated with religious festivals, celebration and worship. Pupils as musicians making music are engaged in a fundamentally revealing, vulnerable and humanising activity, and they are conscious of breath, bodies, emotions and thoughts of both themselves and others (Waligur 2020:52). Thus, it contributes to pupils' spiritual, social, moral and cultural and personal development.

POETICAL RE

Introduction

Poetry is considered an expression of feelings and emotions. Poetry can be, in many cases, an influential means towards spiritual upliftment, faith expression, moral guidance, social reform and political activism. Humans of all persuasions, religious or otherwise, have made huge contributions in this field and poetry has greatly impacted the human consciousness. However, when asked about the relationship of RE and poetry and its potential, students reacted with mixed outlooks and a research task set for them revealed some interesting information about poetry and religion as presented below.

Some attached minor reservations to delivering RE through poetry, as they initially, felt there was no link between the two, unlike others, who thought it had considerable potential, as discussed below. These reactions raise the question of whether poetry in RE was the best use of RE time or was it best done in English lessons. Consider the following:

- ■ I don't like poetry because it is confusing.
- ■ Surprised at how it could be used in RE, as it is about being expressive.
- ■ Poetry is English focussed, so how will they gain a good understanding of RE?
- ■ It is not fully accessible in RE? It is a cross-curriculum thing.
- ■ Poetry can be performed not only read, so it has space in RE and it allows for creativity. It allows for interpretation in RE and English.

■ Is it RE content or English skills? This will be interesting, but what can pupils write about? They might not know anything about religion?

■ It is good for RE as words in poems are far easier to digest than prose.

Poetry and religion

The Rigvedic hymns are devotional poetry in Hindu Dharma, which includes praises to different Aryan gods. There is a huge body of hymns of praise, adoration and supplication found in the main epics and other sacred texts too. Buddhist poetry is found in the songs of the venerable women and venerable men of the Pali canon. Mostly, they consist of their personal experiences which led them to renunciate life. Great poets wrote a biography of the Buddha and hymns to the Buddha as well. In the Jewish traditions, poems can be about the Jewish faith, its people, its history, healing, images, invocations and it is a way of understanding and flourishing faith. Christian poetry is any poetry that contains Christian teachings and references, often of the Bible. The account in the book of Exodus is classified as prose and the Psalms are categorised as poetry. Poems can be didactic in character, portray feelings of individual experience and some urge actions. The Qur'an was revealed in a period when the poetic arts and the beauty of oral expression were at their highest. This influenced the role of poetry in many Muslim societies. The Qur'an is sensitive to the spoken word for its aesthetic qualities and ethical values. Indeed, for Muslims, the inimitability of Qur'anic eloquence serves as proof of its Divine origin. The Sikh religion is embedded in poetry. In the communal memory of the Sikhs, Guru Nanak responded to the Waheguru with poetic eruption and compositions to revere the formless God, the infinite One. The Jain community has produced a large collection of hymns praising chiefly the twenty-four jinas, in addition to some of their ancient teachers.

Thus, it is noted that poetry, both contemporary and of the past, is one way of carrying out theology. However, it is not only theology that is done through poetry, as stated earlier. Poetry offers considerable flexibility and creativity in expressing inner states and feelings. It allows people to grapple with the certainties and uncertainties of life and the afterlife.

RE through poetry

The relationship between religions and poetry is evident. In RE it helps pupils understand and remember facts. That poetry describes common experiences, which many can relate to, it means it is an effective way to introduce a topic, issue or religion. Scriptural texts provide opportunities for pupils to reflect upon and be inspired to write their own from within familiar contexts. It encourages the expression of inner feelings, asks hermeneutic types of questions, open interpretation, examining complex concepts and develops a different kind of understanding. It encourages the use of RE specific vocabulary, and, since it tends to be opinionated it allows pupils to be expressive in their understanding. It helps with retention and remembering significant people and events. However, pupils with SEND and those using EAL may not access them fully, so you will need to secure progress for them as well. Religious, sacred and everyday poetry can be recited from various perspectives including theological, philosophical, literary, linguistic, cultural, psychological and historical to ponder over social and moral issues affecting society, which can be linked to their life experiences. It provokes emotions and soothes the soul, especially when infused with music and sound.

In the classroom

To promote good progress and set high expectations you should use intentional and consistent language that promotes challenge and aspiration. It is suggested that you make good use of expositions using a concrete representation of abstract ideas, for example, by making use of analogies, metaphors, examples and non-examples. You should also use modelling, explanations and scaffolds, as some novices need more structure early in a domain (DfE 2019).

Teachers should scaffold, use and model a range of examples and styles and make it relevant to RE by not only focusing on the nature of poetry itself but also the hidden and deeper meanings and messages. Strong connections must be made to RE instead of tenuous ones. The judgement should be on RE learning not always on English language features and skills.

■ Pupils should also do performance poetry and use a wide range of poetic devices.

■ They should use age and language appropriate poetry.

■ Some poetry is necessary for advanced pupils and to challenge them.

Public performance

This is part of spectator culture in many cultures. The choral play in the primary school provides a controlled and communal space for pupils actively to participate in the emotional workings of the story, which can be presented through a range of media, including performances and recitals.

Spirited Poetry

NATRE runs a project known as Spirited Poetry, which is a creative strategy to enable better and more imaginative RE. Teachers are free to use these poems to inspire further writing and thinking in their classrooms. Schools submit their work for their poetry competition. Atheists, agnostics and believers in God might all respond by expressing their sense of the search for God or finding God to the question: Where's God? From the 2019 submissions, two are illustrated in Table 11.4.

So you might want to consider providing, as and when appropriate, worked examples of poetry that take pupils through the process where a new one or to consolidate previous ones are likely to support pupils to learn. This might mean needing to learn to balance exposition, repetition, practice and retrieval of critical knowledge and skills of poetry when using it to serve RE.

Languages play an important role. Therefore, you will want to plan for and use intentional and consistent language that promotes challenge and aspiration. However, remember it is important to create a positive environment where making mistakes and learning from them and the need for effort and perseverance are part of their daily routine. You should also consider how you will scaffold and support those who need additional support perhaps by providing targeted support to pupils who are struggling to increase their success (DfE 2019).

Table 11.4 Case study: Spirited Poetry	
Leyla (Age 6) **Diwali** Diwali, is a festival of light over darkness and good over evil. I see shining animals. I see a rainbow of fire works. I see happiness and family all together.	Edward (Age 6) **God is …** God is in the plants God is in the ground I find God at the beach God is a friend
Source: NATRE (2019) Spirited Poetry Collection.	

Table 11.5 Case study: Inside my heart	
I know, there's a place of hope for all	To err is human
It lies in a chamber in the heart of all	To forgive is Divine
I know, it's possible to live in peace by all	Words of truth are arms for all
If we found a chamber in our heart for all	'tis the best jihād for all
I know, we need guns and swords	Let's not despair, O fellow, at all
But, isn't the pen mightier?	Cos' you see, the tables will turn soon, all
I know, there's a heart in all	I know, I can be hopeful, O fellow, for all
If there's hope in it, there's hope in us, all	Cos' the Chosen one was hopeful for all
Clean this flesh, all	I know, there is hope for one 'n' all
Reform, the senses and limbs, all	Cos' God promises His hope for one 'n' all
Corrupt this flesh, all	I know, I can hope for all
Corrupt, the senses and limbs, all	I wonder how many hope in a similar hope, none or all.
Source: Inside My Heart (Mogra 2011).	

Finally, practice is an integral part of effective teaching. You should ensure that pupils have repeated opportunities to practise, with appropriate guidance and support, to increase their success. This means you will plan activities around what you want pupils to think hard about, as illustrated in Table 11.5.

Summary

RE through poetry should be more than a collection and marking of literary features. It should bring pupils to bring into being their innermost thoughts and feelings, their hope and feeling, their faith and morals, their aspirations and worries, their sorrow and happiness, the imagination and reality, their spirit and their self.

THEOLOGICAL AND HERMENEUTICAL RE

Introduction

Sacred texts are at the heart of gaining insights into what influences religions, and learning about them is important in RE. Pupils are expected to discuss sacred writings and sources of wisdom and recognise the traditions from which they come. They are to consider how sacred writings or other sources of wisdom provide ethical guidance and spiritual nurture to members of different communities (REC 2013). It has been recommended that pupils are entitled to be taught the role of religious and non-religious foundational texts in both the formation and communication of experience, beliefs, values, identities and commitments and how worldviews have power and influence in societies and cultures, appealing to various sources of authority, including foundational texts (CoRE 2018:12). Young people should develop skills relevant to various disciplinary approaches to Religion and Worldviews, including philosophical enquiry and hermeneutical approaches to texts (CoRE 2018:77). Globally there are debates about the practice of interpretation. Questions are asked about how religious texts should be read and how texts should be written centuries ago guide practice in the contemporary world. There are issues about the 'ownership' of these texts. In addition, about who has and does not have the 'right' to interpret them and how to interpret them.

In learning the tools of interpretation that are specific to the substantive content (parts of the sacred text), pupils can see layers of meaning in texts that interpreters find significant. In addition, they are less reliant on teachers giving them an established meaning to the text (Bowie, Panjwani and Clemmey 2020a). Following this, the Ofsted RE Research Review (2021) noted that when pupils learn about these tools through lots of different substantive content in a sequenced curriculum, they learn: about the usefulness of the methods and tools and knowledge of meanings that previous interpreters have considered important (a receptive expertise). They also learn how to use the tools and methods for themselves (a productive expertise). It is also noteworthy that the interpretation of texts is one aspect of discussions about interpretation in RE. This wider sense of interpretation in RE has been discussed by Aldridge (2018).

You should know that setting clear expectations could help communicate shared values that improve classroom and school culture. A culture of mutual trust and respect supports effective relationships. Moreover, explicitly teaching pupils the knowledge and skills they need to succeed within particular subject areas is beneficial. Every teacher can improve pupils' literacy, including by explicitly teaching reading, writing and oral language skills specific to individual disciplines (DfE 2019). Thus by studying textual sources directly, pupils will see that religions have things to say that are relevant to modern life and the extent to which they have similar and different things to say.

Sacred texts are considered 'buried treasure', so pupils can become explorers to discover 'jewels' from texts of all kinds. The study by Sigel (2009) shows the possibility of the study of sacred texts fostering spirituality and well-being within children and, as such, of growth in self-understanding and self-confidence, and provides a feeling of a valued member of a faith-based community and of the spiritual development of pupils outside the text under study. It is suggested that students' ability to learn in RE depends on their ability to understand sources, such as textbooks, sacred scriptures, images and other forms of discourse. RE teachers' use of text-based learning activities can raise awareness of student positioning and enhance subject content knowledge in RE (Unstad and Fjørtoft 2021).

Selway (2020) has expressed concern about the way the use of hermeneutic has been suggested in the works of Bowie, Panjwani and Clemmey (2020b, 2020c), which ask the question: 'Should schools help students become good interpreters of religion, worldviews, and sacred texts? Should they help students explore what it means to be a sacred text scholar?'

Postulating that the authors expect an affirmative response, Selway (2020:14) questions whether it is the task of a school pupil to be the interpreter of a sacred text or should they be studying how Christians interpret their sacred text. Further, would such a shift in the emphasis put the resource at risk of being accused of a form of confessionalism? Selway (2020:14) acknowledges that religious people interpret their texts in different ways, and it is reasonable to expect pupils to recognise that fact. However, doing the interpretation for themselves, looking for connections between the texts and their own lives and becoming a sacred texts scholar seems to him to be far removed from what was recommended by the Commission on RE: 'The different ways that people interpret and respond to texts and other sources of authority' (sic).

Erricker (2013) has cautioned on approaches to the interpretation of sacred texts that rely on liberalism where there is hermeneutical corruption which seeks to give an interpretation in line with Western liberalism. This kind of reading makes interpretation compatible with an individual's worldview and moral sensitivities, leaving aside what the texts say literally and what believers would believe and hold sacred about their sacred text. On the other hand, it also reveals the pre-modern values system of many believers.

Retrieval practice

Retrieval practice is a strategy, which is most likely to lead to long-term learning and improve memory. It forces pupils to generate answers to questions. It has been proven to be one of the most effective learning strategies (Watson and Bradley 2021). This is because it requires pupils to recall previously learned knowledge, which creates stronger memory traces. This helps secure and embed information into pupils' long-term memory. In the classroom, there are many ways of applying retrieval practice including multiple-choice tests, essay answers, verbal questions and answers and flashcards. It is important not to reduce retrieval practice to a tick box exercise and should not be confused with doing more tests and they should be done in a relatively stress-free manner.

Ask pupils to use the letters of the alphabet to think about words that help them and/or others to think about what God is. As suggested earlier, quotations about the nature of God from different traditions can also be presented to pupils for analysis, and where appropriate, images and artwork can be supplemented to these.

Theologies of Reading

Jenkins (2021) provides useful approaches to deal with what she terms as the 'Theologies of Reading', which describes the idea of meaning and interpretation in texts in RE. The approach is taken from research, faith-based reading and techniques of interpretation and contemplation. Jenkins invites teachers to consider:

- How does engaging with texts support the purpose of the RE curriculum?
- How can 'Theologies of Reading' be implemented across the RE curriculum?
- How could a deeper engagement with texts, interpretation and lenses be implemented across the RE curriculum?

There are several 'desired endpoints' that would result from such work, including:

- Pupils understanding different ways in which texts have been, and can be, interpreted
- Pupils understanding texts have multiple meanings
- Pupils progress in the sophistication of understanding texts
- Pupils are aware of how their own 'reading lenses' effects interpretation
- Pupils show increased religious literacy

Grab your Reading Glasses

Jenkins offers some questions for approaching a text with pupils' by suggesting that pupils put on their 'Reading Glasses' and ask:

- What does it actually say?
- What do I think it means?
- What is clear about it?
- What is questionable?
- What does it remind me of?
- How would…read this?
- What lenses do I bring to the text that affect my reading?

Looking at original manuscripts

Pupils will be fascinated by bringing ancient texts to life by exploring them in original (or ancient) versions. It is always useful to give pupils as much context as possible by showing them images of ancient texts, the original languages they are written in or precious fragments that survive in museums and giving some historical context to these texts, such as the era they were created in, the place, the languages, who created them, and so on.

Several sites exist which can be used. There are brief activities at the Sacred Texts at the British Library (https://www.bl.uk/sacred-texts and at the visual Commentary on Scripture at https://thevcs.org/

Reading as internalisation of the transcendent

In the Muslim community recitation and memorisation of the Qur'an, both individually and in public, is highly valued. The recitation demonstrates the relation between the sound, the rhythm, as well as the pronunciation of the sacred text, and its meaning. It is a highly-skilled discipline, governed by a series of detailed rules to ensure correct pronunciation. By reflecting on the practice of recitation, pupils can be invited to consider how reading is metaphysical in nature, and how the spoken word has power in terms of behaviour and attitude (Ravenscroft and Wright 2018).

In the classroom, Ravenscroft and Wright (2018) suggest that pupils can be encouraged to learn small extracts, poems and text for memory. Teachers can promote the listening and readings of the Qur'an and other texts using available podcasts. They can discuss the importance of recitation for many Muslims. For many Muslims, recitation means 'participation in a divine revelation', and this can sometimes be missed. The power of the Qur'an lies in its oracy. For example, different pupils, where appropriate, could be asked to read a piece of text aloud and to listen for different intonation and sounds within the reading. For example, in groups of three each pupil reads the same short text aloud to one another. They can note emphasis and how words and phrases are spoken and then share their interpretations with each other (Ravenscroft and Wright 2018).

Reading as commentary

Midrash refers to a specific genre of authoritative rabbinic literature within Judaism. It involves a searching and rigorous interpretive practice, seeking theological and practical answers by looking at the meaning of words in biblical and canonical texts. Midrash will respond to contemporary problems and will make connections between the text and lived reality of the Jewish faith (Ravenscroft and Wright 2018).

In the classroom, pupils can undertake silent debates, commenting and asking questions directly on the text. Ravenscroft and Wright (2018) suggest that this can work well with both words and images. Pupils can be invited to use biblical and other commentaries, appropriately, from online sources. Pupils can compare different interpretations of the same text, evaluate these interpretations and decide which is more convincing. Pupils can be helped to create their commentaries. One way of doing this is to use a double-entry journal.

Using a double-entry journal

As shown in Table 11.6, pupils can complete double-entry journals they read and discuss texts, images and their meaning.

In using these different ways of approaching reading and meaning-making within religious communities, it is important to distinguish between their uses as a devotional approach to scriptures. Selway (2020:15) cautions that asking pupils to infer their own meaning from sacred texts could be classed as a literacy skill, but asking them to dwell on individual words and suggest their own meanings for the text might not be a productive exercise when they could be studying how religious individuals and organisations make texts fit with their purposes. According to him, this requires an understanding of the historical and societal influences that shape their interpretations. In other words, for him, theology does not drive textual interpretation or vice versa but sociological pressures bring about the impetus for believers to reassess and redefine meanings and bring emphasis to different parts of their texts.

Table 11.6 Double entry journal	
From the Text	**From Your Mind**
What is the passage about?	What is your reaction?
List some interesting language	What is your theory or idea about this passage? What does it make you think about?
An important quote	What other stories or events does this passage remind you of?
What is the key moment or event in the passage?	What explanation can you give for why this passage/story is still read or retold today?
What is the main idea, theme or concept?	How important do you think this passage is to believers?
Is there a problem or conflict? If so, what is it?	What do other people in your group think about this passage?

Hermeneutical method in RE

The word 'hermeneutics' comes from the Greek 'hermeneuo', meaning 'to interpret'. It is also thought to refer to the Greek god Hermes, who was the messenger of the gods, moving between the divine and the human realms. People were expected to interpret the words of the gods and so Hermes is a fitting symbol for the slippery notion of interpretation.

In the classroom, a hermeneutic question asks pupils to 'unpack' meaning. Accordingly, rather than asking them if they agree with a statement, pupils are asked to say what they think is meant by the statement (Worley 2019:7). Therefore, hermeneutics, conceived at least in a narrow sense, is a methodology for scriptural interpretation (Aldridge 2018:245). It is an investigation into how humans make sense of the world and how humans communicate their ideas to others (Jenkins 2021). It asks questions such as: do we create our own meaning and project it into the world, and does the way we read religious texts reflect our assumptions about religious books, such as whether we believe them to be sacred or not.

In other words, the hermeneutical study looks at the 'lenses' that are brought to reading, which shape the way it is read and the understanding and meaning gleaned from each reading encounter. Sacred texts can be looked at through lenses more formal than individual experiences and beliefs. Discipline is a way of understanding the world. To look through a disciplinary lens is to learn a particular way of seeing, as well as increasing understanding of the world.

The disciplines, as detailed earlier, relevant to reading sacred texts (as well as religion and worldviews generally) are theology, philosophy and the social sciences. These lenses can be formed by life experiences, a belief system, prior experience of sacred texts, knowledge of classical allusions, cultural experiences and so on. The act of reading brings another lens into play; the reader's attempt to understand the meaning as meant by the author of the text. The reader reads through their own lenses but also engages in trying to work out the author's lenses, or experiences, beliefs and culture (Georgiou and Wright 2018; Jenkins 2021).

In the classroom, choose a piece of text, such as Genesis 1 and Genesis 2 and discuss or reflect on how it might change by looking at it through the theological, philosophical and historical lenses.

When teaching the Exodus story, go beyond enslavement and the escape, by teaching what the literature Exodus and how Ezra and Israel in Babylon saw it. Importantly how Jews engage it in modern life. Explore how Christians read it today and how it might speak to pupils and the wider society.

It is also important to show different interpretations of religious text which lead to different conclusions. This way pupils can begin to appreciate the importance of text analysis and how they contribute to the development of different schools, denominations and thoughts which can help them appreciate the diverse practices better.

Hermeneutics and the nature of RE

Aldridge (2018) has discussed the need to attend to the 'double hermeneutic' of religious education because hermeneutics raises a broader set of questions for students of religion than simply those around the interpretation of revealed texts. Each of these emphases (the range of interpretive approaches to texts and the need for religions to be approached interpretively) is a concern in the study of religion. A hermeneutical approach critiques attempt to essentialise religion or engage with 'authoritative' representations of a religious tradition and offers a diversity of its voices (Aldridge 2018:246). In other words, a hermeneutic approach adopted by RE teachers for their subject would not present 'Islam' or 'Christianity', but some of the ways that Christians and Muslims interpret their own faiths. Thus, for Aldridge (2018:254), the educational question concerns what it is in the representation of Islam or Muslims, Hindus or Sanatan Dharma or Judaism or Jews that stands to speak to the pupils.

Hermeneutical learning for teachers

In the context of the subject of RE, it is argued that there is a work of interpretation to be done both by those who profess to adhere to religions and those who would study them (Aldridge 2018:245). Students, both as 'insiders' and 'outsiders', are concerned with discovering the 'perspectivistic' character of each position against (other) religions and worldviews. As such, Pollefeyt (2020:3) contends that, in a quest for value and meaning, nobody is neutral. Therefore, the goal of hermeneutical learning is to find and expose effective interpretations of the world, to achieve a better understanding of things from within, in this case, religions and philosophies of life. Hermeneutics thus involves a movement from the outside to the inside, from description to understanding, from experience to interpretation, from participation to dialogue, from one layer to several layers, from letter to spirit (Pollefeyt 2020:3).

Pollefeyt (2020) explains that students who start from a personal perspective as an insider are not always aware of the interpreted character of their philosophical or religious experience. They often, he maintains, see a kind of unity between their own experience and their own religious or philosophical outlook. For them, therefore, hermeneutical learning means discovering what their philosophical or religious experience carries, establishes and shapes. This is always accompanied by a form of self-reflection, and sometimes also with a critical distance and growing awareness that things could have been different as well. However, to be able to connect the inside perspective pedagogically and dialogically with the outside perspective as a (future) religion teacher, this process of self-reflection is necessary (Pollefeyt 2020:3)

Summary

This section has outlined hermeneutics. It showed how it could be used as a method in RE to study sacred writings or other sources of wisdom. It also discussed the need for teachers of RE to look at the RE, as a subject, hermeneutically. Finally, it analysed how 'insiders' and 'outsiders' should approach religions.

Reference

Abdel-Haleem, M. (1989) Water in the Qur'an, *Islamic Quarterly*, 33, (1), pp. 34–50.

Aldridge, D. (2018) Religious education's double hermeneutic, *British Journal of Religious Education*, 40, (3), pp. 245–256.

Alexander, R. (2008) *Towards Dialogic Teaching: Rethinking Classroom Talk*, York: Dialogos. Fourth edition.

Antonakaki, T. (2007) *Lighting and Spatial Structure in Religious Architecture: a comparative study of Byzantine church and an early Ottoman mosque in the city of Thessaloniki*, Proceeding, 6th International Space Syntax Symposium Istanbul, 2007. [Online] http://www.spacesyntaxistanbul.itu.edu.tr/papers%5Clongpapers%5C057%20-%20Antonakaki.pdf (Accessed 14/07/2021).

Badr, H. (2004) Islamic Identity Recovered: Muslim women after September 11th, *Culture and Religion*, 5, (3), pp. 321–338.

Baumfield, V. (2005) Disciplinary knowledge and religious education, *British Journal of Religious Education*, 27, (1), pp. 3–4.

Beck, G. L. (2009) *Sacred Sound: Experiencing Music in World Religions*, Ontario: Wilfrid Laurier University Press.

Bowie, B., Panjwani, F., and Clemmey, K. (2020a) *Opening the Doors to Hermeneutical RE: The Finding Report*, [Online] https://www.reonline.org.uk/news/teachers-and-texts-report/, (Accessed 19/07/2021).

Bowie, R., Panjwani, F., and Clemmey, K. (2020b) *Opening the Door to Hermeneutical RE*, Canterbury: National Institute for Christian Education Research.

Bowie, R., Panjwani, F., and Clemmey, K. (2020c) *Opening the Door to Hermeneutical RE: The Practice Guide*, Canterbury: National Institute for Christian Education Research.

Chater, M., and Erricker, E. (2013) *Does Religious Education Have a Future? Pedagogical and Policy Prospects*, Abingdon: Routledge.

Clarke, D. (2020) *Developing Chronological Understanding and Language in the EYFS*, [Online] Available at: https://www.history.org.uk/primary/categories/675/resource/9957/developing-chronological-understanding-and-languag (Accessed 12/06/2021).

Cohen, M., and Gerhardt, P. (2014) *Visual Supports for People With Autism: A Guide for Parents and Professionals*, Bethesda, MD: Woodbine House. Second edition.

Connor, D. (2018) *Supporting Children With Autism in the Primary Classroom: A Practical Approach*, Abingdon: Routledge.

CoRE (Commission on Religious Education) (2018) *Religion and Worldviews: The Way Forward*, London: Religious Education Council.

Cooling, T. (1994) http://www.staplefordcentre.org/files/files/Trevor_Cooling-Concept_Cracking-Exploring_Christian_Beliefs_in_School.pdf. Nottingham: Stapleford Project.

DfE (2013a) *English Programmes of Study: Key Stages 1 and 2 National Curriculum in England*, London: Crown Copyright. https://assets.publishing.service.gov.uk/government/uploads/system/uploads/attachment_data/file/335186/PRIMARY_national_curriculum_-_English_220714.pdf

DfE (2013b) *The National Curriculum in England Key Stages 1 and 2 Framework Document*, London: Crown Copyright. Reference: DFE-00178-2013. [Online] https://assets.publishing.service.gov.uk/government/uploads/system/uploads/attachment_data/file/425601/PRIMARY_national_curriculum.pdf

DfE (2013c) *Art and Design Programmes of Study: Key Stages 1 and 2*, London: Crown Copyright. Reference: DFE-00170-2013 [Online] https://assets.publishing.service.gov.uk/government/uploads/system/uploads/attachment_data/file/239018/PRIMARY_national_curriculum_-_Art_and_design.pdf (Accessed 14/07/2021).

DfE (2019) *ITT Core Content Framework*, Department of Education: London. Reference: DfE-00230-2019.

Dobson, T., and Stephenson, L. (2020) Challenging boundaries to cross: Primary teachers exploring drama pedagogy for creative writing with theatre educators in the landscape of performativity, *Professional Development in Education*, 46, (2), pp. 245–255.

English Heritage (2011) Places of Worship Listing Selection Guide, [Online] https://historicengland.org.uk/images-books/publications/dlsg-places-worship/heag124-places-of-worship-lsg/ (Accessed 13/06/2021).

Erricker, C., Lowndes, J., and Bellchambers, E. (2011) *Primary Religious Education – A New Approach*, Abingdon: Routledge.

Erricker, C. (2013) Discourse and dissonance in contemporary paradigm of RE, in M. Chater and C. Erricker (Eds.) *Does Religious Education Have a Future? Pedagogical and Policy Prospects*, Abingdon: Routledge, pp. 74–88.

Freathy, R., Doney, J., Freathy, G., Walshe, K., and Teece, G. (2017) Pedagogical Bricoleurs and Bricolage Researchers: The case of Religious Education, *British Journal of Educational Studies*, 65, (4), pp. 425–443.

Gearon, L. (2013) *MasterClass in Religious Education: Transforming Teaching and Learning*, London: Bloomsbury.

Georgiou, G., and Wright, K. (2018) Re-Dressing the balance, in M. Castelli and M. Chater (Eds.) *We Need to Talk About Religious Education*, London: Jessica Kingsley, pp. 101–113.

Georgiou, G., and Wright, K. (2020) Disciplinarily, religion and worldviews: Making the case for theology, philosophy and human/social sciences, in M. Chater (Ed.) *Reforming RE*, Woodbridge: John Catt, pp. 149–164.

Goldburg, P. (2004) Towards a creative arts approach to the teaching of religious education with special reference to the use of film, *British Journal of Religious Education*, 26, (2), pp. 175–184.

Hammond, J. (2015) Developing experiential RE creatively, in S. Elton-Chalcraft (Ed.) *Teaching Religious Education Creatively*, Abingdon: Routledge, pp. 113–122.

Hackett, R. (1988) *About Art and Religion in Africa*, London: Continuum.

Haider, N. (2011) *The Origins of the Shī'a: Identity, Ritual and Sacred Space in Eight-Century Kufah*, Cambridge: Cambridge University Press.

Harris, D. (2006) *Music Education and Muslims*, Stoke-on-Trent: Trentham Books.

Hassner, R. (2009) *War on Sacred Grounds*, Ithaca, NY: Cornell University Press.

Heathcote, D., and Bolton, G. (1995) *Drama for Learning: Dorothy Heathcote's Mantle of the Expert Approach to Education*, Portsmouth, NH: Heinemann.

Hollander, P., and Houston, R. (2009) *RE and Music Education: Singing from the Same Song Sheet?* Nottingham: The Stapleford Centre.

Homan, R. (2012) Constructing religion, in L. P. Barnes (Ed.) *Debates in Religious Education*, London: Routledge, pp. 183–193.

Hunt, D. (2018) *Addressing Special Educational Needs and Disability in the Curriculum: Religious Education*, Abingdon: Routledge. Second edition.

Hutton, L., and Cox, D. (2021) *Making Every Lesson Count*, Carmarthen: Crown House.

Janes, K. H. (2014) *Using the Visual Arts for Cross-Curricular Teaching and Learning: Imaginative Ideas for the Primary School*, Abingdon: Routledge.

Jenkins, J. (2021) *Theologies of Reading*, [Online] https://www.reonline.org.uk/teaching-resources/theologies-of-reading/ (Accessed 30/05/2021).

Jensen, R. M. (2000) *Understanding Early Christian Art*, London: Routledge.

Jones, L. G. (2012) *The Power of Oratory in the Medieval Muslim World, Cambridge Studies in Islamic Civilization*, Cambridge: Cambridge University Press.

Kueh, R. (2018) Religious Education and the 'Knowledge Problem', in M. Castelli and M. Chater (Eds.) *We Need to Talk About Religious Education: Manifestos for the Future of RE*, London: Jessica Kingsley, pp. 53–69.

Kueh, R. (2020) Disciplinary hearing: Making the case for the disciplinary in religion and world-view, in M. Chater (Ed.) *Reforming RE*, Woodbridge: John Catt, pp. 131–147.

Lucas, B., and Spencer, E. (2017) *Teaching Creative Thinking: Developing Learners Who Generate Ideas and can Think Critically*, Carmarthen: Crown House.

McCreery, E., Palmer, S., and Voiels, V. (2008) *Teaching Religious Education*, Exeter: Learning Matters.

McKain, N. (2018) Religious Education as a safe space for discussing unsafe ideas, in M. Castelli and M. Chater (Eds.) *We Need to Talk About Religious Education: Manifestos for the Future of RE*, London: Jessica Kingsley, pp. 175–176.

Mercier, C., and Long, S. D. (2015) Enriching RE through music and art, in S. Elton-Chalcraft (Ed.) *Teaching Religious Education Creatively*, Abingdon: Routledge, pp. 91–111.

Miller, J. (2003) Using the visual arts in Religious Education: An analysis and critical evaluation, *British Journal of Religious Education*, 25, (3), pp. 200–213.

MoE (2021) *Introduction to the Mantle of the Expert*, [Online] https://www.mantleoftheexpert.com/what-is-moe/introduction-to-moe/ (Accessed 02//2021).

Mogra, I. (2011) Inside my heart, *Interreligious Insight*, 9, (1), p. 80.

Mogra, I. (2018) *Jumpstart RE!*, Abingdon: Routledge.

Mogra, I. (2022) Developing essential values through traditional tales: Voices of Malawian Primary School Teachers, in Y. Matemba and B. Collet (Ed.), *Bloomsbury Handbook of Religious Education in the Global South*, London: Bloomsbury Academic, pp. 273–298.

Moyser, G. (2005) Religion and politics, in J. Hinnells (Ed.), *Routledge Companion to the Study of Religion*, London: Routledge, pp. 423–438.

NATRE (2019) *Spirited Poetry*, [Online] https://www.natre.org.uk/about-natre/projects/spirited-arts/spirited-poetry-2019/spirited-poetry-collection/2019/?ThemeID=83 (Accessed 19/07/2021).

NATRE (2021) *Resources*, [Online] https://www.natre.org.uk/resources/ (Accessed 02/06/2016).

Nes, S. (2006) *The Mystical Language of Icons*, Grand Rapids, MI: Eerdmans.

Ofsted (2007) *Making Sense of Religion*, Manchester: Crown Copyright. Reference no: 070045. [Online] http://www.educationengland.org.uk/documents/pdfs/2007-ofsted-religion.pdf (Accessed 15/11/2020).

Ofsted (2010) *Transforming Religious Education*, Manchester: Crown Copyright. Reference no: 090215. [Online] https://dera.ioe.ac.uk/1121/1/Transforming%20religious%20education.pdf (Accessed 05/12/2020).

Ofsted (2013) *Religious Education: Realising the Potential*, Manchester: Crown Copyright. Reference No: 130068. [Online] https://assets.publishing.service.gov.uk/government/uploads/system/uploads/attachment_data/file/413157/Religious_education_-_realising_the_potential.pdf (Accessed 05/12/2020).

Ofsted (2021) *Research Review Series: Religious Education*, [Online] https://www.gov.uk/government/publications/research-review-series-religious-education/research-review-series-religious-education#fnref:155 (Accessed 18/07/2021).

Ogier, S. (2017) *Teaching Primary Art and Design*, London: SAGE.

Park, C. (2005) Religion and geography, in J. Hinnells (Ed.), *Routledge Companion to the Study of Religion*, London: Routledge, pp. 439–455.

Park, C. (1994) *Sacred Worlds: An Introduction to Geography and the Religion*, London: Routledge.

Parrott, R. (2009) *The Importance of Music in Different Religions*, Oxford: Farmington Trust. WR70.

Phillips, S. (2006) *Making RE Make Sense: Teaching RE Using Theatre of Learning Techniques*, Bristol: SfE Limited.

Phillips, S. (2003) Reflections on classroom practice: The theatre of learning, *International Journal of Children's Spirituality*, 8, (1), pp. 55–66.

Pollefeyt, D. (2020) Hermeneutical learning in religious education, *Journal of Religious Education*, 68, pp. 1–11.

Powell, J. (2021) *Buddhism and Music*, [Online] http://www.personal.utulsa.edu/~john-powell/Buddhist_Music/ (Accessed 02/06/2021).

REC (Religious Education Council of England and Wales) (2013) *A Curriculum Framework for Religious Education in England*, London: REC of England and Wales.

Ravenscroft, R. J., and Wright, K. (2018) *Theologies of Reading New Perspectives on Pupil Engagement with Texts An Introduction*, [Online] file:///C:/Users/id105124/Downloads/Theologies-of-Reading-An-Introduction-Final.pdf (Accessed 30/05/2021).

Reynolds, D., Smith, S., and Vallely, K. (2021) Empowering communication through speaking, reading, and writing, in R. McDonald and P. Gibson (Ed.) *Inspiring Primary Learners*, Abingdon: Routledge.

Rodell, J. (2020) Britain's religion and belief landscape, *Theology*, 123, (1), pp. 28–40.

Selway, C. (2020) *Understanding Christianity and the Study of Religion and Worldviews: How the Church of England Has Gained Control of Religious Education*. London: National Secular Society.

Scriven, R. (2014) Geographies of pilgrimage: Meaningful movements and embodied mobilities, *Geography Compass*, 8, (4), pp. 249–261.

Sigel, D. (2009) Educating for spirituality and wellbeing through learning sacred texts in the Jewish Primary School, in M. De Souza, L.M. Francis, J. O'Higgins-Norman, D. Scott, (Eds.) *International Handbook of Education for Spirituality, Care and Wellbeing. International Handbooks of Religion and Education*, Dordrecht: Springer, Vol. 3, pp. 1157–1171.

Sinclair, J., and Coulthard, M. (1992) Toward an analysis of discourse, in M. Coulthard (Ed.) *Advances in Spoken Discourse Analysis*, Abingdon: Routledge.

Siraj-Blatchford, I., and Mayo, A. (2012) *International Reader Early Childhood Education*, London: SAGE.

Sole, G. (2019) Children's understanding of time: A study in a primary history curriculum, *History Education Research Journal*, 16, (1), pp. 158–173.

Stern, J. (2004) Making time: Using music to create inclusive Religious Education and inclusive schools, *Support for Learning*, 19, (3), pp. 107–113.

Stern, J. (2018) *Teaching Religious Education: Researchers in the Classroom*, London: Bloomsbury Academic. Second edition.

Taylor, T. (2016) *A Beginner's Guide to Mantle of the Expert: A Transformative Approach to Education*, Norwich: Singular Publishing.

TDA (Teacher Development Agency) (2009) *Including Pupils With SEN and/or Disabilities in Primary Religious Education*, Manchester: Training and Development Agency for Schools. TDA0626k/08.09.

Unstad, L., and Fjørtoft, H. (2021) Texts, readers, and positions: Developing a conceptual tool for teaching disciplinary reading in religious education, *Learning and Instruction*, 73, Article 101403. pp. 1–8.

Vygotsky, L. (1978) *Mind in Society*, London: Harvard University Press.

Waligur, S. A. (2020) Sacred sound in world religions: An interreligious teaching and learning experience, *Teaching Theology and Religion*, 23, pp. 49–53. [Online] https://onlinelibrary.wiley.com/doi/full/10.1111/teth.12525?campaign=wolearlyview (Accessed 02/06/2021).

Watson, B., and Thompson, P. (2007) *The Effective Teaching of Religious Education*, Harlow: Longman. Second edition.

Watson, E., and Bradley, B. (2021) *The Science of Learning: 99 Studies That Everyone Should Know*, Abingdon: Routledge. Second edition.

Webster, M. (2010) *Creative Approaches to Teaching Primary RE*, London: Longman.

Webster, M. (2015) Religious Education, in M. Webster and S. Misra (Eds.) *Teaching the Primary Foundation Subject*, Maidenhead: Open University Press, pp. 127–142.

Worley, P. (2019) *100 Ideas for Primary Teachers: Questioning*, London: Bloomsbury.

Wrenn, A., Wilkinson, A., Webb, A., Gillespie, H., Riley, M., Harnett, P., Harris, R., and Lomas, T. (2007) *Teaching Emotive and Controversial History to 3–19 Years Olds: A Report for the Historical Association*, London: The Historical Association.

RE for SEND

FOUNDATIONS

Introduction

The term inclusion features in a variety of contexts, and its history is connected with the history of concepts such as 'poverty', 'equal opportunity' and 'special educational needs' and disability. Stern (2018:75) suggests that the modern concept of inclusion encompasses poverty, social justice and equal opportunities making it a highly significant concept, as poverty would be a social issue and special educational needs and disability an educational issue for children. Thus, there are many meanings of inclusion. This chapter intends to answer the question: what contribution, if any, can Religious Education (RE) make to inclusion through its curriculum and delivery.

There has been a steady increase in the number of pupils with special education needs and disabilities (SEND) across all schools (DfE 2017; Explore Education Statistics 2021). This means that most teachers are very likely to have pupils with additional and specific individual learning needs and others will have significant special needs. In all cases, the ultimate responsibility for both groups is with the class teacher (Hunt 2018:1). As a teacher, you must rise to this challenge and provide opportunities to meet the needs of all pupils and make them appropriately demanding. RE can contribute to inclusion in its curriculum and its pedagogy (the relationship between teacher and pupils) (Stern 2018:75).

Teachers often acknowledge that when RE is delivered appropriately, pupils with SEND enjoy it and gain considerably from its content and experience. Contemporary policies on inclusion have resulted in an emphasis on ensuring that most pupils with SEND are placed in mainstream classes alongside their peers, making it common that the experience and teaching of RE to pupils with SEND will be similar to the experience and teaching of the rest. Within these multifaceted classrooms, there may also be high prior attainers, some of whom may also have SEND, e.g. Autism spectrum disorder (ASD). They too should be challenged and inspired. There are many ways open to you to ensure that RE is challenging and meaningful to all pupils in your care.

This chapter begins with conceptualising inclusion and SEND and its implications for teaching and understanding provision. Before discussing some features from SEND Code of Practice (CoP) (DfE 2015), it outlines foundational principles for RE and SEND. A section is then devoted to inclusion within RE and of all pupils in RE. Statements related to inclusion from the National Curriculum (NC) appear to show how these could be implemented. Thereafter practical suggestions to illustrate how RE can serve these pupils are offered.

DOI: 10.4324/9780429289743-16

Definitions and labels

Wearmouth (2018) has highlighted the significance of recognising the frame of reference within which pupils with SEND are understood. She posits that the frame of reference applied strongly affects how educators treat these pupils and the kind of provision that is made for them. Attaching to pupils the label of 'special educational needs and/or disability' and by referring to them as 'SEND child' or 'additional needs' reveals nothing specific enough about a pupil, so that one can start to think about what could be done to ensure access to the curriculum. As such, they should also be referred to as a 'child with SEND' to recognise individuality and that a child is more than their additional needs – whilst recognising that the use of labels can be really valuable for some parents and children as an explanation for issues. It is important then to find the solution and appropriate approach. Wearmouth (2018:1–10) notes that the label carries with it some ambiguity, as SEND covers many areas including learning, social, emotional, physical, health and sensory. Moreover, it is highly problematic and involves issues of power over decision-making.

These labels carry with them positive and negative connotations. Educators use a variety of frames of reference each implying and influencing the way one thinks about pupils with SEND and the provision to be made for them. The notion of 'need' implies a sense of kindliness. Some use the frame of reference concerned with focussing on what is 'wrong' with them and how this 'problem' can be solved. Others might relate to such pupils as their moral duty to help them with their well-being leading such people to interpret children's experience as a tragedy for the child and their family. Another frame of reference looks at the context in which learning takes place as a potential barrier. Moreover, the term 'needs' is also seen as problematic and sensitive in education. Others identify children's SEND as having a humanitarian aim so that through additional resources and by addressing particular difficulties and overcoming effects of disability, pupils can benefit from their education (Wearmouth 2018:6–9). Therefore, is it paramount that you are aware of the value-laden nature of these terms and other terms used in education as a whole and not just in the context of SEND. Hence, a somewhat different beginning is made in this chapter.

To begin with

It is common to observe many publications on SEND begin with the important CoP (DfE 2015). Instead, this chapter starts with emphasising certain values, facts and expectations before proceeding. These are intended to lay the foundations which ought to inform your thinking about SEND, your role and providing RE.

- Every pupil with SEND has the potential to achieve and benefit from RE.
- Pupils with SEND are found in different contexts and belong to diverse backgrounds.
- All teachers are teachers of pupils with SEND.
- Teachers should be aware of and be sensitive to the backgrounds and personal circumstances of their SEND pupils, as RE sometimes raises sensitive and personal issues.
- RE is a statutory part of the curriculum for pupils with SEND as well.
- Pupils with SEND can be withdrawn from RE should their parents wish to do so.
- Appropriate provisions for pupils with SEND withdrawn from RE should be made.
- RE provision for different groups with SEND should vary.
- Quality teaching involves planning your curriculum carefully for the special and specific needs of all pupils.
- Quality teaching goes beyond simplifying and reducing contents and syllabi.
- Quality learning progresses from previous learning, is coherent and sequential.

Having high expectations that all learners can improve is central to good teaching and a teacher's mindset shapes their teaching practices, which in turn can affect how pupils see themselves (Watson and Busch 2021).

RE and the SEND Code of Practice

Seeking to understand pupils' differences, including their different levels of prior knowledge and potential barriers to learning, is an essential part of teaching (DfE 2019).

Therefore, teachers must plan and provide opportunities for every pupil to achieve. The guidance from the Government about inclusion identifies certain groups who are most likely to experience exclusion and therefore they should be a priority when aiming to promote inclusion. The philosophy, principles and practices reflected in the CoP should be implemented where appropriate for RE as well. In so doing schools would not need to dis-apply a pupil from RE, unless in an exceptional situation such as a pupil with severe learning difficulties.

Specifically, RE contributes towards the SEND policy by ensuring that such pupils can develop their self-confidence and awareness and understanding of the world they live in as individuals and as members of the community. Importantly, they bring their own experiences and understanding of life into the classroom, which can enrich everyone. They learn to develop positive attitudes towards others, respecting their beliefs, feelings and experiences. They have opportunities to reflect on, and consider, their values and those of others and deal with issues that form the basis for personal choices and behaviour. RE helps pupils to understand and appreciate their world and its diversity.

Inclusion within RE

RE can support a wide range of pupil needs. RE can exploit the richness of religious and other traditions and how all those traditions have, in turn, had to meet the needs of the whole range of adherents (Stern 2018:78). Sometimes it can fall short. Nevertheless, researchers in RE have explored how RE can model and contribute to inclusion. Hull (2005) and Ipgrave (2001) were concerned with the 'deep' issues of the nature of humanity. Both of which can be related to theological theories (Stern 2018). In addition, Stern's (2018) own work on inclusion is set in the context of the philosophies about the nature of community and dialogue. He offers a few activities which could be used to analyse the curriculum and the pedagogy of RE to draw out how inclusive RE can be based on inclusive and dialogic models of RE (Stern 2018:76). As you read the models below consider the implications for designing your RE curriculum.

Inclusion of pupils

There are two other important dimensions to be considered for inclusion in education concerning RE. The potential of RE in promoting social inclusion and the opportunities presented to pupils so that they experience and feel included in RE. Of course, this implies that RE should be an inclusive subject itself.

In an ever-changing, complex, multi-cultural and multi-faith society, RE can make a significant contribution to issues of inclusion, especially when one of its core aims is the promotion of respect (Walshe 2020). Unsurprisingly, you will discern that some syllabi and school policies contain many references to the role of RE in challenging stereotypical views, tolerating beliefs, appreciating positive relationships and acknowledging differences, and tackling issues of religious discrimination, prejudice and hatred. Learning and teaching about these can be viewed from the perspectives of what religious traditions have to say as well. However, in the context of disability and RE, for instance, all pupils can consider the impact of their beliefs on their actions, attitudes, behaviour and lifestyles and learn about the response to disability from faith perspectives. You may have heard or observed teachers in schools highlight the importance of pupils' specific religions and beliefs to pupils with SEND and how RE has the potential of developing their sense of belonging. In an inclusive classroom, the confidence and self-esteem of these pupils have to be raised if they are to achieve anything like their potential (Hunt 2018:8).

Stern (2018:78) has shown research that has been concerned with RE and in meeting the range of the needs of pupils. Brown (1996), for example, researched important issues for RE including special needs and bereavement. Krisman (2001, 2008) and Beadle (2006) have written on a range of RE and special needs issues. Moreover, O'Brien (2002) conducted research relating to pupils with autism and those with severe and complex learning difficulties and Orchard (2001) studied challenging pupils aged 11–14. Hunt (2018) has offered a guide exclusively on RE and SEND.

However, it is equally significant to be aware of those who get positioned at the other end of the spectrum. It has been suggested that there are groups who may experience social exclusion which may affect their full educational participation. These include children:

- In the care of the local authorities.
- Living in poverty.
- Who have sought asylum and refuge.
- Living in areas blighted with high rates of crime.
- Suffering long-term illness.
- In one-parent families.
- Living in under-resourced wards.
- From traveller communities.
- Who have recently arrived in this country.
- Sick children, young carers, pregnant schoolgirls, teenage mothers (Ofsted 2000).

Pupil Premium would also be considered within the overall context of inclusion and disadvantage. In designing an RE curriculum for pupils from disadvantaged families it is important to remember that they are not a homogenous group. Therefore, it is important to set high challenges and plan the sequence of learning meticulously. This should manifest in an empowering and enabling environment with avoids low expectations from teachers.

Moreover, pupils should see themselves in the curriculum without regurgitation of what they already know. The curriculum should be enriched by including 'new' knowledge and concepts rather than relying entirely on common and well-known information.

English as an additional language

That said, teachers must avoid generalising and assume that pupils belonging to any of the above categories will necessarily underperform. Equally, it is important to recognise that pupils belonging to these groups are not necessarily children who will have SEND just as children who use English as an additional language will not necessarily have SEND.

The term EAL describes pupils who are in the process of learning English on entry to school. It implies that they are learning English in addition to their existing linguistic skills. Some educators feel that 'EAL learners' implies that these pupils have a weakness to surmount and argue that 'bilingual learners' is a much more positive term for pupils who are developing new language skills by building on existing strengths (Head 2017:183). Monitoring of progress should take account of the pupil's age, length of time in this country, previous educational experience and ability in other languages (DfE 2013:9). Nevertheless, some of these pupils' circumstances may require additional consideration and that some pupils may have more than one additional requirement that needs addressing.

EAL is not a singular label for any pupil who does not speak English as an additional language. The school census states that EAL can range from, 'New to English' to 'Fluent' (DfE 2018). Accordingly, you should be aware of the varying degrees of support that a pupil using EAL may require. It is also important not to confuse the understanding of a language with low ability, which is a misconception that can often become a barrier. Bower (2018) argues that teachers should respond effectively to linguistic diversity and recognise that every pupil arrives in school with useful and potentially transformative knowledge and experience. This might be pertinent in RE, as they may well have an advanced understanding of concepts in RE and have been exposed to religion/s from other sources. Thus, a pupil's bilingualism should not be problematised, rather teachers should seek ways to embrace and capitalise on linguistic diversity. Teachers also need to be mindful that the use of ability group might convey to pupils the message of a fixed mind-set.

Locally agreed syllabi and SEND

The LAS for RE set out what most pupils should be taught at each of the Key Stages and in Special schools and mainstream. Schools and teachers using them are expected to develop the knowledge, skills and understanding in ways that suit the needs of their pupils in their respective schools and settings. To provide effective learning opportunities for all pupils in RE, the statements on inclusion outlined in the NC (DfE 2013:9) are incorporated below.

Setting suitable learning challenges

Setting suitable learning challenges means to:

- Ensure that high standards in RE should be at least equal with other subjects.
- Ensure that pupils gain deep knowledge and understanding of key religious concepts.
- Select material from the programmes of study set out for earlier or later ages.
- Provide appropriate resources for all pupils.
- Plan lessons for pupils who have lower levels of prior attainment or come from disadvantaged backgrounds.
- Plan stretching work for pupils whose attainment is significantly above the expected standard.
- Use a variety of teaching strategies, taking account, wherever possible, of pupils' preferences.
- Use appropriate assessment to set targets.
- Set appropriate targets which are deliberately ambitious.
- Be aware of the pace at which pupils work.
- Be aware of the physical and mental effort required for the work.
- Balance consistency and challenge, according to individual needs.

Responding to pupils' diverse learning needs and overcoming potential barriers to learning and assessment for individuals and groups of pupils

Practitioners and teachers must take account of the diversity represented in their classes, including social and cultural backgrounds, different ethnic groups, linguistic and religious backgrounds and worldviews. The varied and complex experiences, interests and strengths that pupils bring are particularly relevant in RE.

You will need to take the diverse religious backgrounds and worldviews into account and respect the religious beliefs and practices of families and pupils. However, as emphasised earlier, teachers, parents and their children must recognise that it is the responsibility of the family to nurture their children in their own beliefs, lifestyles and values. In a state school, however, RE provides an opportunity for pupils with SEND to learn about a range of beliefs, practices and ways of life.

In RE you will need to take specific actions to respond to pupils' diverse needs by:

- Recognising that some pupils will need access to specialist equipment and different approaches.
- Planning lessons to ensure that there are no barriers to every pupil achieving.
- Creating diverse and enabling learning environments.
- Securing pupil motivation and concentration.
- Providing equality of opportunity through teaching approaches.
- Using appropriate assessment approaches and setting targets for learning.
- Allowing access to practical activities within and beyond the school.
- Catering in all areas and resources of the school for pupils with a variety of learning difficulties.

To make RE lessons inclusive, you will need to anticipate the barriers to taking part and learning that exist and the potential areas of difficulty, which should be addressed at the outset of work. You will then consider the ways of minimising or reducing those barriers in your planning, resources, activities and support so that they can fully take part and learn.

To overcome potential barriers to learning in RE, some pupils may require the following:

- Support to access texts, such as prepared audio-visual material and ICT support programmes, especially when there may be significant quantities of written materials or working at a faster pace.
- Assistance in tasks that require extended writing to communicate their detailed ideas by using video and audio recordings to allow them to demonstrate their understanding and to maintain their concentration and motivation.
- Non-visual means to acquire and access information when researching by using audio materials.
- Non-aural means of expression to communicate ideas and responses by using computers, technological aids, artwork, signing or lip reading.
- Non-sighted methods of reading through Braille.
- Providing support from adults or other pupils when necessary.
- Using specialist aids and equipment.
- Allowing pupils the space, time and freedom to develop skills for themselves.

The above statements provide effective learning opportunities for all pupils. In addition to these specific overarching principles, some general guidelines are offered below.

PROVISIONS

RE in the service of pupils with SEND

The nature of RE is such that it should be accessible and responsive to every pupil. It is expected that all pupils in special schools and pupils with special educational needs, learning difficulties, disabilities and additional physical needs, behaviour challenges and those who with high prior attainment are in mainstream schools receive RE as far as is practicable following an appropriate and modified syllabus or programmes of study based on their circumstances and contexts. For successful inclusion, RE must be taught through a lively, imaginative and inspiring RE curriculum. It is more profitable for it to begin with, build on and be informed by the rich and differing experiences which these pupils themselves bring to RE lessons. Moreover, for effective inclusion, it is essential that a flexible RE curriculum is designed which provides opportunities for appropriate challenge and responds to the complex, diverse and personal needs of pupils in a class and is ambitious.

Pupils with SEND have a lifeworld and life experiences of their own, aspects of which they may share with their peers. As a practitioner, your work with them should complement the diverse experiences brought to RE by the pupils themselves. It should be based on setting suitable learning challenges, responding to pupils' diverse needs and overcoming potential barriers as outlined above. It should enable all pupils to fulfil their potential through incorporating a wide range of teaching methods. Whatever the needs are of the pupils it is important to remember that the activities, resources and areas of study are suitable and appropriate. Pupils with SEND benefit from opportunities, which enable them to reflect on their life experiences with concrete examples, and questions that have personal resonance. Every child with SEND is different. Therefore, a personalised curriculum and an understanding of their learning and progress in non-linear ways is required. Pedagogically consolidation, repetition, rehearsing, scaffolding, modelling and support must be embedded within their curriculum.

Ambitious curriculum

The culture of high expectations and ambition characterises the teaching profession (Hewitt and Wright 2019). The school inspection handbook states that inspectors will judge the quality of education by considering the extent to which its sets out the knowledge and skills that pupils will gain at each stage. An important element within this is the repeated reference to 'ambition' and the extent to which a school's curriculum is ambitious for everyone. The school should not offer disadvantaged pupils or pupils with SEND a reduced curriculum. This means that pupils with lower starting points should not be offered reductive content in RE, instead, they should be provided with appropriately demanding work and the teacher should plan for appropriate scaffolding and support (Myatt 2018). Pupils with learning difficulties do not want to be patronised with too simple and easy tasks. Pupils must be supported with, for example, writing frames and clear examples. They need tasks adapted to their own needs, rather than forcing them into tasks that may be too abstract, complex or demanding. Meeting real people and hearing their views and visiting places of worship, etc. will help pupils to make RE concepts concrete.

Scaffolding

You need to know that pupils are likely to learn at different rates and to require different levels and types of support from teachers to succeed. Also, that adapting teaching in a responsive way, including by providing targeted support to pupils who are struggling, is likely to increase pupil success and that it is less likely to be valuable if it causes the teacher to artificially create distinct tasks for different groups of pupils or to set lower expectations for particular pupils. Importantly, pupils with SEND are likely to require additional or adapted support, so working closely with all those involved to understand barriers and identify effective strategies is essential (DfE 2019).

Differentiation is sometimes thought of as providing different tasks and activities for different groups of children. The CoP makes it very clear that differentiation is an expectation in that high quality teaching that is differentiated and personalised will meet the individual needs of the majority of children and young people (DfE 2015). Some of the RE activities may be based on writing, for example, a letter, story or recount. The differentiation tends to be about supporting a child's writing within a genre rather than the child's understanding of religion or a religious concept. Hence the learning of the child who finds writing difficult can be reduced, as the task becomes a barrier to accessing creativity and understanding (Webster 2010). This conception and practice of differentiation would be considered narrow and limited. To develop Personalised Learning and Thinking Skills (PLTS), Webster (2010) invites teachers to think creatively about differentiation. This means dividing a class into groups that suit the activity that has been planned and support the child's learning in RE (Webster 2010:107).

Gray (2018) proposed a mnemonic to represent widely used routes to differentiation to meet the needs of pupils with SEND, rather than occupying them on tasks. These are liked to seven frequently identified features of outstanding teaching. *MR CHUFFI*, as shown in Table 12.1, delineates a teaching and learning agenda derived from a mixed pedagogical approach, designed to promote the intellectual depth, challenge, curiosity, self-awareness and resilience so apparent in models of excellent teaching practice (Gray 2018:69). It looks to ensure that pupils with SEND do not get trapped at the lower levels of Bloom's Taxonomy but are encouraged to attempt evaluative, creative and analytical tasks.

Thus, pupils with SEND should have more independent opportunities and be encouraged to take risks to ensure their needs are not a barrier to their learning. To lead on differentiation to ensure high-quality teaching and learning experiences for pupils with SpLD and SEND, Gray (2018:71) offers another acronym, DR GOPTA, indicating seven known routes into differentiation, as shown in Table 12.1. In this second framework, differentiation and meeting the needs of pupils are led by the teacher for all children. In any case, you also need to know that adaptive teaching is less likely to be valuable if it causes teachers to create artificially distinct tasks for different groups of pupils or to set lower expectations for particular pupils, and so, you should discuss and analyse with expert colleagues how they decide whether intervening within lessons with individuals and small groups would be more efficient and effective than planning different lessons for different groups of pupils (DfE 2019).

Mastery learning

Mastery of learning is thought of as being advanced performance above expectations or particular teaching and learning strategy, whereby topics are broken down into small units to provide a logical sequence of learning, and depth of understanding is more important than the speed of learning (Harris and Lowe 2018:111). The *Final Report of the Commission of Assessment without Levels* explains that mastery is something that every child can aspire to, and every teacher should promote. It is concerned with deep, secure learning for all, with extension for more able students rather than acceleration (DfE 2015:17). In contrast to differentiation, the assumption here is that every pupil can learn the same content so long as there is appropriate scaffolding and support. Pupils who are working below the level of the rest of the class are supported with intervention strategies, and pupils working above are given tasks that deepen and extend learning rather than moving onto something new (Harris and Lowe 2018:112).

Table 12.1 MR CHUFFI and DR GOPTA	
MR CHUFFI	**DR GOPTA**
Making links	Dialogue
Risk-taking	Resources
Cognitive engagement	Group
Higher-level thinking	Outcome
Checking Understanding	Pace
Frequent Feedback	Task
Fostering Independence	Assessment

Pre-teaching

Pre-teaching can be beneficial for many children with SEND. It involves teaching key knowledge which you intend to cover in future lessons. It develops their knowledge, understanding and familiarity of the foundational vocabulary, concepts and skills. It can support pupils with SEND to participate with greater confidence and better engagement. It is also a way of addressing a potential barrier which holds some pupils from engaging and understanding.

The natural world

A very valuable resource for the teacher of RE is the natural world outside the classroom. Pupils could sometimes explore smells, shapes and textures or to lie down on their backs, if appropriate, and listen to sounds such as a leaf falling, the wind in the trees or a bird singing. Thereafter inviting them to reflect and then talk about the experience. Activities of this kind in RE may be criticised, as they are perceived to offer little in the way of overt learning about religion. Hunt (2018:30–31), accedes to this criticism if the pupils were only to stare at the grass and nothing else happened. However, he maintains that reflections and sharing of responses are essential as the purpose of these activities is to bring pupils closer to the original experiences which probably gave rise to religious impulses in the first place. By doing so, pupils may gain a much greater understanding of the questions and feelings, which form the basis of religious faith.

Children with complex needs have personalities which are to be appreciated in their choices, sounds and movements, however limited these may be. It is not to wait for them to develop personalities to become real people rather they already are in possessions of their personalities. Pupils can roll in a field of long grass; sit on the back of a donkey or pony, splash in a muddy puddle. They can make snowballs, sit still and listen out in the woods or beach, smell flowers and herbs, watch animals/insects move freely, explore shadows, grow and taste fruit and vegetables, observe new life emerging, e.g. chicks, lambs, butterflies and explore ice and observing fire (Longhorn 2019). Pupils with profound and multiple learning difficulties will tend to follow a personalised curriculum based on their individual needs. You will need to tap into this and align it with RE teaching.

Storyboarding

Some pupils with learning difficulties can find it easier to retrieve the details of a story using visual memory based on storyboarding. Hunt (2018:18–19) suggests that teachers do need to avoid becoming too preoccupied with the accuracy with which pupils can recall a religious story. Religious stories are important. However, to him, being able to accurately recall them is of secondary importance compared with having an insight into the messages they have for everyone, or how they may be widely understood by members of the faith for which the stories are of special significance, or how a story may inform our own lives regardless of whether one has a religious faith or not.

Mime and actions

Mimes are used to portray a character, mood, idea or narration by gestures and bodily movements. Some pupils may be hesitant; it may be challenging for some pupils to engage with, e.g. pupils with ASD or might not offer a description of worship and rituals. Mime can help pupils show that they have a body memory of rituals, ceremonies and festivals which is not easily available to them in language. The pupils are given some planning or research time. They then mime the ritual. The rest of the pupils, perhaps provided with a list of choices, guess what ritual is being mimed (Hunt 2018:33).

Religious and spiritual art

Visual images are a powerful medium for RE, especially religious art. Pupils with SEND should be encouraged to study, observe and compare religious and spiritual art. Pupils should ask questions such as 'What is the artist trying to say?' and 'What beliefs is the artist trying to express?' Pupils who may have difficulty with reading and writing can often show a shrewd ability to read an image (Hunt 2018:19).

Sensory experiences

Many pupils with SEND tend to respond positively to sensory experiences, although this can be challenging for pupils with some specific SEND, e.g. ASD. The use of the senses motivates pupils and adds meaning and context to the words making it easier for them to understand. This might include, for example, burning incense sticks when teaching about Hindu puja, whilst ensuring that pupils with asthma are at sufficient distance (McCreery, Palmer and Voiels 2008:24). Plan RE lessons incorporating useful resources such as artefacts and concrete materials through which they can develop their understanding of beliefs, lifestyles, rituals and rites, stories, festivals and celebrations, signs and symbols. Most of these topics provide considerable opportunities for imaginative and creative expressions. As you plan your RE lessons take account of their individual needs by using their pupil profiles and their education, health and care plan (EHCP) and consider their goals and recommendations. This carefully planned work should highlight key areas to be covered and achievable and ambitious steps forward be incorporated.

Quality teaching and learning for all pupils, especially those with SEND, take advantage of multi-sensory strategies and resources based on sight, sound, smell, taste or touch through music, food, light, incense and plants in a sensory garden (Longhorn 2019). These physical, visual and tactile stimuli engage pupils' active participation and response in RE lessons. They may also benefit in minimising the risk of disaffection and assists in the re-integration of pupils with challenging circumstances. Dance, drama and performance should be organised to give personal experiences. Hunt (2018:20) suggests the use of implicit religious images as many pupils have little experience of organised religion.

A conceptual framework is required for pupils with SEND when they are offered sensory opportunities, scaffolding or when adapting the contents of an RE curriculum at a Key Stage below their actual age. The context in such work is important as discussed in Box 12.1.

More than targeted teaching

For some pupils with SEND, repetition might be indispensable and a strategic element of their learning. However, in as much as this could be used for targeted learning, as a teacher, it is

---

BOX 12.1 THE NEED FOR CONTEXTS

It is common for teachers in special schools to attempt wide and varied sensory elements within RE. A Judaism theme could involve spinning a dreidel, touching or eating matzah and wearing a kippah. These disparate experiences, whilst offering positive sensory opportunities, do not truly extend understanding of what it means to be a believer in a particular religion, because they are out of context. Some teachers overlap Personal Social and Health Education 'caring, loving and sharing' activities into special needs RE, missing out on the distinctive elements of RE as a subject and the opportunities for spiritual development and the growth in skills that it offers (Krisman 2013).

Source: https://www.reonline.org.uk/2013/02/01/keys-into-re-anne-krisman/

---

important to ensure that such pupils encounter and are offered alternative methods and approaches of teaching. Exposing pupils to first-hand experience such as meeting visitors, visiting religious buildings and joining in celebrating festivals and special times are significant. Teachers involved in research took a group of 9–11-year-olds from a special school to a mandir. Based on their findings, Stern (2018:81) suggested that engaging and experiential learning enabled them to work at higher levels and meet their needs. Therefore, taking recourse to and using pupil's own experiences of life such as their outdoor experiences, family and communal events, their sharing and caring acts and their feelings are essential aspects of effective and successful RE which contributes to their holistic learning and provide opportunities for developing whole personalities including SMSC. In other words, adapting teaching in a responsive way, including by providing targeted support to pupils who are struggling, is likely to increase pupil success (DfE 2019). Whilst taking into account those pupils who might need any additional support or preparation for changes in routine, new experiences and teaching approaches that are different from typical routines.

Literacy

RE teaching will utilise a wide range of literacy skills. Pupils with SEND can be helped with demonstrating the writing process, joining in composing a shared poem on Eid, supported with writing about a visit to the Gurdwara, helped to generate ideas using thought showers, mind-maps and visualising about birthdays or weddings. They can write a play for Christmas. Design a new cover for a scripture. Identify keywords that are important to them in a religious text. They can make up a song or rap about a celebration. They can select important events in Diwali and convert them into comic strips. They can describe the main characters in the story of Moses or write a thank you letter to a charity. They can talk about pilgrimages, journeys or create a timeline using pictures to explain the order of events in their life and label them.

Teamwork for RE

The CoP explains that local authorities (LAs) must ensure that children, their parents and young people are involved in discussions and decisions about their individual support and local provision (DfE 2015). For teachers in school, this might mean that pupils are also provided with an entitlement to participate safely, in clothing and to adorn artefacts and symbols appropriate to their religious beliefs, within the context of the school policy.

Some pupils may need provisions to be made from the content taught earlier or in later years. These adaptations can be made in consultation with subject leaders, where available or with senior leaders as it can enable individual pupils to progress further. After the adaptation, the content should be presented in contexts and ways suitable to the age of the pupil. To provide continuity and sequence resulting from such changes it would be necessary to communicate this to relevant teachers.

Pupils with learning difficulties can benefit from a caring, respectful and encouraging teacher who values and celebrates their efforts and treats them with dignity. Individual help and focussed support are indispensable to indicate high expectations held for each pupil. Organisationally, they should experience appropriate group work and collaborative learning, practical and oral work with additional resources and time to respond to questions and various stimuli. The classroom environment should be positive consisting of continual encouragement, praise and recognition. Concerning assessment, pupils with SEND will not always meet the same expectations in RE as other pupils. Therefore, appropriate assessments need to be used.

Three-dimensional resources

Objects, artefacts, images promote questioning, reflection and stimulate discussion. The following account in Box 12.2 captures their potential in RE.

BOX 12.2 CASE STUDY: THE POWER OF ARTEFACTS

Arranging the pupils into a circle and placing in the centre of the circle a single object, like an acorn, an expensive cosmetic, a vase of decaying flowers, a fashionable smartphone, a pair of designer-label trainers, can serve as a stimulus to lively discussion. Pupils who sometimes hardly ever speak are suddenly revealed as informed students of globalisation, the power of the media (including social media), materialism, spirituality, human happiness, death and decay. A religious artefact can similarly be used as a stimulus. A quality artefact, for example a Shiva Nata-raja, a crucifix or an image of a laughing Buddha, can provide the prompt for a discussion on what God is like, the purpose of prayer, the role of sacrifice and perhaps in what sense the word salvation might be used (Hunt 2018:20).

Music and sound

Some pupils are particularly responsive to sound and auditory stimuli. The strong association between music and particular religions can be used to establish a memorable theme. Hunt (2018) exemplifies some of these. A teacher might play the song 'To Life' from Fiddler on the Roof as the pupils enter a classroom. This can set the theme of the lesson, which is about the joyous way in which many Jewish festivals like Purim and Simchat Torah are celebrated. In addition, the harmonium and tabla may be used to mark the beginning of a lesson about Sikh worship. Mood music may also be used which has no particular religious associations but may set the appropriate mood to reinforce the lesson. In essence, Hunt (2018:25) posits that the more teachers can make lessons exceptional or different and take pupils by surprise the greater are the chances that learning will take place.

Autism spectrum condition

RE will often have abstract and symbolic concepts which need to be taught to all pupils, including those with autism spectrum condition (ASC), some of whom will be more attuned with the concrete and literate. As discussed above each pupil with SEND is an individual with a personal experience of life, individual need, strengths and personality. Pupils with ASC will have social communication difficulties, language communication difficulties and higher levels of anxiety. They tend to respond particularly well to sensory experiences.

In the classroom

The sequence of the lesson can be shown through a visual timeline. Making your teaching visual will be helpful. This might include using religious artefacts, video clips and images as these support communications without language. You can also use diagrams, tables and charts to show similarities and differences between religions.

Debate, dialogue and discussion are frequently used in RE. For this, pupils with ASC should be addressed by their name to maximise their attention and contributions. They can be provided with sentence frames so that they complete the sentences. Pupils with ASC generally have a specific area of interest. It is for you to tap into these interests and link it to what you are teaching them. Before teaching them a lesson or at the beginning of the topic show them the 'big map' and how the sequence of lessons fits into this 'big map'. In Chapter 11 many strategies have been suggested based on sensory learning where the use of touch, taste, smell and planning of experiential lessons appeared. These are particularly powerful for pupils with ASC as they have a heightened sensitivity to such experiences.

RE in special schools

Pupils in special schools are referred to in the Education Act 1996. It stated that all pupils attending a special school will, so far as is practicable, receive RE unless a child's parents have expressed a wish to the contrary. Therefore, it is for schools to decide what is practicable. In other words, practicability is related to the special educational needs of the pupils and not to the problems of staffing, resources or premises. Pupil's EHCP should be used when making decisions about methodology and content (Richmond 2020).

RE for pupils with Complex Learning Difficulties and Disabilities

■ It begins from the unique individuality of the pupils and provides rich experiences of religion and spirituality.

■ Calm and peaceful space in RE can enable learners to enjoy their RE time individually.

■ It enables pupils with the most complex of needs to develop an awareness of themselves, their feelings, their emotions and their senses.

RE for pupils with Severe Learning Difficulties

■ Multi-sensory approaches bring the possibility of introducing spiritual experiences.

■ It contributes to pupils' social development through story, music, shared experience and ritual.

■ It enables pupils to develop their relationships with other people and their understanding of other people's needs.

RE for pupils with Moderate Learning Difficulties

■ It provides insight into the world of religion and human experience, especially when tough questions are considered.

■ It provides opportunities for pupils to participate in a spiritual or reflective activity.

■ It enables pupils to make links with their own lives.

For pupils with Behavioural Emotional and Social Difficulties

■ It enables pupils to address deep issues of concern in helpful ways through exploring spiritual material and seeing how others have tackled difficult experiences.

■ RE lessons can explore, in the safe space schools should provide, complex emotions or thoughts, and challenging questions.

■ RE assists in the development of pupils' maturity and self-awareness (RE Today 2019:90).

Planning for RE in special schools

To reiterate, pupils in special schools have complex and personal needs which cannot be met within a mainstream setting. Given these needs in special schools, it is therefore important to avoid a 'deficit model' of planning, where the syllabus is watered down, adapting a few units of work, or teaching units for 4–6-year-olds to 7–11s or 11–14s (Manchester 2016). RE in Special schools should explore authentic and central concepts from religions, based on what will connect with pupils' experiences and enable them to respond.

The 'Five Keys' planning model

One of the recommended models devised by Krisman, who advocates five keys for planning in RE for SEND, is shown in Table 12.2. This profound approach enables teachers to use it as a source of information for religious themes and concepts and then to plan RE so that pupils can explore and respond. It promotes their personal development by making connections with core religious concepts and their own experiences. The model below explores 'What does it mean to be a Muslim?' with a focus on Eid ul-Fitr and Ramadan (Manchester 2016:31–32).

Table 12.2 The 'Five Keys' planning model

Key	Focus	Activities
1. Connection *What links can we make with our pupils' lives?* [Creating a bridge between pupils' experiences and the religious theme]	What times are special to us? What food do we like to eat? What does the moon look like?	• Create pictures of pupils with speech bubbles saying what times are special to them, e.g. birthdays, Christmas, holidays. • Ask each other what food they like to eat and tell the class what they have found out. • Look at different pictures of the moon, e.g. surface, crescent, full.
2. Knowledge *What is at the burning core of the religion?* [Selecting what really matters in a religious theme, cutting out peripheral information]	Muslims give up food (fast) during daylight hours during Ramadan. It makes them think of poor people and they give charity (zakat). When the new moon comes, it is Eid-ul-Fitr and they celebrate.	• Act out getting up early in the morning to an alarm, eating, saying no to food, feeling hungry but happy, going home, looking for stars in a sky, eating a date. • Look at pictures of poor people and say how you know they are poor. Make a charity box with the moon and stars on it. • Read Ramadan Moon and talk about what the family does for Ramadan and Eid.
3. Senses *What sensory elements are in the religion?* [Looking for a range of authentic sensory experiences that link with the theme]	Eating of dates to end fast (iftaar). The prayer mat. Listening to Arabic prayers. Washing (wudu).	• Experience eating dates and Indian sweets. • Feel different prayer mats whilst listening to Islamic prayers. Watch a film of children praying. • Show how you wash hands. • Watch a film of children doing wudu before they pray.
4. Symbols *What are the symbols that are the most accessible?* [Choosing symbols that will encapsulate the theme]	The moon and the stars. Word 'Allah'. Word 'Muhammad'.	• Create moon pictures out of silver paper, add them onto Arabic prayers (see Ramadan Moon). • Recognise the words Allah and Muhammad and say how special they are to Muslims. • Create pictures using stencils of the words 'Allah' and 'Muhammad' in Arabic, adding gold and making them look beautiful, whilst listening to nasheeds (devotional songs)
5. Values *What are the values in the religion that speak to us?* [Making links between the values of the religious theme and the children's lives]	Doing things that are hard. Thinking of poor people. Giving to charity (zakat). Being with family.	• Try to complete something that is hard, e.g. a jigsaw puzzle and everyone says well done. • Make a collection around the school or make something to sell for charity, e.g. ice cream or cakes. • Make 3D dolls of happy Muslim families in traditional clothes.

RE for pupils with special needs

Performance descriptors (P levels) have largely been phased out now with different Special schools deciding upon assessment schemes/approaches that are best for them. There are two examples based on Krisman's approach readily available, with supporting material on *Why is the prophet Muhammad inspirational to Muslims?* and the other relates to why was Moses a special leader. These are found at https://www.reonline.org.uk/?s=krisman

RE in the service of pupils with high prior attainment

Education is a devolved issue, and how students are identified, described and supported differs across the UK. In England, there is no national definition of 'more able' or 'gifted' students. Pupil Premium funds allow schools to provide support to highly achieving students, including those from disadvantaged backgrounds. Reports have argued that Ofsted should strengthen its inspection of provision for disadvantaged highly-able students (Loft and Danechi 2020:3). Though these terms are no longer used officially, RE should be seen as one of the core subjects where these pupils can thrive and be challenged further. It is important to recognise that being 'gifted' in RE is not equivalent to being religiously gifted. Kendall and Allcock (2020:13) express concern that 'High attainers' has replaced the term 'gifted' and the latter is ignored. It has been noted that pupils with high prior attainment often do not achieve up to their full potential. In a study of 891 primary school pupils views on desired characteristics of good teachers Bakx, Houtert, van de Brand and Hornstra (2019:49–50) found that the need for relatedness by both high-ability and regular-ability pupils mentioned most often (49–50), competence support was also mentioned regularly and autonomy support was mentioned far less frequently. Earlier mention was made about the important role that mindsets play in the achievement of learners. Those holding more of a growth mindset consistently outperform those who do not, this has been found at every social economical level (Claro, Pauneskub and Dweck 2016).

Anecdotal documents and information provided by schools show that pupils with high prior attainment and talented pupils in RE are identified by some teachers as those demonstrating higher 'levels of insight into and discernment beyond, the obvious and ordinary'. They are 'sensitive to, or aware of, the mysteries of life and have a feeling for how these are explored and expressed'. They 'understand, apply and transfer ideas and concepts across topics in RE and into other religious and cultural contexts'. They are likely to be 'interested in work that exercises thinking skills, philosophical debate and enquiry-based learning, and the examination of topical issues'.

Some talented pupils in RE tend to be eager to ask challenging questions and have a 'heightened spiritual awareness' and 'may also have a strong creative side and flourish when encountering different forms of religious expression'. They may also be eloquent and contribute regularly with profound insight to the discussion.

To meet their expectations, they should be appropriately challenged by the following:

- Using a wider range of deeper questions to explore religious beliefs and phenomena.
- Focussing on the independence of mind and thoughtfulness.
- Setting extension tasks to promote greater depth of knowledge and understanding.
- Attending to complex interpretations of symbol, metaphor and text and how these promote reflection on hidden and apparent meanings and discernment.
- Using appropriate terminology and language needed to grasp complex religious, spiritual and philosophical material and concepts.
- Make greater use of open-ended questions allowing for different responses.
- Developing more opportunities both for independent and collaborative learning.
- Encouraging them to make connections between their work in RE and other subjects.

Some of the elements among some of these pupils indicate they move beyond everyday inter-actions. In RE, their higher level of emotional engagement and deeper spiritual involvement may be discerned. They offer inspiration from the thoughts, actions and ideas of others. They may show the originality of thoughts and meaning with the occasional moment of brilliance. Their outputs and products might exhibit something unique. Nevertheless, some might display socially awkward behaviours, be avid readers and get engrossed in problem-solving which shows that learning can be frustratingly messy (Peacock 2020:55).

Summary

This chapter has stressed the importance of making provisions for pupils with SEND in mainstream schools, in Specialist units and pupils in Special schools as far as is practicable. It has emphasised that you should have high ambitions for all. The quality of teaching is the most important factor in improving outcomes for pupils particularly from disadvan-taged backgrounds and those with additional needs. It is about giving access to intellectually demanding content for pupils whose learning is below age-related expectations and high prior attainment pupils (Box 12.3).

BOX 12.3 VIGNETTE: SEND

I come from a big family. I am half-Irish. I have been brought up as a Catholic which has influenced my interest in RE as I have been intrigued to explore how other religions differ from Catholicism. Therefore, I chose to study Philosophy, Ethics and Religion, which allowed me to learn about different world religions that are not as well known in society, whilst also learning about different philosophers.

I preferred the route of studying for a BA degree before the PGCE route. I should study one degree in greater depth, which then helped me to pick RE as my specialism. In addition, this degree has given me the foundations to teach because it has taught me how religious beliefs shape and influence the world we live in.

During primary school, I experienced difficulties with mathematics as I now think I suffered from maths anxiety. I hope to be able to help children when they struggle by supporting their needs. I feel it is important to be a positive and friendly teacher as this helps to build a relationship with all pupils.

As I enjoyed RE at the undergraduate level, I chose this as my specialism. I have been planning RE lessons with the RE leader. I delivered an RE lesson. I am comfortable teaching this subject as I feel my degree has given me good foundations to do this.

RE is regarded as quite important by my friends and family. I have a mixture of religious and non-religious friends, which has been quite interesting to see how their views differ from mine. I am hoping to build on my RE knowledge and become more confident in teaching RE by learning what pedagogies suit this subject.

A reservation that I have is how to adapt this subject to those who have SEND needs, as I have not seen first-hand in my placement school. This means that I will have to work closely with the class that I am teaching to assess who needs this extra support and how to meet their needs.

In my placement school, RE was a priority as it was a Church of England school. RE is taught once a week to all pupils. The other year 3 teacher is the RE lead which I have found extremely useful, as she has been able to support me in teaching RE and what the expectations are within this subject.

References

Bakx, A., Houtert, T. V., van de Brand, M., and Hornstra, L. (2019) A comparison of high-ability pupils' views vs. regular ability pupils' views of characteristics of good primary school teachers, *Educational Studies*, 45, (1), pp. 35–56.

Beadle, L. (Ed.) (2006) *Steps in RE Onwards and Upwards: Addressing the Additional Support Needs of Students in Key Stage 3 (11–14 Years Olds)*, Birmingham: RE Today Services.

Bower, V. (2018) Promoting a bilingual approach in the primary classroom, in V. Bower (Ed.) *Debates in Primary Education*, Abingdon: Routledge, pp. 142–156.

Brown, E. (1996) *Religious Education for All*, London: David Fulton.

Claro, S., Pauneskub, D., and Dweck, C. (2016) Growth mindset tempers the effects of poverty on academic achievement, *PNAS*, 113, (31) 8664–8668, [online] http://web.stanford.edu/~paunesku/articles/claro_2016.pdf (Accessed 12/12/2021).

DfE (2013) *The National Curriculum in England*, London: Crown Copyright. Ref: DFE-00177-2013.

DfE (2015) *Special Educational Needs and Disability Code of Practice: 0 to 25 Years*, Crown Copyright. Ref: DFE-00205-2013.

DfE (2017) *Special Educational Needs in England: January 2017*, [Online] https://assets.publishing.service.gov.uk/government/uploads/system/uploads/attachment_data/file/633031/SFR37_2017_Main_Text.pdf (Accessed 06/04/2021).

DfE (2018) *School Census: Proficiency in English* [pdf], London: Department for Education. [Online] https://ealresources.bellfoundation.org.uk/sites/default/files/document-files/DfE%20school%20census%20proficiency%20in%20English%20scale.pdf (Accessed 5/01/2020).

DfE (2019) *ITT Core Content Framework*, London: Crown Copyright. Ref: DfE-00230-2019.

Explore Education Statistics (2021) *Academic Year 2020/21 Special Educational Needs in England*, [Online] https://explore-education-statistics.service.gov.uk/find-statistics/special-educational-needs-in-england#dataDownloads-1 (Accessed 24/08/2021).

Gray, A. (2018) *Effective Differentiation: A Training Guide to Empower Teachers and Enable Learners With SEND and Specific Learning Difficulties*, Abingdon: Routledge.

Harris, K., and Lowe, S. (2018) Assessment, in H. Cooper and S. Elton-Chalcraft (Eds.) *Professional Studies in Primary Education*, London: SAGE, pp. 95–120.

Head, C. (2017) Learning and teaching in a multilingual classroom, in D. Waugh and W. Jolliffe, *English 5–11: A Guide for Teachers*, Abingdon: Routledge, pp. 181–193. Third edition.

Hewitt, D., and Wright, B. (2019) *Engaging, Motivating and Empowering*, London: SAGE.

Hull, J. M. (2005) Religious Education in Germany and England: The recent work of Hans-Georg Zieberts, *British Journal of Religious Education*, 27, (1), pp. 5–17.

Hunt, D. (2018) *Addressing Special Educational Needs and Disability in the Curriculum: Religious Education*, Abingdon: Routledge. Second edition.

Ipgrave, J. (2001) *Pupil-to-Pupil Dialogue in the Classroom as a Tool for Religious Education: Warwick Religions and Education Research Unit Occasional Paper 11*, Coventry: WRERU.

Kendall, L., and Allcock, C. (2020) *A Brilliant IQ: Gift or Challenge?*, Dunstable: Brilliant.

Krisman, A. (2001) 'The Yin and Yang' of RE and special needs: Teaching RE to pupils with special needs within a multi-faith community, *SHAP: World Religions in Education: 2000/2001, Living Community*, pp. 83–84.

Krisman, A. (2008) *Growing in RE: Teaching RE in Special Schools*, Birmingham: RE Today Services. [Online] https://shop.natre.org.uk/pdfs/growing_in_RE_final.pdf (Accessed 05/08/2021).

Krisman, A. (2013) *A New Inclusive Way of Planning for Teachers of RE in Special Schools*, [Online] https://www.reonline.org.uk/2013/02/01/keys-into-re-anne-krisman/ (Accessed 06/04/2021).

Loft, P., and Danechi, S. (2020) *Support for More Able and Talented Children in Schools (UK)*, London: House of Commons, Briefing Paper Number 9065. [Online] https://researchbriefings.files. parliament.uk/documents/CBP-9065/CBP-9065.pdf (Accessed 05/08/2021).

Longhorn, F. (2019) *Religious Education for Very Special Children*, Bedfordshire: Flo Publications. *Text updated and revised January 2019.*

Manchester (2016) *Religious Literacy from All: The Agreed Syllabus for Religious Education 2016–2021*, [Online] file:///C:/Users/id105124/Downloads/Manchester_Agreed_Syllabus_abridged%20 (4).pdf (Accessed 06/08/2021).

McCreery, E., Palmer, S., and Voiels, V. (2008) *Teaching Religious Education*, Exeter: Learning Matters.

Myatt, M. (2018) *The Curriculum: Gallimaufry to Coherence*, Melton: John Catt.

O'Brien, L. (2002) *Connecting With RE*, London: National Society.

Orchard, J. (2001) *Raising the Standard, Flying the Flag – Challenging Activities for All in RE at Key Stage 3*, London: National Society.

Ofsted (2000) *Evaluating Educational Inclusion: Guidance for Inspectors and Schools*, London: Stationery Office.

Peacock, A. (2020) Swimming against the tide: Assessment of learning in one primary school, in S. Donarski (Ed.) *The ResearchED Guide to Assessment*, Melton: John Catt, pp. 49–58.

RE Today (2019) *Derbyshire and Derby City Agreed Syllabus for Religious Education 2020–2025*, Birmingham: RE Today Services.

Richmond (2020) *Agreed Syllabus for Religious Education 2020*, London Borough of Richmond upon Thames.

Stern, J. (2018) *Teaching Religious Education: Researchers in the Classroom*, London: Bloomsbury Academic. Second edition.

Walshe, K. (2020) Seeing, grasping and constructing: Pre-service teachers' metaphors for 'understanding' in Religious Education, *British Journal of Religious Education*, 42, (4), pp. 471–489.

Watson, E., and Busch, B. (2021) *The Science of Learning: 99 Studies That Every Teacher Needs to Know*, Abingdon: Routledge. Second edition.

Wearmouth, J. (2018) *Special Educational Needs and Disability: The Basics*, London: Routledge. Third edition.

Webster, M. (2010) *Creative Approaches to Teaching Primary RE*, London: Longman.

13

Assessment and progression

FOUNDATIONS

Introduction

Assessment is a prominent feature of education policy and practice. The Teachers' Standards require teachers to make accurate and productive use of assessment. Teachers must know and understand how to assess the relevant subject and curriculum areas and make use of formative and summative assessment to secure pupils' progress. They must use relevant data to monitor progress, set targets and plan subsequent lessons. Importantly, they must give pupils regular feedback, both orally and through accurate marking, and encourage pupils to respond to the feedback (DfE 2021). Therefore, it is imperative not to isolate assessment from the totality of teaching (Carroll and Alexander 2020). However, making it work is a challenge. Teachers have identified marking, planning and data management as the three biggest challenges that they face, and, therefore there is a moral duty for teachers and leaders alike to reflect upon the efficacy of different assessment approaches (Atherton 2018:4).

Schools are required to assess pupils' attainment and progress in Religious Education (RE). Assessment is essential in what is generally understood to be good educational practice and, there is general agreement, that pupils' achievement in RE must be assessed at every key stage. Second, assessment is important in tracking the learning journey of all pupils. A third point, which is also widely understood, is that assessment in RE must include two main aims (i) knowledge and understanding and (ii) skills development relevant to RE. In addition, a key part of RE is that it should celebrate and praise pupils' positive attitudes to study.

Moreover, it is important to acknowledge that pupils, teachers and carers all carry worries about assessments and making judgments. It is also worth recognising that pupils and teachers take assessments personally (Donarski 2020). Therefore, assessment is a process of judgment. It is about valuing pupils, recognising their work and celebrating their effort. The notion of judgement should remind you of judgement in religious traditions including the Day of Judgment. The fearful nature of such a judgment is a clue, also, to the fearful experience of the mundane forms of assessment in schools (James and Stern 2020:150).

Assessment matters in RE. This can be gauged by the fact that progress, the use of Level Descriptors and assessment was categorical in the *National Non-Statutory Framework for RE* (QCA 2004). However, it is not simple and straightforward (Finch and Hollis 2019). It can create confusion, mistrust and influence negatively some pupils' confidence (Grigg and Hughes 2013:233). Therefore, schools and teachers should ensure they assess RE in the most effective ways to enhance the positive attitudes of pupils towards RE.

Problematic nature of assessment in RE

The policies, practices and issues related to assessment in RE are deep-rooted. Fancourt (2016) illustrated this by studying publications on assessment and RE covering a period of over sixty years. He concluded on the longevity of the issues and the range of different themes within them and found that there was some potential for exploring and refining these vital aspects of RE.

Among religious educators, measuring achievement in RE has been controversial (Blaylock 2012:235; Fancourt 2015:129). Arguments suggest that assessment can be counterproductive. Watson and Thompson (2007:214) maintain that it involves an element of subjectivity on the part of the teacher and the criteria selected. It can be time-consuming and a burden especially with a large number of students. It can also promote comparisons between pupils, which may result in feelings of failure for many. It has been suggested that assessment encourages the wrong kind of motivation and discourages learning for its own sake. However, it is now common for teachers to share their criteria and with each other and with their pupils; develop a shared understanding of these and jointly establish the success criteria. This shared understanding has assisted in demystifying its purpose and process in the class. Schools are now duty-bound to address the workload issues and with the flexibility in the expectations of assessment, the issue of time has been addressed, in theory at least. The reduction in the use of grades and levels is also minimising comparisons, although not every piece of work from every pupil needs assessing in all RE lessons (Webster 2010:119). Technology has an important role in the assessment of RE. Practitioner research by McKavanagh and Robson (2017), while acknowledging the limitation of this study, found that technology saved time, quickened feedback, improved record-keeping, reduced workload and increased pupil engagement.

The concerns of assessment in RE can be addressed by using a rich and varied mix of activities. Blaylock (2012:236) has argued for teachers to be alert to the wide range of interdisciplinary learning opportunities and methods that RE offers including the conceptual, creative, historical, moral, personal, phenomenological, philosophical and spiritual as these are the routes through which evidence of achievement can be gathered and weighed up.

Moreover, researchers and practitioners have called for greater attention to be paid to the meaning of and relationship, between curriculum, pedagogy and assessments. Some have called for greater sophistication in handling assessment. Larkin, Freathy, Doney and Freathy (2020:3) note that the inadequacy of assessment has been evident in the changing methodology (e.g. with or without level descriptors), unclear attainment targets (e.g. the once near-universal 'learning *about* religions' and 'learning *from* religion') and also in terms of articulating precise intended learning outcomes. These are rarely expressed in a language more sophisticated than 'knowledge and understanding', leading to nebulous notions of the cognitive processes necessary for success. They further argue that even where greater precision is evident, how do teachers and pupils conceptualise verbs such as 'interpret', 'evaluate', 'describe', 'explain', 'analyse', 'identify', 'appreciate' and appraise'? Is there clarity regarding the subject's contribution to pupils' mental, cognitive and linguistic development? What are the intentions and expectations of teachers in terms of pupil progression and achievement in RE? (Larkin, Freathy, Doney and Freathy 2020:3). Thus, for them, a way forward is to draw upon generic pedagogical and psychological knowledge drawn from educational studies, educational psychology and cognate disciplines.

Is there something not to assess in RE?

It is recognised that assessing pupils' knowledge, understanding and skills relating to learning from religion is much more difficult than learning about religion. Assessing learning about religion requires the teacher to consider what the pupils know about religion. Assessing learning from religion is considered more difficult to assess as it requires pupils to reflect, interpret, respond imaginatively and discuss a variety of religious concepts including personal opinion (Webster 2010:111). Thus, assessing these skills necessitates a more sensitive approach because measuring emotions and opinions is subjective. Webster (2010) suggests that it is better to be objective when assessing. Being subjective could be problematic as strong religious faith may be interpreted by a non-specialist as an extreme religious view and therefore inappropriately judged. Therefore, it is important to be aware of what should and should not be assessed in RE.

The assessment of attitudes is also contested. Teachers tend to offer feedback to pupils regarding the attitudes demonstrated in their learning in RE. They may comment on their growth in confidence about their own beliefs and identity. They consider the extent to which pupils reflect on their learning and use empathy and imagination. Teachers monitor whether they listen with care to the views of others and consider evidence and arguments thoughtfully. They look to see pupils acquiring deeper impressions and search for meaning in life. Teachers detect whether pupils can recognise concerns for others and whether they appreciate that people's beliefs are often deeply held and felt.

According to McCreery, Palmer and Voiels (2008:117), religious commitment and beliefs should not be assessed as being particularly sensitive to pupils' privacy. Teachers should not attempt to discover the extent to which religion influences their daily life and their particular beliefs about God as well. Other aspects of RE such as pupils' expression of personal views and ideas, although integral to teaching and learning, would not be appropriate for formal assessment (QCA 2004:35), rather the focus should be on pupils' acquisition of knowledge and skills, the development of conceptual understanding and how well pupils to relate to others (Grigg and Hughes 2013:250). On the other hand, Watson and Thompson (2007:214) argue that if an aspect of RE cannot be assessed, can teachers be sure that it can be taught. They admit and acknowledge that there will be difficulties and concerns; however, they suggest that it could be wrong to claim that some things must not be assessed on the grounds that they are personal.

James and Stern (2020:161–162) highlight the issue of commitment. They maintain that the extent of how religiously devout pupils are and which religion or non-religious way of life they follow should not be assessed. In the same vein, pupils should not be assessed on whether or not they agree or disagree with their teacher's views particularly on sensitive issues. For example, schools are expected to promote 'fundamental British values'. However, this does not mean that any teacher can assess pupils according to whether they agree with the teacher and whether or not teachers think that being religious is valuable. Teachers should not be assessing pupils as to whether they are or are not religious. Having said that, most aspects of RE can be and should be assessed.

Teachers also need to be cognisant of their pupils' circumstances. There will be times when pupils would not be able to do well in RE. For example, RE deals with personal issues such as birth, marriage and death ceremonies. A pupil whose family is going through an unpleasant divorce or has had a recent bereavement may not feel good about a project on marriage or death, others may. Someone who has not had a joyous Christmas because of visits from abusive relatives may perform less well in festive projects. These are examples of stubborn problems of assessment in RE, problems that should not be ignored or swept away under the carpet (James and Stern 2020:161–162).

Finally, the assessment in RE can be blurred when it is delivered in conjunction with other subjects. It can become particularly trickier when it includes ethics. In this context, Stern (2018:140) asks, are we to assess pupils' understanding of ethics (e.g. their ability to argue well about ethics), their ability to act ethically (according to their own ethical code) or their ability to act according to a particular (school-based, religious or national) ethical code?

Ofsted and RE assessment

In addition to the subject related polemics and complexity above, assessment in primary RE was found to be weak and poor as some teachers were unclear about what constituted progression (Ofsted 2010). Later, it was reported to be a major weakness and inadequate in a third of primary schools, and, according to Ofsted (2013:6), many teachers were confused about how to judge how well pupils were doing in RE. The extent to which this was related to the use or non-use of the eight-level scale was unclear. Nevertheless, Larkin, Freathy, Doney and Freathy (2020:94) found that none of the participating teachers in their project was using the scale, and many were unaware of it altogether. Although the number of these teachers was small, it does reflect some of Ofsted's findings. Moreover, the project carried out by the Religious Education Council also reported a lack of knowledge of the criteria and use of the eight-level scale (Blaylock, Gent, Stern and Walshe 2013).

The new Ofsted inspection framework focuses on what children learn through the curriculum, rather than an over-reliance on performance data. In Early Years, Ofsted (2019a) will talk to practitioners about their assessment of what children know and can do and how they are building on it (p. 13). Inspectors are expected not to advocate a particular method of assessment but must record aspects of teaching and learning that they observe to be effective and identify what needs to improve (p. 15). To be judged good, practitioners and leaders would be using assessment well to check what children know and can do to inform teaching. This would include planning suitably challenging activities and responding to specific needs. Leaders would understand the limitations of assessment and avoid unnecessary burdens for staff or children (p. 34). Leaders focus on improving practitioners' appropriate use of assessment (p. 40). However, the quality of education is likely to be inadequate if the assessment is overly burdensome and unhelpful in determining what children know, understand and can do. Leaders would not be doing enough to tackle the inappropriate use of assessment (p. 35).

Ofsted (2019b) will not require assessment or recording of pupils' achievements in primary schools in a specific way, format or time (p. 15). Teachers will be expected to use assessment to check pupils' understanding in order to inform teaching and to help pupils embed and use knowledge fluently and develop their understanding, and not simply memorise disconnected facts (p. 44). Inspectors will therefore evaluate how assessment is used in the school to support the teaching of the curriculum, but not substantially increase teachers' workloads by necessitating too much one-to-one teaching or overly demanding programmes that are almost impossible to deliver without lowering the expectations of some pupils. It is recommended leaders should not have more than two or three data collection points a year (p. 45). Importantly, inspectors will ask schools to explain why they have decided to collect whatever assessment data they collect, what they are drawing from their data and how that informs their curriculum and teaching (p. 47). Weak assessment practice means that teaching fails to meet students' needs, and is likely to contribute to the quality of education being inadequate (p. 86).

Having considered the nature and significance of assessment above, the section below discusses policy, principles, planning, features of assessment and progression in RE. It will then analyse the categories and types of assessments.

School policy for assessment

Many schools have a policy for assessment. This policy has implications for how teachers are held accountable for the progress made by pupils. In practice, this should be your starting point as it may well have a statement about the nature and practice of assessment in RE. It is also important to maintain a sense of balance. A total lack of assessment can be just as unhelpful as too much prescription and an obsession with assessment (Watson and Thompson 2007:213). In current thinking, pedagogy and rigorous curriculum design are regaining prominence, where assessment supports learning rather than driving it (Peacock 2020:56).

Key principles

Schools are expected to have an assessment framework that meets a set of core principles. Assessment should:

- set out steps so that pupils reach or exceed the end of key stage expectations;
- enable teachers to measure whether pupils are on track to meet expectations;
- enable teachers to pinpoint the aspects of the curriculum in which pupils are falling behind, and recognise exceptional performance;
- support teachers' planning for all pupils;
- enable teachers to report regularly to parents and, where pupils move to other schools, providing clear information about each pupil's strengths, weaknesses and progress towards the end of key stage expectations (DfE 2013b).

Purposes of assessment

Effective and efficient assessment will be tied to its purpose. Before designing or selecting an assessment method, schools should be clear on why their pupils are being assessed, what the assessment is intended to measure, what it intends to achieve and how the assessment information will be used. Therefore, different forms of assessment may serve different purposes for different people and organisations, including pupils, parents, teachers and support staff, school leaders, school governors, the Government and Ofsted (DfE 2015:18). The purpose of assessment is to show how well the pupils are doing, what they need to do next to make progress and how effective the curriculum and teaching are. Research has found that teachers often failed to assess knowledge of religions, as they were more interested in assessing students' generic skills such as listening or working in groups (Grant and Matemba 2013).

Assessment takes place at various levels. It is used to judge the work of pupils, teachers, schools, clusters of schools and the educational system as a whole (James and Stern 2020:151). Ultimately, it is concerned with advancing the education of individuals. It needs to serve good teaching rather than being driven by goals of comparability and performance. It should lead towards a clear focus on diagnosing what pupils have learned in RE, what is problematic for them, and on prescribing remedies (Blaylock 2012:237). It offers pupils constructive and specific feedback on how and what to improve (Erricker, Lowndes and Bellchambers 2011:158). Therefore teachers should weigh up all the relevant achievements of their pupils concerning the learning outcomes of RE and use the information to enable further learning.

Since the foremost purpose of formative assessment is to improve and develop learning, it should become an integral part of the planning process (Erricker, Lowndes and Bellchambers 2011:154). This means there should also be sufficient and varied opportunities to make judgments about pupil's learning in RE to evaluate the effectiveness of the teaching and learning experiences and to identify where the pupils that are making sufficient progress compared to the progress they make in other areas of learning (Erricker, Lowndes and Bellchambers 2011:156). Importantly, it should help pupils realise, and celebrate the huge amount they are learning (James and Stern 2020:166). In making judgements in RE, Box 13.1 highlights a significant concern.

Assessment helps teachers identify any misunderstandings that pupils may have and address them. It also assists teachers to evaluate the quality and effectiveness of their planning and teaching to inform their future planning of the curriculum and learning opportunities. Assessment assists teachers identify specific learning needs and motivate pupils (Grigg and Hughes 2013:230; McCreery, Palmer and Voiels 2008:118).

Teachers should make their assessments understandable to all parties. Good practice in assessment includes informing parents, carers and other teachers about the pupil's progress (Erricker, Lowndes and Bellchambers 2011). As a two-way process, teachers need to draw more

---

BOX 13.1 VIEWPOINT: MAKING JUDGEMENTS IN RE

Historically there has been a danger that when making a judgement on a pupil's progress in RE, teachers have been unsure how to judge pupils and have ended up making judgments based on a pupil's ability in English (Moss and Pett 2019:8).

Source: RE Today Services.

---

on the views of pupils themselves and integrate assessment within everyday teaching. The key question to ask is what do you want the assessment to inform you of. The new expectation is that before using any assessment, teachers should be clear about the decision it will be used to support and be able to justify its use (DfE 2019).

As discussed above there is a personal dimension to assessment, therefore, good assessment should assist teachers to help build and maintain relationships with their pupils. It will contribute to their developing understanding of religious and non-religious ways of life, it will be fair and timely (James and Stern 2020:152). It involves teachers in addressing difficult issues with sensitivity (and to know when not to assess), to be engaging and celebratory (James and Stern 2020:167).

Over burdensome assessment is now something of the past. Therefore assessments in RE should be manageable, informative, useful, simple and effective (Erricker, Lowndes and Bellchambers 2011:155). Schools need to be clear about where pupils are at a particular point in time or unit of work. This will contribute to the sequence and coherence of pupils' learning and assist in evaluating the success of the planning and curriculum.

It is also important to avoid conceptualising assessment as a bolt to be added to planning later on. It should be an integral part of RE lessons, not as a wholly separate activity (Erricker, Lowndes and Bellchambers 2011; James and Stern 2020:164).

Effective assessment depends on the appropriate progress and the desired high expectations made explicit in the planning. There should be clear intended outcomes identified in each topic. Any assessment should be related to this. It is helpful to decide, in advance, which aspects of the learning experience would be recorded and captured somewhere in terms of assessment. Judgments made about pupils' performance in some of these activities will then provide indicators of pupils' progress in the subject. Such a process provides a coherent picture of development through the key stage (Erricker, Lowndes and Bellchambers 2011:154–155).

Assessment is a continuous process

In practice, schools should continuously identify the development of each pupil based on evidence from a variety of sources. Assessment should be continuous and beyond notions of measurement and testing at the end, nor exclusively quantitative. Nevertheless, end of topic tests may occasionally be appropriate depending on their purpose. It is worth reiterating that the Assessment Reform Group (ARG) many years ago found no evidence that increasing the amount of testing enhanced learning on its own (ARG 1999:2). External tests with very high stakes attached to their results can have very negative effects on students (Wearmouth 2008). Assessment is a powerful educational tool for promoting learning and confidence. However, it does depend on the kind of assessment that is used, and the manner of its use (Wearmouth 2018).

Categories of assessment

There are several categories of assessment, which serve different purposes and are not exclusive to one another. Thus, they are to be used in tandem (Atherton 2018).

1   Formative assessment is also known as Assessment *for* Learning (AfL) (Dann 2014). It involves making regular judgments about current knowledge, understanding and skills

based on the best possible evidence about what pupils have learned and then using this information to decide what to do next (Wiliam 2018:56). It allows teachers to plan further stages in their learning, with common purposes and goals. Formative assessment helps pupils make sense of what they are learning. It should also corroborate with what they have learnt, identifying gaps for future learning through constructive feedback. Moreover, it enables teachers to identify any specific learning challenges and needs experienced by pupils. In the Department for Education's *Final Report of the Commission on Assessment Without Levels*, it was reported that formative assessment was not always being used as an integral part of effective teaching. Some teachers were simply tracking pupils' progress towards target levels instead of using classroom assessment to identify strengths and gaps in pupils' knowledge and understanding of the programmes of study (DfE 2015:13). Closing gaps in learning is vital for development to take place effectively. Pupils need goals to work towards, which should be planned into lessons, through teacher questioning, observation, completion of tasks or pupil's presentations (Christodoulou 2016). The five key strategies are: clarifying, sharing and understanding learning intentions and success criteria; eliciting evidence of learning; providing feedback that moves learning forward; activating learners as instructional resources for one another, and activating learners as owners of their own learning (Wiliam 2018:52). Importantly formative assessment, rather than being a bolt-on feature to regular teaching, ought to be embedded within a self-improving community of teaching and learning (Atherton 2018). Rather than being generic, from the teachers perspective, effective and successful formative feedback is specific and focused (Christodoulou 2016).

2 Diagnostic assessment is about finding out their previous and current learning. It is a process of identifying what aspect of learning a pupil has mastered to enable teachers to plan for the future and decide which aspects need consolidation or repetition. It can be used to ascertain any misconceptions, misunderstandings and gaps before introducing new work. The following can be used for identification and assessment for SEND too:

  O   Individual concept maps.

  O   Group posters.

  O   Peer questioning, group talk and whole-class conversation.

  O   Adult-pupils exploratory conversations.

  O   Visual stimuli by annotating images and pictures.

  O   Imaginary scenarios.

  O   What would I like to know…

  O   Pre-unit tests.

  O   End of unit tests.

  O   Quizzes in pairs, groups or individually at the start, end or during the lesson or topic.

3 In general, summative assessment takes place at the end of a term or unit of work. It sums up the achievement of pupils up to that point. It provides a snapshot summary of where pupils are at any one time. It provides overall evidence and information on the achievements in terms of what they know, understand and can do on the completion of a unit. The use of summative assessment is most profitable when it is used formatively.

4 Assessment as learning (AaL) encourages metacognition and supports pupils to reflect on how they learn and what aids their learning (Webster 2010:111). There has been a recognition that the impact of the processes of formative assessment may be 'deformative' and reduced to a mechanistic approach to AfL, in which assessments become very limited, constraining the focus of learning (Dann 2014:150). AaL offers a process through which pupil involvement in assessment can feature as part of learning and not merely an adjunct

to teaching and learning. Accordingly, understanding the learning gap and the role of assessment in helping teachers and pupils explore and regulate this gap is central. Feedback to pupils requires as much attention to be given to its interpretation by pupils as to how and when it is given (Dann 2014:164). Feedback is effective when it focuses on improvement rather than on a grade (Carroll and Alexander 2020).

5   Ipsative (from the Latin *ipse*, 'of the self') assessment is widely used in education. Claxton et al. (2011) called for more opportunities to be given to pupils to reflect on, talk about or write about themselves as learners, which raises their self-awareness. The use of learning logs, digital records of personal best moments taken by pupils themselves, personal testimonies and self-reports are recommended. The use of a 'learning story' approach based on four Ds: describing episodes of achievement; discussing pupil's assessment and learning with other staff, the children and with their families; documenting learning and assessment and deciding what to do next (Grigg and Hughes 2013:244).

6   Norm-referenced assessments involve assessing the performance of pupils based on the performance of other children to see whether the pupil is below, above or the same as the norm. Criterion-referenced assessment involves assessing pupils learning based on a set of independent criteria.

7   Self-assessment and peer-assessment can contribute to the development of pupils' independence, capacity for critical thinking, reflection and self-evaluation. However, in a Scottish study, Grant and Matemba (2013) found that self-assessment strategies were failing to enable pupils to assess how much their knowledge of religions was developing.

To maximise the potential of self-assessment, the approach adopted would need to be modelled and taught by the teacher so that pupils practise and develop appropriate skills and vocabulary for self-assessment (Erricker, Lowndes and Bellchambers 2011:157). Self-evaluation plays an important role in pupils actively taking charge of their next steps. They need self-evaluation to adjust their goal in time (Kong 2021).

Fancourt (2005) suggested that self-assessment in RE can be broken down into four areas: Self-assessment *of* learning *about* religions; Self-assessment *for* learning *about* religions; Self-assessment *of* learning *from* religions and Self-assessment *for* learning *from* religion. He noted that the third and fourth can be problematic, particularly in terms of possible confusion between 'self-assessment' and 'learning from religions'. In terms of the first area, tools such as quizzes or extended writing tasks (where assessment criteria are clear and communicated to pupils) can be useful in helping pupils understand what they have learned and understood. The second area focuses more on what the pupils know about what they might explore next. Questions such as 'I already know…'; 'I would like to find out…'; 'I need to know more about…' and 'I would like to improve…' are beneficial (Copley and Priestley 1991:140). To these four areas, Larkin, Freathy, Doney and Freathy (2020:95) have added a fifth area, the area of self-assessment of meta-cognition, which focuses on what is in the mind.

These are some processes that involve pupils reflecting upon what they have learnt and making some assessment of what they think they have achieved (Webster 2010:111). Taking ownership of learning and understanding explicitly what is being learnt provides better improvements. It helps them become more reflective and realistic about their work, gaining the confidence to admit when they do not understand something and seeking help to address it. They begin to recognise possible gaps and weaknesses and consider effective forms of addressing them. To enable this, some criteria of learning need to be provided so that they self-assess the extent to which they have understood and learnt the concepts. However, they need to be kept simple, workable and manageable. For youngest pupils, visual clues and informal styles can be used such as faces and thumps (Webster 2010). Pupils assessing themselves is one of the most straightforward and inexpensive ways to increase achievement, (Wiliam 2018:171). Pupils improve most when they understand what they are trying to achieve (Grigg and Hughes 2013:241). It is, therefore, useful to convert learning intentions into personalised targets by using questions such as:

○ What did you find difficult about learning to…?

○ What were you very pleased about learning to…?

○ Can anyone remember what we were trying to learn today?

○ What do you think you have learned today that you did not know before?

○ What do you think you need to do next to improve your learning about…?

○ If you told someone what this lesson was about, what would you say?

8 Peer assessment is giving a role to pupils in the assessment process and means that there should be more dialogue between pupils and teachers in the setting and adaptation of the assessment process. Learners are more aware of what they learn, how they learn and what helps them learn. Therefore, they can assess themselves, learn from themselves and peer assessments, which leads them to reflect on how they learn. In other words, they provide pupils with a key role in learning (Hargreaves, Gipps and Pickering 2018:281).

Peer assessment involves pupils assessing and reviewing the work of one another. It is a process where pupils need to be trained in to understand the criteria that the work is based on so that they can recognise these features within the work of their peers (Webster 2010:112). The process is complex, may take time to be embedded and raises questions of validity and reliability. Therefore, pupils need to be trained in peer assessment with a discussion of the value of peer assessment, how to understand assessment criteria, how to give feedback and how to respond to the feedback (McCreery, Palmer and Voiels 2008:125). Pupils can oftentimes be rather harsh on their peers. Hence, it is important to be alert to unmindful comments and overtly negative feedback on their part. McGrogan and Earle (2019:34) suggest that peer and self-assessment can empower pupils to view learning as a process over which they can exert some control, and enhance teacher assessment and scholarship.

9 Observations are a crucial assessment tool, especially in the Early Years Foundation Stage. It could be used to monitor children's learning when they are learning through play; learning through independent activity; taking part in discussions, practical tasks and collaborative tasks and when using specific skills, experimenting and constructing (McCreery, Palmer and Voiels 2008:122). Nevertheless, observation is a skilled and complex task and you need to be realistic about how much you can observe at any one time. Teachers 'listen in' to pupil conversations, and occasionally question, as they work. This approach is known as continuous dialogue, allowing teachers to observe the 'religious literacy in action' to assess their knowledge, understanding and progress in skills. To aid with this, other adults working in the classroom can be used and technological devices are available for recording.

10 Assessment for planning (AfP), as you read above this is closely related to AfL. In such cases, assessments of learners are used to inform, shape and adapt future planning, which could include using the misconceptions revealed in a task in one lesson to inform the focus of the next lesson. In the second lesson, addressing these misconceptions now becomes the priority (Finch and Hollis 2019).

PROVISIONS

The Education Endowment Foundation (EEF 2021:8–9) recommended five strategies aimed at supporting pupils with SEND: Create a positive and supportive environment for all pupils without exception. Build an ongoing, holistic understanding of your pupils and their needs. Ensure all pupils have access to high-quality teaching. Complement high-quality teaching with a carefully selected small group and one-to-one interventions. Work effectively with teaching assistants.

Assessment techniques and tools

In RE there is considerable freedom in the way that it can be assessed. There are various tools of assessment to assist you to gather information and judge learning. Their use will depend on their purpose, as discussed above. RE lessons taught creatively and using a variety of teaching methods, yield a wide range of evidence which pupils can demonstrate in many ways (Webster 2010:113). Having the freedom and flexibility allows you to make it as imaginative and significant as you want, more suitable to your pupils and curriculum and to evidence achievement. It should involve teaching assistants, subject leaders and other adults. They include the following:

- Sampling pupils' work across year groups.
- Assessing their reasoning and use of evidence.
- Taking video of pupils at work and of their work.
- Selected books scrutinised at the end of the year.
- Setting tasks that require pupils to use certain skills.
- Using images, role play, journals, oral work, computing.
- Day-to-day observations in lessons, especially in EYFS and KS1.
- Carrying self-assessment by using thought showers about their work.
- Using open-ended questions to explore their knowledge and understanding.
- Maintain a record of achievement for each pupil's using their best work for each year.
- Planning activities of assessment into the learning episodes itself rather than at the end.
- Using grids like KWHL (what I Know, I Want to know, How will I find out and I have Learnt).
- Inviting pupils to communicate through drama, artefacts, drawings and concept mapping.
- Elicitation activities to identify misconception, prior learning and common challenges.
- Getting pupils to discuss and explain the meaning of keywords and their usage.
- Display their work to demonstrate their knowledge, understanding or skills.
- Artwork and poems revealing their interpretation, feelings and thoughts.
- Pupils making judgments themselves about how well they have learnt.
- Celebrating pupils' work in whole school events.
- Using photographs of their work for portfolios.
- Listening to how pupils describe their work.
- Producing written work of a various kind.
- Formal testing for specific purposes.

Feedback

To be effective, feedback needs to direct attention to what is next, rather than focusing on how well or poorly pupils did on the work (EEF 2021; Wiliam 2018:143). This can include both oral and written responses. You need to learn that the new expectation about feedback is threefold. To be of value, teachers use information from assessments to inform the decisions they make; in turn, pupils must be able to act on the feedback for it to have an effect. High-quality feedback can be written or verbal; it is likely to be accurate and clear, encourage further effort and provide specific guidance on how to improve. Over time, feedback should support pupils to monitor and regulate their own learning (DfE 2019:23). Feedback is more helpful when it is formative and becomes 'responsive' teaching rather than being associated with marking only (Powley 2020:69). However, live marking allows pupils to amend their work as a teacher goes through the process, it facilitates pupils to compare their work with that of others and encourages them to hand in their work for scrutiny (Odell 2020). It should support pupils moving from their present state to the goal state (Wiliam 2018).

Level descriptions for attainment in RE

Since 1988, all the NC subjects, except RE, had had attainment levels numbered 1–8 across three Key Stages. The eight levels which were generated for RE were produced by the RE community to maintain parity with other subjects (QCA 2004). As RE was not a NC subject, it was not required by the 1988 Education Reform Act to conform to its framework of attainment targets, programmes of study and levels of attainment, like the NC. However, it came under pressure to do so, as a result, all LEAs had done so. Consequently, RE had adopted the same assessment and standards-driven ideology as the rest of the curriculum. One of the pressures that brought RE into the fold of a managerial style of learning was the desire to prevent RE from being marginalised from the rest of the curriculum. Having outlined some predicaments that led to the captivation of RE within a neoliberal framework, Grimmitt (2000:10) stressed that some had argued that if pupils were not subjected to the forms of assessment as in other subjects, then the importance of RE would be hindered. Moreover, practically, teachers were happy to adopt such assessment arrangements for RE as it gave the subject parity with other subjects. Practically, some teachers welcomed the 8-level scale as a solution to some difficult problems at the classroom level, while others rejected the scale, judging it to be a straight-jacket to their work (Blaylock 2000:48), others did not want to cause problems for teachers (Moss and Pett 2019:2). Politically, the inclusion of RE alongside other subjects in national initiatives was welcomed. Nevertheless, the need for more attention to assessment in RE has been highlighted as researchers have given more focus to curriculum development and pedagogy (Blaylock 2012:237; Fancourt 2010; Fancourt 2015). A study drew attention toward identifying the underlying assumptions about the formulation of attainment targets in any subject and that it may be a mistake to assume that one model of assessment will automatically apply across the curriculum equally successfully (Brooks and Fancourt 2012:134).

As you read in Chapter 5, the curriculum framework of REC (2013) embedded the attainment targets of learning about and learning from religion and belief without stating them explicitly. Significantly, it removed the use of the eight levels in line with the new National Curriculum because the DfE had set aside these levels (DfE 2013a). There was a consensus about the need for further future national work in this area for RE and mixed professional views about this. Many teachers wished to continue to use RE levels, while others preferred not to (REC 2013:26). Some suggested that RE teachers might still find them helpful to measure progression in RE (Brooke 2014). However, recently in RE, like in other subjects, a search for clarity is underway and schools are trying different systems (Moss and Pett 2019).

Impediments with using levels

There were theoretical, political and practical issues with the introduction and implementation of Level Descriptions. The development of attainment targets did provide a structure that allowed teachers to find the appropriate level of tasks for pupils (Ofsted 2007:21; QCA 2004). However, over time it seems that the levels became ends in themselves rather than a means to an end. The Commission on Assessment without levels reported that too often levels became viewed as thresholds and teaching became focused on getting pupils across the next threshold instead of ensuring they were secure in the knowledge and understanding defined in the programmes of study. Importantly, it noted that depth and breadth of understanding were sometimes sacrificed in favour of pace. Moreover, levels also used a 'best fit' model, which meant that a pupil could have serious gaps in their knowledge and understanding, but still, be placed within the level. As a result, the exact areas of the curriculum where the child was secure and where the gaps were was unclear (McIntosh 2015:5).

The levels became a label for a pupil, whereas they were intended to identify progress and not static ability (Fancourt 2012:215). Others adhere to the rigidity of the level, and regard them as hierarchical chronological steps, whereas progression is a matter of deepening concepts and not simply increasing vocabulary (Stern 2018:81). Moreover, progress made by pupils is not linear. A related criticism is that progress through the levels is not sequential. For example, Level 1 requires skills of 'recollecting and expressing', while Level 2 focuses on 'identifying and questioning' (Larkin, Freathy, Doney and Freathy 2020:94).

Levels became problematic in the context of differentiation as well and the challenge faced by teachers in helping specific pupils to improve. A common method of detecting differences and needs is through classroom assessment. The diagnostic role of assessment is important. This means that assessment is used to identify pupils' strengths and areas of progress; as such; it informs future lesson planning and delivery. However, to do this effectively criteria for measurement were needed which needed to be accurate. The eight-level scale aimed to provide this model of intellectual progression (QCA 2004). However, this was contested and questions were asked as to whether it was a model of intellectual development in the subject, or simply a set of arranged tasks in a rather haphazard way (cf. Fancourt 2012:219). Such a model based on Bloom's constructivist model was not designed to deal with ethical matters. For instance, Fancourt (2012) asserts that most pupils will have a view on stealing without having to work through a hierarchical set of questions. Second, he cautions that a practical danger is that lower-attaining pupils may only be set basic questions rather than be guided to more advanced questions, especially as each lesson may simply present them with more basic questions on a new topic, rather than being given the opportunity to analyse and reflect at a 'higher' level (Fancourt 2012:219). Whereas, Myatt (2018:142), based on data from pupils, has shown that pupils are capable of a greater level of complexity and challenge than they are given credit as true challenge encourages a deeper engagement with the content.

Levels in new locally agreed syllabi

Previously, schools had to resort to their LAS to find out the requirement of assessment (McCreery, Palmer and Voiels 2008:116). Moving forward, the Department for Education made a policy announcement in 2014 on the removal of the then system of levels for reporting pupil's attainment and progress. As a response to the challenges of assessment 'beyond levels' and with increased freedom, as noted above, SACREs and schools have developed and adopted their own approaches to assessment (Lilly, Peacock, Shoveller and Struthers 2014). It has been noted that these responses are sometimes inconsistent both within and across schools (Larkin, Freathy, Doney and Freathy 2020:95). Consequently, Ofsted inspections will be interested in the rationale and impact of the system adopted by schools. They do not expect specific ways, formats or time for assessment. It is therefore important to be familiar with some of the models being developed in RE.

Unsurprisingly, in the absence of satisfactory assessment procedures to replace the levels, some SACREs had recommended and retained the use of levels to help schools with progress and assessment and expected schools to report to parents using an eight-level assessment scale (Derby 2014). However, currently, this is no longer the case, which is the case with many others (Derby 2020). The Norfolk syllabus provides non-statutory age-related expectations showing examples for Key Stages 1–3 and teachers are expected to ensure that the rationale they use both fits their school context, phase of learning and strives for high standards of attainment for all pupils (Norfolk 2019). Hertfordshire (2017) encourages the use of assessment guidelines set out by schools; for example, working at/expected and above/below age-related expectations. In others, headings of 'emerging', 'secure' and 'exceeding' have been used to indicate three stages of development which can be used to construct meaningful assessment criteria. These are different names for the standards achieved by pupils. However, it has been argued that these categories involve making a summative judgement, and once a word or value-laden statement is used, a summative inference is made (Christodoulou 2016:84).

On the other hand, the framework of Bournemouth and Poole is related to the 8-level scale to help teachers make the comparison and find the benchmarks they are used to using with their previous syllabus. Nevertheless, schools are encouraged to develop their processes, which clearly define progression in RE learning about their schemes of learning (Bournemouth and Poole 2017). Thus, it is clear that the autonomy of schools to determine their assessment processes without the prescription of national level descriptors has offered them the opportunity to restructure and more clearly define their expectations of children and young people's learning. It has also allowed schools to focus more on their programmes of study for RE. At the same time, there is considerable diversity in RE.

The new language

Consequently, schools have preferred to use different assessment terms, including 'Working Towards', 'Expected' and 'Greater Depth'; 'Emerging, Expected and Exceeding', or 'Working towards', 'Working at' or Working beyond', to achieve 'mastery'. You will also find the use of 'Must, Should and Could', a traffic light system of 'Red, Amber, Green' or 'I can ...' statement to show achievement of outcomes, set expectations and map progression. That said, as with the previous eight levels, pupils' learning should not be bound within the three-descriptive system, scope should exist at both ends of the spectrum.

Assessment in Reception

You will also find different models being used in Reception. In the example in Table 13.1, the statements would relate to the aims and outcomes of an RE curriculum, such as the REC (2013). In inquiring about beliefs and teachings, religious stories are used, so pupils would:

Alternatively, since pupils in the Foundation Stage start to explore the world of religion and beliefs in terms of special people, books, times, places and objects, visits and through festivals, rites of passages and celebration, the assessment would form part of their learning journeys, individual profile or portfolios used by practitioners as part of their ongoing assessment process. Teachers collect evidence in the form of observations, photographs, video evidence, class scrapbooks and pupil's work as well as teacher knowledge. Evidence is also captured through conversations in both self-initiated learning and adult initiated learning opportunities and their interaction with the class environment, whereby pupil's comments are written down. These are also known as 'in the moment' assessments to monitor gaps and ensure that a clearer and continuous picture is being built. It is important to remember that the evidence collected for RE focuses on what pupils know, understand or can do about the RE curriculum.

Table 13.1 Assessment in Reception			
Emerging	**Establishing**	**Embedding**	**Enhancing**
Begin to talk about a religious story	Talk about a religious story	Remember a religious story	Retell a religious story

Another approach uses the Early Learning Goals (ELGs) as part of the Early Years Foundation Stage. For example, pupils' comments about the story of Bilal and their questions to clarify their understanding are noted under listening, attention and understanding. When learning about celebration their understanding of their feelings is recorded. In 'Understanding the World' when they talk about the lives of the faith and other leaders around them and their roles in society are captured and their knowledge of some similarities and differences between different religious and cultural communities in this country are documented (DfE 2021).

The mastery approach

This model of assessment requires the existence of a very close relationship between assessment and content. The prerequisite of this approach is that what is taught is identified in the form of key knowledge in all stages until KS3. Key knowledge includes factual knowledge, fundamental concepts, principles, beliefs and ideas and includes certain skills (Hunt 2019). Moreover, it requires that key knowledge is arranged in an appropriate age-related hierarchy to ensure pupils improve continuously and gain progressive mastery in RE.

Hunt (2019:46) asserts that the mastery approach helps pupils gain a deeper understanding of a difficult concept by providing a planned learning journey. They make incremental gains as they progress from one Key Stage to the next. In each Key Stage, the key knowledge that all pupils should master is specified in a program of study with additional guidance provided. He is concerned when RE content is often expressed in generic terms, such as, 'pupils should know why Easter is a special time for Christians'. Unlike fuzzy statements like these, which create discrepancy of what a good answer could be, Hunt (2019:47) maintains that the mastery approach avoids uncertainty, as the content is likely to clarify the kind of answer pupils should give since there is a close relationship between assessment and the content. A summarised version of his sample is given in Table 13.2.

Age-related expectations

At the heart of this model is the close relationship between assessment and pedagogy, which is rooted in a balanced curriculum design. It begins with having a clear purpose of RE. This age-related approach is based on a curriculum for RE which is based on a multidisciplinary understanding of the subject. These disciplinary lenses are theology, philosophy and the human/social sciences. The age-related expectations have been designed to underpin planning as well as assessment. In the illustration in Table 13.3, only one strand from each discipline is used to show age-related expectations of that strand across the years (Norfolk 2019:37–39).

Table 13.2 Summarised version of the mastery approach	
Christianity: The story of Easter	
Key Stage 1 Pupils should be taught to:	**Lower Key Stage 2 Pupils should be taught to:**
Identify and name Easter as a festival that Christians celebrate, and that during the festival many Christians recall the death and resurrection of Jesus.	Identify and describe the main ideas associated with the traditional Christian salvation story, including: the relationship between God and humanity was broken, Jesus sacrifices himself on the cross and restored the broken relationship, as the relationship has been stored humanity has been saved, and because of Jesus' death on the cross 'new life' is possible.
Identify and describe some of the main events associated with the story of Easter, including: Jesus was arrested, he was put on trial, he was crucified on the cross and he rose from the dead.	Identify and describe the main ideas associated with the Christian believe in 'new life', including: there is a heaven; those in heaven live again in 'new life'; 'new life' is not the same as the life that we know and 'new life' involves being changed, made better, made more glorious.

Table 13.3 Example of age-related expectations

Discipline	Strand	Year 1	Year 2	Year 3	Year 4	Year 5	Year 6	Year 7
Theology	Where belief comes from.	Give a clear, simple account of at least one narrative, story or important text used by at least one religion or worldview.	Retell a narrative, story or important text from at least one religion or worldview and recognise a link with a belief. Recognise different types of writing from within one text.	Show awareness of different sources of authority and how they link with beliefs. Identify different types of writing and give an example of how a believer might interpret a source of authority.	Identify different sources of authority and how they link with beliefs. Give examples of different writings and different ways in which believers interpret sources of authority.	Describe different sources of authority and how they link with beliefs. Describe a range of different interpretations of sources of authority and consider the reliability of these sources for a group of believers.	Explain different sources of authority and the connections with beliefs. Begin to discuss the reliability and authenticity of texts that are authoritative for a group of believers.	Begin to analyse and evaluate different sources of authority, considering the writings of key thinkers, and how these have shaped and formed beliefs. Begin to analyse a range of genres and interpretations of sources of authority applying knowledge of reliability of sources when enquiring into religions and worldviews.
Philosophy	How and whether things make sense.	Give a simple reason using the word 'because' when talking about religion and belief.	Give a reason to say why someone might hold a particular belief using the word 'because'.	Decide if a reason or argument based on a religion or belief makes sense to them and is expressed clearly. Use more than one reason to support their view.	Begin to weigh up whether different reasons and arguments are expressed coherently when studying religion and belief. Give reasons for more than one point of view, providing pieces of evidence to support these views.	Explain, using a range of reasons, whether a position or argument is coherent and logical. Link a range of different pieces of evidence together to form a coherent argument.	Begin to analyse and evaluate whether a position or argument is coherent and logical, and show increasing awareness of divergence of opinion. Use well-chosen pieces of evidence to support and counter a particular argument.	Analyse and evaluate whether a position or argument is coherent and logical, explaining with reasons any divergence of opinion. Use principles, analogies and well-researched evidence to support a particular argument and counter this view.

(Continued)

Table 13.3 Example of age-related expectations (*Continued*)

Discipline	Strand	Year 1	Year 2	Year 3	Year 4	Year 5	Year 6	Year 7
Human/ Social Sciences	The ways in which beliefs shape individual identity, and impact on communities and society and vice versa.	Recognise that beliefs can have an impact on a believer's daily life, their family or local community.	Identify ways in which beliefs can have an impact on a believer's daily life, their family or local community.	Identify a range of ways in which beliefs can have an impact on a believer's daily life, their family, community and society.	Describe ways in which beliefs can impact on and influence individual lives, communities and society and show awareness of how individuals, communities and society can also shape beliefs.	Explain how beliefs impact on and influence individual lives, communities and society, and how individuals, communities and society can also shape beliefs.	Begin to analyse and evaluate how beliefs impact on, influence and change individual lives, communities and society, and how individuals, communities and society can also shape beliefs.	Analyse and evaluate how beliefs impact on, shape and change individual lives, communities and society, and how individuals, communities and society can also shape beliefs.

Source: Norfolk SACRE and Diocese of Norwich (2019:37–39).

352

Table 13.4 Descriptor-based assessments	
Year 1 – What happens inside a church?	
Remembering	I can tell you how the community can use the church and recognise some of the church furniture.
Understanding and applying	I can name and explain the purpose of pieces of church furniture and tell you about symbols that I find. I understand how Christians believe the church to be a worldwide family.
Analysing	I can reflect on the purpose, atmosphere and community of a church.
Skills	I can ask 'who', 'what' and 'when' questions.
Source: Moss, F., and Pett, S. (Eds.) (2019) *Assessment in RE: A Practical Guide*, Birmingham: RE Today Services.	

Descriptor-based assessments

Anstice uses descriptor-based assessments, where each unit of work has a specific knowledge-based outcome as well as a skills objective, as shown in Table 13.4. All lesson planning is based on these outcomes and objectives and each unit of work is based on a unit key question. For each unit of work she has a document with statements of her expectations of pupil responses using the headings of *Remembering* (Emerging), *Understanding and applying* (Expected) and *Analysing* (Exceeding). These statements are always positioned at the top of mid-term plans as a reminder of what she wants to achieve by the end of a half-term unit of work. A formal summative assessment is then conducted each term that is then recorded to an online assessment tracker. However, regular formative assessments inform her teaching and content but these are not formally reported on (Anstice 2019:22–23).

Achievement portraits from pupils with SEND

Based on observations with pupils with more complex needs, many who were pre-verbal, Krisman (2019:66–67) categorised their responses and called them markers which indicated points of contact between pupils and RE. She found that these markers often showed significant breakthroughs in understanding. These markers showed pupils making connections, being creative, giving insights, making links, showing a sense of belonging and sense of completion, showing pride, purpose and unique responses, curiosity, wonder, resonance with the natural world, compassion and tree of life. These markers became an enriching two-way process. Krisman showed that she valued their achievements and the pupils responded more strongly in return. Her RE had an impact beyond RE lessons.

Recording and reporting of progress

There is a statutory obligation for schools to provide as part of the annual report to parents the details on the attainment and progress of each child in RE. The recording and reporting can be based upon the assessment structure proposed by the REC (2013) or on a model of their own. The model should enable teachers to know which pupil in their class is working below, within or beyond the expectations of a particular programme of study. Teachers must keep a record of formal assessments and levels of attainment at the end of a key stage. Good RE reporting is individual, accurate, positive, criterion-referenced and formative.

The judgments about pupil's learning need to be recorded in some way. The records provide evidence of how well pupils are progressing and achieving with different concepts in different units and with different teachers (Erricker, Lowndes and Bellchambers 2011:157). A record of attainment can be a useful diagnostic tool to enable teachers to identify where learning and progress might not be as good as anticipated for a variety of reasons, including a concept being too challenging, insufficient resources, inappropriate activities or insufficient focus on the concept. Alternatively, if many pupils are achieving higher, teachers might feel that they can provide more challenges for pupils (Erricker, Lowndes and Bellchambers 2011:157).

Some SACREs request their schools to provide them with a summary of attainment by pupils at the end of Key Stage 2 as part of their responsibility to monitor RE. In addition, some schools may request progress information where pupils transfer between schools. Therefore, you may see systems in place to facilitate the completion of these requirements, and, as a teacher, you may be requested to provide the necessary information.

Reports inform parents and carers about how children have progressed in RE regarding requirements of their syllabus or scheme of work. The report based on evidence may comment on the following (Erricker, Lowndes and Bellchambers 2011:158):

- The content and activities the child has experienced.
- The level of interest, enthusiasm and effort the child has demonstrated.
- A description of what the child has achieved in terms of knowledge, understanding of the concepts and skills.
- Any suggested targets for future work.
- The report should be based on evidence gathered.

Summary

This chapter has discussed some of the issues related to assessment in general and in particular to RE. It has provided you with some practical ideas and models to use in your teaching (Box 13.2).

BOX 13.2 VIGNETTE: CONCERN

My family are from a Pakistani Muslim background. My dad and mum were both born in Pakistan, along with my two elder brothers. For as long as I can remember no one in my family practised Islam daily. However, all members of my immediate family now pray five times a day and have been on Umrah and Hajj.

I went to an Islamic school. We were taught the National Curriculum but within an Islamic environment. We were required to pray during school time and read the Qur'an during school. Our R.E lessons consisted solely of Islamic studies. This allowed me to learn a lot about Islamic history; however, I was uneducated when it came to other religions. I studied R.E at an A level at college. I was hoping to learn more about different faiths. However this A level covered Islam for the majority of the modules. I did briefly learn about Christianity and Hinduism. In addition, I was introduced to the scientific aspect of R.E. I gained most of my education in regards to other religions by asking work colleagues. They would answer any questions I had about their faith. Furthermore, I would also ask atheists to explain what their view of the world is.

I considered applying for a degree in RE but decided against it and pursued English and Business. Either way, my career choice was always to teach, whether that be RE or English. My attitude did not change during my degree.

Teaching is to be able successfully to teach the subject matter to the children. However, I firmly believe that a teacher should primarily teach rules and boundaries to the children, so they realise that a school is a place that they come to learn. In addition,

---

I believe a teacher's role is to have a rapport with all their students allowing them to feel strong emotions when they enter the classroom. I believe people should be educated in all religions so it doesn't lead to people being ignorant of someone else's beliefs.

I am hoping to increase my subject knowledge in R.E and gain a better understanding of all the religions taught. In saying that, I fear that I may make mistakes when presenting information to the children about another religion.

R.E is only taught once a week at my placement. I had only one opportunity to observe an R.E lesson, as this was part of my preliminary visits. Since the start of my block placement, I haven't had the chance to observe another R.E lesson as we have PPA during that time. I feel that R.E isn't a big concern in the school that I am in as there is more of an emphasis on Maths and English. I find this a bit strange because we have had assemblies based on the Christian faith and we have attended church for a service. I feel that the children may feel some passion towards R.E due to the assemblies; however, I think they are more concerned about improving in their Maths and English.

References

Anstice, N. (2019) Descriptor-based assessments, in F. Moss and S. Pett (Eds.) *Assessment in RE: A Practical Guide*, Birmingham: RE Today Services, pp. 22–25.

Assessment Reform Group (1999) *Assessment for Learning: Beyond the Black Box*, Cambridge: University of Cambridge School of Education.

Atherton, C. (2018) *Assessment: Evidence-Based Teaching for Enquiring Teachers*, St Albans, Critical Publishing.

Blaylock, L. (2000) Issues in achievement and assessment in religious education in England: Which way should we turn? *British Journal of Religious Education*, 23, (1), pp. 45–58.

Blaylock, L. (2012) Assessment, in P. Barnes (Ed.) *Debates in Religious Education*, London: Routledge, pp. 235–246.

Blaylock, L., Gent, B., Stern, J., and Walshe, K. (2013) *Subject Review of Religious Education in England, Phase 1: Report of the Expert Panel*, London: Religious Education Council of England & Wales.

Brooke, J. (2014) *The RE Teacher's Survival Guide*, Abingdon: The Bible Reading Fellowship.

Brooks, V., and Fancourt, N. (2012) Is self-assessment in religious education unique? *British Journal of Religious Education*, 34, (2), pp. 123–137.

Bournemouth and Poole (2017) *Any Questions? The Bournemouth and Poole Agreed Syllabus for Religious Education 2017–2022*, Boroughs of Bournemouth and Poole: Bournemouth Borough Council.

Carroll, J., and Alexander, G. (2020) *The Teachers' Standards in Primary Schools: Understanding and Evidencing Effective Practice*, London: SAGE. Second edition.

Christodoulou, C. (2016) *Making Good Progress?: The Future of Assessment for Learning*, Oxford: Oxford University Press.

Claxton, G., Chamber, M., Powell., and Lucas, B. (2011) *The Learning Powered School*, Bristol: TLO Ltd.

Copley, T., and Priestley, J. (1991) *Forms of Assessment in Religious Education: The Main Report of the FARE Project*, Exeter: Fare Project.

Dann, R. (2014) Assessment as learning: Blurring the boundaries of assessment and learning for theory, policy and practice, *Assessment in Education: Principles, Policy & Practice*, 21, (2), pp. 149–166.

Derby (2014) *Derbyshire Agreed Syllabus for Religious Education 2014–2019*, Derby: Derbyshire County Council and Birmingham: RE Today Services.

Derby (2020) *Derbyshire and Derby City Agreed Syllabus for Religious Education 2020–2025*, Birmingham: RE Today.

DfE (2013a) *The National Curriculum in England: Key Stages 1 and 2 Framework Document*, London: Department for Education. DFE-00178-2013.

DfE (2013b) *Primary Assessment and Accountability Under the New National Curriculum*, London: Department for Education.

DfE (2015) *Final Report of the Commission on Assessment Without Levels*, London: HMSO The Stationery Office.

DfE (2019) *ITT Core Content Framework*, London: Department for Education. Reference: DfE-00230-2019.

DfE (2021) *Statutory Framework for the Early Years Foundation Stage*, London: Department for Education.

Department for Education (2021) *Teachers' Standards Guidance for School Leaders, School Staff and Governing Bodies*, London: Department for Education. Reference: DFE-00066-2011. [Online] https://assets.publishing.service.gov.uk/government/uploads/system/uploads/attachment_data/file/1007716/Teachers__Standards_2021_update.pdf (Accessed 19/09/2021).

Donarski, S. (2020) Introduction, in S. Donarski, (Ed.) *The ResearchED Guide to Assessment*, Melton: John Catt, pp. 11–19.

EEF (2021) *Special Educational Needs in Mainstream Schools: Guidance Report*, London: Education Endowment Foundation. [Online] https://educationendowmentfoundation.org.uk/public/files/Publications/Send/EEF_Special_Educational_Needs_in_Mainstream_Schools_Guidance_Report.pdf (Accessed 25/07/2021).

Erricker, C., Lowndes, J., and Bellchambers, E. (2011) *Primary Religious Education – A New Approach*, London: Routledge.

Fancourt, N. (2005) Challenges for self-assessment in religious education, *British Journal of Religious Education*, 27, (2), pp. 115–125.

Fancourt, N. (2010) 'I'm less intolerant': Reflexive self-assessment in religious education, *British Journal of Religious Education*, 32, (3), pp. 291–305.

Fancourt, N. (2012) Differentiation, in L. P. Barnes (Ed.) *Debates in Religious Education*, London: Routledge, pp. 213–222.

Fancourt, N. (2015) Re-defining 'learning about religion' and 'learning from religion': A study of policy change, *British Journal of Religious Education*, 37, (2), pp. 122–137.

Fancourt, N. (2016) Assessment and examinations in religious education: Sixty years of research and analysis, Editorial introduction to VSE of *British Journal of Religious Education*, http://explore.tandfonline.com/page/ed/assessment-and-examinations.

Finch, A., and Hollis, E. (2019) *Assessment*, St Albans: Critical Publishing.

Grant, L., and Matemba, Y. (2013) Problems of assessment in religious and moral education: The Scottish case, *Journal of Beliefs and Values*, 34, (1), pp. 1–13.

Grigg, R., and Hughes, S. (2013) *Teaching Primary Humanities*, Harlow: Pearson Education.

Grimmitt, M. (2000) Introduction: The captivity and liberation of religious education and the meaning and significance of pedagogy, in M. Grimmitt (Ed.) *Pedagogies of Religious Education*, Great Wakering: McCrimmons, pp. 7–23.

Hargreaves, E., Gipps, C., and Pickering, A. (2018) Assessment for learning: Formative approaches, in T. Cremin and C. Burnett (Eds.) *Learning to Teach in the Primary School*, Abingdon: Routledge. Fourth edition, pp. 275–287.

Hertfordshire (2017) *Hertfordshire Agreed Syllabus of Religious Education 2017–2022*, Hertfordshire SACRE: Hertfordshire County Council 2017.

Hunt, D. (2019) Assessment in RE: The mastery approach, in F. Moss and S. Pett (Eds.) *Assessment in RE: A Practical Guide*, Birmingham: RE Today Services, pp. 46–49.

James, M., and Stern, J. (2020) *Mastering Religious Education*, London: Bloomsbury.

Kong, R. (2021) On the potential influence of setting goals on students' future development, *Academic Journal of Humanities & Social Sciences*, 4, (1), pp. 85–91. [Online] https://francis-press.com/uploads/papers/qKbwOmy172RgdNun9JTwG67A30ydo4FJ0CqvVSY3.pdf (Accessed 08/4/2021).

Krisman, A. (2019) Using a religious education achievement portrait with pupils with SEN, in F. Moss and S. Pett (Eds.) *Assessment in RE: A Practical Guide*, Birmingham: RE Today Services, pp. 66–69.

Larkin, S., Freathy, R., Doney, J., and Freathy, G. (2020) *Metacognition, Worldviews and Religious Education: A Practical Guide for Teachers*, London: Routledge.

Lilly, J., Peacock, A., Shoveller, S., and Struthers, d'R. (2014) *Beyond Levels: Alternative Assessment Approaches Developed by Teaching Schools: Research Report*, Nottingham: National College for Teaching and Leadership (NCTL).

McGrogan, N., and Earle, S. (2019) Formative use of assessment by pupils, in S. Earle (Ed.) *Assessment in the Primary Classroom – Principles and Practice*, London: Learning Matters & SAGE, pp. 33–45.

McCreery, E., Palmer, S., and Voiels, V. (2008) *Teaching Religious Education*, Exeter: Learning Matters.

McIntosh, J. (2015) *Final Report of the Commission on Assessment Without Levels*, London: Crown copyright. [Online] https://assets.publishing.service.gov.uk/government/uploads/system/uploads/attachment_data/file/483058/Commission_on_Assessment_Without_Levels_-_report.pdf (Accessed 11/03/2021).

McKavanagh, S., and Robson, J. (2017) *The Role of Technology in the Assessment of RE*, [Online] https://www.reonline.org.uk/research/the-role-of-technology-in-the-assessment-of-re/ (Accessed 13/04/2021).

Moss, F., and Pett, S. (Eds.) (2019) *Assessment in RE: A Practical Guide*, Birmingham: RE Today Services.

Myatt, M. (2018) Making the case for more demanding religious education, in M. Castelli and M. Chater (Eds.) *We Need to Talk About Religious Education*, London: Jessica Kingsley, pp. 133–142.

Norfolk (2019) *Norfolk Agreed Syllabus 2019: A Religious Education for the Future*, Norfolk: Norfolk SACRE (https://www.dioceseofnorwich.org/schools/siams-re-collective-worship/religious-education/age-related-expectations).

Odell, F. (2020) Assessment and feedback a part of a progression model, in S. Donarski (Ed.) *The ResearchED Guide to Assessment*, Melton: John Catt, pp. 123–135.

Ofsted (2007) *Making Sense of Religion Education: A Report on Religious Education and the Impact of Locally Agreed Syllabus*, London: Office for Standards in Education.

Ofsted (2010) *Transforming Religious Education: Religious Education in Schools 2006–2009*, London: Office for Standards in Education.

Ofsted (2013) *Religious Education: Realising the Potential. Religious Education*, Manchester: Office for Standards in Education.

Ofsted (2019a) *Early Years Inspection Handbook for Ofsted Registered Provision*, Manchester: Crown Copyright. No: 180040.

Ofsted (2019b) *School Inspection Handbook*, Manchester: Crown Copyright. No. 190017.

Peacock, A. (2020) Swimming against the tide: Assessment of learning in one primary school, in S. Donarski (Ed.) *The ResearchED Guide to Assessment*, Melton: John Catt, pp. 49–58.

Powley, R. (2020) In pursuit of the powerful: Knowledge, knowers and knowing and the impact of assessment and feedback, in S. Donarski, (Ed.) *The ResearchED Guide to Assessment*, Melton: John Catt, pp. 59–72.

QCA (2004) *Religious Education: The Non-Statutory National Framework*, London: QCA.

REC (2013) *A Curriculum Framework for Religious Education in England*, London: Religious Education Council of England & Wales.

Stern, J. (2018) *Teaching Religious Education: Researchers in the Classroom*, London: Bloomsbury Academic. Second edition.

Watson, B., and Thompson, P. (2007) *The Effective Teaching of Religious Education*, Harlow: Longman. Second edition.

Wearmouth, J. (2008) Testing, assessment and literacy learning in schools: A view from England, *Curriculum Perspective*, 28, (3), pp. 77–81.

Wearmouth, J. (2018) *Special Educational Needs and Disability: The Basics*, Abingdon: Routledge. Third edition.

Webster, M. (2010) *Creative Approaches to Teaching Primary RE*, London: Longman.

Wiliam, D. (2018) *Embedded Formative Assessment*, Bloomington, IN: Solution Tree.

Leadership and life-long learning

CHAPTER

Leadership and management in RE

Introduction

At the outset, you need to understand what the curriculum leadership role entails. Your role is to ensure that learning by the pupils and learning in your subject is continuously improving in your school. It is meeting the expectations of the school. It is to make pupils feel that they are, in Religious Education (RE), continuously progressing and growing. This should be at the heart of everything that you rationalise, decide, implement, evaluate and report. The intent of senior leaders in your school and the intent of your RE curriculum has to be in harmony.

Research conducted into the supply of leaders in schools in England to discover the extent and causes of empty posts in these critical positions showed that schools face challenges in attracting, developing and retaining leaders (Wigdortz and Toop 2016). One of the reasons for this increasing demand has been a growth in leadership positions caused by an increased number of executive head and CEO roles in academy trusts and changes in leadership structures in schools. In other words, you should aspire to be a leader in whatever capacity that suits you, including leading RE.

The value of all subjects has resurfaced after years of pressures of various kinds, which lead to narrowing the approach to curriculum design in some schools. A carefully planned, broad and balanced curriculum is to be implemented by schools. For many schools, this means repositioning the status afforded to each subject to create a broad and balanced curriculum. In addition to your subject, curriculum and pedagogical expertise, to bring your vision to fruition across the school, class teachers at the point of delivery should have the agency to own these as well (Hargreaves and O'Connor 2018). May (2020) suggests three principles for adoption by subject leaders: a deep understanding of the school context and community, a commitment to ongoing professional development in the subject within a supportive network and a commitment to the development of strong subject leadership and management skills set. Ofsted (2019) will gather evidence through discussions with curriculum and subject leaders and teachers about the programme of study that classes are following for particular subjects. Thus, one of the key questions to think about is how to ensure quality subject coverage in RE takes place.

Leader landscape

You will come across several terms used for the person-in-charge of a subject in primary schools. They are known as specialists, subject leaders, subject co-ordinators, curriculum leaders or managers. More recently, however, the term curriculum lead has been in vogue. Perhaps, to emphasise the curriculum rather than the person leading it.

As a leader of your curriculum and classroom practitioner, your ability to know various aspects of your subject is shaped in the landscapes of your practice, both in and outside your school. For instance, the body of knowledge in your profession is not merely the curriculum of your subject. Wenger (2010) suggests that it is a whole landscape of practices. This involves not only the practice of the profession, but also as depicted in research, hub and networks, management, regulation, professional associations and many other contexts, as you will read in the next section. The composition of such a landscape, it is argued, is dynamic as communities emerge, merge, split, compete, complement each other and disappear. Sometimes the boundaries between the practices involved are not necessarily amicable or collaborative. In the landscape of RE, this means that you ought to navigate the regulatory demands, managerial decisions, parental and community expectations, practitioners' preferences, research findings, funding bodies, academic standpoints and your philosophy. Some will chime whilst others may clash in liberating or colonising your subject and practices. Thus, as an advocate of RE, you need to broaden your landscape and actively participate in broader communities of practice, as a supportive professional environment offers better effectiveness and more success.

As a curriculum leader, with the proliferation of social media and the dismantling of boundaries of learning and access to instant information, you are now expected to have a strong network and community. To be an effective leader in the twenty-first century you need to be connected with the RE community in particular. You should maximise social media and technology to network with others to share challenges, opportunities and ideas. In this way, you will take on your responsibilities for your life-long learning. This will inevitably demand time and energy. Once you are connected with the RE community and teachers in general you will notice that sharing is very common. Out of courtesy, however, do inform anyone whose work you use and get copyright clearances. In your school create a culture of teaching and learning walks in RE so that everyone's teaching is invigorated and innovation is continuously promoted. Simultaneously, it is important to keep in mind that these activities should be meaningful, encourage reflection and, importantly, ask all the time, why are you doing what you are doing (McDonagh, Roche, Sullivan and Glenn 2020).

Leadership of RE

In this section, you will be knowing and reflecting upon the significant role that RE curriculum leaders play in maintaining and enhancing the quality of the provision of RE. Some of the features and characteristics are generic, and, therefore, they may apply to non-RE contexts as well. Before proceeding, you may want to pause for a moment and consider what you think education is for and why you entered the teaching profession. You may also want to think about the status of RE in your educational philosophy and its role, if any, in the education of pupils.

Many schools appoint a curriculum leader for most subjects of the NC. In some smaller schools, a single teacher may be responsible for more than one subject. In the context of RE, for a variety of reasons, some Agreed Syllabus Conferences recommend that their schools appoint a subject leader in RE. In an ideal situation, this should be someone who is a subject specialist. However, this is not always practical nor absolute. Many RE subject leaders are not subject specialists. In both cases, someone with good knowledge of the subject and passion and experience for the subject usually leads it.

The nature of the leadership is significant in raising the status of the subject, the quality of teaching and the success in learning, in turn, this impacts the progress and achievement in RE. RE leaders, provide professional leadership by sharing good practice beyond their school.

Leaders exhibit a comprehensive understanding of their responsibilities in addressing barriers to learning in light of key legal and policy requirements and they advance knowledge and understanding of RE within their school and beyond. Critical reflection remains central to the role of RE leaders in addressing issues and provisions for the subject (Sellars 2017).

Vision and mission

Every school has its distinctive ethos, which is usually articulated through the school's vision, mission, values and policies. You may want to pause and ponder for a moment over your vision and mission for RE. Boxes 14.1 and 14.2 show examples from student teachers pursuing leadership in RE:
Now consider the following:

BOX 14.1 A VISION FOR RE

My vision for R.E in school is to have the knowledge and understanding to provide children with a well-resourced, exciting and memorable introduction to RE that they are keen to explore in greater depth, to become open to understanding, appreciative and respectful of all people. R.E. should provide children with the opportunity for spiritual development of self and others, to prepare them for adult life.

BOX 14.2 A MISSION FOR RE

I would want there to be a greater focus on worldviews. In addition, I would want RE to move from being taught through the outdated behaviourism methods to more modern approaches that allow children to experience spiritual and moral exploration. I would focus on the teachers' self-confidence in teaching RE through training, workshops and open conversations. I would engage with the children to see what they wanted from their RE lessons and address issues that are affecting them.

Thus it is useful to think about the extent to which the design of your RE curriculum reflects the school's vision and values. Thought should also be given to the worldviews of the communities and pupils. Moreover, consideration of the local context of the school and the whole school curriculum should feature and the nature and scope of the subject. It might help to share this within your network, if available, to enhance it and clarify your thinking. The APPG (2013) recommended that primary schools provide regular opportunities for RE subject leaders to train their colleagues in their subject. The Chartered College of Teaching stressed that professional learning is more effective when it has an explicit focus on a specific subject area (Scutt and Harrison 2019). Both should also be a regular feature for you.

Understanding the role of the curriculum leader

You will find that role specifications for an RE curriculum leader are varied. To begin with, the role is related to the teacher's professional standards. The precise duties depend on various factors including remuneration, time, resources and the size of the school, its organisation and other roles and responsibilities. It is important to ensure that the role description is realistic and within workload, expectations and the range of activities are contextual. Many job descriptions would expect the descriptions assembled below, from various sources, as a minimum.

Before reading further, perhaps make a list of what you think the role of the RE curriculum lead is. Thereafter, put the items in order of importance. You may want to complete a similar activity on what skills you think are necessary for an RE leader.

The RE leaders will be confident and competent in their subject and pedagogies. They consult their peers and are informative. They design and communicate their rigorous curriculum and coordinate learning to ensure there is progression between the Key Stages. A leader fosters interest and knowledge in RE and promotes it as a serious and enjoyable subject beyond their school. They build on existing good practices and strive for continuous improvement by keeping abreast of developments in RE.

You are likely to experience some challenges, both internal and external, regarding a host of matters linked with RE. Student teachers, as part of an exercise to audit and reflect on existing skills to identify areas of future development, shared potential challenges. For each challenge, list the skills needed as a leader. Thereafter, consider which skill might have the most impact.

- You wish to raise the status of RE.
- You wish to develop subject knowledge and overcome anxieties.
- You wish to extend the repertoire of teaching methods in RE.
- You wish to widen the breadth of RE content.
- You wish to share good practices in your network.
- You wish to change your assessment in RE.

Transparency of RE

All schools must publish their school curriculum by subject online (DfE 2014). Therefore, as an RE leader, you need to ensure that this information is up-to-date and reflects the life of RE in your school. The nature of RE requires public confidence and so its educational basis ought to be transparent to all concerned.

Responsibility for RE

As previously discussed, generally, there are several layers of responsibilities attached to RE. It is part of good practice for you as a leader to have a link governor for RE as a useful resource and point of contact to serve your subject. The APPG (2013) recommended that governors should have a role in supporting all matters of RE including reviewing its strengths and weaknesses. Hence, where applicable, you need to involve them positively and proactively in assisting you to make as best a provision as you can make in your school. Francis and Blaylock (2016) note some of the responsibilities of governing bodies and directors to include that:

- RE is taught and provided.
- The requirements for RE are met in accordance with a syllabus.
- RE is appropriately resourced and staffed to meet the aims.
- Parents receive an annual written report on their child's progress.
- Requests from parents for the withdrawal of their child's from RE are responded to, and alternative arrangements made.
- RE is provided as part of the basic curriculum.
- Sufficient time is devoted to RE to ensure the school meets its legal obligations and provides an RE curriculum of quality.
- Teachers receive appropriate training to deliver RE.

Policy contents

It is highly likely that in a mainstream school you will be responsible for formulating and producing the RE policy of your school, with final approval resting with the head-teacher, trustees and governors. It should set out the rationale, aims and objectives and provide a framework for all teachers and parents (Pett 2015:14). In some academies, an externally produced standardised policy might be in place. In some church schools, the diocese will influence the policy. As with other policies, it is important that you set a cycle of review in consultation with your senior leaders and update it as necessary. It should also reflect current legislation and practice. It is good practice to take account of the voices of all stakeholders in preparing the policy.

The features of an RE policy include:

- Outline of the context of the school community.
- A rationale consisting of a general statement highlighting the aims, importance and value.
- The intent, implementation and impact of the curriculum.
- How it confirms to the Local Agreed Syllabus, where applicable.
- Pupils' entitlement to RE and how it meets this.
- Organisation of the delivery of the curriculum across the years.
- Use of visitors, and how they and their content is vetted.
- Special places to be visited and a rationale for each.
- How assessment, progress and reporting is to be undertaken.
- Explicit reference to the parental right of withdrawal of their children.
- The arrangement for the provisions for pupils whose children are withdrawn from RE.
- How RE meets the learning needs of pupils with SEND and EAL.
- Contribution of RE to the National Curriculum.
- Contribution of RE to the SMSC development.
- Contribution of RE to PSHE development.
- Contribution of RE to Relationship Education.
- Contribution of RE to the well-being of pupils.
- The RE policy can be cross-referenced to other policies including health and safety, safeguarding and anti-bullying. This would show the holistic concern that RE has for pupils.

It is good practice to mention how the monitoring and evaluation of RE take place. This may be through activities such as learning walks, subject audits, reviews of planning and use of resources and quality assurance mechanisms such as team teaching, observation of teaching, scrutiny and moderation of pupils' work and an annual RE report for the senior leaders.

Breadth and progression in RE

As a subject leader, it is important to establish good links with secondary feeder schools to ensure that there is appropriate progression and to minimise unnecessary repetition. As discussed in the previous chapters, schools should ensure that during their school life, pupils should encounter all of the principal religions and worldviews. For some schools, the facilitation and adaptation for such provision rely on the professional judgement of the RE leader. It is recommended that this overview is shown in the school's RE policy and is reviewed regularly. In so doing, all stakeholders will see the journey of RE in the life of learners consisting of a broad and balanced RE curriculum.

SEND and inclusion

School policies set out the entitlement of all pupils and the core principles of inclusion. It is important to recognise that these apply to everything in school including RE, which should be accessible to everyone. Pupils with SEND should be offered the same experiences as other pupils, and beyond this, they should also have experiences that are relevant and appropriate to their needs, aptitudes and personalities. From the subject leader perspective, however, appropriate modifications should be made and opportunities to explore and experience the content in-depth overtime should be set in place.

Newly arrived families

As you welcome newly arrived families into your school, like other aspects of school, in RE, it is particularly important to recognise that some newly arrived families may not be aware that RE, overall in the UK, is an educational endeavour. The subject, unlike in some other countries, is non-confessional. In the interest of transparency and minimising potential misunderstanding, it is useful for such families to have an induction or information provided about the nature and purpose of RE in your school.

Quality assurance

The monitoring and quality assurance role of the subject lead is significant as they are the ones who have a pulse on the state and quality of RE. The education community has produced guidance and resources to support subject leaders in fulfilling their responsibility successfully and efficiently. These should be used to support you in your work. It is also important to work in collaboration with the person in charge of assessment for the whole school should there be one. This assists in aligning subject-specific assessment matters with the rest of the school. It shows tracking of progress as a whole school endeavour. Moreover, support and advice can also be sought from local authorities, although this is diminishing in some quarters. RE related organisations and consultants are also available to access. The quality assurance and monitoring role of the RE leader may include:

- monitoring RE planning across the school.
- monitoring RE delivery in all classes.
- monitoring assessment of RE in all classes.
- moderating, keeping evidence, record keeping and reporting on RE.

Ofsted findings

The initial 101 reports, which mention RE, published under the new Ofsted framework, have provided useful insights to consider by schools (NATRE 2019). These include that pupils need to learn subjects in sufficient depth so that they remember what they have learnt. All pupils need to follow a broad curriculum, which is similar in breadth and ambition to the basic/national curriculum. Where the time for RE and PSHE is contracted into shared provision, this limits pupils' understanding of both areas. They report that planning needs to be sufficiently detailed and sequenced so that pupils develop secure long-term understanding, building on what they have learnt before. Visits to places of worship, handling artefacts and receiving visitors, help pupils to remember what they have learnt and deepens understanding. Learning in RE helps to underpin the development of respect and tolerance and supports school values and the preparation of pupils for life in modern Britain. Where the curriculum is well planned, the interaction between subject content and skills, such as across the Humanities is made explicit which strengthens learning. Well-designed assessment allows teachers to plan more accurately and enables pupils to know and remember more. Effective training leads to primary teachers having good subject knowledge that they use to help pupils learn more effectively. RE makes a valuable contribution to pupil's personal development and to their understanding of the wider world.

Monitoring provides information about the quality of teaching and learning taking place. It celebrates achievement and identifies areas of improvement. The process should be designed in consultation with colleagues and be supportive of class teachers and practitioners. In doing so, a collective and reflective ethos is created in raising expectations. Importantly, any gaps, which may exist in meeting the curriculum coverage, can be revealed. This is essential in securing the full entitlement of each pupil. However, monitoring it is not an end in itself; it needs to be seen as a process having an important role to play in the sharing of good practice and in identifying learning needs for everyone, both pupils and their teachers.

Tools for quality assurance

Some locally agreed syllabi, such as Kent (2017) and others, provide excellent support material to enable RE leaders to evaluate the quality of the provision of RE in their schools. Below are some key questions, which might be asked to gain an overview.

In terms of general/overview monitoring, it is appropriate for subject leaders to ask:

- Is there a planned programme of RE across the school in accordance with the syllabus?
- Is the curriculum time for RE at or above the minimum time required by the syllabus, e.g. over a term, year and Key Stage?
- Are resources for RE adequate and used appropriately? Are resources varied, accurate and authentic?
- Does the taught programme of RE address the key questions from the syllabus appropriately?
- Do teachers have clear objectives and set high expectations in RE?
- Are achievement and standards of attainment in RE promoted through high expectations of pupil progress and a challenging RE curriculum for all pupils?
- Are RE lessons well structured, organised and managed?
- Are teaching and learning focused on appropriate objectives and suitably paced?
- Is there a suitable proportion of direct teaching in RE and is there a balanced variety of opportunities for pupils to respond, e.g. through paired, group and individual work?
- Does whole-class work, discussion and questioning enable all pupils to participate and make progress?
- In what ways does the teaching provide opportunities for the spiritual, moral, social and cultural development of pupils and are these identified, e.g. in planning?
- Is RE teaching providing varied opportunities for pupils to develop ideas, arguments, thoughtful reflections and questions of their own?

■ Are support staff deployed effectively to support learning in RE?

■ Do pupils with a variety of special needs, including those with high prior attainment, make appropriate progress in RE?

School leaders and governors

These selected questions might form the basis of a discussion between headteachers, governors and those responsible for teaching RE in a school.

■ Do all pupils make progress in achieving the learning objectives of the RE curriculum?

■ Is RE well led and effectively managed?

■ Are standards, achievement and quality of provision in RE regularly and effectively self-evaluated?

■ Are those teaching RE suitably qualified and trained in the subject? Do they have regular and effective opportunities for CPD?

■ Are teachers aware of RE's contribution to developing pupils' understanding of religion and belief and its impact as part of the duty to promote social cohesion?

■ Are teachers aware that they do not have to teach RE?

■ Is RE resourced, staffed and timetabled in a way that means the school can fulfil its legal obligations on RE and pupils can make good progress?

■ Where there are insufficient teachers in a school who are prepared to teach RE, does the headteacher ensure that pupils receive their RE entitlement?

The use of self-evaluative tools helps to gauge the state of the subject as a whole on an annual basis. It should result in a clear overview of the current situation of RE and the production of an action plan for progress and improvement.

Resources for RE

RE can be susceptible to an overuse of worksheets, texts and Powerpoints, so it is important to use these thoughtfully, as intimated in Box 14.3. Therefore, it is important that you support an ethos where your RE curriculum is alive.

There are some inspiring and beautiful resources available for RE teaching. Sufficient resources should be provided to deliver the RE curriculum in an exciting, innovative, creative and dynamic way. It should include the provision of human resources to enable educational visits and visitors into the school. In many schools, this is at par with what is provided for foundation subjects.

■ Ensure essential resources are available to support the plans of each year group.

■ Check that resources are up to date and relevant.

■ Continue to collect new resources, artefacts, books, videos, posters.

BOX 14.3 BEAUTIFUL RE

Students need to be in a place of beauty, deep knowledge & understanding in RE (Mary Myatt).

- Contact local faith leaders and the school community to share resources.
- Create resource boxes for each unit of work.
- Keep catalogue resources, share this with colleagues and monitor their use.
- Put recently arrived resources on display in the staffroom.
- Provide brief notes on how to handle some 'sensitive' resources.
- Enable colleagues to use resources for assemblies, worship and RE displays.
- Ensure that planning identifies appropriate and relevant resources.
- Advise and deliver in-house workshops on how to use resources.
- Elicit feedback on the effectiveness of the resources in supporting the curriculum.

Environment for RE

Parents, pupils and visitors to your school should quickly notice the presence of RE in your school. To this end, there has to be an environmental presence of the subject. In addition to considering what, where and why you create RE displays, it is important to consider whose work is and is not displayed, over time. This helps the use of a wider range of pupils' work.

Following a visit to a special place organise a whole school assembly to share this experience and display the learning therefrom. Do the same for any charity work undertaken by the school. Celebrate RE through murals in the playgrounds to show core values. In the main corridor, identify a prominent spot and display a quote from scripture or wise words weekly. Throughout the year, create a dedicated display board for current events of all kinds, perhaps nearest to the reception, contribute to this board regularly for RE, especially about annual festivals and celebrations when they happen. Ensure each class has some general RE books and specific books to enhance the content they cover during the year. Have a good supply of posters, videos, artefacts and devotional utilities to support RE across the year groups.

Organise an RE Day annually for the whole school. Invite parents, carers, representatives from local special places, faith and civic representatives. Organise a student conference on RE in collaboration with secondary schools. In Reception and Year 1 ensure there are costumes, soft toys, games and age-appropriate resources for RE. Suggest content and ideas for RE as cross-curricular work during planning meetings for NC with colleagues. In each classroom, encourage a regular RE working wall display and an area to display artefacts related to the current content being taught.

Religious Education Quality Mark

This is a framework to raise expectations in your RE curriculum and provision. Maintained schools must use the local agreed syllabus and academies and free schools teach a syllabus as per their agreements. The model of REQM is presented as a tool for reflection and critical examination.

REQM was launched in 2013 and has been developed to celebrate outstanding practice in the study of religion and worldviews in all sectors and phases of education in England, Northern Ireland and Wales. The REQM has four strands: Learning, Teaching, Curriculum and Leadership (REQM 2021). Schools applying for the REQM are expected to use the school evidence form and the pupil questionnaire to decide the level of award they would like to aim for. There are three award levels: bronze, silver and gold. The criteria for gold are presented in Table 14.1.

Table 14.1 REQM criteria for gold

Learning		Teaching		Curriculum		Leadership	
1	Learners demonstrate the breadth and depth of their knowledge and understanding, recognising the influence that religious and non-religious worldviews have had on human development and cultures	1	Teachers have high expectations of learners and the subject leader demonstrates exceptional subject knowledge	1	The curriculum is innovative and creative leading to full engagement of all groups of learners across all the age and ability ranges	1	The subject leader demonstrates a deep and robust intention for learning, teaching that flows throughout the planning and implementation of the curriculum design
2	Learners link their knowledge and understanding with ethical and philosophical questions, current global issues and events	2	Teachers build their planning on learners' prior knowledge and this enables all learners to deepen their understanding of religious and non-religious worldviews	2	The curriculum is understood and appreciated across the school and within the wider school community	2	The subject's professional leadership has led whole school improvement and development
3	Learners express their knowledge and understanding about religious and non-religious worldviews, including their own, through a variety of media and forms of communication	3	The quality of teaching overall is recognised as exceptional	3	The curriculum includes space for responses to national and global issues connected with religious and non-religious worldviews and this supports pupils' spiritual, moral social and cultural development	3	The subject leader is embedding high quality systems to ensure sustainability and succession planning for the subject and senior leaders ensure appropriate CPD for all relevant staff
4	Learners show spiritual, moral, social and cultural (SMSC) development through their positive engagement in dialogue about diversity, within and across religious and non-religious worldviews	4	Research based teaching strategies securing an appropriate depth of learning are used by teachers to secure intellectual curiosity and scholarship	4	Curriculum outcomes and impact are shared with other schools and local networks/organisations	4	Senior leaders and governors engage in innovation and creative plans for the future development of the subject in the light of national conversations
5	Learning is regularly reviewed and assessed and outcomes for some groups and individuals are exceptional in relation to their age, ability and prior learning	5	Teachers use agreed criteria in planning and assessment data is well managed to track group and individual progress, and to secure exceptional achievement for specific groups and individuals	5	The curriculum has a discernible, beneficial and lasting impact on the knowledge and understanding of all groups of learners	5	Governors and senior leaders ensure that the subject is secure, and has a high profile in school and in the wider school and local community

(Continued)

Table 14.1 REQM criteria for gold (*Continued*)

Learning	Teaching	Curriculum	Leadership
6 Learners are beginning to co-design their own learning in order to promote their progress and achievement	6 Teachers and learners create appropriate respectful environments where a range of controversial issues and topics are discussed and critiqued	6 The curriculum promotes an understanding of the complexities of religious and non-religious identities	6 The subject leader provides highly effective approaches to whole staff development to support school priorities and to assist other schools locally, nationally and/or internationally
7 Learners celebrate and share what they have discovered within the wider education community	7 Teachers' planning secures high-level thinking and a secure depth of understanding	7 The curriculum is innovative in its approaches to inclusivity and diversity and is effective in its impact	7 The impact of monitoring and overall leadership is a confident and well qualified teaching team
			8 Commitment to support local and/or regional groups
Source: REC (REQM 2021).			

Summary

This section has discussed the importance of a subject leader providing high-quality learning in RE. This involved knowing the local and national landscape within which the school and the subject are located. It illustrated how leadership can operate. The role and responsibility of the curriculum leader were explained and the various features which support the subject such as the policy, resources, environment, planning, curriculum, teaching, assessment and continued training. The criteria used by REQM were offered as a tool for evaluation. As a curriculum leader, you should approach your leadership role with care, attention, high expectation for the wellbeing and growth of RE.

A THRIVING RE COMMUNITY

Introduction

Initially, it may seem to you that there is little support available for RE probably because not much is talked about what is in existence. Over the years, the support mechanisms available to all teachers to enhance their RE provision has increased immensely. This section offers an overview of the main RE organisations, essential documents, reading material and resources rather than subject knowledge content.

Regardless of the level of your expertise, it is crucial that you read about the nature, content and pedagogy of RE, particularly around those topics with which you are less experienced. There is a wide range of books written by leading figures of RE so attempt to read widely and search for books and articles, which have alternative RE perspectives. This will assist you to critically examine and question your understanding of the philosophy, purpose and pedagogy of the subject.

There is now a very good presence of RE communities on social media with whom you can interact. It may be intimidating, as a beginner, to have your presence on social media. However, once you join and interact with teachers, especially those who lead RE in their school, you will find most of them to be generous with their time and very helpful in responding to your questions and will offer guidance and support. A consistent message across all the reviews in the *Developing Great Teachers* paper was that external expertise was crucial in bringing about substantial improvements to pupil outcomes. It also indicated that subject-specific CPD is more effective than generic pedagogic ones (Cordingley et al. 2015:8).

National RE organisations

This section gives a brief description of the main professional organisations that advocate RE.

NATRE

As the name indicates, the *National Association of Teachers of Religious Education* is the subject teacher association for RE professionals. It supports teachers and leaders in all schools at all stages of their careers. It is sponsored by RE Today Services (see below). NATRE provides a focal point for the concerns of RE professionals, a representative voice at a national level for all who teach and lead in RE. It provides publications and courses to support professional development through its networks of local groups. In collaboration with RE Today Services and through its all-inclusive membership service, NATRE provides a comprehensive range of benefits and support for all those who teach RE. Their membership scheme provides members with the termly *REToday* magazine, a curriculum publication, access to the NATRE membership area of the website and support through NATRE-affiliated local groups. It regularly responds to all major government consultations that affect RE (www.natre.org.uk).

NATRE-affiliated local groups

There are over numerous local network groups of teachers and RE professionals. These NATRE affiliated groups come in different forms providing networking opportunities and engagement that is invaluable to teachers. The groups provide lesson ideas and solutions; help the RE network grow, share good practices and resources in the local area and provide opportunities to understand what is happening in the region and across the country. They aim to open up the RE 'world' to class teachers, many of whom are non-specialists. They are run mostly by teachers and support one another but they are also facilitated by diocesan RE advisers, school improvement advisers, independent consultants, local SACRE advisers and university lecturers. They are supported by many organisations and provide a termly newsletter. Local groups can contact NATRE to be affiliated at no cost.

RE Today

They are committed to the teaching of the major world faiths and non-religious worldviews in RE and to an accurate and fair representation of their beliefs, values and practices. They work in the UK and internationally intending to give children a broad and balanced education to support them in the world they live in through the teaching of high-quality RE in schools. RE Today supports teachers in all types of schools through the publication of teaching materials, research papers, a termly *REToday* magazine, curriculum books and other RE publications. They offer RE consultancy services to support Senior Leadership Teams, Local Authorities, SACREs, Dioceses, Funders and Multi-Academy Trusts and Teaching Schools. They provide professional development opportunities regionally, nationally and internationally. They sponsor NATRE, mentioned above. Christian Education is the sister organisation of RE Today (www.retoday.org.uk).

AULRE

The Association of University Lecturers in Religion & Education (AULRE) supports research and teaching at the interface of religion and education. Its members include university lecturers and researchers, and those involved in research and teacher education in a variety of settings. It is for those interested in links between RE and academic disciplines, Religious Education and Religious Studies in all schools and colleges and learning and teaching in theology, religious studies and other disciplines, the professional development and initial teacher education of teachers of RE and the enhancement of public knowledge and understanding of religion and RE. It publishes *The Journal of Beliefs and Values* (www.aulre.org.uk).

The European Forum for Teachers of Religious Education

The EFTRE aims to contribute to the international cooperation of teachers of RE in the theoretical and practical aspects of their work and to develop links between teachers of RE in member countries. It also strengthens and promotes the position of RE in schools in the member countries and Europe in general and lobbies organisations and structures at the national and European level to improve the provision and quality of RE across its member countries and Europe. Members tend to be from associations of teachers of RE, institutes or departments concerned with the preparation of teachers of RE, organisations concerned with supporting the teaching of RE and individuals engaged in RE (www.eftre.net).

AREIAC

The Association of RE Inspectors, Advisers and Consultants (AREIAC) is an organisation for specialist educationalists. Professionally, it is a conduit supporting the trainers, leaders, advisers of RE and the home of expertise for anybody involved in the teaching of RE. It is funded and run by its members and so is independent. Its members represent AREIAC on various bodies, such as the RE Council and are responsible for reporting to the regions on any government-led or curriculum initiatives in RE. In this way, it is involved in policy changes, which may affect RE. They are passionate about high-quality multi-faith RE and inclusive Collective Worship (CW) and seek to promote this. They may work for a local authority or a Diocesan Board of Education or they may be independent or work for a faith community. Many also have responsibilities for their local SACRE.

AREIAC seeks to promote the equal status of RE with other curriculum subjects and the contribution of RE and CW to pupils' spiritual, moral, cultural, mental and physical development. Among other quality and representation related matters, they seek to promote an RE curriculum that challenges disadvantages and inequalities. It promotes CW as an educational activity, which protects and affirms the integrity of all those taking part. It has links with international, national and local faith communities to advance the aims of RE and CW (www.areiac.org.uk).

NASACRE

The National Association of SACREs (NASACRE) is an umbrella organisation for local Standing Advisory Councils on Religious Education (SACRE). They aim to assist SACREs to fulfil their responsibilities and represent their common concerns to other bodies. They assist in the training and mutual consultation of SACRE members and encourage the development of the SACREs. It is a non-profit making organisation, which is financed by affiliation fees from SACREs and subscriptions to public meetings. It offers its members an annual conference considering contemporary RE issues and forums, seminars or workshops to share and discuss a range of issues. An electronic termly newsletter *SACRE Briefing* covers both national issues and news from local SACREs. NASACRE also represents the interests of its members at a national level at meetings of the Department for Education. It holds membership of the RE Council and the Inter-Faith Network UK. The executive committee has close links with AREIAC and NATRE (http://www.nasacre.org.uk).

REC

The Religious Education Council of England and Wales (REC) has a membership of over sixty organisations, together they reflect a national collaborative network comprising different professional interests and religious and non-religious worldviews. They share a common commitment to a richer and stronger provision for RE which ensures a deeper understanding and discernment in beliefs and values throughout the educational system. It provides a multi-faith forum where national organisations with an interest in supporting, improving and promoting RE in schools and colleges can share matters of common concern.

The RE Council clarifies the scope of RE and its relationship to other areas of the curriculum. It works with the government, the media, parents and children, teachers and governors, members of faith and belief communities, to champion RE and raises awareness of its value in the education of all young people. It highlights the importance of high quality, rigorous RE for young people, taught by RE specialists. It promotes a positive public understanding of RE and its value to wider society. It seeks to be a clear national voice for the advocacy RE and influence policy proactively with government and other local, national and international bodies (www.rec.org.uk).

Religious Education Quality Mark

The REQM was developed to acknowledge, celebrate and publicise quality RE. It recognises high quality RE practice, particularly those schools that are providing their learners with authentic experiences and contributing to whole school outcomes. The REQM provides a powerful tool for development. Schools, which have applied for the award, have found that it affirms the work they are already doing, raises the profile of the subject and gives them ideas and confidence for developing their practice even further.

The REC has provided support and has monitored the quality of the award since 2015. The REQM has been set up to raise the profile of RE in schools, celebrate a commitment to excellence in RE and enable the dissemination of quality RE through networking. It also provides a framework for measuring, planning and developing the quality of RE teaching and learning and encourages schools to increase the range and quality of teaching and learning in RE to improve standards. Moreover, it develops pedagogies that have an impact on whole school improvement and provides a structure and framework for dioceses and SACREs to map high quality and outstanding RE (www.reqm.org).

Culham St Gabriel's Trust

The Trust is a charitable foundation with a vision for broad-based, critical and reflective education in religion and worldviews to contribute to a well-informed, respectful and open society. It is committed to providing teachers of religion and worldviews and other professionals with the support, connections, challenges and professional development they need. They want all partners, such as parents, school governors, faith/belief communities and policymakers, to be positively aware of the benefits of a high-quality study of religion and worldviews. They support work that promotes the links between school ethos, values, leadership and school improvement. They are leading agents of change and improvement through their professional development programmes and partnerships with other funders who help fulfil their vision. They give grants to support research, development and innovation in religion and worldviews, as well as providing practical resources through their websites.

The Trust currently runs several programmes for teachers including Teach: RE professional development of all teachers of religion and worldviews through flexible and distance learning courses for teachers at all stages of their career. Research: the trust is committed to enabling religion and worldviews professionals to be research aware, research-informed and research-active. Leadership: equipping leaders of religion and worldviews education for systemic change and building a leadership community. RE ONLINE: a website offering free to use, quality-assured, comprehensive coverage of religion and worldviews. The Trust works with others associated with RE, spiritual and moral development and values-led school leadership (https://www.cstg.org.uk).

RE:ONLINE

An excellent collection of all things RE. This is a major site for teachers and pupils of RE. Free to use, quality-assured, comprehensive coverage of religion and worldviews. Currently divided into five main sections: Knowledge, Resources, Research, Leadership and Professional Development. It has a blog akin to a dialogue between professionals sharing their innovative work and thinking in RE. There are many short accessible articles for all phases of RE (www.reonline.org.uk).

RE infrastructure project

Between 2018 and 2020 an infrastructure of regional support across 10 regions in England through 10 regional ambassadors, under the leadership of a national ambassador had taken place. The project was successful in increasing networking, communication and information gathering across regions. It succeeded in increasing in the number of local groups supporting those teaching RE and practitioners. However, now that the previous national and regional ambassador structures and roles have come to an end, A Theory of Change has been developed to support the next steps for the project for the next three years. The overarching aim and impact is that the RE/R&W community work effectively together nationally (multi-nationally) and across the regions to support all teachers and leaders of the subject in a sustainable way (Joint initiative with CSTG: Progression with the Infrastructure project; natre.org.uk) (Accessed 20/12/2021).

Learn – teach – lead RE

This is a learning partnership project for RE with a focus on creating a community of enquiry and professional development across the regions in hubs. The project aims to support all teachers of RE irrespective of their experience or qualifications through practical support at hub meetings and the opportunity to participate in projects that develop their teaching skills and the learning experiences of those they teach. As a grass-roots movement, they look to collaborate with others and believe that encouragement and collaboration in research projects enable innovative practice and dissemination of best practices. All their hub leaders are teachers themselves who are developing their practice. Some are Specialist Leaders in Education who work with Teaching Schools or support Initial Teacher Education Programmes, others work nationally supporting the teaching of RE. A key strength of their project is that hub leaders are equipped through specialised training giving them skills and expertise. In addition, their annual conference is a springboard for much of their work in schools, offering all those who attend the opportunity to hear national figures in RE. Southwest (https://www.ltlre.org) and North (https://www.ltlre-north.org).

Subject associations

Teachers can join many professional organisations and associations. Almost all subjects have these and their primary purpose is to serve the shared interests of their respective subject among professional members and the public with an authoritative voice. They are also concerned with ensuring their subject is represented in any policy initiatives and school reforms through consultations, for example. One of the ways they maintain the academic rigour and vitality of their subject is through research which is disseminated through peer-reviewed academic journals, professional magazines and digital presence. Some provide high-quality expert CPD to support schools to help them meet their training and development needs. You need to be connected with your subject association; perhaps your school could fund this membership for you as part of your subject budget or CPD activity (https://www.subjectassociations. org.uk/).

Websites for subject knowledge and pedagogy

In this section, some useful websites to support the planning and teaching of the RE are listed. Some of the sites provide useful downloadable resources.

Shap audio glossary

Teachers and student teachers alike are often puzzled as to how to pronounce words they come across when studying religions, or learning about RE. To help overcome this problem, this glossary has an associated sound file, which you can activate by clicking on the word. Of course, this enterprise has some intrinsic difficulties. In the same way that there are differences between how different native English speakers will pronounce a word, depending on regional or national accent, so too with most other languages. Creators of this glossary do not claim to offer the 'right' pronunciation, only a close approximation to a generally recognisable common pronunciation.

The glossary will also be a useful resource to look to when puzzled by the meaning of words found in RE textbooks or other material about religions. More likely, you will just Google the word or expression you are puzzled by. Here too there are likely to be disputed as to whether they have explained some words or expressions accurately or clearly. Then there is the problem of spelling: arti or aarti? Vaisakhi or Baisakhi? Diwali or Divali or Deepavali? Their initial choices are to some extent arbitrary, although as far as possible they reflect the most common usage. http://www.shapcalendar.org.uk/glossary.html

RE-Definitions

RE-Definitions is a new app for RE teachers giving handy access to the pronunciation and meaning of more than 200 key terms. As an app on mobiles and tablets, and as a website on PCs, it is for non-specialists who want to understand the words and how to pronounce them with confidence and for specialists who want to enhance their knowledge. In both audio and text, RE-Definitions provides accurate, clear, resource-linked definitions of key terms in seven religions and beliefs, in ethics and philosophy and the study of religions and beliefs. The App can be downloaded from the Apple App Store or Google PlayStore (www.re-definitions. org.uk).

RE library

This selected list of reading material should enable you as a teacher of RE to meet the requirement of the Teachers' Standards which is concerned with the promotion and value of scholarship (DfE 2021). Together with the literature offered by the RE Research Review by Ofsted

(2021), it contributes to the expectations outlined in the *ITT Core Content Framework* from the viewpoint of RE (DfE 2019). Nevertheless, it is not a definitive list of publications on RE for teachers and the literature is continuously growing, in addition to the regular academic papers being written about RE in the United Kingdom, Europe and internationally. It remains the case that, RE continues to be an important subject in the early years and primary education for children in the UK. Nevertheless, it would be naïve to suggest that the aims and purposes of RE are uncontested. The list below introduces you to some of the seminal works relating to RE including those published most recently.

Barnes, L.P. (2014) *Education, Religion and Diversity. Developing a New Model of Religious Education*, Abingdon: Routledge.

Barnes, L.P. (2020) *Crisis, Controversy and the Future of Religious Education*, Abingdon: Routledge.

Barnes, P., Davis, A., and Halstead, J.M. (2015) *Religious Education: Educating for Diversity*, London: Bloomsbury.

Benoit, C., Hutchings, Y., and Shillitoe, R. (2020) *Worldview: A Multidisciplinary Report*, London: REC. https://www.religiouseducationcouncil.org.uk/wp-content/uploads/2021/01/REC-Worldview-Report-A4-v2.pdf

Biesta, G., and Hannam, P. (Ed.) (2021) *Religion and Education: The Forgotten Dimensions of Religious Education?*, Leiden: Brill.

Chater, M. (2020) *Reforming Religious Education: Power and Knowledge in a Worldviews Curriculum*, Woodbridge: John Catt Publication.

Chater, M. and Erricker, C. (2012) *Does Religious Education Have a Future? Pedagogical and Policy Prospects*, Abingdon: Routledge.

Castelli, M., and Chater, M. (Eds.) (2018) *We Need to Talk about Religious Education: Manifestos for the Future of RE*, London: Jessica Kingsley Publishers.

Conroy, J. C., Lundie, D., Davis, R., Baumfield, V., Barnes, L. P., Gallagher, T., Lowden, K., Bourque, N., and Wenell, K. (2013) *Does Religious Education Work? A Multidimensional Investigation*, London: Bloomsbury.

Cooling, T., Bowie. B., and Panjwani, F. (2020) *Worldviews in Religious Education*, London: Theos. https://www.theosthinktank.co.uk/cmsfiles/Worldview-in-Religious-Education—FINAL-PDF-merged.pdf.

Copley, T. (2005) *Indoctrination, Education and God,* London: SPCK.

Copley, T. (2008) *Teaching Religion: Sixty Years of Religious Education in England and Wales*, Exeter: Exeter University Press.

Erricker, C., and Erricker, J. (2000) *Reconstructing Religious, Spiritual and Moral Education,* London: RoutledgeFalmer.

Erricker, C., Lowndes, J., and Bellchambers, E. (2010) *Primary Religious Education – A New Approach. Conceptual Enquiry in Primary RE*, Abingdon: Routledge.

Felderhof, M.C. (2014) *Teaching Virtue: The Contribution of Religious Education*, London: Bloomsbury.

Felderhof, M.C., Thompson, P., and Torevell, D. (2007) *Inspiring Faith in Schools: Studies in Religious Education*, Abingdon: Routledge.

Gearon, L. (2013) *MasterClass in Religious Education. Transforming Teaching and Learning*, London: Bloomsbury.

Gearon, L. (2013) *On Holy Ground: The Theory and Practice of Religious Education*, Abingdon: Routledge.

Grimmitt, M.H. (Ed.) (2000) *Pedagogies of Religious Education: Case Studies in the Research and Development Good Pedagogic Practice in RE*, Great Wakering, Essex: McCrimmons.

Hannam, P. (2018) *Religious Education and the Public Sphere*, Routledge: London.

Jackson, R. (2004) *Rethinking Religious Education and Plurality,* London: RoutledgeFalmer.

Jackson, R. (2014) *Signposts: Policy and Practice for Teaching about Religions and Non-Religious Worldviews in Intercultural Education,* Strasbourg: Council of Europe Publishing.

Jackson, R., Ipgrave, J., Hayward, M., Hopkins, P., Fancourt, N., Robbins, M., Francis, L.J., and McKenna, U. (2010) *Materials Used to Teach about World Religions in Schools in England*, Research Report DCSFRR197. London: Department for Children, Schools and Families. https://www2.warwick.ac.uk/fac/soc/ces/research/wreru/research/completed/dcsf/reportdcsf-rr197.pdf.

Ofsted (2021) *Research Review series: Religious Education*, [Online] https://www.gov.uk/government/publications/research-review-series-religious-education/research-review-series-religious-education#fnref:155

Shanahan, M. (2017) *Does Religious Education Matter?*, Abingdon: Routledge.

Tharani, A. (2020) *The Worldview Project: Discussion Papers*, London: REC. https://www.religiouseducationcouncil.org.uk/wp-content/uploads/2021/01/The-Worldview-Project.pdf

Thompson, P. (2004) *Whatever Happened to Religious Education?* Cambridge: The Lutterworth Press.

Wright, A. (2000) *Spirituality and Education*, London: RoutledgeFalmer.

Wright, A. (2004) *Religion, Education and Postmodernity*, London: RoutledgeFalmer.

Wright, A. (2007) *Critical Religious Education, Multiculturalism and the Pursuit of Truth*, Cardiff: University of Wales Press.

Wright, A., Schreiner, P., and Craft, F. (Eds.) (2007) *Good Practice in Religious Education in Europe: Examples and Perspectives of Primary Schools*, Berlin: LIT Verlag.

Journals

Many journals publish philosophical reflections, research and position papers on RE. Here are some specifically dedicated to RE.

- British Journal of Religious Education https://www.tandfonline.com/toc/cbre20/current
- Journal of Belief and Values https://www.tandfonline.com/loi/cjbv20
- Journal of Religious Education https://www.springer.com/journal
- Religious Education https://www.tandfonline.com/toc/urea20/current

RE websites

The sites listed below have been selected for their relevance to pedagogy within RE.

Religions of the world – https://www.bbc.co.uk/programmes/articles/1pYRg2f202rqWHrp3ywhTyX/religions-of-the-world

True tube – https://www.truetube.co.uk/

Beginners Bible stories https://www.google.co.uk/search?hl&q=beginners+bible

Holy tales – OT Bible stories https://www.youtube.com/watch?v=TSEkqCXNePM

NATRE resources for all religions https://www.natre.org.uk/resources/

Bar Mitzvah – https://www.youtube.com/watch?v=tEBnpxhb0rc

'My Life, My religion' – diff religions explained https://www.bbc.co.uk/programmes/p02n5wvr

Creation (RE quest) https://request.org.uk/restart/2014/05/29/the-creation-story/

BBC Newsround – Racism in football *(Sikh boy talks re his experiences)* https://www.youtube.com/watch?v=ML_ychlZxMM

Being diff is beautiful – summary of all religions (Little skihs.com) https://www.youtube.com/watch?v=KJ1ygFknjYo

Easter & Lent (RE quest) https://request.org.uk/restart/festivals/easter-fest/

Prayer (RE quest) https://request.org.uk/restart/symbols/prayer-action/

Pilgrimage (RE quest) https://request.org.uk/restart/places/pilgrimage-places/

Apply for RE resources JerusalemTrust.sfct.org.uk/Jersulem.html

Cartoons for RE – everythingfunny.org

Methodistschool.org.uk

Songs https://www.youtube.com/watch?v=pgFT6beutEI (Our God is a great big God)

https://www.youtube.com/watch?v=Br-0-QJptCs (Oh Hallelujah – Jesus is a rock…)

Sikhism – Raksha Bandhan – https://www.youtube.com/watch?v=lW0Z1J-Bjx4 (Rakhi song)

Creation (motions 1234567) https://www.youtube.com/watch?v=nWgC62KGsKM

10 commandments https://www.youtube.com/watch?v=kq4h3Opy-Xc

Good Friday pain to Easter Sunday joy – https://www.youtube.com/watch?v= s7ZJ5D5q54g (Hillsong – Man of sorrows)

Summary

This section has outlined key stakeholders in RE. For teachers and schools, there is the National Association of Teachers of Religious Education, NATRE-affiliated Local Groups and RE Today. The Religious Education Quality Mark celebrates high-quality RE in schools. The Association of University Lecturers in Religion & Education is mainly for academics. The Association of RE Inspectors, Advisers and Consultants exists at a national level and so does The National Association of SACREs is an umbrella organisation for local Standing Advisory Councils on Religious Education. Beyond the education sector, The Religious Education Council of England and Wales reflects a national body of organisation of different professional and religious and non-religious worldviews. A variety of resources was presented to support you in RE. Some of these organisations run regular professional learning and leadership programmes which you can join in (Box 14.4).

BOX 14.4 VIGNETTE: LEADERSHIP

I was brought up in the Latter-Day Saint Church, commonly known as Mormons. I left the church at 18 and no longer practise any religion and consider myself agnostic. My mum was raised in India. Her father, my grandad, was a Hindu, so I was surrounded by strongly contrasting religious views. I was always interested in why people are so passionate about religion. I ended up doing religion and philosophy at University. I enjoyed the course and always wanted to teach it in secondary schools but I ended up deciding to teach primary after experience in a secondary school.

I have wanted to be a teacher since I was 14. Most people in my family are teachers, so I am aware of how difficult teaching can be, so I have always held teachers in great regard. I think the moment I decided to be a teacher was after my dad passed away. Several teachers went to extraordinary lengths for me to make sure I didn't fall behind and was ready for my GCSE's. I, now as a teacher, want to extend that kindness to children who have barriers to learning to ensure they reach their full potential.

It was my degree subject so I'm very passionate about teaching RE. It seems quite a misunderstood subject and I would like to learn more about what can be done to change attitudes towards this subject. I did RE at GCSE, A levels and as my degree, which was a joint honour with philosophy, I have also been very enthusiastic to teach and plan RE at my placement.

My family is very religious so my family has strong opinions of what should and shouldn't be taught in RE. My mum was happy that I was doing RE, but was bothered at some of the things I had to learn about due to her belief; some of it was disrespectful. My friends are mostly atheists but enjoy RE and don't have a problem with it as a subject, but it doesn't affect them due to their age and career path.

I am hoping to become aware of the issues affecting RE in the current climate. I would love at some point to be made head of RE and have a more active role in planning an engaging curriculum that will inspire the children and be child-centred and explorative.

I fear challenging colleagues about their attitudes towards RE and sometimes the lessons they teach. E.g. I find it unprofessional when I hear teachers being negative towards RE or dismissing it or teaching 'RE' lessons which have very tenuous links to RE but I'm unsure of how I would handle this. I have had to teach lessons that I don't consider RE but I didn't want to rock the boat because I'm a student.

I am concerned about cultural sensitivity due to the area we are in. There is a high rate of Islamophobia. The ignorance is so high that parents don't even know the difference between Islam and other Asian religions which has caused a massive issue with the large Sikh population in our school, with various incidents occurring between these children which are always addressed. However, we try to compensate for the ignorance that some of the white children may be learning at home with extensive education on these religions in the hope it may reverse some of the beliefs they have put on them at home. One lesson that occurred involved the children creating Nishan Sahib flags. The lesson was lovely and the children enjoyed it. One mother of one of the Sikh children was incredibly upset because she saw parents putting them in the bin. This did not happen to me but I was unsure of how I would handle the incident. I am concerned about the negativity of other staff members, the lack of respect given to the subject and inadequate curriculums.

I have not interacted with parents concerning religion. The parents of the children in my class seem pretty relaxed in terms of letting the children have RE. However, some children have Islamophobic/racist beliefs that they have picked up from home.

The pupils have a somewhat positive attitude towards their RE. However, I do have quite a nice cohort of children. I have tried to make the curriculum more inclusive for the children of different faiths; for example, one of the Christmas activities was creating angel tea lights. I made a point of talking about how angels appear in other religions as well as Christianity and talked about what they looked like. The children didn't seem to mind and painted their angels in a style of their own regardless of faith.

The teachers whilst not outwardly negative towards RE are not positive either when discussing which afternoon lessons to have for online learning. RE was written off until I offered to do it. The curriculum is not particularly engaging, often supplementing history and geography lessons as RE lessons such as teaching about the poppy because it's a symbol.

References

APPG (2013) *RE: The Truth Unmasked: The Supply of and Support for Religious Education Teachers*, London: REC.

Cordingley, P., Higgins, S., Greany, T., Buckler, N., Coles-Jordan, D., Crisp, B., Saunders, L., and Coe, R. (2015) *Developing Great Teaching: Lessons from the International Reviews into Effective Professional Development*, London: Teacher Development Trust.

DfE (2014) *National Curriculum in England: Framework for Key Stages 1 to 4*, London: Department for Education. [Online] https://www.gov.uk/government/publications/national-curriculum-in-england-framework-for-key-stages-1-to-4/the-national-curriculum-in-england-framework-for-key-stages-1-to-4 (Accessed 13/02/2021).

DfE (2019) *ITT Core Content Framework*, London: Department for Education. Reference: DfE-00230-2019.

DfE (2021) *Teachers' Standards Guidance for School Leaders, School Staff and Governing Bodies*, Crown Copyright. Reference: DFE-00066-2011 [Online] https://assets.publishing.service.gov.uk/government/uploads/system/uploads/attachment_data/file/1007716/Teachers__Standards_2021_update.pdf (Accessed 19/09/2021).

Francis, D., and Blaylock, L. (2016) *Religious Education in Your Academy*, Birmingham: RE Today.

Hargreaves, A., and O'Connor, M. T. (2018) *Collaborative Professionalism: When Teaching Together Means Learning For All*, Thousand Oaks, CA: Corwin Press.

Kent (2017) *Kent Agreed Syllabus for Religious Education 2017–2022*, Kent: Kent SACRE and Birmingham: RE Today. [Online] https://boughton-monchelsea.kent.sch.uk/media/2293/kent-agreed-syllabus197393739.pdf (Accessed 19/6/2022).

May, R. (2020) Leading the primary curriculum: Developing subject leadership and expertise, *Impact: Journal of the Chartered College of Teaching*, Issue 9, May 2020. [Online] https://impact.chartered.college/article/primary-curriculum-developing-subject-leadership-expertise (Accessed 08/03/2021).

McDonagh, C., Roche, M., Sullivan, B., and Glenn, M. (2020) *Enhancing Practice Through Classroom Research: A teacher's Guide to Professional Development*, Abingdon: Routledge. Second edition.

NATRE (2019) *What Are Ofsted Inspectors Saying about Religious Education? The First 101 Reports that Mention RE*, [Online] https://www.natre.org.uk/uploads/Ofsted%20Primary%20and%20Secondary%20Reports%20Autumn%202019%20221119%20final%20final.pdf (Accessed 05/12/2020).

Ofsted (2019) *School Inspection Handbook*, Manchester: Crown copyright. Reference: 190017.

Ofsted (2021) *Research Review Series: Religious Education*, [Online] https://www.gov.uk/government/publications/research-review-series-religious-education/research-review-series-religious-education#fnref:155 (Accessed 18/07/2021).

Pett, S. (2015) *Religious Education: The Teacher's Guide*: Birmingham: RE Today.

REQM (2021) *Recognising Outstanding Learning in Religious Education*, [Online] https://www.reqm.org/ (Accessed 08/03/2021).

Scutt, C., and Harrison, S. (2019) *Teacher CPD: International Trends, Opportunities and Challenges*, London: Chartered College of Teaching. [Online] https://my.chartered.college/wp-content/uploads/2019/11/Chartered-College-International-Teacher-CPD-report.pdf (Accessed 08//03/2021).

Sellars, M. (2017) *Reflective Practice for Teachers*, London: SAGE.

Wigdortz, B., and Toop, J. (2016) *The School Leadership Challenge: 2022*, file:///C:/Users/id105124/Downloads/The_School_Leadership_Challenge_2022.pdf (Accessed 21 June 2020).

Wenger, E. (2010) Communities of practice and social learning systems: The career of a concept, in C. Blackmore (Ed.) *Social Learning Systems and Communities of Practice*, London: Springer, pp. 179–198.

Researching and reflecting whilst religious *educating*

Introduction

This chapter emphasises and illustrates how you, as a teacher, are well-positioned to research pupil's learning in Religious Education (RE). This can be based on your work and ideas, about your classroom and your teaching, both as a trainee and/or as an experienced teacher. You can conduct research within your school community and beyond. You should note that there already is considerable data in your classroom and your pupils are constantly producing information that you can rigorously and systematically gather for research purposes.

However, prior to discussing research in RE, this chapter invites you to consider your identity in relation to teaching with a view to promoting autonomy and reflective practice in a professional context. The chapter will then chart a rationale for engaging in research into teaching and learning in RE. It then illustrates the expected progression in terms of the knowledge, understanding and skills needed for research at three levels: undergraduate, Master's degree and a Doctoral degree. Following this exposition, the discussion moves to present the stages involved in carrying out research, which apply at any of these levels. Thereafter the focus turns to research in RE and your involvement in it. The expected impact is to arouse your interest in research and how it is carried out.

Models for reflection

As a trainee one of the key terms that you may have heard when you attended your selection day or your first lecture may have been that of reflection. The main function of reflection is to learn from both experience and theory by bringing both together to deepen understanding and practice. For seasoned practitioners, this may occur naturally. However, should you not be used to this concept and habit, being reflective, for some, can be a challenge to know where and how to start the process. There are several potential difficulties with reflective practitioner discourse and reflexivity as elucidated by Moore (2012:124–128).

In the context of RE, Hogbin (1983) identified three levels and types of approaches: the curriculum process approach, the teacher-role approach and the personalised approach. There are many generic models which you can use to support your reflection. In this section, three popular models are outlined briefly.

You will notice that each model takes a slightly distinct approach but they all cover similar themes and stages. The main apparent difference is the number of steps involved and how in-depth their developers have chosen to be. Each one has its merits and limitations, and, therefore it is a matter of choosing a model depending on your preferences. Some students alternate between the models depending on their activity.

DOI: 10.4324/9780429289743-20

Figure 15.1 Driscoll's model of reflection.

Source: Created by Author.

Driscoll's model

Figure 15.1 shows a model developed by Driscoll (2011) who proposed that by asking your-selves these three straightforward questions you can begin to analyse your experiences and learn from them.

First, you describe *what* the experience was to contextualise it. This gives you (and others) a clear idea of what the situation, background and activity are. You should then reflect on the experience by asking '*So what?*' In other words, what did you learn because of the experience? The final stage asks, *Now what?* This is an invitation for you to think about the action you will take because of this reflection.

For example, are you going to change a resource, behaviour, teaching method, learn some-thing new or carry on as before? It is important to remember that change is not necessary because of reflection. Sometimes it may result in confirming what you are doing and you may decide to continue following an experience. This is equally valid and you should not be concerned if you cannot think of something to change. Change should have a purpose, as illustrated in Box 15.1.

Kolb's experiential learning cycle

Kolb's model (1984) is based on theories about how people learn and focuses on the concept of developing understanding through actual experiences. It consists of four key stages:

- Concrete experience
- Reflective observation
- Abstract conceptualisation
- Active experimentation

BOX 15.1 CASE STUDY ON USING DRISCOLL'S MODEL

Before I came to my first tutorial, I was not sure how to go about writing reflections for my folder. I was unsure what I needed to include and what to mention. The specific challenge that I faced was not knowing how to structure my reflections and did not know what I needed to mention in my reflections. My tutor suggested a system based on three simple questions when writing my reflections. These were: What? (What is it I am writing about?); So what? (What was the importance or impact of what I had done?) and Now what? (What am I going to do new to continue to develop). I used this to help me write my weekly reflections whilst on school placement and for justifications of evidence in my PDP. It helped me by giving me a basic layout of how to write my reflections and comfort in the knowledge that as long as these three questions were answered, my reflec-tions would be meaningful. It enhanced my reflective skills as now whenever look back on work or lessons, I instantly ask myself those three questions, so that from any point, I can identify my strengths as well as areas for improvement.

The model suggests that you start with an experience, usually not a lecture, either a repeat of something that has happened before or something completely new to you (concrete experience). The second phase invites you to reflect on the experience and record anything about it, which is new to you from multiple perspectives (reflective observation). In the third phase, you develop theories and by looking at patterns (abstract conceptualisation). The last phase invites you to apply what you have learnt (active experimentation).

Brookfield's four lenses model

Unlike the cyclical models of reflection, Brookfield's (2017:61–77) suggests that teaching practice is considered through multiple perspectives: from our standpoint, our learners, our peers and from its relationship to wider theory, as illustrated in Figure 15.2. This will deepen reflection.

The autobiographical aspect of reflection, when considering experiences and feelings, is central to the process of critical reflection. You may draw from your past first-hand experiences and your immediate contexts. It is suggested you re-assess the present and your pasts as a teacher, trainee and learner to reveal the expansive nature of your teaching practice. The second is to use the pupils' perspective/s to yield insights that might otherwise have been ignored if the self-reflection is exclusively upon yourself. It may involve looking back at the work produced by pupils, at their feedback and work. This lens uncovers assumptions and biases and promotes better teaching as positive experiences may be highlighted. The third lens of exploration into yourself involves going beyond pupils and includes taking peers' perceptions and observations into account. They too expose biases and assumptions in your teaching, and highlight areas that you might miss. This is beneficial to all concerned as common and divergent rationales to teaching are shared. For theory, the hardest, Brookfield (2017:72) suggests that teachers need to be engaged with educational theory and research in examining their teaching practice. The training of teachers does not end with your initial teacher education course but is a life-long journey. You need to engage with critical reading, subject scholarship, political and other contexts of contemporary teaching such as pursuing a higher qualification.

These are only three reflective models that are available out of many (Bolton and Deldersfield 2018; Gibbs 1988; Jasper 2013). They are a helpful means of beginning to think about reflection. However, it is important to remember that all models have their limitations and, as such, you should find one which is most suitable for you as reflection is a personal process and students and teachers work towards it in different ways. You may notice that there are some overlaps between them, which is not surprising as the key function of reflection is to learn from both experience and theory to deepen understanding and improve practice. Therefore, you can try different models until you

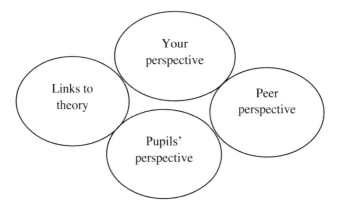

Figure 15.2 Brookfield's four lenses.

Source: Created by Author.

find the one that works best for you. Significantly, over time you should develop as a reflective practitioner and reflection should come naturally and consciously. To be a successful teacher in a climate of performance and accountability you need to be proactive and take ownership of your professional learning for which the skills of critical reflection as tools for self-improvement is essential.

Reflection

■ Which one of them appeals to you?

■ Identify the strengths and limitations of each model of reflection.

■ Is there any other model, which has worked for you?

■ Are such reflective models, in general, helpful or are they restrictive?

Teachers as researchers

In addition to being a reflective practitioner (Schön 1983) and learning through dialogues in schools (Wenger 1998), there is a renewed emphasis on being a teacher-researcher. The evolution of the teacher as a researcher in England has been critiqued. Elliot (2012), for example, had argued that it had become detached from the curriculum development theory advanced by Stenhouse (1981). In the conception of the latter, the 'teacher as a researcher' is at the centre of curriculum development. From this theoretical perspective, the focus of teachers' research should be on how to effect worthwhile curriculum change in their classrooms and schools, through systematic inquiry (Elliott and Norris 2012; Leat, Lofthouse and Reid 2013).

The British Education Research Association and Royal Society for the Encouragement of the Arts, Manufacturing and Commerce (BERA-RSA) inquiry into the role of research in teacher education stressed that research and teacher inquiry was of paramount importance in developing self-improving schools. One of their seven inquiries reported that research can focus teachers' thinking beyond the accountability culture of a performative system, towards a more sophisticated working understanding of an ecology of learning and the development of cultures that permit risk-taking which accompanies the eschewing of the normal routines. They also reported that research can enable teachers to be more accepting of challenges and difficulties, allowing them to step out of their comfort zone (Leat, Lofthouse and Reid 2013:8). Closer working partnerships between teacher-researchers and the wider academic research community were also advocated. As a result, many providers offer professional development programmes through *Alliances, Multi-academy Trusts, Research Schools* (RSN 2021), *Teaching Schools Council* (TSC 2021) and charities such as the *Educational Endowment Foundation* (EEF 2021).

The *Carter Review of Initial Teacher Training* (DfE 2015) made clear that trainee teachers should have access to, and be able to utilise, research evidence as part of their planning and teaching strategies. Later, this was also evident in the education White Paper *Educational Excellence Everywhere* (DfE 2016). Nevertheless, a closer look at the Teachers' Standards will reveal that trainees are required to demonstrate their research competency as part of these standards, except that it stresses reflection, at all careers stages: 'appropriate self-reflection, reflection and professional development activity' (DfE 2021:7), and the opportunities available to them in school to engage with research are sporadic (Philpott and Poultney 2018). However, recently, the *ITT Core Content Framework* (CCF) (DfE 2019a) the *Early Career Framework* (ECF) (DfE 2019b) have established minimum entitlements for trainees. As part of their professional behaviours, it requires trainees to learn that learning from educational research is also likely to support improvement (DfE 2019a:29; DfE 2019b:24). Trainees also need to learn how to develop as a professional by improving at engaging critically with research and using evidence to critique practice (DfE 2019a).

With the publication of the CCF and ECF, the journey of becoming teaching is clear, since in addition to achieving and evidencing the Teachers' Standards, as part of initial teacher education, the former New Qualified Teacher year has been extended to two years. Thus, signally the importance of continuous training and development, beyond a qualification, so that teaching is conceptualised not only as a career-long process but also as lifelong learning for all teachers.

Why research in education?

Research is one way of responding to problems and issues in education (Biesta 2020). It has a utilitarian dimension. It offers 'soft' emancipation, in the sense that research outcomes can be useful in providing educational actors alternative opportunities for decision-making and actions. Research also reveals the hidden workings of power to emancipate educational actors, and through them the 'audiences' they serve. The stronger emancipation is when educational research reveals to educational actors what they themselves cannot see or know about their social situation and, ultimately, about their own thoughts and feelings (Biesta 2020:21–22). In developing programmes of study and enhancing subject knowledge of teachers, the Commission on RE (CoRE 2018:40) report suggests taking account of relevant research. Research has the potential to reconfigure and refresh your practice as a teacher, practitioner, subject leader or senior manager in a school. It can also challenge and strengthen your educational philosophy and value system. Some of the challenges faced by RE are its purpose, curriculum, pedagogy, subject knowledge, confidence, time and assessment.

Research and enquiry are also undertaken for personal, political and school improvement purposes (McLaughlin, Black-Hawkins and McIntyre 2004:7). Often these are tangled, mix and rarely isolated. Therefore, as a teacher for RE, research can provide you with a good opportunity to find out the 'best' teaching methods and approaches possible if you are to provide rich, rigorous, relevant and real RE to your pupils which they can use as a foundation for lifelong learning.

One of the relatively easier and self-contained research that some teachers get involved in is action research, which, at the very least, you can carry out, as it is usually practical. Small-scale research carried out by an individual has the benefit of being related to that individual's practice having exactly the right context and addressing the researcher's main concerns and key question as such it can be powerful research (Williams 2020:169).

Research into Religious Education

In the section below, the expected progression in terms of the knowledge, understanding and skills required for research at three levels: undergraduate, Master's degree and Doctoral degree are illustrated.

Research for an undergraduate degree

An assignment in an honours degree in educational studies and ITE is one of the preferred ways of assessing a final year module for many undergraduates. The requirement is to submit a 'major piece' of work. The name, size and nature of this vary. In some institutes, it is referred to as a project, an assignment, independent study or even dissertation. Regardless of its 'title', there are at least two common features compared to other assignments of such a course. Usually, a supervisor guides and supports this work and, should it be a written piece, then the wordage allocated to it tends to be more than the work submitted in previous years. It may also carry more credits compared to the modules from earlier years. Regardless of these institutional differences, across many undergraduate degrees, there is an expectation that, as an undergraduate, you will have progressively encountered certain benchmarks set by *The Quality Assurance Agency for UK Higher Education*. The benchmarks below are those set for a single honours degree in education studies (QAA 2019:10–11).

These benchmarks may be the most relevant in assisting you to formulate and identify a research question:

■ To understand the underlying values, theories and concepts relevant to education.

■ The ability to analyse educational concepts, theories and issues of policy in a systematic way.

■ The ability to use knowledge and understanding critically to locate and justify a personal position in relation to the subject.

■ The ability to reflect on their own and others' value systems.

These benchmarks may be the most relevant to support you in undertaking a literature review:

■ The ability to select a range of relevant primary and secondary sources, including theoretical and research-based evidence, to extend their knowledge and understanding.

■ To demonstrate a critical understanding of the societal and organisational structures and purposes of educational systems, and the possible implications for learners and the learning process.

■ To understand the diversity of learners and the complexities of the education process.

■ The ability to identify and reflect on potential connections and discontinuities between each of the aspects of subject knowledge and their application in educational policies and contexts.

■ The ability to organise and articulate opinions and arguments in speech and writing using relevant specialist vocabulary.

■ To apply theories and concepts to a range of real-world educational contexts.

These benchmarks may be the most relevant to contributing to the design of the methodology:

■ An understanding of the significance and limitations of theory and research.

■ The extent to which participants (including learners and teachers) can influence the learning process.

These benchmarks may be the most relevant to back your data collection and presentation:

■ To be able to collect and apply numerical data.

■ To be able to present data in a variety of formats.

■ Be able to use technology effectively to enhance critical and reflective study.

These benchmarks may be the most relevant to assist your analysis, evaluation and discussion.

■ To analyse and interpret both qualitative and quantitative data.

■ To process and synthesise empirical and theoretical data, to create new syntheses and to present and justify a chosen position having drawn on relevant theoretical perspectives.

■ To accommodate new principles and understandings.

■ To use a range of evidence to formulate appropriate and justified ways forward and potential changes in practice.

You should also demonstrate an ability to collaborate and plan as a team, to carry out roles allocated to you by your supervisor and to take the lead where appropriate, and fulfil agreed responsibilities. Moreover, you should be able to articulate your own approaches to learning and organise an effective work pattern, including working to deadlines.

Research for a Master's degree

A Master's degree intends to enable practitioners, teachers and students to focus in greater depth on a particular aspect of a broader subject area in which they may have prior knowledge, experience or interest. It enables participants to demonstrate a *systematic* understanding of knowledge, and a *critical awareness* of current problems and/or new insights, much of which is at, or informed by, the forefront of their academic discipline, a field of study or area of professional practice. They should show a *comprehensive understanding of techniques* applicable to their own research or advanced scholarship and *originality in the application of knowledge*, together with a *practical understanding* of how established techniques of research and enquiry are used to create and interpret knowledge in the discipline. They should demonstrate a conceptual understanding that enables them to evaluate *critically current* research and advanced scholarship in the discipline and to evaluate methodologies and develop *critiques* of them and, where appropriate, propose new hypotheses. Typically, they should demonstrate self-direction and originality in tackling and solving problems, and act autonomously in planning and implementing tasks at a professional or equivalent level and continue to advance their knowledge and understanding, and develop new skills to a high level. They should have the qualities and transferable skills necessary for employment requiring the exercise of initiative and personal responsibility, decision-making in complex and unpredictable situations and the independent learning ability required for continuing professional development (QAA 2014:28).

Research for a Doctoral degree

For a Doctoral degree, there are many expectations including the ability to demonstrate the creation and interpretation of new knowledge, through original research or other advanced scholarship founded on a systematic acquisition of a substantial body of knowledge, which is at the forefront of an academic discipline or professional practice. They also demonstrate their general ability to conceptualise, design and implement a project for the generation of new knowledge ... at the forefront of the discipline using applicable techniques for research and advanced academic enquiry (QAA 2014:28).

The research process

What do you want to find out?

If your intent for your research is to provide new insights and further evidence into curriculum and pedagogy, it may be necessary for you to consider the role of the teacher and the role of the pupils in this process because these are, in most cases, inseparable and interact with one another very closely. Having said that, there is no reason for isolating pedagogy and curriculum for research purposes. The subject areas covered in the chapters of this book offer many interesting avenues for further research. Alternatively, you may be interested in exploring the opinions, attitudes and responses about a particular issue among colleagues in school, fellow trainees, pupils, parents, faith leaders or across a MAT. You may be curious about the application of a theory or someone's educational perspective and its impact on learning and teaching in RE across schools. You may want to look at existing research and replicate it within your context. Therefore, the options available to you are many. However, whatever you decide it is important that you have a deep-rooted passion and interest in your enquiry.

Deciding on a research question

Once you have decided on the area of research, you must formulate your research question as precisely as you can. You also need to ensure that the scope of your research is manageable and 'doable' within a certain time scale. The scale for undergraduate and postgraduate research may be influenced by the course, whilst an enquiry in school is usually small scale and focussed. A research question can be about an educational issue, the effectiveness of a specific teaching method or use of resources, or a group of pupils, parents and teachers, or behaviours and interactions in lessons or an initiative across a school or an alliance of schools. All these will generate rich, relevant and ready data for researching RE. There are many benefits of setting such parameters and developing a precise research focus. It helps you determine the field, scale, scope and relevant readings on the area that you need to undertake.

What others have written on the subject

A literature review is what others have written on the topic, issue or subject. It enables you to demonstrate that you are aware of previous publications on the matter and what research others have done. In doing so, you will be able to demonstrate that you are building on the work of others contributions and not replicating it. You will also be able to show that whilst you have identified a gap in your context, nevertheless, you are locating it within what is already known in your field and a scholarship tradition.

Research design and collecting your research data

Not only will you need to carefully formulate your question, but you will also need to select the method which will elicit the appropriate data. You will also need to state why the various research methods were selected and why they were considered to be the 'best' method/s for your research (Williams 2020:152).

You may leave research that tends to gather quantitative data, in preference of research, which provides qualitative data. You could experiment with the effectiveness of a teaching method or the use of a resource. You could use a survey to collect quantitative data. You may prefer to combine the two if they answer your research question more successfully. Qualitative data originates from a case study, interviews, focus groups, observations, action research and documentary analysis. The data might be collected by observing, video recording, visual sources, diaries, reflections and pupils' books. You could carry out action research by identifying a problem in RE, devising a plan to improve the situation, then observing whether the situation improved or not, and then repeating the cycle.

Who will be the participants of your research?

This will depend on your research question. It will also depend on the boundaries set by your context and, in turn, by your research design in terms of who and how many research participants you will involve. For some studies, the method selected may influence the size of your participants. You may decide to choose them randomly or systematically.

Ethical considerations

All research should be conducted ethically and with ethical approval. Universities have their policies, principles, processes and set criteria for scrutinising their research for ethical considerations. With the introduction of The General Data Protection Regulation from 2018 (DfE 2018) schools have tightened up processes including the way they carry out and participate in research to ensure compliance with this regulation. Ethical considerations include, for example, informing the participants the aims and purposes of the research, about anonymity and confidentiality, voluntary and informed consent, opting out at any point, who and how the research will benefit, how it will be disseminated and, if applicable, who funded it. Many researchers use the British Education

Research Association's *Ethical Guidelines for Educational Research*, which is designed to support educational researchers in researching the highest ethical standards in all contexts (BERA 2018).

How will you analyse the data?

Qualitative data is analysed in many ways. Some use a grounded theory approach, content analysis, conversation analysis and larger studies may use computer-aided software. This data can be textual, aural, visual and, essentially, it is about making sense of the data. It involves reading, usually more than once for familiarisation and initial sorting. Thereafter, codes are given to describe the content. Followed by this, themes or patterns are searched within them to locate commonality in the data. Often these themes are refined to create subcategories and names. Finally, the data are presented.

How would you present your findings?

This may be a combination of prose description and numerical data. To present quantitative data you may use pie charts, bar graphs, tables or charts. For qualitative data, word clouds, quotations, images, artwork, transcripts, excerpts from field notes, taxonomies, Venn diagrams and flowcharts are used.

Why do your findings matter?

This is the 'so what' question and why your audience should care about your enquiry. In all research whatever the size, you need to conclude by declaring precisely what you have found. This is where the main ideas will once again be articulated. Based on the evidence, you also need to show how your findings assist in filling the gap, offering an alternative perspective, challenge existing explanations or confirm existing research. You also need to articulate the importance and relevance of your findings and for whom it will be beneficial. Researchers also tend to acknowledge the limitations of their study. You may also want to identify what further enquiries you hope your research will stimulate.

Moving forward: Research in Religious Education

There is a long-standing research tradition in RE in assorted topics using a range of methodologies and paradigms. Frances (2012) provided a broad introduction to the development of empirical research in RE in the United Kingdom during a 50 year period which includes qualitative and quantitative studies.

RE teachers may consider four possible categories of research. *General education research* focuses on teaching, learning, pedagogy and leadership among other topics and *Religious Education research* focus on RE as a discrete curriculum subject and the related types of RE in various faith and community schools. The third category is *religion research* which focuses specifically on religious texts, beliefs, practices or inter-religious dialogue. Finally, *cross-disciplinary research* oscillates between various disciplines such as theology, philosophy, history, sociology and psychology (Cox 2018:219–220). Thus it is evident that the pool of research is extensive. It can therefore be both overwhelming and appealing. Nevertheless, it raises questions of value, relevance and application.

Based on the findings of an informal survey of 186 colleagues, Cox (2018:221) argued that teachers could be involved in and use research at three levels. The evidence-*engaged* level, found to be most demanding, demanded the reading of full research reports, interpreting their use for the classroom and being engaged with academic research methodology. The evidenced-*informed* level involves reading summaries usually by third parties interpreting their use for the classroom whereas the evidence-*based* level involves using teaching strategies and pedagogies recommended by others, based on research findings. After evaluating each one in terms of their implication related to time, accessibility and applicability, Cox (2018) found that evidence-*based* level involvement to be the least time consuming and this is the minimum level, which she suggests should be expected from all RE teachers.

What research areas are most relevant today for Religious Education?

There are many areas of potential research in RE for you to consider. In addition to the broad themes such as pedagogy, assessment, attitudes towards an aspect of RE or religion/non-religions and education, the following are also viable:

- The importance of RE
- RE in special schools
- RE in EYFS
- RE and high prior attainers
- RE and SEND
- RE and 'Worldviews'
- Exploring effective pedagogies for RE
- The right of withdrawal from RE
- The compulsory nature of RE

These are some of the recent publications from the British Journal of Religious Education and Journal of Religion & Values, among many other journals.

- RE and the pandemic: postcolonial perspectives (Gearon 2021).
- Subject knowledge: the 'knowledge-rich' agenda, Buber and the importance of the knowing subject in RE (Jarmy 2021).
- The right of withdrawal from RE in England: school leaders' beliefs, experiences and understandings of policy and practice (Lundie and O'Siochru 2021).
- Seeing, grasping and constructing: pre-service teachers' metaphors for 'understanding' in RE (Walshe 2020).
- A critical policy analysis of local RE in England (Smalley 2020).
- RE of children in interfaith marriages (Kurttekin 2020).
- Religious literacy: a way forward for RE? (Hannam, Biesta, Whittle and Aldridge 2020).

As a teacher, you should be an evaluator of research. This means you should adopt and adapt what applies to your context, as there are many answers to a question related to teaching and learning. In 2017, *Research for RE* was launched by Culham St. Gabriel's Trust to bring together those who teach and research RE to share research reports and encourage collaboration and latest ideas with the expectation that innovative research can have a real-life impact both inside and outside the classroom. The *Research for RE* is a digital and social knowledge exchange tool that also aims to overcome the barriers teachers face in engaging with relevant research by making emergent RE-related research freely available in an easily accessible and relevant format that can be quickly understood and appropriately used as seen here https://www.reonline.org.uk/research/. You may contribute to this ever-growing research in RE in numerous ways since research engagement has now been recognised as a fundamental feature of the teaching profession so that teachers continue to evolve as a learning community. This is shown in Box 15.2.

They also created a network of funded research projects, aimed at targeting the key research issues and questions for RE over the coming years. The projects were distributed across the

---

BOX 15.2 RE RESEARCH COMMUNITIES

RE research communities

Research is one of the main areas of support provided by the https://www.reonline.org.uk/research/ website. You will find free to use, quality-assured, comprehensive coverage of religion and worldviews. Their free research library offers material in four key areas: 'Being an RE teacher', 'nature of RE', 'subject knowledge' and 'teaching and learning.

The *RExChange Resource* page hosts recorded sessions, PowerPoints and articles from research-focused conferences. The *case studies* page illustrates the journey of some current researchers who work in education, as well as details of some current research being undertaken in Religion and Worldviews. These case studies help inspire more people within the Religion and Worldview community to engage in and with research. If you are interested, the site provides links and opportunities to participate in Religion and Worldviews research projects.

Another valuable feature is called the *research of the month*, which features a different piece of research each month with extra resources to support its use by individuals as well as local and regional groups. These are summaries of high-quality academic research that are relevant to classroom practice. You will also discover accounts of collaborations between teachers and researchers, or research projects undertaken by teachers. This feature aims to refresh and develop your professional knowledge and to help you get up to date with what others are doing. Each month, they feature a new piece of research or one chosen from their library to highlight. This monthly focus can be used for personal professional development, as well as a source of reading group material for local or regional groups and hubs.

In the section on *Engaging in and with research*, there are links and resources to use when exploring research undertaken by others as well as carrying out research of your own. Engage with research supports you as you read and explore research through your study or with others. The engage in research part supports you to undertake your research, perhaps inspired by some of the things you have read on their website.

The *Research Bulletin* presents Culham St Gabriel's Masters and PhD students alongside other funded projects. This is expected to be an annual feature consisting of articles based on the work taking place within their master's and doctoral community of practice.

There are *research posters* too. These are a visual representation of data or findings that have been organised in an easily digestible format. Some research posters are available from recent projects to inspire and inform you which have been funded by Culham St Gabriel's Trust. You can access these posters as pdf files.

Source: https://www.reonline.org.uk/research/ [Online] (Access 08/10/2021)

---

country and a range of different institutions to grow and strengthen centres of RE research excellence. A list of the major research areas for RE at that time had been developed as seven projects:

- The challenge of curriculum design in RE.
- Religious literacy.
- Emergent technologies and RE.
- Teachers and texts in the RE classroom.
- Children as scientific and religious reasoners.
- Educational disadvantage, social mobility and religious identity.
- RE teachers' engagement with research.

Summary

This chapter has highlighted the important role of reflection and research for your continued professional learning. It has offered some models to habituate you in becoming a reflective practitioner. It has highlighted the support available to you should you wish to research RE. Your local university and the various RE organisations and charities are some of the options to consider, should you wish to seek funding for research or pursue further studies. You could also join the British Educational Research Association (BERA). Of course, it is not necessary to rely on anyone you can make your school as a starting point (Box 15.3).

Reflection

- How would you respond to the question: why is practitioner research important?
- Is there a role for research in RE?
- What enquiry in RE could you carry out within the cluster of your schools?

BOX 15.3 VIGNETTE: AMBITION

I am a Roman Catholic. My mother and family are religious. She was brought up a Catholic, as I was. My father is non-religious, he does believe in God but does not follow any sort of major religion. My brother and I have been brought up Catholic and I feel this has positively affected my life. It gives me a great sense of hopefulness that I have something great to believe in and somebody to pray to, who I know loves me unconditionally despite faults. Being brought up with the religious views that I have has led me to do certain things in my personal life such as having a partner who is also Catholic as I believe it is an important trait to have. Despite this, I do respect that this is not a necessity to everyday life or even in my family dynamic, as it does not change the view I have of my dad who is not religious at all. As well as this, many of my closest friends of over 10 years are not religious or have a different religion to me but this does not impact my friendships in any sort of way.

I have always had an interest in RE, it was one of my best subjects at secondary school where I got a B in my GCSE, I enjoyed it so much I took up its counterpart 'Philosophy & Ethics' as an A-Level during the sixth form. My main attitude towards teaching before getting into myself was admiration, it was a job that I believed many people thought to be 'easy' or 'just for the holidays' but I knew first-hand the hard work and dedication required to be a teacher as my mom was an instructor at an SEN school.

One reason for choosing RE specifically is that it is a subject that I was interested in and loved learning about when I was in primary and secondary as well as sixth form. However, the main reason is that I want the children I teach to share the same love for the subject as I did at school and do now. This is because RE is not being taught in school as it should be so to me that means that children are missing such vital skills RE can teach them. Skills such as interest, understanding, empathy and so on. This is what I am hoping to achieve during my teaching, giving children the love of knowledge during RE and getting them excited about the subject as well as learning transferable skills that will aid them throughout life. Although my hope does not come without fear or reservations of potential challenges that lie ahead, when teaching RE or as being the subject lead. My main concern is that RE is the subject that will get cut or removed when lessons that others view as being more important are required, more specifically maths and English.

I have seen this happen first-hand in my SBT1 placement. During the 6 weeks, I was there, there was only one lesson of RE taught and that was by myself during my first week

---

of teaching there. In the five consecutive weeks afterwards, RE was always taken off the timetable to make room for 'more important' lessons. As a subject lead, this would worry me greatly because how do you approach a situation where your superiors are telling you to make sure more of another lesson is taught in place of the one you are responsible for. I feel as though this will be the greatest challenge for me as well as others who are leading RE.

During my placement I got the overbearing impression that RE was not a very important subject, however as I am at the same school for my next placement, I am aiming to change this by ensuring I teach RE at least once a week and hopefully give the children lessons to get excited about that piques their interest.

References

BERA (2018) *Ethical Guidelines for Educational Research*, London: British Education Research Association. Fourth edition.

Biesta, G. (2020) *Educational Research: An Unorthodox Introduction*, London: Bloomsbury.

Bolton, G., and Deldersfield, R. (2018) *Reflective Practice: Writing and Professional Development*, London: SAGE

Brookfield, S. D. (2017) *Becoming a Critically Reflective Teacher*, San Francisco: Jossey-Bass. Second edition.

Commission on Religious Education (CoRE) (2018) *Religion and Worldviews: The Way Forward*, London: Religious Education Council.

Cox, D. (2018) Does research matter in the Religious Education classroom? in M. Castelli and M. Chater (Eds.) *We Need to Talk About Religious Education: Manifestos for the Future of RE*, London: Jessica Kingsley, pp. 219–232.

DfE (Department for Education) (2015) *The Carter Review of Initial Teaching Training*, London: Crown Copyright. DFE-00036-2015.

DfE (Department for Education) (2016) *Educational Excellence Everywhere*, London: Crown Copyright. Cm 9230.

DfE (Department for Education) (2018) *Data Protection: A Toolkit for Schools Open Beta: Version 1.0.* Crown copyright. DFE-00119-2018.

DfE (Department for Education) (2019a) *ITT (Initial Teacher Training) Core Content Framework*, London: Crown Copyright. DFE-00015-2019.

DfE (Department for Education) (2019b) *Early Career Framework*, London: Crown Copyright. DFE-00015-2019.

DfE (Department for Education) (2021) *Teachers' Standards Guidance for School Leaders, School Staff and Governing Bodies*, Crown Copyright. Reference: DFE-00066-2011 [Online] https://assets.publishing.service.gov.uk/government/uploads/system/uploads/attachment_data/file/1007716/Teachers__Standards_2021_update.pdf (Accessed 19/09/2021).

Driscoll, J. (2011) *Practising Clinical Supervision: A Reflective Approach for Healthcare Professionals*, Edinburgh: Bailliere Tindall Elsevier. Second edition.

EEF (2021) *Educational Endowment Foundation*, [Online] https://educationendowmentfoundation.org.uk/ (Accessed 07/03/2021).

Elliott, J. (2012) Teaching Controversial Issues, the idea of the 'teacher as researcher' and contemporary significance for citizenship education, in J. Elliot and N. Norris (Ed.) *Curriculum, Pedagogy and Educational Research: The work of Lawrence Stenhouse*, London: Routledge, pp. 84–106.

Elliott, J., and Norris, N. (Eds.) (2012) *Curriculum, Pedagogy and Educational Research: The Work of Lawrence Stenhouse*, London: Routledge.

Frances, L. J. (2012) Empirical research, in L. P. Barnes (Ed.) *Debates in Religious Education*, London: Routledge, pp. 157–167.

Gearon, L. (2021) Religious education and the pandemic: Postcolonial perspectives, *British Journal of Religious Education*, 43, (1), pp. 9–22.

Gibbs, G. (1988) *Learning by Doing: A Guide to Teaching and Learning Methods*, London: FEU

Hannam, P., Biesta, G., Whittle, S., and Aldridge, D. (2020) Religious literacy: A way forward for religious education? *Journal of Beliefs & Values*, 41, (2), pp. 214–226.

Hogbin, J. W. G. (1983) Three approaches to teacher training and the role of Religious Education as a professional subject, *European Journal of Teacher Education*, 6, (2), pp. 107–117.

Jarmy, C. (2021) Subject knowledge: The 'knowledge-rich' agenda, Buber and the importance of the knowing subject in Religious Education, *British Journal of Religious Education*, 43, (2), pp. 140–149.

Jasper, M. (2013) *Beginning Reflective Practice*, Andover: Cengage Learning.

Kolb, D. (1984) *Experiential Learning: Experience as the Source of Learning and Development*, Upper Saddle River: Prentice-Hall.

Kurttekin, F. (2020) Religious education of children in interfaith marriages, *Journal of Beliefs & Values*, 41, (3), pp. 272–283.

Leat, D., Lofthouse, R., and Reid, A. (2013) *Teachers' Views: Perspectives on Research Engagement*, BERA-RSA Research and Teacher Education: The BERA-RSA Inquiry.

Lundie, D., and O'Siochru, C. (2021) The right of withdrawal from religious education in England: School leaders' beliefs, experiences and understandings of policy and practice, *British Journal of Religious Education*, 43, (2), pp. 161–173.

McLaughlin, C., Black-Hawkins, K., and McIntyre, D. (2004) *Researching Teachers, Researching Schools, Researching Networks: A Summary of the Literature*, Cambridge: University of Cambridge.

Moore, A. (2012) *Teaching and Learning: Pedagogy, Curriculum and Culture*, Abingdon: Routledge.

Philpott, C., and Poultney, V. (2018) *Evidence-Based Teaching: A Critical Overview for Enquiring Teachers*, St Albans: Critical Publishing.

QAA (2014) *UK Quality Code for Higher Education Part A: Setting and Maintaining Academic Standards The Frameworks for Higher Education Qualifications of UK Degree-Awarding Bodies*, Gloucester: The Quality Assurance Agency for Higher Education. https://www.qaa.ac.uk/docs/qaa/quality-code/qualifications-frameworks.pdf

QAA (2019) *Subject Benchmark Statement: Education Studies*, Gloucester: The Quality Assurance Agency for Higher Education. Fourth edition.

RSN (2021) *Teaching School Alliances, Multi-Academy Trusts, Research Schools*, [Online] https://researchschool.org.uk/ (Accessed 07/03/2021).

Schön, D. (1983) *The Reflective Practitioner*, London: Temple Smith.

Smalley, P. (2020) A critical policy analysis of local religious education in England, *British Journal of Religious Education*, 42, (3), pp. 263–274.

Stenhouse, L. (1981) What counts as educational research? *British Journal of Educational Studies*, 29, (2), pp. 103–113.

TSC (2021) *Teaching Schools Council*, [Online] https://tscouncil.org.uk/ (Accessed 07/03/2021).

Walshe, K. (2020) Seeing, grasping and constructing: Pre-service teachers' metaphors for 'understanding' in religious education, *British Journal of Religious Education*, 42, (4), pp. 471–489.

Wenger, E. (1998) *Communities of Practice: Learning, Meaning, and Identity*, New York: Cambridge University Press.

Williams, J. (2020) *How to Read and Understand Educational Research*, London: SAGE.

Conclusion

This guidebook should be considered as a foundation for your continued learning journey in Religious Education. It should be a stimulus for reflection and conversations with your peers about the importance of the subject, its place in the school curriculum and its teaching to pupils ages 5–11. Scholarly work in RE continues to grow which is for you to seek further.

The book presented and problematised the historical and legislative framework to assist you to know and understand the present nature and status of the subject. It also offered suggestions on major aspects of teaching such as the curriculum, planning, pedagogy, inclusion, assessment and progression, networking, subject leadership and research to support you to consider how you can become innovative, autonomous and ambitious in your teaching of RE. At the same time, it has invited you to be open-minded to receive new ideas from your peers, experts, research and scholarly works.

Teaching is a complex phenomenon. The complexity is increasing by the day and brings with it opportunities and challenges. Teachers are at the forefront of receiving these opportunities and facing these challenges. It is for you to be resourceful and to flourish with confidence in the world of teaching.

DOI: 10.4324/9780429289743-21

Index

Note: Page numbers in **bold** denote tables.

Printed in Great Britain
by Amazon

18498589R00237